ROMANTIC MUSIC

The Norton Introduction to Music History

ROMANTIC MUSIC

A History of Musical Style
in Nineteenth-Century Europe

LEON PLANTINGA

Yale University

W · W · NORTON & COMPANY
New York · London

The text of this book is composed in Bembo, with display type set in Bembo.
Composition by Vail-Ballou Press, Inc. Manufacturing by The Maple-Vail Book
Manufacturing Group.

First Edition

Library of Congress Cataloging in Publication Data
Plantinga, Leon.
   Romantic music.
   (The Norton introduction to music history)
   Bibliography: p.
   Includes index.
   1. Music—19th century—History and criticism.
I. Title. II. Series.
ML196.P6   1984   780'.903'4   84-4012

ISBN 0-393-95196-0

W. W. Norton & Company, Inc., 500 Fifth Avenue, New York, N.Y. 10110
W. W. Norton & Company Ltd., 37 Great Russell Street, London WC1B 3NU

   6 7 8 9 0

Contents

List of Illustrations

Preface

In this book I seek to give an account of art music in nineteenth-century Europe. The chronological boundaries observed, inevitably somewhat arbitrary, are nearly those of the century itself. The earlier limit, however, falls about a decade before 1800 so as to take notice of certain works, written in the 1790s by the maturing Beethoven and by his more forward-looking contemporaries, that seem to belong more to the new century than to the old. The later boundary, set at 1900, may seem especially whimsical; it cuts Mahler off in mid-career, for example, and surgically separates the tone poems of Richard Strauss from the remarkable operas that follow. But pursuing the tracks of Romantic music into the twentieth century would launch us on a daunting journey with no natural stopping place: Saint-Saëns lived until 1921, Puccini until 1924, Rachmaninov until 1943, both Strauss and Pfitzner until 1949. And if older styles together with their arsenal of aesthetic beliefs had not, with the changing of the century, ceased to be, new ones were clearly present. The language of musical impressionism taking shape in France and the welter of radical experiment in Vienna were distinctly modern in character, and their force and influence were such that they must figure in any balanced account of European music in the last decade-and-a-half before the First World War. How these new ideas and styles comported with the old seems a proper subject in the history of twentieth-century music.

To restrict the discussion here to music in Europe is not to say that the practice of the art elsewhere was fundamentally different in quality or even in kind. It is rather to confess my own limitations in a time of growing specialization. Music in the nineteenth-century Americas alone is a spacious and complex field deserving of a book of its own—written, preferably, by someone versed in the subject.

The explanations of music and musical life offered here deliberately cut a wide swath, incorporating at one extreme modest forays into social and intellectual history, and, at the other, analyses of individual compositions rather more extensive than is usual in historical books on music—this last facilitated by the volume of scores issued as a companion to this one, *Anthology of Romantic Music*. In a memorable essay of

1960, written in refutation of a "scientific" historiography, Sir Isaiah
Berlin returned repeatedly to the metaphor of history as a thick fabric
of elaborately interwoven strands for which no single schematic model
of explanation proves adequate. It is an

> activity of selection and adjustment, the search for coherence and unity,
> together with the attempt to refine it with all the self-consciousness of
> which we are capable, by bringing to its aid everything that we conceive
> to be useful—all the sciences, all the knowledge and skills, and all the the-
> ories that we have acquired, from whatever quarter.[1]

Such a view may prove helpful in the practice of music history as
well, where the sector that produces the most satisfying answer often
depends upon the nature of the question that has been asked—i.e., upon
which "strand" is under examination. A couple of very simple examples may clarify this. If one inquires why it is that certain distinctive
harmonic progressions in Schubert so closely resemble certain exceptional procedures in Mozart, we might note that Schubert had both
motive and opportunity to model his works on those of his predecessor
(that is, he admired them and had access to them); the field that produces this possible explanation is that much-despised one, biography.
Or if we should ask why Beethoven's Opus 105 (Six Themes with
Variations for Piano with optional accompaniment for flute or violin)
is worlds removed in style from his Opus 106 (the *Hammerklavier* Sonata), a plausible reply might point out a clear difference in the intended
audiences—which quickly involves us in elementary issues, at least, of
social history.

Many of the implicit questions posed in this study are of a more
specific kind, such as "What sort of piece is this?" And however one
chooses to characterize the answers to this question—as "criticism,"
"analysis," or whatever—the only extensive and exacting repertory of
terms and concepts that can be brought to the discussion are those of
music theory (broadly considered). The theoretical orientation here is
determinedly eclectic. If the intent at the moment is to show the disposition of thematic matter and tonal areas in a piece, I have used old-
fashioned letter-designations and roman numerals. At other times, as
when the issue at hand is the nature of Chopin's ornamentation of traditional tonal structures, a certain dependence upon the teachings of
Heinrich Schenker (which few American writers on tonal music can
resist these days) will be plain enough.

The present book has been long in coming; for this I apologize to my
friends and colleagues—and publishers—who expected it much sooner.
But rather than to expatiate upon reasons for the delay (the scope and

---

1.   Sir Isaiah Berlin, "The Concept of Scientific History," in W. H. Dray, ed., *Philo-
      sophical Analysis and History* (New York, 1966), 41.

complexity of the subject, the difficulty of writing a synoptic work in a field that is undergoing a sudden explosion of scholarly activity, etc.) it will be more seemly for me at this point to acknowledge those without whose help it would have been much longer. Colleagues to whom I am indebted for suggestions or criticism include Paul Henry Lang, whose voluminous commentary was invaluable, Alan Tyson, Joseph Kerman, Claude Palisca, Allen Forte, David Lewin, Stephen Hefling, and Jan Radzynski. A succession of able students came to my aid at various times; they include Deborah Stein, Irene Levenson, Michael Cherlin, Robin Wallace, Raphael Atlas and, most recently and most extensively, Judith Silber. Carol Plantinga, Elizabeth Dailinger, and Elizabeth Frione helped me prepare a presentable text. People associated with a number of libraries where I worked deserve my thanks for their assistance; of these I wish to mention especially Professor Harold E. Samuel, Kenneth Suzuki, Victor Cardell, Kathryn Mansi, and Warren Call of the Yale Music Library, and Dr. Anthea M. Baird of the Music Library of the University of London. My editor at Norton, Claire Brook, has been both patient and helpful. I am also grateful for a timely research fellowship from the National Endowment for the Humanities in 1979–80. The longest-standing debt of all, however, I owe to my parents, who always encouraged my efforts to do this sort of work; and it was my father, Cornelius A. Plantinga, whose example first awakened in me a love for both music and schoalrship.

ROMANTIC MUSIC

The system of pitch identification used throughout this book is as follows:

C - B   c - b   c' - b'   c" - g"

CHAPTER I

Introduction

The social and cultural roots of Romantic music extend far back into the eighteenth century. Beginning in the mid-1700s profound and irreversible forces were changing the nature of European life. These changes assumed various guises and they occurred at varying rates from one area to another; sometimes by nearly imperceptible stages and sometimes through convulsive upheavals, they ultimately transformed societies, governments, economies, and the mind and sensibilities of an entire continent.

HISTORICAL BACKGROUND

Basic to these changes was an accelerating growth of trade and industry that effected a gradual transferral of power and wealth from a landed nobility to people engaged in commerce. This movement gained momentum earlier in the west than in the east; England led the way, followed closely by France and the Netherlands. England's merchant fleet expanded from about 3,300 ships in 1702 to 9,400 at the time of the American Revolution, and in 1800 the value of her imports and exports was nearly quadruple what it had been in 1750. In France on the eve of the Great Revolution of 1789 the Van Robais textile mills at Abbeville employed some 12,000 workers—an enterprise that contrasted strikingly with the continuing tradition of the small workshop, usually operated by a single family and subject to the restrictions of guilds descended from the Middle Ages.

The Netherlands (or Dutch United Provinces), maritime giant of previous generations, now lagged behind Britain and France in manufacture and trade of goods, but Amsterdam remained a center of banking second to none. In 1777 it was estimated that the Dutch were owed forty percent of England's national debt. There were other centers of political and commercial power in Europe that also shared fully in the new industrial and economic expansion: the free German cities of Frankfurt and Hamburg, and Vienna, imperial center of the Holy Roman Empire, all felt a powerful surge of new commercial activity. Fortunes

The Queen's crystal factory at Creusot, France. Engraving, ca. 1785.

were made and lost very quickly in ventures as diverse as the rum trade, the manufacture of sailcloth, and the printing business.

In past centuries wealth had usually been synonymous with the ownership of land; in the later eighteenth century it became ever easier to join the ranks of the well-to-do through the possession of goods and capital—commodities that change hands readily and flow unhindered around the old barriers of social class systems. A certain power and prestige inevitably attach to wealth, whether it is in the hands of an ancient noble family or of an obscure *ingénu* who has grown rich from, say, the sale of a popular chest ointment. Thus an ever-expanding group of industrialists and bankers, and an even larger class of small merchants, rose to challenge the privilege and prestige of the traditional European aristocracy. For a time there was a tendency for the nobility to absorb, or at least come to terms with, those grown wealthy from business. Merchants' daughters might marry sons of the old aristocracy; in Samuel Richardson's *Pamela, or Virtue Rewarded,* one of the most widely read novels of the time, the middle-class heroine's reward was what society then saw as an ultimate one: she became the wife of a count. There were other paths to amalgamation: in Vienna under the "enlightened monarchy" of Joseph II (1780–90) patents of nobility were sometimes bestowed almost solely on the basis of wealth, and in Venice the names of newly wealthy families were solemnly inscribed into the ancient Golden Book of the city's patrician leadership.

But it was inevitable that social shifts of such magnitude should also sow seeds of discontent with the existing order of things. Governments and laws had seldom been constituted for the benefit of the ordinary citizen—even if he happened to have money. In France the old nobility *(noblesse d'épée)* was immune to the more onerous forms of taxation right up to the Revolution. Only in Britain was the ancient distinction before the law between peer and commoner materially weakened before that time. Throughout Europe there was a spreading discontent among those who felt that government and other existing authority were fundamentally unreasonable, that the old bases for privilege and prestige were simply no longer acceptable.

Such feelings were articulated and powerfully reinforced by the intellectual community of the Enlightenment. The characteristic stance of major writers of the later eighteenth century was one of profound skepticism toward received authority of any kind. Bearing the brunt of their displeasure was the Christian religion with its "irrational" dogma and its clergy whose sensibilities still seemed to be those of the Dark Ages. Edward Gibbon, the greatest historian of the time, could never forgive the Christian Church for its role in undermining and supplanting a pagan ancient civilization. And reflecting upon the centuries when the Church dominated the European landscape, Jean-Jacques Rousseau wrote (this was before his conversion to Catholicism—or his subsequent reconversion to Protestantism), "A revolution was necessary to bring men back to their common sense."[1] The supremely skeptical epistemology of David Hume, however he wished to soften the agnostic consequences of his inquiries, left no rational justification for religious belief, and in America Thomas Paine launched public attacks on Christianity unprecedented in their vehemence.

The principal writers of the Enlightenment agreed less about political theory than they did about religion. Montesquieu, himself a member of the old nobility, declared that

> There are always in a state some people distinguished by birth, wealth or honors; but, if they are confounded with the rest of the people, if they have only one vote like the others, the common liberty will be a slavery for them, and they will have no interest in defending it. . . . Their share in legislation should therefore be proportionate to their other advantages in the state.[2]

Rousseau advanced a very different view in his *Social Contract:*

> Suppose we were to ask: the greatest of all goods, the good that ought to be the goal of every system of laws—of what precisely does it consist?
> It reduces itself, we should find, to two major elements, namely, liberty and equality: liberty, because any personal dependency represents just that amount of resources of which the body of the state is deprived; equality, because liberty cannot subsist without it.[3]

While there is profound disagreement among historians as to the impact of Rousseau's iconoclastic treatise upon subsequent political events in Europe, there can be no doubt that it was very widely read shortly after

1. *Discours sur les sciences et les arts,* in *Oeuvres complètes,* ed. Raymond Gagnebin (Paris, 1959–69), 3, p. 6.
2. *Ésprits des lois,* as cited in R. R. Palmer, *The Age of Democratic Revolution* (Princeton, 1959–64) 1, p. 57.
3. *The Social Contract,* trans. W. Kendall (Chicago, 1954), pp. 75–76.

its publication in 1762, and that it became a kind of secular scripture for the leaders of the French Revolution.

One noted historian has called the last four decades of the eighteenth century the "Age of Democratic Revolution."[4] Struggles for a more democratic form of governance—i.e., one that recognizes a general equality among citizens and professes to operate by the consent of the governed—gathered momentum during this period and came to a climax with the French Revolution and the Revolutionary Wars of 1790–1800. Europe had watched in fascination as the American colonies declared their freedom from the British crown in 1776. And as revolutionary France vowed to lay claim to her "natural frontiers" and to assist "all peoples who rise against their rulers," the tremors of rebellion against constituted government were felt from Naples to Norway, from Amsterdam to Athens.

The assistance offered by revolutionary France consisted more and more of armed invasion, and during the wars that followed, an obscure Corsican army officer, Napoleon Buonaparte, rose meteorically to become France's absolute military commander and ultimately—in direct contradiction to any revolutionary ideals—her Emperor. Resistance to

4.   R. R. Palmer (see n. 2 above).

The storming of the Bastille; a contemporary engraving.

Napoleon's armies as they subsequently spread across Europe was undermined by many who frankly welcomed them as liberators. Although it was short-lived, the French Grand Empire did achieve certain lasting results. Liberals who had been inflamed with the apparent humanitarian ideals of the Revolution, however disillusioned they may have been with the subversion of these ideals by Napoleon, now felt united by a new cosmopolitan bond. So deeply implanted were the new democratic sentiments that efforts of the Congress of Vienna (1814–15) to reconstruct a prerevolutionary Europe were bound to fail. And whatever the temporary successes of a "restoration," the effects of the *Code Napoleon,* a system of laws which struck at the root of old feudal systems of government, were to be seen in the political and social organization of virtually every European nation of the nineteenth century.

MUSIC, PATRONAGE, AND THE PUBLIC

These dramatic alterations in the political and intellectual life of Europe in the later eighteenth century produced a fundamentally new environment for the cultivation of the arts. From time immemorial the arts, as we understand the term, had operated nearly exclusively within the patronage system, and they were subject to both its advantages and its strictures. Painters, sculptors, and even poets had always worked in the direct employ of those having the means to pay for their services. It was only natural that the principal political and ecclesiastical institutions of European society were the leading patrons of the arts. Particularly after the invention of engraving and printing in the fifteenth century, artists, to be sure, had some limited access to a broader clientele. Thus the wood and copper engravings of Albrecht Dürer (1471–1528) were reproduced and sold in modest numbers to his fellow citizens of Nuremberg. But we see this artist in a much more characteristic posture as he paints illuminations for the prayer book of his patron (and friend), the Holy Roman Emperor Maximilian I.

The brilliant flowering of the arts in Renaissance Italy took place under the aegis of two institutions, the Church and the ducal courts. Botticelli and Michelangelo were both in the employ of the Medici family, dukes of Florence; and the work of both can also be seen in the Sistine Chapel in Rome. Torquato Tasso (1544–95), author of *Aminta* and *Gerusalemme liberata,* relied for his livelihood upon the court of the Estes, ruling family of Ferrara. And a century later the fortunes of another writer in another country, the French dramatist Molière, still depended upon his ability to produce satirical comedies that would not prove too offensive to Louis XIV.

Music, perhaps more than any other art, had always been associated with direct patronage. In all but its simplest forms music is a notoriously expensive entertainment: performers must be assembled, instruments procured, parts copied, and, in the case of dramatic music, staging and sets must be arranged. Elaborate musical performances had traditionally enhanced the splendor of festive occasions at court and added solemnity to the great feasts of the Church. In these two institutions, court and Church, European musicians from Machaut to Monteverdi to J. S. Bach necessarily found their places.

Curiously, it was in opera, the most magnificent and costly variety of musical entertainment, that the patronage system first began to disintegrate. In 1637 a public opera house was opened in Venice; here for the first time it was possible for an ordinary citizen to buy a ticket to a staged performance of musical drama, a form of entertainment that was previously the exclusive province of princely courts. The experiment was a success—partly, to be sure, because of heavy support from the affluent local nobility—and by the end of the seventeenth century six opera troupes were simultaneously active in the city. The example set by Venice was followed elsewhere. In the later seventeenth century opera houses opened their doors to the public in Naples, Paris, and Hamburg; in the following century opera became the most popular of all musical entertainments in Europe.

That other most familiar musical institution, the public concert, was longer in coming. Arising from varying forebears in different locations, public concerts were a characteristic product of the changing social patterns of the eighteenth century. In Italy the main progenitors of concert organizations were the academies. These were societies, many dating from the sixteenth or seventeenth centuries, that met to investigate and discuss all sorts of subjects: natural science, history, archaeology, literature, and the arts. A representative scientific academy, for example, was the Accademia del cimento (Academy of Experiment), founded in Florence in 1657. A number of such organizations concerned themselves specifically with music. Among the most famous was Cardinal Pietro Ottoboni's Accademia degli Arcadi (The Arcadian Academy), which met in Rome in the early eighteenth century; among its members were the composers Arcangelo Corelli (1653–1713) and Alessandro Scarlatti (1660–1725). Then there was the Accademia filarmonica of Bologna, which admitted the young Mozart to its membership (upon his completion of certain prescribed compositional exercises) in 1770. As early as 1715 another academy in Rome, this one sponsored by Cardinal Ruspoli, presented weekly concerts under the leadership of the composer Antonio Caldara (c. 1670–1736). In the later eighteenth century it became customary for musical academies to invite audiences to hear regular performances. Thus, by gradual stages, some of these societies were transformed into concert organizations. This patrimony of the public concert was impressed into the Italian language itself; until well into the nineteenth century the ordinary word for "concert" in

A keyboard concert in a Zurich music hall; a 1777 engraving.

Italy (and even in Vienna) was "accademia."

Concerts in the German-speaking states ordinarily arose in more plebeian surroundings. Most prominent among the antecedents of public concerts were the organizations for amateur music making known by the name *collegia musica*. Existing in German and Swiss cities since the beginning of the seventeenth century, these societies gradually began to enlist the aid of professional musicians; and as the quality of their performances improved, they attracted paying audiences as well. In Leipzig in the 1730s J. S. Bach was director of the local *collegium musicum* and provided instrumental music and secular cantatas for its public performances. G. P. Telemann (1681–1767), one of the most admired musicians of his day, founded and directed *collegia musica* in two German free cities, Frankfurt and Hamburg. Both composers became involved in these musical ventures at a time when it became increasingly plain that the future of European music lay not in continuing service to Church and court, but in capturing the interest of the emergent educated, largely middle-class public.

In England, whose commerce and industry outstripped all her competitors in the eighteenth century, a numerous and prosperous middle-class public appeared earlier than elsewhere in Europe, and so did musical institutions designed for it. As early as 1672 public musical performances were organized in various London homes by one John Bannister; shortly thereafter Thomas Britton, a coal merchant, offered regular subscription concerts in his own home. In subsequent years countless concert organizations sprang up as simple exercises in free enterprise:

The Holywell Music Room, Oxford, the earliest public concert hall in Europe, opened in 1748.

the Concerts of Ancient Music in 1710, the Castle Concerts in 1724, and in 1764 the durable series sponsored by the German composers J. C. Bach (youngest son of J. S. Bach) and Carl Friedrich Abel. In addition to these and other concert series (for which admission was normally granted by subscription) there were innumerable individual concerts arranged for the financial benefit of their principal performers. Thus, for most of the second half of the eighteenth century in London, it would have been possible during the height of each season (from January to May) to attend a different concert nearly every evening of the week.

French concerts came into being largely as a substitute for opera. The Concerts Spirituels, most prestigious of all Parisian concert organizations, were founded by the distinguished musician (and chess player) A. D. Philidor in 1725. Originally designed to provide music of a properly devotional nature during Lent and other holy days when opera was prohibited, the Concerts Spirituels soon offered a dazzling variety of vocal and instrumental music, both French and foreign, and continued as a standard of excellence in musical performance until the Revolution. There were many other concerts in Paris. The fabulously wealthy Le Riche de la Pouplinière sponsored a long-lived semipublic series beginning in the 1730s; among his musical directors were the composers J.- P. Rameau, Johann Stamitz, and F.- J. Gossec. Then there were the concerts of the Société des Enfants d'Apollon (beginning in 1784), those of the Loge olympique—this was the organization that commissioned the "Paris" symphonies of Haydn in 1786—and many others.

In the later eighteenth century a "public," in the modern sense of the term, took form. This public not only wielded a distinct political and economic power, but also had certain collective needs, desires, and ideas;

the very expression "public opinion" appeared in several languages at this time. The growth of public opera and public concerts was perhaps the most conspicuous symptom of the response of musicians and musical institutions toward a fundamental shift in the constitution of European society. But there were other signs as well. As increasing numbers of people enjoyed the means and leisure to indulge an interest in the arts in imitation of the nobility, there was a dramatic growth of music making in the home. This in turn encouraged brisk activity in ancillary musical industries such as the manufacture of instruments. Most in demand for the cultivation of home music were the versatile instruments that could serve in either solo or accompanimental roles. One such instrument, the guitar, enjoyed an enormous vogue all over Europe shortly after mid-century. But keyboard instruments exceeded all others in popularity; their great range and adaptability to all kinds of musical textures, thick or thin, contrapuntal or homophonic, had always made them ideal utility instruments. In the second half of the eighteenth century, as the pianoforte gradually supplanted the older harpsichord and clavichord, additional dimensions of expressiveness in the new instrument made it irresistible to amateur players.

There were essentially two types of pianos in the eighteenth century, called (with some imprecision) "Viennese" and "English." Viennese pianos had a light and rapid action, with a very distinct, somewhat

A piano made by Könicke of Vienna in 1798.

piercing, "nasal" sound. Mozart praised these pianos handsomely in 1777 when he tried them out in the Augsburg workshop of Johann Andreas Stein. During the following decades Vienna became the center of a burgeoning industry in the construction of pianos after Stein's model. Some of the makers whose names we know are J. W. Schanz, Anton Walter (who made a piano for Mozart), Stein's son Andreas, and his son-in-law, Johann Andreas Streicher, whose work is said to have benefited from Beethoven's advice. Piano manufacture in England began with the immigration of several German instrument makers who fled Saxony during the Seven Years' War (1756–63); Johannes Zumpe set up shop in London about 1760, and he was followed by a number of his countrymen, best known of whom are August Pohlmann and Burkhart Tschudi (or, as the English spelled his name, Shudi). In 1781 a young Scotsman, John Broadwood, joined Tschudi's workshop; some eight years later he married his employer's daughter, took over the firm, and established the Broadwood piano manufactury, which has survived until the present day. The "English" piano (the mechanism of which really came from Italy by way of Germany) produced a sound more powerful and sonorous but less bright than that of the Viennese instrument. This fundamental design became the basis for a series of developments that ultimately produced the percussive and velvety sound of the nineteenth-century pianoforte—a sound that is among the most vital and pervasive features of Romantic music.

Another business that inevitably benefited from an enlarged literate public and a growing amateur participation in the arts was that of music printing. About 1765 the Leipzig printer Immanuel Breitkopf invented a new method of typesetting that made it possible to publish keyboard music and simple songs in volume at a substantially lower price. This contributed to the decline of the old methods of engraving and of commercial hand-copying by publishers, and to an expanding circulation of printed music for amateur consumption. In the later eighteenth century collections of moderately easy music for voice with keyboard accompaniment, or for keyboard with accompaniment of violin or flute, or for keyboard alone, constituted the bulk of the offerings of all the major music publishers in London, Paris, Leipzig, and Vienna. The publication of "professional" music, such as full orchestral scores, was rare until the second quarter of the nineteenth century.

At the end of the eighteenth century these music publishing houses began to address their clientele in another way: through musical periodicals. The first of this new sort of journal that was to become a familiar feature of nineteenth-century musical life was the *Allgemeine musikalische Zeitung* (General Musical Newsmagazine), founded in 1798 by Breitkopf und Härtel of Leipzig. Its mixture of articles on musical subjects, reviews of published scores and concerts (and, occasionally, books), correspondence reports from other cities, musical supplements, and publishers' advertisements quickly established the pattern for a host of similar journals that sprang up in all the principal cities of Europe. Between 1798 and 1848 some two hundred and sixty such publications appeared. Most of them were put out by music publishers and virtually all were addressed to the new musical public: the growing segment of the population that attended operas and concerts, and that might be persuaded to purchase musical scores and instruments for domestic use.

The alterations we have seen in European society of the later eighteenth century encouraged musicians to shake loose from their courtly or ecclesiastical employers; now for the first time it gradually became possible for them to make a living by offering their services to the public as free agents. Again, this happened earlier in England than elsewhere. In London of the 1770s dozens of players, such as the violinist Wilhelm Cramer, the oboist J. C. Fischer, and the cellist J. Crosdill, carried their instruments from one evening concert to the next; on Tuesdays and Saturdays they played in the orchestra at the opera in the Haymarket, and supplemented their incomes by giving lessons (particularly during off-season). This shift in orientation is plainly visible, too, in the careers of the most famous composers of the age. Mozart's quarrels with his employer, the Archbishop Colloredo of Salzburg, ended with the composer's resignation in the spring of 1781; the remaining ten years of his life were spent in free-lance composing, performing, and teaching in Vienna. But musical life there still depended very largely upon noble or ecclesiastical support, and Mozart's failures in attracting this support led him to a pauper's grave. Beethoven, though dependent upon commissions and stipends from the aristocracy, was never again in the direct employ of anyone after he left the court at Bonn for Vienna in 1792, and for him the venture of living as a free artist was increasingly successful. Haydn lived in both worlds; he continued as kapellmeister for Prince Nikolaus Esterhazy as his published compositions gained him increasing international attention. Then in the 1790s he enthusiastically embraced the life of the public musician as he conducted his symphonies at concerts in London.

The changing pattern of musicians' lives, like that of society as a whole, was irreversible. For the musician living in the Napoleonic era and after, a secure and reasonably lucrative position under the old patronage system was scarcely an available option. There were precious few courts or churches left in Europe with the means or prestige to maintain elaborate musical establishments or to attract important composers. Even the venerable Opéra in Paris, which traditionally operated under the direct control of the crown, was let out in 1831 as a commercial concession to the entrepreneur Louis Véron. There were, of course, some exceptions to the rule: Johann Nepomuk Hummel (1778–1837) spent the latter part of his life as court conductor at Weimar, Louis Spohr held a similar position at the court of Kassel, Liszt spent many of his later years at the Weimar court, and Wagner (without holding an official position) was able to extract lavish financial support from the eccentric King Ludwig II of Bavaria. But even for these four musicians, as for all others of their century, genuine success always meant public success, and all made their reputations in the concert hall and the publicly oriented opera theater.

THE COMPOSER'S TRAINING

The virtual collapse of the patronage system in the arts exerted an influence upon musicians' lives that extended to their earliest education in the craft. Within the court and Church in earlier times, musical establishments had tended to perpetuate themselves by providing early training and experience for aspiring musicians. Given a degree of security by these institutions, fathers would often pass on skills, and sometimes positions, to their sons or nephews. Thus in the seventeenth and early eighteenth centuries we must often distinguish among two or more illustrious composers with the same name: the Gabrielis of Venice, the Scarlattis of Naples and Rome, the Couperins and Philidors in France, and an enormous clan of Bachs in Thuringia and Saxony. Many other highly successful composers born in the eighteenth century, such as Mozart and Beethoven, learned their craft as children within musical families. Most composers in the nineteenth century came to music later in life and by a different route. Schubert's and Chopin's fathers were schoolmasters. Schumann was the son of a bookseller, and his family steered him firmly toward the study of law; Berlioz' father, a doctor, was determined that his son follow in his footsteps. Dvořák's family were innkeepers, and expected him to follow that trade. The identity of Wagner's father is not entirely clear, but in any case neither of his parents was a musician.

One nineteenth-century composer may be mentioned as a prominent exception to the prevailing pattern: Felix Mendelssohn, though descended from distinguished scholars and bankers rather than musicians, received a systematic early training in music, beginning with lessons from his very talented mother. And as late as 1838 Schumann wrote this candid comparison of Mendelssohn's background with his own:

> I know perfectly well how I compare to him as a musician: I could still study under him for years. But he could also learn some things from me. If I had grown up under circumstances similar to his, intended for music from childhood, I would surpass them all.[5]

---

5.   *Jugendbriefe von Robert Schumann,* ed. Clara Schumann (Leipzig, 1886), p. 283.

Schumann's early training was much more typical of the nineteenth-century composers' than was Mendelssohn's. Usually they had much less early exposure to a common body of musical craft and technique than did composers of previous centuries; and therein lies one explanation for the dissipation of a "central style" in the nineteenth century, and for the extraordinary diversity of Romantic music.

MUSICAL AESTHETICS

The intellectual climate of the early nineteenth century urged upon the musician—particularly upon the composer—a new and special view of himself and his work. The notion that music was one of a group of "fine arts," distinct from all the other kinds of activities in which people engage, was of relatively recent vintage. During the eighteenth century the idea of a system of fine arts became gradually more articulate in the writings of Charles Batteux (*Les Beaux Arts réduits à un même principe,* 1746), Alexander Baumgarten (*Aesthetica,* 1750), and Immanuel Kant (*Critique of Judgment,* 1790). In the earlier nineteenth century it was universally assumed that it made sense to talk about "art" or "the fine arts" as if their constituent members—literature, sculpture, architecture, painting, music, and perhaps even landscape gardening—were in some important ways similar. And philosophers of the time, such as Kant, Schelling, Hegel, and Schopenhauer, set themselves in earnest to the task of defining the principles, goals, and significance of the arts as a cohesive community.

For writers of the time aesthetics was a very serious business because art suddenly seemed more important than ever before. After a systematic undermining of the old bases for religious belief by influential figures of the later eighteenth century, the "reasonableness" of sanguine Enlightenment doctrines offered in their stead provided only a temporary refuge. The ravages of revolution and war from 1780 to 1815 left the European intellectual community in considerable disarray and disillusionment. Some, such as Friedrich Schlegel and François Chateaubriand, turned again to religion; at this time the Wesleyan movement made great strides in England. For others, especially in Germany, art took on the status of a kind of secular religion; it was widely thought to provide an access to a level of reality that transcended the accidents and restrictions of a person's ordinary existence. Hegel, in his *Lectures on Aesthetic* (published posthumously in 1835–38), portrayed the arts as the embodiment of *Geist,* for him a primal entity that encompasses the mind of man and of the universe itself. Shelley, in a bold and romantic vision of the poet—himself—as a reincarnation of Apollo, wrote:

> I am the eye with which the Universe
>> Beholds itself and knows itself divine;
> All harmony of instrument or verse,
>> All prophecy, all medicine is mine,
> All light of art or nature;—to my song
>> Victory and praise in its own right belong.[6]

Music came to occupy a central place in such exalted (and occasionally somewhat murky) portrayals of the role of art and the artist. In 1813 E. T. A. Hoffmann declared that instrumental music

> is the most romantic of all the arts—one might almost say, the only genuinely romantic one—for its sole subject is the infinite. The lyre of Orpheus opened the portals of Orcus—music discloses to man an unknown realm, a world that has nothing in common with the external sensual world that surrounds him, a world in which he leaves behind him all definite feelings to surrender himself to an inexpressible longing.[7]

Some six years later, in his *Die Welt als Wille und Vorstellung,* the philosopher Schopenhauer expressed with less metaphor something of what Hoffmann apparently had in mind. Like all philosophers in the Platonic tradition, Schopenhauer believed that the world exhibits various levels of "realness." Objects as we see and hear and feel them around us are mere phenomena—the data of sense perception—and unreliable as indications of the true nature of things. At the other extreme, as the most "real" entity in the universe, Schopenhauer posits a kind of elemental, blind, powerful force called the Will, which is represented in varying degrees of imperfection in the people, objects, ideas, and events we encounter in this world. The most adequate representation of the Will is the traditional Platonic Idea, that original pattern or mold thought to underlie all phenomena we experience. But even this is inaccessible to us—except through art, for art allows us to see beyond the particulars of things to this more fundamental level of reality. And one art, namely music, circumvents even this step; for it is, according to Schopenhauer, the "immediate representation of the Will." Thus in this formulation art does duty for both metaphysics and religion. Truth and beauty, as in Keats's *Ode on a Grecian Urn,* become one. And music offers us a glimpse of the most fundamental nature of the universe, unknowable in any other way.

Now it is unlikely that many early nineteenth-century musicians were very conversant with these literary and philosophical evaluations of their profession (Schopenhauer's work, first published in 1819, was scarcely noticed even by philosophers until mid-century.) Yet Schumann, for one, was an avid reader and admirer of Hoffmann; and ideas about

6. *Hymn of Apollo,* in *The Complete Poetical Works of Percy Bysshe Shelley,* ed. Thomas Hutchinson (London, 1960), p. 613.

7. Oliver Strunk, ed., *Source Readings in Music History* (New York, 1950), pp. 775–76.

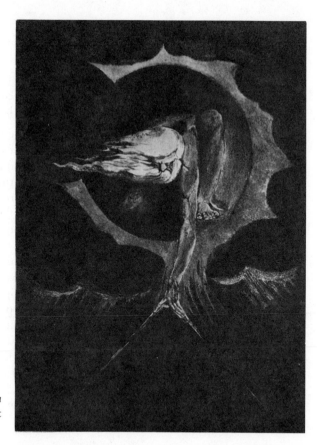

The frontispiece for *Europe, a Prophecy* by the romantic poet and artist William Blake.

music similar to those of Hoffmann and Schopenhauer were heard on all sides, particularly in Germany, from at least 1810 onward. The quotation we have taken from Hoffmann was first printed in the *Allgemeine musikalische Zeitung* in 1810 in a review of the Fifth Symphony of Beethoven; that the composer was at least vaguely aware of Hoffmann's writings about him is shown by a letter he addressed to the author in 1820. But long before that, it is clear, Beethoven entertained lofty—nearly romantic—views about the mission of the composer as artist. In 1801, suffering miserable health and alarming loss of hearing, Beethoven repaired to the rustic village of Heiligenstadt outside Vienna to rest and meditate. Driven in his despair nearly to suicide, he refrained from taking his own life, he tells us in the remarkable "Heiligenstadt Testament," because of the transcendent importance of continuing his work as an artist:

> Oh you men who think or say that I am malevolent, stubborn or misanthropic, how greatly do you wrong me. You do not know the secret cause which makes me seem that way to you . . . I must live almost alone like one who has been banished, I can mix with society only as much as true necessity demands. . . . What a humiliation for me when someone standing next to me heard a flute in the distance and *I heard nothing*, or someone heard a *shepherd singing* and again I heard nothing. Such incidents drove me almost to despair, a little more of that and I would have ended my life—it

was only *my art* that held me back. Ah, it seemed to me impossible to leave the world until I had brought forth all that I felt was within me.[8]

This view of the artist as a kind of Promethean figure in society, as a firebringer from the gods to man—and yet rejected by that society he is bound to serve—gained wide currency among musicians and music critics of the earlier nineteenth century. Flattering in a way to the composer, it also placed upon him a special burden to prove worthy of his calling. Such a view opposed "art" to "entertainment," and contributed in this period to a widening gulf between "serious" and "popular" music. And it forced the composer to think about certain very hard questions: for whom was he writing his works—for himself and a select company of connoisseurs, or perhaps for an enlightened posterity? Or for the anonymous public whose approval could bring popularity and perhaps a living wage? The careers of many leading nineteenth-century composers, Weber, Berlioz, Schumann, Liszt, and Wagner among them, show signs of their struggle with this problem. One sign is the extraordinary volume of apologetic, didactic, and downright propagandistic prose written by composers of the time (all five just mentioned were prolific authors); if success and livelihood depended upon the public, perhaps that public might be swayed by timely appeals and explanations.

HISTORICISM IN MUSIC

Another constituent of intellectual life that exerted a powerful influence upon composers and their music in the earlier 1800s is the phenomenon sometimes called "historicism." During this period many humanistic endeavors reflected an altered perspective on history and a drastic reassessment of the achievements of previous ages. The civilization of the Middle Ages, formerly despised, was subject to appreciative reinterpretations. There was a new admiration for writers such as Dante, Shakespeare, and Cervantes, who stood outside the pale of a central classical tradition canonized by French academic standards. This movement also had profound and permanent consequences for music.

Works of art whose very existence, in the deepest sense, depends upon continual recreation through performance tend to have rather a short life expectancy. Music by its very nature is more fragile than, say, durable objects like sculptures and paintings. In the later Middle Ages musical styles remained current for such a short time that the notation of one generation would often have been difficult for musicians of the next to decipher; musical manuscripts only a few decades old were fre-

---

8.   As quoted in Alexander Thayer, *Thayer's Life of Beethoven,* rev. Elliot Forbes (Princeton, 1964), pp. 304–5.

quently dismembered to make flyleaves and bindings for new volumes. In 1477 the influential composer and music theorist Johannes Tinctoris, chaplain to King Ferdinand I of Naples, wrote:

> Although it seems beyond belief, there does not exist a single piece of music, not composed within the last forty years, that is regarded by the learned as worth hearing.[9]

For the three centuries after Tinctoris, works of musical art remained, on the whole, as ephemeral as he said they were. There were some exceptions. In the Catholic Church the medieval plainsong was preserved in one form or another for everyday use. And the polyphonic compositions of sixteenth-century composers such as Palestrina, approved by the Council of Trent (1545–63), were retained and imitated within the Church—coexisting with current styles—well into the nineteenth century.

But aside from this, Europeans seldom listened to music of earlier generations. Operas, in particular, were typically composed, performed a few times, and forgotten. It is significant that even at so tradition-ridden an institution as the Paris Opéra, early eighteenth-century revivals of late seventeenth-century works entailed extensive revision and modernization. The composer through the eighteenth century characteristically produced his music for Sunday's church service, for the concert next week, or for the opera performance one month hence. Handel in London, Bach in Leipzig, and Haydn at Esterháza were all expected to deliver a continuous succession of new works—or, if necessary, of only slightly used ones, suitably touched up for the occasion.

In the earlier nineteenth century, as the effect of a certain historicism was felt in music, all this was radically changed. Concerts of older music sprang up all over Europe in the second and third decades of the century. Ordinarily they were organized by musical scholars such as François Fétis in Paris, Raphael Kiesewetter in Vienna, and Carl von Winterfeld in Berlin. But more telling in its effect upon the musical public at large was the gradual extension backward in time of the ordinary public concert repertory. Sometimes this happened simply because the works of certain composers, such as Beethoven's symphonies, never dropped from the repertory. In England, the same was true of some of the oratorios of Handel, Haydn's two oratorios, and to some extent, his "London" symphonies.

A more specific exercise of historicism is seen in the systematic nineteenth-century revivals of neglected earlier music. Most spectacular of these recoveries, and most far reaching in its consequences for music in the Romantic era, was the "Bach revival." In his lifetime J. S. Bach was regarded as a provincial organist and choirmaster, little known outside

9.   Strunk, ed., *Source Readings,* p. 199.

An excerpt from the manuscript of Bach's *St. Matthew Passion* used by Mendelssohn for his performance in 1829. His pencil markings reflect nineteenth-century taste.

of Germany. He left behind very few musical publications, and his manuscripts, put up for sale in large lots after his death in 1750, brought next to nothing. The forty-eight preludes and fugues of *The Well-Tempered Clavier* circulated in manuscript copies in the later eighteenth century; the young Beethoven practiced them in Bonn, and Queen Charlotte in London is said to have had a copy made for her use. The publication of this collection about 1800 marked the beginning of a powerful reawakening of interest in Bach's music. Johann Nikolaus Forkel's pioneering biography appeared in 1802, and many of the other keyboard works were resurrected in the first three decades of the new century; then in 1829 Mendelssohn conducted the *St. Matthew Passion*—in a well-doctored version—to celebrate the one-hundredth anniversary of the work's first performance. By this time the Bach movement was a central fact of German musical life. In 1827, C. F. Zelter, Mendelssohn's teacher and musical adviser to Goethe, compared it to the revival of Shakespeare and Calderon.

The recovery of older styles and their injection into the mainstream of musical life in the early nineteenth century had crucial implications for the Romantic composer. In the first place it presented him with an unprecedented challenge: his compositions were forced into competition not only with those of his contemporaries, but with the most revered works of the greatest masters of preceding generations as well. When

Schubert, Schumann, and Brahms expressed discouragement at the prospect of writing quartets and symphonies after Beethoven, there was nothing abstract about their complaint; Beethoven's symphonies still sounded in concert halls throughout Europe, comprising a continuing standard by which all others were measured. To a lesser extent the same held true for composers of organ music after Bach and composers of oratorios after Handel. The traditional categories of instrumental music were not very extensively cultivated by younger composers in the early decades of the nineteenth century. Symphonies, sonatas, and concertos were to a considerable extent displaced by a proliferation of smaller types of indeterminate lineage: music related to the dance, fantasies, ballades, intermezzos, and the like. Most of the earlier Romantics longed to distinguish themselves in the traditional large forms; but the forms which had become traditional still seemed to be the property of the composers who had made them so.

If Romantic composers sometimes felt intimidated by the giants of the eighteenth century, the continuing *actualité* of historical styles also served as a forceful positive stimulus. The influence of the newly revived music of Bach in the Romantic musical consciousness is hard to overestimate. Beethoven, Schumann, and Brahms were strongly indebted to this model for the formation and nurturing of their styles. Composers of the early nineteenth century tended to see Bach as an isolated genius, as a singular and inexhaustible wellspring of technical excellence, but also as an originator of the ineffable poetic qualities they saw in the music of their own time. Commenting upon a collection of keyboard music of the seventeenth and eighteenth centuries, Robert Schumann could not resist invoking comparisons with Bach:

> In a period when all eyes are fastened with redoubled intensity upon one of the greatest creators of all times, Johann Sebastian Bach, it might also be fitting to call attention to his contemporaries. In respect to composition for organ and piano, no one of his century, to be sure, can compare with him. To me, in fact, everything else appears in comparison to the development of this giant figure as something conceived in childhood.[10]

And in a letter to a friend he provided an explicit statement—or perhaps an overstatement—of the Romantic composers' debt to Bach:

> Mozart and Haydn had but a partial and one-sided knowledge of Bach. No one can guess how Bach would have influenced their productivity, had they known him in all his greatness. The profound powers of combination, the poetry and humor of recent music have their origin largely in Bach. Mendelssohn, Bennett, Chopin, Hiller, all the so-called romantics (I mean the Germans, of course) are in their music much closer to Bach than Mozart was; all of them have a most thorough knowledge of Bach.[11]

10. *Neue Zeitschrift für Musik,* 6 (1837): 40.
11. *Robert Schumanns Briefe, neue Folge,* ed. Gustav Jansen (Leipzig, 1904), pp. 177–78.

Schumann and other Romantic musicians made a very specialized, and perhaps self-centered use of the history they knew. They held up historical figures such as Bach, Beethoven, and even Palestrina as mirrors in which they could see little more than reflections of themselves. And in some cases—for example, in the well-known *Ave Maria* of Gounod, based upon the first prelude of *The Well-Tempered Clavier,* or in Grieg's arrangements of piano sonatas of Mozart—historical models have been disfigured through Romantic re-creation. But in the growth of Romantic musical style as a whole, the nourishment provided by older music—particularly by Baroque compositional practice—was healthy and indispensable. The expressive harmonies that were disseminated as a *lingua franca* of nineteenth-century music would have been unlikely without the chromaticism and secondary dominant harmonies of Bach. The integrity of structure and part writing aspired to by composers from Schubert to Reger, from Berlioz to Saint-Saëns, was a natural concomitant of the continuing presence of authoritative models from the past. The collective musical memory of forty years described by Tinctoris was doubled and tripled and quadrupled as the nineteenth century advanced. A heightened consciousness of history informed and in some ways transformed the musical culture of the entire era.

"ROMANTIC"

At several points in the discussion thus far we have made conventional use of the term *Romantic* as a general designation for the dominant strains of music in the nineteenth century. Concepts and names such as these, whether intended as descriptions of style, as canons of taste, or as designations for epochs, are of course blunt instruments whose defects have been amply exposed. This is true not only in music, but also in literary and art criticism, from which most such style and period designations have been derived. In a famous article of 1924 Arthur O. Lovejoy contemplated the checkered history of "romantic" and concluded that, having meant so many different things, it no longer means anything at all.[12] But if attacks such as those of Lovejoy and others urge upon us a salutary caution in using these terms, they are much too firmly implanted in our language to be rooted out. In music criticism the word "romantic" has been in regular use since the very beginning of the nineteenth century, when it often meant something like "abstract" or "indefinite" or "imaginative"—or simply "modern" as opposed to "ancient." Music was almost by definition a romantic art for writers such as W. H. Wackenroder (1773–98), E. T. A. Hoffmann (1776–1822), and G. W. F.

---

12. "On the Discrimination of Romanticisms," *Papers of the Modern Language Association,* 39 (1924): 229–53. Reprinted in *Essays in the History of Ideas* (Baltimore, 1948).

Hegel (1770–1831) because its materials were abstract and its referents indistinct—and because the traditions of European music they knew had no models in antiquity. In the 1830s and 1840s the term was less popular among the adherents of romanticism, such as Schumann and Berlioz, than among its opponents, who carefully preserved its pejorative connotations of "irrationality" and "disorder." Yet from both sides there was at least a modicum of agreement as to the nature of the styles and ideas intended by the word: a preference for the original rather than the normative, a pursuit of unique effects and extremes of expressiveness, the mobilization to that end of an enriched harmonic vocabulary, striking new figurations, textures, and tone colors. In a general way, these are still the attributes in the music of the nineteenth century (and sometimes of the later eighteenth century) that we tend to call "romantic."

"Romantic" is often paired with its supposed opposite, "classic" (from the Latin *classicus,* "of the first class"). This word has been used in literary criticism since the seventeenth century to invoke a complex of established values—particularly the purported norms of antiquity such as balance, restraint, observance of decorum, and the like. "Classic" was installed in the vocabulary of music criticism somewhat later than "romantic"; it was in the 1820s and 1830s, apparently as an offshoot of the "classic–romantic" disputes raging in German literary circles, that this term came to designate the dominant musical styles of the later eighteenth century. In 1836 the influential Leipzig music critic Amadeus Wendt may have been the first to distinguish a "classic period" consisting almost exclusively of the works of Haydn, Mozart, and Beethoven[13]—a formulation that, for better or worse, was to survive until the end of the century and beyond.

But it is probably a mistake to think of a "classic period" in later eighteenth-century music—however constituted—followed by a romantic revolt against it. All attempts at separating and classifying the interwoven strands of history must involve some degree of oversimplification. But the difficulties here lie deeper. It is becoming increasingly clear that stylistic traits we associate with "classic" music—an implied metrical regularity, a circumscribed diatonic harmonic syntax, a largely homophonic texture, and slow harmonic rhythm—persist in large sectors of musical practice in the nineteenth century. And characteristics we think of as "romantic" are easily found in the eighteenth: in the keyboard works of C. P. E. Bach, for example, in Haydn's so-called *Sturm und Drang* symphonies (c. 1768–73), and in some of the instrumental music of Mozart and Clementi of the 1780s. The music historian Friedrich Blume has posited an underlying "stylistic canon" compris-

---

13. *Ueber den gegenwärtigen Zustand der Musik besonders in Deutschland und wie er geworden. Eine beurtheilende Schilderung* (Göttingen, 1836), pp. 3–7.

ing the familiar elements of musical style (metrical ordering, harmony, melody, and formal structure) by which European music of the late eighteenth and nineteenth centuries is fundamentally united:

> Classicism and Romanticism, then, form a unity in music history. They are two aspects of the same musical phenomenon just as they are two aspects of one and the same historical period.[14]

However one may wish to qualify Blume's very positive assertion, there can be little doubt that "romantic" musical styles emanate from and comingle with "classic" ones. There is no isolable time and place where one leaves off and the other begins—and hence no clearly preferable point from which to embark upon a study of Romantic music. Here we shall begin with the compositions of the maturing Beethoven written in Vienna directly after his move there in 1792. Beethoven's works left their imprint upon the precept and practice of music in the nineteenth century as did those of no other composer. Romantic musicians with near unanimity claimed him as their own. Yet in so doing they acknowledged another patrimony; for however tortuous the course of his later style, the roots of Beethoven's music remained firmly imbedded in the compositional procedures of Viennese Classicism.

14.   Friedrich Blume, *Classic and Romantic Music. A Comprehensive Survey,* trans. M. D. Herter Norton (New York, 1970), p. 124.

CHAPTER II

Beethoven in Vienna, 1792–1808

In 1792 the twenty-two year old Beethoven came to Vienna from the provincial Rhineland court town of Bonn to fashion a career as both composer and virtuoso pianist. Only one of many ambitious music students who each year flocked to the political and cultural center of the Holy Roman Empire to pursue their professions, Beethoven might seem to have had no special advantages to recommend him to aristocratic Viennese musical circles. He was the son of an ordinary court musician, and Alexander Wheelock Thayer, his principal biographer, describes a young man of unprepossessing appearance:

> small, thin, dark-complexioned, pockmarked, dark-eyed. . . . His front teeth, owing to the singular flatness of the roof of his mouth, protruded, and, of course, thrust out his lips; the nose too was rather broad and decidedly flattened, while the forehead was remarkably full and round—in the words of Court Secretary Mähler, who twice painted his portrait, a "bullet." [1]

And though he made some effort to acquire the requisite social graces—he bought some fine silk stockings and arranged to take dancing lessons—his behavior was thought at times uncouth, and over the years became increasingly eccentric.

But Beethoven came highly recommended; he was sponsored by the Elector-Archbishop Maximilian Franz of Cologne, uncle of the current emperor, Leopold II, and he arrived with the blessing of another of the most eminent nobility of Bonn, Count Waldstein. Such backing eased his entry into Viennese social circles. It also helped gain him acceptance as a pupil of the most admired composer in Europe, Joseph Haydn, with whom Beethoven studied for about a year (from late 1792 to late 1793) between the older master's two triumphant sojourns in London. These lessons seem to have consisted mainly of the standard didactic fare for musicians of the time, such as species counterpoint in the style of the *Gradus ad Parnassum* (1725) of Johann Joseph Fux. The busy Haydn

---

1. Alexander W. Thayer, *Thayer's Life of Beethoven,* ed. Elliot Forbes (Princeton, 1964), p. 134.

A romantic idealization of Beethoven by Leonid Pasternac.

was apparently not very conscientious about Beethoven's lessons, and Beethoven, for his part, steadfastly avoided any show of gratitude toward his famous teacher; relations between the two remained distant until Haydn's death in 1809. Beethoven had two other teachers during his early years in Vienna: Johann Georg Albrechtsberger, with whom he continued his study of counterpoint, and the court kapellmeister Antonio Salieri, who coached him in Italian declamation.

It was by his extraordinary prowess at the keyboard that Beethoven really made his way in Vienna. His playing was soon applauded by many of the great and powerful of the city: at the home of Prince Lichnowsky, for example, and of the Baron Van Swieten, who was seen as the city's ultimate arbiter of musical taste.[2] Later, in 1795, he began to appear in public concerts as well. As was customary at musical occasions in noble residences, Beethoven performed his own compositions. But even more admired was his marvelous ability to improvise. In 1791, while still attached to the court at Bonn, his keyboard improvisation had made an indelible impression upon the musical author and critic Carl Ludwig Junker:

> I heard him extemporize in private; yes, I was even invited to propose a theme for him to vary. The greatness of this amiable, light-hearted man,

2. Gottfried van Swieten (1734–1803) was a cultivated diplomat and librarian, author of opera librettos, and amateur composer. In 1777, upon his return from assignment in Berlin, he brought with him scores of the music of Handel and Bach—the latter then virtually unknown in Vienna. In succeeding years, he introduced Vienna's leading composers, Mozart and Beethoven among them, to many forgotten masterpieces of the Baroque era.

as a virtuoso, may in my opinion be safely estimated from his almost inexhaustible wealth of ideas, the altogether characteristic style of expression in his playing, and the great execution which he displays. I know, therefore, no one thing which he lacks, that conduces to the greatness of an artist.[3]

A favorite entertainment of the music-loving Viennese nobility of the time was the staging of competitions between famous virtuosos (Mozart had engaged in one with Muzio Clementi in 1781 for the amusement of the Emperor Joseph II). Beethoven repeatedly entered the lists in such contests, pitted against the foremost keyboard players of the day. Soon after his arrival in the Imperial city, he joined combat with the veteran pianist Abbé Joseph Gelinek (1758–1825). According to Carl Czerny (later Beethoven's student), Czerny's father one day "met Gelinek tricked out in all his finery. 'Whither?' he inquired. 'I am asked to measure myself with a young pianist who is just arrived; I'll work him over.' A few days later he met him again. 'Well, how was it?' 'Ah, he is no man; he's a devil. He will play me and all of us to death. And how he improvises!' "[4] In succeeding years Beethoven engaged in similar contests—usually, it is reported, with similar results—with the pianists Joseph Wölfl (1773–1812) and Daniel Steibelt (1765–1823).

The highly placed musical homes in which Beethoven registered his pianistic triumphs were frequently open to him socially as well. One of

The Lobkowitz Palace; an engraving by Vincenz Reim.

3.   Thayer-Forbes, p. 105.
4.   Ibid., p. 139.

the first houses in which he lived in Vienna was that of Prince Lichnowsky, who became his foremost patron. Later he enjoyed both the
friendship and professional support of Prince Joseph Lobkowitz, Count
Andreas Razumovsky, and his young pupil the Archduke Rudolph. As
a piano teacher he was introduced into certain less exalted families with
whom he tended to form strong attachments that often included a
romantic interest in a young female pupil; two such families were the
Brunsviks and the Guicciardis. And the two surviving members of his
own immediate family, his brothers Caspar Carl and Nikolaus Johann,
followed him to Vienna in 1794 and 1795.

EARLY STYLISTIC GROWTH: PIANO SONATAS

Beethoven's musical imagination, in the early Vienna years, was firmly
tied to the newest of the keyboard instruments, the piano. Throughout
most of his career, in fact, the distinctively innovative and characteristic
features of his music were usually first apparent in the piano works.
And if we wish to select a single category of music that best represents
the tortuous and majestic development of his style, it would certainly
be the solo piano sonata.

One modest example of Beethoven's departure, in the 1790s, from
the norms of Classic style, and from his own earliest manner, can be
seen in the piano sonatas of Opus 2, finished in 1795.[5] The second
movement of the first sonata of this set is an adaptation of a movement
from the Piano Quartet in C, WoO 36, for piano, violin, viola, and
cello, composed in 1785. This very early movement consisted of two
statements of the principal melodic material, separated by unrelated
passagework for each of the "accompanying" instruments, followed by
a coda that reverts to scalewise figuration, now given to the piano.
When he set about to revise this piece in 1795, Beethoven was obviously
displeased with the utterly regular construction of the opening melodic
material (Example II–1a): 4 + 4 measures, each group of four subdivid-
ing into 2 + 2, and each set of two measures closing with a routine feminine cadence. In Op. 2, No. 1, that second group of four measures is a

---

5.   This is the first set of sonatas that Beethoven provided with an opus number. Dur-
      ing the eighteenth century the designation of compositions by opus number was
      ordinarily a haphazard business, often left to the whim and fancy of publishers. But
      Beethoven was usually careful in this regard, giving them only to pieces he con-
      sidered deserving, and assigning them for the most part in chronological order.
      Beethoven's works without opus numbers are identified by "WoO" numbers after
      the thematic catalogue of Georg Kinsky and Hans Halm, *Das Werk Beethovens, the-
      matisch-biographisches Verzeichnis seiner sämtlichen vollendeten Kompositionen* (Munich:
      Henle, 1955).

Example II–1

a. BEETHOVEN, Piano Quartet WoO 36, second movement, mm. 1–8

b. BEETHOVEN, Piano Sonata Op. 2, No. 1, second movement, mm. 1–8

seamless unit, bound together by a dramatic rise in register (Example II–1b). By this seemingly minor alteration a very ordinary theme acquires a distinctive profile, and thus transformed serves as the basis for a reconstructed movement whose parts are all clearly related to the whole. The piano quartet was an example of one of the most common musical genres of the later eighteenth century, the "accompanied keyboard sonata," in which the piano is very prominent and the other instruments decidedly subsidiary. When Beethoven remodeled this movement from WoO 36, he eliminated the accompanying string instruments. The accompanied keyboard sonata was falling out of fashion by 1795; in both setting and style, Beethoven's revised movement shows a turning away from the ordinary practices of the eighteenth century.

There are other ways, too, in which the earlier piano sonatas deftly alter the familiar devices of eighteenth-century musical style. In the famous *Pathétique Sonata,* Op. 13, for example, the left-hand accompaniment to the opening Allegro is Beethoven's version of the most humdrum of current keyboard accompaniments, the broken-octave or *murky* bass. Example II–2a shows the *murky* in its native habitat in one of Muzio Clementi's less memorable early sonatas, the first movement of Op. 2, No. 2 of 1779. Example II–2b illustrates how Beethoven adapts this familiar accompanimental formula—an adaptation for keyboard of the orchestral *Trommelbass*—to his own purposes; the harmonic com-

Example II–2
a. CLEMENTI, Sonata Op. 2, No. 2, first movement, mm. 1–11

b. BEETHOVEN, Piano Sonata Op. 13, first movement, mm. 11–19

plication of mm. 17–18 (particularly the striking cross-relation between A♭ in m. 17 and A♮ in m. 18 that refers back to the E♭–E♮ ambiguity in m. 13) adds a dramatic new expressive dimension to a well-worn keyboard idiom.

The piano sonata before Beethoven had typically consisted of three movements (fast–slow–fast) or, after the Italian manner, of only two (usually fast–faster). In his first dozen or so sonatas with opus numbers, Beethoven alternated between the usual three movements and an expanded form with the added minuet or scherzo borrowed from the contemporary symphony and string quartet. Then with the Sonata Op. 26 of 1800–01 he struck out in a radically new direction, beginning with an Andante theme and variations, and substituting a lugubrious funeral march (subtitled "on the death of a hero") for the usual slow movement. The opening movement once again shows Beethoven restlessly experimenting with inherited procedures. Variations were a decidedly popular genre from which little of substance or originality was expected. But here, from the theme with its novel soprano-tenor doubling through one variation after another, Beethoven presents a dazzling array of unorthodox abstractions upon the original material. In the *minore* variation his absorption with the possibilities of a syncopated rising figure[6]

An autograph page from the first movement of Beethoven's Sonata Op. 26, showing the *minore* variation.

6. This rhythmic configuration, in which the tones of the melody consistently fall offbeat, was known in the eighteenth century as *tempo rubato;* in the nineteenth century it came to denote a more irregular, improvisatory freedom in performance.

even leads him to a temporary abandonment of both the melodic and harmonic premises of the theme. And among the several novel keyboard figurations found in this movement, one is particularly deserving of comment: in the final variation the melody is placed in the alto register with a triadic accompaniment below and a measured trill above, in striking prophecy of similar writing in his middle and late keyboard works such as the finales of the sonatas Op. 53, 109, and 111.

In reminiscences about his association with Beethoven, Czerny reports:

> About the year 1800, when Beethoven had composed his op. 28,[7] he said to his intimate friend Krumpholz: "I am not very well satisfied with the work I have thus far done. From this day on I shall take a new way." Shortly after this appeared his three sonatas, op. 31, in which one may see that he had partially carried out his resolve.[8]

Czerny remembered this a good many years after the fact—and his memory was in any event not especially reliable. Yet what he says has about it a certain ring of authenticity. If Beethoven did not literally embark upon a "new way" of composition around 1800, at least the processes of experiment and maturation we have noted in his work of the 1790s accelerated noticeably. At the end of 1798 the central body of his oeuvre was heavily weighted toward his own instrument: two piano concertos, two cantatas, four string trios, three piano trios, two sonatas for piano and cello, three for piano and violin, and about ten for piano solo.[9] But now, as one indication of the change in Beethoven's course, the piano began to relinquish its grip on his musical imagination. The String Trios Op. 9, published in 1798, were described by Beethoven himself in a dedicatory letter as "la meilleure de ses oeuvres"—a not altogether unbelievable claim, for these trios, unlike most contemporary compositions of the genre, are works of weight and substance. Then between 1798 and 1800 Beethoven embarked upon an ambitious new project that obviously was for him a matter of the utmost consequence: the composition of the six String Quartets Op. 18.

THE STRING QUARTET OP. 18, NO. 6

Of all genres of chamber music current in the last decades of the eighteenth century, the string quartet bore the exclusive connotations of seriousness, learning, and lofty connoisseurship. It had first been invested

7.   The Piano Sonata in D major, the *Pastorale*.
8.   O. G. Sonneck, ed., *Beethoven. Impressions of Contemporaries* (New York, 1926), p. 31.
9.   This list does not include a considerable number of very youthful works, such as the Piano Quartets, WoO 36, the *Kurfürsten Sonaten* for piano, WoO 47, and a good many songs and variations for piano.

with these associations in Haydn's remarkable Quartets Op. 20 (1772), with their profound new expressiveness and (in three of them) earnest, elaborate fugal finales. In much of his Opus 18, however, Beethoven was apparently less indebted to these or to any of Haydn's quartets than to the mature works of Mozart, particularly the six quartets that he published in 1785 with a dedication to Haydn. It seems clear that the A-major Quartet of Beethoven's Opus 18 was modeled after Mozart's Quartet in A major, K. 464, which Beethoven is known to have copied out in its entirety.[10]

The sixth quartet of Opus 18 is thought to have been composed last, partly because sketches for it are found in Beethoven's papers in conjunction with those for the large-scale Piano Sonata Op. 22 of 1799–1800. It differs from the other quartets in this collection in the surprising addition of an Adagio introduction to the Allegro finale (in chamber compositions and symphonies of the period, slow introductions to first movements were much more common). And this is no ordinary Adagio. Subtitled "La Malinconia" ("melancholy"), it proceeds in audaciously intense harmonies that threaten the limits of the tonal system;

10.   Cf. Joseph Kerman, *The Beethoven Quartets* (New York, 1967), pp. 58–63.

Example II–3: BEETHOVEN, String Quartet Op. 18, No. 6, fourth movement, mm. 1–20

long-held chords played alternately *piano* (or *pianissimo*) and *forte* combine with extreme registral shifts to produce a maximum of strain and discontinuity (see Example II–3). The first twenty measures describe a circuitous movement from B♭ major to the dominant of E minor, the crucial shift occurring in mm. 11–12, where the outer tones G and F expand by semitone to F♯.[11] Though the following diminished seventh chords create a certain tonal chaos, there are threads of continuity: alternating in different octaves between the first and second violins is an ascending line F♯–G–A–B–C, while the F♯ itself reappears in mm. 14 and 16, preparing to anchor the following B-major sound, dominant to E. This bold harmonic excursion shows only one facet of the broad range of Beethoven's musical exploration around 1800. In the same movement fragments of the Adagio are abruptly inserted into the mainstream of the following effervescent Allegro, creating a juxtaposition of vividly contrasting materials falling well outside the usual norms of Classic style.

THE *TEMPEST SONATA,* OP. 31, NO. 2

Such violent contrast becomes an explicit principle of structure in the Piano Sonatas Op. 31 of 1801–2; these are the first compositions, we will remember, that Czerny mentioned specifically as representative of Beethoven's "new way." The Sonata Op. 31, No. 2 in D minor, called *The Tempest*[12] (ARM 1),[13] reveals its spirit of nonconformity at the very beginning: Beethoven sets diametrically opposed Largo and Allegro snippets side by side, separated only by questioning fermatas. The initial Largo statement is nothing more than an arpeggiated A-major chord in first inversion; the Allegro is a nervously agitated eighth-note figure with alternating repeated tones and stepwise motion, aiming first toward D minor, then G minor, and finally resting upon the dominant of D

11. The harmony in m. 11 is a dominant seventh to C minor. But Beethoven resolves the chord as if it were an augmented sixth—as if the topmost F were written as an E♯. This produces a B-minor chord that easily becomes, by sharping the D, a dominant of E minor.

12. Of the various programmatic titles appended to Beethoven's piano sonatas only two, *Pathétique* (Op. 13) and *Lebewohl* (Op. 81a) originated with the composer. The name *Tempest,* applied to Op. 31, No. 2, derives from a report of Beethoven's younger friend and amanuensis Anton Schindler: "One day when I was telling the master of the great impression that Carl Czerny's playing of the D minor and F minor sonatas opp. 31 and 57 had made upon the audience, and he was in a cheerful mood, I asked him to give me the key to these sonatas. He replied, 'Just read Shakespeare's *Tempest.*'" Anton Felix Schindler, *Beethoven as I Knew Him,* ed. D. W. MacArdle (Chapel Hill, 1966), p. 406.

13. The acronym ARM, which is used throughout this volume, refers to the *Anthology of Romantic Music,* edited by Leon Plantinga and specifically created to serve as a score resource for this book.

The title page of the first edition of Beethoven's Sonatas Op. 31, Nos. 1 and 2, printed by Nägeli of Zurich.

minor. But the following Largo, now a C-major arpeggio in first inversion, contradicts our rapidly forming orientation toward D minor, suggesting instead, by analogy, a turn in the direction of F major. This too is wiped out in the ensuing Allegro, which proceeds with great energy and increasing resolution toward a cadence in D minor in m. 21. Everything so far sounds improvisatory, as if Beethoven were sitting at his piano, tentatively exploring the potentialities of his two bits of material now in one tonality, now in another.

We shall understand better what happens next if we explore for a moment what Beethoven's listeners would ordinarily *expect* of such a movement. The term "sonata form" (or "sonata-allegro form") was adopted in the nineteenth century to denote a usual sequence of events in the first movement, and sometimes in other movements, of eighteenth-century compositions of the sonata type that included trios, quartets, symphonies, and other multimovement intrumental pieces. In descriptions of sonata form beginning in the mid-nineteenth century, the events defining this form were usually thought to be melodies or themes.[14] Thus, the first movement of a sonata was typically said to consist of three parts: an exposition, in which two principal themes—preferably contrasting in character—are stated, a development, in which these themes are subjected to various transformations, and a recapitulation, in which they are restated. Of less importance to such a definition by themes, as this explanation goes, are certain harmonic characteristics. The principal theme in the exposition defines the key of the piece; the subsidiary theme is in a contrasting key, normally dominant or relative major; and in the recapitulation both appear in the original tonic. The development is expected to modulate from one key to another with relative freedom.

14. The music theorist most influential in the formulation of this "textbook" description of sonata form was Adolph Bernhard Marx, in his *Die Lehre von der musikalischen Komposition* (Leipzig, 1837–47).

It has become increasingly clear in recent years that this traditional formulation misrepresents both the theory and practice of the musical repertory it is designed to describe. Sonata form is a linear descendant of the much older binary form common to many types of dance music (until well after Beethoven's death it was routinely said to consist of two parts, not three). What is reasonably predictable about both is a general *harmonic* scheme, as the following diagram of a usual binary structure shows:[15]

$$\|: I \quad \mathord{\sim\!\!\sim\!\!\sim}V \quad :\|:(V)\mathord{\sim\!\!\sim\!\!\sim\!\!\sim}I \quad :\|$$

Much less reliable, in both binary and sonata-form movements, is the number, type, and placement of themes; Mozart's sonata-form movements often dispense them by the handful, while Haydn frequently contents himself with variants of one. A sonata-form movement with several themes, melodies, or motives—these are designated here by lower-case italic letters—might have a shape such as this, for example:

(Introduction)$\|: I \quad \mathord{\sim\!\!\sim\!\!\sim}V \quad :\|:(V)\mathord{\sim\!\!\sim\!\!\sim\!\!\sim} I \qquad\qquad :\|$ (Coda)

 a, b   *c, d, e   c, a, d, e*   *a, b, c, e*

 Exposition   Development   Recapitulation

An introduction to such a movement is normally in a slow tempo and thematically little related to what follows; the coda usually has the same tempo as the movement as a whole, and is constructed of materials drawn from it. The modulatory section in the exposition that leads to the contrasting tonality is often called the bridge.[16]

After his improvisatory, harmonically errant beginning, Beethoven continues the first movement of his Sonata Op. 31, No. 2, in m. 21, with the first harmonically stable material so far presented. But this music soon turns modulatory, leading to A minor (the dominant minor—the relative major, F, would have been more usual), in which three other well-defined motives appear (in mm. 41, 55, and 75). When the exposition is restated, the listener discovers that the opening material is included in the repetition; hence it is no ordinary introduction. But Beethoven has woven this introductory music into the fabric of his movement in more conclusive ways: for all the subsequent motives,

---

15.   The roman numerals refer to key areas; the wavy lines indicate modulatory passages.

16.   There are a considerable number of descriptions of sonata form from the late eighteenth century; fullest and most carefully worked out is that of Heinrich Christoph Koch, *Versuch einer Anleitung zur Composition* (Leipzig, 1782–93). Good summaries of views of musical form in this period can also be seen in Leonard Ratner, "Harmonic Aspects of Classic Form," *Journal of the American Musicological Society*, 2 (1949): 159–68; and William Newman, *The Sonata in the Classic Era* (Chapel Hill: 1963), pp. 26–35.

one in D minor, and three in A minor, are related to the beginning Largo or Allegro or both. The D-minor one (let us call it *a*) is divided between the bass and soprano registers; the figure below derives directly from the Largo arpeggio, the one above (more distantly) from the conjunct motion of the Allegro. In mm. 41 ff. *(b)* the right hand plays a motive obviously derivative of the Allegro, while in the left hand an apparently accompanimental figure subtly refers back to the upper motive from *a*. This winding stepwise motive, derived from the Allegro, is then explicitly stated in m. 55 *(c)*, and both the arpeggiated Largo figure and the conjunct Allegro motion can be seen in the upper part of m. 75 *(d)*. This accounts for all the thematic matter of the exposition, and it all proceeds from those enigmatic opening measures.

As if to emphasize once again the germinal character of his double-motive beginning, Beethoven starts both the development and recapitulation with this material (mm. 93 and 143). In the latter case the Largo arpeggio is twice extended with an expressive single-line, recitative-like melody (mm. 144–48 and 155–58) that dwells upon the descending stepwise movement characteristic of the Allegro motive (note especially the striking juxtaposition of the two in mm. 147–49). This produces a further implicit interpenetration of materials, this time between those thoroughly unlike the opening motives. The second appearance of the Allegro at this point is also transformed (mm. 159–70), and to the same end: it has taken on the chordal and arpeggiated motion of the Largo. Now, as the original key of D minor is reestablished, Beethoven thought it unnecessary to recapitulate *a*—partly, no doubt, because it had figured prominently in the development section, but also, it seems, because its function of fusing together the two original motives had just been well taken care of. The entire movement could be represented this way:

m. 1	21		41	55	75		93		99		122	143		171	185	205	
‖:(i)〜〜 i		〜〜〜v				:‖	〜〜	♯III	〜〜(i)		〜〜〜〜〜i						‖
L A	*a*		*b*	*c*	*d*		L		*a*		*c*	L recit.	A	*b*	*c*	*d*	
a l							a					a	l				
r l							r					r	l				
g e							g					g	e				
o g							o					o	g				
r													r				
o													o				
Exposition							Development					Recapitulation					

What is new and striking about this movement from a formal point of view is the substitution of harmonically erratic, heterogeneous bits of material for a tonally stable first theme, and the use of these unpromising fragments as the structural basis for a movement of a marvelously integral design. If any doubt remains about Beethoven's intentions as to the function of those opening materials, the beginning of the second movement (shown in Example II–4a) should dispel them: once again

Example II–4: BEETHOVEN, Piano Sonata Op. 31, No. 2
  a. second movement, mm. 1–5

  b. third movement, mm. 1–8

  c. third movement, mm. 43–51

an arpeggio in a low register is answered by a conjunct figure above. And in both this movement and the finale (see Examples II–4b and c) the music is persistently haunted by references to these seminal motives.

Beethoven's piano music and piano playing from this period never failed to impress his listeners with the novelty of its keyboard figurations. The *a* motive in the first movement of Op. 31, No. 2, for example, in which the melodic matter is divided between lower and upper registers with a rapid oscillating accompaniment in the middle, is quite unlike standard Viennese piano writing of the time; it sounds to us— and probably sounded to contemporary local audiences—characteristically "Beethovenian." But many of his special figurations were anticipated in the music of an older keyboard virtuoso much admired by Beethoven, Muzio Clementi. A passage from Clementi's Sonata Op. 13, No. 6, published in 1785, shows a configuration markedly similar to that of Beethoven's *a* motive (see Example II–5).[17] Certain other hallmarks of Beethoven's earlier pianistic style may be traceable to Clementi. One is the extensive use of melodies and passages in octaves and broken octaves, as in the Clementi Sonatas Op. 2, No. 2 (1779) and Op. 7, No. 3 (1781), and in Beethoven's Op. 2, Nos. 1 and 3 (1795), Op. 7 (1796–97), Op. 10, Nos. 1 and 2 (1796–98), and many others.

Example II–5: CLEMENTI, Piano Sonata Op. 13, No. 6, third movement, mm. 24–32

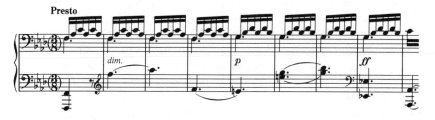

Having survived his intense personal crisis at Heiligenstadt in 1802, Beethoven, now thirty-one years old, moved back into Vienna and entered upon a period of productivity as rich as any artist has ever enjoyed. This was a time of frenetic activity for him. He moved restlessly from one apartment in Vienna to another, even living for a time in the opera house, the Theater-an-der-Wien, as lodging was included in his contract to produce an opera for performance there. Summers were regularly spent in the country near Vienna. Whether in the city or country, and whatever the season, Beethoven took long daily walks during which he ruminated over his compositions, sometimes jotting down ideas in a pocket-sized sketchbook. His pupil Ferdinand Ries describes a country hike that must have occurred about 1805:

> Once we were taking a walk and lost our way so completely that we did not get back to Döblingen, where Beethoven lived, until eight o'clock. Throughout our walk he had hummed and, in part, howled, up and down the scale as we went along, without singing any individual notes. When I asked him what it was he replied: "The theme for the final Allegro of the Sonata [in F minor, Op. 57] has occurred to me." When we entered the room he ran to the piano without taking off his hat. I sat down in a corner and soon he had forgotten me. Then he raged on the keys for at least an

17.   The melody shown in Example I–5 in its original form at the beginning of Clementi's movement is remarkably like the theme Beethoven published as a contradanse (WoO 14 of 1800–1,) and then used in his *Prometheus* ballet music, his Piano Variations Op. 35, and the finale of the *Eroica* Symphony.

hour, developing the new Finale of this Sonata [which appeared in 1807] in the beautiful form we know. At last he rose, was surprised to see me still there and said: "I cannot give you a lesson today; I still have work to do."[18]

During this period Beethoven's music was often heard in the salons of the Viennese nobility, sometimes with the composer at the piano. And in April of 1803 a "benefit concert" consisting entirely of his music was given at the Theater-an-der-Wien; the works performed included the First and Second Symphonies, the Third Piano Concerto, and the first version of the oratorio *Christus am Oelberg*. Finding his music ever more in demand, Beethoven was continually in negotiation with publishers in several cities, frequently quarreling with them about publication rights, correctness of editions, and payments to the composer.

During these years, Beethoven produced a prodigious series of masterpieces. In 1803–4, he wrote the *Kreutzer Sonata,* Op. 47, the Third Symphony *(Eroica),* and the *Waldstein Sonata,* Op. 53. The following two years were even more productive: they saw the first two versions of the opera *Fidelio,* the *Appassionata Sonata,* Op. 57, the *Razumovsky String Quartets,* Op. 59, the Fourth Piano Concerto, Op. 58, the Fourth Symphony, and the Violin Concerto, Op. 61. And in 1807–8, he completed the *Coriolan Overture,* the Fifth and Sixth Symphonies, the Cello Sonata Op. 69, and the Piano Trios Op. 70.

THE *EROICA SYMPHONY*

In the works produced during this period of six years, the most salient features of Beethoven's "middle" style were established, and a standard, unassailable in its authority, was set for all composers of large-scale instrumental pieces for the rest of the nineteenth century and beyond. The *Eroica Symphony,* composed in 1803–4, may be considered the first of that series of imposing monuments that so inspired and intimidated Beethoven's followers. Heroic even in its physical proportions, this was probably the longest symphony written up to that time. It was also without precedent in rhythmic energy, in the scope of its developmental procedures, and in its protracted building of powerful climaxes.

The first movement of the *Eroica Symphony* (ARM 2) begins with an enigmatic, seemingly fragmented exposition. Its harmonic direction, at least, is vaguely what we might expect. After unarguably establishing the tonic key of E♭ with two statements of the opening motive (mm. 3 and 15), Beethoven feints toward the dominant (mm. 18 ff.), only to reestablish the original key in m. 37 with another resounding assertion of the original melody. In m. 45 an abrupt shift is made to the dominant

18. Sonneck, pp. 52–53.

B♭ in conjunction with contrasting new material, but we are not yet allowed to rest comfortably in the new key: the active, brilliant, modulatory passage beginning in m. 65 sounds exactly like bridge material, and its inexorable conclusion in B♭ (m. 83) establishes this point as the "real" beginning of the dominant key area. From here to the end of the exposition no other key challenges the supremacy of B♭; the sequence of events might be represented this way:

m. 1		3	23		37	45	56	65		83	109	117		123		133	
I	‖: I	(V)—			I	V	V	wwwwwwww		V	V	www	www		wwwwV :‖
(Introduction)		*a*	*b*		*a*	*c*	*d*	*e*		*f*	*a′*	*g*		*h*		*i*	

More unorthodox than its harmonic scheme is the number and nature of melodic motives in this exposition. Two brusque *forte* tonic chords do duty for an introduction, followed by the triadic first melody played in the bass range by the cellos. An unobtrusive accompanimental G in the violins gradually becomes melody in m. 10, but this melodic strand is virtually absorbed into the cadence that follows.[19] If this opening thematic material seems curiously incomplete and without definition, it is followed by eight or nine other bits of material that sound equally inconclusive. After the enormously energetic introduction to the dominant key area (mm. 73ff.), for example, we are given only eight measures of stability and calm (motive *f*); immediately the tonality shifts toward minor, and another section of powerful registral and dynamic build-up begins.

Another salient feature of this exposition is a determined disruption of meter. Beginning in m. 25 harmonic and melodic interest are minimal, and the listener's attention is focused upon powerful accents falling regularly in patterns of two beats in contradiction to the 3/4 meter. The effect of this rhythmic displacement is hemiola, a metrical ambiguity in which a group of six beats (two measures here) is implicitly divided two ways: into two groups of three, and three groups of two. At one other place in the exposition (mm. 128ff.) Beethoven again indulges in this kind of disruption, now utterly suppressing all other constituent elements of the music as the hemiola rhythm is hammered out upon a single repeated chord. Such rhythmic and metrical disturbances are all the more keenly felt in that they occur against a background of surprisingly regular metrical periodization. Four-measure phrases predominate strongly in this exposition. The first clear violation of this pattern (discounting the opening chords) occurs with the addition of two "extra" measures, mm. 35–36, in order to increase the tension of a dominant preparation for the return of the original melody in its original key.

---

19. Most satisfying as a conclusion to the melody might be the F–E♭–D–E♭ in the second oboe; in his sketches for this movement, however, Beethoven showed the line ascending from B♭ to E♭ in the flute and clarinet.

Two other occurrences of six-measure groups serve similar purposes: in mm. 77–82 and 103–8 they prolong the dominant preparation for triumphant points of arrival in the tonic key (now B♭).

Beethoven's development section makes extensive use of those cryptic melodic and rhythmic ideas broached in the exposition. Sometimes they appear in combination: in mm. 198ff. the motive a goes with e, and in the disappointingly abbreviated fugato passage in mm. 236ff. a leaping figure reminiscent of b is heard in conjunction with the rhythm of c. This b motive is then continued in the violins as harmonic motion comes to a virtual standstill, the entire orchestra playing harmonically unstable repeated chords (six measures each) with powerful offbeat accents (mm. 248ff.). Twenty-six measures of this generates excruciating tension. But Beethoven goes one step further: in mm. 276ff. the offbeat chords, mercilessly repeated in alternation between the wind and string sections, become sharply dissonant (the pitches are A–C–E–F). Some thirty-five years later the decidedly avant-garde composer and critic Hector Berlioz (1803–69) still found such procedures shocking:

> The rhythm is particularly remarkable by the frequency of syncopation and by combinations of duple measure, thrown, by accentuation of the weak beat, into the triple bar. When, with this disjointed rhythm, rude dissonances come to present themselves in combination, like those we find near the middle of the second repeat, where the first violins strike F natural against E (the fifth in the chord of A minor)[20] it is impossible to repress a sensation of fear at such a picture of ungovernable fury. It is the voice of despair, almost of rage.[21]

Abruptly in m. 280 all this tension is dissipated in a deft resolution to the remote key of E minor, where we hear a placid, seemingly new, sololike melody in the first oboe. It is unusual for Beethoven to present entirely new material in his development sections, and here all the more so in that the oboe melody is ushered in with such titanic uproar and urgency. But the very full sketches that survive for this movement show us that Beethoven had something else in mind. One such sketch is of the sort sometimes called a "continuity draft"—it consists of a single-line (or occasionally double-line) notation of considerable stretches of the movement. At the point of the "new oboe melody" Beethoven writes not that melodic line, but the one heard simultaneously in the second violins and cellos (Example II–6).

20. This sonority might better be described as a Neapolitan sixth (i.e., a ${}^6_3$ chord on the lowered second degree, F) with the E retained as a suspension from the previous chord. Thus the entire passage makes harmonic sense:

m. 278 280 284 286 288

e: ♭II⁶   V⁷   i

21. Hector Berlioz, *A Critical Study of Beethoven's Nine Symphonies*, trans. Edwin Evans (London, 1958), p. 42.

Example II–6

This melody is readily identifiable as a "filled-in" version of motive *a,* and the oboe line is then only a prominent counterpoint to it. Once more, a most audacious gesture has in the last analysis a solid rationale—and contributes again to an overriding goal of musical unity.

This development section is more than one hundred measures longer than the exposition, and as if in whimsical reference to the players' eagerness to be done with it, Beethoven anticipates the recapitulation with the famous "false entrance" four measures early in the second horn.[22] Once the recapitulation is underway it proceeds in fairly orthodox fashion, with material originally presented in dominant now transposed into tonic. But the size and momentum of the development were altogether too overwhelming to allow this monumental movement to end with such a simple restatement. With an extraordinary tonal slide from E♭ to D♭ to C,[23] Beethoven launches into a coda nearly as long as the exposition. Full of developmental procedures, this coda continues to exploit the potentialities of the original materials of this movement—now prominently including the "filled in" version of *a* together with its singular counterpoint—until the movement closes with the same startling abruptness with which it began.

For the second movement Beethoven writes another piece of unprecedented weight and proportions, in this case with a descriptive title, *Marcia funebre* (Funeral March). Audiences of Beethoven's time would have had no trouble recognizing the style of a movement such as this: it is plainly modeled after grand dirges played at the funerals for heroes

22. While the violins play a persistent tremolo on the dominant, the horn enters tentatively with motive *a* in tonic (m. 394). Ferdinand Ries describes a rehearsal of the symphony at Prince Lobkowitz's palace with Beethoven conducting:
     In the first Allegro occurs a mischievous whim *(böse Laune)* of Beethoven's for the first *[sic]* horn; in the second part, several measures before the theme recurs in its entirety, Beethoven has the horn suggest it at a place where the two violins are still holding a second chord. To one unfamiliar with the score this must always sound as if the horn player had made a miscount and entered at the wrong place. At the first rehearsal of the symphony, which was horrible, but at which the horn player made his entry correctly, I stood beside Beethoven, and, thinking that a blunder had been made I said: "Can't the damned hornist count?—it sounds infamously false!" I think I came pretty close to receiving a box on the ear. Beethoven did not forgive the slip for a long time.
     As translated in Thayer-Forbes, p. 350.

23. The motion to C major further cements a relationship with the development section, whose initial stable tonality is also C major. Beethoven seems to have recalled this passage eighteen years later when he virtually quoted it in the first movement of the Piano Sonata Op. 110.

Example II–7
a. GOSSEC, *Marche lugubre,* piano transcription, mm. 1–16

b. BEETHOVEN, *Eroica Symphony,* second movement, mm. 1–8

of the Revolution and Napoleonic wars. These marches, as well as the music for elaborate Republican *fêtes* staged in Paris in the 1790s, were written by the leading French composers of the day such as François Joseph Gossec (1734–1829), Étienne-Nicolas Méhul (1763–1817), and Luigi Cherubini (1760–1842). Example II–7a is the beginning of Gossec's *Marche lugubre,* composed for a memorial service for soldiers killed putting down an antirevolutionary uprising in Nancy in 1790; Example II–7b is the opening of Beethoven's *Marcia funebre.* Both show the very slow tempo, minor mode, imitations of drumrolls, and pervasive dotted rhythms—related ultimately to the solemn grandeur of the French overture—characteristic of Republican funeral music.[24] But Beethoven's movement goes far beyond its prototypes; a secondary motive in E♭ (the relative major to the principal key, C minor) and a contrasting middle section in C major provide additional materials for a movement of intricate and imposing architectural design.

After a lightning-swift Scherzo–Trio featuring precarious solo roles for the three horns and some very insistent hemiola effects, Beethoven begins his finale with an outraged flurry in the strings, coming to a dead stop on a series of dominant chords. Once more he shows a proclivity for extravagant introductory gestures, and once more that which follows is fragmentary in the extreme, consisting of what we later recognize as only a skeletal bass line to the principal melody. A couple of leisurely variations of this bass line prolong the mysterification until the "real" melody at last enters in m. 75. Beethoven was apparently fond of this melody and bass; he had already used both as thematic material for his Piano Variations Op. 35 of about one year previous and for several earlier pieces.[25] A transformed and vastly expanded revision of the piano piece, this energetic movement, combining elements of theme-and-variations and rondo, makes a fittingly forceful conclusion to this unique symphony.

The "hero" Beethoven originally intended to celebrate in the *Eroica* was Napoleon. Schindler claims that Count Bernadotte, Marshal of France and later King of Sweden and Norway, while in Vienna first suggested to Beethoven that he compose a musical work in honor of the French commander.[26] Both Ries and Schindler relate the now-famous anecdote about Beethoven's subsequent disillusionment upon learning that Napoleon had arranged to have himself crowned Emperor in May 1804. Here is Ries' version:

> In this symphony Beethoven had Buonaparte in his mind, but as he was when he was First Consul. Beethoven esteemed him greatly at the time

---

24. The funeral march in Beethoven's Piano Sonata Op. 26 is in a very similar style, and at some points bears a startling resemblance to Gossec's piece.

25. See above, p. 37, fn. 17.

26. Schindler, pp. 11–12. Schindler's account apparently does not agree with the actual dates of Bernadotte's stay in Vienna.

An autograph title page for the *Eroica,* on which the dedication to "Bonaparte" has been erased.

and likened him to the greatest Roman consuls. I as well as several of his more intimate friends saw a copy of the score lying upon his table, with the word "Buonaparte" at the extreme top of the title page, and at the extreme bottom, "Luigi van Beethoven," but not another word. Whether, and with what the space between was to be filled out, I do not know. I was the first to bring him the intelligence that Buonaparte had proclaimed himself emperor, whereupon he flew into a rage and cried out: "Is he then, too, nothing more than an ordinary human being? Now he, too, will trample on all the rights of man and indulge only his ambition. He will exalt himself above all others, become a tyrant!" Beethoven went to the table, took hold of the title page by the top, tore it in two and threw it on the floor. The first page was rewritten and only then did the symphony receive the title: "Sinfonia eroica."[27]

Whatever credence we wish to grant this story, it is clear that the title of the symphony was changed at some point before the parts were published in 1806 under the title *Sinfonia eroica.* A surviving autograph title page (apparently for a set of parts made by a copyist) reads as follows: "Sinfonia grande / intitolata Bonaparte / 804 in August / del Sigr. / Louis van Beethoven" (Grand Symphony entitled Bonaparte 1804 in August by Mr. Ludwig van Beethoven). The words "intitolata Bonaparte" have been so assiduously erased that a hole was torn in the paper. It may be that the change in title was partly dictated by reasons less idealistic than those Ries suggests. For in 1805 Napoleon's troops captured Vienna, scattering the nobility and occupying their palaces—including that of Beethoven's faithful patron Prince Lobkowitz, to whom the symphony

27. As translated in Thayer-Forbes, pp. 348–49.

was dedicated. At this time and even after the withdrawal of the French it would hardly have been politic for Beethoven to pay such a handsome tribute to the invader. But like so many Europeans with liberal sentiments, the composer seems not to have lost all admiration for Napoleon. In a letter to the Leipzig publisher Breitkopf und Härtel of August 26, 1804—i.e., about three months after the incident Ries reports—Beethoven writes, "the title of the symphony is really Bonaparte."[28]

FIDELIO

The French occupation of Vienna had a direct bearing on another of Beethoven's major musical projects from this period: the production of his only opera, *Fidelio*. Republican France even provided the source for its libretto. *Léonore, ou l'Amour conjugal* was a dramatic "rescue opera" with text by J. N. Bouilly; it was performed in Paris in 1798 with music by Pierre Gaveau. This libretto was translated into German by Joseph von Sonnleithner, and Beethoven began setting it to music early in 1804. Various *contretemps* forced postponement of work on the opera until mid-1805, however, and it was not until late autumn of that year that it was staged at the Theater-an-der-Wien. Meanwhile Napoleon's troops were advancing steadily eastward across Bavaria; Salzburg fell on October 30, and early in November the nobility of Vienna, from the empress

The Theater-an-der-Wien, where Beethoven's *Lenore* was first performed; a contemporary engraving.

28.   Emily Anderson, ed. and trans., *The Letters of Beethoven* (New York, 1961), p. 117.

downward, began to flee. On November 11 the French entered the imperial city, and Napoleon himself took up residence in Schönbrunn Palace on the 15th. Beethoven's opera opened on the 20th and played for only three nights to almost empty houses, the audience consisting mainly of a few French soldiers wandering in and out.

The plot of *Fidelio* reflects the French appetite for terrifying tales of dungeons, executions, and hairbreadth escapes—events that were all too real in the days of the Revolution. Jean-François Lesueur's *La Caverne* (1793) and Luigi Cherubini's *Les Deux Journées* (1800) are earlier operatic examples of the type. In *Fidelio,* the hero Florestan, languishing in a dungeon, is about to be murdered on orders of the prison commander Don Pizarro, by the jailer Rocco. But Florestan's wife Leonore, assuming the name "Fidelio" and masquerading as Rocco's male assistant, interposes herself between Pizarro and the intended victim. At this crucial moment the minister of the state, Don Fernando, arrives and sets all things aright. Other events and characters are subsidiary; there is the usual pair of ingénu-servants (Jacquino and Marcellina) and the inevitable amatory confusion owing to the ambiguity of Leonore's gender.

The opera adheres in many ways to the conventions of French opéra comique and German Singspiel.[29] Spoken text alternates with closed-form arias and ensembles, and two of the three acts in the 1805 version end with multisectional finales. We cannot help but note certain dramatic weaknesses. Almost nothing happens in the original first act; the spoken dialogue tends to be grimly and unrelentingly serious, the alternating set pieces lightheartedly amorous or even comic; Don Pizarro is a featureless villain, and Don Fernando is unknown to the audience until he enters as a *deus ex machina* in the last act. Contemporary critics were also displeased with Beethoven's music: "As a rule there are no new ideas in the vocal pieces," complained the correspondent for the *Allgemeine musikalische Zeitung* of Leipzig; "they are mostly too long, the text repeats itself endlessly, and finally the characterization fails remarkably."

At the end of 1805 Beethoven's friends Prince Lichnowsky, Stephan von Breuning, the tenor Joseph August Röckel, and others met with the composer to persuade him to revise the opera. Capitulating only after some resistance, Beethoven shortened the first two acts, combining them into one, and substantially rewrote parts of the original third act with the necessary textual revisions done by von Breuning. On March 29 and April 10, 1806, this second version of the opera was given, and this time the critics were somewhat kinder. But Beethoven, displeased with the performances and suspecting deliberate sabotage of his work by certain "enemies," withdrew it from the stage. It was not until 1814

---

29. These varieties of opera are described below in Chapter VI.

A scene from *Fidelio* in an engraving published in 1815.

that he was able to face once again the sore subject of his opera. In May of that year, with yet many more revisions (new text this time was provided by Georg Friedrich Treitschke) the opera was revived with Beethoven conducting at the first performance, and it was a resounding success. It is this revision that is regularly performed today.

One point in *Fidelio* that seems to have been problematic for Beethoven in all three versions is the first appearance of Florestan, near death in the dungeon. Though necessarily a principal character (and a tenor at that), he is not seen until the beginning of the final act. Here he sings a few measures of recitative, followed by an aria, "In des Lebens Frühlingstagen," whose importance the composer emphasized by incorporating its melody into three of the four overtures intended for this opera. Beethoven's sketches show how mightily he struggled with this melody, and all the versions he wrote leave an impression of a certain tentativeness (Example II–8). Both the movement from A♭ to C♭ (mm. 8–10) and the cadences on "meine Pflicht hab' ich getan" sound vaguely awkward. Nor can this cantabile, reflective aria be expected to satisfy the lead tenor for whom it is almost the only time he holds the stage alone in the entire opera. In the 1805 and 1814 versions, Beethoven solved this problem by writing different bravura second sections to the aria, even adding eighteen measures of concluding orchestral music in 1814 during which, according to Treitschke, the tenor might be applauded for his efforts. The second section, in F major, of the 1814 version of the aria, seems eminently successful; a soaring obbligato oboe melody set off against a vocal part of almost frenzied rhythmic motion is an apt musical vehicle for the dying Florestan's delirious vision of his beloved.

Example II–8: BEETHOVEN, *Fidelio,* "In des Lebens Frühlingstagen"

For many listeners, the best vocal writing in *Fidelio* is found in the ensembles. The familiar Prisoners' Chorus, for example, is an impressive adaptation of Männerchor singing (something like a German men's glee club) and the memorable trio between Leonore, Florestan, and Don Fernando in the last Finale ("O Gott! O Gott! Welch' ein Augenblick") plainly had a special meaning for the composer. For this scene of exultation at the liberation of an innocent man, Beethoven reached into his past and used music from his *Cantata on the Death of Joseph II* (1790). The text there is "Da stiegen die Menschen ans Licht" (Then mankind ascended to the light), an affirmation of the "enlightened" emperor's— and Beethoven's—sanguine faith in justice and the future of humanity.

Beethoven never wrote another opera or, as far as we know, ever even contemplated doing so. *Fidelio* had cost him enormous effort and agony, and it was clear that great victories were more easily achieved on other battlegrounds. But the work stands as a monument to the composer's genius for succeeding in the face of enormous odds. The primary obstacles in this case were the weaknesses in the musical-dramatic structure of the opera; what is most remarkable about *Fidelio*, perhaps, is how well it works despite them. For some, however, the most valuable legacy of *Fidelio* may be its instrumental music. In all, there were four overtures written for this opera: the *Leonore Overture* No. 2 for the 1805 version, No. 3 for the 1806 version, No. 1 for a projected revival in 1807, and the *Fidelio Overture* for the 1814 revision. The *Leonore Overtures* Nos. 2 and 3, though judged even by Beethoven too overwhelming for an operatic introduction, hold a central place in the canon of his works from these splendid years of orchestral composition. In this arena, his triumph was complete.

CHAPTER III

Beethoven: The Late Years, 1809–27

In May 1809 Napoleon's armies once more moved against Vienna. This time, unlike 1805, the decision was taken to resist the invaders, and it is reported that even the swords and lances from the property rooms of local theaters were pressed into service for the defense of the city. But all was in vain; once more the nobility packed their bags for a hasty exit, and after a brief but intense bombardment, the *Grande Armée* marched through the city gates on May 12. Beethoven, according to the testimony of Ries, spent the fearful night of May 11 in the cellar of his brother Caspar Carl's house, covering his head with pillows to shield his sensitive ears from the heavy explosions.

The renewed French occupation of Vienna with its attendant hardships was only one of a series of factors adversely affecting the composer's productivity for the next years. Beethoven's health, already bad, gradually became worse; he suffered constantly from colitis, recurrent bouts with bronchitis, and innumerable local infections. His deafness, first evident as early as 1797, increased inexorably. For a time he took

Vienna under attack from Napolean's troops, 1809. A gouache by Franz Jaschke.

recourse to "ear trumpets," and, from about 1816 onward, to conversation books—tablets of paper upon which his interlocutors wrote down their sides of conversations with the composer. From this time until his death Beethoven was by all accounts nearly totally deaf. In the midst of these difficulties, in 1815, his brother Caspar Carl died, leaving a young son, Karl, to be cared for under a joint guardianship of his mother and Beethoven. Beethoven considered the mother unfit as a guardian for the child, and launched a series of protracted and bitter legal actions to gain custody for himself. These efforts were ultimately successful in 1820. But in the meantime it became increasingly clear that the composer's mercurial temperament and chaotic bachelor household were not very suitable for child rearing, and both uncle and nephew suffered greatly from the relationship. And a reclusiveness, attributed as early as the Heiligenstadt Testament to his deafness, came ever more to dominate Beethoven's life; in 1818 he wrote in his diary, "Sacrifice once and for all the trivialities of social life to your art . . ."[1]

The economy of the Hapsburg empire virtually collapsed during its losing encounters with Napoleon, and Beethoven's sources of income from concert appearances, performances in the homes of nobility, and publication in Vienna were sharply curtailed. In 1809 three of his most loyal patrons, the Archduke Rudolph and Princes Kinsky and Lobkowitz, fearful that Beethoven might forsake the city, took the extraordinary step of settling upon him a very considerable lifetime annuity of 4000 florins. But two years later the currency was devalued by eighty percent, leaving Beethoven (who was in any event once improvident enough to rent three different lodgings at the same time) again in financial straits. Lobkowitz ceased to pay his part of the annuity in 1811; Kinsky died in 1812, and his share was also cut off. So in a typically forthright maneuver Beethoven went to court again to recover what he considered rightly his.

It is not surprising that in the face of these mounting troubles the composer's forties (corresponding roughly to the second decade of the new century) were vastly less productive than his thirties. The year of the "second invasion," 1809, was still a good one for him: it saw the completion of the Fifth Piano Concerto (the *Emperor*), the String Quartet Op. 74, most of the Piano Sonata Op. 81a *(Das Lebewohl),* and several other substantial works. But thereafter it was apparent that the first flood tide of towering masterpieces was clearly past. In 1812 both the Seventh and Eighth Symphonies were finished, but not until 1823 was there another year in which Beethoven finished more than one major composition (that was the date of the completion of the *Missa solemnis* and the *Diabelli Variations).* The leanest year of all was 1819, in

1.   Maynard Solomon, "Beethoven's Tagebuch of 1812–1818," in *Beethoven Studies 3,* ed. Alan Tyson (Cambridge and New York, 1982), p. 284.

Autograph fragment from "Clärchens Tod" in Beethoven's *Egmont*.

which Beethoven completed nothing that he felt merited an opus number.

Until 1813 Beethoven continued to register his most visible triumphs in symphonic composition. The Fifth Symphony, finished in 1808, with its heaven-storming crescendos and echoes of French Revolutionary music, continues the "heroic" manner of the Third. The Sixth Symphony (the *Pastoral*), completed the same year, is utterly different. Provided by the composer with programmatic titles for each movement ("The awakening of happy feelings upon arriving in the country," "Scene at the brook," "A jolly meeting of country folk," and the like,[2]) this composition evokes appropriate pastoral impressions through musical imitations of a murmuring brook, country music, bird calls, and a brief storm. But its overriding effect, especially in the first and last movements, is achieved by the leisurely, long-term repetition of quiet motives, providing thus a static melodic surface that focuses the listener's attention upon delicate variations in harmony and tone color. The two symphonies of 1812 are again a thoroughly unlike pair. The Seventh returns to the urgency and energy associated with Beethoven's odd-numbered symphonies, while the Eighth (in F major like the Sixth) is an intentionally slighter work, overflowing with an almost Haydnesque grace and wit.

In the summer of 1812 Napoleon embarked on his disastrous Russian campaign, to return the following spring with his army in tatters. After a hasty regrouping and even a few minor victories, the French were decisively beaten by Wellington at Vittoria in Spain on June 21, 1813. It now seemed safe for the Hapsburg government to join the nations

2. Beethoven apparently had certain misgivings about attaching these verbal referents to his instrumental music. Among the autograph materials for this symphony he included remarks such as: "A person who has any idea whatever of country life can discern for himself the composer's intention without much in the way of titles," and "More the expression of feeling than tone painting."

united against Napoleon, and with the participation of Austrian troops, the allies dealt the *Grande Armée* what appeared to be its final defeat at Leipzig in October. The Viennese were delirious with joy and patriotism. And in this heady atmosphere Beethoven, the man who once composed a symphony in honor of Napoleon, now provided the public with a little something to commemorate his downfall. In collaboration with Johann Nepomuk Mälzel, inventor of numerous mechanical devices,[3] Beethoven wrote a "battle piece"—a most fashionable musical genre at this time—called *Wellington's Victory*. It was originally designed for performance on Mälzel's "Panharmonicon," a kind of elaborate barrel organ that could simulate the sound of various band instruments. But at Mälzel's urgings, Beethoven rewrote the piece for full orchestra.

The *Battle Symphony* is—and probably quite intentionally on Beethoven's part—a musical absurdity: a mishmash of battle music, patriotic songs, and even a parodic pseudo-fugal treatment of *God Save the King*. At its first performance, with Beethoven conducting, many leading musicians of the city participated, some playing unaccustomed instruments—the composer-pianists Moscheles, Hummel, and Meyerbeer, for example, were in charge of the percussion instruments. The audience was so enraptured that the program had to be repeated a few days later. From the point of view of the Viennese public, always fickle and

The last remnants of the Grand Army en route to Smolensk, November 1812, by Faber Du Four.

3.   The one for which he is chiefly remembered, the metronome, was invented not by Mälzel, but by one D. N. Winkel.

Title page of *Wellington's Victory* in the first edition arranged for piano.

sometimes, as Beethoven and others complained, shallow in their judgment, the *Battle Symphony* was the composer's finest triumph. Income from subsequent performances was to have financed a lucrative tour of England for Beethoven and Mälzel. But, predictably enough, the two quarreled over rights to the music and the trip did not materialize. From this high water mark of his popularity with the Viennese public, however, Beethoven realized certain genuine benefits: his Seventh Symphony was given repeated performances, and the way now stood clear for the 1814 revival of *Fidelio*.

During Beethoven's relatively fallow years in the 1810s he produced some other "occasional" compositions about as ephemeral as *Wellington's Victory*. He provided incidental music to two plays by August von Kotzebue, *König Stephan* and *Die Ruinen von Athen,* performed at the dedication of a new theater in Pest in 1811. For the glittering assemblage of dignitaries attending the Congress of Vienna in 1814–15, Beethoven wrote a flattering cantata, *Der glorreiche Augenblick* (The Glorious Moment); this piece, together with *Wellington's Victory,* was wildly applauded by the elegant international audience at a special concert in November, 1814. Also in 1814 Beethoven worked on the *Namensfeier* (Nameday Celebration) *Overture* to celebrate the patron saint's day of Emperor Franz, not completing it, however, until the following year. When the new Josephstadt Theater was opened in Vienna in 1822, Kotzebue's play of ten years earlier, *Die Ruinen von Athen,* was dusted off and suitably revised by one Carl Meisl—the original author having been assassinated in the meantime by a radical German student. Beethoven adjusted his music to the altered text and provided a new overture, all under the new title *Die Weihe des Hauses*. Like other composers of his time, such as Haydn, Clementi, Pleyel, and Kozeluch, Beethoven produced his share of "amateur music" intended for home performance and quick sale. Examples of this music are the arrangements of Scottish Airs (some published by George Thomson of Edinburgh in 1818) and the Variations for piano with optional flute or violin, Opp. 105 and 107.

FORMATION OF THE LATE STYLE

In his earlier years, Beethoven had worked out compositional problems at the piano. Now in his mid-forties, chronically ill, deaf, and engulfed in personal difficulties, he once again showed glimmerings of a major shift in style, and once again such signs were first detectable in his music for keyboard. Almost five years intervened between the *Lebewohl Sonata,* Op. 81a, and the next piano sonata, Opus 90 in E minor, finished in 1814. The muted dynamics of this piece, together with a leisurely continuity of ornamentation—especially trill-like figures in a middle register—create a reflective tranquility prophetic of an important facet of the composer's late music. The second of the two Sonatas for Cello and Piano, Op. 102, from the following year demonstrates another of Beethoven's growing proclivities: it ends with a thoroughly worked-out Allegro fugato whose first subject is clearly derivative of Baroque contrapuntal practice (Example III–1). That dramatic downward leap from the sixth degree to the seventh below is characteristic of numerous fugal themes from the eighteenth century; they occur more usually in minor, as in the subject of J. S. Bach's *Musical Offering* of 1747. (Mozart used one for the Kyrie of his *Requiem,* and Beethoven had written a similar contrapuntal subject as early as 1795 in the first movement of his Piano Trio, Op. 1, No. 3.)

Example III–1: BEETHOVEN, Sonata for Cello and Piano, Op. 102, No. 2, third movement, mm. 4–13.

Some of Beethoven's older contemporaries had at critical junctures in their compositional careers turned to musical styles of the Baroque for enrichment and sustenance. Haydn in the early 1770s, Clementi in about

1780, and Mozart some three years later all plunged into concentrated study and imitation of the contrapuntal art of the earlier eighteenth century; in all three cases the effects upon their work were decisive and lasting. Though well schooled in J. S. Bach's *Well-Tempered Clavier* while yet in Bonn, Beethoven's formal education in contrapuntal writing seems to have begun only after his move to Vienna in 1792, when he studied species counterpoint in the tradition of J. J. Fux, first with Haydn and later with J. G. Albrechtsberger. Though he had proved a somewhat recalcitrant student, Beethoven later showed that at least in retrospect he approved of this sort of traditional instruction. In 1809, when his faithful patron the Archduke Rudolph became his composition student, he set about compiling teaching materials solidly based upon Fux and his own lessons with Haydn.

Example III–2: BEETHOVEN, Piano Sonata Op. 101, third movement, mm. 123–37

From about 1815 a renewed fascination with contrapuntal procedures becomes increasingly clear in Beethoven's work. The last movement of the Piano Sonata Op. 101 in A major (1816) includes a determined and dramatic fugato passage whose subject is again very Baroque in construction (Example III–2).[4] Moreover the material set against this subject (or the countersubject) shows characteristic Baroque homogeneity of motion—a feature that will permeate much of Beethoven's late style, fugal or not. For Beethoven, as for Mozart and Haydn before him, contrapuntal writing was closely associated with the medium of the string quartet. He composed some fugal exercises for this ensemble as early as 1795; the Op. 18 Quartets contain considerable genuine coun-

---

4.   The rhythm of this subject is similar to that of the Gigue of J. S. Bach's Fifth Partita, BWV 829.

Ludwig van Beethoven in 1818. Pencil drawing by August von Klöber.

terpoint, and there are fugues in Op. 59 (1806) and Op. 95 (1810). There was also a separate Fugue in D for string quintet (Op. 137), written in 1817. The following year saw the completion of the *Hammerklavier Sonata*,[5] a gargantuan piano piece ending with a fugue whose relentless length, difficulty, and violence have been the despair of pianists ever since. (With a bow toward traditional strict style, Beethoven carefully labels this movement "Fuga a tre voci, con alcune licenze,"—i.e., "fugue in three parts, with certain freedoms taken.") From this time to the end of his life, fugal and contrapuntal procedures are tightly woven into the entire fabric of Beethoven's compositional practice.

THE *DIABELLI VARIATIONS*

Another proclivity that comes strongly to the fore in the composer's late career is a fascination with formal variations. As early as 1801, in his Sonata Op. 26, we have seen that Beethoven invested the theme-and-variations with an unaccustomed weight and inventiveness; shortly after, in the Piano Variations Opp. 34 and 35, and in the finale of the *Eroica*, variations again became the vehicle for important steps in the maturation of his style. Now in his later years, variation movements are more in evidence than ever. Two of his last three piano sonatas, Op. 109 and Op. 111, end climactically with variations (the finale of the other one, Op. 110, is fugal). There are variation movements as well in two of the late string quartets, Op. 127 in E♭ and Op. 131 in

5. Beethoven specified that both the Op. 101 and Op. 106 sonatas were intended for the *Hammerklavier*—this being merely a modish German equivalent for the Italian *pianoforte*. But the name has continued to adhere only to Op. 106.

C♯ minor. And the most prominent architectural principal of the finale of the Ninth Symphony, for all its grandiose complexity, is again theme-and-variations.

In 1819 the Viennese publisher Antonio Diabelli invited a number of leading composers to submit one variation each on a waltz theme he had written; these were to form a marketable collection with a patriotic name, *Vaterländischer Künstlerverein* (Patriotic Society of Artists), to be published by his firm, Cappi and Diabelli. According to Schindler, Beethoven at first refused, ridiculing Diabelli's tune with its absurd *Schusterflecke* ("cobbler's patches").[6] But this unprepossessing melody evidently stuck in Beethoven's memory and kindled his imagination. He sketched several variations early in 1819 and proposed to Diabelli that his composition be published separately from all the other variations. Progress on the *Diabelli Variations* (as they are now known) was slowed during the following three years as Beethoven struggled with his monumental *Missa solemnis*. But as time passed, his conception of this music expanded enormously from a projected seven or eight variations to twenty-five, and ultimately thirty-three. Again and again the jaunty little theme is transformed into something original and profound. There are two imitative contrapuntal variations that Beethoven calls *fuga* and *fughetta,* and one that even incorporates a quotation from the opening music of Mozart's *Don Giovanni.* Variation 30 (shown in part in Example III–3 together with the corresponding section of Diabelli's waltz) illustrates the degree of abstraction to which Beethoven sometimes progressed.

Example III–3: BEETHOVEN, *Diabelli Variations*
    a. Theme

6.   Schindler, *Beethoven as I Knew Him,* ed. D. W. Mac Ardle (London, 1966), p. 253. "Cobbler's patches" refer to successive bits of melody repeated at different pitches.

b. Variation 30, mm. 1–8

   The only clear melodic connections with the theme here consist of the opening two tones of the variation with their repetitions, and the sequentially repeated figures in mm. 5–6—these corresponding of course to the *Schusterflecke* in Diabelli's mm. 8–12. Beethoven's variation is persistently contrapuntal, though informally so, as an extraneous fourth voice occasionally enters simply to reinforce sonorities of the three-voice texture. An extreme uniformity of rhythm is broken only by the dotted-note figures that allude to the beginning of the theme. Besides these hallmarks of his late style Beethoven provides us with a sample of his most taut and dense harmonic syntax. The first eight measures of Diabelli's waltz contain only two harmonies: four measures of tonic and four of dominant. Beethoven's harmonies shift very rapidly. A maze of nonharmonic pitches sometimes obscures the tonality and produces abrasive dissonances, as on the first beat of m. 8. When modulation occurs, as in m. 2 from C minor to D♭ major, it is done with extreme abruptness. But however eccentric the harmonic plan of this variation may seem, it reflects, in an abstruse way, the structure of the theme: Diabelli's first introduction of a dominant sound in m. 5 corresponds to Beethoven's *modulation* to the lowered second degree (D♭), and the internal cadence of the waltz theme in the dominant key (m.16) is reflected in an arrival at A♭ (m.8) in the variation. Beethoven's tough, compact writing is in a style worlds removed from its model, but the essential idea of a variation upon a theme is never lost.
   When late in life Beethoven plunged headlong into the techniques of fugue and of variation, he was operating at both extremes of a stylistic spectrum. Fugue meant rigorous, strict style, associated often with church music and sometimes bearing connotations of dry academicism. Theme-and-variations, on the other hand, suggested amateur music—music for

polite diversion and even for pleasing background noise. What these very unlike types had in common is that they placed severe restrictions upon the composer, and therein, perhaps, lay their attraction for Beethoven. The myriad prescriptions for fugue were well documented and widely taught. Convention governed theme-and-variation procedures—variations ordinarily presented easily recognizable elaborations of the melody of the theme, and its harmony and phrasing were expected to remain essentially intact. Beethoven subjected these rules and conventions to severe strain; nonetheless, in essential ways he submitted to their strictures as he created the uniquely potent and concentrated language of his late style.

That late style, gradually forged in the teens of the new century, remains something of a puzzle.[7] Whatever his continued allegiance to the sonata, fugue, and theme-and-variations, Beethoven now bends their shapes to radically new ends. Sometimes traditional patterns appear enormously concentrated: the first movement of the Piano Sonata Op. 109 compresses all the essential traits of a sonata-allegro exposition into just sixteen measures. At the other extreme, familiar procedures (especially fugue and theme-and-variations) achieve unheard-of size and weight, as in the *Grosse Fuge,* Op. 133, and the *Diabelli Variations.* Boundaries between forms grow indistinct. Sonata-allegro and theme-and-variations types are elaborately mingled (first and last movements of the String Quartet Op. 132) and fugues show the development of motives associated with sonata movements. Themes may appear on the surface more fragmentary and disjunct; but their elements are transformed and abstracted to yield a musical coherence more profound than ever.[8] And here, as nowhere else in the repertory, we feel the force of the Romantic notion of music as a "speech above verbal speech," as an expression of the inexpressible.

THE *MISSA SOLEMNIS* AND NINTH SYMPHONY

The two biggest compositions of Beethoven's last years, the *Missa solemnis* (finished in 1823) and the Ninth Symphony (finished in 1824), were both long in preparation. When in June 1819 it was announced that the Archduke Rudolf was to be appointed Archbishop of the Moravian city Olmütz, Beethoven wrote to him, "The day on which a High Mass composed by me will be performed during the ceremonies solemnized for your Imperial Highness will be the most glorious day of my life."[9]

---

7. Particularly so is its apparent discontinuity with the style of the middle period.

8. The music historian Carl Dahlhaus (*Die Musik des 19. Jahrhunderts* [Wiesbaden, 1980], p. 69) suggests that in Beethoven's late style the development of themes as such gives way to the free treatment of a "subthematic stratum" of musical materials.

9. Emily Anderson, ed. and trans., *The Letters of Beethoven* (New York, 1961), pp. 814–15.

But there was little chance that the sort of Mass Beethoven had in mind—a large work for four soloists, chorus, and large orchestra—would be ready by the installation date in March of 1820; the final revisions in fact were not made until about three years later. In preparation for his task, Beethoven apparently buried himself in antiquarian studies. The Archduke's library provided examples of polyphonic Masses from the sixteenth century to his own time. Beethoven also took pains to acquaint himself with the church modes of medieval plainsong, sought out traditional theoretical works on church music, such as the *Istitutioni harmoniche* (1558) of Gioseffo Zarlino, and studied the text of the Mass in a German translation. When he began actual composition, titanic combat with this relatively unfamiliar genre ensued. A narrative of Schindler, though it must be accepted with caution, is too vivid to exclude:

> Towards the end of August I arrived at the master's rooms in Mödling accompanied by the musician Johann Horzalka. . . . From behind the closed door of one of the parlours we could hear the master working on the fugue of the Credo, singing, yelling, stamping his feet. When we had heard enough of this almost frightening performance and were about to depart, the door opened and Beethoven stood before us, his features distorted to the point of inspiring terror. He looked as though he had just engaged in a life and death struggle with the whole army of contrapuntists, his everlasting enemies. His first words were confused, as if he felt embarrassed at having been overheard. Soon he began to speak of the day's events and said, with noticeable self-control, "What a mess! Everyone has run away and I haven't had anything to eat since yesterday noon."[10]

This account is probably inaccurate in one point at least. It more likely would have been the fugue at the end of the Gloria ("in gloria

An early nineteenth-century painting of the village of Mödling, where Beethoven worked on the *Missa solemnis* and Ninth Symphony.

10. Schindler, p. 229.

Dei patris, amen"), and not part of the Credo, that he overheard Beethoven working on that summer in Mödling. This fugue (mm. 440ff.) is a technical tour-de-force whose first nineteen measures are set over a dominant pedal. But it is only one extreme example of a pervasive feature of this work. Fugal and (more broadly) contrapuntal writing are its ordinary language; imitative openings are standard for both chorus and soloists in all movements. Other techniques are used for specific purposes. At the "Et incarnatus est," a point in the Credo traditionally singled out for special treatment,[11] Beethoven writes an imitation of medieval plainsong in the Dorian mode which upon repetition is subjected to another fugal development.

In the Agnus Dei, the last of the five Mass movements, he again resorts to exceptional procedures. The text consists of three invocations:

Agnus Dei, qui tollis peccata mundi, miserere nobis.	Lamb of God, who takes away the sins of the world, have mercy on us.
Agnus Dei, qui tollis peccata mundi, miserere nobis.	Lamb of God, who takes away the sins of the world, have mercy on us.
Agnus Dei, qui tollis peccata mundi, dona nobis pacem.	Lamb of God, who takes away the sins of the world, grant us peace.

By m. 96 Beethoven has used up all his text except "dona nobis pacem," and with these three words, following the usual custom, he begins a new section. But he shows that they have special importance for him by setting above them a highly personal rubric: "Bitte um innern und äussern Frieden" ("Prayer for inner and outer peace"). After some seventy measures of appropriately pastoral music, however, the idea of peace is summoned up by invoking its opposite. Military trumpet calls are heard in the orchestra, and the soloists, one after another, sing a telescoped recapitulation of the first two sentences of the Agnus Dei in the dramatic style of accompanied recitative. Thus the earlier portions of the text, especially the "miserere nobis," are associated with war and tribulation and struggle, those constant companions of Beethoven's life. But now pastoral music returns with "dona nobis pacem," leading to a triumphant fugue whose subject has apparently been borrowed from the Hallelujah Chorus of Handel's *Messiah*. Peace, in its broadest sense, Beethoven evidently saw as a positive, powerful thing; the prayer for

---

11. In the sixteenth century it was usual to cast this statement of the Incarnation into bold relief by a homophonic, chordal style, in a context that was largely contrapuntal.

its realization constitutes a fitting climax to the composition he once singled out as his greatest work.

The other monumental work of Beethoven's late years, the Ninth Symphony, underwent a gestation period longer even than that of the *Missa solemnis*. It seemingly resulted from a gradual coalescence, over many years, of ideas Beethoven had for three different compositions. In June 1817 Beethoven's erstwhile student Ferdinand Ries, now in London, conveyed to him a handsome proposal from the London Philharmonic Society. Like Haydn before him, Beethoven was asked to spend the coming winter season, beginning January 1818, in England, and supply the society with two new symphonies for its concerts. The composer promptly accepted, with a characteristic request for a larger fee than the 300 guineas specified. Though this project, like a number of other plans for visiting England, never materialized, for some years Beethoven apparently clung to the notion of writing two more symphonies—a new pair after the models of the Fifth and Sixth and the Seventh and Eighth. In 1822, when the prominent Leipzig music critic Friedrich Rochlitz visited him, Beethoven still mentioned among his works contemplated or in progress "two great symphonies . . . each different from the other, and each also different from all my other ones,

Title page of the first edition of Beethoven's Ninth Symphony.

and an oratorio."[12] The Ninth Symphony was apparently to have been a wholly instrumental work, while in the Tenth, according to random jottings Beethoven made about 1818, "vocal parts would enter gradually—in the text of the Adagio Greek myth, *Cantique Ecclesiastique*—in the Allegro, feast of Bachus [*sic*]."[13]

An entirely separate idea that merged eventually with these plans for symphonies was Beethoven's intention, as early as 1793, to compose music to Friedrich Schiller's poem *An die Freude*. In a sketchbook from 1811 appear certain cryptic notes ("Freude schöner Götterfunken, Tochter. Work out the overture") suggesting that the sort of work he had in mind for this text may have been a cantata. In 1818–19, and again in 1822–23, the composer worked earnestly at the first three movements of the Ninth Symphony, making use of material (i.e., the fugal subject of the Scherzo, originally planned for a string quartet) entered in the sketchbooks as early as 1815. And in late 1822 he agreed to sell rights for this symphony—surely without a finale set to a German text—to the London Philharmonic Society. It was not until about mid-1823 that the three projects, i.e., an entirely instrumental symphony, another one incorporating voices, and a setting of Schiller's poem, finally became one composition. This accomplished, Beethoven was still sorely troubled about finding a convincing method of introducing vocal parts into the finale, after the singers had sat mute upon the stage during all the first three movements. Schindler recalls an event from October, 1823:

> The working out of the fourth movement, however, began a struggle seldom encountered before. The problem was to find a suitable introduction to Schiller's ode. One day he burst into the room and shouted at me: "I have it! I have it!" He held his sketchbook out to me so that I could read: "Let us sing the song of the immortal Schiller"; then a solo voice began the Hymn of Joy.[14]

This transition was yet to undergo considerable elaboration. In the final version of the score, finished in 1824, Beethoven opens the fourth movement with an outraged flurry of sound in all the wind instruments (beginning with a sharply dissonant B$\flat$ set against the D-minor tonic triad).[15] The cellos and basses then play an unmistakably clear imitation

12. O. Sonneck, ed., *Beethoven. Impressions of Contemporaries* (New York, 1926), p. 127. The "oratorio," which was never written, may refer to the request that Beethoven received for such a work from the Handel and Haydn Society in Boston.

13. Alexander Thayer, *Thayer's Life of Beethoven,* ed. Elliot Forbes (Princeton, 1964), p. 888.

14. Schindler, p. 269. A sketchbook this time bears out Schindler's report.

15. Wagner called this opening a *Schreckensfanfare* ("terror fanfare"). Two instructive (and very different) discussions of Beethoven's Ninth Symphony are Ernest Sanders, "Form and Content in Beethoven's Ninth," *The Musical Quarterly,* 50 (1964): 59–76; and Leo Treitler, "History, Criticism, and Beethoven's Ninth Symphony," *19th Century Music,* 3 (1980), especially pp. 193–202.

Example III–4: BEETHOVEN, Symphony No. 9, fourth movement, mm.
          8–16

of dramatic recitative, hinting at some sort of rapprochement between
instrumental and vocal music (Example III–4). After this procedure is
repeated Beethoven quotes in turn the beginnings of his first three
movements, each cut off abruptly by the imperious recitativelike statements from the cellos and basses. Finally a new theme, hesitantly
advanced by the orchestra, is accepted and played in full by those seemingly tyrannical low strings (Example III–5). Little by little the other
instruments join in, ending with a triumphant statement of the new
theme in D major.

Example III–5: BEETHOVEN, Symphony No. 9, fourth movement, mm.
          92–107

This is all very mysterious. And Beethoven now begins anew, as if
to explain himself. A shortened repetition of these proceedings (omitting the quotations from previous movements) is offered; but the recitativelike parts are now real recitative, sung by the baritone soloist. His
text is apparently of Beethoven's own invention: "O friends, not these
tones; instead let us sing more pleasing and joyful ones." (Berlioz calls
this a "treaty of alliance entered into between chorus and orchestra.")
The "more joyful tones" are, of course, that new theme, which the
baritone now sings to the first lines of Schiller's poem:

Freude, schöner Götterfunken,	Joy, thou divine spark,
Tochter aus Elysium,	Daughter of Elysium,
Wir betreten feuertrunken,	Fire-drunken we approach,
Himmlische, dein Heiligtum.	Heavenly one, thy holyness.
Deine Zauber binden wieder,	Thy enchantments bind together
Was die Mode streng geteilt,	What fashion has rent asunder;
Alle Menschen werden Brüder,	All people become brothers
Wo dein sanfter Flügel weilt.	Where thy gentle wing tarries.

This becomes the first in a magnificent series of variations on the *Freude*
theme with ever-changing antiphonal effects between soloists, chorus,
and orchestra. And when Beethoven comes to a bit of text with the
exhortation "Follow your path with joy, Brothers, like a hero march-

ing to victory," he seizes upon these military associations to write a variation in the style of "Turkish Music."[16] This first large section of the movement is concluded with an orchestral development of the *Freude* theme followed by one more ecstatic statement using the opening text, by chorus and orchestra.

Up to this point Beethoven had not used the concluding four lines of Schiller's first stanza:

Seid umschlungen, Millionen!	Be embraced, ye millions!
Diesen Kuss der ganzen Welt!	This kiss to the whole world!
Brüder—überm Sternenzelt	Brothers—above the starry canopy
Muss ein lieber Vater wohnen.	A loving Father must dwell.

Such expansive sentiments of mingled humanism and religiosity might be expected to appeal to the composer, and he uses this text for the second principal theme of the movement, a soaring melody in triple meter (Example III–6). Then in the third major section—perhaps predictably—the Joy and Brotherhood themes are mingled (the meter of the former having now become triple); and an appended coda, written in a very high tessitura and marked *fortissimo* nearly throughout, ends the symphony on a note of triumphant exultation.

Schiller wrote his *An die Freude* in 1785 at the age of twenty-six. A few years later he confessed to a friend that he considered it a "bad poem that signifies a level of cultivation that I of necessity left behind."[17] Its sanguine celebration of the glories of universal brotherhood must surely strike us as a bit naïve, and sometimes the poem sounds perilously like a students' drinking song:

Wem der grosse Wurf gelungen,	Let him who has ventured
Eines Freundes Freund zu sein,	To be a friend of a friend,
Wer ein holdes Weib errungen,	Let him who has embraced a pretty girl,
Mische seinen Jubel ein!	Add his joy to ours!

Yet it was altogether characteristic of Beethoven that he should be attracted to such homely expressions of humane impulses. Indeed the *Freude* theme itself seems intentionally "common." Its earthy, foursquare rhythm is probably meant as an imitation of popular music, such as the songs to be heard among amateur *Männerchöre* throughout the German-speaking states. Mozart also wrote imitations of folk music, as in the peasant scene from the first act of *Don Giovanni* (Scene 7); but

---

16. "Turkish" bands with fifes and bass drum, cymbals, and triangles were a familiar feature of military establishments in eighteenth-century Europe.

17. *Schillers sämtliche Werke,* ed. Eduard von der Hellen (Stuttgart and Berlin, 1904), 1, p. 288.

Example III–6: BEETHOVEN, Ninth Symphony, fourth movement, mm. 603–10

Mozart seems to give us an eighteenth-century sophisticate's tongue-in-cheek rendition of how rustic music probably sounds. Beethoven, however, is in earnest. That the uncomplicated liberal humanity urged by Schiller's poem was part of Beethoven's continuing creed can be seen in the *Joseph* cantata, in *Fidelio,* and perhaps even in the "Dona nobis pacem" from the *Missa solemnis.* The ordinary generous sentiments of ordinary people, Beethoven seems to be saying in the finale of the Ninth, offer the best hope for mankind.

In the view of musicians of following generations, Beethoven seemed to be saying something else as well—that with this composition he had exhausted the expressive resources of the instrumental symphony, that he had burst its restraining boundaries by introducing text and voices. Berlioz, for example, explains,

Beethoven had already written eight symphonies before this. What means were open to him, in the event of his proposing to go beyond the point at which he had already arrived, by the unaided resources of instrumentation? *The junction of vocal with instrumental forces.*[18]

And likewise Wagner:

With this opening of the last movement Beethoven's music takes on a more definitely *speaking* character: it quits the mould of purely instrumental music, observed in all the three preceding movements, the mode of infinite, indefinite expression; the musical poem is urging toward a crisis, a crisis only to be voiced in human speech. It is wonderful how the master makes the arrival of Man's voice and tongue a positive necessity, by this awe-inspiring recitative in the bass-strings.[19]

Such assessments of the step Beethoven had taken were evidently taken rather seriously by later composers; many, such as Mendelssohn, Berlioz, and Mahler, followed his example in writing symphonies with vocal movements.

There is no denying that the use of soloists and chorus in a symphony was per se new and startling in 1824. Yet in several respects the Ninth is reminiscent of Beethoven's work of former years. The first movement and Scherzo extend the "heroic" tradition of the Third, Fifth, and Seventh Symphonies. Even the finale shows signs of its origins in the ponderings of the young Beethoven (and the young Schiller): in both style and idea it retains certain echoes of the massive musical celebrations of the French Revolution. Only the slow movement, with its subtle alternation of two marvelous themes, with variations, in B♭ and D, seems to belong wholly to the composer's final period. The one in D soars effortlessly, constantly renewed by veiled cadences and an overlapping of instrumentation; it is a supreme example of the composer's late "contemplative" style, and one of the finest melodies Beethoven ever wrote. (In Example III–7, it is played by second violins and violas.)

THE LATE QUARTETS

In November 1822, Prince Nicholas Galitsin took steps to become the second member of the Russian nobility (after Count Razumovsky, the dedicatee of Op. 59) to attach his name to Beethoven's string quartets. In a flattering letter he offered to commission "one, two, or three new quartets," and Beethoven, though deeply engrossed in the *Missa solem-*

18.   Hector Berlioz, *A Critical Appreciation of Beethoven's Nine Symphonies and his Only Opera, Fidelio, with its Four Overtures,* trans. and ed. Ralph DeSola (Boston, 1975), p. 104.

19.   From a program written by Wagner for his performance of the Ninth Symphony at Dresden in 1846; quoted from *Richard Wagner's Works,* trans. W. A. Ellis (London, 1898), 7, pp. 251–52.

Example III–7: BEETHOVEN, Ninth Symphony, third movement, mm. 25–34

nis and Ninth Symphony, quickly accepted. A remark in a letter from the previous June suggests that Beethoven was already contemplating a new quartet; so even though a dozen years had passed since his last work in this genre, Galitsin's proposal evidently fell in nicely with his own plans. Unfinished business delayed serious work on the new commission until the summer of 1824, but from that time until his death, Beethoven devoted himself with rare single-mindedness to composing for this most demanding and sophisticated of ensembles.

The three quartets for Galitsin, composed between mid-1824 and late 1825, are Op. 127 in E♭, Op. 132 in A minor, and Op. 130 in B♭. (Op. 127 was the only one of these—and indeed the latest of Beethoven's compositions—to be published during the composer's lifetime.) But it was plainly more than the commission that prompted this concentrated devotion to quartet composition. Two more quartets followed: Op. 131 in C♯ minor and Op. 135 in F, finished respectively in July and November, 1826. Then Beethoven decided to make a momentous change in the last of the Galitsin quartets, Op. 130 in B♭. This work, like the *Hammerklavier Sonata* in the same key, ended with a herculean, apocalyptic fugue. After its performance in the spring of 1826, the ailing Beethoven allowed himself to be persuaded by Artaria, his publisher, that such a fugue was simply out of place. In autumn of the same year, shortly before taking to his deathbed, he wrote a new finale and authorized separate publication of the *Grosse Fuge* (as it was now called) in two versions: for string quartet (Op. 133) and for piano four-hands (Op. 134). Though the composer's thoughts were yet awash with ideas for major new compositions (a quintet, perhaps a symphony, and an ora-

A view of Beethoven's work room, drawn three days after the composer's death by J. N. Höchle.

torio), this substituted finale for Op. 130 was to be his last finished work. Early in December, 1826, on a journey from his brother Johann's home in Gneixendorf back to Vienna, he fell seriously ill; he subsequently underwent four operations and finally died, apparently from collapse of liver function, on March 26, 1827.

It is entirely consistent with the progress of Beethoven's late work that he should entrust his final musical utterances to the four frail vessels of the string quartet. The restrictions of tone color, dynamics, and density of texture imposed by this austere ensemble required just that distillation of resources that marks so much of his later music. The string quartet is thoroughly amenable to contrapuntal writing, and it provides an uncluttered medium for the exposition of Beethoven's most advanced ideas in harmonic motion and thematic transformation.

The Quartet in C♯ minor, Op. 131 (ARM No. 3), Beethoven's last large-scale composition (Op. 135 is of modest dimensions), can stand as representative of the unbroken series of masterpieces of his late years. According to the composer's own numbering this piece would appear to have seven movements of diverse types and tonalities:

No. 1. Adagio ma non troppo e molto espressivo (fugue, C♯ minor)

No. 2. Allegro molto vivace (shortened sonata-allegro, D major)

No. 3. Allegro moderato (introduction to No. 4, B minor—V of A)

No. 4. Andante ma non troppo e molto cantabile (theme-and-variations, A major)

No. 5. Presto (scherzo and trio, E major)

No. 6. Adagio quasi un poco andante (introduction to No. 7, G♯ minor–C♯ minor)

No. 7. Allegro (sonata-allegro, C♯ minor)

We note immediately that Beethoven's No. 3 serves as a brief introduction to the extended theme-and-variations that follows, and No. 6 performs a similar function for the finale. That leaves five ostensibly independent movements, three of which are of relatively standard types: the "slow movement" (No. 4), the scherzo (No. 5), and the finale. Much less to be expected in a sonata-like composition are the unremittingly severe opening fugue (see Example III–9a) and No. 2, a short, idyllic, nearly monothematic piece in D major that seems to neutralize its effect. That this movement should be heard as a sequel (or perhaps an antidote) to the fugue is made quite plain. The ending of the fugue never manages to reach its home key of C♯ minor; a final C♯-major sound is heard as dominant to F♯ minor. In this atmosphere of uncertainty a questioning octave leap on C♯ is unceremoniously nudged up a semitone in true Beethovenian fashion, and the second movement in

Example III–8: BEETHOVEN, String Quartet Op. 131, first movement,
mm. 117–end; second movement, mm. 1–8

D major is already underway (Example III–8). Only forty-four measures into the movement, moreover, we are given another backward
glance at the fugue as if Beethoven were obsessed with showing that
this D-major movement indeed belongs in a piece in C♯ minor.

At its close this movement is yet again grafted into the composition
by means of an F♯; that tone abruptly shifts from the third of the final
D-major chord to the dominant of B minor—the tonality of the beginning of No. 3. Again there is no pause between movements. Such
rhythmic continuity becomes a norm in this quartet, supplementing the
careful harmonic transitions that bind one movement to the next. In
this way Beethoven mitigates the potentially disruptive effects of a
multiplicity of movements cast in four different tonalities. (The usual
sonata-type composition uses only two: one for the outer two movements and the minuet or scherzo, and another for the slow movement).
And when the long odyssey from C♯ minor through D major, A major,
E major, and back to C♯ minor is complete, we note faint glimmerings
of another kind of striving toward unity. In a finale that is utterly unlike
the first movement, there can be heard, nonetheless, unmistakable

Example III–9: BEETHOVEN, String Quartet Op. 131
  a. First movement, mm. 1–8

  b. Seventh movement, mm. 1–5

  c. Seventh movement, mm. 21–25

melodic echoes of that opening fugue. The abrupt gesture with which the finale begins restates the fugue's emphasis of the semitones B♯–C♯ and A–G♯ (Example III–9b); a few measures later the connection becomes explicit (Example III–9c).

Movement No. 3, as we have said, serves an introductory function. Its peremptory opening chords sound like the orchestral interjections of dramatic accompanied recitative. The subsequent meanderings of the first violin over a sustained dominant of the dominant harmony resemble a melodic ornament emphasizing a specially significant word, with extended range and speed because the instrument is more agile than the voice it imitates. And finally, in the next-to-last measure, we hear the everyday cadential formula that in opera, oratorio, or cantata signals the end of a recitative and the beginning of an aria.

The "aria" that follows is a spacious theme-and-variations in which Beethoven has accepted nearly in toto the conventional restrictions of that type. The movement falls into the following divisions:

	m.
Theme	1
Var. 1	33
Var. 2	65
Var. 3	98
Var. 4	130
Var. 5	162
Var. 6	187

The theme itself is cast in the most regular binary form: two segments of eight measures each, both immediately repeated. The first goes from tonic to dominant (without actually modulating), and the second from dominant back to tonic:

‖: I   (V)   :‖‖:   (V)   I :‖

This metrical and harmonic regularity is maintained to an astonishing degree nearly throughout the movement. Only minute exceptions occur, such as the extra measure at the beginning of Variation 1 and the omission of one measure upon repetition of its first segment (cf. mm. 68–69 and 77–78); then in Variation 6 the repetition of the second segment leads to a cadenzalike passage (mm. 220ff.) and, at last, the dissolution of all this iron-clad orderliness. The variations differ in duration because they have different meters and tempos; their internal proportions remain almost precisely the same.

Having chosen to impose these strictures upon himself, Beethoven explores textures, extreme ranges, and kaleidoscopic instrumental combinations. In the theme and in all but one of the variations he writes out the repetitions, thus providing an opportunity each time for yet further variation. Thus the theme includes, in effect, the first variation. Its homely little melody, initially alternating between the first and second violin in the same register, exchanges parts upon repetition (beginning in m. 9), this time with the second violin put down an octave. In the second segment (m. 17), the melody is initially all in the first violin with the second violin doubling at the tenth below; in the repetition (m. 25), these melodic parts are initially given to the second violin and viola; but soon the main tune passes easily back, once more, to the first violin.

The first variation shows a kind of progressive rhythmic elaboration as the double-dotted note figure ♪.♪ at the beginning comes to dominate the second segment (beginning in m. 49), occurring either as ♫ or ♫ . And upon repetition Beethoven shows one of his favorite means of building climax: in mm. 60–61 all the instruments insistently play the same rhythmic figure (the second one shown above) as the registral ranges of the first violin and cello are expanded to their utmost. Another kind of extreme registral extension is shown in Variation 4, where the cello is constantly called upon to play in the highest possible tessitura; it even begins the variation above the viola, well up in the violin range, inevitably producing a thin, strained sound. Beethoven in all probability wrote such parts with one very able player in mind—his friend Joseph Linke, cellist of the Schuppanzigh Quartet.

One might reasonably expect a set of late-Beethoven variations of such proportions to include at least one fugal or contrapuntal section. This expectation is fulfilled in Variation 3: an austere canonic exercise that sometimes sounds—perhaps intentionally—labored. Part of the reason for this lies in the mercilessly repeated dotted rhythms of the first segment. In the second (beginning in m. 114), Beethoven introduces a new idea made up of a scale figure with short trills. While in the first segment only two voices at a time participated in the canonic imitation, here all four eventually join, producing finally an almost unbearable density of texture.

Of all the variations, the sixth is by far the longest—not, of course, because it has more measures, but because the measures are larger (9/4) and the tempo slow (Adagio ma non troppo). Its first section provides a placid, hymnlike fulcrum for the entire quartet, a release for the moment from all the rhythmic vigor and dynamic and registral extremes that govern this composition. The rhythmic configuration of its simple close-position quarter-note chords is hard to grasp (this off-beat beginning is borrowed from the opening of the theme), and it is not until m. 192 that we hear an unequivocal melody, in the first violin. The serenity of the piece is disturbed when the first segment is repeated (m. 195); Beethoven introduces an energetic sixteenth-note figure in the cello that throws additional weight upon the second group of three quarter notes in each measure, and the violins once more soar high in their range in a potently expressive climax.[20]

In the second half of this variation that peculiar sixteenth-note figure, ever more insistent, seems to derail the harmonic progress of the piece; in m. 205 it leads the music abruptly into the distant key of C major—one of the rare instances up to this point where the simple tonal plan stated in the theme is violated. What had begun as a pure example of the late Beethoven's static, contemplative style by degrees takes on an air of great urgency and expressive force. This is really the last variation. What follows loses the thread of the theme-and-variations idea, dissolving into cadenzalike episodes and partial statements of thematic material—some exaggerately simple but off key (mm. 231 and 254) and one (m. 243) intentionally raucous. Finally in m. 266 the lofty cadential phrases of the theme's ending are invoked again, and the movement comes full circle to the serenity with which it had begun.

CONTEMPORARY ASSESSMENT

Throughout much of his adult life Beethoven was the most respected composer in Europe. His music routinely commanded high prices from both aristocratic patrons and publishers in several countries; his orchestral works quickly became standard fare at concerts everywhere except in France. Artists and intellectuals flocked to Vienna to visit him at his deathbed; Louis XVIII sent him a gold medallion out of simple admiration; the London Philharmonic Society—earlier the victim of the composer's somewhat questionable business dealings—contributed a good sum of money to ease his final suffering. And at the funeral procession for this reclusive and misanthropic man the crowd in attendance was estimated at between 10,000 and 20,000 persons.

This is not to say that Beethoven was popular in the sense that, say, his younger contemporary Rossini was. Beginning with the first works of his maturity, shortly after 1800, Beethoven's music evoked from some quarters a continuing litany of exasperated criticism. The charges were nearly always the same: his compositions were too long, difficult, obscure, eccentric, and bizarre (or, according to contemporary usage, "baroque"). A private concert in Vienna of 1805, in which both the First Symphony and the *Eroica* were played, elicited these remarks from the correspondent for the Leipzig *Allgemeine musikalische Zeitung:*

> Beethoven's Symphony in C major [the First Symphony] was performed at Herr von Würth's with precision and ease. A splendid artistic production . . . in which an uncommon richness of beautiful ideas are charmingly and

---

20. Much of the special sound of mm. 199–200 results from the close spacing of tones in the cello and its isolation (by two octaves' distance) from the other instruments.

splendidly developed, and overall pervades continuity, order and light. An entirely new symphony by Beethoven [the *Eroica*] is written in a completely different style. This long composition, extremely difficult of performance, is in reality a tremendously expanded, daring and wild fantasia. It lacks nothing in the way of startling and beautiful passages, in which the energetic and talented composer must be recognized; but often it loses itself in lawlessness. . . . The reviewer belongs to Herr van Beethoven's sincerest admirers, but in this composition he must confess that he finds too much that is glaring and bizarre. . . . The Symphony in E-flat by Eberl again was extraordinarily pleasing.[21]

At the first public performance of the *Eroica,* it is reported, someone in the audience shouted "I'll give another kreutzer if the thing will but stop!"[22]

Even in London, where there was a special fondness for Beethoven, similar complaints were heard for many years. When the Seventh Symphony was performed at a Philharmonic Society concert in 1828, a reviewer remarked,

> The almost interminable symphony of Beethoven in A has one redeeming movement, that in A minor, which cannot be too highly praised; but judging from the practice of the Philharmonic Society, it may be compared to a pleasant member of a disagreeable family, who cannot be invited without asking the whole party.[23]

Beginning about 1804, however, a very different strain of Beethoven criticism made an appearance. In that year the *Allgemeine musikalische Zeitung* of Leipzig printed a technically competent and highly sympathetic review of the *Eroica Variations,* Op. 35; this was followed in 1805 and 1807 by similar assessments of the Third Piano Concerto and the *Eroica Symphony.*[24] In all three of these reviews the anonymous author (or authors) makes a strong attempt to penetrate the aesthetic obscurities of Beethoven's music, finding musical justification for even his brashest *bizarreries* (such as the fugue of the Variations, Op. 35). Then in the *Allgemeine musikalische Zeitung* of 1810–13, E. T. A. Hoffmann inaugurated a new chapter in formal music criticism as well as in critical appraisals of Beethoven with extensive reviews of five works: the Fifth Symphony, the *Coriolan Overture,* the Piano Trios Op. 70, the C-major Mass, and the music to *Egmont.* These reviews present a singular mixture of close technical description and flights of metaphor in which Beethoven's music is compared to an "infinite spirit-kingdom" quite removed from ordinary human experience and modes of thought. In these reviews—most particularly in the introduction to that on the Fifth

21.   As translated in Thayer-Forbes, p. 375.
22.   Ibid.
23.   *The Harmonicon,* No. 6 (June, 1828): 138.
24.   *Allgemeine musikalische Zeitung,* 6 (1804): 338; 7 (1805): 445; 9 (1807): 321.

Symphony—Hoffmann provides a new approach to understanding Beethoven, as well as a central document in Romantic musical aesthetics.[25]

As Beethoven grew older his music diverged even more markedly from the practices of his contemporaries, inspiring in his listeners a curious blend of awe and puzzlement. In 1824, in a review of the Piano Sonata Op. 109, a writer for the *Berliner allgemeine musikalische Zeitung* articulated a widely held view:

> It cannot be denied that he withdraws increasingly within himself, and thus ever more absents himself even from the pursuits and interests of other music lovers. He reveals only his own subjective thoughts, and in his composing pays heed to nothing but his own inspiration.[26]

In a less charitable piece a few issues later in the same journal, a critic expounds at length upon the impossibility of reviewing a composition so eccentric as Beethoven's Sonata op. 111:

> Perhaps you, dear Editor, can establish a position from which criticism and the commonly accepted rules of aesthetics can be defended against these novelties, these attacks upon first principles. For when the primary conception of a work of art is divorced from reason, when feeling alone determines every basis for judgment, when works that scorn all our rules gain such passionate admirers—then I must be silent.[27]

If Beethoven deviated ever more from rule and fashion, this seemed not to detract from the devotion of his admirers or the authority of his oeuvre. A paradox of the genuine masterpiece is that it must be in important ways *unique*—quite unlike other works of its kind—and at the same time *exemplary,* comprising a lasting standard of achievement and a model for others to emulate. Beethoven's instrumental compositions were seen as both for the entire nineteenth century. In the view of many he held proprietary rights for vast areas of composition—the symphony, the sonata, the string quartet, and perhaps the piano concerto. And the man himself, a voluntary exile from society who seemed to follow inner lights of extraterrestrial origin, easily became a prototype for the Romantic artist, and the founder, by general consent, of Romantic music.

---

25.   See J. Schnaus, *E. T. A. Hoffmann als Beethoven-Resenzent der Allgemeinen musikalischen Zeitung* (Munich and Salzburg, 1977) and Robin Wallace, *Contemporaneous Criticism of Beethoven: Implications for Musical Analysis* (Ph.D. diss., Yale Univ., 1983).

26.   *Berliner allgemeine musikalische Zeitung,* 1 (1824): 37.

27.   Ibid., 1: 99.

CHAPTER IV

Beethoven's Contemporaries: Instrumental Music

Beethoven devoted his enormous energies to traditional large-scale instrumental compositions—sonatas, string quartets, and symphonies—in a time when this sort of music was passing out of fashion. In public concerts there was, to be sure, a continuing demand for symphonies; they still played their traditional role as "overtures" or opening numbers. But many of the symphonies heard during the early 1800s were written in the previous century. The works of Haydn and Mozart predominated at first; only Beethoven's symphonies rivaled theirs in international popularity. Orchestral works by other composers were usually presented under special circumstances: symphonies of Clementi were heard at the Paris Concerts Spirituels when he visited that city in 1816–17, and the violinist and composer Louis Spohr (1784–1859) conducted his own symphonies in London in 1820. But a growing preference for Beethoven's symphonies over all others, even those of Haydn and Mozart, can be seen in the concert programs of the major musical centers except Paris by the third decade of the century. During the first three years of its existence (1813–15) the London Philharmonic Society, for example, programmed seven performances of Beethoven symphonies; in 1824–27 there were 21—far more than the symphonies of any other composer.

The orchestral music of Beethoven's contemporaries, even the younger ones, was for the most part strikingly conservative. Ferdinand Ries, Beethoven's faithful pupil, wrote a series of symphonies for London performances in 1813–24 that recall his master's earliest style, or even that of late Haydn and Mozart. Another younger German contemporary of Beethoven, Carl Maria von Weber (1786–1826), primarily a composer of opera and piano music, produced two symphonies in 1806–7, both in C major. Those delightful pieces, too, show the transparent textures, regular phrasing, and circumscribed harmonic syntax of Classic instrumental style. Yet for fleeting instants we hear harbingers of things to come in Weber's music: in the first movement of the second symphony, for example, an atmospheric solo-horn melody evades its anticipated diatonic conclusion and dissolves into a sea of mysteriously

An orchestral "Sunday Concert" in the Hague, the Netherlands; sepia print, ca. 1820.

chromatic harmonies (Example IV–1).[1]

Example IV–1: WEBER, Symphony No. 2, first movement, mm. 51–59

Other composers who carried the style of the Classic symphony into the first two decades of the nineteenth century were Adalbert Gyrowetz (1763–1850) in Vienna and Peter Winter (1754–1825) in Munich. In

1.   The rising chromatic line in mm. 55ff. culminates with an enharmonically spelled German augmented-sixth chord in m. 58; this chord resolves typically to the octave A–a, which functions as dominant of the new tonality, D. While D *minor* is normal for such a resolution, here a particularly luxuriant sound results from a progression to D *major*.

most respects the four surviving late symphonies of Muzio Clementi (1752–1832),[2] composed in 1813–24, are stylistically more advanced. All are scored for an expanded ensemble including three trombones; the resulting fullness of texture resembles the orchestral sonorities of composers such as Johannes Brahms, from a half-century later.

The popularity of traditional types of chamber music also suffered a precipitous decline in the new century. In the 1810s and 1820s there was still some enthusiasm in Paris for chamber music for strings and winds. Anton Reicha (1770–1836), a native of Bohemia who associated with Beethoven in both Bonn and Vienna, and later established himself as an important music pedagogue and theorist in Paris,[3] wrote some twenty competent and conservative string quartets, and about two dozen wind quintets. Perhaps more interesting is the early chamber music of his student André Georges Onslow (1784–1852). The String Quintets Opp. 17–19, for example, published in 1823, move with an easy fluency and indulge in the sort of harmless chromaticism that scarcely disguises regular and traditional structural plans. The famous and prolific Louis Spohr also wrote a good bit of estimable chamber music in the first decades of the nineteenth century. Twenty-six of his 36 string quartets were composed before 1830. Best known of all his chamber music, both in his time and ours, is the Nonet, Op. 31, of 1813. Its opening measures show the ornamental chromaticism and regularly recurring feminine

Example IV–2: SPOHR, Nonet, first movement, mm. 1–8

2.   These symphonies are preserved in incomplete form in Clementi's manuscripts in the Library of Congress, Washington, D.C., and in the British Library, London. Two of them were edited (very extensively) and published by Alfredo Casella in 1938, and all four were published in a less-than-reliable edition by Pietro Spada in 1975–78 (Milan: Zerboni).

3.   Reicha's principal theoretical works are the *Cours de composition musicale* (1818) and *Traité de haute composition musicale* (1824–26). In these works he gives methodical instruction in composition in various styles. For the "modern" style his principal models are Haydn, Mozart, and early Beethoven.

cadences that leave the impression—a familiar one in this period—of a decorated but weakened Classic style (Example IV–2). Even in these early works Spohr was nonetheless a superb craftsman, perhaps somewhat too comfortable in his easy command of an inherited musical language.

SCHUBERT

The greatest composer among Beethoven's contemporaries was Franz Schubert (1797–1828). The only one of the celebrated Viennese composers of the time actually to have been born in Vienna, Schubert was vastly more responsive to the sights and sounds and habits of the city than the reclusive and deaf Beethoven. Vienna just after the Congress of 1814–15 was a place of celebration and easy gaiety. Countless coffee houses and inns were filled day and night with people who had time to relax, read, and talk. There were five principal theaters in the city where spoken drama and opera were presented, and about a half-dozen halls used for concerts. Since few of the nobility could now maintain private orchestras, professional musicians were hired for special occasions. But amateur musical ensembles flourished among the bourgeoisie. In 1781 Mozart had called Vienna "the land of the clavier," and in the earlier nineteenth century convivial music making around a keyboard instrument—now almost invariably a pianoforte—was a ubiquitous entertainment. There was a great deal of amateur part singing, often for men's chorus, much of which would remind us today of the special sound of the barbershop quartet. Informal chamber-music groups abounded; even small orchestras were assembled by those who enjoyed spending their leisure hours making music. Among all classes dancing was a veritable rage. It is reported that on one evening in carnival time in 1821 there were sixteen hundred balls in private homes in Vienna. An indigenous dance, the waltz, gradually became the favorite, replacing the more stylized, aristocratic, and foreign minuet and polonaise.

Schubert wrote music of great charm for amateur consumption. And his compositions in all categories—even the sonata, quartet, and symphony—tend to slip easily into the sonorities and rhythms of current Viennese music: the part song, the dance, and the march. But in his large-scale instrumental music, Schubert was nonetheless uniquely successful in progressively expanding the structure of the sonata from within, in accommodating an imposing architecture with lyrical expression.

The son of a schoolmaster in the suburb of Liechtenthal, Schubert received excellent general and musical training first at his father's school, and from 1808 at the Vienna Stadtkonvikt (a boarding school with spe-

Franz Schubert, 1825. A watercolor by Wilhelm August Rieder.

cial emphasis on music) and as a member of the Imperial choir. In 1813, at the age of sixteen, he left the Konvikt and the choir, entered a course in teacher's training, and taught as assistant to his father. All his spare hours were spent at music, and at the beginning of 1817, with little hope of a secure position or even of substantial commissions, he gave up teaching to devote himself exclusively to composition. He spent his dozen remaining years working feverishly, gradually winning a certain degree of recognition in the city to whose musical enrichment he dedicated his life. A portion of his music, mostly songs and short piano pieces, was published during his lifetime, but the bulk of it, particularly his large-scale compositions, remained unknown until after mid-century.

In his thirty-one years, Schubert produced a very sizable corpus of works in traditional categories: included are eight operas and Singspiele, seven Masses, eight symphonies, about a dozen string quartets, and fifteen piano sonatas. Less to be expected was his stupendous production of songs with piano accompaniment—some six hundred of them. Schubert, like most of his contemporaries, wrote orchestral music with the painful awareness that he worked in the shadow of Beethoven. Yet in his earlier works for orchestra, especially in his first six symphonies of 1813–18,[4] he seems to have plunged back into Vienna's past, to the

4. There is some ambiguity as to the numbering of Schubert's symphonies. A fragment of a symphony in D major (c. 1812) precedes the first six numbered ones of 1813–18, and there are sketches for two later symphonies. The famous *Unfinished Symphony* in B minor (1822) is sometimes called No. 7, and the "Great" C-major (1826), No. 8. For positive identification of all Schubert's music, it is best to use the "D" numbers established by Otto Erich Deutsch; the most recent edition of his thematic catalogue is *Franz Schubert. Thematisches Verzeichnis seiner Werke in chronologischer Folge* (Kassel, 1978). Here the *Unfinished Symphony* is assigned the number D. 769, and the "Great" C-major, D. 944.

music of Haydn and Mozart, for his most general stylistic models. In these symphonies Schubert's orchestration is that of the late eighteenth century: the standard four string parts, pairs of woodwinds and horns (except for the Fourth Symphony in C minor, which requires four horns) and, in two cases, trumpets and drums. The type and order of movements is also standard and invariable: two outer fast movements (the first may have a slow introduction), a slow movement, and a minuet with trio.

In several respects the early Schubert symphonies are closer to Mozart than to Haydn. Schubert normally eschews the tight-knit thematic unity of much of Haydn's instrumental music; like Mozart—and much more than Mozart—he dispenses his melodies with almost reckless largesse. And specific similarities in style to Mozart's music are not hard to find. The melodic and harmonic motion at the opening of the Fifth Symphony in B$\flat$, for example, is characteristically Mozartian. Examples IV–3a and b compare the first theme of this symphony with a very similar passage from the final movement of Mozart's Symphony in G minor, K. 550. Each consists fundamentally of a series of descending sixths; at the crucial descent from V^6 to IV^6 (mm. 72–3 in Mozart, mm. 8–9 in Schubert) each composer underlines this special harmonic motion with a striking gesture to the upper B$\flat$, as shown in the reductions in Example IV–4.[5] Another of Schubert's early symphonies, the *Tragic* (No. 4 in C minor), begins with a chromatic, dissonant introduction reminiscent of that of Mozart's String Quartet in C, K. 465. Yet much in these early symphonies is unlike the style of either Mozart or Haydn, and even more unlike that of Beethoven. For the last movement of the C-minor Symphony, for example, Schubert writes a "perpetual motion" piece with almost continuous movement in eighth notes. Against this he repeats regular, dancelike, almost trivial melodies; what is captivating here are the kaleidoscopic shifts in harmony and instrumentation. Such innocent and leisurely repetition of material is a hallmark of Schubert's music. To see how far removed such writing is from Beethoven's manner one need only compare it with the perpetual-motion finale of the latter's Fourth Symphony; instead of rollicking Viennese dance tunes, terse motives and mere fragments of melody punctuate the unvarying rhythmic motion. These gather momentum and make tense climaxes. Schubert's movement, by comparison, sounds lyrical, placid, and agreeably static.

5.   We have reliable testimony that Schubert was already well acquainted with this Mozart symphony during his days at the Konvikt. Joseph von Spaun, his fellow student, reported that "The Adagios from the Haydn symphonies moved him profoundly, and of the G-minor Symphony by Mozart he often said to me that it produced in him a violent emotion without his knowing exactly why." O. E. Deutsch, ed., *Schubert: Memoirs by his Friends* (New York, 1958), p. 126.

Example IV–3
  a. SCHUBERT, Symphony No. 5, first movement, mm. 5–19

  b. MOZART, Symphony No. 40, K. 550, fourth movement, mm. 70–
  78

Example IV–4: Mozart and Schubert Reductions

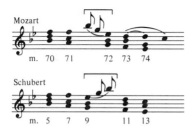

Best known today of all Schubert's symphonies is the *Unfinished* in B minor, composed in 1822. The work consists of two movements, an Allegro and Andante in contrasting keys—types perfectly usual for the first two movements of a symphony—and there can be no question but that the work is incomplete. Schubert actually began to write the third movement, a Scherzo, but gave it up for reasons that have never been fully explained. It is clear, however, that in this work the composer struck out in a direction quite different from that of his first six symphonies. It starts with a lugubrious eight-measure statement in octaves by cellos and basses, the distinctive modal sound of which is mainly due to the A♮ (the lowered seventh degree in B minor) in m. 4 (Example IV–5a). With unaccustomed economy Schubert offers only two other distinct melodies in this movement: the "real" first theme (Example IV–5b) and the famous dancelike music in G major shown in Example IV–5c. These themes are moreover related by distinct motivic connections; disjunct melodic motion with prominent leaps of a fourth or fifth, as well as a rising three-note stepwise motion are important features of

Example IV–5: SCHUBERT, *Unfinished Symphony*, first movement
a. mm. 1–8

b. mm. 13–20

c. mm. 42–47

all three. Then in the development section, he confines himself to a studious working out of the first of these melodies.

Surely Schubert is not following his natural inclinations here; the development, in particular, with its tense climaxes and insistent bela-boring of melodic cells, looks like an imitation of Beethoven. That this music in fact turns out sounding so little like Beethoven is surely not for want of effort on Schubert's part. His materials simply do not lend themselves very well to Beethovenian treatment. All three melodies of this movement have a lyrical, "closed" character; they are more like finished products than raw material suitable for rigorous development. Even in his strongest climaxes Schubert is led by the nature of his mel-odies (and his own nature as a composer) to repeat rhythmically regu-lar, neatly partitioned segments of music, thus checking the generation of any long-term forward momentum. The glories of this symphony, whatever Schubert's intentions, lie in the grace of its individual parts: its irresistible melodies, its exquisite instrumental coloring and surpris-ing harmonic turns.

Schubert grew up in a Viennese household which, like many others, cultivated chamber music as a normal domestic diversion. From early childhood the young musician took the viola or violin part in music making at home, and he did the same on a more formal basis while enrolled at the Stadtkonvikt. It was only natural that as a composer Schubert should devote himself persistently to the special problems and

A Family Concert, ca. 1800; engraving by Meno Haas.

special advantages posed by small ensembles. Fragments of string quartets as well as separate minuets, *Deutsche Tänze,* and one "Ouverture" written for quartet survive from as early as 1810. Most of these pieces apparently saw their first performance in the Schubert home. The same is true of the first six of the ten complete quartets written in 1812–15: all this music was intended for pleasant evenings of amateur playing. Reminiscent alternately of Mozart (or Haydn) and of popular Viennese idioms, they show only occasional flashes of Schubert's more personal and serious manner. Several movements have double secondary tonalities. The first movement of the D-major Quartet of 1813 (D. 74), for example, modulates as expected to its dominant, A; but in the recapitulation a new key area, the subdominant, G, usually only touched upon in the return of the bridge, is extensively explored. Here, at the age of sixteen, Schubert is innocently experimenting with the sort of extension of standard tonal plans that will come to characterize much of his large-scale instrumental composition.

Of the numerous fragmentary string quartets Schubert left us, one, the estimable *Quartettsatz* (Quartet Movement) of 1820, has become a lasting part of the Schubert repertory. Of the complete quartets, most ambitious and impressive are the three latest works of 1824–26, the Quartets in A minor (D. 804), D minor (D. 810), and G major (D. 887). The D-minor Quartet (called *Death and the Maiden*), like the

Example IV–6: SCHUBERT, String Quartet D. 810, first movement, mm. 61–66

Unfinished Symphony, often falls self-consciously into Beethovenian mannerisms. But the result, especially in the first movement, is altogether satisfying. A harsh, peremptory opening motive paired with a subdued *pianissimo* response resembles many Beethoven themes (two in particular are the opening of the String Quartet in E minor, Op. 59, No. 2, and the beginning of the third movement of the Quartet Op. 131, ARM 3). In the course of the movement Schubert manages to reconcile such imposing opening materials with ingratiating—and eminently Schubertian—tunes of perfect harmonic and metric regularity (see Example IV–6).

This quartet derives its subtitle *Death and the Maiden (Der Tod und das Mädchen)* from its slow movement, a set of variations on music from the composer's own lied of that name composed in 1817. Schubert used only the piano introduction to his song; its unchanging chordal structure, repeated melody tones, and homogeneous rhythm are the stuff of which processional music for funerals are made.[6] From these somber materials Schubert constructed an extended binary form to serve as his theme, and added four variations plus a short coda. For the most part the variations are conventional. Stylized figurations accompany integral presentations of the melody in one or another of the instruments. But the third variation, the *minore* one, leaves a different impression: relentless *sforzati* on every beat in the first section and an energetic double diminution of the rhythm of the theme inject a note of vehemence that effectively checks a certain threat of monotony in this melancholy movement.

In addition to his ten complete string quartets and numerous fragmentary ones Schubert produced various other kinds of chamber music: two string trios, three compositions for string quintet, an octet for strings and winds, four piano trios, one piece for piano quartet, and one piano quintet called *The Trout (Forellen-Quintett).* Both the Octet (D. 803, 1824) and the *Trout Quintet* (D. 667, 1819) feature odd assemblages of instruments and were created for specific groups of players. Undoubtedly influenced by Beethoven's Septet, the Octet is a sprawling six-movement divertimento-like piece for string quartet plus double bass, clarinet, horn, and bassoon. In his Piano Quintet, instead of simply adding a piano part to a string quartet (the usual later arrangement),[7] Schubert also deleted one violin and added a double bass. Such an ensemble is potentially bottom-heavy. But Schubert habitually puts the

6.   As in the funeral march to Beethoven's Piano Sonata Op. 26; an example from Beethoven more strikingly like Schubert's music is the Andante con moto from the Seventh Symphony. The poetry of Schubert's song is cast in the form of a dialogue in which Death extends his macabre invitation to a reluctant young maiden.

7.   Historical accuracy might require us to speak of adding parts for a string quartet to a piano sonata; all the genres of chamber music with piano in this period are descended from the "accompanied keyboard sonata."

Example IV–7: SCHUBERT *Trout Quintet,* fourth movement, mm. 128–35

piano parts of his chamber compositions in a high tessitura; in fact he often writes simple octaves as in the *primo* part of ordinary four-hand keyboard music—in this case to the clear advantage of the overall texture.

Throughout its five movements the *Trout Quintet* echoes strains of Viennese popular music. This is true even of the fourth movement (ARM 4), the theme-and-variations that gives the piece its name. The theme is fashioned once again from one of Schubert's own Lieder, *Die Forelle* (D. 550, 1817), this time incorporating almost the entire vocal melody. And once again the variations that follow tread well-worn paths: the entire melody appears consecutively in the various instruments while the others weave figurations around it. For the listener who knows *Die Forelle,* however, the final variation offers something special. The square-cut melody is given back its original accompaniment—a lilting figure in triplets that is the chief glory of the song—and the movement ends with distinctively Schubertian simplicity and elegance (see Example IV–7). Both this movement and the corresponding one in the *Death and the Maiden Quartet* show how strikingly Schubert's notion of theme-and-variations differed from Beethoven's. In the *Diabelli Variations* and the variations of the Quartet Op. 131, as we have seen, Beethoven indulges in radical thematic transformation and audacious novelties of figuration and rhythm. Schubert's variations are by comparison formally conventional. Their charm lies elsewhere: in ever-fresh rhythms and inexhaustible melodic inventiveness.

In March 1824, Schubert wrote to his friend Leopold Kupelwieser,

> Of songs I have not written many new ones, but I have tried my hand at several instrumental works, for I wrote two Quartets for violins, viola and violoncello[8] and an Octet, and I want to write another quartet, in fact I intend to pave my way towards grand symphony in that manner.—The latest in Vienna is that Beethoven is to give a concert at which he is to produce his new Symphony, three movements from his new Mass and a new Overture.[9]—God willing, I too am thinking of giving a similar concert next year.[10]

Any mention of his own efforts at large-scale instrumental composition invariably invoked the spectre of Beethoven. Throughout his career as a writer of quartets and symphonies Schubert vacillated between acts of capitulation to Beethoven's overpowering influence and the musical habits that came to him more naturally: adherence to an older Viennese Classic style, an uninhibited response to the dances, marches, and tavern music of bourgeois Vienna, and experiment with the leisurely pace and expanded harmonic pallette that mark his most personal compositional manner. At the end of his life he was to achieve a magnificent synthesis of these divergent tendencies in a series of masterpieces in large forms, all composed in 1827–28: the Piano Trios in B$\flat$ (D. 898) and E$\flat$ (D. 929), the C-major String Quintet, D. 956, the "Great" C-major Symphony, the last three Piano Sonatas, D. 958, 959, and 960, and—in quite a different vein—the last of his six Masses, D. 950 in E$\flat$.

MUSIC FOR PIANO: CLEMENTI, DUSÍK, AND FIELD

The musical instrument that Schubert and most other nineteenth-century composers played best was the piano. Immensely versatile, this instrument could be used as an equal partner in chamber music, it could provide an accompaniment for other instruments or voice, or it could be played all by itself. It was and is the only instrument regularly heard in a solo capacity in public. As pianos are rather large and complicated

---

8. The String Quartet in A minor (D. 804) and the *Death and the Maiden Quartet* (D. 810).

9. This concert took place on May 7, 1824, at the Kärnthnerthor Theater. The works of Beethoven to which Schubert refers are the Ninth Symphony, the *Missa solemnis,* and the overture *Die Weihe des Hauses.*

10. Otto Erich Deutsch, ed., *Schubert: a Documentary Biography,* trans. Eric Blom (London, 1946), p. 339. Schubert's own concert—the only one of his entire life—took place on March 26, 1828.

machines, dependent upon sophisticated technology and hard to move about, it is only natural that the great urban centers should enjoy something of a monopoly in their cultivation and use. In the late eighteenth and early nineteenth centuries three cities were preeminent in the manufacture of pianos and in attracting pianists: London, Vienna, and Paris.

In the rich concert life of London the piano was well known since J. C. Bach began to play public solos on small English square pianofortes in the late 1760s. Beginning in the 1780s and 1790s a splendid succession of young pianists was heard on the London stage: Muzio Clementi, J. L. Dusík (1760–1812), J. B. Cramer (1771–1858), John Field (1782–1837), and Ignaz Moscheles (1794–1870). In addition to these long-term residents of England, others appeared for brief engagements: J. N. Hummel, Daniel Steibelt, Friedrich Kalkbrenner (1785–1849), and the boy Franz Liszt (1811–86), who made his London debut in 1824. Only one of these pianists, John Field of Dublin, was born in the British Isles. In the itineraries of the more peripatetic of these musicians we can detect the beginnings of that familiar nineteenth-century phenomenon, the touring virtuoso.

Until the mid-nineteenth century, public pianists for the most part played their own music; in this branch of music making the traditional identity of composer and performer lingered on. Concertos, sonatas, variations, rondos, and pieces of uncertain lineage with names like "capriccio," "fantasy," "impromptu," and the like were performed by the composer on stage and then promptly offered for sale (often in simplified versions) to a receptive public. Perhaps the earliest pianist-composer to practice this diversified profession on an international scale was the cosmopolitan Clementi, who was born in Rome, but lived in London from about 1774 and made his first European tour in 1781–84. Clementi's piano music, first published in London, Paris, and Vienna, was quickly pirated by a host of unauthorized printers (this was an accepted eighteenth-century practice) and disseminated throughout Europe. His powerful, tight-knit sonatas of the 1780s and 1790s, as we have seen, influenced Beethoven from about the turn of the century.

Another facet of Clementi's variegated keyboard style, however, was more decisive in its impact upon subsequent piano writing and upon the whole of nineteenth-century musical practice. As early as his Opus 2 of 1779 he wrote melodic lines lavishly decorated with double-note turns and chromatic altered tones astonishingly like those of Parisian piano style two generations later (see Example IV–8). And some twenty years afterwards he composed music that seems comfortably at home in the new century: in his Sonatas Op. 40 (1802) and Op. 50 (c. 1805) and the Capriccios Op. 47 (published in 1821) Clementi characteristically indulges in luxuriant melodic ornament, strong chromaticism, far-flung tonal relationships, and long stretches of mellifluous passage-

Example IV–8: CLEMENTI, Sonata Op. 2, No. 4, first movement, mm.
1–7

work. These are all familiar traits of Romantic piano music. In Clementi's works they are present, full-grown, from the beginning of the nineteenth century. The pattern of Clementi's career prefigured that of many nineteenth-century pianist-composers in another way as well. From the late 1790s he became increasingly involved in the "music business": in manufacture and sale of pianos and in music publishing and editing. From 1798 until 1830 Clementi and Co. was one of the world's major vendors of these necessities of musical life.

Jan Ladislav Dusík, some eight years Clementi's junior, was born in Bohemia and practiced his craft as pianist and composer in Germany, Holland, and France before coming to London (as a refugee from the French Revolution) in 1789. There he resided as a pianist, composer, and publisher until 1810, when the collapse of his business ventures (for which he showed less talent than Clementi) forced his departure. Moving restlessly during the Napoleonic years from Hamburg to the service of Prince Louis Ferdinand of Prussia (himself an ambitious composer), and then to Paris as music director to Prince Talleyrand, Dusík gained wide international recognition as a virtuoso pianist and composer. Yet the crucial segment of his career, that in which his mature style took shape, was the decade spent in London. Dusík produced the usual profusion of "commercial" music in some sixty accompanied keyboard sonatas and a great many salon pieces; one is the morbidly programmatic *La Mort de Marie Antoinette,* complete with a descending glissando to depict the falling of the blade of the guillotine. But like his older colleague Clementi, he devoted his most serious and fruitful efforts to his solo piano sonatas, some thirty-two in all.

The earliest surviving solo sonata of Dusík, according to the best

Example IV–9: DUSÍK, Piano Sonata Op. 5, No. 3, first movement, mm. 45–54

information now available[11] is his Opus 5, No. 3 (C 43), in A♭ major, apparently first published in 1788. This composition, like more than half of Dusík's sonatas, is in two movements. The first is an extended sonata-allegro form in which classic keyboard writing is mingled with clear harbingers of Dusík's mature style: long stretches of wide-ranging keyboard figuration, splotches of chromatic ornament, and abrupt shifts into foreign tonalities. Example IV–9, taken from the exposition of this movement, shows one of Dusík favorite harmonic stratagems: a sudden move from the tonic through tonic minor (A♭ minor) to the major key on the lowered sixth degree (enharmonically spelled E major). The effect is brilliant and rhetorical; overuse in years to come by Dusík and his followers made this procedure almost a staple of Romantic keyboard music.

A characteristic late sonata of Dusík's, his Opus 61 (C 211) in F♯ minor, was written in memory of his patron Prince Louis Ferdinand, who had recently been killed in the battle against Napoleon at Saalfeld. This two-movement sonata (ARM 5) was published in Paris by Pleyel in 1807 under the title *Élégie harmonique sur la mort de son altesse royale, le Prince Louis Ferdinand de Prusse, en forme de sonata pour le piano forte.* . . . The work exudes a rhetorical pathos, employing extremes of dynamics, register, and harmonic tension to achieve its expressive ends. An introductory Lento patetico opens with a low-lying two-voice figure in tempo rubato (in the eighteenth-century sense), set over a tonic pedal. This gives way, in m. 11, to a somewhat distant imitation of accompanied recitative in which exclamatory diminished seventh chords in a

---

11. The dissertation by Howard Allen Craw, *A Biography and Thematic Catalogue of the Works of Dussek (1760–1812)* (University of Southern California, 1964). This work arranges Dusík's compositions in chronological order.

high register alternate with quiet melodic tones below. Chromatic harmonies obliterate any sense of tonality in this section, until in m. 37 the music finds its way back to the tonic, F♯ minor, in preparation for the "arioso" (m. 43) that follows the "recitative." This new melodic passage now reestablishes the harmonic bearings of the Introduction and leads quickly to the opening of the movement proper.

The exposition, marked Tempo agitato, begins with a single-line melody accompanied by an intrusive off-beat figure below—a keyboard texture strongly reminiscent of certain minor-keyed, "impassioned" sonatas of Haydn, Mozart, and Clementi.[12] After fewer than a dozen measures the music turns toward G minor, and then, more decisively, to the dominant, C♯ major. This is the true secondary key of the movement, but Dusík characteristically conceals this fact by means of two further excursions, still within the exposition, to D major (the sixth degree) and B minor (the subdominant)[13]—in both cases in conjunction with new thematic material. Finally in m. 96, a striking new two-handed figuration, securely in C♯, drives to the end of the exposition. An approximate plan of the entire movement might be constructed thus:

	Introduction					Exposition							
m.1	11		37	43			53	63	71	75	83	88	96	
x	y			z	‖		a		b	c		d		:‖
i	i ~~~~~~~		i	i	‖:		i	(♭ii)	V	VI	iv	~~~~	V	‖

	Development						Recapitulation		
113		121	126	136	144	150	161	174	181
b		c		d	c		a	c	d
V/iii		iii	~~~~	♯vii ~~~~~~~		(i)	i	i	i

Several enduring traits of Romantic keyboard styles may be seen here. A weakening of the traditional tonic–dominant axis of sonata-type movements results from the introduction of foreign tonalities that function as ornamental neighboring keys to the principal ones; in the exposition ♭ii is thus related to I, and both VI and iv act as temporary diversions from V. But perhaps even more innovative are the substantial stretches of genuinely indeterminate tonality effected by ubiquitous diminished-seventh chords and chromatic shifts. And in this piece the special skills of the professional nineteenth-century keyboard virtuoso are everywhere evident: fast figurations for both hands requiring large leaps and intricate changes of direction, and even faster multi-octave arpeggios and scales reflect the predilections of a new breed of "public" pianist.

12. Haydn, Hob. XVI: 20 in C minor, first movement; Mozart, K. 310 in A minor, finale; Clementi, Op. 7, No. 3, first movement. This movement also shows a fascinating similarity in musical materials and procedures to Clementi's Op. 50, No. 3 (first movement), not published until 1821, but apparently largely finished by 1805.

13. These two keys are introduced, respectively, in mm. 75 and 83.

The overall effect of such a piece is one of grandiloquent, theatrical expressiveness; it is equally far removed from the heroic middle style of Beethoven and the terse, introverted musical speech of his late period—and it is more representative of the times than either.

A younger piano composer within the London orbit was Johann Baptist Cramer, a member of a musical family that moved from Mannheim to London in 1774 when he was three years old. Cramer studied briefly with Clementi (apparently only in 1783—the protracted hostilities between the two musicians may have begun this early) and then with the aging C. F. Abel. About 1788 he made his debut both as a composer (with the publication of his Sonatas Op. 1) and as a concert performer. In subsequent years he appeared regularly on English and European concert stages and produced an unceasing stream of music, much of it consisting of sonatas (some 120 in all) and most of it of rather an old-fashioned cast. His keyboard etudes were praised by Beethoven, and they alone of all his music are still used for study today.

Of more intrinsic and historical interest is the piano music of John Field, the native of Dublin who came to London in 1793, became under the tutelage of Clementi a recognized virtuoso at an early age, and accompanied his teacher to Russia in 1803, there to remain for most of his life. Pictured in contemporary accounts as an awkward, tractable young man[14]—and later as a dissolute alcoholic—Field was nonetheless an almost legendary performer whose style of writing and playing for the piano exerted a decisive effect upon the virtuosos of the next generation: Chopin, Liszt, Thalberg, and others. Immediately striking in Field's music, in comparison with that of his older London contemporaries, is the dramatic reduction of the proportion of sonatas and sonata-like pieces in his oeuvre. He wrote only four solo keyboard sonatas, three of them early compositions published in 1801 and dedicated to Clementi. The bulk of Field's keyboard music consists of shorter pieces adorned with all sorts of names, some old, some new: there are the familiar-sounding rondos, variations, polonaises, and etudes; more avant-garde are the designations "waltz," "romance," and "pastorale." But one type of piano piece became Field's special province: his fifteen nocturnes for piano were apparently the first such pieces, and served as a model for Chopin and other Romantic keyboard composers. Field's nocturnes characteristically present a lyrical, sometimes lavishly ornamented melody for the right hand supported by a wide-ranging arpeg-

---

14. In his autobiography, Louis Spohr writes vividly of Field's first months in St. Petersburg, "I still keep in my memory a picture of the pale, overgrown youth, whom I never saw again. When Field, who had outgrown his clothes, sat down at the piano, stretched his long arms toward the keyboard so that the sleeves pulled up almost to his elbows, then the whole figure appeared awkward in a most English way; but as soon as his soulful playing began, one forgot everything and was all ear." *Louis Spohr's Selbstbiographie* (Cassel and Göttingen: Georg H. Wigand, 1860), 1, p. 43.

giated accompaniment. Most often the harmonic motion is slow, as individual sonorities are sustained through extensive tonic pedal points.[15] This allows for special "atmospheric" effects by lavish use of pedal—it was this trait of Field's music, in fact, that Robert Schumann singled out in 1835 as the Irishman's signal contribution to Romantic musical style.[16]

When pianists appeared in public concerts from the time of Mozart until the middle of the nineteenth century, the sort of piece they most often played was the piano concerto. Almost invariably in three movements, and featuring dialogue with the orchestra that amalgamated the tutti–solo exchanges of the Baroque concerto with tonal and thematic elements of the sonata, such concertos were the most characteristic type of public piano music. But publishing concertos was always an expensive and risky business. Each pianist came with his own—so there was no need for concert managers to buy anyone else's—and difficult music with orchestral accompaniment was never in much demand in amateur circles.[17] As a result, a great many concertos by leading pianists from this period have been lost—or, as in the case of works by both Clementi and Dusík, preserved only in more salable arrangements as sonatas.

It is thus fortunate that all seven of Field's known concertos were published in full score during his lifetime (five of them by the Leipzig firm Breitkopf und Härtel in 1815–17). These compositions illustrate certain characteristic tendencies in the Romantic piano concerto: the exquisite balance of forces that is the glory of Mozart's and Beethoven's concertos is tipped in favor of the solo instrument, the orchestral writing is rather primitive, and the extended harmonic and tonal syntax we have seen in sonatas of the period is exploited. In the first movement of his Third Concerto, in E♭, for example, Field writes a remarkably conservative-sounding, chordal introduction for an orchestra of Mozartean proportions. The piano then enters as from a different world with a stentorian pronouncement that becomes ever more chromatic and ornamental, all over a tonic pedal point. Later, en route to the dominant (B♭ major), there is an abrupt detour to the lowered third (G♭ major), where the piano once more embarks upon an elaborate lyrical excursion, as shown in Example IV–10.

This music, without the minimal orchestral accompaniment, might have come from a Field nocturne. It has all the hallmarks of his most

---

15. The opening of Clementi's Sonata Op. 2, No. 4, shown above in Example IV–8, is remarkably prophetic of Field's most characteristic keyboard texture. There is good reason to think that Field studied and played this sonata.

16. *Neue Zeitschrift für Musik,* 2 (1835): 127.

17. The London correspondent for the Leipzig *Allgemeine musikalische Zeitung* wrote in 1805 (7: 473), "Large-scale music, full scores and the like, no one can print here, for they would only remain on the shelves."

Example IV–10: FIELD, Piano Concerto No. 3, first movement, mm. 113–30

characteristic solo piano style; a sonorous accompaniment is effected by wide-ranging arpeggios or expansive bass-note-plus-chord figures, in addition to generous use of pedal facilitated by the slow-moving bass. The single-line melody above is laden with ornament, particularly the ubiquitous appoggiaturas on strong beats (11 of the piano's 15 measures in Example IV–10 begin with one) that will become a cliché in piano music of the 1830s and 1840s. A passage such as this will inevitably remind modern listeners of Chopin; but its salient traits were in fact to be the common property of a whole generation of pianist-composers.

Nearly all the leading pianists of Beethoven's generation (not including Beethoven himself) performed at one time or another in Paris, and all had their music published there. But few were born in France, or were educated there during the tumultuous Napoleonic years or the uncertain Restoration (1815–30), or lived there for any length of time.

When the music historian and critic François Fétis took stock of the musicians active in Paris in 1830, he named the pianists Kalkbrenner, Herz, Zimmerman, Woetz, Mme. de Mongeroult, and some other extremely obscure figures.[18] Of these only Friedrich Kalkbrenner and Henri Herz (1803–88) achieved international standing, and neither was originally French. Fétis might conceivably have added to his list the names of the venerable piano pedagogue Louis Adam (1758–1848)[19] and François-Adrien Boieldieu (1775–1834), the opera composer who began his career as a pianist-composer. But in general, Paris during the Beethovenian years was more a consumer than a producer of pianists and piano music.

Beethoven's own city of Vienna surely produced more distinguished pianist-composers during the early decades of the nineteenth century than any other. Most of these musicians, like Beethoven himself, were born elsewhere, a remarkable number of them in nearby Bohemia. One such, the prolific Abbé Joseph Gelinek, we have already met in his role as the young Beethoven's competitor. Gelinek was best known for his sets of variations on popular tunes—so well known that Carl Maria von Weber was moved to write a bit of unkind doggerel on the subject:

Kein Thema auf der Welt verschonte dein Genie,	No theme on earth has escaped your genius;
Das simpelste allein—dich selbst—variirst du nie.	But the simplest one of all—yourself—you never vary.

However formulaic and conventional most of Gelinek's variations may be, some provide a striking (if not altogether pleasant) foretaste of the virtuoso figurations in which more than one future generation of pianists was to indulge. His Variations on "Là ci darem la mano" from Mozart's *Don Giovanni* (the beginning of the tenth one is shown in Example IV–11) may well have provided a model for Chopin's similar elaborations of the theme, written in 1827.

Example IV–11: GELINEK, Variations on "Là ci darem la mano," Variation 10

---

18. François Fétis, *Curiosités historiques de la musique* (Paris, 1830), p. 146.
19. Adam wrote a widely used pedagogical treatise, *Méthode nouvelle pour le piano* (Paris, 1802).

CZERNY, MOSCHELES, HUMMEL

Beethoven's faithful pupil and friend Carl Czerny (1791–1857) was born of Bohemian parentage in Vienna and spent virtually his entire life there playing, teaching, and compiling some 1000 musical *opera,* nearly all of them for piano. Most valued among pianists for his prodigious output of keyboard exercises, and by scholars for his observant reminiscences of Beethoven, Czerny is always seen as the archetypal pedagogue, as a transmitter—despite those 1000 opus numbers—rather than a creator. Much more cosmopolitan, and more influential as a composer, was the Bohemian-born pianist Ignaz Moscheles who was instructed by Albrechtsberger and Salieri in Vienna, and befriended by Beethoven. In 1820 his playing caused a sensation in Paris; the next year he took up residence in London, and after numerous concert tours collaborated with his former student Mendelssohn and with Schumann in the founding of the Leipzig Conservatory. Like many of his generation, Moscheles seemed to vacillate between the attractions of frothy salon-style composition and the hard work of serious artistic production. In his eight concertos and four sonatas for piano, Moscheles shows his more earnest, craftsmanlike—and conservative—side. With certain exceptions, such as the single-movement *Sonate melancholique* in F♯ minor (c. 1822), Moscheles's efforts in these genres reflect a continuing adherence to the manner of middle-period Beethoven, plus some more modern ornament. Moscheles to some extent shared the fate of Cramer and Czerny. Most of his compositions, both the frankly *à la mode* ones (such as his *Alexander Variations*) and those that were more seriously motivated, passed quickly out of fashion; his piano etudes alone enjoyed a longer currency.[20]

The career of Moscheles's older colleague, Johann Nepomuk Hummel, was, if anything, even more cosmopolitan and variegated. He was born in Pressburg (now Bratislava), but came to Vienna early enough to study with Mozart and Haydn, as well as with the entrenched musical pedagogues of the city, Albrechtsberger and Salieri. Developing at a phenomenal rate, Hummel as a child charmed audiences in Vienna with his elegant, fluent style of playing, and did the same in London as early as 1791. Later, while continuing his life as a touring virtuoso and maintaining long-term employment at the courts of Stuttgart and Weimar, he produced an unceasing stream of compositions: church music, several operas, chamber music of various kinds (best-known is his Septet, Op. 74), and a great mass of piano music. There is the usual profusion of fashionable rondos, variations, and fantasies which include generous doses of conventional piano figuration, especially mellifluous

---

20. In 1838 Schumann declared that Moscheles's Etudes Op. 95 had something of the "romantic coloring" of the "most recent" piano style. *Neue Zeitschrift für Musik,* 8 (1838): 202.

A Bösendorfer piano, made in Vienna in 1828.

passagework that is bound to strike modern ears as superficial. Hummel's seven piano concertos, though to an extent similar in style, have a higher specific gravity; particularly the Fourth Concerto in B minor (Op. 90) and the Sixth in A♭ major (Op. 113) are in harmony and figuration more inventive than the common run of such pieces of the period.

Like many piano composers of his time, Hummel wrote a proportionately small number of solo sonatas—there are nine—but invested them with his best efforts. The earlier ones (Op. 2, No. 3 in C, Op. 13 in E♭, Op. 30 in C) show clear signs of the young Hummel's Mozartean patrimony, along with a Clementi-like interest in bravura passagework, and occasional splashes of the decorative chromaticism in which virtually every keyboard composer but Beethoven indulged during the first two decades of the new century. The F♯ minor Sonata, Op. 81 (c. 1819), is a different sort of work; the driving intensity of its figurations and its insistent terse motives may remind us of the Beethoven of the *Appassionata Sonata,* Op. 57 (see Example IV–12a). But other characteristics of this composition point to Hummel's central position among the most *au courant* denizens of the concert stage and salon. The first movement proceeds from F♯ minor to the extremely remote lowered fifth (C major), and then promptly compromises all the previous drama and passion with a repetitious dancelike passage of the most conventional sort (see Example IV–12b). Much lost ground is regained as Hummel works out the rest of the movement, often in impressive fashion. The piece is a good illustration of the ever-present contradictions in style and intent among public musicians of this time: popular success and serious artistic attainment often proved immiscible. But in this instance posterity judged well; Hummel's F♯ minor sonata is a worthy work, and one of the few of his compositions that remained in the

Example IV–12: HUMMEL, Piano Sonata Op. 81, first movement
a. mm. 1–12

b. mm. 43–46

repertories of succeeding generations.[21]

The pianist-composer Václav Jan Tomášek (1774–1850) was described by his famous student Eduard Hanslick as the "musical Dalailama" of Prague. Tomášek spent his entire career in his native city, composing, teaching, entertaining famous guests, and making pronouncements about the musical life around him, including some disapproving remarks about the late style of Beethoven.[22] Tomášek was widely regarded as a musical conservative, and he produced his full quota of compositions in traditional categories: operas, church music, symphonies, and sonatas. But what has attracted most attention, in his time and ours, are his numerous smaller piano pieces with the intriguing names "eclogue," "dithyramb," and "rhapsody." On the strength of these compositions (or perhaps of their names), Tomášek has often been pointed to as a foun-

---

21. The two compositions that, judging from his diaries, the young Schumann practiced most assiduously were Hummel's A-minor Concerto and F♯-minor Sonata.

22. Most of Tomášek's reflections on the music of his time are to be found in his *Memoirs*, which appeared in Prague in 1845–50 (excerpts are translated in *The Musical Quarterly*, 32[1946]: 244–64).

der of the Romantic "character piece"—a composition with its own special personality and expression, as opposed to one that is merely representative of a genre. The names he chose are all poetic terms from classical antiquity. An eclogue is a pastoral poem, a dithyramb a kind of poetry in praise of Bacchus; rhapsody was the name for a selection for recitation from epic poetry—this last being the only one of these titles adopted by later Romantic composers. Most of Tomášek's character pieces are in style and shape somewhat old fashioned. Nearly all fall into the formal pattern of the Minuet-Trio (two binary sections ending with a repetition of the first), and the music is simple and diatonic. When Tomášek sets out to write more dramatically and expressively (as in the Rhapsodies Op. 41, c. 1813), he resorts to the disjunct textures and imitations of recitative typical of the *empfindsam* style of C. P. E. Bach in the previous century. In a few pieces, however, we hear suggestions of a more modern manner of piano writing. The Eclogue Op. 66, No. 6 (c. 1819) has the long atmospheric tonic pedal points and the resonant arpeggiation that were becoming a commonplace among Tomášek's younger contemporaries (see Example IV–13).

Example IV–13: TOMÁŠEK, Eclogue, Op. 66, No. 6, mm. 1–4

SCHUBERT'S PIANO MUSIC

Among all the pianist-composers contemporary with Beethoven, the one now recognized as greatest was once again the Viennese Schubert. If any single external factor distinguishes Schubert from all the other pianists mentioned here, it is that he was not a public virtuoso, and the kind and quality of his keyboard music reflect this crucial distinction. The technical showpieces that were *de rigueur* in every virtuoso's repertory had little place in the life of Schubert, who performed at the keyboard only for groups of his friends, or at most, provided music for the ubiquitous Viennese balls. His keyboard compositions fall roughly into two categories: modest pieces with a host of different names, appropriate for domestic amateur performance; and large-scale compositions in several movements, most of them sonatas, in which Schubert patiently explored the most profound and intricate possibilities of his art.

Much of Schubert's "amateur" music for piano has great charm. There are ländler and waltzes, marches, rondos, and variations; eight pieces were published with the evocative title "Impromptu," and one set appeared (ungrammatically) as *Moments musicales* (D. 780, c. 1823).[23] Throughout these pieces, as in most of Schubert's instrumental compositions, one hears adumbrations of Viennese popular music: the rhythms of the dance and the melancholy close-position chords of the part-song. The second of the *Moments musicales* shows one characteristically Schubertian piano texture, together with a poignant chromatic coloring of flatted thirds injected into both tonic and dominant sonorities (see Example IV–14).

Example IV–14: SCHUBERT, *Moment musical* No. 2, mm. 1–8

Among Schubert's latest and finest compositions are the three expansive piano sonatas, D 958 in C minor, 959 in A, and 960 in B♭, written during the last months of his life. The last of these is a masterpiece in which Schubert develops to the full his unique gifts for melodic invention, captivating piano sound and figuration, and striking key relationships. And in all four movements can be heard, once again, Schubert's habitual evocation of the dance. But however clearly this music displays the composer's personal stamp, it is nonetheless a sonata, and for Schubert that category had special implications: it carried with it the inviolable compositional traditions of Haydn, Mozart, and especially Beethoven. In both outer movements Schubert is at pains to engage in determined developmental procedures that are not really native to his style, but which in this case succeed brilliantly.

---

23. How casual publishers were about the names for such music can be seen in the alternate titles for the third number of this collection: *Air russe* and *Plaintes d'un troubadour*.

The first movement of the Sonata in B♭ is a splendid example of Schubert's reconciliation, in his late music, of the demands of tradition with his own special gifts. It starts with a theme that captures the best of Romantic piano sound: octave-plus-sixth doubling diffuses the shape of the melody throughout the entire texture as it creates sonorities of special warmth and resonance (see Example IV–15).[24] And the overall shape of this spacious movement shows Schubert's characteristic expansion of the sonata-allegro structure. An extended sojourn in the tonality of the lowered sixth (F♯ minor) assumes the status of a second subsidiary key before the dominant is reached—in Schenkerian analysis it would be regarded as an upper-semitone embellishment of the dominant. And that large-scale semitone motion from ♭VI–V is reflected in many details of the movement, particularly in a mysteriously recurring "leitmotif," a trilled G♭–F in a very low register, with which Example IV–15 ends.

Example IV–15: SCHUBERT, Sonata in B♭, D. 960, first movement, mm. 1–9

In the finale of this sonata, there is a specific gesture of homage to Beethoven, just recently deceased. This dancelike movement begins enigmatically with a long-held octave G, the major sixth degree of the tonic, B♭. This G turns out to be dominant to C minor, whose statement delays the entrance of the true tonic until m. 10, as is shown in Example IV–16a. The harmonic similarity to the opening theme (also dancelike) of the finale of Beethoven's String Quartet Op. 130 in the

24.   Earlier approaches to this sort of texture can be seen in the soprano–tenor doubling at the beginning of Beethoven's Sonata in A♭, Op. 26, and the opening piano statement of his Fourth Piano Concerto.

same key, completed just before his final illness and death, is unmistakable (see Example IV–16b). Thus, in his last major composition Schubert acknowledged the sort of debt to his older contemporary that was to prove a burden to nearly every composer of instrumental music of the nineteenth century. But he did so in a composition that fully establishes his own greatness in the very traditions to which Beethoven seemed to have gained a proprietary claim.

Example IV–16
   a. SCHUBERT, Piano Sonata D. 960, fourth movement, mm. 1–10

   b. BEETHOVEN, String Quartet Op. 130, fourth movement, mm. 1–10

CHAPTER V

The Lied: Schubert and His Predecessors

A prominent thread in the tangled skein of ideas and attitudes that led to the full maturation of Romanticism was a growing admiration for the "primitive." In the later eighteenth century primitivism appeared under two separate guises. Certain writers evinced a new liking for whatever seemed untamed and irregular, as in the eighteenth-century English garden or, as some saw it, in the plays of Shakespeare. As early as 1740, in his poem *The Enthusiast*, Joseph Wharton inquired:

> What are the lays of artful Addison
> Coldly correct, to Shakespeare's warbling wild?

Others saw simplicity, naïvete, and spontaneity as the most desirable attributes in works of art and literature. Thus the sensibility of the unspoiled peasant, the "noble savage," and the child were held up as models for the artist by Jean-Jacques Rousseau and his contemporaries in England. "Many a genius probably there has been which could neither write nor read," exclaimed Edward Young.[1] Gaining access to human nature and its products unsullied by the corrosive effects of civilization became a favorite pursuit of the educated classes; thus from about 1750 there was enormous enthusiasm throughout Western Europe for folk poetry, and for works of folk art and music.

In the British Isles, Bishop Thomas Percy (1729–1811) edited his very popular *Reliques of Ancient English Poetry* in 1765. Even more influential were the remarkable works of the Scot James MacPherson, who from 1760 to 1765 published a series of supposed translations from a shadowy third-century Gaelic bard, Ossian. Though Ossian and his verses were mainly the product of MacPherson's imagination, he was promptly acclaimed in England and Germany as a newly discovered "natural genius"—as another Homer or Shakespeare.[2] In Germany the influential litterateur Johann Gottfried von Herder (1744–1803) came under

---

1. *Conjectures on Original Composition*, 1759.
2. Samuel Johnson soon challenged the authenticity of MacPherson's "discovery" (*Journey to the Western Islands of Scotland*, 1775), and MacPherson challenged him to a duel that never materialized.

Anne-Louis Girodet-Trio-son, *Ossian Receiving Napo-leonic Officers,* 1802.

the spell of Percy's *Reliques* and the Ossianic poems and began to collect systematically what he believed to be German folk poetry—the unspoiled utterance, according to primitivist doctrine, of the voice of the people. Many of these poems were published in 1788–89 as *Stimmen der Völker in Liedern.* Others wrote verses (with no intent to deceive) frankly based on folk models. Best known of these were the work of August Gott-fried Bürger (1748–94), who devoted his energies to a special type of primitive poetry, the ballad: a narrative form often arranged in many stanzas, and showing a preference for supernatural, sometimes grisly subjects.

It was widely believed that modern folk or primitive poetry, like the epics of Homer, was meant to be sung; the German word "Lied" referred interchangeably to a poem with music or without. As the melodies assumed to accompany the folk or folklike poems were hardly avail-able, composers set their hands to providing them. As early as 1736 a little volume of simple poems set to simple tunes appeared in Leipzig under the imposing title *Die singende Muse an der Pleisse* (The Singing Muse on the Pleisse River). The poet-composer-compiler, identified as "Sperontes," was really one Johannes Sigismund Scholze (1705–50). In subsequent years similar collections appeared all over Germany. Plainly intended for amateurs, they consisted almost uniformly of unpreten-tious poetry in regular stanzas set to simple strophic music. Most often the music was printed on two staves with the text in between; that way it could be performed at the keyboard by a single person, or even as a keyboard solo.

THE BERLIN SCHOOL

From the mid-eighteenth century there grew up about the Lied a body of theory with a full arsenal of prescriptions and proscriptions. The principal center for Lied composition and theory was Berlin, and the first influential treatise on the subject appeared there in 1753: Christian Gottlieb Krause's *Von der musikalischen Poesie.* Here the simplicity and "singableness" of the Lied (or, as it was often somewhat incongruously called, the "ode") were raised to the level of dogma. One of the primary distinguishing features of this category of song, said Krause, was that the music should be strophic: "For each stanza of an ode only one melody will usually be provided."[3] Another was that repetition of words and extensive melismas were to be avoided. Almost precisely a half century later the influential music theorist Heinrich Christoph Koch defined the Lied similarly:

> A lyrical poem of several stanzas, intended to be sung, and united with a melody that is repeated for each stanza and that also is of such a nature that it can be sung by anyone who has a normal and reasonably flexible voice, whether he has any training in the art or not.[4]

The agreed-upon simplicity and amateur status of the Lied seems to have kept most of the leading eighteenth-century German composers at a distance—even Krause had admitted that the genre hardly represented "the most elevated sort of poetry set to music."[5] Haydn and Mozart both contributed some examples, none of which either reflects very serious intent by the composer or constitutes an important part of the Lied repertory. Mozart's well-known *Das Veilchen* (The Violet), for example, composed to a text by Goethe, is a charming tongue-in-cheek exercise in triviality that shows how foreign this composer's orientation was to the central practice of the German Lied. For the most part the Lied in the late eighteenth century remained the province of minor North German composers. Rather typical was the Berliner Johann Abraham Peter Schulz (1747–1800), whose self-consciously artless volumes, *Lieder im Volkston,* appeared from 1782 to 1790. As had been true earlier in England, songs of this type, whether of genuine folk origins or specifically composed for the purpose, were also put to good use in the indigenous music drama, in Germany called Singspiel.[6] Central figures in the cultivation of this "opera for the bourgeoisie," and hence in the

---

3.   C. G. Krause, *Von der musikalischen Poesie,* p. 112.
4.   H. C. Koch, *Musikalisches Lexikon* (Frankfurt am Main, 1802), p. 901.
5.   Krause, p. 112.
6.   In England the music for the ballad opera was largely drawn from popular ballads and songs. The chief source for the tunes in the *Beggar's Opera,* for example, was Thomas D'Urfey's six-volume collection *Wit and Mirth: or Pills to Purge Melancholy* (1719–20).

dissemination of the Lied, were Johann Adam Hiller (1728–1804) and his student Christian Gottlob Neefe (1748–98), from about 1780 the teacher of the young Beethoven.

Johann Wolfgang von Goethe (1749–1832), the literary figure who towered over German letters for several decades around the turn of the nineteenth century, showed a lively interest in the Lied from about 1770, when he came to know Herder in Strassburg. How seriously he often took the old prescriptions for "folklikeness" in this genre can be seen in his *Trost in Thränen,* written in March 1803. This little poem in dialogue form is directly modeled after a supposedly genuine folksong first printed with music in C. F. Nicolai's *Eyn feyner kleiner Almanach* of 1777–78 (see Example V–1). Goethe's poem, later set by about thirty-

Example V–1: *Wie kommt's,* mm. 1–8

five composers, including Schubert, Loewe, and Brahms, begins as follows:

Wie kommt's dass du so traurig bist,	How is it that you are so sad
Da alles froh erscheint?	When all appears cheerful?
Man sieht dir's in den Augen an,	One can see in your eyes,
Gewiss, du hast geweint.	Surely, that you have wept.

Goethe's influence upon the fortunes of the German Lied is hard to overestimate. In his well-publicized pronouncements on the subject he always threw in his lot with the old doctrines of simplicity: little in the way of melismas, melodic ornament, or word repetition was permitted, and strophic poems required strophic music. He also expressed his preferences in composers: Johann Friedrich Reichardt (1752–1814) and Karl Friedrich Zelter (1758–1832), his "musical advisers," won his approval; he criticized Beethoven and Spohr, and virtually ignored Schubert.

Reichardt and Zelter were both solid members of the North German school of composers and music theorists. Reichardt was an enormously prolific author of musical travel books and benign music criticism, editor of journals, and composer of Singspiele and more than 1000 Lieder. He published a great many Goethe settings from 1780 on, including the four-volume collection *Goethes Lieder, Oden, Balladen und Romanzen*

Autograph of C. F. Zelter's song, *Wonne der Wehmuth.*

(1809). Few of Reichardt's Lieder are musically very ambitious; a fairly representative one is his setting of Goethe's *Wandrers Nachtlied* I[7] (see Example V–2). The setting is nearly syllabic (one note to a syllable in the vocal part), with the accent of each trochaic foot given a half-note's duration at the beginning of 3/4 measures. Simple, homophonic three-part writing dominates the keyboard part. The harmony alone offers some relief from the mundane; passing chromatic notes in m. 4 form a fleeting secondary dominant function to the submediant, and in m. 7 to the dominant.

Example V–2: REICHARDT, *Wandrers Nachtlied* I, mm. 1–8

Zelter, Goethe's confidant and the teacher of Felix Mendelssohn, was long a leading figure in the musical life of Berlin. From 1800 he directed the famous Singakademie, a musical organization that regularly pre-

7. So named to distinguish it from Goethe's better-known *Wandrers Nachtlied* II begin-
    ning "Über allen Gipfeln." *Wandrers Nachtlied* I was written in 1776 and first set to
    music by Philipp Christoph Kayser the following year. In America the poem is
    known in Longfellow's translation as a Protestant hymn: "Thou that from the heav-
    ens art." At least one Reichardt setting of a text by Goethe, *Rastlose Liebe,* could be
    cited as a song of some musical consequence.

sented works of major importance, including the revival of Bach's *St. Matthew Passion* in 1829, conducted by the young Mendelssohn. Zelter wrote some 200 Lieder, many of them to texts by Goethe. Often a bit more adventurous in text setting than Reichardt, Zelter also tended to allow the piano part a greater degree of independence, as can be seen from his setting of *Wandrers Nachtlied* I (see Example V–3). Instead of the monotonously recurring trochaic meter of Reichardt's song Zelter writes flexible speech rhythms that, together with the sparse chords in the piano, at first suggest recitative. He allows himself a modest expressive melisma on the word "Schmerzen" (pain), and in mm. 7–8 introduces some rudimentary imitation in contrary motion between voice and piano.

Example V–3: ZELTER, *Wandrers Nachtlied* I, mm. 1–10

The so-called Berlin Lieder school was perpetuated by two younger composers, Ludwig Berger (1777–1839) and Bernhard Klein (1793–1832). Berger, another teacher of Mendelssohn, had for a time studied with Clementi; he was a brilliant pianist and was well known as a composer of keyboard music and about 160 Lieder. Among the latter is a collection called *Gesänge aus einem gesellschaftlichen Liederspiele, Die schöne Müllerin,*[8] published in Berlin in 1818. This series of songs, set to texts by Wilhelm Müller and others, forms a loose dramatic narrative meant for domestic performance; it may have served as a model for Schubert's

8.   "Songs from a sociable Lieder-play, The Lovely Mill-Maid."

later Lieder cycle *Die schöne Müllerin*. Most of the numbers in Berger's *Liederspiel* are utterly unpretentious and consistently strophic. In the last one, however, he attempts something different. Here, as the millstream sings its consolation to the despondent protagonist (now drowning in it), the words are intoned ominously on a single pitch while the piano plays dramatic arpeggios over a tonic pedal (see Example V–4); this setting shows some of the theatricality that was much more usual in the contemporary ballad.

Example V–4: BERGER, *Die schöne Müllerin: Des Baches Lied,* mm. 1–4

Klein's Lieder hardly swerve from the Berlin traditions of aggressive simplicity. How well he struck the popular mood can be seen in his collection *Neugriechische Volkslieder* (Modern Greek Folksongs) of 1826.

Example V–5: KLEIN, *Neugriechische Volkslieder* I:*Gyphtakis,* mm. 1–8

All things Greek were of great interest in Germany because of their classical implications; if they were Greek folksongs, so much the better. The song texts in this collection (translated by Wilhelm Müller), furthermore, related to the Greek struggles for independence from the Turks; this added modish overtones of both exoticism—anything Turkish was exotic—and interest in national liberation. The music Klein provided for these poems consists of plain, square-cut melodies with an occasional modal cast, and the sparest of piano accompaniments (see Example V–5).[9]

SOUTHERN GERMANY AND VIENNA

In southern Germany, far removed from the somewhat ponderous influence of the Berlin School, Lieder had more variety. Johann Rudolf Zumsteeg (1760–1802), kapellmeister at the court of Stuttgart, published seven volumes of Lieder and ballads around the turn of the century; the latter became models for their genre. He set to music most of the widely known ballad texts of the time: Goethe's *Colma,* for exam-

9.   The text in this example can be translated: "The meadows all thirst for water, the mountains thirst for snow, the sparrow-hawks for little birds, but the Turks—for heads."

Leonore, or "The Dead Go Fast." Painting by Ary Scheffer, ca. 1830.

ple, *Ritter Toggenburg* of Schiller, and *Leonore* of Bürger. *Leonore* (translated by Sir Walter Scott as *William and Helen*) is a very long poem, much of it verging on doggerel, about a girl waiting for her betrothed to return from war. Having died in battle, he finally appears in ghostly form and gallops off with her to their nuptial bed—a grave. Zumsteeg provides 950 measures of constantly shifting styles of music for this tale: recitative, simple song, arioso, and dramatic piano interludes. Such a through-composed setting became a norm in the ballad repertory.

Goethe's *Colma* appeared as a poetic insertion in his lacrymose and overwhelmingly popular novel *Die Leiden des jungen Werthers* (The Suf-

Example V–6: ZUMSTEEG, *Colma,* mm. 1–13

ferings of the Young Werther). Werther, a prototype for the familiar Romantic hero, his delicate sensibilities cruelly bruised by an unfeeling world, is an avid admirer of Ossian—to the point of exclaiming, "In my heart Homer has been replaced by Ossian." Near the end of the novel, "his eyes full of tears," he reads aloud his own translation of a selection from Ossian in which the heroine Colma finds herself abandoned at night on a desolate mountaintop. This section of text Zumsteeg set as a ballad; this too is a long, sprawling structure with recitative (both the accompanied and simple varieties), tuneful song, and theatrical musical effects. Often the piano part is used for dramatic representation, as is shown in Example V–6.[10] Here tremolo figures in the right hand imitate the howling of the wind, and a precipitous downward scale depicts a waterfall. Such procedures are "melodramatic" in the most literal sense. They are much like the devices of melodrama, a popular type of entertainment with spoken text and pictorial accompanying music cultivated by Georg Benda (1722–95), for example, and by Zumsteeg himself.

In the last decades of the eighteenth century, Lieder were also vigorously cultivated in and around Vienna. Here, in compositions by Joseph Anton Steffan (1726–97) and Leopold Kozeluch (1747–1818), for example, the incursion of features from dramatic music—from the opera, cantata, and melodrama—is again much more in evidence than in North Germany. In his more than fifty German songs with piano accompaniment Beethoven reflects this and other traditions in song writing to which he fell heir. Sometimes operatic models seem near at hand, as in his early setting of Bürger's *Seufzer eines Ungeliebten* (Sighs of an Unloved One), which consists of two sections, recitative and arioso. Quite different are the innocuous *Geistliche Oden und Lieder,* Op. 48 (1803), to texts by Gellert. Here, in the year of the *Eroica,* Beethoven writes straightforward homophonic accompaniments to four-square melodies of which any North German theorist would have approved.

As a Lieder composer Beethoven is best known for his *An die ferne Geliebte* (1816), often described as the first Lieder cycle. This work actually exhibits a good deal more cohesion than virtually all succeeding examples of the genre. The six poems by one Alois Jeitteles remain clearly on one subject, the longing of the persona for his distant beloved (the clouds, streams, and breezes can go to her, but he cannot; the swallows happily build their nests together, but he remains alone). Like the varying sections of the extended ballads of Zumsteeg and others, moreover, all the individual songs of this cycle are connected by modulatory piano interludes. And for the last stanza of the last poem, Beethoven returns to the music of the first, presented now in an elaborated version in its

---

10.   The text of this example consists of Colma's words, "The wind howls among the peaks; the stream roars down from the rocks."

original key. Most telling as a unifying device, however, is his consistent use of an old practice, strophic variation, for the successive stanzas of individual poems. Most often, what is varied from one strophe to the next is simply the figuration in the piano. But sometimes key and mode are changed as well, and in the second stanza of the second song the melody is in the piano while the singer declaims the text on a single pitch, the dominant—thus borrowing, again, from the tradition of the ballad. Whatever the ingenuities of *An die ferne Geliebte,* this music is, by Beethoven's standards, primitive; as a composer of Lieder he never reached the heights he achieved in his instrumental music. But *An die ferne Geliebte* stood very high in the estimation of the Romantics and provided an important precedent for the growth of the song cycle.

SCHUBERT

Franz Schubert inherited exactly the same traditions in Lied compositions that Beethoven did, but in his more than six hundred Lieder he explored and expanded the potentialities of the genre as no composer before him. A number of Schubert's earliest Lieder are exercises in the dramatic ballad style of his time. Several are frankly modeled on particular ballads of Zumsteeg: his very first songs, *Hagers Klage* (D. 5, 1811), *Die Erwartung* (D. 159, 1815), and *Ritter Toggenburg* (D. 397, 1816) are based on Zumsteeg ballads with the same titles and texts. Even when a direct model is not discernible, as in the case of *Der Taucher* (two versions, D. 77 and 111, 1813–14), composed on a text of Schiller, Schubert shows his youthful allegiance to the prevailing ballad style. This is an extended composition with constant shifts of texture and tonality, from recitative to arioso, and from one sort of pictorial keyboard figuration to another.

In 1814 and 1815 the teenaged Schubert composed the first two Lieder that were to be widely admired in his own time and by all posterity, both to texts by Goethe: *Gretchen am Spinnrade* (D. 118) and *Der Erlkönig* (D. 328).[11] (Both songs appear in ARM 6a and b.) The text for *Gretchen am Spinnrade* is a ten-stanza poetic insertion in Goethe's monumental drama *Faust,* Part I; here the servant girl Gretchen, while spinning, sings of her infatuation with Faust. Schubert writes a dramatic musical setting that mostly ignores the strophic arrangement of the poem in favor of a three-part organization with successively more emphatic climaxes. The poem itself suggests such an organization: each of the three sections (starting with stanzas 1, 4, and 8) begins with the opening lines of the poem, "Meine Ruh' ist hin, / Mein Herz ist schwer," and Schubert begins each of his three sections with the same music (mm. 1,

---

11.   These two songs were published in Vienna in 1821 as Opus 1 and Opus 2.

Autograph of Schubert's famous song, *Heidenröslein*.

31, and 73). Not suggested by the poem is a final rounding-off statement of this text and its music, added by Schubert. An onomatopoetic device like those common to the ballad repertory is used consistently here. The sound of the spinning wheel (the figures in the left hand suggest the treadle) is heard in the piano throughout, except at the climax of the second section, where Gretchen, overcome with emotion, forgets to spin. Immediately striking in this song is a sophistication of harmonic style that sets it well apart from the expectations of its genre. Each of the three main sections begins in the tonic D minor and proceeds, almost entirely by seconds and thirds, through a remarkable constellation of keys that seems congruent with the psychological journey of the protagonist. In the second section, the invocation of Faust's personal attractions ("Sein hoher Gang, sein' ed'le Gestalt") is accompanied by a magical shift from A minor to F major, accomplished simply by positing the new tonic. In the final section, Gretchen's mounting emotional excitement is underscored with a stepwise rising sequence from E♭ through F, G, and finally to A minor. And even on a small scale Schubert's special harmonic procedures are immediately evident; the first two lines, heard four times in the song, move from D minor to C major, with little more of harmonic syntax than pedal points on the two successive tonics.

The text for Schubert's second famous Goethe song, *Erlkönig,* is also taken from a dramatic work, the Singspiel *Die Fischerin,* performed at the Weimar court in 1782. For that performance unprepossessing strophic music for this ballad was supplied by the actress who sang the part, Corona Schröter. In succeeding years many composers set the poem: Reichardt, Zelter, Tomášek, and even Beethoven (whose effort remained only a sketch). Schubert left us four versions, of which the last has remained standard (ARM 6b). Many familiar features of the ballad are to be seen in this text: a father and son gallop through a nocturnal, stormy landscape until the son is snatched away to his death by a malevolent supernatural being, the Erlking.[12] The poem is literally dramatic in that four characters speak directly: the narrator, the father and son, and the Erlking. Shorter than many ballads, it has eight four-line stanzas; the meter is a typically free mixture of iambs and anapests, almost invariably with four accents to a line; this is the first stanza:

Wĕr réitĕt sŏ spät dŭřch Nácht uňd Wínd?	Who rides, so late, through the night and wind?
Eš iśt dĕr Vátĕr mĭt séinĕm Kínd;	It is the father with his child;
Ĕr hát dĕn Knábĕn wóhl ĭn dĕm Árm,	He has the boy firmly in his arm,
Ĕr fásst ĭhn síchĕr, ĕr hält ĭhn wárm.	He holds him safely, he keeps him warm.

Schubert matches this poetic meter to a 4/4 musical meter (6/8 would have been more usual). Accented syllables fall regularly on the accented first beats of the measures; for the words of the faster-speaking Erlking, they also fall upon the secondary accent, i.e. the third beat. Although the poem is unvaryingly strophic, that organization is overlaid with another created by the dramatic interchanges among speakers; this can be shown as follows:

I (m. 15)
Narrator   g–B♭–g

II (m. 36)   III (m. 56)
Father   g–C   Erlking   B♭
Son   c (–b♭)
Father   B♭

IV (m. 70)   V (m. 83)
Son   g (–b)   Erlking   C
Father   b–G

VI (m. 94)   VII (m. 113)
Son   a (–c♯)   Erlking   E♭–d
Father   c♯–d   Son   b♭–g

                                 VIII (m. 129)
                                 Narrator   g (–A♭) g

12. There was some confusion about this Erlkönig (literally "Alder king"). Goethe evidently borrowed the character and name from Herder's poem *Erlkönig;* but Herder had mistranslated it from the Danish "Ellerkang," which means "king of the elves," or, in German, "Elvenkönig."

It was mainly this dramatic organization rather than the simple arrangement in stanzas that guided Schubert in his setting of the poem.

The song as a whole could perhaps be called through-composed, as
there are no sections literally repeated. But intricate congruities of melody and tonality powerfully reinforce its dramatic plan. The characters
of the father and son, in their exchanges in stanzas II, IV, and VI, for
example, are distinguished through the consistent use of low versus
high vocal tessitura. And the relationship between them is subtly
underlined by tonal continuities: when the child responds to the blandishments—or the mere presence—of the Erlking, the tonality is
obscured; the father each time answers reassuringly, takes up the tonal
syntax where his son had left it, and resolves all ambiguities. Schubert
also characterizes the personae of the poem through the nature of the
melodic material he assigns them. The Erlking is given seductive,
familiar-sounding tunes of utmost rhythmic and tonal regularity—until,
finally dropping his facade (m. 116), he sings "und bist du nicht willig,
so brauch ich Gewalt" ("and if you are not willing, then I shall use
force"). Here, with telling effect, the tonal center is wrenched from E♭
to D minor, and the folklike, harmless nature of his music comes to an
abrupt stop. In setting the successive entreaties of the son (stanzas IV,
VI, and VII) Schubert approaches most closely the literal restatement
of musical materials. Three times the son cries "Mein Vater, mein Vater,"
using the same motive beginning with a poignant semitone dissonance,[13] but the mounting urgency of the situation is vividly portrayed
by introducing these cries in successively higher tonalities.

In this song the voice seems to plunge *in medias res;* when it enters
the drama is already underway in the extraordinary keyboard part.
Illustrative piano accompaniments were by 1815 perfectly familiar to
those who listened to ballads. But this one is special; the repeated octave
triplets in the right hand, representative of the galloping of the horse,
are extremely difficult to play and effectively remove this piece from
the useful repertory of amateur musicians.[14] This virtuoso figuration
persists nearly throughout the song, quite unlike the local pictorial effects
of most ballads. Its disappearance at certain points only heightens the
drama: when the Erlking speaks in stanzas III and V the accompaniment
softens to a lilting rhythmic figure that for a moment obliterates the
realities of the wild ride and the child's threatened fate. Then, when the

---

13. The dissonance results from the simultaneous sounding of a semitone upper neighbor
with the principal tone to which it resolves. The harmony of mm. 71–2 could be
shown thus:

14. The third of the four versions of this song exists in Schubert's own manuscript with
straight eighth notes instead of triplets in the accompaniment. And Schubert himself
is said on good evidence to have remarked that others could play the triplets if they
wished—for *him* they were too difficult.

Erlking drops his benign mask in stanza VII, the two types of accompaniment blend; his intentions are now clearly sinister and the threat and fate are real.

It has often been said that Schubert was not particularly discriminating in the poetry he chose to set. And it is true that a fair number of the texts to his Lieder were by third-rate poets, or simply written down by versifying friends: for example, Johann Senn, Joseph Kenner, and Franz von Schober. But the poets to whom he turned most frequently were the most distinguished of his day, notably Goethe (some sixty-five settings) and Schiller (about forty). Schubert was also one of the first composers attracted to the poetry of Heinrich Heine; six poems of Heine's *Buch der Lieder* (1827) were included in Schubert's collection *Schwanengesang* (1828). One poetic source Schubert found irresistible was Goethe's great novel *Wilhelm Meisters Lehrjahre*. This novel, like *Faust* and *Werther,* includes a number of poems, in this case sung by the characters Mignon, the Harper, and Philine; in the first edition music by Reichardt is conveniently included for each of these nine songs. Schubert set all but one (the single song of Philine); some he set more than once and one, Mignon's *Nur wer die Sehnsucht kennt,* seven times.

The remarkable catholicity of Schubert's taste in poetry has given rise to much discussion as to the nature (or even the possibility) of a genuine amalgamation of poetic and musical values in the Lied. This problem would seem especially acute when the poem in question is either particularly good or particularly bad. As an example of the former we may consider Goethe's *Wandrers Nachtlied* II (1780), probably the most praised poem in the German language:

Über allen Gipfeln	Over all the mountain peaks
Ist Ruh,	There is rest,
In allen Wipfeln	In all the treetops
Spürest du	You can feel
Kaum einen Hauch;	Scarcely a breath;
Die Vögelein schweigen im Walde.	The birds in the wood are silent.
Warte nur, balde	Wait a bit, soon
Ruhest du auch.	You too will rest.

The elegance of language, the artful enjambments whereby syntax is continuous between lines, and the congruence of sound and sense ("Ruh," for example, is a long, dark sound forcing a pause, a "rest")—all these show a level of sophistication far removed from the mode of "folklikeness" then current. And profound implications lurk beneath the surface; the pervasive restfulness of nature invoked here becomes a symbol not only for the imminent rest of the human observer, but also for his ultimate rest in death. Yet by its very delicacy of diction and meaning, its metrical irregularity and brevity, the poem creates serious problems for the composer.

Schubert was one of more than a hundred composers in the nineteenth century who rose to the challenge posed by this poem (ARM 6c). His setting (c. 1823), despite some text repetition and three measures of introduction and postlude for piano, is a mere fourteen measures long. One reason for this is that Schubert shows considerable respect for Goethe's irregular poetic meter, reproducing it with remarkable faithfulness in a nearly syllabic setting. With almost perfect consistency he manages to place accented syllables at accented points in the 4/4 measures; the result, particularly in the first six measures, is a declamation of the text in recitative-like irregular rhythms. Later, distinct rhythmic patterns emerge; the dotted figure first heard with "Über al[-len]" becomes a persistent motive used for "warte nur," and (less happily) for "Walde" and "balde." Schubert's sensitivity to the uses of rhythm can also be seen in the "smoothing out" of m. 1 as it approaches the word "Ruh"; and the reiterated "warte nur," beginning in m. 9, occasions an appropriate cessation of rhythmic activity in the accompaniment.

The style of music first heard in the piano is of a familiar sort: repeated close-position tonic chords proceeding to an accented subdominant sonority suggest the manner of the *Männerchor*. But when the voice enters on the tonic B♭ instead of the expected D, the melodic center of the piano introduction, it is clear that Schubert had special intentions for this piece. The surprising and altogether satisfying dissonance (dominant over a tonic pedal) on "Gipfeln" together with a bit of contrary motion between voice and piano (tenor register) complete the transformation of an everyday musical idea into something extraordinary. Prevailing tonic sounds create a static effect perfectly in keeping with the sentiments of the poem; "Gipfeln" is singled out for specific attention without disturbing that effect. Later in the song Schubert indulges in illustrative devices well known to future generations—but hardly hackneyed in 1823—to enhance the congruence of music and text. The moving figures in the accompaniment beginning in m. 9, especially when they include prominent hollow fifths, are suggestive of the hunting horn, with its association of outdoor sylvan scenes. From this point to the end of the song, as the *Singverein* style reasserts itself, the mood is all comfort and repose: for Schubert "Ruh" in Goethe's verse implied nothing more than it says.

A very different Schubert Lied set to a very different sort of text is *Auf dem Wasser zu singen* (D. 774, 1823). The poet is Friedrich Leopold, Graf zu Stolberg (1750–1819); the poem is jingly doggerel, three stanzas worth, in absolutely regular dactylic tetrameter. This is the first stanza:

Mitten im Schimmer der spiegelnden Wellen	Amidst the shimmer of the glittering waves

Gleitet, wie Schwäne der wan- kende Kahn;	The wavering boat glides like swans;
Ach, auf der Freude sanftschimmern- den Wellen	Oh, upon gently shimmering waves of joy
Gleitet die Seele dahin wie der Kahn;	The soul glides thence, like the boat;
Denn von dem Himmel herab auf die Wellen	For from heaven down to the waves
Tanzet das Abendroth rund um den Kahn	The red evening glow dances about the boat.

In all three stanzas straight repetition of words substitutes for rhyme—a most novel procedure—and further internal repetitions abound: "gleitet" and "Schimmer" are examples in the first stanza.

Schubert wrote unvarying strophic music to this poem (see ARM 6d). In his setting the repetitiousness of the poetry is intensified as lines 3 and 4 and line 6 are immediately restated. Thus, while our patience is strained by three appearances of the word "Kahn" in the first stanza of the poem, Schubert lets us hear it five times; the same is of course true for the repeating words of the other stanzas (those corresponding to "Kahn" are "Schein" and "Zeit"). All this repetition, we might think, would be unendurable. But the song is a delightful thing, a clear success, and the repetitions seem of little consequence. For here, quite unlike the case of "Über allen Gipfeln," the text is submerged in music to the extent that the listener is scarcely aware of any poetic infelicities. How differently Schubert approaches his task in this Lied compared with "Über allen Gipfeln" can be heard from its opening measures. The piano has a downward "cascade" figure whose sixteenth-note motion is to continue intact (except for the close of the introduction in m. 8) from the first note to the last. Like the other continuous accompanimental figures we have seen in Schubert's Lieder, this one has an obvious connection with the text, representing, as it does, the shimmering waves of the first stanza. In the piano interludes between stanzas this figure subtly changes its shape, perhaps to signify the "dancing" in the final line of the first stanza. In its rhythm the vocal part is nearly as homogeneous as the accompaniment. It has three rhythmic motives, all of which appear in its first two measures: the dotted figure on "Mitten im," the even eighths of "Schimmer der," and the "wave" music borrowed from the piano. The single (and marvelous) digression from this uniformity is the long-held dominant tone at the repetition of the final line of each stanza (as in mm. 26–27). A good deal of the musical attraction here lies in the playing off of these rhythmic figures of the vocal line against the continuous motion in the piano; whenever both have the "wave" figure the parts move, momentarily reconciled, in harmonious parallel thirds.

The harmonic plan of the song shows another kind of uniformity. There are only momentary deflections from the tonic, A♭, but these are managed with splendid effect. In m. 13 there is a characteristically Schubertian shift from a dominant sonority to the mediant (C♭) and to its dominant. This turns out to be part of a cadential pattern leading directly back to A♭; it could be reduced as follows:

Schubert appears to have been pleased with his cadential figure and repeated it in mm. 17–20, accompanying the repetition of lines 3 and 4 of the poem. There follows in mm. 21–24 another feigned tonal digression, toward the subdominant, but this too is quickly subsumed in a motion back to A♭. Most pleasing of all of Schubert's harmonic ploys in this song, perhaps, is the mode change to major at the end of each stanza (first appearing in m. 27); the extraordinary effect of the C♮ here is largely attributable to the powerful emphasis upon the C♭s in those cadence patterns in mm. 13–16 and 17–20.

In *Auf dem Wasser zu singen* Schubert shows that it is possible to compose a most satisfying song to an undistinguished poem. The poetry is scarcely disregarded: its metrical regularity is well preserved in the vocal part, and its dominant ideas give rise to Schubert's dominant musical figurations. A general impression of the words and meanings of the poem surely comes through. But the music is simply of a much higher order than the text, and its insistent activity attracts the major share of the listener's attention. This music, like so much of Schubert's writing, echoes the familiar sounds of the dance—particularly in the accompanimental figures in the left hand; the unceasing cascade figure above, subjected to exquisite shifts in harmony, however, and intricate rhythmic relationships between voice and accompaniment make it something quite out of the ordinary.

Among Schubert's finest accomplishments in any genre are his two Lieder cycles on poems of Wilhelm Müller: *Die schöne Müllerin* (D. 795, 1823) and *Winterreise* (D. 911, 1827). (One further "cycle," *Schwanengesang*, D. 957, is a compilation whose contents and ordering were determined after Schubert's death by his brother and the publisher Haslinger.) The poems of *Die schöne Müllerin* originated in 1816–17 as part of a "Lieder play" severally written by a group of young literary enthusiasts in Berlin of whom Müller was a member. Probably inspired by Paisiello's opera *La Molinara*, then current in Germany under the title

Die schöne Müllerin, the text forms a narrative of unrequited love and
suicide: the young miller is rejected by Rose, the lovely maid of the
mill, in favor of a hunter, and in despair drowns himself in the millstream. A version of this Lieder play, as we have seen, was composed
by Ludwig Berger in 1818. Müller then expanded it to twenty-three
poems and included it in the first volume of his fancifully titled collection 77 *Gedichte aus den hinterlassenen Papieren eines reisenden Waldhornis-
ten* (77 Poems from the Posthumous Papers of a Traveling Hunting-
Horn Player), published in 1821. This was the source Schubert used.

In Schubert's composition three of Müller's poems are omitted, but
the thread of the narrative, somewhat diffuse to begin with, is not really
disturbed. We see the young hero in a series of tableaux depicting various episodes of the story: setting out on a journey, arriving at the mill,
doubting that the maid of the mill—as yet unnamed—returns his love,
realizing her preference for the hunter, and drowning as the mill stream
sings its consoling lullaby (here Schubert seems perfectly aware of the
double significance of the word "Ruh"). In these twenty songs we have
a rather full anthology of Schubert's methods of text setting: from the

Schubert and his friends, a watercolor by Leopold Kupelweiser, 1821.

A Schubertiad at the home of Joseph von Spaun by Moritz von Schwind. In this sepia drawing, Schubert is at the piano, the singer Vogl on his right and Spaun at his left.

purely strophic *Das Wandern* (No. 1) to the through-composed *Eifersucht und Stolz* (No. 15), with its intermittently recitativelike vocal part and evocations of hunting-horn sounds in the piano. And as the millstream winds its way through the narrative, sometimes even taking an active role in its events, Schubert finds ever new ways of making its motion and meaning felt in the music.

Schubert's songs were not intended for concert performance, as they are most often heard these days. In his lifetime they were typically sung at private salons or at gatherings of the composer's friends called "Schubertiads." Franz von Hartmann records in his diary the details of a specially gala occasion of this sort on December 15, 1826, at the home of Joseph von Spaun. He names some twenty-five people who were present and records that Schubert played four-hand music with Joseph von Gahy, and then accompanied his singer friend Michael Vogl in the performance of "almost 30" of his Lieder.[15] (This Schubertiad is represented in a famous drawing by an artist of the group, Moritz von Schwind.) At Schubert's only concert, given on March 26, 1828, he and Vogl in fact performed a half dozen of his songs; but both the concert and the public airing of his Lieder were altogether exceptional events in this composer's career. The Viennese press took no notice of either—an imminent appearance in Vienna of the virtuoso Paganini absorbed most of their attention—and the possibility of another concert never arose, since he died only a few months later.

15.   Otto Erich Deutsch, *Schubert: a Documentary Biography,* trans. Eric Blom (London, 1946), p. 571.

CHAPTER VI

The Rise of Nineteenth-Century Opera

During the second half of the eighteenth century the opera remained the most popular form of public musical entertainment. It was more specifically the Italian opera that, despite all barriers of culture and language, dominated European stages everywhere except in France. Two distinct types of Italian opera flourished—opera seria and opera buffa—each with its own special character and practices. Opera seria was firmly identified with the works of its magisterial librettist, Pietro Metastasio (1698–1782), and the conventions he established.[1] Still a court entertainment, it derived its elevated subjects from ancient history and legend: from well-known episodes in the chronicles or myths of the Assyrians, Babylonians, Athenians, Romans, and others. With only a few exceptions (one is Metastasio's *Didone abbandonata,* the story of Dido and Aeneas after Vergil) these operas end happily. This usually occurs when, after a series of complicated intrigues, a magnanimous monarch—in a thinly disguised homage to the ruler of the court sponsoring the opera—forgives all villainies and effects a universal reconciliation.

A satirical but fairly accurate recipe for the construction of an opera seria was provided in the 1760s by the German-turned-French litterateur Friedrich Melchior Grimm:[2] there must be three acts with one change of scene in each; six main characters including two pairs of lovers; several "confidants" are required; each of the principals must be assigned two arias per act and must always exit immediately after singing each of them (to allow for applause). A typical scene in opera seria was built from recitative—simple or accompanied[3]—in which the drama

---

1. Metastasio's tenure as court poet in Vienna from 1730 until his death demonstrates the international character of the opera seria.
2. "Du Poème lyrique" in *Correspondance litteraire* (Paris, 1882), pp. 388–90.
3. In his *Dictionnaire de musique* (Paris, 1768), Jean-Jacques Rousseau accurately described three varieties of recitative: *recitatif ordinaire* (with continuo accompaniment only—often called "simple" or *secco*), *recitatif accompagné* (with a sustained chordal accompaniment in the strings), and *recitatif obligé* (with orchestral accompaniment and, typically, strong rhythmic interjections between vocal phrases). Both of the latter two types are often simply called accompanied recitative; they were usually heard at dramatically tense moments: upon the appearance of a god, for example, or at the announcement of a death.

was propelled forward, and which culminated in an aria that expressed the emotions or the reflections of one character. The text for recitative was normally in regular meter but unrhymed. Poetry for arias was both metrical and rhymed, the most common meter being iambic tetrameter. Aria texts usually had two stanzas, one each for the first two sections of the characteristic da capo aria, an elaborate *ABA* structure in which music and text were repeated for the second *A*. Further conventions attached to the singers of these roles: the male hero was normally sung by a castrato soprano or alto, and the bass voice was seldom used. Ensembles of soloists and choruses were rare. The supremacy of this kind of opera was virtually uncontested until about the 1760s, and all the leading opera composers contributed to it: Alessandro Scarlatti, Handel, Johann Adolf Hasse, Gluck, and Niccolò Piccinni. A splendid late example, reflecting the ceremonial use of the genre at the end of the century, is Mozart's *La Clemenza di Tito,* composed for the coronation of Leopold II in 1791.

As opera became increasingly the province of public theaters late in the century, opera seria progressively lost ground to the several types of comic opera, particularly the Italian opera buffa. Far less rigidly codified than opera seria, opera buffa admitted a wide variety of subjects, and its characters included everyday people like lawyers, soldiers, shopkeepers, servants, and music teachers. Certain stock roles emerged; one was the *basso buffo,* a clownish figure, usually a servant, who characteristically sang fast syllabic music, clearly an ancestor of the patter songs in Gilbert and Sullivan. The more humble characters often sang in dialect, especially the Neapolitan variety. Simple recitative and arias of varying types and proportion dominated the sequence of events. But ensembles of soloists were commonplace, particularly in the increasingly elaborate finales of the acts. As the eighteenth century wore on, elements from opera seria were seen in opera buffa with growing frequency: counts and countesses—often treated satirically—sang "high style" da capo arias, and serious dramatic situations came to be seriously presented. Especially in the works of the librettist Carlo Goldoni (1702–93), the leading characters were often a pair of lovers who overcome all obstacles to achieve their ultimate happy union. Such librettos increasingly attracted the best-known composers of the time—Baldassare Galuppi (1706–85), Niccolò Piccinni (1728–1800), Domenico Cimarosa (1749–1801), Giovanni Paisiello (1740–1816), and Mozart. Simple domestic virtues were celebrated in these works, and many (such as Goldoni-Piccinni's *La buona figliuola* after Richardson's *Pamela*) exuded a cozy bourgeois sentimentality.

As opera buffa underwent fundamental alterations in the later eighteenth century, the opera seria, seemingly on the wane, also changed markedly. Especially in the hands of composers working outside the

Italian states—Gluck in Vienna and Paris, Niccolò Jommelli (1714–74) in Stuttgart, and Tommaso Traetta (1727–79) in Parma and St. Petersburg—the Metastasian model was subjected to a deluge of foreign influences. Foremost among these were the generous use of chorus, an element originally borrowed from French models, and a partial abandonment of the standard alternation of recitative and set arias. Thus composers of Italian opera at the beginning of the nineteenth century inherited two distinct but subtly shifting traditions, and it is in the light of these that the course of early Italian Romantic opera can best be understood.

A central figure in the transitional period in opera around the turn of the century was the thoroughly Italianized Bavarian Johann Simon Mayr (1763–1845), who, after learning his musical craft in Venice, settled just to the west in Bergamo and remained there as a church musician, opera composer, and conservatory teacher until his death. Mayr wrote some seventy operas; they were widely performed throughout Europe, and the importance and influence of his music cannot be gauged from the tiny proportion of it that is known today. Many of Mayr's operas fall rather easily into the old classifications of seria and buffa. His first one, *Saffo,* produced in Venice in 1794, is recognizably an opera seria; there is a heroic castrato role, a generally Metastasian organization of scenes, and a predominance of familiar opera-seria arias. But the presence of a chorus and preponderance of accompanied recitative suggest French influences. This early in his career Mayr already shows an uncommon interest in orchestral elaboration and color; a prominent role given the English horn and the other woodwinds sets this work somewhat apart from the traditional representatives of its genre.

One of Mayr's last operas was *Medea in Corinto,* composed for the Teatro San Carlo in Naples in 1813. Specifically commissioned by the theater to write an opera "in the French manner," Mayr and his librettist Felice Romani (1788–1865) apparently modeled their work after the immensely successful *Médée* (Paris, 1797) of Luigi Cherubini. The Medea story, a particularly grisly episode in the Jason legend,[4] had been a recurrent subject for operatic treatment since the *Giasone* (1649) of Francesco Cavalli. Cherubini's composition recalls the modified or "reformed" opera seria of Gluck, Jommelli, and others. What Romani and Mayr produced, however, was in several respects closer to the central Metastasian tradition; it first included simple recitative, and the part of Giasone seems to have been planned as a castrato role. Both of these hallmarks of eighteenth-century opera seria, outdated by 1813, were altered during the Naples performances. But the familiar Metastasian

4. Medea, spurned by Jason, murders the two children she has had by him, as well as his proposed bride, Creusa. There is a good recording of this opera conducted by Newell Jenkins.

intrigues, the role of the confidants, and the high proportion of recitative, whether simple or accompanied, show how persistently some composers clung to elements of the old opera seria. Other traits of this work seem more at home in the serious opera of the nineteenth century: a great variety of aria forms, many in several sections separated by choral interjections, for example, and extended ensemble finales. And in one respect Mayr again appears individual and inventive: his writing for orchestra, always brilliant, includes satisfying solo parts for clarinet, French horn, and bassoon.

By the second decade of the nineteenth century the most distinguished composers of Italian opera were growing old. Mayr's Neapolitan colleague Nicolò Zingarelli (1752–1837) had virtually finished his operatic career, and Giovanni Paisiello, perhaps the most admired of them all, died in 1816 at the age of seventy-six. Others began their careers in Italy, but sought greener pastures elsewhere at the first signs of success. Luigi Cherubini saw his early operas staged in Florence and Venice; after a brief stay in London he took up permanent residence in Paris just on the eve of the Great Revolution of 1789. His younger colleague Gasparo Spontini (1774–1851) achieved his first operatic successes in Rome, Naples, Venice, and Palermo, but in 1803 he too settled in Paris. The Italian operatic stage clearly needed rejuvenation of some sort if it was to retain its European hegemony. There was, in fact, such a rejuvenation, and it was almost exclusively the achievement of one man, Gioacchino Rossini.

ROSSINI

Rossini was born in Pesaro, on the Adriatic coast of the Papal States, in February 1792. Both his parents were employed by the theater there, his mother as a singer and his father as a horn player. Rossini's boyhood was repeatedly disturbed by the chaos of Napoleon's Italian campaigns: first subdued by the French in 1797, Pesaro changed hands frequently in the years that followed. After the family moved to Bologna in 1804, young Rossini was enrolled in the venerable Liceo Musicale, where he received systematic instruction in singing, solfeggio, piano, and cello. By 1809 he was accompanying from the keyboard at various theaters around Bologna and had produced a fair number of rather tentative compositions, both vocal and instrumental. Then in 1810, at the age of eighteen, he made his debut as an opera composer with the one-act *farsa, La Cambiale di matrimonio,* presented at the Teatro San Moisè in Venice. Its success was immediate and Rossini's meteoric career was underway. Two years later his *La Pietra del paragone,* called a *melodramma giocosa* (another of the rather fluid collection of names the Italians applied to their comic opera), was performed at La Scala in Milan;

Luigi Lablache as Figaro in a nineteenth-century performance of Rossini's *Il Barbiere di Siviglia*.

the resulting acclaim prompted a run of fifty-three performances and made Rossini Italy's leading composer.

Rossini's music, set to both serious and comic librettos, now resounded from the principal operatic stages from Venice to Naples. *Tancredi,* an opera seria with a libretto by the much admired Gaetano Rossi, premiered to great applause in Venice in 1813; one of its numbers, the lilting "Di Tanti Palpiti," quickly became popular all over Europe (it is mentioned in Byron's *Don Juan*). The same year saw *L'Italiana in Algeri* (a comic opera) and *Aureliano in Palmira* (an opera seria). In 1814 and 1815 there were four new operas, including *Elisabetta, regina d'Inghilterra,* based on Sir Walter Scott's *Kenilworth. The Barber of Seville (Il barbiere di Siviglia),* destined to become one of the most popular operas of all time (in 1825 it became the first opera ever sung in Italian in New York), opened in Rome in 1816 to a tumultuously hostile audience that threatened to stop it dead at its premiere. Voices from the gallery delighted in loud mimicry of certain lines of Cesare Sterbini's libretto, and the

Adelina Patti costumed as Rosina in a nineteenth-century performance of Rossini's *Il Barbiere di Siviglia.*

whistling and howling drowned out some of the numbers. The composer, as was the custom at premieres, presided from the cembalo in the orchestra; he seemed unperturbed by the uproar, and, it is said, stood to applaud his singers at the conclusion.

The Roman audience resented this opera as an act of impertinence, since Paisiello's opera on the same subject (adapted from Beaumarchais's *Le Barbier de Séville* by Giuseppe Petrosellini), first performed in 1782, was still regarded with special reverence there. Rossini's work seemed to provoke a direct confrontation between the old and the new—i.e. Rossini's—style of opera buffa. Sterbini and Rossini evidently took pains to avoid any obvious similiarities between the two operas; the first performances of Rossini's work were even given under a different title: *Almaviva, ossia l'inutile precauzione*. The verse was all newly written, a chorus was used (Paisiello's opera had none), and a new servant character, Berta, was added and assigned a substantial aria in the second act. Yet the dramatic situations are nearly all the same: a young count (Almaviva) resorts to two subterfuges, first disguised as a soldier and then as a music teacher, to approach and win Rosina, ward of the jealous doctor Bartolo, who intends to marry her himself. The plot is abetted at every step by Bartolo's wily barber and factotum, Figaro. Substantially similar types of musical numbers are used at corresponding dramatic points; a brief comparison of one or two of these places in the two scores may illumine ways in which Rossini was faithful to eighteenth-century traditions in opera buffa as well as his departures from them.

Both operas, after the overture, open with Almaviva's appearance under the window of Rosina; there he meets Figaro, and the two recognize each other as former acquaintances. Paisiello begins with short songs for each character, which are then intermixed with simple recitative, leading to a duet in two sections. Rossini's opening scene is appreciably more elaborate. A chorus of serenaders assembled and instructed by Almaviva's servant Fiorello appears, sings a bit, and pretends to accompany the count's serenade to Rosina ("Ecco ridente"). Then comes a short exchange in recitative between Almaviva and Fiorello, leading to a full ensemble number sung by the two soloists and the chorus. The chorus is dramatically quite superfluous (its members are only slightly more useful when they reappear as guards in the finales to the two acts): these "serenaders" sing their admonitions to each other to be quiet, feign an instrumental accompaniment to Almaviva, are paid off, sing "thank you," and leave. All this suggests that the chorus is there to fulfill a convention rather than a function. Rossini's operas, both serious and comic, in fact regularly begin with an *Introduzione* consisting of (1) a section for chorus, often with solo interjections by minor characters, (2) a slow section, frequently an aria for a major character, and (3) a final fast section for chorus and soloists.[5] The striking differences between Paisiello's and Rossini's opening scenes reflect not so much divergent individual approaches to a dramatic situation as altered operatic conventions.

Although both operas feature a good deal of dialogue in simple recitative, there is substantially less of it in Rossini's work. By 1816 simple recitative was nearing the end of its useful life, and composers including Rossini showed their disregard for this stock commodity by hiring assistants to write it. At one point in the first act Rossini seems to run counter to his usual practice and composes a passage in recitative that we might expect to hear as an ensemble. This is the broadly comic scene in which Bartolo's two servants, having been given sneezing and sleeping powders by Figaro, respond to their master's enquiries with nothing but yawns and sneezes. Paisiello, however, had composed a memorable little trio at this point; Rossini probably felt that a similar trio for so distinctive a situation would be unnecessarily provocative to his Roman audience.

Extended, many-sectioned ensemble finales had become standard in opera buffa at the time of Paisiello's *Barbiere;* its second act has a fully developed one. In the first decades of the nineteenth century ensembles within acts (as well as solo arias) also tended to take on such a sectionalized form. This can be seen in a comparison of the quintets in the second acts of the two operas (see ARM 7 for the quintet from Rossini's *Barber*). They occur at the same dramatic moment: Almaviva is masquerading as a substitute music teacher for Rosina when her real teacher, Don Basilio, appears; during the quintet Almaviva, Figaro, and Rosina manage to get rid of the unwelcome arrival—convincing him that he is ill—without arousing the jealous Bartolo's suspicion.

The novelist Stendhal wrote in his biography of Rossini, "Paisello's quintet . . . is a masterpiece of grace and simplicity, and no one was more acutely aware than Rossini of the veneration in which it was held throughout the length and breadth of Italy."[6] This piece is a fairly representative ensemble number for the opera buffa of its period. The characters sing alternately much of the time while continuity is provided by distinctive motives in the orchestra. At climactic moments, as when all wish the befuddled Don Basilio a good evening ("Buona sera"), they sing together. The quintet proper is a closed composition united by tempo, tonality, and musical materials. Rossini instead makes two sections from the corresponding part of his libretto. The first, in E♭,

5.   See Philip E. Gossett, *The Operas of Rossini: Problems of Textual Criticism in Nineteenth-Century Opera* (Ph.D. diss., Princeton Univ., 1970; Ann Arbor: University Microfilms 71-1603), p. 95.

6.   Stendhal [Marie Henri Beyle], *Life of Rossini,* trans. Richard N. Coe (Seattle, 1972), p. 198.

consists mostly of singing in dialogue; it is accompanied by a great deal of continuous motion in the orchestra (as in mm. 5ff.) and an infectious two-part motive shared by the first violins and clarinets, first heard in mm. 5–7. Beginning with the repetitions of "Buona sera," Rossini constructs a new section with a different style of music and a different tonality (G major). In an exaggeratedly *affettuoso* manner the other characters bid Don Basilio farewell[7] and then speed him on his way with a breathless ensemble *stretta,* a very fast closing section that was a hallmark of Rossini's operatic style. Now after Don Basilio's exit there is further ensemble singing in both operas. But while Paisiello makes a full stop at that point, Rossini effects a transition to the reduced ensemble, and ultimately back to the original key and the genuine *stretta* of this entire complex. Thus Rossini's ensemble scene consists of more sections than Paisiello's, but nonetheless leaves an impression of greater continuity.

Immediately noticeable in a comparison of these two operas is the altered style of melody and singing in Rossini's composition. All the soloists, for one thing, are called upon to sing a great deal more coloratura figuration, which in traditional opera buffa had been reserved for the more "exalted" characters. Rosina, to whom Paisiello gave charming, unpretentious music, becomes a coloratura mezzo-soprano; upon hearing Rossini's opera, the Roman audience, Stendhal tells us, objected that he had "transformed an *ingénue* into a virago."[8] Another feature that distinguishes Rossini's music from the "classic" style of the previous century is his obsessive rhythmic repetitions that can be both exhilerating and comic. At the last of the "Buona sera" section of the Quintet (beginning with "Maledetto seccatore"), soloists in pairs, supported by the woodwinds, sing long stretches of sixteenth triplets with minimal melodic or harmonic interest. All other factors of the music are suppressed in favor of mere bustling motion. The *stretta* to the entire ensemble, in 3/8 meter, is an even more extreme case; the four soloists sing unbroken triplets at a terrific rate—all having adopted the manner of the *basso buffo*—as a rhythmic thumping and jangle from the bass drum and triangle add to the titillation.

However *The Barber of Seville* may differ from the classic opera buffa in style and structure, it remains faithful in spirit to the genre cultivated by Cimarosa, Paisiello, and the Mozart of *Così fan tutte*. Sharply drawn comic characters and situations and perfectly calculated pacing contribute to a musical drama whose essence is wit and parody, with scarcely a sign of the earnestness and sentiment that had begun to color much of comic opera in the waning eighteenth century.

7. The trifling melody of "Buona sera" became another favorite throughout Europe; when Rossini visited Paris in 1823, a gala celebration in his honor ended, predictably enough, with its rendition.

8. Stendhal, p. 177.

When the Kärntnerthortheater in Vienna sponsored a lavish Rossini Festival in 1822, the Italian took advantage of his presence there to visit the ailing Beethoven. In a much later reported conversation with Wagner, Rossini recalled the advice Beethoven had given him on that occasion: "Never try to do anything but *opera buffa;* wanting to succeed in another genre would be trying to force your destiny."[9]

By 1822, however, Rossini had already composed a good number of opere serie. Nor did he heed Beethoven's advice thereafter. He was often bound by contract to compose whatever libretto a theater management provided him; at least partly as a result of this some twenty-five of his thirty-nine operas are of the seria type. In the year after his visit to Beethoven, in fact, Rossini composed two new serious operas for Venice; the second of these, *Semiramide,* was his last work written for an Italian stage. This is the bloodcurdling narrative of Semiramis, queen of Babylonia, who, having poisoned her husband, is slain (after much confusion) by her son Arsace, who becomes the new king. The libretto by Gaetano Rossi follows Metastasio's venerable *Semiramide* in certain ways, and Rossini's composition bears a clear family resemblance to the opera seria of the eighteenth century. Except for the *Introduzione* and the two finales, the sequence of events consists mostly of recitative (now all accompanied) leading to extended virtuoso arias or ensembles designed less to further the drama than to display the powers of the singers. And we even see something of the old anomalies as to the genders of the characters, formerly typified by the castrato singer: the part of the young hero Arsace was written for coloratura contralto and was sung at the first performance by the renowned Teresa Mariani. Singing the title role was the Spanish soprano Isabella Colbran, who was the composer's wife.

Even in this dark tale of murder, revenge, and terrifying supernatural intervention, we are sometimes treated to the lighthearted verve of Rossini's most ingenuous melodic style. The second section of Semiramide's aria from the first act, "Bel raggio lusinghier," begins with the rollicking music shown in Example VI–1. The aria falls into two parts, often called "cavatina-caballetta," a form that became customary in this period; the caballetta is normally the more animated and vigorous of the pair, as it is in this excerpt. Elsewhere in the opera Rossini indulges in certain complexities of harmony and instrumentation not usually associated with this composer. These were in all likelihood the traits that sounded "Germanic"—and unpleasing—to Stendhal:

9.   As reported in Edmond Michotte, *Souvenirs: La Visite de R. Wagner à Rossini* (Paris, 1860), trans. Herbert Weinstock (Chicago, 1968), p. 44. In 1824, Beethoven is reported to have said, "Rossini is a talented and melodious composer; his music suits the frivolous and sensuous spirit of the times, and his productivity is so great that he needs only as many weeks as the Germans need years to write an opera." Alexander Thayer, *Thayer's Life of Beethoven,* ed. Elliot Forbes (Princeton, 1964), p. 804.

Example VI–1: ROSSINI. *Semiramide,* Act I

But the degree of Teutonism revealed in *Zelmira* is nothing compared with that which is displayed in *Semiramide* . . . Rossini, I fancy, must have been guilty of a slip in his geographical calculations, for this opera, which in Venice escaped ignominy only by grace of the composer's sacred and untouchable reputation, would probably have been hailed, in Königsberg or in Berlin, as a miracle straight from heaven.[10]

After a rather uneventful but supremely lucrative stay in London in 1824, Rossini and his wife settled in Paris, where he was showered with honors and official recognition. His first efforts at opera there were French adaptations of Italian works: *Maometto II* (a timely story about Greeks fighting Turks) became *Le Siège de Corinthe* in 1826, and the following year *Mosè in Egitto* was recast as *Moïse et Pharon.* A successful comic opera followed, *Le Comte Ory,* made from a French libretto and a good bit of reused music. After having negotiated an astonishing contract with the French State (signed in person by King Charles X) granting him an unconditional lifetime annuity of 6000 francs, Rossini at the age of thirty-seven produced his last opera, *William Tell* (1829), and proceeded to live in semiretirement for another forty-odd years. There is good evidence that Rossini had for some time contemplated abandoning the operatic stage after *William Tell;* this opera was expected to be his ultimate dramatic achievement, and in more than one sense it was.

10. Stendhal, p. 395.

Jacques-Louis David, *Oath of the Horatii*, 1784.

Constructed upon a libretto rather clumsily adapted from Schiller's play *Wilhelm Tell* by Etienne de Jouy (with abridgements and revisions by others), this opera offers a wealth of fashionable dramatic themes and scenes: the heroic struggle for freedom of an oppressed people, the local color of Swiss Alpine villages, the spine-tingling episode in which Tell shoots the apple from his son's head, a tempest on a mountain lake, and ever-present throngs of emotionally charged citizenry. Rossini makes the most of these opportunities. In the first act the *ranz des vaches* (a Swiss cowherd's horn call) echoes among the mountains. Act II ends with a spectacular choral rendition of the ceremonial vow of the Swiss freedom fighters—a scene with classical overtones that may remind us of Jacques-Louis David's painting *The Oath of the Horatii*. In massed crowd scenes, in its sensational spectacle and dancing, in its expanded orchestral forces and virtual abandonment of coloratura singing, *William Tell* belongs more to the history of French opera than Italian.

DONIZETTI AND BELLINI

Opera composers of a slightly younger generation in the meantime were coming to dominate the stages of Italy; foremost among them were Gaetano Donizetti (1797–1848), Saverio Mercadante (1795–1870), and Vincenzo Bellini (1801–35). Donizetti, born in Bergamo, was a partic-

Gaetano Donizetti (left) and his teacher, Simon Mayr; a contemporary engraving.

ularly promising student of Simon Mayr in that city in 1815–17. During this time he began to write instrumental music and compositions for the church with astonishing ease. An opera of his, *Enrico, conte di Borgonia* was heard in 1818, and before his career was effectively ended in 1844 he had more than seventy musical dramas to his credit. With the production of *I Pirati* in Milan in 1822 began his long and fruitful collaboration with the librettist Felice Romani (1788–1865). First among Donizetti's operas to attract international attention was *Anna Bolena* (1830), composed to one of Romani's most estimable serious librettos. In quick succession followed the opera buffa *L'elisir d'amore* (1832), and the serious operas *Lucrezia Borgia* (after Victor Hugo) and *Lucia di Lammermoor* (after Sir Walter Scott), all but the last to Romani librettos. Like all the most noted Italian opera composers of this period, Donizetti accepted an invitation to the Théâtre Italien in Paris, and the best known of his late works were all composed for the Parisian stage: *La Fille du regiment, La Favorite* (both 1840), and his final buffa masterpiece *Don Pasquale* (1843).

If Rossini had been little inclined to heed Beethoven's advice to confine his efforts to comic opera, this younger generation was even less attached to that genre. Increasingly they turned to a variety of opera seria, just taking shape in the 1820s and 1830s, that without essential modification was to dominate Italian opera for the remainder of the century. *Anna Bolena,* in both its text and music, is representative of this type. The plot is derived from modern—i.e., post-classical—history rather than from the deeds and myths of the ancients so persistently celebrated by Metastasio. Anna (Anne Boleyn) is the second wife of Henry VIII; her stormy life and eventual beheading provide splendid scenes of tumultuous love, pathetic madness, and violent death so favored in the Romantic Italian opera. Gone are the clockworklike conflicts and intrigues and the ultimately rational act of amnesty granted by a benign sovereign. Scourged by war and disruption, and excited by the stirrings

of democratic and revolutionary sentiment in political movements leading to the Risorgimento, Italian audiences were attracted to a drama
governed less by decorum and reason than by strong action and passion.

In the new opera seria, however, we can still discern something of
the skeleton of the old. Internal scenes, i.e. those other than the *Introduzione* and finale, now typically consist of structures called *scena ed aria*
(an ensemble of soloists sometimes being substituted for the aria). The
scena, while much more flexible and changeable than the recitative of
Metastasian opera, resembles it in function and to some extent in style.
Here the music is largely one or another type of accompanied recitative
(interrupted occasionally by choral interjections) in which the dialogue
takes place and dramatic situations are developed. In *Anna Bolena* these
sections show great variety and force. Often a character sings with no
accompaniment whatever—the ultimate in secco recitative—while in
more highly charged situations the orchestra takes a very active part
and the singer sometimes breaks into real arioso melody.

Example VI–2: DONIZETTI, *Anna Bolena,* "Nel veder la tua costanza"

The arias proper in *Anna Bolena,* and throughout Donizetti's operas, are often stereotyped and musically less satisfying. Orchestral introductions end on *sforzato* dominant chords with considerable predictability, and many accompaniments effect a strumming resembling the proverbial "big guitar." Donizetti's melodies themselves, whatever their dramatic surroundings, often sound much the same. In the second act of *Anna Bolena,* Percy, Anna's former lover, and Rochford, her brother, both condemned to death, declare their indissoluble friendship. Under these grave circumstances Percy launches into the robust, swinging melody shown in Example VI–2. That inevitable curtain-raising dominant stroke in the orchestra, the obsessive dotted-note rhythms, the absolute regularity of periodization, and the primitive harmony of this example suggest that at this point, at least, attractive singing was more the objective than dramatic veracity.

Vincenzo Bellini was a student of another eminent opera composer active at the turn of the nineteenth century, Nicolò Zingarelli. Born in Sicily in 1801, and educated largely in Naples, Bellini achieved popularity in Italy during the 1820s. In the remaining five years of his life his operas came to be known internationally; he moved to Paris in 1833, and like Rossini and Donizetti composed his last important work *(I Puritani)* for the French stage. In other ways Bellini's career differed sharply from those of his best known Italian colleagues. He produced only ten operas—a small number by contemporary standards even if allowance is made for the brevity of his life—and all of them are of the serious type.[11] All except the first and last (*Adelson e Salvina,* 1824–25, and *I Puritani,* 1835) were composed to librettos by Romani. The subjects are the familiar ones of Romantic Italian opera: tales of hopeless love and violent death drawn from turbulent episodes in European history or from the dramas of Shakespeare, Scribe, or Hugo. Bellini's *Puritani* are the Puritans of the seventeenth-century Cromwell insurrection; his *I Capuletti e i Montecchi* (1830) is one of many operas after *Romeo and Juliet;*[12] *Ernani* (1830), left incomplete by Bellini, but later famous in the setting by Verdi, was based on Victor Hugo's controversial play *Hernani* of the same year.

For *Norma* (1831), the best known of Bellini's operas today, Romani provided a kind of inverted classical theme: it depicts the Roman invasions of Gaul, but almost exclusively from a Gallic point of view. The heroine, Norma, is a Druidic high priestess who is betrayed by Pollione, a Roman soldier and the father of her children; she eventually

---

11. Two of Bellini's operas, *Adelson e Salvina* (1824–25) and *La Sonnambula* (1831), are usually classified as opere semiserie and the rest as serie.

12. Zingarelli's *Giulietta e Romeo* had been produced in Milan in 1796; other composers attracted to the tale of star-crossed lovers were Franz Benda and Nicola Vaccai, and, later in the century, Charles Gounod and Richard D'Ivry.

Aquatint of the "sacred forest" scene from Bellini's *Norma* designed by Alessandro Sanquirico for the premiere in 1831.

dies with him upon a funeral pyre. For this intense drama Bellini writes music that is often impressively inventive and apposite. In the *scene,* those portions dominated by recitative, arioso style often intrudes to fine effect, as in the opening of the second act where Norma contemplates murdering her two children. Her hesitation and revulsion are expressed in accompanied recitative with a numbly monotonous harmonic and melodic pattern. Then as she recalls happier days there is a temporary shift to untroubled arioso music (see Example VI–3, p. 142).

The arioso section (beginning with "Teneri") shows a rather standard Bellini melody. Its opening is divided into two half phrases whose symmetry is offset by a characteristic ornamented extension of the second. A well-known and representative example of Bellini's melodic style in a full-fledged aria can be seen in "Casta diva," sung by Norma in the first act as an incantation to the moon goddess (see Example VI–4, p. 143). Its first eight measures are built from exactly symmetrical two-measure modules, each finishing with a feminine cadence whose resolution (except for the last one) is decorated with typical ornamentation. The vocal part as a whole is also laden with ornament. The first two measures of melody are at root only a descent from A to F, the second two an ascent from A to B♭; the rest is all embellishment. Harmonically the example is simplicity itself. A temporary diversion from F major toward G minor is safely checked in mm. 7 and 8, where F major is firmly reinstated. There is nothing here to distract the listener's attention from sensuous, eminently singable melody, a commodity that was Bellini's special domain.

Example VI–3: BELLINI, *Norma,* Act II, "Non posso"

Bellini and Donizetti represent somewhat differing strains of a common style. Both make generous use of chorus, which comments upon the proceedings during both recitativelike and arioso sections, and at climactic moments often joins the soloists in unison singing at very high volume. Both write music designed mostly to offer audiences the pleasures of brilliant singing. But there are also consistent differences between these composers. Donizetti's recitative shows more variety and

Example VI–4: BELLINI, *Norma,* Act I, "Casta diva"

flexibility than Bellini's, and there is proportionately more of it, since Bellini breaks more readily into arioso style. Bellini's arias are much more variable than those of Donizetti—whose tunes are often uniformly rousing and rhythmic—and they frequently seem more congruent with the dramatic situation at hand. And that sinuous, decorated melody of Bellini's most expressive manner, widely imitated in subsequent vocal and instrumental music, came to figure prominently in the future of Romantic musical style.

OPERA IN FRANCE

In the eighteenth century only France maintained a native operatic practice of sufficient vitality to resist the Italian domination in force everywhere else in Europe. Though some of its roots can easily be traced to seventeenth-century Italian practice, French opera grew in its own way, and was to a large degree molded by specifically French sensibilities. Like the Italians, the French had two distinct classes of opera, serious and comic (the *tragédie lyrique* and the *opéra comique*), and two separate theaters for their performance. Tragédie lyrique, as established by Jean-Baptiste Lully (1632–87) and his librettist Philippe Quinault (1635–88), was for more than a century the official French opera, sanctioned by the Crown and regulated through the Académie Royale de Musique. It was at least as stylized as the Metastasian opera seria: the subjects were mainly from classical myth, there were invariably five acts and a prologue, and every work was preceded by the requisite standardized French overture. Dramatic niceties and style of language were always more of an issue than in Italy. The music, too, was invariably decorous; there was none of the gymnastic virtuosity of Italian arias. Recitative in tragédie lyrique was measured—free secco recitative, it was widely believed, was suitable only for the Italian language. And instead of the predictable alternation of recitative and aria, French serious opera presented a fluid procession of measured recitative, arioso, short arias, and choruses and dances, these last often as *divertissements* unrelated to the central drama. This pattern remained nearly intact for generations: in the works of Jean-Philippe Rameau (1683–1764) that dominated much of the eighteenth century, in those of his rather pale successors, and even in the French serious operas of the reform-minded Christoph Willibald von Gluck (1714–87).

Comic opera in France grew up with much less official sanction and restraint, and it was always more subject to Italian influence than the courtly tragédie lyrique. The most popular of eighteenth-century Italian comic operas, such as Pergolesi's *La serva padrona,* were regularly mixed into the standard indigenous repertory at the Théatre de l'Opéra Comique. After the mid-eighteenth century, French comic opera, like its Italian counterpart, came to be treated in a more serious fashion. Librettos of considerable literary substance were provided by Charles Simon Favart (1710–92), Michel Sedaine (1719–97), and others; estimable composers such as Egidio Romoaldo Duni (1708–75), François André Philidor (1726–95), Pierre Alexandre Monsigny (1729–1817), and André Ernest Modeste Grétry (1741–1813) were attracted to the genre and created a repertory that came to be known well beyond the boundaries of France.

The subjects of this "elevated" comic opera were varied. Often they presented middle-class people given to middle-class virtues and vices: ingenuous young heroes frequently triumphed over all adversity to defeat noble oppressors and win the hands of their beloveds. Certain operas of this type, such as Sedaine-Monsigny's *Le Déserteur* (1769), were bathed in modish bourgeois sentimentality. Other librettos indulged in pointed social commentary. Not only the nobility, but the clergy and other people of the educated classes, physicians in particular, were objects of broad satire.[13] A type of plot rife with political implications gradually rose to prominence: the "rescue opera." A model for this genre was Sedaine-Grétry's *Richard Coeur-de-lion* (1784), in which Richard the Lion-hearted is rescued from an infidel prison by his faithful servant-minstrel, Blondel. More often, however, as the winds of revolution blew ever stronger over the land, royalty and others of the privileged classes were seen as villains, not victims. Bouilly's *Leonore,* set in German translation by Beethoven, represents a rather older species of rescue opera in which the villainy of one highly placed personage (Don Pizarro) is corrected by the intervention of a higher-placed one (Don Fernando).

The opéra comique, like all non-Italian comic opera, made use of spoken dialogue rather than recitative.[14] Especially dramatic points (as, for example, the moment when Florestan is first seen in the dungeon in the second act of *Leonore*) were intensified by the use of accompanied recitative. Other momentous or frightening events were sometimes set as melodrama, as in *Leonore,* once more, and in Cherubini's *Faniska* (1806). Solo vocal numbers, often called by the generic name "ariette," occurred in widely varying forms, from elaborate da capo pieces resembling those of opera seria to humble strophic songs. A favorite type of ariette was cast in an *ABA* form with the middle section in the parallel minor. Choruses were frequent, as was that diversion which always seems *de rigueur* in French opera, the dance. Single-movement overtures were most usual, though the three-movement type common to opera buffa was also heard.

With certain modifications this sort of dramatic musical entertainment continued to dominate the French stage from the revolutionary period through the Napoleonic era, and up to the July Revolution of 1830. While Italian opera seria of the eighteenth century seemingly exerted a determinant influence upon the destiny of Italian nineteenth-century opera, the historical continuity in French opera unmistakably followed the course of opéra comique. One reason for this difference is that tragédie lyrique, the official opera of the French crown, and always subject to ponderous supervision, was unable to adjust to changing times and tastes. Another was that during the revolutionary period the various successive regimes made use of the popular and traditionally liberal opéra comique as a powerful instrument of propaganda. The composers of opéra comique were the same musicians who provided music for the spectacular republican *fêtes,* and the opera, in both style and idea, came to resemble them.

These festivals were conceived as outdoor public spectacles in which

13.   As, e.g., in Sedaine's *Roi et fermier* (1762) and *Felix* (1777).
14.   An exception is Monsigny's *Les Aveux indiscrets* (1759), which consistently uses French-style recitative.

the entire populace theoretically should participate; vows of allegiance to republican principles were to be renewed, military and political events celebrated, and the fires of revolutionary fervor kindled anew. One of the most elaborate of these celebrations was the *Fête de l'Etre Suprème* of 1794. Wind instruments and singers numbering literally in the thousands united to celebrate the new official revolutionary religious doctrine with overwhelming éclat. On another occasion, in 1791, the percussion section consisted of 130 pieces of field artillery. Music, such as F. J. Gossec's *Hymne à l'Etre Suprème,* E. N. Méhul's *Chant du départ,* and the *Marseillaise* itself (by Rouget de Lisle) was expressly composed for use at these events. The government took care that such political songs were widely distributed among the populace; thus the rhythms of military band music and the plain but rousing sounds of what one contemporary observer called the "hymnic" style[15] were heard on every side. In the theater, audiences were treated to a series of dramatic musical productions on current subjects whose style and format drew heavily on the festivals. There was Gossec's *Offrande à la liberté* (1792), as well as dramatizations of specific events such as *Le Siège de Thionville* (1793) and *La Réunion du 10 Août* (1794). Opera proper responded quickly

Inauguration of Robespierre's *Fête de l'Etre Suprème* before a large crowd in the Tuilleries gardens, June 8, 1794. Engraving by Swebach-Desfontaines.

15.   J. B. Le Clerc, "Essai sur la propagation de la musique en France, sa conservation et ses rapports avec le gouvernement" (1796).

to the same impulse. Many librettos were advertized as *faits historiques* (actual events), and something of the musical manner of the festivals—a profusion of brass instruments, military marches, massive male choruses singing "hymnic" music—quickly made its appearance.

Foremost among the composers of revolutionary opera was the newly arrived Italian, Cherubini. His *Lodoiska* (1791), composed on a libretto by C. F. Fillette, has rather a standard rescue-opera plot, with the action set at a discreet distance in Poland. Lodoiska, the young heroine, imprisoned in the castle of the evil Baron Dourlinsky, is rescued by her beloved, Floreski, with the aid of a horde of benevolent tartars led by a sort of noble savage, Titzikan.[16] Identified curiously as a "comédie heroique," *Lodoiska* clearly shows its patrimony in the opéra comique in a comic drinking scene and its use of spoken dialogue. Orthodox rev-

Example VI–5: CHERUBINI, *Lodoiska,* Act I

16. Several writers have suggested that Floreski and Lodoiska may have been dramatic models for the characters Florestan and Leonore in Beethoven's *Fidelio.*

olutionary sentiments abound in the opera, as in the oath-taking scene in the first act, where Floreski and Dourlinsky swear their alliance to the death in defeating the enemy. Revolutionary music, too, appears promptly; the first aria of the opera, sung by Titzikan, shows the square triadic melody, characteristic upbeats, and aggressively simple harmony of the best hymnic style (Example VI–5). Ubiquitous male ensemble singing, moreover, an enlarged orchestra, and a spectacular conflagration at the end show clearly the direction French opera was to take during the ensuing decade. Cherubini himself wrote two more revolutionary rescue operas—*Faniska* (1806), again set in Poland, and the celebrated *Les Deux Journées* (1800), in which the innocent prisoner escapes hidden in a water cart; this last, its libretto by Bouilly, was said to be a *fait historique*. Much admired by Haydn and Beethoven, and in a later generation by Schumann, Cherubini exerted an influence upon the music of his time far more powerful than his present near-eclipse would suggest.

During the years of the Napoleonic empire another resident Italian musician, Gasparo Spontini, rose to great prominence. Officially named "Composer to the Empress" in 1805, he provided cantatas for the celebration of such events as Napoleon's victory at Austerlitz (December, 1805) and the birthday of the empress. In 1807 his first full-scale work for the French stage, *La Vestale,* was a popular triumph. It also won official approval: the Institut de France pronounced it the "best opera of the last decade." A variation of the rescue opera, de Jouy's libretto for *La Vestale* depicts a Roman vestal virgin, Julia, beloved of a young soldier, Licinius. Having violated her vows and allowed the sacred flame on the altar to go out, she is condemned to be buried alive, only to be saved at the last moment by a supernatural bolt of flame that relights the fire. The opera requires enormous forces and presents every opportunity for massed choruses, spectacle, and pageantry. Long stretches of instrumental music are provided for processions and ceremony; in the finale of the first act the orchestra plays continuously as groups of senators, priests, vestal virgins, battalions of soldiers, and vast portions of the populace assemble themselves on stage. As the victorious warriors appear, an Allegro marziale is sounded; for this piece Spontini adds to his already oversized orchestra the bass drum, triangle, and cymbal— the military associations of these traditional janissary instruments apparently qualify them to accompany the Roman legions.

If this spectacular display of victorious Romans appealed to French Republican taste in a time of Napoleonic triumphs, Spontini's next opera, *Fernand Cortez* (1809), was even more overtly political. It was at the instigation of the emperor himself that the composer collaborated with J. A. Esménard and de Jouy to produce this glorification of Mexico's Spanish conquerors, and particularly of Cortez himself—the intended analogy to contemporary events and persons being plain enough. In

Drawing by Karl Friedrich Schinkel of Vesta's temple for an 1818 performance of Spontini's *La Vestale* in Berlin.

both these works Spontini writes recitative for the dialogue and rather Italianate arias; but the main attraction seems to be the massive choruses and ensémbles. In these last, sheer volume seems often to substitute for musical interest. A paucity of harmonic invention is likely to disappoint listeners acquainted with the choruses of Mozart's *Idomeneo,* say, or those of Gluck's French operas. But Spontini's manner—particularly that impression of overwhelming spectacle and power—was to set a standard for much of the later operatic practice of the nineteenth century, including that of Wagner.

In the French opera of revolutionary and Napoleonic times, certain familiar Romantic themes and scenes began to emerge with growing frequency. Both Jean-François Le Sueur (who was to be Berlioz's teacher) and Étienne Méhul set a libretto by P. Dercy entitled *La Caverne* (1793 and 1794); the story, modeled after Alain René Le Sage's *Gil Blas de Santillane,* glorifies a band of noble and romantic outlaws who occupy a picturesque underground grotto. *Paul et Virginie,* the romantic novel of Bernardin de Saint-Pierre, was adapted for operas composed by Rodolphe Kreutzer (1793) and Lesueur (1794). And episodes from the bogus Ossianic sagas were seen on stage in Lesueur's *Ossian, ou les Bardes* of 1804; here the savagery of the warlike Scandinavians is evoked with the well-used device of "Turkish music." Picturesque and exotic landscapes, storms at sea, violent political struggle, mass crowd scenes, and musical forces of great power and variety were the stuff of French opera in the first two decades of the century. During this period the foundations for Rossini's *Guillaume Tell* and for French grand opera of the 1830s and 1840s were firmly laid.[17]

17. A fuller picture of Paris as a musical and intellectual center will be drawn in Chapter VII.

GERMAN ROMANTIC OPERA

Before the nineteenth century there was no indigenous tradition of German opera, either serious or comic, to compare with those of Italy and France. There were scattered attempts to establish something like a German version of opera seria in both the seventeenth and eighteenth centuries. The public opera theater in Hamburg produced German operas on serious subjects from 1678 to 1737. And a century later, amidst stirrings of nationalistic fervor, theaters were opened in many German-speaking centers specifically for the cultivation of German drama, with and without music. Thus in 1777 the Mannheim court saw an opera on a German historical subject, *Günther von Schwarzburg,* with a libretto by Anton Klein and music by Ignaz Holzbauer. The event was thought important enough to have the music printed, and *Günther* became the first German opera published in full score. But the style of both its libretto and music is 'manifestly borrowed from opera seria. This undertaking proved largely sterile; the future of German opera was little furthered by the simple presentation of Italian courtly conventions in the German language.

Of much greater consequence was the adaptation, mainly in North Germany, of the modest English ballad opera; in the 1740s and 1750s German audiences showed enthusiasm for translations of pleasant and unprepossessing works such as Charles Coffey's *The Devil to Pay* and *The Merry Cobbler.* In such Singspiele, as they were now called, the dialogue was spoken, and the interpolated songs were fitted with translated texts and sometimes provided with new music as well. Christian Felix Weisse (1726–1804) of Leipzig, a prime mover in the adaptation of such English musical plays, was also influential in the ensuing phase in the growth of German comic opera. In the 1760s and 1770s he collaborated with musicians such as Johann Adam Hiller, also of Leipzig, in a series of Singspiele that set the genre firmly upon a familiar path toward seriousness and respectability. Some of these productions were simply translations from current French comic opera: C. S. Favart's *Ninette à la Cour,* for example, became *Lottchen am Hofe,* with new music by various composers. As time passed, simple tales about farmers, merchants, and journeyman laborers gradually gave way, as in the opéra comique, to romantic plots of ill-fated love, magic and enchantment, and adventurous rescues. The composer Georg Benda (1722–95) at the court of Gotha marked this progressive "elevation" of subject matter with his *Der Dorfjahrmarkt* (The Village Fair) of 1775 and *Julie und Romeo* of 1776. And in his melodramas (i.e., dramatic plays with spoken dialogue and instrumental accompaniment) some of the old classical subjects again made an appearance, as in *Medea* and *Ariadne auf Naxos,* both of 1774.

In Vienna the Singspiel, both indigenous and borrowed, was well known from about mid-century, and Joseph II officially established a German opera company at the court theater in 1777. Mozart's two mature Singspiele were supreme examples of the genre as cultivated in Vienna. *Die Entführung aus dem Serail* (The Abduction from the Seraglio), presented there in 1782, showed the Viennese taste for exotic subjects[18] and for a profuse mixture of styles: an overture of the *ABA* type most common in French opéra comique and spoken dialogue characteristic of all comic opera except Italian mix easily with the inevitable "Turkish" music. Then there are accompanied recitatives and show-stopping coloratura arias reminiscent of opera seria in full bloom. *The Magic Flute (Die Zauberflöte)* of 1791, the work that contributed more than any other to Mozart's reputation in the nineteenth century, shows specific traits of the nascent German Romantic opera. It began as one of a growing class of "magic" operas that was to include Carl Maria von Weber's *Der Freischütz.* Another example, performed in Vienna in the same year as *The Magic Flute,* was *Der Fagottist, oder die Zauberzither* (The Bassoonist, or the Magic Zither), with music by the prolific Wenzel Müller (1767–1835).

In the subsequent two decades Italian opera regained its supremacy in Vienna, climaxing with the triumphs of Rossini that began in 1812. One native son of the city who labored persistently to stem this tide by producing German opera was Schubert. However little we may associate his name with opera, in the years 1814–23 he composed no fewer than nine complete German operas, as well as some half dozen attempts that were never finished. Schubert's labors as an opera composer won him less recognition than his instrumental music and songs. Only two of them, *Die Zwillingsbrüder* (The Twin Brothers, 1819) and *Die Zauberharfe* (The Magic Harp, 1819–20), were performed during his lifetime. His most extensive work, *Fierrabras,* though completed in 1823, was first staged in 1829 shortly after the composer's death; two other operas, *Alfonso und Estrella* (1821–22) and *Die Verschworenen* (The Conspirators, 1823), were not heard until 1854 and 1861 respectively.

All these works show an allegiance to established modes of Viennese musical drama. *Die Zauberharfe,* with a libretto by Georg von Hofmann) is based on a stylish medieval subject about enchanted musical instruments so beloved of audiences in Vienna. Schubert's musical numbers also follow certain well-known procedures. Six of the fourteen are melodramas after the manner of Georg Benda; hence the piece is sometimes considered a melodrama rather than a Singspiel. Choruses of troubadours and knights reflect the *Singverein* style, and the instrumental music, like so much in Schubert, carries unmistakable echoes of

---

18. The scene is set in Turkey, where the European Belmonte after various reverses manages to rescue his beloved Constanze from the harem of a pasha.

the dance.[19]

Die Verschworenen (The Conspirators,[20] 1823) has a libretto constructed by Schubert's (and Beethoven's) friend Ignaz Castelli upon two comedies of Aristophanes, *Ecclesiazusae* and *Lysistrata,* with the action transferred from ancient Greece to medieval Europe. The libretto is a rough-hewn thing to which Schubert wrote music of considerable charm. In the second number, a Romanze sung by the conspirator Helene, there is an ornamented melody about as Italianate as anything Schubert ever wrote. But an atmospheric clarinet obbligato and certain Lied-like turns of phrase—such as a surprising move from minor to major in the final measures—shows the composer working in his native habitat of the German song. And the frequent ensembles usually sound like indigenous part song; a march and chorus of the male characters (No. 5) has the close-position triads and emphasis on the subdominant characteristic of music for German men's chorus (see Example VI–6).

Example VI–6: SCHUBERT, *Die Verschworenen,* Act I, "Nun ruh' mein Schwert!"

Chor der Ritter
Allegro moderato

Nun ruh' mein Schwert! Es weicht das Kriegs-ge-wühl dem sanf-tern, süs-sern Min-ne-spiel!

Schubert understandably felt despondent about the fate of his operas; in a letter of March 1824 he wrote to Leopold Kupelwieser, brother of the librettist for *Fierrabras:*

> The opera by your brother . . . has been declared unusable, and thus no claim has been made on my music. Castelli's opera, *Die Verschworenen,* has been set in Berlin by a local composer[21] and received with acclamation. In this way I seem once again to have composed two operas for nothing.[22]

19. The overture in C that Schubert wrote for *Die Zauberharfe* is the one that has come to be known as the *Rosamunde Overture;* it was published under this title in 1827, apparently with Schubert's consent. The composer's incidental music to *Rosamunde,* a play by Helmina von Chézy, was performed in 1823 with a different overture, viz. that written for his opera *Alfonso und Estrella.*

20. Later also known as *Der häusliche Krieg* (The Domestic War).

21. Georg Abraham Schneider (1770–1839).

22. O. E. Deutsch, ed., *The Schubert Reader: a Life of Franz Schubert in Letters and Documents,* trans. Eric Blom (New York, 1947), p. 339.

The poor reception of Schubert's operas has often been attributed to bad librettos. In plot and language they seem mediocre, to be sure, but so do the texts of many successful operas of the period. A symptom of Schubert's difficulties as a dramatic composer may be seen in his own words: "The opera by your brother" and "Castelli's opera." He seems to have thought of opera as a play with added musical numbers. His music, however attractive, usually comes in discrete, closed sections that reflect the static quality of German song and contribute little to dramatic movement. His operas were no match for the quick wit and sure dramatic pacing of Rossini's musical comedies.

In 1813 the peripatetic composer Louis Spohr freed himself from the ducal court at Gotha to become musical director at a prestigious Viennese theater, the Theater an der Wien. Within the same year he had composed a three-act opera on the Faust legend to a libretto by J. C. Bernard.[23] Spohr's *Faust* achieved no more success in Vienna than Schubert's operas: it was first given several years later, and survived only a few performances. Viennese audiences at the time seemed to care little for German opera by local composers. Later, however, in his years as music director at the court of Kassel (from 1822), Spohr produced a successful series of German stage works: *Zemire und Azor* (composed in 1819), *Jessonda* (1823), *Der Berggeist* (1825), *Die Kreuzfahrer* (1845), and others. In *Faust* Spohr shows some accommodation to Italian taste by including both recitative and spoken dialogue. The music of *Zemire und Azor*, adapted from the French libretto of J.-F. Marmontel,[24] is more Italianate, reflecting something of the manner of Rossini, whose operas Spohr claimed to dislike. His autobiography relates:

> Little as I was an admirer of *Rossini's* music . . . yet the applause which "Tancred" had met with in Frankfort was not wholly without influence on the style of my new opera. . . . This explains why the music to "Zemira and Azor" has so much colouring and vocal ornamentation.[25]

Spohr's best-known opera, *Jessonda*,[26] remained standard fare in Europe throughout the nineteenth century. Set in Malabar, the principal action takes place amid splendidly exotic choruses of Brahmins, Indian soldiers, and temple dancers (bayaderes). The musical setting is nearly as remote from German Singspiel as is the dramatic action. Sung throughout, the opera presents several varieties of accompanied and simple recitative, as well as extended ensemble numbers and arias. Spohr's music

---

23. This libretto appears unrelated to Goethe's *Faust,* well known in Germany since the publication of *Faust: ein Fragment* in 1790.

24. Composed in 1771 by Grétry.

25. *Louis Spohr's Autobiography* (London, 1878), 2, pp. 58–59.

26. The libretto by Eduard Gehe is adapted from A. M. Lemierre's tragedy *La Veuve de Malabar* (1710).

is typically well crafted and of a conservative cast, similar to, say, Cherubini's style at the turn of the century. Example VI–7 shows the beginning of the second part of the heroine Jessonda's long aria in Act I. Here

Example VI–7: SPOHR, *Jessonda,* Act I, "Bald bin ich ein Geist geworden"

chromatic passing tones continually add bits of vivid coloring to music that never strays from the home key. Generous vocal ornament and inviting high notes, moreover, show that Italian operatic models, even more so than in *Zemire und Azor,* lay close at hand.

A figure of considerable importance in the growth of German Romantic opera and Romantic attitudes toward music was Ernst Theodor Wilhelm Hoffmann (he substituted Amadeus for Wilhelm around 1808 out of admiration for Mozart), whom we previously met as a music critic. E. T. A. Hoffmann's output as an opera composer was neither large nor particularly successful. He wrote five Singspiele and some incidental music—most of these works were never performed—as well as one estimable opera, *Undine* (1813–14, first staged in Berlin in 1816). But in his life and work Hoffmann became a prototype, almost a caricature of the Romantic artist-musician. Trained for a career in law, he cared only for the arts, and in 1808 became musical director of the theater in Bamberg by placing an advertisement in a newspaper. Having virtually no experience conducting, he was utterly unsuited to the post and stepped down after about two months. Nonetheless he stayed on for a time as a scene painter and an occasional provider of incidental music. A later stint as conductor for an opera company based in Dresden was scarcely more successful; in 1814 Hoffmann became a court assistant in Berlin and remained nominally in the legal profession until his death.

While Hoffmann always preferred to think of himself as a musician, he suffered grievously from that malady common to Romantic artists, a lack of systematic early training. In both music and painting he always retained certain marks of the amateur. But he came early under the spell of contemporary Romantic authors, especially Ludwig Tieck (1773–1853) and W. H. Wackenroder, and from about 1810 he turned increasingly to the sort of prose writing that made him famous: extravagantly metaphorical music criticism—though often fortified with careful analysis—and fanciful tales and novels. Music and musical subjects are woven into all his writings. A recurrent figure in his works is the half-mad kapellmeister Johannes Kreisler, who represents at once the consummate Romantic musician's sensibility and something of Hoffmann himself. In the author's first presentation of Kreisler we are told,

> Johannes was drawn constantly to and fro by his inner visions and dreams as if floating on an eternally undulating sea, searching in vain for the haven which would grant him the peace and serenity needed for his work.
>
> Thus it was that even his friends couldn't bring him to finish a composition or to prevent him from destroying what he had written. Occasionally he composed at night in extreme excitation, waking his friend whose room was nearby to play him the compositions he had written with incredible speed in this inspired state of mind. He would shed tears of joy over his

success, holding himself to be the luckiest of men. But the next day the splendid composition would lie in the fire.[27]

In Hoffmann's portrayal the artist is guided by forces inaccessible to others, and he is often ill-suited to existence in ordinary society. His life and his art—or, as with Kreisler and Hoffmann, a synaesthetic amalgam of the arts—are indivisible; the exoticism and otherworldliness in Hoffmann's tales are seen as the real experience of the artistic mind. Such notions were immensely attractive to succeeding generations of writers and musicians. Robert Schumann adopted much of Hoffmann's manner in his earlier prose writings and memorialized Hoffmann's mythical kapellmeister in the *Kreisleriana* for piano (1838). Wagner described himself in his sixteenth year as "on fire with the maddest mysticism, chiefly from perusing Hoffmann's works";[28] in his maturity he drew on Hoffmann's tales in the librettos of *Tannhäuser* and *Die Meistersinger*. Hoffmann's story *Don Juan, eine fabelhaftige Begebenheit* (1813) influenced a whole century of views about Mozart's masterpiece, including Kierkegaard's famous exposition in *Either / Or* (1843).

Undine, the only one of Hoffmann's operas to achieve any public notice, clearly belongs to that somewhat elusive genre German Romantic opera. Characteristic of the type are subjects of chivalry or enchantment associated with medieval romance, picturesque landscapes with a deliberate juxtaposition of the realistic and supernatural, and certain recognizably "German" elements in both libretto and music. The libretto of *Undine* is based on a German fairy tale of the same name by Friedrich de la Motte Fouqué. Set alternately in unspoiled nature and scenes of medieval splendor, it is peopled with an easy mixture of realistic and supernatural characters, including the appealing water-spirit Undine. Hoffmann's music is for the most part unremarkable. Four-square melodies of a somewhat Mozartian cast are harmonized with a generous sprinkling of diminished-seventh and augmented-sixth sonorities that serve little structural purpose; the many choruses consist largely of straight homophonic singing. Inventive instrumentation, especially the use of certain colorful accompanimental figures in the winds, tends to relieve an overall impression of routine simplicity—an impression far removed from the flights of fancy we associate with the literary Hoffmann.

Hoffmann's opera was applauded at its Berlin performances in 1816 by Carl Maria von Weber, the composer often described as the originator of German Romantic opera—though Hoffmann, Spohr, Schubert, and perhaps Wenzel Müller and even Mozart might have an equal claim to this distinction. Weber's early life and training were rather like

27. From the *Kreisleriana,* published in the *Phantasiestücke in Callots Manier* (1814). This translation is from R. Murray Schafer, *E. T. A. Hoffmann and Music* (Toronto, 1975), pp. 113–14. The character Kreisler may be modeled after another fictional musician, W. H. Wackenroder's Joseph Berglinger.

28. Richard Wagner, *Autobiographische Skizze,* as translated in Schafer, ibid., p. 185.

A design for the stage setting of E. T. A. Hoffmann's opera, *Undine*, by Karl Friedrich Schinkel (1816).

Hoffmann's: an unsettled childhood in a traveling theatrical family[29] effectively precluded early systematic education in anything. Weber nonetheless showed marked abilities from an early age in both music and writing; at fourteen he published his first essay, a spirited rejoinder to a review of his first opera, *Das Waldmädchen* (Freiberg, 1800). In later years he continued to write prose: music reviews beginning about 1809, an unfinished autobiographical novel called *Tonkünstlersleben* (Life of the Composer), and, after 1813, explanatory treatises on the operas he conducted. But Weber's career took a very different course from Hoffmann's. Early on he attracted noble patronage and came into contact with important musicians such as Michael Haydn and later Gottfried Weber. Even his first operas enjoyed multiple performances, and he managed to gain enough experience as a conductor to function successfully as a director of major opera houses. Weber's life as a composer and musician seemed a realization of all Hoffmann had hoped for himself.

After *Das Waldmädchen* and *Peter Schmoll* (1803), youthful works that survive only in fragments, Weber's next major operatic projects were *Silvana* (1810; in large part it was a reworking of *Das Waldmädchen*) and *Abu Hassan* (1811). *Silvana,* with a libretto by one Franz Carl Hiemer, is in some ways a concatenation of Romantic elements already familiar from French opera: an innocent child of nature (Silvana) lives in a rocky cave surrounded by a sylvan landscape in which horn calls of roaming hunters can be heard. Such scenery provided ample occasion for the exercise of Weber's most colorful and evocative orchestration—particularly for horn parts similar to that we have noted in his nearly contem-

29. Weber's family was related to Mozart's in-laws.

poraneous Symphony No. 2.[30] In the one-act *Abu Hassan*, set to a libretto adapted by Hiemer from *The Thousand and One Nights*, Weber reverted to a nearly unalloyed Classic style, producing a delightful "Turkish" comedy with a clear debt to Mozart's *Die Entführung aus dem Serail*. Signs of this can be seen in occasional Italianate coloratura, as in the duet of Abu Hassan and Fatime (No. 4), the buffo music sung by Omar (something of a counterpart to Mozart's Osmin), and the similarity in accompaniment between Weber's "Aengstlich klopft" and Mozart's "O wie ängstlich."[31] Planned as an amusing courtly entertainment—in 1811 it was staged in quick succession at the courts of Munich, Stuttgart, and Württemberg—*Abu Hassan* is scarcely indicative of the direction Weber's career as an opera composer was to take.

Nearly ten years elapsed before Weber composed another opera. During this time most of his energies were channeled into conducting, first as opera director at Prague (1813–17) and then at Dresden (1817–26). But these years also saw the gradual maturation of Weber's thoughts about music and its relationship to drama and the other arts. He was strongly affected by exposure to prevailing winds of Romantic aesthetic doctrine. In Heidelberg he associated with Clemens Brentano and Achim von Arnim, compilers of that collection of supposed folk poetry that fired the imagination of generations of German Romantics, *Des Knaben Wunderhorn* (The Youth's Magic Horn); he had first met the poet and novelist Ludwig Tieck in Baden-Baden in 1810, and in 1825 appointed him *Dramaturg* (dramatic director) at the Dresden Opera. His contacts with E. T. A. Hoffmann began in Bamberg in 1811 and continued until Hoffmann's unfavorable review of his *Der Freischütz* (1821) had a cooling effect on their relationship. Many episodes of Weber's *Tonkünstlersleben*, whose hero Felix resembles both Weber and Kapellmeister Kreisler, show Hoffmann's influence. And a Hoffmannesque penchant for mingling reality with fantasy can be seen in the secret *Harmonischer Verein* (Musical Society) Weber attempted to found in 1810, in which the members were to adopt bizarre pseudonyms and do battle against all philistinism in music.[32]

The composer's artistic theories were concentrated largely in opera, and in his review of Hoffmann's *Undine* he airs some of them by quoting from his own *Tonkünstlersleben*:

30. See above, p. 80.

31. Some seven years later, Weber expressed admiration for Mozart's opera: "To my own artistic sensibility this joyful creation, glowing with abundant youthful strength and maidenly gentleness, is especially attractive." *Sämtliche Schriften von Carl Maria von Weber*, ed. G. Kaiser (Berlin and Leipzig, 1908), p. 303.

32. In the statutes for this society, drawn up by Weber, he names as founding members himself and his friends Jakob Beer (later Giacomo Meyerbeer), Gottfried Weber, and Alexander von Dusch. Article 14 explains that the principal goal of the society is "to exalt and promote what is good [in music], wherever it is found, and especially to take notice of young and rising talents." *Sämtliche Schriften*, p. 13.

> In no variety of artwork is this [fragmentation of parts] so difficult to avoid—and consequently so often present—as in the opera. By opera I understand, of course, the opera which the German desires—an artwork complete in itself, in which the partial contributions of the related and collaborating arts blend together, disappear, and, in disappearing, somehow form a new world.
>
> As a rule a few striking musical numbers determine the success of the whole. Only rarely are these numbers, agreeably stimulating in the moment of their hearing, finally dissolved, as they properly should be, in the great general impression. For one must come first to admire the whole; then, on closer acquaintance, one may take pleasure in the beauty of the separate parts of which the whole is composed.[33]

There is nothing very new or surprising about Weber's objection to the "detached number" construction in opera; similar criticism had been leveled at the standard recitative–aria structure well back in the previous century by Francesco Algarotti, Gluck, and others. But eighteenth-century opera theorists usually criticized this arrangement because it encouraged the hegemony of the aria; what they wanted above all was dramatic integrity, an opera in which music was a "handmaid of poetry." Weber advocated instead a thorough amalgamation of the constituent arts in opera to produce a whole greater than the sum of its parts. This view grows directly from tenets of German Romantic aesthetics, and its influence upon the future of opera in the nineteenth century was decisive.

Lurking in the quotation above and in most of Weber's opera criticism are pronounced sentiments of nationalism. They became much more explicit when he took up his duties at the court of Dresden as director of German opera, in direct competition with Francesco Morlacchi, who produced Italian opera for the same theater. In the first of the *Dramatisch-musikalische Notizen* written after assuming his new post Weber explained,

> The Italians and French have created for themselves a form of opera which they practice contentedly. Not so the German. Always curious, and always in search of progress, he seizes for himself the best features of the others—but uses them in a more profound way.[34]

Such declarations sounded well to German ears in 1817, when the Napoleonic disorders had finally been put to rest and feelings of national pride began to grow strong.

When Weber finished *Der Freischütz* in 1821, he had produced, in the opinion of many, the quintessential German Romantic opera (he certainly had produced the most popular one; it has been performed more

---

33. *Allgemeine musikalische Zeitung*, 19 (1817): 203. This translation, with emendations, is from O. Strunk, *Source Readings in Music History* (New York, 1950), p. 803.
34. *Sämtliche Schriften*, p. 277.

Nature is seen as other-
worldly and threatening
in Caspar David Fried-
rich's *Two Men Looking
at the Moon*.

often than any other opera in the German language). *Der Freischütz* is
laden with recognizable strains of German Romanticism. Its libretto by
Friedrich Kind was fashioned on an old Germanic myth as recounted in
a book of ghost stories by Johann August Apel. It takes place in the
expansive green German forest, a place at once both hospitable and
threatening. And as the story unfolds, gruesome otherworldly forces
continually impinge upon the ordinary lives of common people. The
ingenuous hunter Max, who according to custom must win a shooting
match to gain the hand of his beloved, Agathe, is persuaded by Caspar,
a hunter in league with the Underworld (represented by the shadowy
Samiel), to use "free bullets" which can be directed magically to their
targets. Making these bullets involves forbidden black rites that in this
version of the story take place in the fearsome Wolfschlucht (Wolf's
Glen). One bullet remains in Samiel's possession; Caspar believes it will
be directed against Agathe, but he himself is its target. Max is banished
for conspiring with evil forces, but then pardoned after a mysterious
hermit (representing benevolent supernatural powers) speaks in his favor.
The opera ends with general rejoicing and the anticipation of Max's
impending marriage.

Such a libretto provided the composer with an abundance of usable
picturesque scenes—something like a series of landscapes by the German painter Caspar David Friedrich: the great virgin forest, a shooting
contest, an innocent girl fearing for her intended husband (there is, oddly,
no love scene), but above all, a harrowing episode in the Wolf's Glen.
Weber's musical realization abounds with the instrumental effects that
were his special province and with a studied use of folklike melodies.
In his later conversations with the critic J. C. Lobe he provides some
specific commentary about this:

> There are in *Der Freischütz* two principal elements that can be recognized
> at first sight—hunting life and the rule of demonic powers as personified

by Samiel. So when composing the opera I had to look for suitable tone colours to characterize these two elements; these colours I tried to retain and use not only where the poet had indicated one or the other element but also where they could be made effective use of. The tone colour of the scoring for forest and hunting life was easy to find: the horns provided it. The difficulty lay only in finding for the horns new melodies that would be both simple and popular. For this purpose I searched among folk melodies, and I have careful study to thank if this part of my task is successful. I did not even shrink from using parts of these tunes—shall I say, as far as the actual notes are concerned? . . . The most important part, to my mind, is in Max's words, "mich umgarnen finstre Mächte" ["I am entrapped by sinister forces"], for they showed me what chief characteristic to give the opera. I had to remind the hearer of these "dark powers" by means of tone-colour and melody as often as possible . . . I gave a great deal of thought to the question of what was the right principal colouring for this sinister element. Naturally it had to be a dark, gloomy colour—the lowest register of the violins, violas and basses, particularly the lowest register of the clarinet, which seemed especially suitable for depicting the sinister, then the mournful sound of the bassoon, the lowest notes of the horns, the hollow roll of drums or single hollow strokes on them.[35]

The words of Max that Weber quotes are from his aria in the first act, "Durch die Wälder, durch die Auen," sung shortly before his visit to the Wolf's Glen. In this aria Max vacillates between expressions of horror at his coming ordeal and happier thoughts of Agathe and times past. The words "Doch mich umgarnen finstre Mächte" ("But dark forces ensnare me") mark a turn from pleasant nostalgia to the sinister, and Weber provides music for this according to his own formula. As Samiel appears mysteriously in the background, there is a sustained diminished triad in the bottom register of the clarinets, bassoons, and violas, followed by a rushing, low-lying, syncopated string figure in C minor that becomes the accompaniment to Max's singing (see Example VI–8). Horns symbolizing the uncomplicated hunter's life sound ubiquitously (as in the Act I chorus "Lasst lustig die Hörner erschallen"), and folklike music, especially choral textures reminiscent of the *Singverein,* abound—examples are the Hunters' Chorus and the Bridesmaids' Chorus in Act III. The two main dramatic motifs of the opera, rustic innocence and supernatural malevolence, are given two distinct types of music; something of this is clear from the beginning, when the principal musical themes of the opera are directly juxtaposed in the overture.[36]

In the first of his *Dramatisch-musikalische Notizen* written in Dresden[37]

35. J. C. Lobe, *Gespräche mit Weber in fliegende Blätter,* 1 (1853). This translation from John Warrack, *Carl Maria von Weber* (2nd ed., Cambridge, 1976), p. 221.

36. The use of music from the body of an opera in the overture was not new: this practice was familiar, for example, from Mozart's *Don Giovanni* and Spohr's *Faust.*

37. Quoted above.

Example VI–8: WEBER, *Der Freischütz,* Act I

Weber seems to say that the foremost trait of German opera is eclecticism—the appropriation of "the best features of the others." *Der Freischütz* illustrates the principle well. Its realistic out-of-door scenes, both picturesque and violent, had been known in French opera since the last years of the previous century. The frequent choruses and the dances are reminiscent of French forebears, and many of the characters, particularly Max and Agathe's cousin Aennchen, are familiar types from opéra comique. That Weber should look to this repertory for his models is not surprising: the majority of productions he conducted at Prague and Dresden were German adaptations of French operas. Nor are Italian traits entirely lacking in *Der Freischütz,* whatever Weber's professed bad opinion of Italian opera.[38] This is especially clear in the Romanze und Aria of Aennchen (who in all other respects seems a refugee from *French* opera), "Einst träumte meiner selgen Base." The beginning of the aria proper has the sort of lively and uniform rhythmic figure, as well as the harmonic simplicity one expects of, say, Donizetti (see Example VI–9).

One of Weber's notable achievements is his construction of extended, unified musical scenes. A famous example is the Wolf's Glen episode. This is the finale to Act II, and finales are invariably set to continuous music. But Weber presents a fluent mixture of techniques—choral writ-

Example VI–9: WEBER, *Der Freischütz,* Romanze und Aria

38. In his *Tonkünstlersleben,* Weber gave a satirical description of Italian orchestration: "Oboi coi Flauti, Clarinetti coi Oboi, Flauti coi Violini, Fagotti col Basso. Viol. 2e col primo. Viola col Basso. Voce ad libitum. Violini colla parte." ("The oboes double the flutes, the clarinets double the oboes, the flutes double the violins, and the bassoons double the bass part. The second violins double the first, the violas double the bass. The vocal part is optional. The violins double the voice.")

tau - gen_ ei - nem   hol - den_ Braut- chen nicht.

ing, several types of recitative, melodrama, arioso song, and a continuous and prominent participation of the orchestra—for which it is hard to find a contemporary parallel. The paired keys of C minor and F♯ minor provide a tonal anchor for the entire scene and cement an obvious association of C minor with things demonic that is observable throughout the work. However familiar many of Weber's musical devices, in this opera we can see at work certain remarkable principles of large-scale construction: musical themes, tonalities, and orchestral timbres come to represent specific dramatic and scenic motifs. If the individual elements are well known, the consistent attempt to create intricate interconnections between them is novel.

In the remaining five years of his life after the premiere of *Der Freischütz* Weber wrote two more operas, *Euryanthe* (1823) and *Oberon* (1826), as well as incidental music to the drama *Preciosa* by Pius Alexander Wolff; a comic opera he began during this period, *Die drei Pintos,* survives only in part.[39] Weber conceived of *Euryanthe* as a massive production after the manner of Spontini's *La Vestale,* but based on a medieval subject and colored with a generous admixture of supernatural events. The libretto by Helmina von Chezy—with many contributions and suggestions from others, including Weber—turned out as a rough and unmanageable adaptation of the old romance earlier adopted by Shakespeare in *Cymbeline.* Opportunities for conventional spectacle and excitement abound here: there is a medieval festival, a large and menacing serpent, a rustic wedding, a mad scene, and a chorus of hunters with their inevitable horns and *Männerchor* singing. Weber's music often follows patterns familiar from *Der Freischütz.* But all the dialogue has been set to music, and some scenes show an impressive maturing of his efforts toward continuous musical realizations of large-scale dramatic events. One such is the beginning of Act III, where the heroine Euryanthe is led into the wilderness by Adolar, her beloved, who is charged with executing her for certain rather obscure offenses (of which she is of

39. It was completed by Mahler in 1887.

course innocent). The ferocious serpent appears and Adolar kills him. Unable to carry out his orders, he leaves Euryanthe to die in this inhospitable place; she then sings of her grief and desolation. The music for these events is uninterrupted. It is a seamless web of subtly shifting styles of recitative, arioso, and ensemble singing enlivened by inventive coloristic orchestral accompaniments. But *Euryanthe* hardly fulfills Weber's prescriptions for an opera whose individual parts are dissolved in an overall artistic effect; any such effect is spoiled by the ineptness of its libretto.

Der Freischütz gained Weber an international reputation. Staged throughout Germany and in notoriously mutilated versions in France and England, this opera won him a commission from London in 1825 to conduct three of his works: *Der Freischütz,* the music to *Preciosa,* and a new opera, *Oberon, or the Elf-king's Oath.* Never in very robust health, and now suffering from tuberculosis, Weber nevertheless set off for England in January 1826, and after a reasonably successful series of performances died there the following summer. If good intentions were thwarted by weaknesses in the libretto of *Euryanthe,* this problem is even more acute in *Oberon.* Adapted once again from a medieval chivalric tale (this one, too, had been used by Shakespeare, in *A Midsummernight's Dream*), the English text for *Oberon* was constructed by J. R. Planché with an eye to pleasing the London public. As Weber himself complained, there are a great many characters who do not sing, and important dramatic events take place with no music whatever; at points the piece seems less an opera than a play with incidental music. Some of this music has great charm; the overture and one aria, Reiza's "Ocean, thou mighty monster," are still familiar to concertgoers. But, through little fault of Weber's, *Oberon* stands for the most part outside the traditions of Romantic opera.

German opera in the earlier nineteenth century followed familiar patterns. In the latter part of the eighteenth century the Singspiel had been progressively enriched by the absorption of foreign influences, especially elements of the opéra comique. In the first three decades of the nineteenth century, German Romantic opera was fashioned in large part from practices born in France of revolutionary and Napoleonic times, together with certain strongly indigenous elements. In its narrowest definition the genre appears a short-lived thing; Wagner's *Tannhäuser* (1845) is often described as the last one. But certain of its characteristics, especially a tendency toward musical continuity and large-scale unity, were to become fixtures in European operatic practice for the remainder of the century.

CHAPTER VII

Paris from 1830 to 1848

As the resplendent Congress of Vienna celebrated his downfall early in 1815, Napoleon escaped from exile, ousted the recently enthroned Louis XVIII, gathered an army of 350,000, and set out to renew his conquests. The Hundred Days of his return ended decisively with the battle at Waterloo in Belgium. But what is astonishing about this episode is that it could have occurred at all, that Napoleon, the wrecker of peace and stability in all Europe, still commanded powerful support in war-weary France and elsewhere. The success of this campaign, however temporary, underscored the profound political divisions in Europe. Napoleon still represented for many certain abstract doctrines of the French Revolution: notions such as the "sovereignty of the people," the *a priori* illegitimacy of monarchy, and the equality of all persons before the law. The overriding concern of the Congress System and Prince Metternich of Austria, its main architect, was to prevent revo-

The Congress of Vienna, 1814–15. Far left, the Duke of Wellington. Prince Metternich is pointing at Lord Castlereagh. At right of table, Prince Talleyrand.

lution. The means adopted to that end, such as the reseating of monarchs, and internal measures to stifle dissent, ran counter to widespread liberal and nationalistic sentiment. The acts of the Congress of Vienna and subsequent meetings of the Allies at Paris, Aix-la-Chapelle, and Troppau from the first rested upon shifting sands of divided public opinion and a widespread new belief in the effectiveness of rebellion.

By 1820 revolutionary movements had toppled the governments of Spain, Naples, and the Ottoman Empire, and in 1825 the tremors of rebellion were felt in Russia. But it was in France, once more, that the issues of governmental prerogatives and the rights of the several classes of citizens were most sharply drawn. Louis XVIII had been deposited on the French throne (twice—both before and after the Hundred Days) by the victorious Allies, but he was subject to a *charte* that provided for a bicameral legislature and placed considerable limits on the power of the king. Louis, moreover, had become a cautious man and did nothing to disrupt an uneasy truce between the old nobility, the powerful bourgeoisie, the "intellectuals," laborers, and peasants. But his death in 1824 brought to the throne Charles X, the former Count of Artois, an unbending believer in the principles of the Old Regime and a champion of the most conservative faction of the nobility. Charles set about to indemnify these nobles for their losses in the Revolution, to reinstate the clergy as guardians of French education, and to restore gradually

The July Revolution, Paris, 1830. Charles X was overthrown in favor of Louis Philippe, the "citizen king."

the old hegemony of the monarchy and church. This was an impossibility in postrevolutionary France; but Charles, as it was said, marched straight toward disaster "with the crown over his eyes." The collapse came in 1830, in response to the July Ordinances that dissolved the legislature, imposed censorship of the press, and severely limited suffrage. The morning after their proclamation barricades went up once more in the streets of Paris. Two days later Charles had abdicated and fled to England. This July Revolution was almost bloodless, but its effects were momentous.

The government that followed was a product of intricate compromise. There was a new king, Louis Philippe, who had served in the republican army of 1792, and later had lived for a time in the United States. Calling himself the "citizen king," he wore ordinary clothing; as a symbol of his democratic leanings he moved about Paris unattended, carrying an umbrella. Louis understood that the balance of power had shifted decisively into the hands of the ascendant bourgeoisie, and it was mainly to the newly wealthy bankers, manufacturers, and merchants that he appealed for support. A new "capitalist nobility" was given a free hand to speed France's participation in the nascent Industrial Revolution. At the same time, many repressive measures of previous regimes were abolished, and France for a time showed a greater toleration for liberal ideas than any other nation on the continent.

GRAND OPERA

In Paris the new governmental and social order exerted an immediate and profound effect upon the arts. While the old nobility, traditionally patrons of artistic institutions, sulked in the background, the theaters and opera houses were populated increasingly by the well-to-do bourgeoisie. The venerable Opéra (the Académie royale de musique) was let out as a concession to the entrepreneur Louis Véron, a methodical businessman who set about adjusting the offerings of the institution to the tastes of its audience. He assembled a cohesive group of directors, designers, and performers whose every effort was coordinated to produce the sensational genre of musical entertainment known specifically as grand opera.[1] The efforts of others were enlisted to ensure its success. Véron's close ties with journalistic circles insured a flood of favorable publicity for his product. A well-organized and well-paid claque, directed by one Auguste Levasseur, led the audience in timely and enthusiastic applause.

---

1.   A thorough and perceptive description of the grand opera may be found in William L. Crosten's *French Grand Opera; an Art and a Business* (New York, 1948). The discussion here is indebted to this book.

The principal librettist for the grand opera, Eugène Scribe (1791–1861), drew on several traditions for his texts. Most of his subjects, like those of contemporary Italian serious opera, were loosely adapted from post-classical history. *La Muette de Portici* (The Mute Girl of Portici), performed with music by D. F. E. Auber in 1828, depicts a seventeenth-century revolution in Naples, though the title role was newly invented. The action of *La Juive* (The Jewess), composed by Jacques Halévy in 1835, takes place against the backdrop of the Council of Constance (1414–18); the sixteenth-century St. Bartholomew's Day Massacre supplies the setting for *Les Huguenots* (The Huguenots, 1836), the operatic triumph of Giacomo Meyerbeer (1791–1864). These librettos usually have a noticeable liberal bias in keeping with the prevailing sentiment of their audience; the nobility are generally made to look bad, and anticlerical sentiment runs strong—the Catholics in *Les Huguenots* are portrayed as murderous fanatics.

But historical events, however interpreted, are little more than occasions for the real business of grand opera, the creation of great excitement and spectacle. The massive pageants and processions were already familiar from the operas of Spontini; added to these is the titillation of grisly and terrifying events. Sometimes they are menacing and supernatural in the best traditions of the Gothic novel and the German Romantic opera; in the Cloister Scene in the third act of *Robert-le-Diable* a group of deceased nuns rise from their graves, cast off their habits, and execute a macabre dance; other horrors are realistic, as the massacre scene of *Les Huguenots*. Of crucial importance for all such spectacle in the grand opera were advanced methods of stagecraft; lavish set designs by Pierre Cicéri, Edmond Duponchel, and Louis Daguerre (known for

Cicéri's design for the cloister scene in Act III of Meyerbeer's *Robert-le-diable*, 1831.

the early photographic process that bears his name) were calculated for the maximum in novelty and realism. For the production of Hérold's *La Belle au bois dormant* in 1829, for example, Cicéri devised an undulating stage decoration to simulate the deck of a moving boat. Many of these dramatic and scenic effects were already well proven in the smaller popular theaters of Paris, where the principal architects of the grand opera had learned their craft. The dramas and melodramas seen in playhouses of "the Boulevard"—roughly equivalent to modern-day Broadway—furnished a ready fund of techniques that were simply adapted to the scale and magnificence of the Opéra.

The beginnings of grand opera are discernible as early as Spontini's *La Vestale* (1807). Auber's *La Muette de Portici* of 1828 and Rossini's *Guillaume Tell* of the following year speeded its development; but it first appears in full flower in the 1830s in two works of the German-born composer whose name is inseparably linked with the genre, Giacomo Meyerbeer. After the brilliant success of *Robert-le-Diable* in 1831, Meyerbeer collaborated with Scribe and the concerted personnel of the Opéra five years later to produce one of the most popular operas of all time, *Les Huguenots*.[2] Nothing was spared in preparation and publicity for this spectacular work. The most glittering and moneyed of Parisian society were in attendance; the Baron James de Rothschild, perhaps the richest man in Paris, even timed the inaugural ball at his opulent new palace to coincide with the *Huguenots* premiere, so that at the final curtain the guests could go directly to a resplendent spectacle of their own.

Surely *Les Huguenots* provided its audience with all they expected. In addition to the final massacre of the Protestants, there is a wedding procession, a grand ball, a bathing scene regarded by some as licentious, a ceremonial consecration of swords, and two raucous drinking parties. Meyerbeer was quick to seize all such opportunities for grandiose or "characteristic" music. The opera abounds with massive choral singing supported by full orchestra. And even the principals sing as often in ensembles as alone; there is only one large-scale virtuoso aria, "O Beau Pays de la Touraine," sung at the opening of Act II by Marguerite de Valois, a relatively minor character. Neither this nor any other solo singing occurs as the climax of a scene. Instead, Meyerbeer constructs shifting kaleidoscopic tableaux of soloists and chorus that culminate in full deployment of all forces at hand. Scenic splendors are matched by music of great volume and inventive orchestral color. The least subtle element of Meyerbeer's style is rhythm. Time and again the listener is bombarded with simple rhythmic patterns mercilessly repeated, as in the "orgy" scene from Act I (Example VII–1); this ensemble sounds like a rousing Rossini chorus with echoes of the can-can, a dance just

---

2.   First performed on February 29, 1836, it had been given at the Opéra one thousand times by May 1906.

Example VII–1: MEYERBEER, *Les Huguenots,* Act I

gaining currency in Paris at that time.[3]

The critical reaction to *Les Huguenots* in Paris—clearly encouraged by financial connections between the Opéra and the press—was unanimously favorable. Even Heine and Berlioz, both of them later critical of Meyerbeer, wrote admiringly of the work. German critics, however, were unanimously contemptuous; particularly so were the

3.   Very similar rhythmic and melodic patterns can be found in later Italian opera, as in the first chorus of Verdi's *Rigoletto.*

Achille Devéria's 1836 lithograph depicting the final scene of Meyerbeer's *Les Huguenots*.

redoubtable Ludwig Rellstab in Berlin and Robert Schumann in Leipzig, who saw in Meyerbeer's opera a glorification of the contrived effect, unrelieved musical eclecticism, and, not least, a libretto that was an affront to Protestant sensibilities.[4] What Schumann and the other Germans appreciated least was a heightened dramatic realism in *Les Huguenots:* a willingness to show scenes of violence and horror directly and to supply them with music that was deliberately unlovely. And they failed to recognize what is surely Meyerbeer's principal virtue, a radically experimental orchestration employing new instruments such as the bass clarinet, and producing novel timbres that influenced the sound of the orchestra from Berlioz and Wagner to Richard Strauss.

The public furor over *Les Huguenots* proved impossible to duplicate. Though Meyebeer accepted another Scribe libretto in 1838, *L'Africaine* (based on the explorations of Vasco de Gama), the work was abandoned when he returned to his native Berlin in 1842. After producing several modest works for the court there, he returned to Paris in 1848 for the very successful staging of *Le Prophète,* again composed to a libretto by Scribe. In 1865, shortly after the composer's death, *L'Africaine* was at last performed. By this time, new influences were being brought to bear on the Parisian stage (Wagner's *Tannhäuser* had been seen there in 1861). Parisian grand opera was tailor-made for a special moment in history; the theatrical and musical forces at the Opéra and the social ambiance of Paris were exactly right for *Les Huguenots* in 1836, and, whatever the acclaim won by *Le Prophète,* this high-water mark was not to be repeated.

One significant effect of grand opera is that it confirmed the place of Paris as the musical center of Europe. As a century earlier aspiring musicians flocked to Naples and Rome, now even the leading Italian opera composers sought their fortunes in Paris. Opera there had become a visible triumph of the commercial revolution, complete with an

4.　See Leon Plantinga, *Schumann as Critic* (New Haven, 1967), pp. 160–64.

An autograph page of Paganini's *Caprices,* Op. 1.

expensive product, substantial investments in advertising, and sizable profits. Scribe produced librettos on something like an assembly line, sketching the plots himself, but leaving all the details to be worked out by his employees. Other facets of music making in Paris were soon influenced by the special orientation of the opera toward its public; one of the first of these was the rise of the virtuoso instrumental performer.

THE VIRTUOSOS

A correspondence report from Milan in the Leipzig *Allgemeine musikalische Zeitung* of 1814 called attention to an astonishing Italian violinist:

> On the 29th of October [1813] Mr. Paganini of Genoa, generally regarded in Italy as the first violinist of our time, gave a musical academy in the Scala Theater. He performed a violin concerto of Kreutzer (E minor), and, finally, Variations on the G string . . . His playing is simply unbelievable. He has special runs, leaps, and double stops that have never been heard from any violinist, whoever he may be. He plays the most difficult two-, three-, and four-voiced passages using his own unique fingering. He imitates many wind instruments, and presents the chromatic scale in the very highest register, right up by the bridge, so purely that it is hardly to be believed. He amazes his listeners with the most difficult passages played on one string, and, as in jest, plucks an accompanying bass on the other.[5]

---

5.   *Allgemeine musikalische Zeitung,* 16 (1814): 231–32.

Niccolò Paganini (1782–1840) began to dazzle Italian audiences in about 1805 when he became solo violinist for Elise Baciocchi, the sister of Napoleon who was the newly installed ruler of Piombino and Lucca. After 1809 he gave up this post to make his way as a touring virtuoso and occasional composer. Paganini's violinistic acrobatics became legendary. Word of his breathtaking speed, spectacular multiple stops, strange harmonics, left-hand pizzicatos, and single-string playing spread so rapidly that during his great European tour in 1828–34 he was a celebrity everywhere by the time he arrived.

A concert in this period nearly always still meant an elaborate evening's entertainment with orchestra, at least one singer, and assorted other soloists. So Paganini's meteoric course across Europe was in fact a cumbersome business. In every city performers had to be assembled, parts provided, programs printed, and advertising arranged. Accompanied by a manager who shielded the maestro from all these humdrum details, Paganini became a model of the nineteenth-century traveling virtuoso: an urbane public figure always surrounded by eager admirers and public furor.

Paganini, like other concert givers, ordinarily played his own music, tailored to display his special technical strengths. Concertos were a staple in the repertory, and audiences could usually count on hearing one of his. (When he played a Kreutzer concerto at the Milan concert noted above, he had not yet written one of his own.) The other compositions most often repeated were sets of variations, particularly those on current opera tunes like Rossini's "Di tanti palpiti" from *Tancredi* or "Non più mesta" from *Cenerentola*. The "Variations on the G string" heard at the Milan concert were composed on an operatic theme of Franz Xaver Süssmayr; another piece with which he startled audiences by playing entirely on the lowest string of the violin was his *Napoleon Sonata*. But most influential of Paganini's compositions, perhaps, were the *24 Capricci* for solo violin, Op. 1, published in Milan in 1818. A compendium of his most stunning effects, they became a sort of textbook of virtuosity for the rest of the nineteenth century. Nor was their influence confined to violin music; both Schumann and Liszt made widely admired transcriptions of these pieces for piano.

Number 24 of the *Capricci* is a miniature theme-and-variations. The theme, familiar to many from Rachmaninov's *Rhapsody on a Theme of Paganini* and Brahms's Variations, Op. 35, is a rhythmically active, evenly periodicized binary tune that strongly emphasizes the tonic and dominant degrees (A and E), both playable on open strings of the violin (Example VII–2 shows the theme and Variations 8 and 9). In Variation 8 the three-part polyphonic texture clarifies certain harmonic details that were not explicit in the theme, such as the bass motion by descending fifths in mm. 9–12. Here the violinist must overcome sticky problems of coordination and intonation as he plays on three strings

Example VII–2: PAGANINI, *24 Capricci,* Op. 1, No. 24: Theme, Variations
         8 and 9

From 24 CAPRICES by N. Paganini, revised by Emil Kross. Copyright © 1912 by Carl
Fischer, Inc., New York. Used by permission.

throughout. Variation 9 shows Paganini's famous "fingered pizzicato";
the notes marked with a small circle are to be plucked with the left hand
(for technical reasons they usually occur in downward scalewise or
arpeggiated figures). While some of Paganini's virtuoso devices were
anticipated by eighteenth-century violinists, particularly Pietro Antonio Locatelli (1695–1764) and Giuseppe Tartini (1692–1770), this one,
it seems, was wholly new.

   In the making of Paganini's public image, his person figures as much
as his playing. The Italian's reputation as an implausibly brilliant performer was soon colored with another impression: the French critic
F.-J. Fétis recalled,

> The extraordinary expression of his face, his livid paleness, his dark and
> penetrating eye, together with the sardonic smile which occasionally played
> upon his lips, appeared to the vulgar, and to certain diseased minds,
> unmistakable evidences of a Satanic origin.[6]

---

6.   F.-J. Fétis, *Biographical Notice of Nicolo [sic] Paganini* (London, n.d.), p. 59.

Paganini in a portrait by Eugène Delacroix.

As Paganini toured Europe in triumph, these indistinct rumors of a dark and gruesome past pursued him, and his extraordinary technical feats were often put down to some Faustian pact with the Devil. Willingly or not, in the popular imagination Paganini became a sort of musical "fatal man," related to fictive personages such as Schiller's robber Karl Moore, Byron's Giaour, and Caspar of *Der Freischütz*. His instrument was the right one (fiddles had been shown in the hands of Death and the Devil since the Middle Ages), and he showed hints of special qualities thought appropriate to the genre: "mysterious (but conjectured to be exalted) origin, traces of burnt-out passions, suspicion of a ghastly guilt, melancholy habits, pale face, unforgettable eyes."[7] Paganini benefited from a climate in which the public fancied something of the demonic in its heros, of whom the principal model was Napoleon. In a recorded conversation with J. P. Eckermann in 1831 Goethe said quite specifically, "Napoleon appears to have been a demonic type through and through, and to the highest degree, such that almost no one can be compared with him. . . . In Paganini it [the demonic] can be seen very clearly, and it is this that enables him to produce his marvelous effects."[8]

In February 1831, Paganini first appeared in Paris and proceeded to take the city by storm. At this time Louis Philippe had occupied his throne for some seven months and was still busy reorganizing his regime along egalitarian lines. The Opéra had just been entrusted to Véron,

7.   From Mario Praz, *The Romantic Agony* (London, 1933), p. 59.
8.   Johann Peter Eckermann, *Gespräche mit Goethe* (Leipzig, 1868), 2, pp. 201–2.

who soon decided (with some persuasion from Paganini's countryman Rossini) that a series of dazzling concerts by the newly arrived virtuoso would be a perfect stop-gap until a new opera could be mounted. Paganini played ten times during a five-week period; the enthusiasm of both audiences and critics knew no bounds. Castil-Blaze, music critic for the influential *Journal des débats,* exclaimed of the first concert,

> This is the most amazing of events, the most astonishing, marvelous, triumphant, stupifying, singular, extraordinary, incomprehensible, unforeseen. . . . This first piece, sparkling with engaging melodies that hurl out passages of scintillating originality, of extreme audacity for which Paganini alone possesses the secret since he alone can play them, was greeted with thunderous applause. . . . Sell, pawn everything to go and hear Paganini.[9]

While some critics sometimes credited Paganini with certain gifts as a composer, his works in the main seem but vehicles for his extraordinary prowess as a performer. The concertos in particular are in harmony and instrumentation decidedly pedestrian.

Paganini's success in Paris was a powerful stimulus to the growing cult of virtuoso solo playing. Violinists like the prodigious Henri Vieuxtemps (1820–81) and the cellist Auguste Franchomme (1804–84) helped satisfy the Parisian appetite for brilliant performance. But most prominent of the virtuosos were the battalions of pianists, most of them from central or eastern Europe, who gathered in the City of Light to establish their credentials and seek their fortunes. Friedrich Kalkbrenner went there at age fourteen in 1799; Joseph Wölfl arrived in 1801. Henri Herz entered the Paris Conservatory in 1816 and remained a resident of the city. In 1823 the eleven-year-old Liszt moved there with his family to make his mark as a child prodigy. Chopin came in 1831, and about that time many others appeared, such as Ferdinand Hiller, Theodor Döhler, J. P. Pixis, and Alexander Dreyschock. All of these musicians came to Paris simply because in music, as in other things, it was the world's center of fashion. Parisian styles in music were watched and imitated throughout Europe; success there almost guaranteed success everywhere.

At the center of French musical life was the opera, and musicians of every sort contrived to share its glory. Even more than Paganini, the piano virtuosos specialized in musical embroideries on the most popular operatic tunes. They dazzled audiences in concerts or at resplendent salons with their fantasias, variations, rondos, and capriccios on favorite morsels from Rossini and Meyerbeer, and then sold their handiwork, very often in simplified form, for people to play for themselves. Characteristic of this repertory is the "fantasia with theme-and-variations," an example of which may be seen in Döhler's *Fantasia and Bra-*

9. *Journal des débats,* March 13, 1831.

vura Variations on a Theme of Donizetti, Op. 17 (c. 1836). This piece is
in fact based upon two tunes from Donizetti's *Anna Bolena,* one for the
fantasia and one for the variations. The fantasia begins with characteristic juxtaposition of fast and slow sections containing fragmentary bits
of the two melodies to come (Example VII–3a). When the improvisatory, harmonically far-flung fantasia gives way to the variations, we
hear first the unadorned theme for this section, taken from Percy's aria
"Nel veder la tua costanza" (its beginning is shown on page 139). The
The very regular variations present one standard virtuoso figuration
after another. First is a scintillating rapid-fire alternation of the two
hands playing chords in the same register (Example VII–3b). In Variation 3 Döhler employs a favorite device of the time: a melody in a
middle register, here written in octaves, is festooned with brilliant
arpeggios above and below (Example VII–3c).

Example VII–3: DöHLER, *Fantasia and Bravura Variations on a Theme of
Donizetti,* Op. 17

a. Introduction

b. Variation 1

c. Variation 3

This last pianistic figuration was popularized mainly by Sigismund Thalberg (1812–71), the urbane Viennese-trained pianist who burst upon the Parisian scene in January 1836. The opening measures of his first concert, wrote Hector Berlioz, demonstrated that he was one of the world's premier pianists. And like many others Berlioz was impressed with the special Thalberg keyboard texture that left a clear impression, he said, of "three-handed" playing.[10] Early reviews of Thalberg's playing also speak of an unprecedented resonance and fullness of sound. The "three-handed" texture itself is conducive to such an effect: the arpeggios above the melody powerfully reinforce its upper partials. But Thalberg also benefitted decisively from recent developments in the construction of pianos. The beginning of his career coincided almost exactly with the appearance of a potent new instrument; the seven-octave grand piano with felt-covered hammers and metal plates and braces, in most essentials like the present-day concert instrument, just at this time made a new kind of playing possible.

Like the grand opera, the piano virtuosos were surrounded by a distinct aura of commercialism. Some of them (beginning with Clementi) made use of their reputations as piano players to further their careers as piano manufacturers. In 1824 Kalkbrenner entered into partnership with the Parisian piano firm of Pleyel (whose founder, Ignaz Pleyel, had been an estimable composer); Herz collaborated with the Klepfer piano manufactury and subsequently founded his own. Music and business mingled easily at the premises of the piano makers. The most prosper-

---

10. *Revue et gazette musicale,* 3 (1836): 38.

ous of them provided instruments to leading pianists as an inducement to use their product exclusively; Pleyel, Érard, and Herz even maintained concert halls for the exhibition of pianos and pianists. Nearly all the leading virtuosos published lucrative piano methods. And the dubious academies J. G. Logier founded in London and elsewhere after 1814, which purported to teach piano to twenty pupils at once, found a ready collaborator in Kalkbrenner. Kalkbrenner also helped sell Logier's patented mechanical device for assuring correct hand position at the piano, the *Chiroplast* (its manufacturer was Clementi and Co.); a similarly useless contraption called the *Dactylion* was put on the market by Herz.

LISZT

Franz Liszt (1811–86), often regarded as the greatest pianist of all time, made his Parisian debut in 1824 as a boy of twelve. Born in Raiding, Hungary, he soon showed such talent for music that his ambitious parents moved to Vienna to find him a teacher. In the spring of 1823, after a year's study with Czerny, he gave a concert in the Kleines Redoutensaal that attracted considerable notice. At this early age the boy already composed music—rondos, fantasias, variations, and even two concertos, according to his father—for his own performances. And one little composition of his, a variation on the waltz by Diabelli that also gave rise to Beethoven's monumental *Diabelli Variations,* was published in 1823 before the Liszts left for Paris.[11]

Once in Paris the young virtuoso was left largely to his own devices; though he made use of Kalkbrenner's piano method and undertook studies in music theory from Ferdinando Paër (1771–1839) and Reicha, he apparently had no more lessons on his instrument from anyone. But brilliant concerts in France and England in 1824–26 soon made him widely known. The pieces he played were at first mainly his own contributions to standard virtuoso fare; *Sept Variations brillantes sur un thème de G. Rossini, Impromptu brillant sur des thèmes de Rossini et Spontini,* and an *Allegro di bravura* were all played and published in 1824–25. In quite a different vein he managed to write an opera, *Don Sanche;* it was a brave effort, but the production closed after three performances at the Opéra.

When Paganini cast his spell over Paris in 1831 and 1832, the impressionable twenty-year-old Liszt was stunned. In an often-quoted letter of May 1832 he wrote,

> "And I too am a painter!" cried Michael Angelo the first time he beheld a *chef d'oeuvre.* . . . Though insignificant and poor, your friend cannot leave off repeating those words of the great man ever since Paganini's last per-

11. In the volume *Vaterländischer Künstlerverein;* see above, p. 58.

Franz Liszt

formance. . . . What a man, what a violin, what an artist! O God, what pain and suffering, what torment in those four strings!

According to his own testimony he now plunged into an almost frenzied regime of technical work at his instrument: "I practice four to five hours of trills, sixths, octaves, tremolos, repeated notes, cadenzas and the like."[12] Liszt had shown a keen interest in the raw elements of virtuoso playing well before he heard Paganini: his earliest concert pieces show this, and in 1827 he had published his *Étude en quarante-huit excercises dans tous les tons majeurs et mineurs,* an ambitious collection of exercises (despite the claims of the title there are only twelve) in brilliant and difficult keyboard figurations. The influence of Paganini added direction and focus to a proclivity already in evidence.

A sign of the Italian's influence appeared promptly in 1831–32 in Liszt's *Grande Fantaisie de bravoure sur la Clochette de Paganini,* based upon the "bell" theme *(La Campanella)* from Paganini's Violin Concerto No. 2 in B minor. Paganini was honored again in his *Etudes d'execution transcendante d'après Paganini* (1838), a collection of piano transcriptions of numbers from the Caprices, Op. 1, and, once more, a reworking of the "bell" theme. This famous etude, often called simply *La Campanella,* presents a series of dazzling pianistic figurations on Paganini's tune; two of them, together with the original melody (transposed for easier comparison) are shown in Example VII–4a, b, and c. In both of these variations, as often happened, Liszt places the melody in the pianist's left

12. *Letters of Franz Liszt,* ed. La Mara, trans. Constance Bache (New York, 1894) 1, pp. 8–9 (quoted with corrections).

Example VII–4 a. PAGANINI, *La Campanella, mm.* 1–4

b. LISZT, Etude, *La Campanella,* mm. 42–46

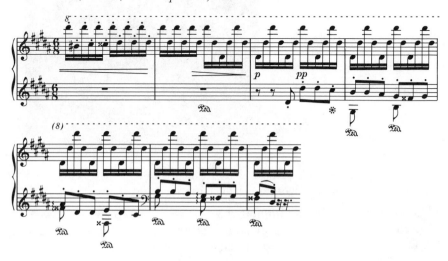

c. LISZT, Etude, *La Campanella,* mm. 79–83

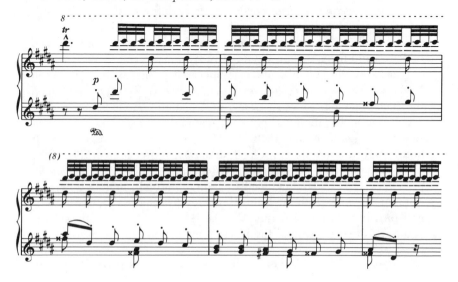

hand (but in a high range) with an added filigree above. To execute the "upper pedal" on the dominant in mm. 44ff. the pianist must pivot his right hand around the middle finger so as to encompass two full octaves. The effect is scintillating and altogether novel. In mm. 79ff. another ostinato on the dominant is sustained through a trill and repeated tones an octave lower. There are clear precedents for keyboard figurations that mix continuous trills with other materials in the same hand, as in the last movement of Beethoven's *Waldstein Sonata,* Op. 53. But in both these passages the sound is strikingly new, owing in part to the very high tessitura recently made available on the nineteenth-century piano.

During the 1830s Liszt was the preeminent Parisian virtuoso, and he played the role well. Even the customary commercial connections were not entirely lacking: the piano maker Pierre Érard had conscripted young Liszt for his stable of performers in 1824, and immediately arranged for his first visit to England, where he played Érard pianos at the Érard concert rooms in London. Mutually beneficial arrangements with this firm continued for most of the pianist's career. And when in 1836 Thalberg threatened to unseat him as the public's favorite, Liszt participated energetically in the ensuing rivalry, a spectacle marked by inflated journalism and, in 1837, a face-to-face "contest" between the two at the salon of the Princess Belgiojoso. Liszt now seemed once more without peer among the pianists of Paris, and in 1838–47 he proceeded to conquer the rest of Europe in a series of triumphant concert tours that took him from Constantinople to Scotland and from Spain to Sweden. In his native Hungary he was presented with the sword of nobility and declared a national hero (though he spoke barely a word of Hungarian); in 1842 in Berlin, where Liszt gave twenty-one concerts in ten weeks, King Friedrich Wilhelm IV of Prussia conferred upon him the order *Pour le Mérite,* an honor hitherto reserved for that country's military heroes.

During much of his career as a public pianist Liszt's concert programs largely conformed to the usual pattern: several soloists participated, and an orchestra was on hand to accompany singers and instrumental concertos and sometimes to play an overture. Liszt's solo contributions typically included such perennial favorites as his *Grande Valse di bravura* (1836), the *La Campanella* etude, and his fantasies on tunes from *Robert-le-Diable* and Pacini's *Niobé.* But he also soon presented the public with quite different sorts of transcriptions. He made piano versions of Lieder by Beethoven, Schubert, and others (a particular favorite was the *Erl-könig*). And in a concert of December 1836, he played his ingenious arrangement for piano of two movements from Berlioz's *Symphonie fantastique.* This was only one of his professed attempts to make the solo piano, under his hands, a rival of the orchestra. In later years, he created a profusion of such transcriptions as he set about to turn all the Beethoven symphonies, Berlioz's *Harold en Italie,* and the overtures to *William Tell, Oberon, Freischütz,* and Wagner's *Tannhäuser*[13] into gigantic piano pieces. Liszt finally took the unprecedented step of doing away with an orchestra or other soloists in his concerts. In a letter of 1839 to the Princess Belgiojoso he described such a solo concert as a "musical soliloquy" and offered a sample program:

1. Overture to William Tell, performed by M[onsieur] L[iszt].

2. Reminiscences of the *Puritani.* Fantaisie composed and performed by the above-mentioned!

3. Etudes and fragments by the same to the same!

4. Improvisation on themes given—still by the same.[14]

In the Berlin concerts of 1842, most of which were solo recitals, Liszt's programs featuring some eighty compositions reveal another of his innovations that was to become common practice: in addition to his own music and transcriptions he performed works by Bach, Handel, Scarlatti, Beethoven, Weber, and others. This is a decisive move from the characteristic posture of the earlier nineteenth-century virtuoso, for whom the music performed has little purpose but the exhibition of his own lightning speed and thundering octaves; in his serious presentation of serious music by other composers—Beethoven's *Hammerklavier Sonata,*[15] for example—Liszt became a new sort of public soloist, the *interpreter* typical of the later nineteenth century and the twentieth.

From about 1830 Liszt eagerly attached himself to the close-knit Parisian coterie of Romantic litterateurs and artists that included Balzac, Victor Hugo, Alfred de Vigny, Alfred de Musset, George Sand, the painter Eugène Delacroix, and the musicans Chopin and Berlioz. He was also quickly drawn into a variety of Saint-Simonism (an early form of socialism tinged with Christian mysticism) by the maverick priest and political writer H. F. R. de Lamennais. Largely lacking in formal education, Liszt developed an appetite for visionary conversation and voracious reading, guided, often, by the tastes of his more experienced friends. One of this group, the Countess Marie d'Agoult, who in 1835 left her family to become Liszt's mistress and the mother of his three children, described her first impression of the virtuoso in familiar-sounding terms:

13.   ARM 8.
14.   *Letters,* 1, p. 31. The term "recital" was apparently first used in its modern sense by Liszt in London about two years later.
15.   Liszt had performed the *Hammerklavier* in Paris as early as 1836. The common belief that he played Beethoven's *Emperor Concerto* there in 1828 has been laid to rest by Emile Haraszti in "Le Problème Liszt," *Acta musicologica,* 9 (1937): 126–27.

An imaginary assemblage of musicians and writers painted by Joseph Dannhauser in 1840. Liszt is at the piano with Marie d'Agoult at his feet. Seated behind him are George Sand and Dumas père. Standing are Victor Hugo, Paganini, and Rossini.

> A tall figure, thin to excess, a pale face with large sea-green eyes . . . an ailing and powerful expression, an indecisive walk that seemed rather to glide over than to touch the ground, a distracted air, unquiet and like that of a phantom about to be summoned back to the shades, this is how I saw the young genius before me.[16]

Like Paganini, Liszt was transformed by the Romantic imagination into a particular sort of hero: mysterious, sickly, and bearing the faint marks of dark associations which another world.

On other occasions, Liszt's personality became a subject for literary elaboration. The Countess d'Agoult (under the name Daniel Stern) later wrote a novel about Liszt, *Nélida,* and he appears again in Balzac's *Béatrix ou les Amours forcés;* neither portrait is favorable. The pianist himself came to be known as a writer. Most of the essays published under his name are about music; some are in a highly "literary" style, and most were really written by the Countess or by Liszt's subsequent mistress, the Princess Sayn-Wittgenstein. In the 1830s and 1840s Liszt showed increasing interest in relating his music to literary ideas and images, to works of art, and to scenes from nature as they strike the artistic sensibility. Piano compositions appear with the titles *Apparitions* (1835), probably borrowed from Lamartine's poem *Apparition, Harmonies poétiques et religieuses* (1835 and 1853), and *Consolations* (1849–50), after Sainte-

---

16. Maria d'Agoult, *Mémoires,* as translated in Eleanor Perényi, *Liszt: the Artist as Romantic Hero* (Boston, 1974), p. 80.

Beuve's second volume of poems. The *Album d'un voyageur* and *Années de Pèlerinage* (Parts I and II)[17], which include some of the most impressive of Liszt's "evocative" piano compositions, are products of his sojourns in Switzerland (1835–37) and Italy (1837–39). The individual pieces of these collections nearly all have titles referring to places, scenes, poems, or paintings, or bear epigraphs from Byron, Sénancour, and others. His three *Sonnets of Petrarch* are transcriptions of his songs to those texts, and in a piece called *Les Cloches de Genève* the bells are clearly audible. The relation of the music to its title is in other cases more subjective, as in *Le Mal du pays* (Homesickness) and *Après une Lecture du Dante: fantasia quasi sonata* (After Reading Dante: Fantasy like a Sonata). Keyboard writing in these pieces is as diverse as their titles. Some, such as *Au Bord d'une source* (Beside a Spring), have a texture something like a Field nocturne: a lyrical melody with an arpeggiated accompaniment. Others, like the *Dante Sonata,* as it is called, engage in heaven-storming virtuosity that strains the physical limits of both player and instrument. Liszt's harmonic style in this music is often startlingly advanced; portions of *Vallée d'Obermann,* for example, verge on atonality.

The first piece, *Sposalizio,* from Part II, *Italie,* of the *Années de Pèlerinage* (ARM 9) is a fairly representative specimen of Liszt's writing for piano in the late 1830s. At the outset we are presented with an alternation of two contrasting motives in the tonic E major, *a* (mm. 1–2) and *b* (m. 3), that in various transformations permeate the entire composition. While the single-line falling figure in *a* seems to be used mainly for accompanimental patterns (sometimes in powerful bravura octaves), its harmonic properties have serious implications for the entire composition. This figure is made from the pitches of the dominant triad on B plus upper neighbors. All the neighbor-note motion is by major second; another interval of which we become aware at the opening of the piece is the minor third (see Example VII–5). The dotted rhythm and

Example VII—5: LISZT, *Sposalizio,* motive *a*

escape-tone motion of *b* (related to *a* in its stepwise upward motion) will yield several varieties of stable thematic material. At m. 9 another motive, *c* (in G♯) introduces two new elements: the sustained chords in the lower range and even eighth-note motion above (at mm. 10, 12,

---

17.   Some of the individual numbers of the *Années de Pèlerinage* (not published until 1855 and 1858) are revisions of pieces from the *Album d'un voyageur* (published in 1842).

16, etc., the left hand plays a figure from *a*). In this first section the melodies are fragmentary and, before the extended dominant preparation in mm. 18–28, the tonality is unstable; mm. 1–29, which function much as an introduction to the rest of the piece, could be represented thus:

m.	1	3	9	18
	a	*b*	*c* (+*a*)	*a* (+*c*)
	I		III	V/$_{\mathrm{I}}$

In the main body of this composition reasonably stable melodic areas (designated by upper case letters) made up of elements of *b* and *c,* and sometimes accompanied by *a,* occur as follows:

m.	30	38	77	109	120
	B	BC	BC (+*a*)	B	(+*a*)
	I	♭III	I	VI	I

At m. 38 and m. 77 Liszt combines the sustained chords of *c* with the upward motion of *b* (rhythmically displaced and augmented, and with the leap of a third filled in) as shown in Example VII–6. The occurrence of *c* in G♯ (m.9), *BC* in G major (m. 38), and of *B* in C♯ major (m. 109) is part of an overall harmonic plan built upon the thirds-relationship prepared at the very outset. At a more local level this plan is further elaborated. After *BC* is stated a minor third above the tonic (m. 38), the tonality moves further by minor thirds to B♭ (m. 60), D♭ (m. 64), and (enharmonically) back to E (m. 66). Also contributing to this pattern is the very strong emphasis upon the sixth degree, C♯ (a minor third below the tonic) from m. 109 to the end; the final cadential phrases simply repeat the vi–I motion in which the alternation of C♯' and b recall the first measures of the piece.

Example VII–6: LISZT, *Sposalizio,* motive *b* and melodic area *BC* compared

Liszt's harmonic style here is inventive and varied. Abrupt shifts, especially by thirds, from one tonality to another are sometimes mediated only by the common pitches involved. In mm. 37–38, for example, the motion from the dominant of E major to G major pivots upon the common B. The modulation down a third from G♯ to E is a very much more elaborate procedure in mm. 9–30. Here the bass descends by whole steps from G♯ (m. 9) to C (m.17), and then via D♯ to B, the dominant of E. An overlapping line in the treble moves, also by whole steps, from B♭ downward to the tonic E. The entire progression could be reduced as shown in Example VII–7. While the whole-tone motion in mm. 9–19 virtually obliterates any sense of tonality, the measures that follow reestablish E major through the most usual of tonal procedures, an extended dominant pedal.

Example VII–7: LISZT, *Sposalizio,* mm. 9–30 reduced

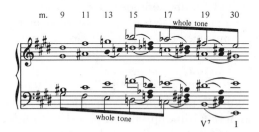

Sposalizio takes its title from the Raphael painting that portrays the betrothal of Mary and Joseph. Liszt had seen this painting in Milan and instructed that a drawing of it (together with one of Michaelangelo's statue *Il Penseroso,* the inspiration for the second number of *Années de Pèlerinage*) be included in the first edition of the music. The nature of the reference of this music to its title, to the painting, or to the subject of the painting is surely less than obvious. About a year before this piece was written, Liszt himself (or was it the Countess d'Agoult?) had something to say about the relationship of music to titles or explanations:

> But his [the musician's] language, more arbitrary and less defined than all the others, submits to a multitude of different interpretations. . . . it is not useless, and certainly not ridiculous, one must repeat, that the composer should give in a few lines a psychic sketch of his work, tell what he wished to do . . . and express the fundamental idea of his composition. Then the critics are free to praise or blame the embodiment of the idea, whether it is beautiful and successful or not; this way, at least, they will avoid making a host of false interpretations.[18]

This statement reflects a characteristic Romantic view of musical expressiveness. While music without words cannot be said to have any precise "meaning," the impressions or feelings it evokes find analogues, it was thought, in other areas of human activity: language (especially poetry), the visual arts, or the contemplation of nature. Thus by invoking an appropriate "poetic counterpart"[19] the composer can

---

18. "Lettre d'un bachelier ès-musique," *Revue et gazette musicale,* 4 (1837): 55.

19. This was Robert Schumann's term. For a discussion of a Romantic review of musical reference see my *Schumann as Critic,* pp. 114–29.

Lo sposalizio della Virgine by Raphael.

convey a general idea of the sort of musical expression he intended. Liszt apparently felt that Raphael's intimate betrothal scene, leaving impressions, say, of tenderness and ardor, suggested feelings similar to those he thought his composition would convey. In later years he was to demonstrate a continuing interest in this sort of rapprochement of music and "poetic counterparts" in his cultivation of the symphonic poem.

Some of Liszt's finest and most enduring works, however, achieve their effect without literary programs or evocative titles. One such is the Sonata in B minor for piano (1852–53), a masterpiece of nineteenth-century keyboard music that shows Liszt in command of remarkably advanced formal techniques. The three "movements" are combined in one, connected by elaborate motivic interrelationships. This procedure, which we have seen in tentative fashion in *Sposalizio,* came to be known as "thematic transformation." The result in the B-minor Sonata is a work of rare structural unity and dramatic power.

CHOPIN

One element in Liszt's enormous attraction for western European audiences was his "exotic" Hungarian origin. However tenuous his actual connections with his birthplace, he celebrated them repeatedly in the composition of nationalistic music such as the *Hungarian Marches* for piano (1840s) and their revisions for orchestra (1860s and 1870s). Other works, such as the formidable Sonata in B minor, induce an air of exoticism with Eastern-sounding scales and harmonic configurations. A virtuoso whose origins seemed even more splendidly outlandish was Louis Moreau Gottschalk (1829–69) of New Orleans; his elaborations of Creole melodies first excited French audiences in 1844. Something of this sort of appeal also attached to Frédéric Chopin (1810–49), the supremely gifted Polish pianist and composer who settled in Paris in the fall of 1831. Poland had shortly before fallen under Russian domination, and Chopin was sometimes imaginatively portrayed as a refugee from a heroic national struggle, though he had in fact left Warsaw before the fighting began, with the express intent of furthering his musical career in Vienna and Paris. But though he never again set foot in Poland, Chopin's attachment to his homeland was lasting, and the composition of music in a Polish idiom, particularly the polonaises and mazurkas, was one of the most serious endeavors of his life.

Unlike Liszt, Chopin received a systematic general and musical education. At the secondary school in Warsaw where his father taught he was given rigorous instruction in Latin, Greek, mathematics, and other subjects. Then in 1826 he entered the newly founded Warsaw Conservatory to study composition and music theory with the estimable German composer Joseph Elsner (1766–1854). His musical horizons were broadened by visits to Berlin (1828) and to Vienna, where in 1829 he played his piano music in two concerts. Like almost all young virtuosos he was fired with enthusiasm by Paganini, who appeared in Warsaw in 1829. In this environment Chopin's musical development proceeded with astonishing rapidity. By the time he came to Paris at the age of twenty-one he had well over fifty piano compositions to his credit (including his two piano concertos, Op. 11 in E minor and Op. 21 in F minor) and central elements of his style were already fixed.

Chopin's role in the musical life of Paris was very unlike that of the other celebrated virtuosos. The delicate nuances of his playing had a much more telling effect in the intimate salon than on the concert stage, and during his career in Paris he was heard in public only about seven times. Never subjected to the glare of publicity that surrounded Liszt and Thalberg, he first associated mainly with his fellow Polish emigrés; then from 1838 to 1846 he lived quietly with the novelist George Sand (Mme. Dudevant), spending winters in the city and summers at her estate at Nohant, some miles south of Paris. He nonetheless became a

A portrait of Chopin by Eugène Delacroix.

great favorite of the moneyed aristocracy. Engaged in 1832 as a piano teacher for the wife and daughter of the banker Rothschild, he soon found himself abundantly supplied with well-to-do pupils, and their expensive lessions provided him with a very comfortable living for more than a dozen years.

At the end of 1831 Chopin made some observations about social conditions and continuing political dissent in Paris:

> You meet with crowds of beggars with menacing looks on their faces, and you often hear threatening remarks about that imbecile Louis-Philippe who is still only just hanging on to his Ministry. The lower classes are completely exasperated and ready at any time to break out of their poverty-stricken situation. . . . There are the medical students, the so-called "Young France" group, who wear beards and have a special way of tying their scarves . . . The Carlists have green waistcoats; the Republicans and Bonapartists, *i.e.* "Young France," have red ones; the Saint-Simonians or "New Christians" (who are devising an original religion of their own and have already a huge number of converts—they too preach equality) have blue ones, and so on. Well, a thousand of these anti-government agitators made their way through the town with a tricolour banner to salute Ramorino [an Italian revolutionary].[20]

Louis Philippe succeeded in "just hanging on to his Ministry" until February 1848, when an unlikely confluence of antigovernment forces—such as Chopin describes—overwhelmed the Bourgeois Monarchy. Ironically, a series of shifting alliances resulted in a military government

20. *Selected Correspondence of Fryderyk Chopin,* ed. and trans. A. Hedley (London, 1962), p. 105–6.

none of these groups wanted, and, by 1852, in the elevation of Louis
Napoleon (a nephew of Napoleon Bonaparte) as Napoleon III, Emperor
of France. The chaos of the 1848 revolution left the aristocratic society
that provided Chopin with his livelihood in disarray. His halcyon days
of teaching and composing clearly at an end, and his health broken, he
undertook a desperate concert tour of England and Scotland that probably hastened his death from consumption in 1849.

Like Domenico Scarlatti and Clementi, Chopin is known almost
exclusively as a composer of music for his own keyboard instrument.
The Piano Trio, Op. 8 (1828–29), the Piano and Cello Sonata, Op. 65
(1845–46) and some nineteen Polish songs represent his only significant
efforts in other genres. In addition to the two piano concertos there are
several other works with orchestral accompaniment: Variations on "La
ci darem la mano" from *Don Giovanni,* the *Grand Fantasia on Polish Airs,*
Op. 13, the *Krakowiak Rondo,* Op. 14, and the *Andante Spianato,* Op.
22. All these are early works written for Chopin's own performances
in Warsaw and Vienna. The great majority of the solo piano compositions come in neat musical categories—Chopin was always wary of the
uncertain genres and extramusical associations that so attracted Liszt.
There are only three multimovement works for solo piano: the sonatas
in C minor (Op. 4, 1828), B♭ (Op. 35, 1839), and B minor (op. 58,
1844). Two sorts of works he arranged in sets: the twenty-four Preludes, Op. 28 (1836–39), written in all the major and minor keys in
conscious imitation of J. S. Bach's *Well-Tempered Clavier;* and the two
sets of Etudes, Opp. 10 and 25 (1829–36). Throughout his life Chopin
cultivated three varieties of music derivative of the dance, viz. the Polish Mazurka and Polonaise, and the Austrian (or, by now, European)
Waltz. His twenty-two nocturnes, three impromptus, and Fantaisie-

Autograph page of Chopin's Waltz in E♭, Op. 18, showing an opening that
differs from the published version.

Impromptu derive their mildly evocative genre names and some of their stylistic traits from the "lyric" piano pieces of Chopin's immediate predecessors, particularly Field and Tomášek. His four extended ballades are the first known piano pieces of that name. There are also pieces belonging vaguely to traditional categories of instrumental composition: four elaborate and virtuoso scherzos, the Fantaisie in F minor (Op. 49, 1841), and two rondos.

Chopin's efforts in the "serious" genres of the concerto and sonata have been much criticised, and it seems clear that like many of his generation he fared better with single-movement compositions. The piano concertos show a rather casual approach to overall structure and to the interplay of solo and orchestra. In the E-minor Concerto, Op. 11 (though published as his First Piano Concerto, it was written in 1830, after the Concerto in F minor, Op. 21) Chopin writes relentlessly in the tonic key: in both expositions of the first movement the secondary material occurs in the parallel major, and the second movement is in E major as well. The orchestral part, written without much skill, usually provides only an unobtrusive accompaniment to the piano music and the requisite tuttis. There is little attempt at the sort of dialogue between forces that enlivens the piano concertos of Mozart and Beethoven, and it is probably significant that in Vienna, Chopin played his own concertos

Example VII–8: CHOPIN, Concerto No. 1, first movement, mm. 222–30

as solos. His approach to the structure of the concerto, resembling that of such immediate predecessors as Weber and Hummel, is altogether standard among his own generation of pianist-composers. Leisurely stretches of ornamental keyboard figuration based on sequential (and very regularly periodized) harmonic progressions also recall concerto writing of the 1810s and 1820s. But the lyrical cantilena Chopin writes in these compositions is often identifiably his own. Example VII–8 shows such a melody from the first movement of the E-minor Concerto; the initial prolonged tonic harmony, the widely spaced accompaniment implying an inner line in thirds and sixths with the melody, and the deft chromatic shifts at the end from V/vi to V are vintage Chopin.

In 1841, Robert Schumann, an early champion of Chopin, expressed certain reservations about his Sonata in B♭ minor, Op. 35 (1839):

> He calls it a "sonata." One might regard this as capricious if not downright presumptuous, for he has simply tied together four of his most unruly children—perhaps to smuggle them under this name into places they otherwise could never have reached.[21]

There is indeed something odd about the assemblage of movements comprising this sonata. For the slow movement Chopin used the now-famous Funeral March that he had composed some two years before; its unrelenting dotted rhythms and dronelike bass (see Example VII–9) place it squarely in the tradition of funeral marches born in the French

Example VII–9: CHOPIN, Sonata Op. 35, third movement, mm. 1–4

Revolution and perpetuated in Beethoven's Sonata Op. 26 and *Eroica Symphony*.[22] Most controversial of the movements in this sonata is the last. It is a lightning-fast Presto only seventy-five measures long, consisting exclusively of a tuneless single-line figuration, doubled at the octave, that moves in unvarying eighth notes. Schumann called it "unmelodious and joyless". Its very shortness is startling: in a sonata of some twenty minutes' duration it accounts for only about a minute

---

21. *Neue Zeitschrift für Musik*, 14 (1841): 39.
22. See above, p. 42.

and a half. And it offers nothing of the usual kinds of development or climax associated with finales to large-scale compositions in a post-Beethovenian era.

But whatever troubled Schumann and other critics about this sonata, it has proved irresistible to all the generations of pianists and audiences from Chopin's time to our own. One reason for this, surely, is that (except for the finale) it abounds with the ornamented melodies with sonorous accompaniments for which Chopin is famous. In the beginning of the contrasting central section from the Funeral March (see Example VII–10), slow-moving harmonies are sustained by the pedal throughout each measure to enhance the resonance of both the melody

Example VII–10: CHOPIN, Sonata Op. 35, third movement, mm. 31–34

and its wide-ranging arpeggiated accompaniment. This is an example of Chopin's gift for making the most of romantic piano sonority, and not the least of the attractions of this sonata is the opportunities it provides to hear the instrument at its best. But certain structural factors in the piece surely also contribute to our appreciation of it. The development section of the first movement concentrates on a working of materials from the first thematic area of the exposition; the recapitulation then begins, happily, with the main secondary theme in the tonic key (this procedure also occurs in the first movement of the B-minor Sonata, Op. 58). This sonata also shows satisfying motivic connections between movements; one such is the insistent B♭–(C)–D♭ motive common to the opening melody of the first movement (Example VII–11) and both bass and treble of the Funeral March (see Example VII–9, above).

Example VII–11: CHOPIN, Sonata Op. 35, first movement, mm. 9–12

Chopin's two sets of Etudes, Op. 10 and Op. 25, are universally regarded as the finest of all such studies for the piano. While exhaustively exploring the various brilliant and difficult new keyboard figurations with which the modern virtuoso was expected to be conversant, they maintain an uncompromisingly high level of musical interest. The first section of the Etude Op. 25, No. 10 in B minor, for example, is an exercise in bravura chromatic runs in octaves for both hands simultaneously—a powerful figuration Chopin wrote much less often than, say, Liszt. But the slow middle section, with the right hand now in legato octaves, presents an *espressivo* ornamented melody that lends considerable musical weight to this virtuoso composition. These etudes, like most in this genre, are usually all of a piece, showing only one sort of figuration. The Etude in A♭, Op. 25, No. 1, consists entirely of a common nineteenth-century keyboard texture: both hands play arpeggiated figures from which a soprano line emerges as melody. But occasionally the piece is enriched by a tenor or alto line that takes on melodic shape; Chopin writes the important notes large so the pianist will not overlook them (Example VII–12). From the seventeenth century onwards "serious" music with a didactic intent was common in keyboard composition. Chopin's etudes stand in a venerable tradition: that of Clementi's *Gradus ad Parnassum,* for example, and the various *Büchlein* of J. S. Bach.

Example VII–12: CHOPIN, Etude Op. 25, No. 1, mm. 40–44

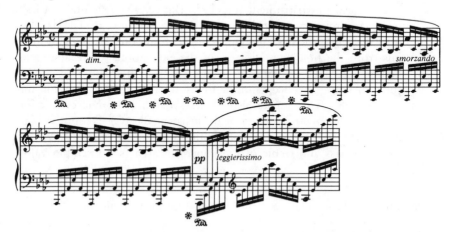

Though the etudes are sometimes performed as cycles, they show no consistent overall design of key or character, and there is little reason to think that Chopin wanted them heard together (etudes were in any case seldom played in public). The 24 Preludes follow a very clear tonal plan: like their model, the preludes and fugues of J. S. Bach's *Well-Tempered Clavier,* they encompass the 24 tonalities of the major–minor system. But the unity conferred by this arrangement hardly means that these pieces were intended for performance at one sitting any more than the etudes—or than the *Well-Tempered Clavier*. Written-down preludes emerged from the ancient habit of improvising or "preluding" before playing a real composition; providing them in a large variety of keys enhances their usefulness in such a context.

Most of the preludes are very short, some occupying only a single printed page. In these brief pieces the episodic structures (*ABA, ABACA,* etc.) that predominate very strongly in this composer's music are little in evidence. Characteristically, they consist of one homogeneous section in which Chopin explores a single musical idea. The collection shows an astonishing variety of keyboard textures, harmonic style, and mood. Stormy virtuoso pieces are juxtaposed with the most ingenuous lyrical statements, and extremes of harmonic ambiguity (as in the Prelude No. 2 in A minor) contrast with the purest diatonic writing (Prelude No. 7 in A major). A celebrated example of Chopin's proclivity for obscuring tonal syntax by means of linear chromatic motion is the Prelude No. 4 in E minor, the first half of which is shown in Example VII–13.

Example VII–13: CHOPIN, Prelude Op. 28, No. 4, mm. 1–13

Here the single line in the treble moves down stepwise (with prominent upper neighbor tones) from B to F♯ while the left hand descends by ⁶₃ chords, through a thicket of suspensions and anticipations, from E (tonic) to B⁷ (dominant); this construction can be simplified as follows:

Example VII–14: CHOPIN, Prelude Op. 28, No. 4, reduced

At several points the motion of the voices produces dominant-seventh sonorities that suggest a safe resolution in an identifiable key: E in mm. 2 and 6, A in m. 4, and G in m. 7. But none of these chords actually turns out to function as a dominant, and there is no point of harmonic stability until the second beginning of the theme in m. 13.

When Chopin first wrote polonaises at the age of seven, this Polish dance had already been well absorbed into European art music. Examples can be found in the works of Couperin, Telemann, Handel, and J. S. Bach (the French Suite in E major includes a well-known one). At the turn of the nineteenth century the genre was further popularized in widely known programmatic polonaises of Count Michael Oginsky, and it may well have been these pieces that served as the young Chopin's first models. By 1825, however, when he composed the Polonaise in D minor, Op. 71, No. 1, Chopin had clearly struck out on a course of his own; here the polite, domesticated dance of the eighteenth century has become an impassioned virtuoso composition. Characteristic rhythms of the dance are a propulsive force in all of Chopin's polonaises. The familiar principal theme of the Polonaise in A♭, Op. 53 (1842), for example, is animated by the distinctive accentuation or lengthening of the second beat of a 3/4 measure (see Example VII–15). Occasionally the power and urgency of these pieces are relieved by lyrical episodes that would almost be at home in a Chopin nocturne. But in such a passage in the Polonaise in C♯ minor, Op. 26, No. 1 (1834–35; ARM 10 and Example VII–16), a vigorous rhythm typical of the dance is

Example VII–15: CHOPIN, Polonaise in A♭, Op. 53, mm. 17–18

present in the bass and imparts some of its energetic motion to the cantabile melody above.

Example VII–16: CHOPIN, Polonaise in C♯ minor, mm. 5–8

While the polonaise was danced by the Polish aristocracy in the seventeenth and eighteenth centuries, the various forms of the mazurka (the mazur, oberek, and kujawiak) remained folk dances and were seldom heard in European art music before Chopin's time. Some of his early efforts in this genre closely resemble folk models; for one, the Mazurka Op. 68, No. 3 (1829), a specific model has been identified.[23] Example VII–17 is an excerpt from the Mazurka Op. 17, No. 3 that shows several characteristic features of the original dance: an accented third beat (sometimes it is the second) in a 3/4 measure, an ambiguity between a natural and raised fourth scale-degree (the E♭ and E♮), a phrase structure made up of single-measure slightly varied cells, and a drone bass. (All four Mazurkas of Op. 17 comprise ARM 11.) Many of the composer's later mazurkas are highly stylized and abstract; a lifelong preoccupation of Chopin's, this miniature genre became a vehicle for his most individual and advanced musical ideas.

Example VII–17: CHOPIN, Mazurka Op. 17, No. 3, mm. 16–20

Chopin's four ballades—Op. 23 in G minor, Op. 38 in F major, Op. 47 in A♭, and Op. 52 in F minor—are apparently the first instrumental compositions to appear with that name. Though little is known about

23. See Maurice J. E. Brown, *Chopin: An Index of His Works in Chronological Order*, 2nd ed. (London, 1972), p. 37–38.

Chopin's reasons for using this title, it is apparently intended as a reference to the eighteenth-century English or German ballad (certainly not the medieval ballade), and it is probably meant to evoke associations with an idealized folklike, narrative style of poetry and music.[24] Specific points of similarity between these pieces and any known repertory of ballads are not easy to find. An overwhelming predominance of compound binary meters (6/8 or 6/4, however, corresponds to the most usual rhythm of declamation in the Lied and ballad of the turn of the century, and simple melodies, sometimes with a "strumming" accompaniment, are woven into an extended and dramatic structure in a way vaguely congruent with the story-telling ballad.

The Ballade in G minor (ARM 12) was composed in 1835, though some preliminary drafts survive from 1831. Like the others, this ballade is a many-sectioned virtuoso piece of intricate construction. First, an enigmatic introduction of seven measures built initially upon the Neapolitan-sixth triad leads to a full-measure pause on the dominant with the characteristic motion $^{6-5}_{4-3}$, to which a poignant 9–8 suspension is added, as shown in Example VII–18a.[25] Both the Neapolitan sonority and the suspensions, as we shall see, lay the groundwork for elaborate motivic correspondences between the seemingly disparate sections of this composition.

The overall shape of the piece can be shown roughly as follows:

m.	1	8	36	67	94	106	138	166	194	208
	Intro.	A	x	B	A	B	γ	B	A	Coda
	($^\flat$II^6)	i	i	VI	ii	II	VI	VI	i	i

The A melody, which occurs only in minor, has the single-line simplicity and strumming accompaniment reminiscent of balladlike recitation. B is a more impassioned statement, always in major, and balanced delicately between E$^\flat$ and its dominant, B$^\flat$. This mild tonal ambiguity is underscored as the melody is introduced by way of the dominant of its dominant, viz. F. Between the several fixed points of A and B there are passages that function as transitions or extensions. The two episodes at mm. 36ff. and 138ff., however, have a harmonic and metric stability

---

24. See above, pp. 108 and 114–15. Schumann reported in 1841 that Chopin claimed his ballades were inspired by certain poems of the Polish nationalist writer Adam Mickiewicz (1798–1855). *Neue Zeitschrift für Musik,* 15 (1841): 141.

25. Certain early editors changed the highly dissonant e$^\flat$' in m. 7 to d'. Later, the influential music theorist Heinrich Schenker argued for d', claiming that the voice leading must proceed d'–c'–b$^\flat$. Heinrich Schenker, *Neue musikalische Theorien und Phantasien III: Der freie Satz* (Vienna, 1935), pp. 108–9. But both Chopin's autograph and the first French edition show an unequivocal e$^\flat$'. The passing c' in m. 8 simply appears "prematurely" (though it is still sounding at the time of its proper occurrence); the progression in the alto voice here can be read as: e$^\flat$'–(c')–d'–c'–b$^\flat$

Example VII–18: CHOPIN, Ballade in G minor
a. Mm. 7–11

b. Mm. 7–9, reduced

c. Mm. 67–69, reduced

d. Mm. 67–71

that confers on them a certain degree of thematic identity; here they are called *x* and *y*. A striking feature of the large design of this ballade is the occurrence of two very distinct secondary keys, neither of them the expected relative major (though the passages in E♭ typically incline toward B♭) or the dominant. While one secondary key, E♭ (VI), occurs only in major, the other one, A (II), is heard in both modes.

In *A*, the beginning of the theme consists of the resolution of the suspension in mm. 6–8; upon its repetition in m. 10 the suspension and resolution are repeated as well (see Example VII–18a). Thus a downward motion by step is built into the harmonic fabric of this music, and it is confirmed by the contours of the melody in mm. 9–10, 13–14, and

15–16 (mm. 11–12 shows its inversion). The fundamental harmonic structure of mm. 7–9 is V $^{6-5}_{4-3}$ (Example VII–18b); Chopin has elaborated this common harmonic motion by adding a 9–8 suspension and by anticipating the passing seventh (c′) in m. 8. Now let us compare the same progression, set in E♭ over a dominant bass (Example VII–18c), with the beginning of B in Chopin's Ballade (Example VII–18d). Though its elements are very much displaced, this theme is clearly built upon the same cadential figure as A. Immediately noticeable is the absence of the 6–5 resolution in the treble, resulting in the distinctive leap of a third from g′ to e♭′. But the expected f is present in the tenor range on the fourth beat of m. 68, and has been prominently featured in the soprano at the beginning of the measure. The passing seventh, a♭, is also anticipated in the tenor. In Chopin's somewhat casual voice leading the treatment of the dissonant c′ of mm. 67–68 may seem puzzling; it appears to resolve upward, 9–10. But its rhythmic context forces us to hear it as a suspension, and the c′–b♭ at the end of m. 68 effects its actual resolution, 9–8, as well as a subtle correspondence to the 9–8 suspension in A. An interrupted motion from c″ to b♭′, moreover, recurs in the treble in mm. 70–71 as Chopin repeats his elaborated cadential formula on the dominant.

Other parts of the composition show a similar preoccupation with suspensionlike shapes and their stepwise downward motion. Episode y in mm. 138ff has a persistent 6–5 or 7–6 motive in the left hand. This figure is even more pronounced in x (mm. 36ff.), which consists of parallel tenths in the outer voices with ubiquitous 7–6 motion in the alto register doubled at the octave above. In its stepwise downward journeys the upper voice in this passage also shows a curious ambiguity between the natural and flat supertonic, a′ and a♭′, recalling the emphasis upon the Neapolitan sound, and its subsequent "naturalization", at the very opening of the piece. One might recognize one more harmonic connection between the introduction and the body of this composition: the distinctive and very insistent secondary key E♭ seems an echo of the e♭′ whose resolution to d′ propels the music of the introduction into the beginning of theme A. The recurrence of B in E♭ in m. 166 is in any event extraordinary. And when the prolonged E♭ pedal point of its continuation (mm. 180ff.) is followed by the reappearance of A with an extended pedal on D—something no previous statement of that theme had—the large-scale motion E♭–D is made quite explicit. Interrelations of this sort, even if only partly perceived, contribute to the listener's sense of harmony and "rightness" in such a composition.

Like many large-scale virtuoso piano pieces of the period, this ballade seems to pursue musical ideals of two very different kinds; we might describe them as "lyrical expressiveness" on the one hand, and "brilliance," "power," or "rhetorical passion" on the other. Chopin's favored episodic construction works admirably to this end: strongly contrasting musical statements can simply be placed side by side. The Ballade in F major, Op. 38, presents an extreme example of this strategy. In the G-minor Ballade the lines are much less sharply drawn; x (m. 36) first prolongs the subdued quality of A, and then, gradually gaining force and speed, dissolves into glittering, wide-ranging passagework. At its first appearance B is spare-textured and *pianissimo*. When it recurs in m. 106 (in A major), and again in m. 166 (in E♭ major), it has been transformed into a *fortissimo* declaration: the texture has been reinforced, the register extended, and (in mm. 170–73) the melody laced with one of Chopin's favorite kinds of emphatic ornament. Through devices such as these the sectional nature of the piece is mitigated, and one is left with an impression of the organic growth that was highly prized in all Romantic theories of art.

Chopin's career in Paris turned out quite differently from Liszt's. An apparent aversion to the concert stage really left him only a single means of addressing the musical public: through the printing of his works. But even the reception of these works depended largely upon a reputation he made as an exotic celebrity of the salon, as the musical favorite of a society that set the fashion for all Europe. That his music has strengths far transcending its cultural origins was at first seen by only a few such as Liszt and Schumann. But these strengths have subsequently made it the backbone of the piano repertory.

FRENCH ROMANTICISM

An identifiable Romantic movement was slow in coming to France. The German Romantic writers Novalis, Tieck, Wackenroder, and the brothers Schlegel did their most characteristic work and issued their newly minted literary theories as young men around the turn of the nineteenth century. Wordsworth's Preface to the *Lyrical Ballads,* widely seen as a seminal document of English Romanticism, appeared in 1801. In France a certain cultural isolation and the tenacious influence of the academies held newer views in literature and the arts at bay well into the nineteenth century. Another factor, however, was probably of greater importance for the progress of the arts in France: from 1789 until at least 1815 the country was in a state of perpetual uproar. While the Revolution, contemplated from across the channel, awakened new impulses to poetry in the breasts of young Englishmen, leading writers in France (like André Chénier) went to the guillotine or (like René de Chateaubriand) into exile. The best minds of the revolutionary period were usually absorbed by political and public affairs. Mme. de Staël's book on Germany *(De l'Allemagne),* sympathetic to the tenets of Romantic literature, was suppressed by Napoleon in 1810. Dictatorship, whether revolutionary or Napoleonic, proved inimical to artistic unorthodoxies.

In 1828 Victor Hugo's preface to his play *Cromwell* challenged the Classical prescriptions for language and manners in drama held sacred in France since the days of Racine and Boileau. Then in 1830 his revolt became public with the performance of *Hernani*. For forty nights after February 25, cabals of radical young litterateurs (led by the poet Théophile Gautier in a blazing red waistcoat) and their opponents, whom they called *perruques* (wigs), attempted to out-shout each other at the Comédie française. The issues were Hugo's violation of the "unity of place," his defilement of the sacrosanct Alexandrine with enjambements and neglected caesuras, and his assignment of ordinary-sounding speech to exalted personages. The battle was now joined, and the Romantic coterie formed an alliance (called a *cénacle* after the scene of the Last Supper of Christ and his disciples) that included Hugo, Sainte-Beuve, Gautier, Gérard de Nerval, Alfred de Vigny, Alfred de Musset, various painters, and the musicians Berlioz and Liszt.

The role of music in the "Classic–Romantic" dispute in France was always somewhat equivocal. Indeed, the seventeenth-century formulators of the Classic doctrine of the arts had had difficulty placing music at all: music in the French view meant mainly opera, which was by definition a mixture of genres and for this alone, according to Classical dogma, suspect. By 1830 French audiences had become quite familiar with musical drama (through the operas of Cherubini, Spontini, Rossini, and even Weber) that was vastly more antithetical to the Classical canon than anything of Hugo's. Opera seemed exempt from the regulations imposed upon spoken drama; even the most "romantic" sorts of events and behavior were acceptable if presented in music. While opera was a constant subject for dispute in Paris from the seventeenth century to the nineteenth, this was not to be the arena for a Classic–Romantic debate in music.

The progress of literary Romanticism in France can be rather accurately measured by a gradually increasing receptivity to the plays of Shakespeare, which for nearly two hundred years had been scorned in France as barbarous. As late as 1822, when an English troupe presented *Othello* in Paris, they were hissed off the stage; an actress was even wounded (while curtseying, it is said) by a projectile thrown from the pit. But five years later *Hamlet* and *Romeo and Juliet* played at the Odéon theatre to an audience that was at least attentive—and to a claque of young Romantics who were jubilant in their approval.

In the musical life of Paris one might see an analogous process in an increasing acceptance of the music of Beethoven. Though scarcely known in France before the 1820s, Beethoven had a reputation for extravagance, disorder, and *bizarrerie* strikingly like that of Shakespeare. In

1810 the Parisian composer-critic Giovanni Cambini recorded his impression of a movement from a Beethoven symphony:

> The composer, often bizarre and baroque, sometimes sparkles with extraordinary beauties. Now he takes the majestic flight of the eagle; then he creeps along rock-strewn paths. After penetrating the soul with a gentle melancholy he immediately lacerates it with a mass of barbarous chords. I seem to see doves put in together with crocodiles.[26]

Beethoven's foremost champion in France was François Antoine Habeneck (1781–1849), the musical director at the Opéra, and conductor for the distinguished Conservatory Concerts. In 1821 he conducted a performance of the Second Symphony at the Concerts Spirituels. For the slow movement, however, he inserted the Allegretto from the Seventh Symphony; while the audience did not care for the symphony as a whole, we are told, they demanded an immediate repetition of this movement. When Habeneck was put in charge of reorganizing the Conservatory Concerts in 1828, he dedicated them almost exclusively to the performance of Beethoven's works, and noisy enthusiasm for this "untamed genius" grew by leaps and bonds. After a performance of the *Eroica Symphony* the redoubtable critic Castil-Blaze wrote,

> Why do we allow ourselves to be outdone by foreigners? How does it happen that this masterwork, which the Germans have known by heart for twenty years, should have been introduced here only last week? . . . I shall not attempt to describe the transport of admiration and enthusiasm that followed the last chords of each movement of this work. Seven or eight salvos of applause served to accompany the finale; even composers and players took part in this fitting show of generosity.[27]

BERLIOZ

A rapt member of the audience for the performances of Shakespeare in 1827 and Beethoven in 1828 was a mercurial medical student-turned-composer, Louis Hector Berlioz (1803–69). Of *Hamlet* he exclaimed in his *Memoirs:*

> Shakespeare, coming upon me unawares, struck me like a thunderbolt. The lightning-flash of that discovery revealed to me at a stroke the whole heaven of art, illuminating it to its remotest corners. I recognized the meaning of grandeur, beauty, dramatic truth, and could measure the utter absurdity of the French view of Shakespeare which derives from Voltaire.[28]

26. *Tablettes de polymnie* (1810), pp. 310–11, quoted in Éduard Herriot, *La Vie de Beethoven* (Paris, 1929), pp. 211–12.
27. *Journal des débats,* March 19, 1828.
28. *The Memoirs of Hector Berlioz,* trans. David Cairns (London, 1969), p. 95.

Portrait of Berlioz by
Gustave Courbet.

Berlioz had scarcely recovered from this encounter when he confronted
Beethoven: "The shock was almost as great as that of Shakespeare had
been. Beethoven opened before me a new world of music, as Shakespeare had revealed a new universe of poetry."[29] Such a reaction to
Shakespeare was not in the least unusual among the members of the
Romantic circle; Alexandre Dumas on the same occasion announced
that he felt like a blind man who was suddenly able to see. But it was
Berlioz's particular accomplishment to have introduced musical issues
firmly into the gathering revolution in the arts; his tireless campaigning
on behalf of Beethoven, Weber, and Gluck—as well as his extraordinary compositions—soon established him as the leading spokesman for
musical Romanticism in France.

Born in La Côte-Saint-André, a village in the foothills of the French
Alps, Berlioz was the son of a physician under whose influence he entered
medical school in Paris in 1821. But almost from the beginning his time
was spent mainly at the Opéra and in the library of the Convervatory.
When he formally forsook medicine to become a student at the latter
institution in 1826, he had already studied for some time with Lesueur
and had to his credit a good number of compositions, including a full
Mass that had been performed in public. Another regular activity he
had taken up, partly out of conviction and partly to support himself,
was musical journalism; beginning with a little piece called "Polémique
musicale," published in 1823, he supplied the periodical press of Paris
with a steady stream of witty and often substantive articles, reviews,
and feuilletons for some forty years. Berlioz gathered many of these

29. *Ibid.*, p. 104.

writings into his "composite" books: *Les Soirées de l'orchestre* (Evenings with the Orchestra, 1853) and *A travers chants.*[30] Berlioz was perhaps better known in his time for these partisan and brilliant essays than for his music; as late as 1856, when he was elected a member of the Institut, the *Revue des deux mondes* complained, "The Institut has chosen not a musician, but a journalist."

As a young composer with a very original bent of mind, Berlioz had difficulty making progress in the static and institutionalized musical life of Paris. Having failed three times to win the Prix de Rome, the conservatory's official blessing upon composers, he finally succeeded, just as the July Revolution of 1830 broke, with his cantata *La Dernière Nuit de Sardanapale.* By this time he had already completed substantial works such as the *Waverley Overture,* the overture to his incomplete opera *Les Francs-Juges,* and *Eight Scenes from Faust,* as well as his first major work, the *Symphonie fantastique.* After spending fourteen months of the required two-year stay at the Villa Medici in Rome, the composer returned to Paris in November 1832, armed with several new works, including the *King Lear* and *Rob Roy* overtures and the "melologue" *Lélio,* a sequel to the *Symphonie fantastique.*

Like most French musicians, Berlioz directed a large share of his thoughts and aspirations toward opera. His earliest public and private writings reflect this preoccupation, and from about 1824 he always had an operatic project before him. The monopolies and cabals at both the Opéra and the Théâtre Italien, however, proved too much for him. It was not until 1838 that a work of his, *Benvenuto Cellini,* was performed at the Opéra; it failed badly and came to be remembered only in the familiar *Roman Carnival Overture,* constructed in 1844 from its themes. His small-scale comic opera *Béatrice et Bénédict,* with a libretto after Shakespeare's *Much Ado about Nothing,* was presented with success to a resort audience at Baden-Baden in 1862. But despite his persistent efforts Berlioz could not get an opera performed in Paris again until 1863, when a radically truncated and altered version of his epic *Les Troyens* (based on his own libretto after Vergil's *Aeneid*) was presented at the Théâtre Lyrique. The staging and performance were inadequate; while some critics saw value in his most ambitious work, Berlioz's detractors carried the day—one devastating cartoon depicted a slaughterhouse where cattle were felled with blasts of music from *Les Troyens.* As the composer Charles Gounod later remarked, "One may say of him, as of his namesake Hector, that he died beneath the walls of Troy."[31]

In the 1970s, *Les Troyens* was revived; performances were given in several of the world's major opera houses and a full recording was issued.

30. The title of the latter work, published in 1862, is an untranslatable pun on the expression *a travers champs, i.e.* "across open country."
31. *Memoirs of Hector Berlioz,* p. 11.

This work has revealed a new side of Berlioz to modern audiences. The huge sweep of dramatic action, from the warnings of Cassandra in Troy (Acts I and II) to the doomed love of Dido and Aeneas in Carthage (Acts III, IV, and V), reveal a classical control and inevitability while in scenes such as the Royal Hunt and Storm (reminiscent of Weber's Wolf's Glen scene) and the Garden scene, Berlioz gives full rein to his talents for pictorial, expressive music. In this opera we have a nineteenth-century masterpiece that the nineteenth century scarcely knew.

In the face of his bleak prospects as an opera composer Berlioz utilized and created other vehicles for dramatic musical expression. He composed cantatas and "scenes," a "dramatic legend," programmatic overtures, and two symphonies with texts and voices (*Roméo et Juliette,* 1839, and the *Symphonie funèbre et triomphale,* 1840). Scarcely any of his works, in fact, is without a literary text or title, or a specified dramatic association. The most famous among his programmatic instrumental pieces, and surely Berlioz's most influential composition, is his earliest major work, the *Episode de la vie d'un artiste, Symphonie fantastique en cinq parties,* first performed on December 5, 1830. That evening, as the audience entered the concert hall of the conservatory, they were handed leaflets presenting the "story" of the symphony together with an explanatory introduction: "The outline of the instrumental drama, which lacks the help of words, needs to be explained in advance. The following program should thus be considered as the spoken text of an opera, serving to introduce the musical movements whose character and expression it motivates."[32]

The narrative, an extravagant, disjointed outpouring of Berlioz's own making, tells of a temperamental young musician who falls desperately in love, and in a series of separate scenes is tormented by visions of his beloved: he sees her at a ball, in the country, at his own execution, and finally in the midst of a frightful Witches' Sabbath (these last two scenes are represented as a dream of the hero under the influence of opium[33]). From the beginning this program had distinct autobiographical associations. Berlioz had been stricken with a passion for Harriet Smithson, the Ophelia and Juliet of the Shakespeare performances in 1827; as his letters and memoirs show, the young musician and his beloved are a representation of himself and the actress—a fanciful one, to be sure, as they had not yet met when the symphony was first performed.

The music of the symphony is related to the program in various ways. Foremost is the representation of the appearances of the beloved with a

---

32. Trans. Edward T. Cone in the Introduction to *Berlioz: Fantastic Symphony* (New York, 1971).

33. In a later version of the program the entire sequence of events is represented as an opium dream. For a good discussion of the various forms of the program see Nicholas Temperley, "The *Symphonie fantastique* and its Program," *The Musical Quarterly,* 57 (1971): 593–608.

melody that recurs in each movement. Berlioz specifies this association in the program: "Whenever the beloved image appears before the mind's eye of the artist it is linked with a musical thought. . . . This melodic image and the model it reflects pursue him incessantly like a double *idée fixe.*" Then there are "onomatopoetic" devices—musical imitations of nonmusical sounds—such as the sounds of a storm in the third movement, *Scene in the Country,* and the famous stroke of the guillotine and falling head in *March to the Scaffold.* Another connection is established by musical imitation of music: the third movement includes a *ranz des vaches* (a Swiss cowherd's horn call); Berlioz evokes the ball scene of the second movement with a vigorous waltz; and in the final movement the *Dies irae,* the sequence from the Mass for the Dead, represents the hero's dream of his own death.

Berlioz hoped that another connection between the music and the story would be effected through the ordinary operations of musical expression, as he understood them. The musical *idée fixe* represented for him a "state of melancholy reverie," and its character, "passionate but at the same time noble and shy" seemed fitting as a musical symbol for the beloved. In a version of the program from 1836 Berlioz appended a long footnote in response to a criticism in the *Revue musicale* (the writer was very likely F.-J. Fétis); here he offered a clarification of his views as to musical reference:

> He [the author] knows very well that music can take the place of neither word nor picture; he has never had the absurd intention of expressing *abstractions* or *moral qualities,* but rather passions and feelings. Nor has he had the even stranger idea of painting *mountains:* he has only wished to reproduce *the melodic style and forms* that characterize the singing of some of the people who live among them, or *the emotion* that the sight of these imposing masses arouses, under certain circumstances, in the soul.[34]

Berlioz speaks of two sorts of connections between the music and its program: that brought about by the imitation of musical sounds that already have fixed associations, and that produced by a musical expression of emotions. Like other romantics, Berlioz saw such expression of feelings as the principal way in which music achieves its effect. Musical sounds cannot ordinarily denote scenes, events, or people; it can, however, convey (and perhaps arouse) feelings like those associated with them. The history of the first movement serves to illustrate the composer's view on this matter. Both the opening adagio melody (Example VII–19a) and the first part of the *idée fixe* theme (Example VII–19b) had been used in earlier works with other literary or programmatic associations. The twelve-year-old Berlioz first composed the adagio melody for some mawkish verses from Jean Pierre Claris de Florian's pastorale

---

34. Trans. Edward T. Cone, *op. cit.,* p. 28.

Example VII–19: BERLIOZ, *Symphonie fantastique,* first movement
  a. Mm. 3–10

  b. Mm. 71–86

Estelle et Némorin. In these lines a young lover laments that he must
leave his homeland and his beloved, Estelle. According to the *Memoirs,*
the boy Berlioz strongly identified this figure with a real-life eighteen-
year-old Estelle with whom he was infatuated. It was in the cantata
Herminie, composed for one of his unsuccessful attempts to win the
Prix de Rome in 1828, that Berlioz first wrote down the distinctive first
section of the *idée fixe* melody. Taken from a scene in Tasso's *Jerusalem
Delivered* (1574), the libretto depicts the despairing love of a Saracen
woman, Erminia, for the Christian knight Tancred. These melodies,
then, finally united in the first movement of the *Symphonie fantastique,*
had been associated in the composer's mind with a remarkable procession of different situations and scenes, some autobiographical and some
literary. What they had in common was an association with emotions
attendant to hopeless love—just the sort of thing that Berlioz felt his
music could express.

  Critics of the *Symphonie fantastique,* sympathetic or not, were quick
to note the originality of Berlioz's orchestration. Even the disapproving
Fétis relented on this point:

> In a word, I saw that he lacked melodic and harmonic ideas, and I came to
> the conclusion that he would always write in a barbarous manner: but I
> saw that he had an instinct for instrumentation, and I thought that he might
> perform a real service by discovering certain combinations that others could
> use better than he.[35]

35. Ibid., p. 217.

Something of Berlioz's novel writing for orchestra can be seen in a comparison of three occurrences of the *idée fixe* theme in the first movement:

Example VII–20: BERLIOZ, *Symphonie fantastique,* first movement
  a. Mm. 71–79

  b. Mm. 234–48

The melody upon its initial appearance (Example VII–20a) is played, almost unaccompanied, by the violins and flutes in unison; important points are punctuated by the detached eighth-note figure seen in mm. 78–79. Example VII–20b shows the same melody as it appears in the development section of the movement. Against a sustained d' (sounding an octave lower than notated) in the third horn, a distinctive quickleaping accompanimental pattern is gradually assembled; the melody then enters, played by the first flute, first clarinet, and first bassoon in three separate octaves—a scoring that invests it with extraordinary resonance and a most individual tone color. The recapitulation (see Example VII–20c) presence yet another radically different setting of the theme, this time for full orchestra. While the flutes, piccolos, cornets, and violas play the melody, the divided violins present a kind of scurrying paraphrase of it in a high register. The effect is one of frenzied activity and great brilliance.

Before Berlioz, the functions of orchestral instruments associated with the Classic style (melody and harmony mainly in the string choir, with winds used for occasional reinforcement and soloistic color) had remained standard; exceptional instrumentation, as in certain passages in the operas of Gluck, Weber, and Spontini, was reserved for special dramatic effects. For Berlioz the invention of particular tone colors for individual passages was a part of the normal process of composition. In his comprehensive *Grand Traité d'instrumentation et d'orchestration*[36] he gave rather a

36.   Published in 1844; edited and expanded by Richard Strauss in 1904.

c. Mm. 412–15

full account of his discoveries in this area. But what is new about Berlioz's writing for orchestra does not all fall easily under the rubrics
"instrumentation" and "orchestration." The three occurrences of the
idée fixe theme in Example VII–20 show not only an original deploy-

ment of instruments, but also a most unconventional musical texture. Instead of melody and bass lines with filled-in harmony, he presents an extremely prominent (and in Example VII–20c, lavishly ornamented) melody with only the sketchiest bass and inner voices. In all three cases it remains somewhat unclear, in fact, whether the implied bass moves from a sustained tonic up one step to effect a weak second-inversion dominant sonority, or up a fifth to the root of the dominant triad. But in these passages such questions as to harmony and voice leading seem secondary: the melody and the color of orchestral sound make almost exclusive claims upon our attention.

Berlioz's music was first heard in public when he conducted his early Mass at the Church of St. Roch in 1825. At this time Charles X was restoring the official sanctions that church and church music had not enjoyed since the Revolution of 1789. The musical scholar and pedagogue Alexandre Étienne Choron (1771–1834) was named director of the newly established École de Musique Religieuse in 1826, and established composers such as Cherubini and Lesueur began composing sacred texts with renewed vigor. French church music, like opera, had taken on something of the pomp and grandeur of the revolutionary *fêtes;* in the oratorios, Masses, and psalms of Berlioz's teacher Lesueur, for example, the multiple choruses and expanded brass sections of the fervent republican days were now bent to a new purpose. Berlioz's best-known sacred composition, the *Requiem* (Grande Messe des morts, Op. 5), was a clear extension of this tradition. Originally commissioned to commemorate the fallen defenders of Louis Philippe in an assassination attempt of 1835,[37] it was intended as a massive celebration of patriotism and piety. Some four hundred singers and players gathered in the church of Les Invalides for its first performance in December, 1837: in addition to a mammoth orchestra with twenty woodwinds and twelve horns there were four brass ensembles variously positioned in the church to add special éclat at certain points—notably for the vision of the Day of Judgment evoked by the "Tuba mirum" in the *Dies irae.*[38]

Elaborate concerts of his own works became the forum in which Berlioz presented his music to the public. His compositions, few of which fall into traditional musical categories, were always controversial, and in general fared much less well in Paris than elsewhere. He enjoyed considerable success in German cities, particularly in Weimar, where his cause was enthusiastically promoted by Liszt, director of music at the local court since 1842. Berlioz's concerts in Russia in 1847, how-

---

37. This commission was withdrawn, and the *Requiem* was first heard at another national pageant, the funeral service for one General Damrémont, recently killed in a campaign in Algeria.

38. In his *Memoirs* (p. 231) Berlioz claims that the conductor Habeneck nearly ruined the first performance by pausing at this crucial juncture to take a pinch of snuff.

ever, failed miserably, and after the Revolution of 1848 Paris offered him fewer opportunities than ever. He finally died there in obscurity and near-poverty in 1868.

Late in 1846 Berlioz hired the theater of the Opéra comique for two Sunday-evening performances of his recently completed "dramatic legend," the *Damnation of Faust*. Like many of his large-scale works this composition originated in literary and musical conceptions of his seminal years just before 1830. In 1828 he had fallen under the spell of Geothe's *Faust*, Part I, in the recently released translation of Gérard de Nerval: "I could not put it down," he recounts in his *Memoirs,* "I read it incessantly, at meals, at the theater, in the streets."[39] Berlioz promptly produced his *Eight Scenes from Faust,* a collection of settings of songs and ballads of the play as they appear in Nerval's translation, scored for voice and varying small groups of instruments. Like Schubert before him, Berlioz sent his work to Goethe for his approval, but received no reply. The following spring he published the *Scenes* at his own expense, but shortly after thought better of it and withdrew them from distribution. Some seventeen years later, having recently returned from Weimar where the memory of Goethe loomed large, Berlioz returned to

39. *Memoires,* p. 125.

Delacroix lithograph of the tavern scene in Goethe's *Faust.*

his youthful music, refashioned it for voice and orchestra, and incorporated it in his new dramatic work, the *Damnation of Faust*.

The *Damnation* still has about it much of the character of separate scenes. We are shown Faust in the peaceful countryside, in his study, in a beer hall, in Marguerite's room, in a natural setting that is inhospitable and threatening, and finally in his descent into the underworld (this last is quite independent of Goethe, whose Faust met with no final damnation). Berlioz's composition is as ill-suited for dramatic staging as Goethe's play, and for the same reasons: the frequent and drastic scene changes can better be followed by flights of the imagination than shown on the stage. During his ill-fated London sojourn of 1847–48 the composer made abortive plans to present his work as an opera; that he never revived these plans may show a growing confidence in his various genres of "semidramatic" music.

The three major personae in Berlioz's *Damnation* are Faust (tenor), Mephistopheles (bass), and Marguerite (mezzo-soprano). Berlioz presents considerable musical delineation of these characters. The childlike Marguerite sings the "King of Thule" in a very simple setting (adapted from the *Eight Scenes*) with "folk-like" raised fourth and lowered sixth degrees. Mephistopheles's appearance, as in Scenes 5 and 10, is accompanied by a jarring chromatic motive in the trombones (traditionally an "other-worldly" instrument) and portentious tremolos in the strings; for Faust himself Berlioz writes music of the sort associated with heroic operatic tenors, but with a wealth of original and expressive detail in the orchestral accompaniment. A large chorus plays an integral part in the drama: the singing of shepherds, carousers, students, and Spirits in Hell provide a note of operatic immediacy to some scenes, and at one point (Scene 4) Faust refrains from committing suicide when he hears a choral Easter hymn (originally from the first of the *Eight Scenes*). Instrumental interludes also serve the composer's dramatic ends. The Minuet of the Will-o'-wisps in Scene 12, for example—particularly the skittering Presto section—shows Berlioz's special proclivity for musical characterization of things elfin and diminutive.[40] Another evocative instrumental piece, the well-known Rákóczy March that had been written earlier for the composer's visit to Hungary, actually influenced the course of the narrative. That Faust is shown in Hungary at all, Berlioz candidly admits in the preface to the first edition, resulted simply from the composer's eagerness to make use of this music.

Berlioz's independence from Goethe's text is seen further in Scene 16, "Invocation to Nature" (ARM 13). Here, just before sealing his fateful pact with Mephistopheles, Faust repairs to the forests and caves and waterfalls—to a nature sublime and unfathomable—and delivers a

---

40. Another striking example of this is the Queen Mab music from *Roméo et Juliette*.

remarkable pantheistic soliloquy written by Berlioz himself:

FAUST

Nature immense, impénétrable et
    fière,
Toi seule donnes trêve à mon ennui
    sans fin.
Sur ton sein tout puissant je sense
    moins ma misère,
Je retrouve ma force, et je crois vivre
    enfin.
Oui, soufflez ouragans, criez, forêts
    profondes,
Croulez rochers, torrents, précipitez
    vos ondes!

A vos bruits souverains ma voix aime
    à s'unir.
Forêts, rochers, torrents, je vous
    adore! mondes
Qui scintillez, vers vous s'élance le
    désir
D'un coeur trop vaste et d'une âme
    altérée,
D'un bonheur qui la fuit.

Nature, immense, unfathomable,
    proud,
You alone quiet my unending ennui;

On your omnipotent breast I feel my
    misery less keenly,
I regain my strength and believe finally
    that I shall live.
Yes, blow, hurricanes! Roar, you deep
    forests,
Crash down, you rocks, and tor-
    rents, hurl headlong your
    waters!
My voice delights to mingle with your
    majestic sounds.
Forests, rocks, torrents, I adore you!

Glittering worlds above, to you cries
    out the longing
Of a heart too vast and a soul tor-
    mented by
A happiness it cannot seize.

Berlioz's vocal setting of this text is syllabic and scrupulously faithful
to its rhythms and accents. Line endings with the mute "e" *(fière, misère,
profondes)* are consistently set to feminine cadences—in classical declamation and virtually all vocal music these are pronounced but unac-
cented—and strong-syllable endings *(fin, unir)* occur on strong beats.
The rhythms of the vocal line as a whole are mainly those of a meticulous declamation of the poetry, as here:

Crou-lez,   crou-lez, roc-hers,___   tor-rents,   pre-ci-pi-tez vos on-des

The harmonic style in this scene is, for Berlioz, strongly chromatic.
Fluent linear motion leads from the tonal centers of C♯ minor and F♯
minor as far afield as F major (mm. 23ff.) and B minor (mm. 44ff.).
Radical tonal shifts (and highly charged rhetorical effects) are repeatedly
achieved by means of a particular harmonic ploy: six times (mm. 22–
23, 27–28, 31–32, 41–42, 43–44, and 46–47) Berlioz treats a seventh
chord enharmonically as an augmented sixth sonority, thus propelling
the music in quite unexpected directions. The occurrences of this device

in mm. 41–42 and 43–44 may be seen in Example VII–21. The implied movement toward D♭ in m. 41 is aborted as the A♭ dominant seventh moves to a C-major sound; in mm. 42–43 an expected resolution in C (minor) leads instead to B minor. These striking harmonic motions accompany some of Faust's more grandiloquent utterances: "Je retrouve ma force," "Criez, forêts profondes," "Torrents, précipitez vos ondes," and the like; long associated with musical and dramatic moments of special force,[41] they underscore the strength and boldness of the protagonist's address to nature at its most overwhelming.

Example VII–21: BERLIOZ, *Damnation of Faust,* "Invocation to Nature," mm. 41–44

Berlioz's ample orchestra provides a supple accompaniment to the vocal line: a fluid, shifting chordal texture in the strings is reinforced at climactic prints and at cadences by the upper winds. Such a backdrop for vocal declamation is strongly reminiscent of the most dramatic type of operatic recitative, the accompanied or obbligato recitative used for scenes of special gravity or supernatural import by composers of serious opera since the seventeenth century; the resemblance is particularly striking in the central section where the chords are played tremolo.[42] In such recitative it was usual for the orchestra to heighten the tension by injecting occasional vigorous, sharply profiled motives. In this scene the bass instruments do so insistently; the rising and falling, swelling, and diminishing figure first heard in mm. 11–12 cuts through the static orchestral texture nine times to become the most identifiable motive of

41.   As in the sextet in *Don Giovanni,* Act II, at the point where Donna Anna and Don Ottavio enter, and in Beethoven's Fifth Symphony, second movement, upon introduction of the heroic theme in C major (mm. 29–30).

42.   Berlioz gained early exposure to this style of recitative in his study of the operas of Gluck.

the piece. This bass motive apparently had a prior programmatic association for Berlioz: in the movement *Scene in the Country* of the *Symphonie fantastique* (mm. 87ff.) a very similar bass figure, again with tremolo strings above, signals the gathering of a storm and the threatened destruction of the protagonist by the irresistible powers of nature. Berlioz showed extraordinary sensitivity to the ways in which music can be associated with scenes, ideas, and emotions; without ever achieving a clear success in opera he became one of the century's most notable composers of dramatic music.

CHAPTER VIII

Schumann and His German Contemporaries

At the time of the Napoleonic wars present-day Germany was still a crazy-quilt of some 300 independent states, each with its own system of government, tariffs, and army. Some states, moreover, lay entirely within the boundaries of others; Prussia contained no fewer than thirteen such enclaves. For centuries the dukes and princelings who ruled these realms had exhausted themselves in diplomatic and economic intrigue with and against one another, and at the beginning of the nineteenth century the prospect of a united Germany would have seemed impossible. The instrument for changing all this, paradoxically, was the utter defeat and humiliation visited upon the German states by Napoleon in 1806–9. In 1812 the disastrous retreat of the French armies from Moscow provided the German powers with an opportunity for a concerted act of revenge: Austria and Prussia, previously always at odds, combined forces to deliver the *coup de grâce* to Napoleon and his armies in the battle of Leipzig in October 1813. While the confederation of German nations established at the Congress of Vienna in 1815 was a feeble thing, the war of liberation against Napoleon had roused German-speaking people to a sense of common nationality; a strong liberal opposition to the restored princes now demanded both personal liberties and national unification.

The most vocal sector of the liberal movement consisted of young people and students; a national student society, the *Burschenschaft*, celebrated an ardent love of Fatherland and longing for freedom. Insecure heads of state became alarmed at some activities of the young radicals. The murder of the reactionary dramatist August von Kotzebue by a fanatical student clinched the matter: a meeting of German ministers in 1819 issued the repressive Carlsbad Decrees that provided for the supervision of the universities, imposed strict censorship, and forbade the framing of any constitution opposed to the principle of monarchy. From that time until the collapse of the old German order in the revolutions of 1848, the restoration governments fought a rear-guard battle against the forces for liberalism. The liberal or radical opposition coalesced in the movement known as *Junges Deutschland* (Young Germany) and found an effective voice in the writings of Ludwig Börne (1786–1837), Karl Gutzkow (1811–78), and, above all, in the satirical prose of Heinrich Heine (1797–1856).

SCHUMANN

In the autumn of 1830 Robert Schumann (1810–56), then a somewhat desultory law student, decided to pursue a career in music. A native of the Saxon town of Zwickau near the present-day border with Czecho-slovakia, he had spent one year each at the Universities of Leipzig and Heidelberg, and now returned to Leipzig to devote himself to the piano. His teacher, Friedrich Wieck (later his father-in-law), promised to make of him within three years "one of the greatest pianists now living"—a most ambitious proposal, considering that the twenty-year-old Schumann had not yet studied piano very systematically and had next to no experience as a public performer. Although in 1831–32 his studies in piano were supplemented with some lessons in counterpoint from the local conductor Heinrich Dorn, Schumann suffered a common deprivation of nineteenth-century composers: a lack of early professional training in music.

The son of a book dealer and publisher with marked literary inclinations,[1] Schumann was immersed at an early age in literature ranging from the Greek classics to Byron and Scott. His year of ostensible study of law at Leipzig University is described thus by his classmate Emil Flechsig:

> In Leipzig . . . he never entered a lecture hall. . . . But there was always the newest literature: Heine's travel essays, Menzel's German history, and especially a great deal of Jean Paul, whose style and manner he unfortunately imitated too much in his own writing—which he practiced several hours every day.[2]

Some of Schumann's writings from this period have survived: aphorisms, fragments of novels, and essays on various subjects. These, as well as his letters to his family, are often written in an extravagantly ornate style in apparent imitation of the fanciful and diffuse novels of his literary idol, Jean Paul (Johann Paul Friedrich Richter, 1763–1825). Even after his decision to pursue a career in music, Schumann's literary interests continued to absorb him; in a letter of December 1830, he

---

1.   August Schumann was well known in Germany as the translator of the works of Sir Walter Scott.

2.   W. Boetticher, ed., *Robert Schumann in seinen Schriften und Briefen* (Berlin, 1942), p. 14.

A portrait of Schumann bearing his autograph.

wrote, "If only my talent for music and poetry would converge into a single point, the light would not be so scattered, and I could attempt a great deal."[3]

The following year Schumann hit upon a way to effect such a convergence of his talents for music and literature. In the *Allgemeine musikalische Zeitung* of December 1831, he published a review of Chopin's variations for piano and orchestra on "Là ci darem la mano" from *Don Giovanni*, cloaking his work in an elaborate, novelistic, Jean-Paulian guise; the review begins this way:

> Not long ago Eusebius walked quietly in through the door. You know those pale features and that ironic smile with which he tries to excite curiosity. I sat at the piano with Florestan. Florestan, as you know, is one of those rare musical individuals who seems to have understood long in advance anything that is progressive, new, or unusual. What is extraordinary seems to him so only for a moment; he grasps the unfamiliar instantly. Eusebius, on the other hand, enthusiastic but composed, plucks his blossoms one at a time; he comprehends with more difficulty, but more surely; he is less often delighted, but his enjoyment is longer lasting. He studies more rigorously, and his piano playing is more intellectual, gentler, and mechanically more perfect than Florestan's. This time, however, even he [Forestan] was to be surprised. With the words "Hats off, gentlemen, a genius!" Eusebius laid down before us a musical score.[4]

3. *Jugendbriefe von Robert Schumann,* ed. Clara Schumann (Leipzig, 1886), p. 136.
4. *Allgemeine musikalische Zeitung,* 33 (1831): 805–6.

The cast of characters thus introduced[5] he then engages in a highly metaphorical discussion of Chopin's music. In this colorful fashion Schumann presented both Chopin, an unknown composer, and himself, an unknown critic, to the musical public. That Schumann should have singled out the young Chopin in 1831 as "a genius" is remarkable; that he should have done so solely on the basis of the "Là ci darem" Variations—similar in most respects to countless other sets of variations on the market—is even more so.

Although Schumann intended this review as a first installment in a series of such essays, the editor of the *Allgemeine musikalische Zeitung,* G. W. Fink, wanted no more to do with criticism of this sort. And Schumann was no more successful in publishing his fanciful prose in any other established musical journal. One editor, however, proved receptive to the young critic's unorthodoxies: Carl Herlosssohn, a radical social activist and stalwart of the *Junges Deutschland* movement, printed two articles of Schumann's in 1833 in his literary journal *Der Komet.* These essays, which appeared under the collective title *Der Davidsbündler,* portray Schumann's half-imaginary figures Florestan, Eusebius, Raro, and the others as a group of young artists and musicians, a "band of David," doing battle with the Philistines of contemporary culture. Thus, in this organ for social and political dissent of the German youth movement, Schumann launched his own campaign of dissent against the prevailing musical taste in German society.

Since the later years of Beethoven, Schumann felt, the German concert and opera stage had been awash with superficial music from abroad. "Rossini reigned supreme in the theater," he later reminisced, "and among pianists Herz and Hünten had the field pretty much to themselves."[6] So pervasive was the influence of Italian and French opera and of the Parisian piano virtuoso that it was, in his opinion, next to impossible for a serious native composer to get a fair hearing. The rather extensive German musical press, and particularly the local *Allgemeine musikalische Zeitung,* showed little interest in changing the status quo. In response, Schumann and a group of like-minded friends founded their own journal in 1834, the *Neue Zeitschrift für Musik* (New Journal for Music). For nearly ten years Schumann presided over the twice-weekly issues of this journal, conducting its correspondence, taking charge of proofreading, and contributing in the neighborhood of 1000 pages of copy, consisting of reviews of published music, editorials, and articles on a wide range of musical subjects. At first Schumann wrote

5. The narrator is called Julius, and another character introduced is Meister Raro. Schumann thought of Florestan and Eusebius as representing two sides to his own nature, one impetuous and fiery, the other more calm and deliberate. Meister Raro most often seems to represent Friedrich Wieck.

6. Robert Schumann, *Gesammelte Schriften über Musik und Musiker* (Leipzig, 1854) 1, p. iii.

Neue Leipziger Zeitschrift für Musik. Herausgegeben durch einen Verein von Künstlern und Kunstfreunden. Erster Jahrgang. № 1. Den 3. April 1834.

The first page of Schumann's music journal, launched on 3 April 1834.

nearly everything in his unorthodox novelistic style. Reviews were cast as discussions among members of the *Davidsbund,* and one even pretends to be a description of a dream about a country fair. But the press of his duties as editor and writer soon precluded such literary flourishes, and Florestan, Eusebius, and their shadowy friends gradually disappeared from the pages of the journal. In his writings Schumann consistently excoriated the grand opera and its fashionable appendages, deplored all things Italian, and exalted the canon of Romantic musical heroes from Bach to Beethoven, Schubert, and contemporaries such as Chopin and Mendelssohn. Like Berlioz, Schumann was for much of his career better known as a critic than as a composer; upon his death in 1856 a notice in the *Neue Zeitschrift* recalled that "until his retirement from this journal [i.e. in 1844], he was admired, by the overwhelming majority, primarily as an author."[7]

Schumann's initial hopes of becoming a piano virtuoso foundered quickly. In the spring of 1832 he reported to his family a 'curious misfortune" with his right hand, and from that time on the hand was partially paralyzed.[8] But by 1832 his life seemed in any case pointed in other directions. He had already published his review of Chopin's variations, and his compositions were beginning to see the light of day: his variations on the pitches ABEGG (Op. 1) had appeared in 1831, and

7.   *Neue Zeitschrift für Musik,* 40 (1856), No. 7.

8.   There has been a good bit of speculation to what was wrong with Schumann's hand. A usual explanation has been that he injured it with a mechanical device intended to improve his piano technique. But recently discovered information suggests that the root of the problem may have been mercury poisoning brought about in the treatment of syphilitic infection.

the collection *Papillons* (Op. 2), in the spring of 1832. The *Etudes after Caprices of Paganini* were finished in June of 1832, and the *Intermezzi,* Op. 4, one month later. By the time he suffered his hand injury, his career as composer and critic seems to have been decided.

During the 1830s Schumann composed a splendid body of piano music, and virtually nothing else. Almost all his famous compositions for piano were written in this decade; in addition to those just mentioned there are (in approximately chronological order) the Toccata, Op. 7, the Symphonic Etudes, Op. 12, *Carnaval,* Op. 9, the three piano sonatas in F♯ minor (Op. 11), G minor (Op. 22) and F minor (Op. 14), the *Scenes from Childhood,* Op. 15, the *Kreisleriana,* Op. 16, and others. Most of the collections consist of a series of shorter movements, and some have elaborate programmatic associations.

Papillons, Schumann's first major publication, provides an example of his early manner of assembling a longer composition by combining small modules; it illustrates as well something of the flavor of the literary and programmatic allusions that attach to his early piano music. This collection consists of a six-measure *Introduzione* and twelve movements; most of them are very short, and all show the rhythms and textures of dance music. Some of these individual numbers had been composed before Schumann left Heidelberg in 1830. These were apparently conceived as individual dances; several survive in Schumann's sketchbooks under the title "waltz." Schumann composed the remaining movements in Leipzig in 1831–32, interspersed them among the dances he had already written, and gave the collection its title. While the beginning and end are bound together by a very clear thematic and tonal connection, the inner movements show the strong contrasts of key and character that we might expect of a composition thus assembled.

The published score of *Papillons* contains in addition to the title one other mystifying programmatic reference; in the final number, above six occurrences of the pitch a″ this note appears in the score: "The tumult of the Carnaval-night ceases. The tower clock strikes six." Schumann provided some much-needed clarification of his meaning in letters to his family and to the editors who were to review the composition. To the former he wrote,

> And tell them all to read, as soon as possible, the final scene of Jean Paul's *Flegeljahre,* and that the *Papillons* are in fact meant as a transformation of this masked ball into music. And then ask them if the *Papillons* accurately reflect, perhaps, something of Wina's angelic love, Walt's poetic nature, and Vult's lightning-sharp spirit.[9]

9.   *Jugendbriefe,* pp. 166–67. Jean Paul's characters Walt and Vult may be models for Schumann's Florestan and Eusebius. In his own copy of *Flegeljahre* (Years of Adolescence) Schumann marked some specific passages with numbers that are thought to correspond to individual movements of the *Papillons.*

The Emperor entertains at a masked ball in the Hofburg, Vienna, 1815.

But how can we square Schumann's description of the *Papillons* as a musical counterpart of a masked ball in Jean Paul's novel with the pre-history of the set as a disparate group of keyboard pieces, many of which apparently were written quite independently? Whatever their origins, they were all suitable in this context, Schumann seems to have thought, because they are all dance music, just of the sort that would have been heard at a Carnival ball. Some of the numbers, (such as 1, 2, 6, and 10) even have the introductory sections that announce the tonality and tempo of the next dance of the ball. So one sort of musical reference that Schumann evidently expected to operate in the *Papillons* is the well-known one in which music imitates music. And when in the letter quoted above he spoke of specific connections between this music and a scene from Jean Paul's novel, he did not claim that the *Papillons* portray Wina, Walt, or Vult, or their activities, but rather "something of Wina's angelic love, Walt's poetic nature, and Vult's lightning-sharp spirit." Here he subscribes, seemingly, to a central tenet of Romantic musical aesthetics: rather than describing scenes, events, or actions themselves, music communicates the feelings, the "states of the soul" attendant to them. The title *Papillons* (French for "butterflies") also plays a role in these layers of subtle reference and allusion. Schumann's word for "masked ball" is *Larventanz*. *Larve* means "mask," but also "larva," the premature form of moths and butterflies in which the insect—like a reveler at a masked ball—assumes an appearance very unlike its usual one.

Example VIII–1: SCHUMANN, *Papillons* No. 1, mm. 1–8

Most of the numbers of the *Papillons* have the extreme metric regularity of social dance music of the time; almost all are in triple meter and fall into unvarying patterns of four, eight, and sixteen measures. Many show the keyboard textures of amateur "party music." In the very first one, for example, there are clear echoes of a popular sort of four-hand piano playing in which the upper part has the melody in octaves while the lower one provides a waltzlike accompaniment (see Example VIII–1). The chromatic inflections and shapely conjunct motion of the bass line, however, betray a degree of sophistication not often found in the collections of dance music of the period. And stretches of very felicitous keyboard writing by this budding composer are prophetic of good things to come; one instance, shown in Example VIII–2, is the sonorous arpeggiation adorning a stepwise rising sequence of parallel tenths in *Papillon* No. 7. Our enjoyment of this ingratiating bit

Example VIII–2: SCHUMANN, *Papillons* No. 7, mm. 1–16

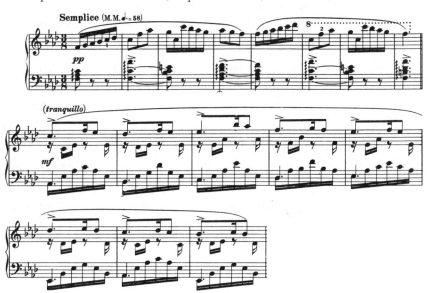

of piano music is fleeting; like many good ideas in the *Papillons,* it disappears after a mere 16 measures.

Schumann returned to the carnival revels of his fervid imagination and to the modular construction of *Papillons* in his most famous composition for piano, *Carnaval: Scènes mignonnes sur quatre notes,* completed in 1835. All twenty numbers of *Carnaval* have titles; most of them are programmatic. There are musical characterizations of the familiar members of the *Davidsbund,* Florestan and Eusebius as well as Chiarina (Clara Wieck, whom Schumann was to marry in 1840) and Estrella (Ernestine von Fricken, to whom he was briefly engaged in 1834). Chopin and Paganini are represented, each with a deft imitation of his style of composition, and in this imaginary celebration they rub elbows with the traditional figures of pantomime, Pierrot, Arlequin (Harlequin), Pantalon, and Colombine. Another gossamer thread binding the composition together is a musical acrostic upon which nearly all the numbers are based, ASCH (in German *Es,* pronounced "s", is E♭, and H is B♮). Halfway through the collection Schumann writes out the notes represented by these letters in several permutations under the title "Sphinxes," with the instruction that they are not to be played. And we learn from a letter to his friend Henriette Voigt that those letter names had for him a double significance: Asch was the hometown in Bohemia of his fiancée, Ernestine, and these letters are the only ones in his own name that designate musical pitches.[10]

The individual numbers of *Carnaval* are in many cases more extended than those of *Papillons,* and the musical ideas are better developed. *Carnaval* is nonetheless permeated with dance rhythms, particularly waltz-like ones, that fall into regularly recurring periods of eight and sixteen measures. Where Schumann exercises his invention is in the shapes of the patterns themselves; *Carnaval* presents one artful variation after another upon the ordinary textures and rhythms of dance music for piano. In *Estrella* (Example VIII–3), the regularly recurring bass notes

Example VIII–3: SCHUMANN, *Carnaval: Estrella,* mm. 13–20.

10. *Robert Schumanns Briefe,* Neue Folge, ed. F. Gustav Jansen (Leipzig, 1904), p. 57.

on the third and first beats are distantly reminiscent of the waltz; the tones of the melody are played above in octaves, but staggered in such a way that they always occur on the second beat in the alto voice (thus supplying the missing second beat of the bass pattern) and on the third in the soprano. Rhythmic displacement such as this is pervasive in *Carnaval* and became a permanent feature in Schumman's style as a whole.

Another Schumannesque trait in *Carnaval* is the splendidly resonant sound of its chordal passages, as in the beginning of the final *Marche des Davidsbündler contre les Philistins,* (Example VIII–4). It is not entirely obvious what makes the effect of this passage so extraordinary. Surely it is due partly to the long-held pedals (Schumann indicates "pedale grande") permitted by the slow harmonic motion; the low bass tone that begins each two-measure group resounds through the passing chordal changes above so as to add great weight to the principal harmonies.

Example VIII–4: SCHUMANN, *Carnaval: Marche des Davidsbündler contre les Philistins,* mm. 1–8

In 1839 Schumann prefaced a review of three recently published piano sonatas with some melancholy remarks about the health of that genre:

> It is strange, for one thing, that sonatas are written mainly by less well-known composers, and, further, that the older living composers who grew up in the heyday of the sonata (the most important of these, surely, would be Cramer and then Moscheles) have cultivated the category the least . . .
>
> It was first of all Hummel who vigorously built upon the Mozartian manner; his F-sharp minor sonata alone would suffice to perpetuate his memory. But Beethoven's example was followed mainly by Franz Schubert, who sought after new terrain and won it. Berger contributed individual things of excellence, but without decisive effect, and the same with Onslow. C. M. von Weber quickly achieved a telling effect with the individual style he developed; more than any other, he still has disciples who

follow his example. Thus the sonata stood ten years ago, and thus it stands now. Individual beautiful examples of this category will surely show up here and there, and already have, but in general it appears that the form has run its course.[11]

One of the "less well-known composers" who had recently composed sonatas was Schumann himself. By 1839 he had published all three of his full-scale piano sonatas, and for him, at least, the form seemed to have "run its course," for he never wrote another.[12]

Schumann's piano sonatas show something of the modular approach to composition that we have seen in his programmatic collections. Individual movements were often composed at very different times, and one was frequently substituted for another. The first movement of the Sonata in F minor (1835), for example, was apparently written as an independent dance, a fandango. For the Sonata in G minor, Op. 22, published in 1839, Schumann wrote the first and third movements in 1833, the second in 1830 (it is based on his song *Im Herbste,* composed in 1828), and the original finale in 1835 to be replaced, in 1838, with a new one. The changes and substitutions made in the Sonata in F minor, Op. 14 (published in 1836), were such as to call in doubt even the genre of the composition; at least partly at the suggestion of his publisher, Haslinger, Schumann deleted the two scherzos of this five-movement work, substituted a new finale, and called the piece *Concert sans orchestre* (Concerto without Orchestra). In the second edition of 1853, with one of the scherzos restored, it is called a sonata. And within movements, as has recently been shown, Schumann made many changes "by extracting, moving about, omitting, and substituting large blocks of finished material, while at the same time leaving intact the surrounding musical text."[13]

The results of these compositional procedures vary. The Sonata in F minor, particularly the restored scherzo and the new finale, is leisurely in the extreme; very long sketches of discursive (if highly original) figuration tend to deny the piece any consistent forward momentum. By comparison the Sonata in G minor is terse, tight-knit, and formally regular. Easily recognizable motivic correspondences create a strong sense of unity within and between movements. Chief among these is a distinctive stepwise melodic line that figures prominently in both the first and last movements. Example VIII–5 a and b shows two occur-

11. *Neue Zeitschrfit für Musik,* 10 (1839): 134.

12. In 1853 he wrote three miniature sonatas, published as *Drei Sonaten für die Jugend,* Op. 118.

13. Linda Correl Roesner, "Schumann's Revisions in the First Movement of the Piano Sonata in G Minor, Op. 22," *19th Century Music,* 1 (1977): 107. See also the same author's "The Autograph of Schumann's Piano Sonata in F minor, Opus 14," *The Musical Quarterly,* 61 (1975): 98–130.

Example VIII–5: SCHUMANN, Sonata in G minor, Op. 22, first movement
a. Mm. 1–9

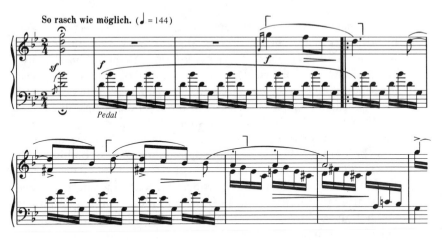

b. Mm. 82–90

rences of it in the first movement, viz. at the very beginning of the
piece and as the initial motive in the secondary key. The descending
melody in G minor (Example VIII–5a) falls into two similar interlocking tetrachords, g″–d″ and d″–a′, in which the semitones are the bottom
intervals. The interlocking tetrachords F–B♭ and B♭–E♭ that appear
later (Example VIII–5b) are exact inversions of the original ones, with
the semitones on top. The headlong motion in sixteenth notes seen in
both excerpts is consistent enough in this movement to constitute another
significant unifying device. And in the opening measures of this move-

ment we hear another of Schumann's euphonious piano sonorities: the wide-spaced accompaniment in the left hand, reaching above the melodic line, produces a splendidly resonant sound.

Schumann's *Fantasiestücke,* finished in 1837, is a collection of eight piano pieces with individual programmatic titles: *Des Abends* (In the Evening), *Grillen* (Whims), *In der Nacht* (In the Night), *Warum?* (Why?), *Fabel* (Fable), and others. The second number of the set, *Aufschwung* (Soaring), is among the five pieces from *Fantasiestücke* included in ARM 14. The title may refer particularly to the second principal theme, first heard in mm. 16ff., in which the soprano melody moves upward in sixths with the tenor voice, and "soars" to an accented upper appoggiatura (bb'') in mm. 18 and 20 before descending again smoothly in mm. 20–23. The other main theme, that with which the piece begins, consists of two quite different subsections: the very opening is energetic and sharply rhythmical (mm. 1–4) while its sequel (mm. 5–8) smooths out and glides downward with a motion that might also remind us of flying or soaring.

There is another complex of musical ideas in the middle of the piece that is united by an interrupted motion in eighth notes, such as we had already heard in the second part of the first theme (mm. 5ff). This large middle part begins in m. 53 and includes related ideas at mm. 61ff., 71ff., and 93ff. The entire composition, in fact, falls into easily perceptible sections and subsections that can be shown thus:

m:	1	16	40	53	114	123	147
	A	*B*	*A*	*C*	*A*	*B*	*A*
	abab	cdc	ab	wxywz	ab	cdc	ab
key:	(f)–A♭	D♭	(f)–B♭	B♭	(f)–A♭	A♭	(f)–f

In the central section, *C*, the subsections *x, y,* and *z* are all less stable tonally than other areas of the piece; this and the dynamic buildup in *z* to the return of *A* in m. 114 invests *C* with something of the character of a development section. And the appearance of secondary material *(B)* toward the beginning and toward the end in two related keys suggests kinship with the exposition and recapitulation of a sonata-allegro movement. The fourfold appearance of *A,* however, leaves the impression of a refrain, and the entire structure takes on the shape often called sonata-rondo.

Individual sections in this composition seem highly schematic and regular. The factor most responsible for this impression is its severely symmetrical periodization. Almost the entire piece falls into clear four-measure phrases, many of which are further divided neatly in half. The "soaring" theme *(B)* can serve as an example: mm. 16–20 are a pair of identical half-phrases, and those in mm. 20–24 are rhythmically symmetrical. These eight measures are then followed by two more pairs of perfectly symmetrical half-phrases (mm. 24–32) with the form *abab*, after which we hear the original eight again. The metrical regularity of this piece is as ironclad as it is in the dancelike movements of *Carnaval* and *Papillons;* here, as there, the composition seems constructed of modules of uniform size.

Within the overall orderliness of this metrical scheme Schumann indulges in certain favorite local irregularities. One welcome ambiguity results from frequent beginning and ending of phrases at mid-measure. In *A* this takes the form of a consistent two- or three-beat anacrusis, while in *B* the strong beginnings on the second halves of the measures generate real uncertainty as to the location of the downbeat. This local rhythmic displacement later necessitates a couple of adjustments. Because *C* begins squarely on the downbeat of m. 53, the preceding phrase must be lengthened by one-half measure—and in such a regular rhythmic context the change is decidedly noticeable. There is a readjustment in m. 104 when the anacruses of *A* appear in the fourth measure of the current phrase. There are only three other disturbances of the reigning pattern of four-measure phrases: mm. 69–70 are "added," as are mm. 83–84 and 112–13.

Within individual measures we hear much of Schumann's beloved hemiola. In *A,* the "answering" phrase *b,* pits an implied 3/4 meter in the melody against the prevailing 6/8 below. And in *B* a similar ambiguity is created at a more minute level: in mm. 26–28 and 30–32 the melody in the soprano subdivides the measure into two groups of three (these melody notes could be more accurately written as dotted eighths), while in the tenor below, the usual ternary division prevails. The distinctive staggered effect that results is particularly striking because the tenor has the same melody as the soprano an octave below, and seems, as the eighth notes fail to coincide, to follow hard in its footsteps.

However regular and lucid its large-scale formal design, this composition shows, right up to the end, one monumental ambiguity: until the last two measures we cannot be sure of its tonality. The piece's structural similarities to sonata-allegro form would suggest $A\flat$ as its key. Section *B,* its principal secondary material, is presented in $A\flat$ in the "recapitulation" after having been heard in a contrasting key, $D\flat$, in the "exposition."[14] And the two statements of *A* at mm. 1 and 114

14. $D\flat$ is, of course, the subdominant of $A\flat$; the more usual contrasting key would be the dominant. The two contrasting keys in this piece, $D\flat$ and $B\flat$, reflect the two most prominent pitches of the opening motive. In restating *B* in $A\flat$, Schumann encounters a problem that had long confronted sonata composers: transposition at the fifth (or fourth) results in a radical change in register, and music often simply doesn't sound as well when put up or down by such a large interval. *B* is vastly more effective in $D\flat$ than in its later occurrence a fourth lower.

Example VIII–6: SCHUMANN, *Aufschwung*

end in A♭. But the beginning of *A* is rather noncommittal as to key. The very opening suggests B♭ minor, which is soon contradicted by the g♮ in m. 1 and the dominant seventh over C in m. 2; upon repetition of these two measures the C in the bass is present from the beginning, and we are led to reinterpret all the initial sounds in the context of a dominant sonority over C (see Example VIII–6). But the key of F minor thus implied never materializes, as each statment of *A*, up to the last one, leads elsewhere. Only in the final *A*, two measures before the end, is that dominant C resolved, when b takes an abrupt detour from its usual path toward A♭ and ends the piece positively in F minor.

As in much of Schumann's piano music, a good share of the interest here lies in felicitous keyboard textures. Configurations such as those at the beginning of *B* and *C* produce a most sonorous effect by means of chord spacing, use of inversions, and arpeggiation in the middle register. A considerable degree of activity in the lower and middle voices, in fact, is a consistent feature of the keyboard writing in this piece. The melodic motion of the opening theme is in the alto, and in two subsequent appearances (mm. 44 and 114) Schumann rewrites this music with satisfying snatches of imitation. But the typical occupation of active lower voices is in doubling the soprano (or sometimes each other) at the third, sixth, or octave. We have already seen that the tenor line at the beginning of *B* doubles the soprano a sixth below, and later, in mm. 26ff., at the octave. Just after that, at m. 29, the alto and bass move in parallel tenths. Such internal activity adds an impression of ever-changing mobility to piano writing in which the harmonic motion and metrical organization are for the most part square-cut.

For Schumann the 1830s were a decade of splendid accomplishment. He directed his journal at Leipzig with imagination and energy, establishing it as the principal organ for Romantic music in Germany. As his journalistic reputation grew, he also continued to write music with unremitting vigor, compiling during this decade twenty-three opus numbers, all for solo piano. But his life, outwardly productive and convivial, was repeatedly clouded by attacks of anxiety and paranoia; the winter of 1833–34—the period of planning for the *Neue Zeitschrift*—saw Schumann on the verge of suicide. During the later 1830s he was increasingly absorbed in a love affair with Clara Wieck, his teacher's

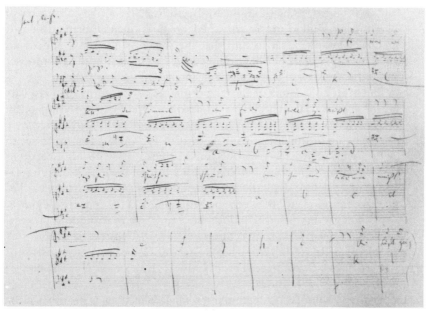

The first page of Schumann's *Mondnacht* from the Eichendorff *Liederkreis*, Op. 39.

teenage daughter, who was gaining international fame as a pianist. Her father's adamant opposition to their union was finally overcome—through recourse to the courts—and they married in September 1840.

That year marked another change of direction for Schumann. Up until that time he had written almost exclusively instrumental music; the only exceptions are a few tentative songs on texts of J. A. C. Kerner, composed in 1827–28. In an oft-quoted letter of June 1839 to Hermann Hirschbach he even said, "All my life I have considered vocal composition inferior to instrumental music—I have never regarded it as a great art. But don't tell anyone about this!"[15] Nonetheless in the following year he unleashed a veritable torrent of Lieder for solo voice and piano: in 1840 alone he wrote over 125 of them, more than half of his entire output in the category. These include many of the most admired Lieder ever written: the collection *Myrten*, Op. 25, the Heine *Liederkreis*, Op. 24, the *Liederkreis von Eichendorff*, Op. 39, the *Dichterliebe*, Op. 48, the *Frauenliebe und -leben*, Op. 42, and many others. Several reasons have been advanced for Schumann's about-face. It is possible that love lyrics now had for him an intensely personal significance. This was also a time when Schumann seemed to reevaluate certain of his most cherished ideals as to the progress of contemporary music as a whole. He had long taken for granted that the real future of Romantic

15. *Briefe,* ed. F. Gustav Jansen, p. 158.

music, founded, as he thought, by Beethoven, lay in the cultivation of Beethoven's kind of music, viz. the large instrumental forms. But as it gradually became clear to him that the sonata, symphony, and string quartet simply were not developing as he had hoped, both as composer and critic he showed a new surge of interest in the Lied.

The great collections of Lieder Schumann produced in 1840 are variously constructed. The Heine *Liederkreis,* Op. 24, is a setting of an integral series of nine poems from Heine's *Buch der Lieder,* united by a clear scheme of tonalities. And the text of *Frauenliebe und -leben,* set to eight poems of Adalbert von Chamisso (1781–1838), forms a coherent narrative that Schumann invested with a further coherence of key relations and (recalling Beethoven's song cycle *An die ferne Geliebte*) a thematic correspondence between the beginning and the end. But *Myrthen,* an anthology that Schumann presented to Clara as a wedding present, consists of twenty-six songs composed to texts by such diverse authors as Friedrich Rückert (1788–1866), Goethe, Heine, and (in translation) Robert Burns, Byron, and Thomas Moore; it shows little in the way of poetic or musical unity.

The most admired of Schumann's song collections is his other cycle composed to verses of Heinrich Heine, *Dichterliebe* (The Poet's Love). Written at white heat during the last week of May 1840, *Dichterliebe* consisted in the original autograph of twenty songs, four of which were omitted when the work was first published in 1844. All the poems were chosen from the section *Lyrisches Intermezzo* in the first edition of Heine's *Buch der Lieder* (1827). The poetry of *Lyrisches Intermezzo* again and again addresses the theme of unrequited love, proceeding from a slightly questionable innocence and lyricism to a tone of abrasive cyncism that shows Heine's famous "romantic irony" at its most extreme. Here we are offered both the expected outpouring of feeling of lyrical verse and a mischievous mockery of it. The conventions of Romantic poetry are held up to ridicule in verse that itself seems to operate by those conventions. In the first poem, *Im wunderschönen Monat Mai,* a confession of love is presented with all the appropriate metaphors of budding flowers and birdsong in springtime; in the last, *Die alten, bösen Lieder* (The Old, Wicked Songs), the protagonist proposes to drown his love, his dreams, his suffering—and his poems—in the sea.

In his criticism Schumann laid down some rather demanding prescriptions for the Lied: it should seek "to recreate in a subtle musical realization the most delicate effects of the poem."[16] And he praised the Danish Lieder composer J. P. E. Hartmann (1805–1900) for striving to reflect in music "the sense of the text, down to the individual words."[17] In his own settings of Heine's verses, nonetheless, Schumann has often been accused of misunderstanding or ignoring much of the poet's

16. *Neue Zeitschrift für Musik,* 13 (1840): 118.
17. Ibid., 17 (1842): 9.

Drawing dated 1837 by Kaspar Karsen, showing the far-from-completed Cologne Cathedral that Heine would have seen from across the Rhine.

meaning—most particularly those sardonic turns of phrase that color so much of his poetry.[18] There can be little question but that Schumann sought to neutralize the cynicism and despair of the ending of Heine's *Lyrisches Intermezzo.* After providing appropriately "troubled" chromatic music for the sinking of the poet's sorrows and songs in the sea in *Die alten, bösen Lieder,* he appended a delicate seventeen-measure piano epilogue borrowed from the twelfth song, *Am leuchtenden Sommermorgen* (In the Radiant Summer Morning); there this music is associated with expressions of forgiveness and reconciliation, and it is on this note that Schumann's cycle ends.

There is reason to think that where Schumann adjusted the emphases of Heine's poetry he did so quite deliberately. The poet's disingenuousness would hardly have escaped Schumann, who, upon meeting Heine in 1828, described him in his diary as "an ironic little man," and took note of "the bizarre, the burning sarcasm, the caricaturing of grandeur and dignity" in his poetry. And in some of the songs of *Dichterliebe* Schumann seems bent on offering sophisticated musical equivalents for Heine's double meanings and insincerities. The sixth song, *Im Rhein, im heiligen Strome,* is an example. This is Heine's first stanza:

Im Rhein, im heiligen Strome,   In the Rhine, in the holy river,
Da spiegelt sich in den Well'n,   There is mirrored in the waves
Mit seinem grossen Dome   The great, holy city,
Das grosse, heilige Köln.   Cologne, with its great cathedral.

18.   An extreme critic of Schumann on this score is Eric Sams in *The Songs of Robert Schumann* (London, 1969), p. 3.

Example VIII–7: SCHUMANN, *Dichterliebe: Im Rhein,* mm. 1–7

Such puerile repetitions of the unpoetic words "gross" and "heilig" and the ungainly rhyme "Well'n"—"Köln" effectively undercut any ostensible reverence shown the river, the city, or the church. Schumann gave this poem a musical setting in which constant dotted rhythms in the accompaniment invoke, according to the ordinary musical rhetoric of the time, fitting impressions of grandeur and majesty (see Example VIII–7). But that rhythmic pattern, uncharacteristically for Schumann, persists from the beginning of the song to the end, and then on and on throughout a sixteen-measure piano epilogue. Surely the musical imagery here, like the poet's veneration, is intentionally overdone.

Schumann usually had reservations about accompaniments constructed from a single illustrative figure like that in *Im Rhein.* In an otherwise laudatory review of a collection of Lieder by Norbert Burgmüller (1810–1836) he expressed disappointment in a setting of Goethe's song of the Harper, *Wer nie sein Brot mit Thränen ass,* because of its constant strumming accompaniment:

> This figure, though it can be explained as a reference to the Harper, strikes me as too external and arbitrary; it tends to obscure the life and sensitivity of the poem. With Franz Schubert the use of a single continuous figure from the beginning of a Lied to the end appeared as something new. But young Lieder composers should be strongly warned against this mannerism.[19]

Schumann the critic favored a more flexible accompaniment for the Lied, and in 1843 he prescribed a kind of division of labor for the piano and voice:

> The singing voice is hardly sufficient in itself; it cannot carry out the whole task of interpretation unaided. In addition to its overall expression, the finer shadings of the poem must be represented as well—provided that the melody does not suffer in the process.[20]

19. *Neue Zeitschrift für Musik,* 11 (1839): 69.
20. Ibid., 18 (1843): 120.

Thus the piano part is expected to be responsive to minute shifts of meaning and mood in the text, and—much more than in the traditions of Lieder composition from C. P. E. Bach to Schubert—it is regarded as a full partner in the interpretive process.

In his Eichendorff *Liederkreis,* composed, like the *Dichterliebe,* in May 1840, Schumann seems to have achieved a particularly happy union of music and poetry, and one largely in harmony with his own theoretical prescriptions. Schumann's source for these verses was the *Gedichte* (1837) of Joseph Freiherr von Eichendorff (1788–1857). He ranged through this volume, selecting single poems in no easily discernible order from the various categories (*Wanderlieder, Sängerleben, Zeitlieder,* etc.) under which they are grouped. Yet the twelve poems of the *Liederkreis* show great regularity of structure and theme. Each consists of two to four metrically regular four-line stanzas,[21] and they depict again and again the playing out of human drama, often an internal one, in intimate contact with nature—nature seen as benign and hospitable, or, especially in nocturnal sylvan settings, as mysterious and vaguely threatening. Schumann's settings of these poems (the first five are given in ARM 15) show the extraordinary range and aptness of his musical expression in this genre.

In the fifth song of this collection, *Mondnacht* (Moonlit Night; ARM 15e), Schumann creates a marvelously sensitive musical realization of a poem whose lyrical celebration of nature is untouched by darker passions; its three stanzas are as follows:

Es war, als hätt' der Himmel
Die Erde still geküsst,
Dass sie im Blütenschimmer
Von ihm nur träumen müsst!

It was as if heaven had
Quietly kissed the earth.
So that in glimmering blossoms
She must dream only of him.

Die Luft ging durch die Felder,
Die Ähren wogten sacht,
Es rauschten leis' die Wälder,
So sternklar war die Nacht.

The breeze went through the fields
The corn swayed softly
The woods rustled lightly
So clear and starry was the night.

Und meine Seele spannte
Weit ihre Flügel aus.
Flog durch die stillen Lande,
Als flöge sie nach Haus.

And my soul spread
Wide her wings,
Flew through the silent land
As though she were flying home.

For the first two stanzas Schumann writes only slightly differing versions of the same music. In seeming illustration of the initial ethereal metaphor the piano introduction and the music for the first poetic line

21. *Wehmut,* the ninth number of the *Liederkreis,* is a longer poem; Schumann used only the first three-stanza section.

are artfully suspended upon the dominant: in mm. 1–4 the piano twice proceeds from a dominant-ninth sound to a dominant triad, and in mm. 5–9 this dominant sonority moves fleetingly toward the supertonic before it is restored. Only with the beginning of the second line, upon mention of "earth," do we hear the tonic chord; and then for three measures the music is all tonic as the bass strides downward in fourths and fifths. The vocal line also moves appropriately up and down for "heaven" and "earth"; the upward motion is reinforced by a poignant cross relation between E♮ and E♯ (the leading tone of the supertonic). In the third stanza, the "unfolding of wings" and the "soul's flight" are given a setting that is largely new; released from its restricted harmonic plan, the music moves strongly to the subdominant—a most telling gesture within so static a context—before sinking back to the placid, "homelike" dominant and tonic of the piano epilogue.

The third song, *Waldesgespräch* (Conversation in the Forest; ARM 15c) is composed to a very different sort of poem. A brief dramatic vignette, it presents two characters who meet in the forest: a knightly rider and a lovely young woman who is revealed to be the witchlike Lorelei, here displaced from her usual perch above the Rhine. Its four stanzas are spoken alternately by these two characters:

Es ist schon spät, es wird schon kalt,
Was reitst du einsam durch den Wald?

Der Wald ist lang, du bist allein,
Du schöne Braut! Ich führ dich heim!

"Gross ist der Männer Trug und List,
Vor Schmerz mein Herz gebrochen ist.
Wohl irrt das Waldhorn her und hin,

O flieh! Du weisst nicht, wer ich bin."

So reich geschmückt ist Ross und
        Weib,
So wunderschön der junge Leib,
Jetzt kenn ich dich—Gott steh mir bei!
Du bist die Hexe Lorelei.

"Du kennst mich wohl—von hohem
        Stein
Schaut still mein Schloss tief in den
        Rhein.

It is already late, it is already cold,
Why are you riding alone through
        the wood?

The wood is vast, you are alone,
You pretty bride, I'll lead you home!

Great is men's deceit and cunning,
From pain my heart has broken.
The wandering hunting horn
        sounds here and there,
Oh flee, you do not know who I am.

So richly adorned is horse and
        lady
So enchanting is your young body,
Now I know you—God be with me!
You are the witch Lorelei!

You know me indeed, from a
        high rock
My castle looks silently deep into
        the Rhine;

| Es ist schon spät, es wird schon kalt, | It is already late, it is already cold, |
| Kommst nimmermehr aus diesem Wald!" | You will nevermore leave this wood! |

The sections of Schumann's song are arranged in accord with the dialogue of the poem: stanzas one and three, spoken by the man, have one melody, and stanzas two and four, spoken by the Lorelei, another. A striking shift of tonality from the tonic E major to C major marks the introduction of the Lorelei's voice in stanza two; then in the final stanza (perhaps because she is no longer so mysterious) her music is presented in the home key. The song begins and ends with a memorable stretch of piano music whose initial progression, with a prominent open fifth, (b–f♯') echoes the strains of hunting horns. Rhythmically and harmonically placid, it serves both as an idyllic frame for the entire composition and as an equal participant, at least, with the voice in the music for the first poetic line.

Schumann's prescription that the accompaniment should reflect "the finer shadings of the poem"[22] seems well fulfilled in this song. After setting an unruffled, picturesque tone for the beginning of the composition, the piano part shifts easily to a figure with urgent repeated chords for the question and warning of the following two lines. Something analogous happens when the Lorelei speaks in the second stanza. A gentle arpeggiated figure accompanying her expressions of rejection and sorrow in the first two lines gives way again to a repeated-note pattern for *her* warnings in the succeeding lines. And within those bland arpeggios, all over a tonic pedal, a local chromatic disturbance in m. 22 is a response to the Lorelei's "suffering" mentioned in the second line—there is no such harmonic deflection at the corresponding point (m. 52) in the fourth stanza where she speaks of her castle silently surveying the Rhine. At the moment of recognition, too, in the third stanza (mm. 40–44), the piano part momentarily adopts a new guise: its isolated chords combine with the declamatory style of the voice for a dramatic if fleeting simulation of recitative.

The textual change in the accompaniment for the second line of poetry at m. 9 is complemented by a vivid shift in harmonic style. Up to this point the music of the "frame" had sounded nothing but tonic and dominant chords in E major. Now, as the text describes a lonely, directionless trek through the forest, the music embarks upon an extended tour of the circle of fifths, from A♯ to D♯, G♯, C♯, F♯, B, and, as the poem speaks of a homecoming, back toward E (the arrival at which is thwarted by a deceptive cadence). In the equivalent passage in the second stanza it is hunting horns that are heard to "wander" (m. 25), and here too Schumann introduces a harmonic excursion. From the local

---

22. See above, p. 238.

Example VIII–8: SCHUMANN, *Waldesgespräch*, reduction

tonic, C major, a chromatic descent in tenths and sixths leads back to E major (see Example VIII–8). In the last stanza, the corresponding music accompanies the Lorelei's sudden pronouncement of doom; here its chromatic course is much shortened, matching the swift denouement of the poem.

For the final line of the poem, "and never again will you come out of this forest," Schumann delays the conclusion of a standard cadential pattern with unstable passing sonorities and repeated text (mm. 61–63); then all is resolved and the piano swings once more into the quite untroubled "frame" music. Understandably enough, this ending has been thought inappropriate: the sylvan picturesqueness of the opening of the song is hardly the right note to strike when the man has just been told he will die in the woods. But for Schumann and his German contemporaries the Lorelei was not a seriously threatening figure, and Eichendorff's poem conveys a certain sense of fairy-tale unreality (nothing whatever, for example, is known about the identity of the man fated to remain in the forest). The "framing" device of Schumann's song effectively puts this miniature tragedy at a safe distance and allows us to see it for what it is: woodland lore, not human drama. Whether Schumann's musical realization of the poem is convincing or not, it is clear that he brings new forces to bear on the process of Lied composition. An intensified and flexible accompaniment and an enriched harmonic language are marks of a new style of Lied in Schumann's generation. The old prescriptions for this genre of simplicity and folklikeness fell before new artistic requirements that brought the Lied much more into the mainstream of Romantic composition. In 1843 Schumann referred to this: "The Lied, in fact, is perhaps the only genre which has shown significant progress since Beethoven."[23]

At the end of 1840, nevertheless, Schumann turned his attention firmly toward a very different sort of composition. In 1839 he had helped arrange the first performance of Schubert's Great C-major Symphony; how strongly this work affected him is evident from his correspondence and from an inspired article on the symphony in the *Neue Zeitschrift,* where he wrote:

---

23. *Neue Zeitschrift für Musik,* 19 (1843): 34.

For here, besides masterful technique of musical composition, there is life in every fiber, color in the finest gradations, significance everywhere, sharply cut detail. And finally, over the whole there is poured out that romanticism we know to be characteristic of Franz Schubert. And those heavenly lengths, like a great novel in four volumes by one such as Jean Paul . . .[24]

The "heavenly lengths" of Schubert's symphony were for Schumann one example, at last, of an extended instrumental composition in a genuinely Romantic style. Then in 1841 he set about attempting something similar himself. During that year alone he composed his Symphony

Example VIII–9: SCHUMANN, Symphony No. 3, first movement, mm. 1–9

24. Ibid., 12 (1840): 82.

No. 1 in B♭, Op. 38 (the *Spring*), the first version of the Symphony No. 4 in D minor (revised and published ten years later as Op. 120), the Overture, Scherzo, and Finale Op. 52, and preliminary drafts of a symphony in C minor that was never completed. Thus, having written more than half of his Lieder in 1840, during the next year Schumann produced half of his symphonies. The other two, the Symphony No. 2 in C major, Op. 61, and the Symphony No. 3 in E♭, Op. 97 (the *Rhenish*), were completed in 1846 and 1850 respectively.

Schumann's abilities as a composer of orchestral music have been much impugned. Conductors from the later nineteenth century to the present day have made adjustments in his instrumentation, the best known of which are Gustav Mahler's extensive emendations of the symphonies. Most problematic, surely, of Schumann's orchestral compositions are the later ones, including the third and fourth symphonies (the latter in its revised form of 1851). These works are for the most part heavily orchestrated. Woodwinds routinely double the strings and are almost never heard in a solo role; horns and trumpets very often play filler material in a middle register, sometimes to the detriment of textural clarity. The first violins, however, are frequently left unsupported as the second violins engage in harmonic figuration; the result, as in the otherwise splendid, soaring first theme of the Third Symphony, is, for many ears, too little melody and too much accompaniment (see Example VIII–9). But the problem is not that such thick scoring is always disagreeable; it is that Schumann wrote it too consistently—perhaps, it has been thought, to mask unreliable playing by the orchestra he conducted in Düsseldorf.

From the standpoint of orchestration the First Symphony and the early version of the Fourth show much more variety than their succes-

Example VIII–10
  a. SCHUMANN, Symphony No. 1, first movement, mm. 1–3

  b. SCHUBERT, Symphony No. 9 in C major, first movement, mm. 1–2

Autograph of the opening page, Schumann's First Symphony *(The Spring)*.

sors. Light-textured passages and flashes of woodwind color often relieve Schumann's full orchestral sound. The First Symphony, in fact, given the composer's nearly total inexperience in the medium, is a startlingly successful effort. The slow introduction to its first movement begins with a stentorian pronouncement in the horns and trumpets that Schumann said "should sound as if from on high, as a call to awaken"[25] (see Example VIII–10a). This horn call, which seems indebted to the very similar beginning of Schubert's Great C-major Symphony (Example VIII–10b), provides the motivic basis for most of the tight-knit movement that follows. (An earlier version of this figure, written a third lower, but rejected as unperformable by the horn players in the Leipzig Gewandhaus Orchestra, has yet a closer thematic connection with both Schubert's symphony and the remainder of Schumann's movement.) Schumann follows Schubert's example, too, in connecting the slow introduction to the movement proper by means of a portentous accelerando and crescendo, a device Schumann specially praised in his review of his predecessor's symphony.[26] Schumann's slow movement is dominated by a flowing cantabile melody, inventively assigned in the cen-

25. *Briefe,* ed. F. Gustav Jansen, p. 224.
26. In the Symphony No. 4, Schumann makes two such connections: between the slow introduction and the body of the first movement, and between the third and fourth movements.

tral section to unison solo oboe and solo horn. The scherzo with two trios that follows again shows facile contrasts of theme and color. Only the finale suffers from sameness and predictability: its running, *scherzando* eighth notes fall into the even metrical patterns that for Schumann were always something of a danger.

In the following year, 1842, Schumann once again addressed himself to a new specialty, viz. the composition of chamber music. His three String Quartets (Op. 41), the Piano Quartet (Op. 47), the Piano Quintet (Op. 44), and the *Fantasiestücke* for piano, violin, and cello were all produced during this single year. Of these the compositions with piano are generally thought most successful; the Piano Quintet (for string quartet and piano) is a universally admired work in which Schumann's characteristically inventive (though often metrically four-square) musical ideas are masterfully adapted to their medium.

In the midst of his relentless pursuit of new achievements in the early 1840s, however, Schumann felt that one significant goal, the composition of a successful opera—that is, a *German* opera—remained elusive. The considerable popularity of his secular oratorio, *Das Paradies und die Peri* (1843), seemed an encouraging sign of his talent for dramatic music. After considering a host of different subjects for an opera, he finally settled upon an adaptation of two plays on the medieval legend of Geneviève of Brabant by Ludwig Tieck and Christian Friedrich Hebbel. With his friend Robert Reinick, Schumann fashioned the libretto, and the music was finished by 1848. After vexing delays the premiere of *Genoveva* took place in Leipzig in the autumn of 1850, with Schumann conducting. The opera was not a success. Generally described as dramatically inert, it closed after only three performances and has seldom been revived since.

In 1843 Schumann (together with Mendelssohn and Moscheles) was appointed professor at the newly founded Leipzig Conservatory. But by the following year, at the age of thirty-four, he had suffered further mental disturbances, given up the *Neue Zeitschrift,* and moved his family to Dresden. From that time on there was no regaining anything like the astonishing productivity of the earlier years. Then in 1850, the assumption of a post in Düsseldorf saw him miscast as the conductor of a civic orchestra and chorus, and professional setbacks were added to the gathering storm of his nervous disorders. A few notable works were written between 1850 and his commitment to a mental hospital near Bonn, where he died in 1856: the Third Symphony, for example, the Cello Concerto, the two Violin Sonatas Opp. 105 and 121, and sections of *Scenes from Goethe's Faust.* But Schumann, the archetypal Romantic musician, like many Romantic artists made his most characteristic contribution when he was young. The best that he left us was, in a sense, his less ambitious and less studied music, most notably the inspired piano pieces and songs of earlier years.

The *Gewandhaus* concert hall in Leipzig, drawn by Mendelssohn.

MENDELSSOHN

In the summer of 1835 Schumann's *Neue Zeitschrift* carried a notice that a new conductor and composer, Felix Mendelssohn-Bartholdy (1809–47), was to become director of the Gewandhaus Orchestra of Leipzig. Mendelssohn's background was very different from Schumann's; a former child prodigy whose family had provided him the best of education, travel, and contacts from his earliest years,[27] Mendelssohn seemed to Schumann urbane and supremely accomplished. Born into a prominent Berlin Jewish family (his grandfather was the philosopher Moses Mendelssohn), he had music lessons with the pianist Ludwig Berger and the violinist Eduard Rietz. Most influential of his early musical training, however, was his study with Friedrich Zelter, the dour director of the Berlin Singakademie, who put him through a rigorous regime of figured bass, chorale harmonization, counterpoint, canon, and fugue. Zelter's teaching followed North German traditions in musical instruction that derived from J. F. Kirnberger, F. W. Marpurg, and ultimately from their teacher, J. S. Bach. Mendelssohn thus received what was essentially an eighteenth-century musical education, and the extraordinary facility (and sometimes conservatism) of his music reflects this early training.

By the time the twenty-six-year-old Mendelssohn came to Leipzig he had presided over the revival of the *St. Matthew Passion* in Berlin, had made a name for himself in London and Paris, and had an impressive roster of compositions to his credit. These included two youthful operas,[28] a dozen string symphonies, three symphonies for full orches-

---

27. See above, p. 12–13.
28. *Die Hochzeit des Camacho* (1825) and *Die Heimkehr aus der Fremde* (1829). There were also several shorter operettas from an even earlier time.

In *Titania and Bottom*, an illustration for *A Midsummer Night's Dream*, Henry Fuseli enters the realm of the irrational and the fantastic.

tra,[29] four concert overtures,[30] two piano concertos, many solo piano pieces, and about a dozen chamber works. The best known of all his compositions, the *Overture to A Midsummer Night's Dream*, had, in fact, been finished in 1826 when the composer was only seventeen.

Mendelssohn wrote his *Overture to A Midsummer Night's Dream* under the spell of his reading of Schlegel and Tieck's German translation of Shakespeare (published in 1801). The most deliberately programmatic of all his compositions, it presents scurrying *pianissimo* violin figures for the elfin inhabitants of Oberon and Titania's fairy kingdom, solemn chordal strains for the court of Duke Theseus, and rambunctious "peasant music," with open-fifth drones and a fairly realistic imitation of the braying of the donkey, for Bottom and his brutish companions.[31] All this is done with a sure and light touch; the *scherzando* "elfin" music in particular (see Example VIII–11) seems perfectly suited to that diminutive enchanted world of Shakespeare's imagination. This passage illustrates Mendelssohn's special proclivity for transparent *leggiero* musical textures with very rapid surface motion. (Two later examples, both also in the key of E, are the Fantasy [or Capriccio] in E minor for piano,

29. I.e. the Symphony No. 1 in C minor, the Symphony No. 5 (the *Reformation*), and the Symphony No. 4 (the *Italian*).

30. *Overture to A Midsummer Night's Dream*, *The Hebrides* (or *Fingal's Cave*), *Meeresstille und glückliche Fahrt*, and *Die schöne Melusine*.

31. Mendelssohn's friend Adolf Bernhard Marx (who later became well known as a music theorist) claimed to have induced the composer to include all these illustrative effects. A. B. Marx, *Erinnerungen aus meinem Leben* (Berlin, 1865), 2, p. 231.

Example VIII–11: MENDELSSOHN, *Overture to A Misummer Night's Dream,*
    mm. 8–15

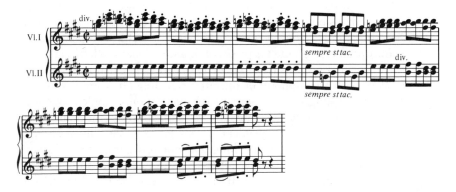

Op. 16, and the finale of the Violin Concerto.) This theme in *A Mid-summer Night's Dream* is bound together with almost all the other melodies of the overture by its initial descending diatonic scale-figure; this unifying device contributes strongly to a certain impression of rightness and inevitability.

All the illustrative music in Mendelssohn's overture, furthermore, fits comfortably into a sonata-allegro structure that is entirely regular except for its alternation between E major and E minor (major for the music of the "real world" and minor for that of the fairy kingdom). Metrically, too, the piece is highly regular; there is little sign of the local displacements of rhythm that so often relieve the symmetry of phrase construction in Schumann's music. And the ensemble for which Mendelssohn wrote this overture is, in all respects but one, that of the mature Haydn; the exception is his use of the ophicleide, a bass-keyed bugle (replaced in the modern orchestra by the bass tuba), that adds heft to the drones in the peasant music.[32] Mendelssohn manages this eighteen-century orchestra—adding a modern extension of range and the use of divided strings—with consummate skill. The winds contribute vivid patches of individual color and balanced reinforcement to the orchestral sound, and all the instruments are deftly handled with respect to idiom and register. This composition seems to show that Mendelssohn was in possession of nearly his full powers as a composer at the age of seventeen; when some seventeen years later he provided complete incidental music for a performance of Shakespeare's play at the Royal Theater in Berlin, the numbers he added—the Scherzo, Intermezzo, Notturno, and

32. The earliest ophicleides had been built only about ten years earlier in Paris by J. Halary. Spontini used the instrument in his opera *Olympie* (1817).

the familiar Wedding March—are stylistically of a piece with his youth-ful Overture.

In composing the *Overture to A Midsummer Night's Dream* Mendels-sohn, perhaps unwittingly, provided a notable example of a new genre, the programmatic concert overture. There was a clear and practical need in European concert life for pieces of this sort. Since the later eighteenth century it had been usual to begin a concert (and often its second half as well) with a symphony or operatic overture. The former was often thought too long for this purpose (frequently only single movements were played), and the latter was drawn from an irrelevant dramatic and musical context. An independent work created specifically as an open-ing orchestral sally—not too long and not too complicated—seemed just what was needed, and Mendelssohn's example was soon followed by other composers such as Berlioz and Schumann.[33] Mendelssohn himself composed three more programmatic overtures, *The Hebrides* (or *Fingal's Cave*), 1830–32, *Meeresstille und glückliche Fahrt* (after two poems of Goethe), 1832, and *Die schöne Melusine* (after a play of Grill-parzer), 1833. These pieces typically present mildly illustrative musical materials (such as the wavelike melodic motion at the beginning of *The Hebrides*) within very regular sonata-allegro structures. They abound in the attractive melodies and effortless mastery of instrumentation that are Mendelssohn's specialty.

The composer's four mature symphonies (No. 1 in C minor, com-posed in 1824, is an early work) form two pairs: the *Reformation* (No. 5) and *Italian* (No. 4) from 1832 and 1833, and the *Lobgesang* (No. 2) and *Scottish* (No. 3) from 1840 and 1842.[34] Only one of these, the *Ital-ian,* has achieved a secure place in the orchestral repertory. According to Mendelssohn's own testimony, the inspiration for this work derives from his travels in Italy in 1830–32. The journey was suggested by Goethe. Like Goethe before him, Mendelssohn responded to Italy by embracing the classical values of clarity and regularity that came so easily to him; this symphony is the very model of formal and metrical orderliness, enlivened with Mendelssohn's own melodic grace and sharply delineated orchestral color. The *Lobgesang* is one of many symphonies of the nineteenth century strongly indebted to Beethoven's Ninth. Its first three movements are wholly instrumental, while the last, longer than the others combined, is an extended oratoriolike structure for soloists, chorus, and orchestra.

During Mendelssohn's first years in Leipzig the composition of his that attracted the most attention in Germany was his oratorio *St. Paul,* completed in 1836. Mendelssohn's friend Julius Schubring, with the aid

---

33. Berlioz's *Waverley, King Lear,* and *Roman Carnival* overtures, for example, and Schumann's *Manfred* and *Hermann und Dorothea* overtures.
34. The numbering of the symphonies follows the order of their publication.

of the composer, fashioned the libretto from Acts and other books of the Old and New Testaments. The story of St. Paul, from the stoning of Stephen to his missionary travels, is narrated not by the traditional *testo,* but by various solo voices and even the chorus; only St. Paul himself is consistently subject to dramatic impersonation. All essentials of the Handelian oratorio—accompanied and unaccompanied recitative, aria, and both homophonic and fugal choruses—are present here. In addition, at many points Mendelssohn introduces chorales, harmonized approximately in the style of Bach, as reflective commentary upon the drama. Quite foreign to the traditions of the extraliturgical oratorio, this usage is a familiar one of North German Protestant church music and probably reflects Mendelssohn's fascination with Bach's church cantatas and the *St. Matthew Passion.*[35]

The musical idiom of this oratorio, especially in its recitative and choruses, seems, like many nineteenth-century works in this genre, very derivative of Handel. In the arias the writing is less consistently Baroque. The harmonic style of the familiar contralto solo *Doch der Herr vergisst der Seinen nicht* (But the Lord is Mindful of His Own) belongs wholly to the nineteenth century, as does that of *Jerusalem! die du tötest die Propheten* (Jerusalem, Thou that Killest the Prophets). As we would expect, furthermore, even where Mendelssohn's antiquarianism appears to be in full command there are clear elements of a more modern style. In his fugues the voices frequently enter at regularly spaced intervals of two or four measures; these patterns underline that metrical regularity that often holds for even the most contrapuntal of this music. And certain turns of harmony in the most Handelian of his choruses echo the sounds of nineteenth-century parlor music. The concluding chorus of Part I, *O! welch eine Tiefe* (Oh, How Great Are the Depths), ends with a massive "Amen" (see ARM 16). Here the slow-moving chord changes and the liberal use of weak first-inversion triads are harmonic mannerisms indigenous to the polite music of Mendelssohn's own time.

St. Paul was quickly translated into English and performed at Liverpool in October 1836. It became an immense favorite of the oratorio-loving British, whose numerous choral societies were always eager to supplement their standard repertory of Handel and Haydn. Ten years later, in 1846, Mendelssohn produced his other oratorio, *Elijah,* again to a text compiled by Schubring and himself. In this case the popularity of the English version far outstripped that of the German original; *Elijah* became and has remained a staple for singing societies throughout England and the United States. In Germany Mendelssohn's oratorios were regarded as the most prominent representatives of a diminishing

35. Mendelssohn had undertaken exhaustive studies of chorale harmonization in the style of Bach with his teacher Zelter. See Larry Todd, ed., *Mendelssohn's Musical Education: A Study and Edition of His Exercises in Composition* (Cambridge, 1983).

but hardy breed. Other Biblical oratorios occasionally heard were Spohr's
Das jüngste Gericht (The Last Judgment, 1812), and Friedrich Schneider's *Das Weltgericht* (The Judgment of the World, 1819). In 1841 Mendelssohn's erstwhile friend Adolf Bernhard Marx produced his oratorio
Moses;[36] Schumann in his *Das Paradis und die Peri* of 1843 and Carl Loewe
(1796–1869) in *Gutenberg* (1835) broke new—but apparently not very
fertile—ground with the secular oratorio.

Mendelssohn seems most consistently at his best in his chamber music.
The most conspicuous of his virtues, a splendid facility in part-writing
and an unfailingly idiomatic handling of instruments, are particularly
noticeable in the four later string quartets (Opp. 44 and 80), the early
Octet, Op. 20, and in the two Piano Trios in D minor, Op. 49, and C
minor, Op. 66. Of all these pieces only the Octet and the Piano Trio in
D minor have survived the vicissitudes of changing tastes to become a
standard part of the current chamber repertory. The trio, an ambitious
work in four movements, demands a virtuoso pianist; yet its string
parts are much more substantial and better integrated than was usual
for this genre, whose lineage in the accompanied keyboard sonata was
often still highly visible. As is frequently the case in Mendelssohn's
music, its "fast and light" movement, the Scherzo (ARM 17), comes
off best.

This Scherzo in D major features the quick, close-spaced staccato
chords and fleet running figurations for which Mendelssohn had a special affinity; the opening statement of the piano presents two such figures, in eighth notes and sixteenth notes respectively, and the entire
Scherzo moves without pause in these patterns. The usual contrasting
trio is missing, and the expected binary form of the scherzo is subject
to expansion and clever manipulation. Its overall shape can be shown
thus:

m.	1	28	47	118	156
key	I	V	I ⩘⩘⩘⩘ I		I
	a		a	a	Coda

An arresting irregularity appears almost immediately, in the modulation to the dominant key. In m. 13 a V of V harmony (characteristically in first inversion) duly makes its appearance; but the expected arrival
in A major is delayed until m. 28. The intervening fifteen-odd measures
suspend the listener's expectations of resolution with a great deal of
bustle and activity within an unstable harmony—even a clear statement
of the dominant in root position is withheld until the second half of m.
27. A more fundamental ambiguity comes to light a few measures later.

---

36. Mendelssohn, though he was himself the author of the libretto, refused to perform
   this composition in Leipzig; this precipitated a permanent falling out of the two
   musicians.

When the first part of the binary form ends Mendelssohn pretends to repeat it as one would expect: an abrupt modulation in m. 44 leads from A major back to the tonic and a restatement of the opening music (m. 47). Then at m. 54 the pattern breaks, successive modulations set in, and the listener suddenly discovers that this is in fact the beginning of the second section of the movement. In the metrical disposition of its phrases, too, this movement is much less straightforward than much of Mendelssohn's music. It begins with a three-measure phrase whose rhythmic profile is somewhat obscured by the repetitious turning figure in mm. 2 and 3. When a new phrase on the dominant enters in m. 4, successively shorter rhythmic units are repeated; this blurs the overall metrical pattern, so that even when the phrase turns out to be four measures in length, it does not sound particularly regular. And when motivic repetition in this movement takes the form, as it often does, of imitation between voices, the implications for metrical structure are the same: there is a uniformity and continuity of movement somewhat akin to the "spun-out" phrasing of Baroque instrumental music.

Much of the attractiveness of this Scherzo results from Mendelssohn's felicitous writing for the three instruments, singly and in combination. The fast passages for piano invariably fall easily under the fingers, and the preponderant use of the middle and upper resisters of the instrument makes for clarity and brilliance appropriate to the genre and provides for a very striking contrast in sonority when the lower bass range is used, as in mm. 101 ff. The highly articulated *scherzando* melodic materials of this movement are equally well suited to the violin. Though often consigned to the role of providing harmonic support, the cello adds sharp rhythmic definition to the texture. And when in mm. 57–58 and 61–62 it is assigned the sixteenth-note turning figures, the motive in this piece that seems least appropriate for a bass instrument, Mendelssohn writes it in such a low register that the effect is distinctly comic.

From a modern perspective it is easy to underestimate Mendelssohn's influence in his own century. He was one of Europe's busiest conductors, traveling ceaselessly between the major cities of Germany and England to present his own works and those of his revered predecessors Haydn, Mozart, and Beethoven. Almost equally in demand as a pianist, he was a powerful exponent of the concertos of Mozart and Beethoven—and of Mendelssohn—as an antidote to the fashionable virtuoso keyboard music to be heard on all sides. In another sense Mendelssohn was himself a fashionable musician. Particularly in England, where even Queen Victoria memorized his songs, he was the favorite of a musical culture that placed a high premium on decorum and propriety. His music was thought as impeccably well mannered as the composer himself, strongly rooted in tradition and quite free of the disturbing iconoclasm of, say, Berlioz, and later, Wagner. His settings of Protestant religious texts conveyed a further reassuring sense of stable morality to a society that often found its artists eccentric and troublesome. But these very qualities of amenity and regularity made Mendelssohn's music seem pallid by the end of the century, when the potently expressive musical language of Wagner and the Wagnerians had become the norm. In the later twentieth century, when all the styles of the nineteenth seem historical, there are clear signs of a reawakening interest in the work of this extraordinarily gifted composer.

OTHER CONTEMPORARIES

Two women in the Mendelssohn-Schumann circles in Leipzig and Berlin made a decisive mark on the musical life of the time, attaining a remarkable success in view of European society's general disapprobation of women in professional roles. Clara Schumann (1819–96) was one of the genuinely great pianists and piano teachers of the century. As a very young performer she ran counter to ordinary practice by playing a good bit of Beethoven on her programs, well before Liszt did the same. And in her mature years she was a tireless champion of the works of Schumann and, later, Brahms. Widely acclaimed for technical brilliance at a time when glittering pianism was everywhere to be heard, she was still more admired as a musicianly interpreter of the best in the

Clara Schumann and Joseph Joachim in performance; a print after a chalk drawing by Adolf von Menzel (1854).

piano repertory. Fanny Mendelssohn Hensel (1805–47), Mendelssohn's older sister, early showed a musical talent comparable to that of her brother, and, like him, was provided with instruction in piano and music theory from Berger and Zelter. She was by all accounts a splendid pianist, and her songs and piano pieces, while similar in style to her brother's early music (six songs of hers appeared under his name in the collections of Opp. 8 and 9), show certain individual traits in texture and figuration. The majority of her works, including large-scale cantatas and oratorios, remain unpublished.

A German composer whose fame and influence in the second quarter of the century were second only to Mendelssohn's was Louis Spohr, who ceased his travels in 1822 and settled down to a lifetime tenure as kapellmeister at the court of Kassel. During these years, major works of his were premiered, such as *Jessonda* (1823) and the oratorio *Die letzten Dinge* (1826). As a conductor, he was an early advocate of the music of both Bach and Wagner, and as a violinist he attracted students from all over the world. In his instrumental music from this period he showed a certain experimental streak. He composed four double string quartets and three programmatic symphonies that were very widely performed: No. 4, *Die Weihe der Töne* (Dedication of the Tones, 1832), No. 6, *Historische Sinfonie* (1840), and No. 7, *Irdisches und Göttliches in Menschenleben (The Earthly and Godly in Human Life, 1841)*. In the *Historical Symphony,* successive movements are imitations of "the period of Bach-Handel, of Haydn-Mozart, of Beethoven, and of most recent times." But in all this music, Spohr's own even, sweet-sounding—and largely

Carl Heinrich Arnold's drawing of *A string quartet at Spohr's house.* The composer-violinist is seated at the center of the gathering.

conservative—manner can be plainly heard.

A very different mid-century German composer with conservative leanings was Carl Loewe (1796–1869). A student of theology and music from the area of Halle, Loewe became a church musician in 1820, and shortly afterward municipal music director, in the town of Stettin on the Baltic Sea, where he remained for some forty-five years. Though he wrote five operas and a number of oratorios, his only compositions to win lasting attention are his ballads for voice and piano. As a student he was much attracted to the late-eighteenth-century ballads by Bürger and Stolberg, set to the music of Zumsteeg,[37] and it was upon this rather old-fashioned style that he modeled his own efforts. Loewe's favored poets were Goethe and Herder, and later Johann Ludwig Uhland (1787–1862). He showed a special fondness for the horrific and super-natural elements of the genre. His first published collection (Op. 1, 1823) includes his best-known song, *Edward*. The text, a translation

Example VIII–12: CARL LOEWE, *Edward,* mm. 54–67

from a Scottish source by Herder, is a grisly dialogue between a young man and his mother. The young man has slain his father; he answers his mother's inquiries with a curse, for, as we learn in the final line, it was she who had put him up to it. Loewe sets the fourteen stanzas of this poem in a series of informal sections that move easily between arioso and recitativelike declamation. The piano contributes a good bit of illustrative music; especially dramatic points, such as that in which the son reveals that he has killed his father, are underlined with stormy tremolos.

While this music contains certain harmonic refinements that one would not find in its eighteenth-century models (such as the ambiguity between F♯ and F♮ toward the end of the excerpt above), the style is essentially similar to the ballads of Zumsteeg and to Schubert's early efforts in that genre. Loewe continued to write in this manner for about fifty years; his music, even in his own lifetime, became something of an anachronism. The musical idiom of the dramatic ballad, however, had a clear issue in popular forms of the later nineteenth and early twentieth centuries, for example in the puppet theater and American silent films. In *The Perils of Pauline* we can hear distinct echoes of the terrible Erlkönig and of Edward and his mother.

In 1843 another musician from Halle, Robert Franz (1815—92), published his Opus 1, a collection of Lieder set to texts by various contemporary German poets and (in translation) by Robert Burns. In his *Neue Zeitschrift* Schumann declared enthusiastically that these songs represented a modern, "more artistic and more profound kind of Lied,"[38] and some dozen years later Liszt concurred with this estimation.[39] Schumann found Franz's harmonic style novel, and it is easy to understand that the tonal characteristics of a song such as *Die Lotosblume*,[40] Op. 1, No. 3, would have seemed striking in 1843. It begins quite unambiguously in B♭ major, but modulates almost immediately to establish the poles of G♭ major and E♭ minor as a genuine double tonal center (Example VIII–13, p. 258).

Certain turns of phrase in this song, as in mm. 7–10 of the example, may well sound faintly cloying to modern ears. The progression downward in parallel first-inversion triads moves twice to the measure with great predictability, and in mm. 9–10 the melody falls from the fifth to the third degree in a closing gesture that has since become a cliché of lacrymose popular and religious music. Many of Franz's Lieder carry on traditions of simplicity and *Volkstümlichkeit* long associated with the genre; but their popular features—a decorative, somewhat sentimental-sounding chromaticism within a rhythmic structure of great regularity—are distinctly those of his own generation. And Franz's commit-

---

38. *Neue Zeitschrift für Musik,* 19, (1843): 35.
39. Franz Liszt, *Gesammelte Schriften* (Leipzig, 1882), 9, pp. 221ff.
40. The poem *(The Lotus Flower)* is by Emmanuel Geibel, 1815–84.

Example VIII–13: ROBERT FRANZ, *Die Lotusblume,* Op. 1, No. 3, mm. 1–10

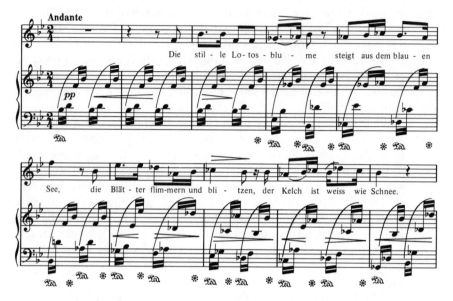

ment to the musical practices of his time led him to prepare many "modernized" editions of the music of J. S. Bach; it is for this unfortunate work that he is now best known.

According to a commonly held view, the political uprisings in a number of German cities at mid-century marked a watershed in the intellectual life of the region. This held true for music in some ways as well.[41] The German musical traditions that looked to Beethoven (and more distantly to Bach) for models and inspiration seemed to have reached something of an impasse. Symphonies and sonatas were no longer very viable genres; the luxuriant flowering of the Lied and of character pieces for piano appeared to have passed its peak. One musical field, however, lay relatively fallow. There had been no very convincing successors to the German operas of Weber; but now, as the tide of nationalism rose ever higher, the most significant developments in German music were to occur in that sector.

41. The life-work of Schumann and Mendelssohn was finished. Spohr lived only until 1859, and the young Brahms was as yet wholly unknown.

CHAPTER IX

Wagner and the Music Drama

After the tumultuous success of *Der Freischütz* (1821), German opera took a provincial turn. New works were for the most part presented at court theaters, and their effect was often only local. Operas such as *Die Felsenmühle zu Estalières* (1831) of Carl Gottlieb Reissiger (1798–1859) and *Der Vampyr* (1828) of P. J. von Lindpaintner (1791–1856) were scarcely known outside the courts of Dresden and Stuttgart, respectively, where their composers were active. Spohr's operas, particularly *Jessonda* (1823), received a somewhat wider hearing, but neither they nor any other dramatic music set to German texts could rival the popularity of the French and Italian imports.

A conspicuous new figure on the German operatic scene in the 1820s and 1830s was Heinrich Marschner (1795–1861), whose two successes at Leipzig with *Der Vampyr* (1828; the libretto is not the same as the one set by Lindpaintner the same year) and *Der Templar und die Jüdin* (1829) gained him a considerable reputation. His *Hans Heiling*, first performed at Berlin in 1833, is often regarded as most significant of the proximate precedessors of the Wagnerian music drama. Like Marschner's other works, it shows many characteristics associated with the German Romantic opera. Here, as in *Der Freischütz*, supernatural forces intrude into the lives of ordinary people, and the action is advanced through spoken text, square-cut Lieder and choruses, portentous melodrama, and, at the beginning of the second act, one full-dress *Szene und Arie* after the Italian manner, sung by the heroine. The stylistic eclecticism suggested by such a mixture is very real in this opera. Yet all of its music shares in the unity conferred by a certain simplicity and popularity of style. Straight diatonic harmonies are disturbed only by the sort of coloristic chromaticism that abounded in amateur music of the time, and long sections (such as the finale to the first act) move with the most regular and unabashedly popular dance rhythms.

Another strain in German opera toward mid-century was a kind of musical comedy that showed a clear patrimony in eighteenth-century German comic opera and in the comedies of Rossini; it appears almost as clearly to prefigure the later operettas of Johann Strauss, Jr., and

Gilbert and Sullivan. Gustav Albert Lortzing (1801–51) provided a model for this genre in his *Zar und Zimmermann* (Leipzig, 1837) with its absurd situations, fast pacing, and rather old-fashioned music.[1] In Berlin Otto Nicolai (1810–49) produced a lasting masterwork in this style in *Die lustigen Weiber von Windsor* (The Merry Wives of Windsor, 1849). Much of its music would be quite at home on the operatic stage of, say, 1790, while its patter-songs seem indebted to works such as *The Barber of Seville*.

A very minor participant in the operatic life of provincial Germany in the later 1830s was the volcanic young composer-conductor who was to bring about a profound revolution in the dramatic music of all Europe, Richard Wagner (1813–83). Born into a theatrical family,[2] the boy Wagner had an early introduction to the German stage in Dresden, where he lived from his childhood until 1828, and in Leipzig, the city of his birth to which he returned in that year. His early interests leaned strongly toward drama and literature, and it was not until he returned to Leipzig that he began formal training in music; for some three years he studied harmony with the composer and conductor Gottlieb Müller and counterpoint with Theodor Weinlig, cantor at the Thomaskirche in Leipzig. His first compositions began to appear in 1829; by 1834 they included two symphonies (one incomplete), four concert overtures, two piano sonatas, and music for several parts of Goethe's *Faust*. During those student days in Leipzig Wagner also embarked on some tentative dramatic projects. One was prophetic of things to come: in 1832 he wrote his own libretto for an opera, *Die Hochzeit* (The Wedding). The music for it was begun the same year, but never completed.

During adolescence Wagner was a voracious reader of musical scores, particularly those of Beethoven. Evidently this self-instruction proved beneficial when, in 1834, he took over the duties of second conductor (and the following year, first conductor) of the opera company in the town of Magdeburg. Though he did his work creditably enough, the opera troupe fell into bankruptcy, and Wagner was forced to move in quick succession to similar positions farther east, first in Königsberg (1836) and then in Riga (1837–39). These moves were also prompted by the insurmountable personal debts that Wagner invariably contracted wherever he went.

As music director in the small theaters in these cities Wagner conducted the standard Italian and French repertory (Rossini, Bellini, Auber, Cherubini) as well as the favorite operas by Weber and Marschner. His

---

1.   Lortzing also made a serious attempt at German Romantic opera in *Undine* (1845); *Der Wildschütz* (1842) is an amalgam of the two types.
2.   Wagner grew up in the home of his mother and stepfather, the actor Ludwig Geyer. His mother's first husband, the police clerk Friedrich Wagner, died soon after his birth, and it is widely thought that Geyer may have been his actual father.

Richard Wagner in a photograph of 1860.

own earliest completed operas, written at this time, were frank imitations of the works he knew. *Die Feen* (1833), like all of Wagner's operas composed to his own libretto, was a German Romantic opera modeled after the later works of Weber. Quite a different impulse underlay *Das Liebesverbot* (The Ban on Love, 1834–35); it derives its subject matter from Shakespeare's *Measure for Measure,* and its music is determinedly imitative of Rossini and Bellini. At this time Wagner showed a powerful but temporary preference for the Italian style. In two essays published in 1834 he sang the praises of Italian vocal writing, singing, and musical characterization, all at the expense of the pedantic and bungling Germans.[3] Most of his later theories about art and music were to be predicated upon an assumed centrality of the German nation, its culture and language; this short burst of Italophilism may serve as a warning that no single statement of his on any issue can be taken as his settled opinion.

In the summer of 1839 Wagner and Minna, his wife of three years, her small daughter, and their large dog left Riga under cover of night to escape his creditors. Their goal was Paris, where Wagner hoped to produce his grand opera in the French style, *Rienzi,* for which the libretto

---

3. *Die deutsche Oper* in *Zeitung für die elegante Welt,* and *Pasticcio* in the newly founded *Neue Zeitschrift für Musik.*

and much of the music were complete. A fearful storm drove their ship into a tiny Norwegian port, suggesting to the composer the idea of a drama about ships and storms at sea; these imaginings were to come to fruition in his next major opera, *The Flying Dutchman*. Prospects in Paris, however, turned out to be miserable. Despite Meyerbeer's provisional endorsement, and meetings with Habeneck, conductor at the Opéra, and its new director Léon Pillet, Wagner was unable to get his works produced at that august institution. He was further humiliated when he sold the libretto of *The Flying Dutchman* for translation and setting by another composer. The proceeds from this transaction, however, bought him the free time to complete his own music to this opera. For the rest, he and his small family kept body and soul together through commercial composing and arranging, and occasional prose essays for the periodical press. Then in the fall of 1842 there was a dramatic reversal of the young composer's fortunes: *Rienzi,* the grand opera planned for Paris, was produced in Dresden, and with such success that Wagner was appointed Hofkapellmeister at the court there.

The following year the Dresden audience heard the premiere of *The Flying Dutchman* under Wagner's direction. This, the first of the composer's works to show something of his growing originality and dramatic power, met with but faint success. Whereas *Rienzi* was a brilliant but mainly derivative work modeled after Spontini, *The Flying Dutchman* was a less imposing but more original German Romantic opera. Its

The final scene of Wagner's *The Flying Dutchman,* as depicted in the *Illustrirte Zeitung* of Leipzig, 1843.

libretto, adapted by Wagner from a story by Heine, *Memoiren des Herrn Schnabelewopski,* tells of a mythical Dutch sea captain condemned to wander eternally in the oceans except for one visit ashore every seven years. Only the true love of a maiden can free him from this odious immortality; this he finds in the heroine Senta, with whom he finally ascends in spirit to the heavens as his ghostly ship sinks to the bottom of the sea. This story provides all the titillation of the supernatural and the charm of local color (in this case supplied by the stormy sea) required of the genre. And it shows the first clear example of a nearly ubiquitous theme in the Wagner operas, redemption through love.

Instead of the hunters' or peasants' music typical of German Romantic opera, *The Flying Dutchman* presents sailors' songs and a chorus of the maidens who attend Senta. Also intentionally naïve in character is Senta's famous ballad in Act II. In his autobiography, Wagner tells us that this was one of the first numbers he composed,[4] and it forms something of a crux for the entire work. As in the purported folk ballads and in those of Schubert or Zumsteeg, the text setting here is mainly syllabic, and the accompaniment is often of a vivid illustrative character. Each strophe falls into two parts; the first, in G minor, tells of the Dutchman's dreary wandering of the oceans and of frightening storms at sea (this is accompanied with rushing chromatic scales in the strings), and the second, in B♭, holds out the promise of his redemption. The ballad is represented as an old song known to Senta and her companions; the story of the entire opera, thus, is seen to grow out of it. And musically too, much of the work is bound up with this piece. The sailors' cry with which it begins, with its distinctive leaps of fourths and fifths (see Example IX–1), is the motive associated throughout the opera with the Dutchman. The chromatic "storm music" accompanies other references to storms, and the "redemption" theme occurs at the very end—juxtaposed with the "Dutchman" motive—when the he is released from his bondage. The elaborate use of motivic reference to characters, objects, events, and ideas that Wagner develops later is seen here in embryo.

Example IX–1: WAGNER, *The Flying Dutchman,* Act II, Senta's Ballad, mm. 11–15

4.   Richard Wagner, *My Life,* ed. Mary Whittall, trans. Andrew Grey (New York: Cambridge University Press, 1983) p. 201. This highly readable document, while often tendentious and misleading, reveals much of the flavor and texture of the composer's tumultuous life.

In other ways, too, *The Flying Dutchman* shows significant innovations. The distinction between recitative and arioso is often blurred—
very much more so than in a typical *scena* of Bellini or Donizetti—and,
though this is ostensibly a "number opera," the music is sometimes
perfectly continuous between numbers. Harmonically the opera clearly
belongs to Wagner's early career: its predominantly diatonic syntax is
disturbed by little other than patches of diminished-seventh sonorities
in moments of high emotional or meteorological agitation.

During his tenure as conductor at Dresden (1843–49) Wagner composed two more operas, *Tannhäuser* (1845) and *Lohengrin* (1848). The
poem of *Tannhäuser und der Sängerkrieg auf Wartburg* (Tannhäuser and
the Song Contest at Wartburg) recounts the medieval legend of the
Christian knight who is torn between the carnal delights offered by
Venus, Goddess of Love, and the pure and ultimately redeeming love
of the saintly Elizabeth.[5] Wagner designated this work a "Romantic
opera." Though its medieval theme, its setting in the picturesque German countryside, and its *Männerchor*-like Pilgrim's Chorus fit that genre,
it also has the éclat and pageantry of grand opera, as in the opening
scene in the Venusberg (added for Paris in 1861) and in the courtly
procession in the second act. The solo singing, ensembles, and choruses
usual in both varieties of opera are all there, but the lines of demarcation
between them are further obscured to produce a new fluidity of events
and music.

The proportion of clearly identifiable recitative is much smaller in
Tannhäuser than in *The Flying Dutchman*. In its place there is a good bit

Example IX–2: WAGNER, *Tannhäuser,* Act I, Pilgrims' Chorus, mm. 16–
24

Ach, schwer drückt mich der Sün - den Last, kann län - ger

sie nicht mehr er - tra - gen:

---

5.   The song contest added by Wagner in the second act derives from an unrelated
      medieval source.

of flexible arioso singing in which the orchestra assumes a heightened importance. And in the third act, where Tannhäuser tells of his pilgrimage to Rome and his intention to return to the Venusberg, Wagner creates an intensely dramatic style of declamation enlivened by significant orchestral motives, notably the magical shimmering of the Venusberg music from the first act. Also pressed into the service of dramatic expression is Wagner's expanding harmonic technique. In the Pilgrims' Chorus in the first act, for example, at the words, "O, the burden of sin oppresses me sorely, I can no longer bear it"—just the sort of text that had always elicited chromatic motion—Wagner provides a foretaste of his own famous chromatic polyphony (Example IX–2). Here and elsewhere in *Tannhäuser* we are aware of a palpable strengthening of the composer's powers of musical characterization; situations and persons, even secondary figures such as the Landgrave and Wolfram, begin to have their own distinctive melodies and textures in this work.

The final scene of *Tannhäuser* as shown in the *Illustrirte Zeitung* of Leipzig, 1853.

Title page of *Lohengrin,* published at Weimar in 1850.

Similar in several respects to *Tannhäuser* is the other opera of the Dresden period, *Lohengrin.* Also named a "Romantic opera," this work again combines characteristics of that genre with those of grand opera. Its story presents a subtle mixture of medieval legend and history, rife with symbolism: Lohengrin, son of Parsifal and a guardian of the Holy Grail,[6] intervenes in the tangled affairs of the German king Henry the Fowler (c. 876–936) and of the nobility of Brabant. He weds Elsa and then forsakes her to return to his own realm because her mortal love proves insufficient. The clear movement toward musical continuity in *Tannhäuser* is carried further here. Except for certain set pieces such as the familiar Bridal Chorus in Act III, the music moves from event to event in an almost unbroken progression, dominated by melodious and dramatic declamation with very full participation of the orchestra. And Wagner's vocal writing in *Lohengrin* shows some advances in refinement; awkward passages for the singers, such as the song in praise of Venus at the beginning of *Tannhäuser,* are much less in evidence.

6. Wagner's version of the legendary material is taken mainly from *Parzival* of Wolfram von Eschenbach, the real poet of the late twelfth century who appears in fictionalized form in *Tannhäuser;* in his final opera, *Parsifal,* Wagner returns to the Grail legend. The principal source for the historical events in *Lohengrin* is Jakob Grimm's *Deutsche Rechtsaltertümer* (Antiquities of German Law).

Wagner's association of distinctive musical motives with particular elements of the drama is extended in *Lohengrin*. The major characters Lohengrin, Elsa, and Ortrud all have their identifying music. Events and ideas are given similar musical referents. Lohengrin's injunction that Elsa shall never inquire as to his name or origin—the better to demonstrate her unconditional love for him—is associated with the motive shown in Example IX–3. The very regular metrical construction of this melody (2 + 2 + 4 measures) points to Wagner's continuing predilection for periodized phrases; much of the music of *Lohengrin* is rhythmically symmetrical, often even falling into traditional patterns of antecedent and consequent phrases and showing a strong preference for duple meter. Harmonically, too, this music is conservative as seen against the emerging backdrop of Wagner's development as a composer; traditional diatonic procedures and clearly established tonal areas predominate strongly.

Example IX–3: WAGNER, *Lohengrin,* "Frageverbot," mm. 1–8

A major innovation in *Lohengrin* is the substitution of a homogeneous prelude leading into the drama for the usual overture that presents a kind of musical synopsis of it. This prelude has a dramatic significance that is revealed only in the third act when its music accompanies Lohengrin's narration about his origins: its otherworldly shimmering tremolos and slow-moving harmonies refer to the land of the Holy Grail, the Templars who guard it, and the dove who descends each year to renew its miraculous powers. Another prelude introduces the third act; this brilliant orchestral piece, often performed independently, is now one of Wagner's most familiar compositions. The power and prominence of the orchestra's music in *Lohengrin,* when it plays alone and when it acts as an equal partner with singers, is symptomatic of the direction in which Wagner's art is moving: toward a unification of forces and a homogeneity of texture designed to serve new dramatic ends that were just now taking shape in his mind.

The premiere performance of *Lohengrin* was scheduled at the Dresden court theater for the autumn of 1849, but this was not to be: the score was finished amidst the rumblings of revolution, and when the Dresden revolt broke in full force in May of that year, the court conductor Wagner, already much irritated by friction with his superiors, took to the barricades. In any case the opera theater went up in flames, and when the insurrection was defeated, Wagner was forced to flee from the authorities. With the aid of Liszt in Weimar he made his way to Zurich and then to Paris, beginning a period of forced exile from the German states that lasted until 1862. From 1849 to 1853, deprived of any base of operations, Wagner composed next to nothing. During this time he wrote the poems for his epic cycle *The Ring of the Nibelung,* as well as a series of essays in which he expounded his rapidly evolving theories about society, politics, art, and music. Most significant of these are *Art and Revolution, The Artwork of the Future* (both 1849), and *Opera and Drama* (1850–51).

These were Wagner's years of iconoclasm and revolutionary fervor. During the uprising in Dresden he had fallen under the spell of the Russian anarchist Michael Bakunin, whose plans for destroying the existing social and political systems struck a responsive chord in the frustrated composer—perhaps, he imagined, once society was dismantled it could be reconstructed along lines more favorable to his own artistic aims. In *Art and Revolution* Wagner set forth a fanciful view of history in which the ancient Greek tragedy, the communal, all-embracing art of a free and robust society, was destroyed during succeeding epochs; only its feeble constituent parts survived in modern drama, music, the dance, painting, etc. Nothing short of revolution, he cried, could restore art to its true unity and efficacy:

> Each of these single arts, abundantly nourished and tended for the pleasure and entertainment of the wealthy, has now richly filled the world with its products. Great spirits have achieved delightful results in them. But genuinely effective art has not yet been born again, either during or since the Renaissance. For the perfected artwork, the great single expression of a free and beautiful public life, the *drama,* the *tragedy*—though great poets have here and there composed tragedies—is not yet born again, for the reason that it must not be *born again,* but *born anew.*
>
> Only the great *Revolution of Mankind,* whose beginnings once shattered Grecian Tragedy, can also win for us this artwork.[7]

The Artwork of the Future presents a much fuller airing of Wagner's thoughts on these expansive subjects. He gives a kind of psychology of art in which the three "purely human arts"—dance (or more broadly, "gesture"), tone, and poetry—address themselves respectively to the faculties of vision, hearing, and intellect. Just as these human faculties realize their full potential when they act together, so do the three sorts of art to which they correspond. This could be seen to come to pass in musical history, he claimed, when Beethoven added text and singing

7.   Richard Wagner, *Gesammelte Schriften und Dichtungen,* ed. W. Golther (Berlin, Leipzig, c. 1926), 3, p. 29.

to the finale of his Ninth Symphony, thus taking a decisive step toward the "great universal artwork of the future."[8] But it is not only the three "purely human arts" that will join forces to produce the desired result; the plastic arts as well—architecture, sculpture, and painting—must be pressed into service to produce the universal artwork, as well as to realize (or regain) their own full potential. What it is, precisely, that the plastic arts are expected to contribute to the artwork of the future is not entirely easy to extract from Wagner's verdant prose. But it seems no more complicated than that they are to provide the theater and the stage design. The function and future of sculpture, for example, he describes this way:

> Only when sculpture no longer exists, or when it has taken a direction other than that of [representing] the human body, as sculpture ascending into architecture, when the rigid loneliness of this stone-hewn person shall have been released into the endlessly streaming multiplicity of actual living people . . . when we out of this stone erect for ourselves the edifice that shall contain the living artwork, no longer needing therein to represent to ourselves the living human [form], only then shall we have before us genuine plastic art.[9]

Wagner's mind during this period was a welter of confused ideas drawn from diverse and incongruent sources. A Rousseau-like primitivism led him to decry the corrosive effects of civilization and exalt the natural, unspoiled man, who merges easily into that most elusive product of the Romantic imagination, the Folk:

> Not you, the intelligentsia, therefore, are truly inventive, but the Folk, for it was need that drove them to invention. All great inventions are the deeds of the Folk, as opposed to the exploitations and perversions, indeed the splintering and mangling by the intelligentsia of the great inventions of the Folk. You did not invent *speech,* but the Folk; you have only spoiled its sensuous beauty, broken its force, and lost its inner coherence—that can

8. *Das grosse, allgemeine Kunstwerk der Zukunft,* in *Gesammelte Schriften und Dichtungen,* 3, p. 63. A commonly used word for Wagner's notion of the universal artwork is *Gesamtkunstwerk.* Some have recently dismissed the notion of the *Gesamtkunstwerk* as a later distortion of his thought. Thus Curt von Westernhagen points out that the term occurs, apparently only once in Wagner's writings, in *The Artwork of the Future* (*Gesammelte Schriften und Dichtungen,* 3, p. 156). Curt von Westernhagen, *Wagner: a Biography,* trans. Mary Whittall (Cambridge, 1976), 1, p. 146. But Wagner's use of that word is surely no issue. In the surrounding passages in "The Artwork of the Future" alone, the very similar term "gemeinsames Kunstwerk" (collective artwork) abounds; another term Wagner uses is "künstlerisches Gesammtwerk" (artistic collective work). In general, Wagner stood by the opinions and predictions in the essays of 1848–51. Some twenty years later he republished them in his *Gesammelte Schriften und Dichtungen* under prefatory remarks that offer some explanations about his earlier dependence upon Ludwig Feuerbach and repudiate any kinship with the "communism" of the Parisian communes; the substance of these writings, however, is untouched. *Gesammelte Schriften und Dichtungen,* 3, pp. 1–7.

9. *Gesammelte Schriften und Dichtungen,* 3, p. 140.

now only be laboriously searched out again. Not you are the inventors of
religion, but the Folk. . . . Not you are the inventors of the *state,* but the
Folk; from the natural bond of those with a common need you have made
an unnatural forced unity of those without common need, from a benevolent common defensive pact a malevolent means of protecting the privileged.[10]

Under the spell of revolutionary political sentiment he advocated overthrow of the state for the sake of art, and castigated all materialism and
privilege as the chief opponents of art and the Folk. But at the same
time, under the influence of the atheist philosopher Ludwig Feuerbach
(1804–72),[11] he singled out the Christian religion as the real enemy, the
force mainly responsible for the present degradation of art and the
enslavement of man. And only shortly thereafter, in his scurrilous essay
Judaism in Music (1850), the villain is Jewish control of the arts.

In the essays of 1849–51, Wagner was very much influenced by
determinist historical views, stemming from Hegel and disseminated
by Hegel's followers, such as Feuerbach. From this group emanated
confident predictions about the "religion of the future," the "philosophy of the future, " the "state of the future," and the like. Seen in this
setting Wagner's formulations appear somewhat less eccentric. But most
powerful and consistent of the factors affecting Wagner's theories always
seemed to be his own personal concerns of the moment: society and its
institutions are corrupt because they do not further his current aims;
material goods and luxury are the bane of mankind because he is now
destitute; the influence of Jewish musicians is deplorable because, still
largely unappreciated himself, he cannot bear the successes of Meyerbeer and Mendelssohn; the individual arts can be cheerfully dispensed
with because his own attention is riveted upon the music drama. His
thought was governed by a near-perfect solipsism: his cares were the
world's problems, and society at large should bend all its efforts for
their solution.

In the book-length *Opera and Drama* Wagner serves up more tendentious history and tedious bombast about the insufficiencies of the modern arts and about their imagined future. But this essay also presents
rather specific prescriptions for the music drama that prefigure in a
remarkable way Wagner's own future practice. This new genre will
differ fundamentally from all contemporary opera, he claims, for opera
contains the fatal flaw "that a means of expression (music) has been
made the end, while the end of expression (the drama) has been made a

10.   Ibid., 3, p. 53.
11.   Feuerbach's principal work, well known to Wagner, was *Das Wesen des Christentums*
      (The Nature of Christianity), 1841. *The Artwork of the Future* was dedicated to
      Feuerbach.

means."[12] The constituent arts—poetry, music, and dance (or "gesture")—and to a lesser extent the subsidiary plastic arts, are all to operate equally as means to a central end, the living, visible drama. And the subject of this drama, he determines, must be myth rather than, say, history—evidently because mythology enjoys the great advantage of having its origins among the Folk.

Wagner rejects the various species of modern poetry with their meters and end rhymes in favor of a free verse organized according to *Stabreim* ("stem rhyme"), by which he means both assonance and alliteration occurring between "root syllables"—a procedure validated by his current beliefs about the origins of speech. As an example of verse with *Strabreim* he gives the following:

Die Liebe bringt Lust und Leid	Love brings delight and pain,
Doch in ihr Weh auch webt sie Wonnen	But into its sadness it also weaves rapture

A musical setting, he explains, should emphasize both the connectedness of the stem-rhymed words *Lust* and *Leid* ("delight" and "pain"), as well as their opposed emotional force, by involving them in a process of modulation in which the new key is reached at the word *Leid*. The second line would be delivered in the new key, until at the word *webt* ("weaves") a modulation begins that leads back to the original key at *Wonnen* ("rapture"). Thus both the contrast between the two emotions implied by the text, and their essential unity (both having their origins in "love") are reinforced by musical means.[13]

The best-known feature of Wagner's later works is their use of the so-called leitmotif (leading motive), a device that had already made fitful appearances in the operas of Cherubini and Spohr, among others. It was first named and codified in relation to Wagner's works by the master's younger friend and disciple Hans von Wolzogen.[14] With the full deployment of the leitmotif, events, persons, objects, and ideas in the drama are signaled by specific musical motives, so that there emerges an elaborate system of musical reference reinforcing and complementing the dramatic text. Wagner's own anticipatory description of this practice in *Opera and Drama* is much more limited than what later commentators were to make of it. He does describe the "reminiscence," i.e.

---

12. *Gesammelte Schriften und Dichtungen*, 3, p. 231. This, Wagner's principal complaint about the genre, sounds much like those of earlier opera reformers such as Gluck and Francesco Algarotti. See O. Strunk, ed. *Source Readings in Music History* (New York, 1950), pp. 657–86.

13. *Gesammelte Schriften und Dichtungen*, 4, pp. 152–55.

14. In *Thematischer Leitfaden durch die Musik von Richard Wagner's Festspiel "Der Ring des Nibelungen"* (Leipzig, 1876) and other works.

the appearance in the orchestra of a motive that recalls an earlier event or emotion, thus revealing unspoken thoughts of the actor. And on rare occasions he attaches specific dramatic referents to specific motives.[15] More frequently he seems to say that his musical motives are positioned simply to provide, in a traditional fashion, unity of design. In a later essay, *Über die Anwendung der Musik auf das Drama* (On the Use of Music in Drama, 1879), he specifically compared his use of motives to those in a movement of a symphony, with the exception that "here the progress and playing out of the dramatic action provide the basis for separations and connections."[16] That the musical signification of the "reminiscence" should ordinarily occur in the orchestra is important in theory and practice alike: "Here," Wagner exults, "the musician's power, when employed for the highest realization of the poetic aim, is, by means of the orchestra, made boundless."[17] But that other accountrement of opera, the chorus, as normally employed "will only confuse us: none but clearly distinguishable individualities can engage our sympathies."[18]

THE RING OF THE NIBELUNG

Much of the theory of dramatic poetry expounded in *Opera and Drama* was related to Wagner's struggle, at that time, with the beginnings of a new dramatic project which was to result in his monumental cycle *The Ring of the Nibelung* about a quarter-century later. As early as 1848, while yet in Dresden, Wagner had made a sketch for a drama based on his extensive reading of Germanic myth in the *Nibelungenlied* and the *Edda*.[19] And by the end of the year a poem for an opera treating the final portion of that complex of legend had emerged under the title *Siegfried's Death*. Later, living in exile in Zurich, he felt that an understanding of the saga demanded some knowledge of its earlier events; accordingly he wrote a prefatory poem, *The Young Siegfried* (1852), and by a similar process produced yet two more librettos, *Die Walküre* and *Das Rheingold* (both 1852). Then *Siegfried's Death* and *The Young Siegfried* were revised and renamed, respectively, *Götterdämmerung* (Twi-

---

15.   See John Deathridge in *19th-Century Music,* 5 (1981): 84.
16.   *Gesammelte Schriften und Dichtungen,* 10, p. 185.
17.   Ibid., 4, p. 84.
18.   *Ibid.,* 5, p. 162.
19.   These two bodies of literature represent, respectively, the German and Icelandic versions of a common fund of northern European legend. According to responsible opinion this network of tales has an ultimate historical basis centering about the overthrow of the kingdom of Burgundy by the Huns in the fifth century— a conclusion that probably would not have appealed to Wagner's German nationalist sentiments.

light of the Gods) and *Siegfried*. By 1853 this giant literary project was finished, and the four librettos were printed privately. Almost immediately, after over five years in which he wrote next to no music, Wagner plunged into the setting of these texts to music. Working forwards this time, he finished the scoring of *Das Rheingold* by May, 1854, and the music of *Die Walküre* was nearly complete by the end of that year. A season as conductor of the Orchestra of the Philharmonic Society in London in 1855 hardly slowed his pace:[20] by April of 1856 *Die Walküre* was completely scored, and a little over a year later he had finished the music, except for the orchestration, through the second act of *Siegfried*. At this point, discouraged about the prospect of ever seeing his huge tetralogy performed or published, he abandoned work on it for a dozen years. It was not until 1874 that he put the finishing touches on *Götterdämmerung*.

The *Ring of the Nibelung* is an involved tale of the doings of Germanic gods, demigods, giants, dwarfs, and other creatures more difficult to classify. Almost all are greedy for the gold controlled by the dwarfish race of the Nibelungs, and particularly for the ring fashioned from it by Alberich, the Nibelung referred to in the title. Desirous of the ring, but fearful of its curse, the god Wotan begets a pair of twins, Siegmund and Sieglinde. The son of their incestuous love, Siegfried, is destined to retrieve the ring from the giant Fafner, who has taken on the form of a dragon. Siegfried succeeds, and also wins the love of the Valkyrie Brünnhilde, the favorite daughter of Wotan (she is the *Walküre* of the second drama of the cycle). Possession of the ring, however, proves fatal: Siegfried is finally slain by Hagen, son of Alberich. Brünnhilde joins him on the flaming funeral pyre; those two, the gods, and their home Valhalla are all consumed in a general conflagration, and the ring is returned to the Rhinemaidens, its rightful owners.

The music of the entire *Ring,* like the dramatic action, is conceived as a unified whole. Musical motives are used consistently from beginning to end, and—particularly in view of the twenty-year span over which the work was composed—its style is astonishingly uniform. In *Das Rheingold,* especially, occasional skeletal outlines of recitative and arioso persist; but vocal writing in *The Ring* as a whole is dominated by a style of declamation that moves easily between two poles: rhythmically regular melody and a kind of disjunct vocal counterpoint to the music in the orchestra. The orchestral part is powerful, flexible, vividly expressive, and coherent in its own right. And in this, Wagner's mature style, his famous chromatic idiom operates within a harmonic framework that, however intricate, remains solidly tonal.

In the final portion of Act III of *Die Walküre* (ARM 18), often known as Wotan's Farewell, the God Wotan visits punishment upon his daugh-

---

20. This visit brought Wagner into frequent contact with Berlioz, who that season conducted the competitive New Philharmonic Society Orchestra of London.

"Wotan's Farewell" from *Die Walküre* in a recent Bayreuth production.

ter, the Valkyrie Brünnhilde. He had ordered her to intervene in the combat of Siegmund (father of the hero Siegfried) and Hunding (husband of Sieglinde, Siegmund's beloved—as well as his sister) on behalf of Hunding. Instead, she had protected Siegmund, and now Wotan proceeds to divest her of her godly status and puts her into a deep sleep. He conjures up about her a circle of magic flame which can be penetrated only by the true hero who will come to rescue her (this, of course, is to be Siegfried). After his opening farewells Wotan sings the following lines (mm. 536ff.):

Muss ich dich meiden	If I must leave you
und darf nicht minnig	and never more lovingly
mein Gruss mehr dich grüssen;	extend you my greeting;
sollst du nun nicht mehr	if you shall no more
neben mir reiten,	ride with me,
noch Met beim Mahl mir reichen;	or give my mead at the table;
muss ich verlieren,	if I must lose
dich, die ich liebte,	you, whom I loved,
du lachende Lust meines Auges:	the laughing delight of my eye:
ein bräutliches Feuer	then a bridal fire
soll dir nun brennen	shall now burn for you
wie nie einer Braut es gebrannt!	such as never yet burned for a bride!
Flammende Gluth	Flaming fire
umglühe den Fels;	shall glimmer around the rock;
mit zehrenden Schrecken	with devouring fear
scheuch es den Zagen;	it shall terrify the timorous;
der Feige fliehe	the coward shall flee
Brünnhilde's Fels!	Brünnhilde's rock!
Denn einer nur freie die Braut,	For only one shall free the bride,
der freier als ich, der Gott!	one freer than I, the God!

Such a mixture of very short lines with slightly longer ones is characteristic of Wagner's verse. This poetry, intentionally archaic in flavor, frequently has two or three strong accents per line and is loosely organized by means of *Stabreim* ("dich meiden—darf minnig," "Met beim Mahl," "lachende Lust," etc.). Wagner gives this text a musical setting that is almost entirely syllabic and that places textual accents with great consistency on strong beats (in the first lines, these occur on "Muss," "mei[den]," "darf," "min[nig]," "Gruss," and "grüs[sen]").

Short poetic lines serve Wagner's purposes well. Their lengths are directly coordinated with the phrases of the vocal part, so that single lines can comprise very brief exclamations ("Flammende Gluth," and "umglühe den Fels," for example), or combine, usually in pairs, to produce longer phrases. Sometimes the phrases fall into symmetrical patterns. Beginning with "Muss ich dich meiden" a very regular and common type of melodic sequence is made up of two sets of two phrases, each set comprising 2 + 4 measures. This arrangement follows the clear parallelism of syntax and meaning in the three-line groups "Muss ich . . ." and "sollst du." Beginning with "muss ich verlieren," there follows another symmetrical sequence of 2 + 2 + 4 measures. And even the fragmented melody starting from "Flammende Gluth" has a strongly sequential character, for the initial one-measure phrases form pairs, and the following three-measure ones all have the same shape. Wagner's vocal melodies are often thought to be flexible almost to the point of amorphousness. Many, as here, are in fact meticulous as to declamation and rich in underlying symmetries that accord with both poetic form and significance.

The harmonies of this passage, though they often steer a tortuous modulatory course, play a vital role in establishing its symmetries. "Muss ich dich meiden," for example, begins in F♯ minor, tilts immediately toward C♯ minor, and in the course of the first set of two phrases (2 + 4) modulates through E to the dominant of G at "grüssen." The corresponding set of two phrases starting at "sollst du nun nicht mehr" then begins in G minor and pursues a parallel harmonic course, a half step above the first pair, through F to the dominant of A♭ at "reichen." What follows is another three-line group set as three phrases (2 + 2 + 4). Here, however, there is a clearer harmonic goal: a rising bass line drives toward the emphatic dominant of E major in preparation for the "bridal fire" and its characteristic music in that key.

Wagner's mature harmonic style is often described, with some ambiguity, as chromatic. Seldom, however, does his music show much of the chromatic inflection and decoration of a traditional diatonic structure such as that common in piano music of the 1830s and 1840s (and often in the music of Chopin). Nor does it eschew the ordinary syntax of diatonic harmony. Rather, on both a local and long-range level, it expands upon the usual relationships of tonal harmony. An instructive example is the sixteen-measure passage in Wotan's Farewell (ARM, pp. 359–60) from "Wenn Kampfeslust" to "Letztem Kuss." Beginning and

Example IX–4: WAGNER, *Die Walküre,* Act III, Wotan's Farewell,
harmonic reduction

ending in E, this music thoroughly explores some of the possible relationships of that key, as can be seen in Example IX–4.

Starting in E minor, this passage moves directly into G, its relative
major, and then, after a fleeting reference back to E minor, to C, the
subdominant of G. A tonally unstable passage centering around A minor
(relative minor of C) completes this exploration of the "natural" keys
in the orbit of E minor. Then, at "webendem Bangen," a plunge in the
sharp direction brings a series of harmonies pointing toward B minor,
which in the major mode becomes the dominant leading back to E. But
before the final cadence is reached, another brief excursion brings sonorities based on C and F that we heard before in a very similar configuration in the C-major section. Now they have the effect of digressive
Neapolitan sounds in B minor and E major, and they seem an encap-
sulated reference to that earlier, more extended tour of the keys related
to E minor on the "natural" side. Such an insertion of parenthetical
sonorities before a cadence is only one method Wagner employs to avoid
or delay an arrival at the tonic. Another is simply a determined evasion
of the expected movement from dominant to tonic. In the C-major
section two elaborate progressions lead to the dominant and no further,
and the final passage in B and E presents a series of dominants that find
no resolution until the very end.

The key of E, which dominates the passage just discussed, is the principal one in the second half of Act III and the key in which the entire work ends. The persistent return to this tonal home base can be seen in this diagram of the whole of Wotan's Farewell:

Measure:	518	536	555
Text:	"Leb' wohl"	"Muss ich dich meiden"	"Ein bräutliches Feuer"
Key:	D〜〜〜〜〜	f#〜〜〜〜〜	E〜〜〜〜〜
Motive:	Brünnhilde's slumber		Fire, Siegfried

Measure:	573	577	602
Text:	"Denn Einer nur"	[Orchestral]	"Der Augen"
Key:	e, E	E	c, e〜〜〜E
Motive:	Siegfried	Brünnhilde's justification	Brünnhilde's slumber

Measure:	631	638	672
Text:	"Denn so Kehrt"	[Orchestral]	"Loge hör"
Key:	e, c	(A♭)〜〜〜E〜〜〜E	〜〜〜g〜〜〜
Motive:		Magic sleep, Brünnhilde's slumber	Compact, Fire

Measure:	691	714	721
Text:	[Orchestral]	"Wer meines"	[Orchestral]
Key:	E〜〜〜E	〜〜〜E	E〜〜〜E
Motive:	Fire	Brünnhilde's slumber, Siegfried	Brünnhilde's slumber

As the opera nears its end the magnetic attraction to the key of E becomes ever stronger. And in the motion from D major of the previous section to this key there is a reflection in miniature of the tonal movement of the entire work from D to E.

The musical motives mentioned in the diagram are the celebrated leitmotifs of the *Ring*, designated by their customary names. Sometimes they refer to dramatic events in the most obvious possible way (Debussy once contemptuously called them "calling cards"): when Wotan speaks of the "bridal fire" the orchestra plays music associated with fire and with Loge, the god of fire in *Das Rheingold* (Example IX–5a). At other times the reference is more subtle. "For only one shall free the bride" is accompanied by a motive that signifies Siegfried, who has not yet been born (Example IX–5b). The exultant music called "Brünnhilde's justification" (Example IX–5c) follows Wotan's reference to "one [i.e. Siegfried] freer than I, the God!" This motive had occurred earlier when Brünnhilde spoke of Wotan's actual desire as to the outcome of the Siegmund-Hunding duel (he had been forced to favor Hunding by Fricka his wife). Now this music reappears as Wotan contemplates the ultimate fulfillment of his will through Siegmund's son Siegfried.

Example IX–5: Motives from *Die Walküre*
   a: Fire

b. Siegfried

c. Brünnhilde's Justification

d. Brünnhilde's Slumber

e. Magic Sleep

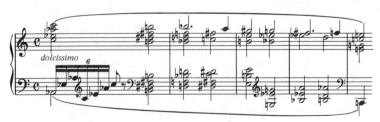

f. Compact[21]

But the referential function of these motives is often overemphasized, as if their detection and labeling alone provide a useful account of Wagner's musical drama. They are the very stuff of his music, and they are subject to the sort of development, transformation, and combination that one expects in large-scale instrumental compositions. The music to Wotan's final words, "Wer meines Speeres Spitze fürchtet durchschreite das Feuer nie!" ("He who fears the point of my spear shall never cross the fire!") provides an example. Wotan sings these words to a single statement of the "Siegfried" motive in augmentation while the fast, even-note motion of the fire music is played above. At the same time repetitions of "Brünnhilde's slumber" pursue a serpentine modulatory course dictated by the harmonic requirements of the "Siegfried" theme. Such an elaborate working-out of musical materials stands solidly in the German traditions of Bach and Beethoven to which Wagner fell heir.

The orchestra Wagner demanded for this work is a very large one. In addition to the usual strings it includes six harps; the normal woodwinds (in threes) are augmented by the English horn and the bass clarinet (an instrument much favored by Wagner). The giant brass ensemble requires eight French horns, four tubas (tenor and bass) modified to Wagner's specifications, four trumpets, a bass trumpet, three trombones, a contrabass trombone, and one contrabass tuba. Among the percussion instruments are a tenor drum, a tantam (or gong), cymbals, triangle, and glockenspiel. Wagner's infinitely inventive and flexible management of this expanded ensemble, producing effects ranging from overpowering brilliance to the most fragile and delicately colored orchestral commentary, though in some particulars indebted to Berlioz and Meyerbeer, was in his time a unique achievement.

Example IX–6 shows in full score the ending to Wotan's Farewell that was just discussed. The vocal line is powerfully reinforced through approximate doublings by four horns and the bass trumpet.[22] In a sense,

21. The compact refers to an agreement made in *Das Rheingold* whereby Freia, goddess of youth, is given to the giants in exchange for their having built the mansion of Valhalla for the Gods. This agreement is engraved on Wotan's spear; the motive appears in Wotan's Farewell as he points his spear at a large rock to summon fire.

22. This instrument, now largely obsolete, is often replaced in modern performances with the similar valved trombone. Mixing such an instrument with the horns provides a sharpness of attack that the horns themselves lack.

however, it is the *vocal* part that does the doubling. The horns and bass trumpet present the "Siegfried" motive exactly (in augmentation), while Wotan sings but an approximation of it: the anacrusis has been lengthened to accommodate Wagner's text, and rests have replaced some notes to allow the singer to breathe—at one point ("Speeres Spitze fürchet") to the clear detriment of melodic continuity. Changing combinations of flutes, oboes, and clarinets with reinforcement at points by the English horn, meanwhile, play the repetitions of "Brünnhilde's slumber" with continual minute shifts in tone color. Two sorts of motion comprise the "fire" music: the even sixteenths in the harps and the thirty-second-note filigree in the divided violins. Embedded in the first violin part is an outline of the "slumber" motive that coincides with the melody above in the woodwinds. And a more telling doubling of that melody occurs alternately in the two harps as they define its contours with sharp, metallic points of sound.

Those adjustments Wagner apparently thought necessary in the assigning of a significative motive to the vocal part are symptomatic of the immense importance of the orchestra in his works. Musical continuity and his famous "endless melody," like the enunciation and development of motives, are more often than not the business of orchestral instruments; the singers become no more than equal participants in creating the complex polyphonic fabric of his music. With a great burst of metaphor Wagner compared his ideal musical texture with the sounds a solitary visitor hears in the forest on a summer's evening:

> Thus he perceives ever more clearly the endless diversity of voices awakened in the forest; new and different voices, ones he believes he has not heard before, are continually added. As they grow in number their special strength increases; the sound rings louder and louder. And however numerous the voices and their individual melodies that he hears, the tones, though grown overwhelmingly brilliant, seem to him again but one great forest-melody. . . . This melody will eternally echo in him. But he cannot hum it; to hear it whole again, he must return to the woods, and on a summer evening.[23]

23. *Zukunftsmusik* (Music of the Future), in *Gesammelte Schriften und Dichtungen,* 7, p. 131.

Example IX–6: WAGNER, *Die Walküre,* Act III, from Wotan's Farewell,
Mm. 1032–41

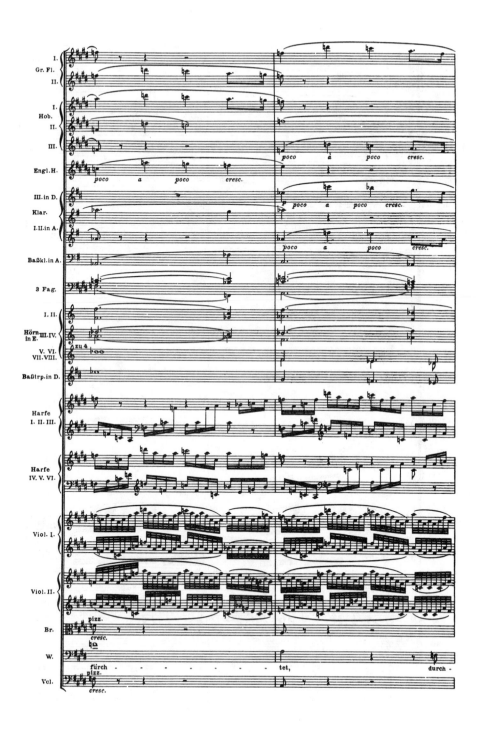

TRISTAN UND ISOLDE

In 1857, the year in which he broke off work on *The Ring,* Wagner set himself a new operatic project. For its subject he delved once again into medieval myth, into the same web of Arthurian legend, in fact, that had supplied the story of *Lohengrin* and that was to reappear in *Parsifal.* This was the tale of Tristan and Isolde, those victims of circumstance and fate whose love was as perfect as it was hopeless. Drawing mainly from the early thirteenth-century epic *Tristan* by Gottfried von Strassburg, Wagner selected from the many episodes of this story only three central elements that were to comprise the three acts of his work. First, Tristan, nephew of King Mark of Cornwall, returns from Ireland with Isolde, the Irish princess he has secured as wife for his uncle. On board ship they accidentally drink a love potion that confirms the emotion growing between them. Then, as queen of Cornwall, Isolde is surprised in a nocturnal meeting with Tristan, who is mortally wounded by a courtier of King Mark. Finally, having returned to his own ancestral home in Brittany, Tristan dies just before Isolde arrives to care for him. King Mark has declared his forgiveness and his intention to unite the two lovers; but it is too late, and Isolde in an ecstatic delirium sinks upon Tristan's body, joining him in death.

In Wagner's hands this concentrated narrative becomes an intensely psychological drama. Action in any traditional sense is severely limited, though when it does occur, as, for example, when King Mark and his followers discover the lovers in the second act, its force seems all the greater. For the most part the subject at hand is the states of mind of the two principal characters, who seem to live in a world of feeling all their own. Wagner at first intended this as a drama of modest proportions, something much more manageable for the contemporary European stage than the gigantic *Ring.*[24] But as composition of the work progressed in 1857 and 1858 it expanded to immense proportions, and what resulted was perhaps the most difficult and taxing—and, for some, the most profound—of all musical dramas. It is often said that outside circumstances contributed to the *furor poeticus* that held Wagner in its grip: the earlier work on *Tristan* coincided with his celebrated love affair with Mathilde Wesendonck (wife of his benefactor in Zurich, Otto Wesendonck, who at the time provided most of the composer's material support). But whatever importance such connections between art and life may have had for the creation of *Tristan,* they hardly seem to have been its sustaining force. The major portion of the work was composed in 1858–59, after the affair with Mathilde had come to its disastrous conclusion, and Wagner was in Venice, far from the scene of the scandal.

24. He even thought for a time of having *Tristan* performed in Italian in Rio De Janeiro, as he had been told that the emperor of Brazil was a great admirer of his.

View of Zurich with the Wesendonck villa at the left, in a watercolor of 1857.

The music of *Tristan* represents a decisive extension of the stylistic innovations in the first parts of *The Ring*. Development and transformation of characteristic motives is carried to new heights. There is exhaustive orchestral exposition and exegesis of musical materials, and single melodic ideas can serve as the basis for page after page of the score. As in *The Ring,* the motives have dramatic associations. But even more than before, their identification is an uncertain and risky business: the drama is largely an internal one, whose events lend themselves poorly to specific names or labels. The very familiar opening of the Prelude to *Tristan* (Example IX–7) illustrates several aspects of the musical style of the work:

Example IX–7: WAGNER, Prelude to *Tristan und Isolde,* mm. 1–18

Three times the cellos, playing in a very high register, present a descending chromatic figure that is answered by the woodwinds with a rising one. These three statements together form an ascending sequence in which the final tones in the bass are E, G, and B. Then the last part of the final statement, from the entry of the winds, is repeated an octave higher, followed by a twofold repetition of its last two tones. This successive fragmentation is finally countered as the violins enter for the first time and energetically guide the rising chromatic figure to a recognizable cadence (a new melodic figure in the cellos, however, already underway, dispels any strong impression of arrival). Each member of the rising sequence (plus the repetition of the last in mm. 12–13) has a most inconclusive sound, as each ends with an unresolved dominant-seventh chord. Together with the strong dominant seventh (and ninth) in m. 16, then, we hear dominant sounds successively on E, G, B, and E. Only the last of these is resolved, as it moves upward by semitone (mirroring the initial bass motion in m. 2) in a deceptive cadence from E to F. This segment of music, for all its harmonic elusiveness, projects E as the principal dominant, B as dominant of the dominant, and the initial tone A as tonic—from the conclusive concert ending in A that Wagner provided for the Prelude it is clear that he thought of it in that key.

In mm. 2 and 6 the woodwinds enter with the much-discussed "Tristan chord," or $^{6+}_{4+}_{2+}$, which in each case is resolved almost entirely by chromatic motion[25] to a dominant seventh. Of the various explanations given for this sonority, perhaps the most common describes it as an altered ii$^4_3$ chord (see Example IX–8a), in which the G♯ and D♯ are appoggiaturas to A and D♮. Another analysis considers the G♯ as a principal tone and only the D♯ as an appoggiatura,[26] making the chord as a whole an altered diminished seventh (see Example IX–8b).

---

25. The exception is the leap of the first bassoon, in the tenor range, from b to g♯. This motion can, however, be interpreted as part of a voice exchange with the oboes:

This reading is suggested by William Mitchell in his very detailed analysis "The *Tristan* Prelude: Techniques and Structure," *The Music Forum,* 1 (1976): 162–203. The three members of Wagner's sequence (mm. 1–3, 5–7, and 8–11) are not symmetrical; the b in m. 4 would be c' (or b♯) in an exact transposition, and the third statement in mm. 8–11 is very much altered. These changes, like tonal answers in fugues, seemingly came about because of a collision of linear and functional considerations. Wagner arranged his sequence so that the resolutions occur successively on the dominant of the tonal center A minor, of C (its relative major), of E (its dominant), and finally, again, of A. The adjustments he made in the sequence also permit an unbroken chromatic line in the upper voice (in which the anacruses in the cello in mm. 4 and 8 participate) from g♯' in m. 2 to a" in m. 17.

26. Mitchell, p. 176.

Example IX–8: WAGNER, the Tristan chord
  a. As an altered II$_3^4$ chord

b. As an altered diminished seventh

c. GOTTSCHALK, *The Last Hope*

d. Comparison of Wagner and Gottschalk (transposed)

But Wagner's progression was not so singular an occurrence in his time as most people who are puzzled by this passage seem to assume, and similar harmonic constructions in other works may shed some light on the matter. Example IX–8c shows such a progression from a very popular piano composition of Louis Moreau Gottschalk, *The Last Hope,* published in Paris in 1854, some three years before Wagner began work on *Tristan*.[27] In the first two sequential statements of this passage, strikingly like those of Wagner, a "French" augmented sixth appears in the place of the Tristan chord—a "French" sixth also results when the

27. See Robert Offergeld, *The Centennial Catalogue of the Published and Unpublished Compositions of Louis Moreau Gottschalk* (New York, 1970), p. 22.

The Max Bruckner stage design for Act III of the 1886 production of *Tristan und Isolde*.

uppermost voice in the Tristan chord moves to a′—and resolves to a dominant just as the example from *Tristan* does. (Example IX–8d compares Wagner's progression with Gottschalk's, here shown for convenience in transposition.) This shows Gottschalk's readiness to resolve an augmented sixth chord in an unorthodox way: the essential interval of the augmented sixth resolves in similar downward motion to a seventh rather than by contrary motion to an octave.[28] This is exactly what the augmented sixth of the Tristan chord does, and in neither case does such an unusual resolution of the chord affect its essential function as a pre-dominant sonority.The example of Gottschalk, of course, proceeds augmented sixth—dominant—tonic, while Wagner characteristically halts his progression at the dominant.

Wagner marks the beginning of his Prelude *Langsam und schmachtend* ("slow and languishing"). Contributing to a languishing effect is a certain amorphousness of rhythm: consistent resolutions on the very weak second beat (mm. 3, 7, 11, etc.), and suppression of the stressed points of the measure (m. 9) create an impression of uncertainty and irresolution. At other times Wagner uses rhythmic means to a very different expressive end. In Act II, as Isolde awaits Tristan's arrival, the orchestra reflects her mounting excitement with a steady crescendo and rising sequential figures whose rhythm is sharp, insistent, and regular. And

28. This motion can be heard as an elision of the normal progression in which the seventh is passing:

In the third member of the sequence Gottschalk writes the usual resolution for an augmented sixth (this time the "German" variety), in which that interval expands outward by semitone to the octave.

in Isolde's final *Liebestod,* the closest approximation there is in this work to a set aria, there are strong elements (particularly in the orchestra) of symmetrical, periodic phrasing.

When *Tristan und Isolde* was finished in the summer of 1859 Wagner had written three and a half operas for which there was no good prospect of performance. The public knew nothing of his music after *Tannhäuser* and *Lohengrin*—the latter work had never even been seen by the composer, its only performances having taken place in Germany where he was banned. And the following five years were exceedingly hard for Wagner as he moved restlessly from one European city to another, attempting to arrange for performance and publication of his works and for large loans from his acquaintances. None of these efforts met with much success. A performance of *Tannhäuser* at the Paris Opéra in 1861 was hooted and whistled off the stage by a vocal portion of the audience who missed the ballet by arriving too late; *Tristan* was not to be seen in performance until 1865.

DIE MEISTERSINGER

In the midst of these troubles Wagner launched another major dramatic work, *Die Meistersinger von Nürnberg.* The poem, for which he had made a prose sketch as early as 1845, was written at top speed in Paris in December 1861–January 1862; the music was finally finished in 1867. Like *Tristan, Die Meistersinger* was first conceived as a modest, practicable work, as a pendant, in fact, to *Tannhäuser.* But it grew to ever vaster proportions, finally requiring six major soloists and a large orchestra and chorus; in performance it lasts some five hours. But except for size and grandeur of conception, there are few major points of resemblance between *Die Meistersinger* and Wagner's other mature works: its libretto is historical and comic, it has arialike singing and imposing choral scenes (contrary to Wagner's theoretical tenets), as well as substantial stretches of solidly diatonic harmony.

Set in the narrow, crooked streets and high-gabled buildings of sixteenth-century Nuremberg, this opera presents an amused but sympathetic view of the highly codified art of the Meistersinger. Their maze of strictures and prescriptions for poetry and song, represented by the pedant Beckmesser, is held up to ridicule, while the true poetic impulse is embodied in the prize song of the young hero Walther von Stolzing. The opposition between the two is mediated by Hans Sachs, a Meistersinger who represents both tradition and inspiration—and, what is more, the ultimately reliable judgment of an enlightened populace. Wagner's music participates intricately in this allegory of artistic creation. The rapid *fioritura* with which Beckmesser decorates his songs are made to sound appropriately absurd, and Walther's contest piece comes off all the better by comparison (he is also given a very helpful orchestral accompaniment that Beckmesser is always denied). But Wagner makes it clear through musical means that this is no simple triumph of the moderns over the ancients. A poem of the historical mastersinger Hans Sachs, *Wach auf, es nahet gen den Tag* (Act III), is set in a consciously archaic style; an actual Meistersinger melody is used for the "guild march" (and as the second principal theme of the overture); the opera opens with a chorale reminiscent of church music in the German Reformation. These features, together with a polyphonic combination of themes in the overture, pay sincere tribute to genuine tradition in art, to the real foundations upon which innovation must rest.

LATER TRIUMPHS

In 1863 Wagner published the text of *The Ring,* together with a preface offering some bold suggestions as to how its performance might be arranged and supported:

> Two ways occur to me.
>
> An association of wealthy art lovers, men and women, formed for the specific purpose of raising the necessary funds for a first performance of my work.—When I think of the usual pettiness of the Germans in such matters, I do not dare to expect success from an appeal addressed to this end.
>
> On the other hand, the thing would be very easy for a German prince, who would need to make no new demands upon his budget, but simply use the funds that he previously devoted to the maintenance of that worst of all public artistic institutions, utterly compromising and ruinous to German musical taste, his opera theater . . . and thus he would found an institution that would gain a permanent influence upon German taste for art, upon the development of German artistic genius, upon the nurture of a genuine rather than arrogant national spirit, as well as indestructible fame for himself.
>
> Will such a prince be found?[29]

The advertisement, astonishingly, paid off: the eighteen-year-old Wagner-partisan Ludwig II ascended the throne of Bavaria in March of 1864; in May he sent for Wagner, paid off his mountainous debts, and installed him with a handsome annuity in a villa on Lake Starnberg and then in a great house in Munich. Wagner quickly became the impressionable young monarch's constant companion and almost sole advisor. Feeling unlimited power in his grasp, he launched ambitious plans for renewed work on *The Ring,* for construction of a theater for its performance, for founding a German Music School to train Wagnerian

---

29. *Gesammelte Schriften und Dichtungen,* 6, pp. 280–81.

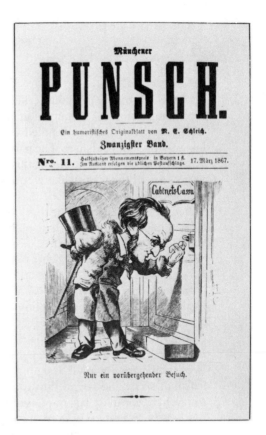

A caricature of Wagner at the royal treasury; the caption says "Just a passing visit." (Punsch, Munich, 17 March 1867)

musicians, and for bringing certain of his friends to Munich by adding them to the royal payroll. One of these was the pianist and conductor Hans von Bülow, whose wife Cosima (daughter of Franz Liszt) deserted her husband for Wagner and in 1870 became his second wife.

The luxury and irregularities of the composer's life, however, and particularly his tendency to meddle in political matters for his own benefit, soon raised a storm of protest among influential circles in Munich. Ludwig was forced to send him away—without, however, cutting off his salary. In 1866 he settled at Triebschen, a villa on Lake Lucerne in Switzerland, where he spent seven relatively carefree and very productive years. *Die Meistersinger* was finished there in 1867, *Siegfried* in 1871, and the principal work on *Die Götterdämmerung* in 1872. Wagner began meanwhile to act upon his long-cherished dream of founding a theater to his own specifications for the performance of his works. With scanty financial backing from a few patrons the foundation stone was laid in 1872 in the Bavarian town of Bayreuth. When the project foundered, King Ludwig once more came to the rescue; the theater was finished in 1873—together with a handsome new house for the Wagners—and the first Bayreuth Festival took place in August of 1876 with a full performance of *The Ring*.

Wagner was to write only one more opera: *Parsifal*, finished in 1882, one year before his death. This revisiting of the legend of the Holy Grail now turned sharply religious: called a "festival-drama of consecration," it presents a story of renunciation and redemption in which symbols of Christian mysticism are mingled with reflections of the pessimistic philosophy of Schopenhauer. The naïve and unblemished hero Parsifal, by renouncing the temptations of this world, is enabled to effect a miraculous cure of the Christ-like wounds of Amfortas, king of the Knights of the Grail, thereby himself becoming the sacerdotal guardian of the sacred vessel. Redemption, that ubiquitous Leitmotif of the operas, is here achieved not through the "healthy sensuality" (Ludwig Feuerbach's phrase) of a Siegfried, nor through the pure love offered by Wagnerian heroines from Senta to Isolde, but through sacrifice and self-abnegation.

In the composition of *Parsifal* Wagner drew upon varied techniques from his past. No longer feeling obsessed by the theories that affect much of *The Ring* and *Tristan,* he wrote a poem organized mainly by end rhyme. Much of the drama is arranged in static *tableaux* somewhat reminiscent of the grand opera. But the intent and effect are very different: they are not at all designed to overwhelm the listener with brilliance of scene and sound, but to present ritual and epic narration and to lay bare complex layers of symbolism. A referential use of musical motives once again works to elucidate the actions and thoughts of the characters. And the nature of the motives themselves seems more than ever finely tuned to their dramatic significance: in accordance with age-old traditions of Western music, suffering and adversity are expressed through chromaticism, while purely diatonic constructions convey the simplicity of the character Parsifal or the sublimity of the Holy Grail.

From June of 1868, when *Die Meistersinger* had its triumphant premiere in Munich, Wagner's fame in Germany grew by leaps and bounds. And after his death in 1883 debate over his works and his theories virtually overwhelmed all other issues in European music. For each of the festivals the devoted streamed into Bayreuth with the air of pilgrims, the religious overtones of their undertaking seeming all the more vivid if *Parsifal* was on the boards. Among those in attendance in the late 1880s were Debussy, Hugo Wolf, Gustav Mahler, George Moore, and George Bernard Shaw.[30] While seeking support for the Festival Theater Wagner had publicly advocated the forming of societies for the advancement of Wagnerian causes. By 1886 there were more than 200 such worshipful Wagner Societies in cities from New York to St. Petersburg. Some issued journals devoted to veneration of the artist and discussion of the oeuvre; there were the *Bayreuther Blätter,* founded under Wagner's own aegis, *The Meister,* established in London by William Ashton Ellis, and *La Revue Wagnérienne* of Paris, directed by Edouard

---

30. In his *The Perfect Wagnerite* (1898) Shaw interprets *The Ring* as an elaborate socialist allegory.

Richard Wagner at Home in Bayreuth, oil painting by W. Beckmann, 1882. From the left are Cosima and Richard Wagner, Liszt, and Hans von Wolzogen.

Dujardin. And well into the present century, the spirit of Wagnerism continued to flourish at Bayreuth, now presided over by the magisterial Cosima.

Opposition to Wagner and Wagnerism was sometimes spirited. The Viennese music critic Eduard Hanslick (1825–1904), Wagner's most articulate and effective detractor, adamantly opposed all his works after *Lohengrin.* In his *Vom musikalisch-Schönen* (On Beauty in Music, 1854) Hanslick had advanced a musical aesthetic strongly opposed to the common idea that the "subject" of music was feeling, or that it achieved its main effect through the expression of feeling. Instead he embraced an older notion of beauty—understood roughly in the sense of Kant's *Critique of Judgment* as embodying design, order, or fitness—as the most desirable attribute of music as of all the arts. To him Wagner's later works seemed to aim for an apotheosis of exaggerated feeling (though their effect was often one of numbing boredom), and to lack essential natural requirements of both drama and music. After attending the premier of *The Ring* at Bayreuth in 1876, he freely expressed admiration for certain individual passages and effects—he considered Wagner unrivaled in the composition of pictorial orchestral music, for example. But the overall verdict was predictably negative; three musical traits are singled out for special disapproval:

First: the lack of independent, separate vocal melody, replaced here with a kind of heightened recitative, with the "endless melody" in the orchestra as a basis. Secondly: the dissolution of all form, not only the traditional forms (aria, duet, *etc.*), but all symmetry and musical logic, governed by laws, in general. And thirdly: the exclusion, with a few fleeting exceptions, of polyphonic vocal numbers, the duet, trio, chorus, and finale.[31]

The young Friedrich Nietzsche, for a time an ardent disciple of Wagner, became disaffected about the time of the opening of the Festival Theater. Wagner had progressively succumbed, he concluded, to the unhealthiest forces in contemporary society. The bold beginning of *The Ring* was perverted by its author's conversion to Schopenhauerian pessimism: "It was only the philosopher of decadence who enabled the artist of decadence to discover himself."[32] The phenomenon of Wagnerism he found perfectly congruent with the spirit of Bismarck's new Reich: both reflected an obsession with unquestioned authority and absolute obedience. And of Wagner's final work, *Parsifal,* he declared: "Richard Wagner, apparently the most triumphal, while in truth become a decayed, despairing *décadent,* sank down suddenly, helpless and disjointed, before a Christian cross."[33] Others spoke even more directly. Mark Twain, who heard *Tristan* at Bayreauth, reported, "I know of some, and have heard of many, who could not sleep after it, but cried the night away. I feel strongly out of place here. Sometimes I feel like the one sane person in the community of the mad."[34]

The public took little notice of other German composers of opera in the last third of the century. Wagner's faithful younger friend Peter Cornelius (1824–74) composed two worthy dramatic works, *Der Barbier von Bagdad* (1858) *Der Cid* (1865); both achieve a fair degree of independence from the nearly irresistible influence of the master, but neither survived a few performances. More successful was Wilhelm Kienzl's *Der Evangelimann* (1895). Followers of Wagner such as Heinrich Zöllner (1854–1941) and the conductor-composer Felix von Weingartner (1863–1942) made a futile attempt to carry forth the Wagnerian tradition. At the close of the century Richard Strauss began his operatic career unobtrusively with a work for which he supplied his own libretto, *Guntram* (1894). But the only opera other than those of Wagner that strongly appealed to the German public's fancy before the turn of the century was *Hänsel und Gretel* (1893) by Engelbert Humperdinck (1854–1921), for a time an assistant of Wagner's at Bayreuth. With its remarkable mixture of innocent melody and Wagnerian orchestral textures, this

31. Eduard Hanslick, *Musikalische Stationen* (Berlin, 1880), p. 231.

32. *The Case of Wagner,* in *The Works of Friedrich Nietzsche,* ed. Alexander Tille (London, 1896), 11, p. 16.

33. *Nietzsche contra Wagner, loc.cit,* 11, p. 82.

34. Quoted in Edward Lockspeiser, *Debussy: His Life and Mind* (London, 1962) 1, p. 95.

work scored an instant and lasting success. This, however, was an isolated occurrence. For the most part Wagner exerted an influence upon German opera composers much like that of Beethoven upon writers of symphonies early in the century: his example seemed to demand adherence, while by its very magnitude it paralyzed any hope of similar achievement.

CHAPTER X

Italian and French Opera
in the Later Nineteenth Century

In Italy, as in Germany, national unification was a slow and troubled process that lasted for much of the nineteenth century. But the formation of an Italian nation faced the additional obstacle of foreign domination. According to the treaties of the Congress of Vienna in 1815, Austria directly governed the northern provinces of Lombardy and Venetia, and Austrian princes were installed in Modena, Parma, and Tuscany. Ferdinand, the restored Bourbon king of Naples, had secretly agreed to conduct his government in a manner compatible with Austrian designs. Victor Emmanuel I, king of Sardinia, was the only native ruler on the peninsula. Throughout Italy, despised French administrations and French systems of law from the Napoleonic conquests were replaced by retrogressive regimes that the Italians found even more odious; an antiquated feudalism designed for the benefit of the aristocracy (and a foreign aristocracy at that), strict censorship, and oppressive police systems were the rule.

Opposition was not long in coming. Semisecret organizations of "Carbonari" (so-called because they pretended to be sellers of charcoal), devoted to the expulsion of foreign tyrants, sprang up throughout Italy. Feelings of national identity were fostered by writers such as Ugo Foscolo (1778–1827) and Giacomo Leopardi (1798–1837). The Genoese Giuseppe Mazzini founded a secret patriotic society, *La Giovine Italia* (Young Italy), that, like its counterpart in Germany, sought to rally the youth of the land to the cause of nationalism and freedom. Organized insurrections occurred in Naples in 1820, and Italy was shaken by the tremors of rebellion that spread across Europe in 1830–31.

A powerful movement toward independence, known as the Risorgimento (Reawakening), was clearly underway. In 1848 there was widespread war on the peninsula. The center of the fighting was Rome, where the pope had long ruled as both temporal and spiritual leader; in 1849 revolutionists had just managed to take the city and declare a Roman republic when a French army came to the pope's aid, and after a month-long siege restored him to power. During this conflict there emerged an able and colorful military leader who was to inflame the imaginations of Italians everywhere, Giuseppe Garibaldi (1807–82). In 1859–

The Battle of San Martino, June 1859, was a decisive victory for the forces favoring Italian unification.

60, under his inspired leadership and now with the active connivance of the French, the forces of liberation finally drove the Austrians from all the Italian states except Venetia. Now all the peninsula, except for the Patrimony of St. Peter, was united as the Kingdom of Italy under the titular leadership of Vittorio Emanuele II, the constitutional monarch of Sardinia.

VERDI

A figure of enormous importance in this struggle was the greatest Italian opera composer of the century, Giuseppe Verdi (1813–1901). Born in the village of Le Roncole in Parma (at the time under French domination), Verdi undertook his first formal study of music in 1825 with the organist and conductor Ferdinando Provesi in the nearby town of Busseto. Except for three years' study of composition with Vincenzo Lavigna in Milan (1832–35), he remained in Busseto, playing the organ at the local church and directing the concerts of the town's Philharmonic Society until 1839, when he took up residence in Milan. In 1836 he had married Margherita Barezzi from Busseto; she and two children born to them all died by 1840. These years saw the completion of a good number of early compositions, including two sinfonias, several pieces to sacred texts, and his earliest opera, *Oberto,* first performed at La Scala, Milan, in November of 1839. *Oberto* was well received and led to a commission for three more operas at La Scala. One of these was *Nabucco* (or *Nabucodonosor*), 1842, Verdi's first great triumph. In both Milan and Parma the populations of those cities were exceeded by the number of tickets sold to *Nabucco* in its first full season.[1]

1. George Martin, "Verdi and the Risorgimento," in *The Verdi Companion,* ed. William Weaver and Martin Chusid (New York, 1979), p. 22. Much of the discussion here is indebted to this essay.

Giuseppe Verdi; an engraving from an 1861 photograph.

Politics was a prime factor in the spectacular success of *Nabucco*. In this story, adapted from the Old Testament by Temistocle Solera (who was once imprisoned by the Austrians for revolutionary activity), Hebrews of the sixth century B.C. long for release from their captivity in Babylon. A chorus in chains and at hard labor in Part III sings:

Oh, mia patria sì bella e perduta! Oh, membranza sì cara e fatal![2]	Oh, my land so lovely and lost! Oh, memory so sweet and despairing!

Italians in 1842 were not slow to associate sentiments such as these with their own situation. Audiences all over Italy roared their approval and demanded repetitions of the chorus, often against specific prohibitions by the police. Verdi's opera of the next year, *I Lombardi,* gives an account of the First Crusade in which a rousing chorus calls the Lombards to battle against the Saracens (identified by the audience with the Austrians), who are defilers of the Holy Land (i.e. Italy). Verdi and his librettists collaborated to introduce political and patriotic themes in opera during all the years of the Italian struggle for independence. They appear

2. This chorus begins "Va, pensiero, sull'ali dorate" ("Go, thought, on golden wings"); it appears to be a loose adaptation of Psalm 137, "By the rivers of Babylon, there we sat down, yea, we wept."

The interior of La Scala; aquatint, ca. 1850.

even in so unlikely a dramatic work as *Macbeth* (1847), where a chorus of Scottish exiles sings warmly about their fatherland. During the insurrection of 1848–49, Verdi and his music were again much in evidence. Living at the time in Paris, he returned to Italy twice to be close to the action; in 1849, when liberated Rome was temporarily a republic, its new status was celebrated by a frenzied audience at a performance of Verdi's *La Battaglia di Legnano,* a drama about the defeat of Frederick Barbarossa by the Lombardic League in the twelfth century—the connection with current events again being plain. Later Verdi's very name became an acronym for a revolutionary battle cry ("Vittorio Emanuele Re D'Italia"), and when the first national parliament was formed in 1861, he was elected a deputy and performed his duties faithfully.

While much of the attention accorded Verdi's early operas, up to about 1850, can be attributed to their topical significance, it was soon apparent that a powerful new musical personality had burst upon the operatic scene. In his earliest works Verdi is clearly a pupil of the current school of Italian opera: his fast-paced ensembles are often reminiscent of Rossini, and a preference for suave, exactly regular melody surely reflects the influence of Bellini and Donizetti. But there is a new simplicity and energy to much of his writing. The proportion of recitative is reduced and the standard *scena ed aria* tends to be more compressed. Starkly plain marchlike rhythms abound, and the chorus very often sings simple melodies in unison. The choruses, nonetheless, show a great range in style. Part III of *Nabucco,* for example, opens with a chorus of Babylonian high priests, soldiers, and the populace, who sing an

Example X–1: VERDI, *Nabucco*, Part III

elemental unison melody (shown in Example X–1) accompanied by an unrelenting marchlike tread of the instruments. The famous chorus of the Hebrews, "Va, pensiero," occurs near the end of this part (or act); though also sung in unison (except at climactic points), here the music is very different: a wide-ranging cantabile melody is given a special lilt by cadential ornament in triplet motion. Rossini described it as a grand aria sung by sopranos, contraltos, tenors and basses[3] (see Example X–2).

The sixteen operas Verdi composed from 1839 through 1850 may be said to comprise his early style. Four of them are still occasionally performed, and these four seem particularly significant in the development of his individual manner: *Nabucco* (1842), *Ernani* (1844), *Macbeth* (first version, 1847), and *Luisa Miller* (1849). *Ernani,* produced at La Fenice

3.   Julian Budden, *The Operas of Verdi* (New York and Washington, 1973) 1, p. 107. A similarity between these two melodies is a strong emphasis of the third scale degree.

Example X–2: VERDI, *Nabucco,* Part III, "Va pensiero"

theater in Venice, was Verdi's first opera composed for a theater other than La Scala of Milan, and in several respects it marks a departure from his earliest practice. For the first time the composer was in a position to dictate his own terms. His contract with La Fenice allowed him to choose the subject, the librettist, and the singers. After considering a number of literary sources, most of them English, he settled upon Victor Hugo's controversial play *Hernani.* To the French this work was revolutionary as literature, while in Italy it was thought politically sensitive—in 1830 Bellini had given up his opera on the subject for fear of the censors. The librettist Verdi chose was the unknown writer Francesco Maria Piave (1810–76), who over the next twenty-five years was to supply him with nine additional librettos, including those for *Macbeth, Rigoletto, La Traviata,* and *La Forza del destino.* Verdi did not hesitate to urge his own ideas upon his collaborator; the dramatic form and even the language of the librettos were often strongly influenced by the composer.

In *Ernani* the characteristic conflicts surrounding love and honor are played out in most extravagant fashion. Ernani, a dispossessed nobleman living as an outlaw, loves Elvira, who is also loved by the King Don Carlo, as well as by her aging uncle, Don Ruy Gomez de Silva. Silva allows Elvira to be taken hostage by Don Carlo rather than violate his obligation as a host by turning Ernani over to the law. Ernani swears to give his life as forfeit if Silva will allow him temporary freedom to conspire against Don Carlo; Silva agrees and later exacts payment—an arrangement with which, as honor requires, Ernani complies. Ernani's role as a bandit chief allows for an opening scene (not in Hugo's play)

Example X–3: VERDI, *Ernani,* Act IV, trio

that is a conflation of the "romantic outlaw" motif of revolutionary opéra comique and the drinking chorus familiar in comic opera of both the French and Italian traditions. Yet in the course of this *Introduzione* Ernani is revealed as less a bandit than a characteristic Verdian tenor consumed with love. Two other character-types that are to become standard in Verdi's operas also emerge in this work: the powerful dramatic baritone (Don Carlo) and the older *basso cantante* (Silva)—the latter a serious singing role that up to this time had been rare for the bass voice.

The last of the four acts of *Ernani* illustrates Verdi's talents for compression of action and economy of means. Ernani and Elvira are to be married. The celebration of their happiness at a masked ball, however, is disturbed by the sound of the horn that Ernani has given Silva as a token of his pledge to relinquish his life to him upon command. Presently Silva actually appears and presses his demand. Ernani after some hesitation stabs himself, sings his farewells and dies as Elvira falls senseless upon his body. All this transpires in the course of a ball scene and a *gran scena e terzetto*—altogether twenty minutes of music. The final trio (which Verdi told Piave "should be the best piece in the opera") is dominated by a melody that might seem a bit ingenuous for this grave dramatic situation (Example X–3). The regularly recurring dotted rhythms together with the simplest rhythmic accompaniment in 9 / 8 meter are a part of Verdi's heritage from the previous generation of Italian opera. One recurring harmonic device in this trio, however,

Example X–4: VERDI, *Ernani,* Act IV, trio

shown in Example X–4, is much more individual and dramatically effective: a sudden diversion toward the parallel minor (D minor) touches briefly on *its* relative major (F major).

Verdi was always powerfully drawn to the plays of Shakespeare. Again and again he contemplated an opera on *King Lear,* a project he never realized. When he agreed to provide a new opera for the carnival season in 1847 at the Teatro della Pergola in Florence, he settled upon an equally challenging Shakespearian subject, *Macbeth.* Piave was again the librettist, and Verdi bombarded him relentlessly with instructions and reproof; in the end some parts of the libretto were rewritten by the composer's friend Andrea Maffei. Verdi's gathering strength as a dramatic composer is clearly visible in this opera: in the eerie supernatural atmosphere of the witches' scenes, and in the impressive power of the title role, now a full-fledged dramatic "Verdi baritone." But the most memorable single feature of the work, perhaps, is Lady Macbeth's sleepwalking scene in Act IV, in which the effect of the potently expressive arioso vocal part is redoubled by an obsessively repeated rhythmic figure in the orchestra (Example X–5).

Verdi's reputation toward mid-century began to spread well beyond

Title page of the first piano-vocal score of Verdi's *Macbeth* (Milan, 1847).

Example X–5: VERDI, *Macbeth,* Act IV

Italy. After the production of *Macbeth* early in 1847, he set out for London to oversee the production there of his new opera, *I Masnadieri.* It was performed at Her Majesty's Theatre in the summer of 1847 before a glittering audience that included Queen Victoria, Prince Louis Napoleon, and the Duke of Wellington. The opera itself was less favorably received than its leading singer, the great Swedish soprano Jenny Lind (1820–87), who was in the midst of her first triumphant year in London. Immediately thereafter Verdi lived for a time in Paris, where his *Jerusalem,* a revision of *I Lombardi,* was performed at the Opéra. Then in the summer of 1849 he returned to Italy with the singer Giuseppina

Strepponi, who was to be his second wife; the couple settled in Busseto, the town of Verdi's youth where he lived for the rest of his days.

During the following four years Verdi composed five operas for various Italian stages: *Luisa Miller* (1849), *Stiffelio* (1850), *Rigoletto* (1851), *Il Trovatore* (1853), and *La Traviata* (1853). The last three, still among the best loved of all operas, are normally thought to mark the beginning of Verdi's middle period. Of these three, the composer himself regarded *Rigoletto* as a particularly important milestone in his career—on one occasion even referring to it as "revolutionary."[4] This opera was once more composed to a libretto of Piave adapted, with the generous aid of the composer, from a play by Victor Hugo. The original *Le Roi s'amuse* (The King Amuses Himself) presents scenes of royal profligacy such that in 1832 it was banned even by the comparatively liberal regime of Louis Philippe. Verdi's appetite was once more whetted by a subject that was bound to be politically sensitive. But in this work he was also attracted by a dramatic situation in which a doting father (Rigoletto) unwittingly participates in the destruction of his daughter (Gilda), and in which the two male leads, Rigoletto and the Duke (the King in Hugo's play), both of them in a sense villains, show attractive human emotions in the course of the action.

Immediately striking in *Rigoletto* is the juxtaposition of the grave, menacing prelude (in C minor, with tremolando lower strings and accented diminished-seventh chords) and the opening scene that exudes good-humored energy. This ball scene begins with the rousing strains of the *banda* (an on-stage band), and gradually develops into a finale-like concerted ensemble. Its bland harmony and rhythmic vivacity, though, take on an ironic coloring as the Duke is shown to be a profligate in search of amorous conquests among the wives and daughters of his courtiers. His hunchbacked jester Rigoletto, moreover, furthers his designs and ridicules the reproaches of the outraged husbands and fathers. A *stretta* of ensemble singing and dancing is then broken off by a return of the ominous manner of the prelude as Monterone, father of one of the Duke's victims, pronounces a curse upon Rigoletto. This curse and its consequences were the central theme of the play according to Hugo's preface to the work; the opera, dramatically and musically, shows the inevitable unfolding of its results amidst scenes ranging in tone from merriment to horror.

A great portion of the drama in *Rigoletto* is carried on in duets. A particularly effective specimen of the genre is the *scena e duetto* between Rigoletto and Gilda in Act I, scene 2. It opens with Rigoletto's soliloquy (beginning "Pari siamo") in which he agonizes over his deformity and his station in life as a clown. This section is set in a powerful

4.   Ibid., p. 483.

Example X–6: VERDI, *Rigoletto,* Act I, Scene 2

declamatory style making use of various devices of accompanied recitative that change with the protagonist's shifting moods: energetic
orchestral interjections, chordal tremolando accompaniment in the strings,
and, when Rigoletto reflects on the carefree life of the Duke, a jaunty
figure shared by pizzicato lower strings and clarinet. The overriding
gravity of the soliloquy then gives way to animated music in the orchestra
that turns out to be an obbligato accompaniment to the first section of
the duet proper. Characteristic of earlier nineteenth-century Italian
operatic style, the orchestration creates a special air of animated frivolity by doubling the tune in the violins with all the treble winds (Example X–6). With the remaining two sections of this number (Andante
and Allegro moderato assai) Verdi carries out the fast-slow-fast form
for duets that he inherited from Rossini. But here the structure is
extremely flexible: the sections are interrupted by recitativelike declamation, and singing by two other characters (Gilda's governess Gio-
vanna and the Duke) intervenes in accordance with the swiftly moving
dramatic situation.

Arias have proportionately less importance in this opera. There are only three numbers designated as *scena ed aria* (one for each of the three principal characters), and none of these has a full multisectional form such as the cavatina-cabaletta. Gilda's well-known "Caro nome" in Act I, scene 2, for example, is a single-movement song of a type often called a *romanza*. The most familiar solo in *Rigoletto* and perhaps the best-known tune in all Verdi opera is not an aria proper; it is "La Donna è mobile" ("Woman is fickle"), sung by the Duke twice in Act III, in the *Preludio, Scena, e Canzone,* and again in course of a *Scena, Terzetto e Tempesta.* This rousing song has several characteristics of Verdi's earlier style and that of his predecessors: it falls into unvarying two-measure half-phrases with an emphatic martial rhythm (each half-phrase is energetically marked off with a dotted-note figure), while the orchestra plays a steadily throbbing guitarlike accompaniment with nothing but tonic and dominant harmonies. (Example X–7) But this ingenuous music, an ordinary vehicle for the earnest and high-minded Verdian tenor, now

Example X–7: VERDI, *Rigoletto,* "La Donna è mobile"

Rigoletto, Act I, Scene 2. A watercolor sketch by Giuseppe and Pietro Bertoja, 1856.

carries strong overtones of irony: the character who thus sings of the fickleness of women is the rakish Duke, a complex figure who is himself the very soul of inconstancy. And there is something askew about the music itself: its metrical regularity is upset by the "extra" measure in the accompaniment just before the melody enters, and by the whimsical interruption in m. 9. Thus in this middle-period opera Verdi uses the most standard of musical manners—with adjustments—in the service of somewhat convoluted dramatic ends.

In several of Verdi's operas of the late 1840s and early 1850s he brings his dramatic and musical forces to bear upon the exposition of individual personalities or the exploration of specific human relationships such as the father-daughter interaction in *Rigoletto*. This is the case in *Macbeth*, in *Luisa Miller* (after Schiller's play *Kabale und Liebe*), and especially in the domestic drama *La Traviata* (The Fallen Woman), in which the primary relationship, that between the lovers Violetta and Alfredo, has been seen as a reflection of Verdi's own involvement with Giuseppina Streponi.[5] In the next years Verdi showed an increasing interest in more grandiose subjects, where the collusions and conflicts among the principals are explicitly representative of the relations among large social groups or nations. Something of the monumental scale of the French grand opera is increasingly apparent, and it is significant that most of the works from 1855–71 were written for theaters outside of Italy: *Les Vêpres siciliennes* (1855), *Don Carlos* (1867), and a revision of *Macbeth* (this version of 1868 is the one known to modern audiences) were first staged in Paris, *La Forza del destino* (1862) in St. Petersburg, and *Aida* (1871) in Cairo.

5. See, e.g., Gerald A. Mendelssohn, "Verdi the Man and Dramatist," *Nineteenth-Century Music,* 2 (1978): 129–31.

Les Vêpres siciliennes is a violent and bloody tale about the massacre of the French by the Sicilians in the thirteenth century. The five-act libretto is the work of Eugène Scribe, Meyerbeer's librettist,[6] and the work as a whole is a curious amalgam of the brilliant spectacle, massed choruses, and ballet of grand opera invested with Verdi's own Italian style. A greater work after the plan of the Parisian grand opera is *Don Carlos,* composed to a libretto adapted from Schiller's play of that name by F. J. Méry and C. du Locle. Here the drama of a love triangle among father, son, and stepmother unfolds before the backdrop of larger struggles among nations and between church and state. Massive crowd scenes and religious pageantry provide for the tableau-like construction that is reminiscent of Meyerbeer's *Huguenots* and *Le Prophète*. Verdi's personal stamp, however, is everywhere evident: in lyrical solo melodies such as Don Carlos' aria "Io la vidi" in the first act, in King Philip's famous and dolorous aria in the fourth act, "Ella giammai m'amò," and above all, in the magnificent scene between the King and the Grand Inquisitor in the same act—a memorable duet for two basses who represent the collision of ecclesiastical and temporal powers. Other influences may be felt in the work. About this time, Verdi showed an interest in Wagner's prose writings, and in 1871 he wrote, "For these operas *[Don Carlos* and the forthcoming *Aida],* whether they are good or bad, one superior intelligence is needed to direct the costumes, the décor, the props, the production, *etc.* in addition to an exceptional musical interpretation."[7]

Despite exhaustive preparations, enormous expense, and the compulsive attentions of the composer, *Don Carlos* was not a great success in Paris. Verdi himself was eventually less than satisfied with the work; he revised it for a production at La Scala in 1884, in the process eliminating the first act. This version, with the first act of 1867 restored, is the one most often performed today.[8] In the meantime, in *Aida,* Verdi achieved a brilliant success in every respect: this work represents a crowning synthesis of the best of the Italian and French traditions that Verdi had been cultivating so assiduously, and it can be seen as the inauguration of the final period of his creative career.

Aida was first commissioned as a part of the celebrations in Cairo for the opening of the Suez Canal in January, 1871. Though the disruption of the Franco-Prussian War forced the postponement of its premiere until December of that year, the work is appropriately grand in concep-

6.   Andrew Porter has recently shown how large a part Verdi had in determining the final form of the libretto.

7.   Quoted in Andrew Porter, "The Making of *Don Carlos,*" *Proceedings of the Royal Musical Association,* 98 (1971–72): 81.

8.   In 1983 in London, the Paris version of 1867 was revived; this is only one sign of a resurgence of interest in this neglected work.

Aida, Act I, Scene 1 from the 1976 Metropolitan Opera production. Left to right: Donaldo Gaiotti (Ramfis); Marilyn Horne (Amneris); James Morris (The King); and Leontyne Price (Aida).

tion and rich in festive pageantry. The libretto, constructed by the French Egyptologist Mariette Bey, with reworking by du Locle (one of the librettists for *Don Carlos*), the Italian versifier Antonio Ghislanzoni, and Verdi himself, once again tells the story of harrowing conflict between love and honor played out in a context of struggle between nations. Ancient Egypt and Ethiopia are at war. Aida, an Ethiopian princess held prisoner in Egypt, and the Egyptian general Radames are in love; each must choose to follow the dictates of patriotism or passion. In the end, however, they choose another alternative, death; at the close of the opera they are immured, still alive, in their common tomb.

Though ostensibly a "number opera," *Aida* has a continuity of action and music that is new in Verdi's works. Recitative as such is scarcer than ever; the drama is advanced mainly through a potently expressive declamation that shifts easily to arioso, both being supported by a rich and flexible orchestral accompaniment. The ensemble scenes and "divertissements" are monumental beyond anything in Verdi's earlier operas. Most imposing of all is the second scene of Act II, a mammoth act-finale involving a brass band, choruses of the populace, high priests and prisoners, a huge victory procession, and extensive dancing. Verdi handles these forces with a practiced eye for effective theater. Solo singing by the principals in a contrasting middle section provides timely relief from the power and brilliance of the massed forces, while manipulating

Example X–8: VERDI, *Aida,* Act II, Processional March

the dramatic situation toward an even more climactic end. Two sections from this finale have become famous in their own right. One is the familiar trumpet tune in the victory procession whose beginning is shown in Example X–8. Its energetic martial rhythms and insistent emphasis of the third scale-degree are reminiscent of early Verdi; a novel intensifying effect, however, is achieved when the second time around this music is peremptorily shifted a minor third higher, to B major. The other famous section is the choral passage "Gloria all' Egitto" ("Glory to Egypt"), which was adopted for a time as the Egyptian national anthem.

The harmonic language of *Aida* is distinctly more elaborate than is usual in the Italian tradition to this point. Even Radamès' well-known romanza "Celeste Aida" ("Heavenly Aida") at the opening of Act I shows a rather advanced harmonic complexity. The initial two sets of two half-phrases in the first eight measures proceed to the third (D major) of the tonic (B♭ major) instead of its dominant. In a metrically irregular continuation (beginning with "tu sei regina"; see Example X–9) the bass line descends in parallel fourths with the melody, forming a series of V_3^4 sonorities that suggest in turn dominants of C, B♭, G minor,

Example X–9: VERDI, *Aida*, Act I, "Celeste Aida"

and F; and the resolution of a final dominant, F, is accompanied by an extended decorative chromatic figure in the violins. From the very outset real chromaticism and counterpoint in the brief Prelude to this opera must have alerted Verdi's audience to unaccustomed levels of musical complexity. Critics were quick to note these developments and some, to the chagrin of the Germanophobe Verdi, attributed it to Wagner's influence.

After the brilliant success of *Aida* in Cairo and Milan in 1871–72, the fifty-eight-year-old Verdi showed little inclination to work on any new opera, and was content to spend long stretches of time tending his crops and horses at Sant' Agata, his villa near Busseto. In the spring of 1873, however, the death of the poet Alessandro Manzoni, whom Verdi intensely admired, led him to undertake a composition of quite a different sort: by April of the following year he had completed his great Requiem Mass in memory of Manzoni, and soon began traveling extensively to conduct performances of it throughout Europe. Despite occasional complaints that this gigantic work for chorus, orchestra, and soloists was too theatrical for a Requiem mass, its performances in Milan, Paris, London, and Vienna were for Verdi another popular triumph.

It was not until 1879 that Verdi seriously entertained a new operatic venture. In that year his lifelong fascination with Shakespearian tragedy was quickened by a meeting with the young poet and composer Arrigo Boito (1842–1918), formerly a Wagner partisan, some of whose public statements had greatly angered Verdi. In 1868 Boito's opera *Mefistofele,* with a libretto after Goethe written by the composer, had failed miserably at La Scala; a revised version performed at Bologna in 1875 inaugurated its long and honorable career. Meanwhile Boito, very much impressed with Verdi's *Aida,* proposed through intermediaries that he and Verdi collaborate on an opera after Shakespeare's *Othello.* Other projects intervened: a revised version of Verdi's *Simon Boccanegra* (originally 1857) with new text by Boito was produced at La Scala in 1881, and the new four-act *Don Carlos* played there three years later. But the collaboration of the two artists intensified during these years, and in 1887, when Verdi was seventy-three, *Otello* was finally performed before an ecstatic audience at La Scala.

The text of *Otello* is a supreme example of the librettist's art. Because events in opera move more slowly than in spoken drama, the action of the original play needed to be drastically compressed. Boito's most severe cut was virtually to eliminate the first act of *Othello,* which takes place in fifteenth-century Venice and introduces the principal characters Othello and Desdemona. The opera begins instead with a ferocious storm on the island of Cyprus, in the midst of which the Moorish general Otello arrives to take charge of the war with the Turks; he is welcomed by the jubilant populace in a great choral scene. These events, taken from Shakespeare's second act, provide for a spectacular operatic open-

Verdi and baritone Victor Maurel, who created the role of Iago, backstage at the Paris Opera, 1894.

ing. But the first act of the play is not entirely discarded: key elements from it are artfully introduced at various points so that its contribution to the development of the characters is not all lost. Many of Shakespeare's poetic excursions are severely shortened or omitted, making room for a new kind of poetry: the lyrical flowering of Verdi's music. For some of the integral musical pieces new text had to be made; for the choruses, for example, for the splendid love duet in Act I, and for Iago's famous "Credo" in Act II. But in nearly every case the new words were based upon strategically chosen passages in the play, so that these lyrical sections might make a clear contribution to the progress of the drama.

From the beginning both Verdi and Boito were specially fascinated with the villainous Iago. Verdi, who for a time even proposed to call his opera "Iago," left a vivid account of his conception of this character:

> But if I were an actor and had to play Iago, I would rather have a long and thin figure, thin lips, small eyes set close to the nose like a monkey's, broad, receding brow, and the head developed behind; an absent, *nonchalant* manner, indifferent to everything, witty, speaking good and evil almost lightheartedly, and having the air of not even thinking of what he says; so that, if someone were to reproach him: "What you say is vile!" he could answer: "Really? I didn't think so . . . we'll say no more about it! . . ."[9]

But because opera cannot afford the spoken drama's leisurely exposition of so elusive a character, Iago reveals his true colors all at once in his monologue "Credo":

9. Quoted from Martin Chusid, "Verdi's Own Words," *The Verdi Companion* (New York, 1979), p. 158.

> I believe in a cruel God, who has created me after his
>   image, and upon whom in hate I call.
> From some vile germ or base atom I am born.
> I am evil because I am a man.

Verdi sets these words at first as impassioned declamation akin to the most dramatic sort of accompanied recitative; powerful orchestral interjections punctuate the recitation of the baritone in the upper reaches of his vocal range (Example X–10). This heightened declamation later takes on a melodic regularity as Iago's various "articles of disbelief" (all beginning with the word "credo") are given the same head-motive in a chromatically rising sequence. And the entire monologue is bound together with subtly recurring instrumental motives, particularly by a sixteenth-note triplet figure that in the first scenes of Act II is as prominent in the orchestra as the personality of Iago is on the stage.

Example X–10. VERDI, *Otello,* Act II, "Credo"

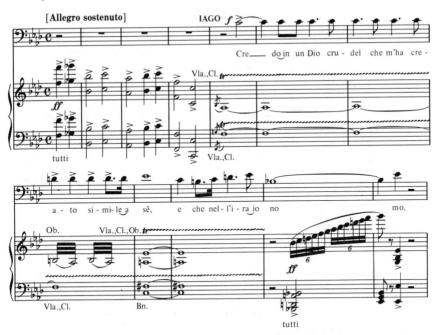

If there was a single governing principle in opera of the later nineteenth century it was a striving for continuity. The old succession of recitative and aria had provided a convenient vehicle for alternate action and reflection—as well as for timely stops for applause. But the shifting textures and tempos of events were in large part governed by operatic

Engraving by A. Bonamore of a scene from Act II of Verdi's *Otello* at La Scala, 1887.

convention, not by requirements of the unfolding drama. This became less and less acceptable to composers of the nineteenth century for whom realism *(verismo)*—a supposed similarity to spoken drama and to life itself—was a cherished ideal. In Italian opera earlier in the century the substitution of a somewhat fluid *scena* for recitative was a step toward flexibility and homogeneity. Another operatic convention, however, worked at cross-purposes with this new freedom: the rousing, show-stopping, often irrelevant cabaletta regularly closed off a good number of arias and ensembles in the operas of Bellini, Donizetti, and the young Verdi. In later years Verdi worked systematically toward a continuous musical fabric whose changing textures responded to the dramatic purpose at hand. The cabaletta was all but banished; set arias and ensembles were less frequent and often contributed significantly to the flow of the drama. There was a growing preponderance of a declamatory style that merged easily into arioso, or, on occasion, in the opposite direction toward recitative. And the orchestra increasingly became a binding force, developing its characteristic motives in ways that lent continuity and force to large sections of dramatic action.

The first two scenes of Act III of *Otello* (ARM 19) provide an example of the superb skill with which Verdi was able to manage a complex bit of musical theater. At this point Iago has engineered the demotion of Cassio, captain in Otello's forces; he has also persuaded the young man to appeal to Otello's wife Desdemona to intercede with her husband. Meanwhile, he has sowed the seeds of suspicion in Otello's mind concerning Cassio's relationship with Desdemona and arranged for Otello to see them together. Iago further convinces Otello that Desdemona

Example X–11: VERDI, *Otello,* Act II

has given Cassio a handkerchief that was Otello's first gift to her. Act II ends with Otello in a fury, swearing vengeance. The third act begins with an orchestral introduction built upon a motive that had been introduced in Act II when Iago hypocritically warned Otello against jealousy—that "dark hydra, livid, blind, poisoned with its own venom" (Example X–11). This introduction will alert the listener to Otello's state of mind as he is discovered onstage conversing with Iago. A herald enters to report the arrival of Venetian ambassadors, but the preoccupied Otello takes no notice and listens receptively to a plan Iago proposes to test Desdemona's faithfulness. Desdemona enters and confronts her troubled husband. In the ensuing scene Otello at first behaves kindly toward her, partly (upon Iago's advice) to conceal his suspicions, and partly because she seems guileless to him at the moment. But Desdemona persists in untimely pleas on behalf of Cassio, gradually stirring Otello to new heights of rage that he largely conceals beneath an icy, malevolent calm. Desdemona's ingenuous innocence gives way to alarm and then to bewildered terror as she senses Otello's mood.

The task Verdi set himself was to provide continuous music that would delineate these shifting emotions and attitudes while carefully controlling the pace at which they unfold. The first scene, consisting entirely of recitative, is quickly dispatched. As the orchestral prelude finishes its exposition of the "jealousy" motive in F♯ minor, a sudden shift to E major for the herald's speech is heard as a tonal interruption—just as attending to affairs of state is an interruption of Otello's dark musing. As the herald leaves, the F♯ tonality immediately resumes, and Iago continues to outline his plan for testing Desdemona. In this scene the orchestra provides the barest of accompaniments for the recitative: the strings play continuo-like chords, give unobtrusive support here and there to a vocal line, and provide snatches of connective material.

In the second scene we see the harrowing confrontation between Otello and Desdemona. This scene may be divided into four sections; each begins with a lyrical melody whose calm is then destroyed by the agitated music accompanying Otello's mounting rage. The four sections are as follows:

	I	II	III	IV
Measure:	4	70	128	196
Text:	(D.) "Dio ti giocondi"	(D.) "Tu di me"	(D.) "Io prego"	(O.) "Datemi ancor"
Motive:	(x) a	b	c	a
Key:	E	G	F	E

As Desdemona enters in the first section the orchestra plays a quiet falling figure in even eighth notes *(x)* whose distinctive ornamented cadence in sixteenth notes is taken up as a punctuating device in the vocal music that follows. Desdemona then sings the first strains of a very regular melody *(a),* which is presently taken up by Otello (who, with an edge of irony, returns her affectionate greeting), much as in a conventional duet. This music unfolds as a binary form followed by a short *parlante* interjection that approaches G♯ minor ("Eppur qui annida," m. 18), and a codalike extension rounded off with the orchestral strain *(x)* that had accompanied Desdemona's entrance.

This passage, formally closed off and tonally stable, is followed by a snatch of unaccompanied recitative in which Desdemona makes an ill-advised attempt to introduce the subject of Cassio ("Ma riparlar di debbo di Cassio," m. 32). The easy lyricism of the preceding music vanishes: the tonality turns to A minor, and an agitated figure in sixteenth notes—related to the opening of the Prelude to this act—is heard in the violins. This becomes a persistent accompaniment to the declamation that follows in which Otello begins to expostulate about Desdemona's handkerchief. The tonality here veers in quick succession toward D minor, C♯ minor, and in a striking move (as Desdemona finally registers alarm at Otello's manner: "Mi fai paura!", m. 111) from an implied F♯ minor to F major.

All this excitement abruptly dies down as Desdemona decides that Otello is after all not serious ("Tu di me ti fai gioco," m. 70), and the second main section of the scene begins, like the first one, with an untroubled lyrical melody *(b).* But almost immediately she unluckily broaches the matter of Cassio again, and Otello's anger once more begins to mount: his detached declamation ("Il fazzoletto!", m. 77), with an agitated accompaniment in the lower strings, is now distributed between the phrases of Desdemona's melody (it is *b*) as she continues to sing about Cassio. When at last she understands Otello's mood ("Gran Dio! nella tua voce," m. 83) both of them sing in short bursts of declamation; a new version of the troubled sixteenth-note figure is constantly present in the strings, and the tonality moves restlessly from C minor through D♭ major, F major, D minor, and E minor. A climax is reached as Otello condemns Desdemona for her supposed faithlessness ("Giura e ti danna!", m. 96), and Desdemona, now quite terrified, replies in a quietly desperate monotone over a tense, crackling rhythm in the orchestra (mm. 115ff.).

For the third time Desdemona initiates a new episode with a soaring melody *(c)* as she addresses heaven on Otello's behalf ("Io prego il cielo per te," m. 128), and once again Otello seems for a moment to concur in her sentiments as he fits his declamation to an orchestral statement of that melody ("S'or ti scorge il tuo démone"). But his agitation again takes over; after Desdemona makes a last desperate plea of innocence ("E son io l'innocenta") to a strain of melody *c,* irregular declamation with no tonal center accompanied by portentous string tremolos leads to Otello's climactic accusation, "Non si forse una vil cortigiana?" ("Are you not then a vile strumpet?", m. 232). Desdemona's very dramatic negative reply, "Ah! non sono ciò che esprime quella parola orrenda" ("Ah! I am not what that horrible word expresses," m. 238), descends through a twelfth from b♭″ to e♭′, seemingly adding a note of finality by establishing E♭, at last, as the tonic. But this certainty is swept away as E♭ becomes D♯, the third of the dominant of E major, where, astonishingly, Desdemona's untroubled melody *a* from the opening of the scene is heard in the orchestra. Even more astonishingly, it is Otello who sings its continuation, as he seems inexplicably mollified and asks for Desdemona's pardon. But this, the beginning of the final and shortest section of the scene, is only the most extreme of his seeming reverses; the melody is brutally broken off as Otello hurls his final accusation and forces Desdemona out the door.

In this crucial scene Verdi's music performs marvels of characterization. Otello's volatile anger and erratic shifts of position, real and feigned, are finely delineated in the movement between arioso singing and emotionally charged declamation. The orchestra is a sort of gauge of his feelings: changes in motion and intensity are intimated there first. Desdemona's naïve innocence takes the form of lyrical song in which Otello sometimes (and sometimes reluctantly) joins. He wishes to believe her innocent and to *appear* to believe her innocent, but both wishes are consistently overpowered by his explosive anger; each time the "innocent" melody associated with Desdemona asserts itself, it is eroded or broken off before coming to completion. All this transpires in a seamless web of music whose fluctuations respond to dramatic forces rather than operatic convention. But the scene nonetheless takes on a certain abstract unity and closure by virtue of the final repetition of *a* in its original key—Otello's malevolent irony at this point turns out to serve a traditional formal end.

The musical language in *Otello* shows an impressive enrichment of Verdi's earlier style. Inventive diatonic procedures and elements of chromaticism in this work seem quite at home in the late nineteenth century. Even harmonically stable song such as the melody *c* (beginning "Io prego," ARM 19, p. 382) is subjected to chromatic inflection that is rare in Verdi's music, at least before *Aida*. The first phrase of that melody is exactly four measures long and ends with a standard feminine cadence, ostensibly on the dominant. In its second measure it bends toward the third degree, A, providing that sonority temporarily with its dominant, as shown in Example X–12. But a tonic pedal underlies the entire phrase, effectively misting over such harmonic functions, and sharpening the jangling tritone between f' and b'. In the second half of the phrase a perfectly usual extension of the dominant in which bass and soprano ascend in parallel tenths to a dominant chord in first inversion (still, of course, over a tonic pedal) is given elaborate chromatic decoration. The net effect of the tonic pedal and chromatic inflections in this phrase is only an embroidery upon standard harmonic progressions whose outlines remain perfectly perceptible.

Example X–12: VERDI, *Otello,* Act III, "Io prego," reduction

Verdi was quite right to object to imputations of "Wagnerism" in his operas of this period; his music regularly retains the underpinnings of an implied metrical regularity, and his elaborations of the inherited tonal language are characteristically more decorative than substantive. Verdi's orchestra, for all its importance, never assumes the dominant role it plays in the music dramas of Wagner; to the end his operas focus attention upon very human *dramatis personae* who are revealed and developed through their singing. This was also true of Verdi's final masterpiece, *Falstaff* (1893), composed to Boito's libretto after Shakespeare's *The Merry Wives of Windsor*. In this, only his second comic opera, Verdi brings his mature powers of musical characterization to bear upon a work that stands in the best traditions of the opera buffa of Mozart and Rossini. It finishes with a bubbling fugue to the words "Tutto nel mondo è burla" ("All the world's a joke"); here Verdi ends his career with a display of musical virtuosity full of the vigor and dramatic cogency that were consistent hallmarks of his art.

ITALIAN CONTEMPORARIES AND FOLLOWERS

For a great many years Verdi effectively overshadowed all other Italian opera composers. Occasionally a single work by a contemporary would gain public recognition, such as Boito's *Mefistofele* upon its revival in 1875. A younger contemporary, Amilcare Ponchielli (1834–86), produced a series of operas of which only one, *La Gioconda* (1876), with a libretto by Boito after Hugo, was an unqualified success. This violent story of an implausibly magnanimous heroine (La Gioconda) caught up in impossibly evil circumstances has many outward traits of middle-period Verdi: though distinctly a number opera, it has few formal arias, and much of the drama transpires in the course of ensembles. There are impressive choruses and engaging divertissements, such as the famous Dance of the Hours in Act III. But the effective pacing and brilliant musical characterization to which Verdi accustomed his audiences are largely missing, and there is a certain dwelling on pathos that the older composer was careful to avoid.

In 1888 the Milanese publisher E. Sonzogno sponsored a competition for single-act operas. First prize was won by the unknown young musician Pietro Mascagni (1863–1945) for his *Cavalleria rusticana* (Rustic Chivalry). From its first performances in Rome in 1890 this work achieved a dazzling success: it created an instant furor throughout Italy, and by 1891 had been performed in German, Swedish, Hungarian, Czech, Danish, and Lettish. Its libretto, fashioned after a story by Giovanni Verga, tells a rough-hewn and lachrymose tale of passion and revenge amidst the local color of a Sicilian village. Mascagni's music is generally old fashioned; its simple harmonic idiom and emphasis on strongly doubled melody with spare accompaniment are reminiscent of Bellini and Donizetti. Every effort is bent toward investing melody with the utmost poignancy of expression; the best-known tune in the work occurs in an orchestral Intermezzo (Example X–13). Here the melody descends from an obsessively repeated f″ (tonic) to the f′ below while the bass descends stepwise from f to G, before moving to the dominant and tonic. Although the only functional harmonies are I–vi–IV–ii⁷–V–I,

Example X–13: MASCAGNI, *Cavalleria rusticana*, Intermezzo

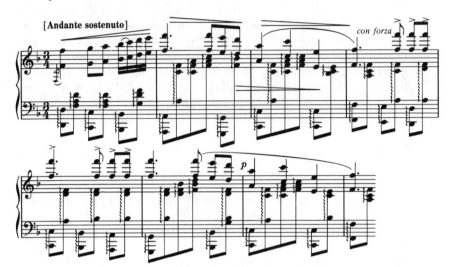

the holding fast of the high f″ throughout the descent of the bass creates a formidably grandiloquent effect—all the more so in that the progression is immediately repeated twice. This opera, with its stark depiction of violence and passion among ordinary people, and its superheated musical effects, was promptly hailed as the epitome of *verismo* in music.

Mascagni produced fourteen other operas during his long life. *L'Amico Fritz* (1891) and *Iris* (1898), a "Japanese" opera, attracted some attention; but even in his lifetime he was regarded as a one-opera composer. His brilliant triumph with that one opera moved an older contemporary, Ruggiero Leoncavallo (1858–1919), to compose a similarly short work in a similar style, *I Pagliacci* (The Clowns); first performed in Milan in 1892 under the baton of Arturo Toscanini, it quickly became the companion piece for *Cavalleria rusticana* in opera programs throughout the world. The libretto and music of *I Pagliacci,* both by Leoncavallo, exude a heightened pathos like that of *Cavalleria rusticana.* But the drama is more artful. Canio, leader of a troupe of *Commedia dell'arte* players, performs in a play-within-a-play, acting the part of the traditional clown Pagliaccio, the ostensible buffoon who is inwardly sensitive and suffering. But he finds himself acting out a situation painfully similar to the awful circumstances of his real life. Abruptly he sheds his assumed identity and murders his wife, who plays the faithless Columbine. Such violations of the boundaries between art and reality had already been intimated in the prologue, where an actor in the opera appeals directly to the audience.

The music of *Pagliacci* also seems more sophisticated, and more of its time, than that of *Cavalleria rusticana.* It is more continuous, it shows

Enrico Caruso as Canio in *Pagliacci*.

less distinction between recitative and arioso styles, and its harmonic language is richer. The famous and lugubrious tune "Ridi, Pagliaccio," that occurs three times in the opera, illustrates something of Leoncavallo's writing (Example X–14a). As in the excerpt quoted from *Cav-*

Example X–14

   a. LEONCAVALLO, *I Pagliacci,* "Ridi, Pagliaccio"

b. "Ridi, Pagliaccio" reduced

alleria rusticana (Example X–13), a certain prolongation of harmonic tension (here the persistent reiteration of a supertonic seventh chord) abruptly yields to an easy passage from dominant to tonic in a routine, familiar cadence (Example X–14b). But the ubiquitous use of seventh chords (especially secondary dominants and diminished sevenths) and harmonic movement by thirds gives Leoncavallo's music a distinct late-nineteenth-century sound. Like Mascagni, Leoncavallo made persistent but vain efforts to repeat his initial triumph. His *La Bohème* (1897) was no match for the opera on the same subject by Puccini, and his *Roland* (1904) was known only in Berlin, where it was said to be a favorite of Kaiser Wilhelm. During a sojourn in London beginning in 1911 he conducted a series of successful performances of *Pagliacci;* but attempts at English musical theater (such as the operetta *Are You There*) were a public disaster.

A third composer who leaped into prominence through Sonzogno's opera competitions was Giacomo Puccini (1858–1924), scion of four generations of musicians in Lucca. His entry in 1883, *Le Villi,* failed to win a prize, but attracted the attention of Boito and Ponchielli, who arranged to have it performed in Milan. Its great success there led to contracts with Ricordi, Verdi's publisher in Milan, for additional operas: *Edgar,* after a verse-drama by Alfred de Musset, was first staged at La Scala in 1889, and the premiere of *Manon Lescaut,* Puccini's first international triumph, took place in Turin in 1893. Like the earlier *Manon* of Jules Massenet (1842–1912) (see pp. 334–35), *Manon Lescaut* takes its subject from the novel of that name by A. F. Prévost. The libretto, concocted by a whole procession of writers (the first was Leoncavallo), tells of the decline and demise of the lovable courtesan Manon; exiled for her sins, she dies pathetically on a dry and endless plain, "on the borders of New Orleans."

The music of *Manon Lescaut,* while clearly revealing its Italian patrimony in a profusion of sensuous melodies, shows some genuinely individual traits. Most striking, perhaps, is an almost continuous activity in the orchestra; obbligato bits of melody and splotches of instrumental color accompany almost everything that occurs on stage. At points the endlessly busy orchestra sounds ponderous; it threatens to compete with the singing without achieving the dramatic import of Wagner's orchestra or that of the late Verdi. Puccini's harmonic style, too, is in some particulars unlike that of his contemporaries. There is little of the characteristic ornamental chromaticism of late-nineteenth-century music. Instead, Puccini experiments with expansions of tonal language that have a basically diatonic sound. One technique he favors is a nonfunctional, coloristic use of seventh chords. Another features various modal constructions, such as the aeolian tonal cast in the orchestral opening to Act II (Example X–15). Both of these traits suggest an awareness of the nascent impressionistic style just beginning to take shape in Paris.

Example X–15: PUCCINI, *Manon Lescaut,* Act II

Puccini's greatest success, and one of the most popular operas of all time, was *La Bohème* (1896). This engaging drama of starving but high-spirited artists in the Latin quarter of Paris, and particularly its portrayal of the guileless consumptive Mimi, has held a universal charm for opera audiences since its premiere. The libretto, written by Giuseppe Giacosa and Luigi Illica, who became Puccini's regular collaborators, is tight-knit and cogent in comparison to the jerry-built story of *Manon Lescaut.* Its narrative is simple in the extreme: Rodolfo and Mimi meet and fall in love; they are unable to get on together and separate, to be reunited just as Mimi dies of consumption. All else—a subsidiary love affair, portrayals of life in the garrets and streets of Paris—is only a scenic backdrop.

The musical style of *La Bohème* shows a new sure-handedness and economy of means. The orchestral part, lighter and less frenetic than that of *Manon Lescaut,* now participates more smoothly with the voices in the central dramatic pursuit. At the celebrated point in Act I where Rodolfo sees Mimi's face framed in a halo of moonlight, the orchestra plays a melody with which he had earlier sung of his new-found love for her. Rodolfo's words (together with a facetious remark of his friend Marcello) are at first delivered in a flexible declamatory style; then, as passions flare, he and Mimi join in the melody that is already underway in the orchestra, singing in octaves at high volume and pitch (Example X–16). Aria-like singing often emerges this way in *La Bohème:* it occurs in the context of ensembles, and often wells up first in the orchestra. The declamation with which Rodolfo begins in Example X–16 is also

Example X–16: PUCCINI, *La Bohème*, Act I

distinctive. It is a kind of understated, unaccentuated recitative typical
of Puccini that again suggests the influence of current French models.
It is harmonically straightforward and moves rather routinely between
A major and E major, providing special interest only in unexpected
bass movement to the third and sixth degrees (mm. 2 and 5 of the
example). Harmonically, *La Bohème* seems in general less adventurous
than both earlier and later music of Puccini.

As *La Bohème* scored its triumph, Puccini was already at work on a
new collaborative effort with Giacosa and Illica; the subject was taken
from *La Tosca,* Victorien Sardou's violent play set in Rome during the
Napoleonic wars at the turn of the nineteenth century. Some aspects of
this drama of heroic struggle against an oppressive regime are reminiscent of the *risorgimento.* But there is a powerful new realism as well: in
Act II of the opera there is a torture scene just off stage but within
earshot, and the heroine Tosca murders the villainous Scarpia in full
view of the audience. The music of *Tosca* (the title of the opera omits
the definite article) is a somewhat uneasy mixture of various earlier
strains of Puccini's style. Nonfunctional uses of traditional sonorities,
such as the sequence of root-position major triads on Bb, Ab, and E at
the very opening (these chords come to be associated with the character
Scarpia) rub elbows with an old-fashioned sort of harmonization, rife
with secondary dominants, that had been common in parlor music since
early in the century. The duet for Tosca and Cavaradossi in the first act
includes such a passage (see Example X–17). Music like this,[10] sometimes bordering on triviality, appears in diverse contexts in the opera.
But such passages are often particularly felicitous for the singer; Puccini's operas, including those written in the twentieth century (notably
Madama Butterfly, 1904; *La Fanciulla del West,* 1910; *Gianni Schicchi,* 1918;

10.   There is evidence that this duet was composed before it context was determined.
      See William Ashbrook, *The Operas of Puccini* (London, 1968), pp. 70–71.

Adolfo Hohenstein created this poster for Puccini's *Tosca*, 1899.

Example X–17: PUCCINI, *Tosca*, Act I

and *Turandot*, 1926) always include enough of these memorable tunes to gratify both singers and audiences and to reassert a continuity of an Italian operatic tradition reaching back at least to Rossini.

FRENCH OPERA OF THE LATER NINETEENTH CENTURY

During the second half of the nineteenth century France had no opera composer comparable in stature or influence to the giants Wagner and Verdi. Meyerbeer's *Le Prophète* was a great success in 1849, but at the time of the posthumous debut of *L'Africaine* (1865) it was clear that grand opera after the old model was declining. A new strain of opera was in the ascendant, mainly at the Theater of the Opéra comique, from about mid-century. Called *opéra lyrique,* works of this genre had little of the pomp and panoply of grand opera; their subjects were mainly poignant stories of love derived from modern literature, and violence of any sort—theatrical or musical—was for the most part excluded. The oldest composer associated with opéra lyrique was Ambroise Thomas (1811–96), who had competed with Berlioz as a student at the Conservatoire in the late 1820s and was still at that institution as its director when Debussy studied there a half-century later. His first opera, *La Double Echelle,* was produced at the Opéra comique as early as 1837; his reputation was made by *Le Caid* (1849) and *Le Songe d'une nuit d'été* (Midsummer Night's Dream—the plot, however, is about Shakespeare, not by him) of 1850. His most famous work, *Mignon,* after Goethe's *Wilhelm Meister,* followed in 1866, and *Hamlet* in 1868. The shape and style of these works seem deliberately retrospective: there is a good bit of recitative—faithful to French tradition, it is usually on the

Example X–18: THOMAS, *Mignon,* "Connais-tu le pays"

tuneful side—and solo singing often falls into easily recognizable forms. Thomas's music sounds sweet and well bred. Lilting, repetitious rhythms in compound meters abound, and the touches of chromaticism here and there are purely decorative. In the *romance* in Act I of *Mignon*, "Connais-tu le pays"[11] (see Example X–18), the music seems patterned and predictable, showing a clear kinship with the sentimental romances sung in Parisian salons.

Best remembered of the composers of opéra lyrique is Charles Gounod (1818–93), another product of the Paris Conservatoire. In his very active career Gounod wrote a great quantity of church music, a good many pieces for piano and instrumental ensembles, and some 200 songs to texts in various languages (his familiar *Ave Maria,* constructed as an obbligato melody to the first Prelude of Bach's *Well-Tempered Clavier,* was first written in 1852 to a poem of Lamartine; it was given its present text in 1859); his first stage work, *Sapho,* was produced at the Opéra in 1851. Gounod's initial and greatest triumph was *Faust,* first heard (with spoken dialogue) at the Théâtre lyrique in Paris in 1859. The composer and his librettist, Jules Barbier, shared the growing fascination Goethe's *Faust* held for Frenchmen of the later nineteenth century. But a decision was made to limit the action essentially to one episode, i.e. Faust's liaison with Marguerite (Gretchen). Extensive cuts and changes made before the first performance, moreover, sometimes threaten the intelligibility of this limited narrative. A decade later Gounod made further substantial changes, most significant of which was the substitution of recitative for the spoken dialogue and the addition of a ballet. In this form the opera met with acclaim throughout Europe and remained a staple of the repertory well into the present century.

The declamatory singing in *Faust,* including the recitatives the composer added later, is perhaps the most satisfying part of the work. Faust and Mephistopheles, particularly, converse in a style that is faithful to natural speaking accents and reflects something of the pace of actual dialogue, despite the French penchant for a certain measuredness and tunefulness. The set pieces—arias, songs, ensembles, and orchestral music—tend to be attractive but, to some ears, a bit superficial. As in Thomas's music, drawing-room rhythms in compound meters are very usual, and the harmonic style reflects little of recent developments in the art. An instance of such writing occurs very early in Act I. Faust is assured by Mephistopheles (in flexible, dramatically convincing declamation) that he can yet experience youth, joy, and love, whereupon the two of them break into a lilting, ingenuous tune (see Example X–19). Many Germans have felt that the towering intellect and visionary imagination of Goethe, and of his character Faust, were not accorded proper

---

11. The original version of this poem from Goethe's *Wilhelm Meister,* "Kennst du das Land," was set to fine effect by Schubert.

Example X–19: GOUNOD, *Faust,* Act I

respect in Gounod's opera; to the present day in German-speaking countries the work is called *Margarethe.*

In his *Roméo et Juliette,* first performed at the Théâtre lyrique in 1867, and at the Opéra in 1888, Gounod's overriding lyricism seems more appropriate than in a work with the grave philosophical and religious implications of Goethe's masterpiece. In the two duets of the principal characters at the end of Act II and the beginning of Act IV, the sweet sound of singing in parallel sixths (and in the latter case, gentle movement in 12 / 8 meter) seems right for the situation. And if in *Faust* Gounod seemed little affected by the musical treatment of that theme by his older compatriot Berlioz,[12] his *Roméo et Juliette* betrays signs of an

12. Some of the situations presented in Gounod's opera correspond to those in *The Damnation of Faust:* Faust in his study, a drinking scene, and a scene in Marguerite's room in which she sings *The King of Thule.*

The grand staircase of the Paris Opera (Salle Garnier).

acquaintance with Berlioz's "Symphonie dramatique" *Roméo et Juliette:* both works, for example, begin with a prologue set to measured recitative sung by the chorus.

Youngest of the three principal composers of opéra lyrique was Thomas's student at the Conservatoire, Jules Massenet, whose operatic career began with the performance of his *La Grand' Tante* at the Opéra comique in 1867. A great crescendo of public acclaim greeted his subsequent productions, *Le Roi de Lahore* (1877) and *Hérodiade* (1881), culminating with *Manon* (after Prévost's novel)[13] in 1884. *Manon* is the epitome of opéra lyrique. All attention is focused on Manon herself, the lovable coquette who finally expires while yet singing sweetly (in this libretto, written by H. Meilhac and P. Gille, the end comes not in Louisiana, but on the road to Le Havre). The mood is not one of tragedy but of bittersweet pathos, and the music is for the most part facile and mellifluous. There is a certain characteristically French restraint to Massenet's approach. Spoken dialogue[14] often takes the form of melodrama—i.e., the text is recited against a musical background; but there is little of the intensity of expression associated with that genre. And when the lovers meet for the last time after a long separation, the hero, Des Grieux, calls out to Manon in an impetuous outburst that within four measures subsides to pianissimo followed by silence (Example X–

---

13. See above, p. 326–27.
14. Spoken dialogue was customary at the Opéra comique, where *Manon* was first performed.

Example X–20: MASSENET, *Manon,* Act V

20) and a resumption of gentle, soothing music in 9/8 meter. How radically the sensibility reflected in this scene differs from that of the increasingly dominant Wagnerian music drama can be shown by recalling a similar dramatic situation in Act II of *Tristan und Isolde.* As the lovers meet there, rising sequences build to a frenzied climax in the orchestra, and they sing to each other in frenetic disjointed phrases at the top of their ranges. Massenet's scene seems by comparison suave, understated, and decidedly Gallic.

The sweetness and gentle pathos of opéra lyrique so completely won the hearts of "le tout Paris" that comic opera, as such, almost disappeared. Then, in 1855, an enterprising young musician from Cologne, Jacques Offenbach (1819–80), established a tiny new theater called Les Bouffes parisiens at the exhibition grounds of the Champs Elysées. Formerly a virtuoso cellist and for seven years director of music at the theater for spoken drama, the Comédie française, Offenbach now applied his talents to composing, directing, and conducting a new breed of musical theater: fast-moving, lighthearted productions bristling with satire, and set to energetic music in a popular vein. These operettas revive something of the format of the old *vaudeville,* in which spoken dialogue is interspersed with songs, choruses, and dances. The music abounds with the rhythms of current dances: the waltz, the gallop, the quadrille, and the can-can.

Offenbach's first great success was *Orphée aux enfers* (Orpheus in the Underworld, 1858); this was followed by an unbroken series of triumphs, including *La Belle Hélène* in 1864, and his most popular work of all, *La Vie parisienne,* in 1866. These comedies often rely for their effect upon preposterous breaches of decorum: barons seem hopelessly foolish and Olympian deities dance the can-can. A booter and a glover sing of the merits of their respective professions in a coloratura duet of high style.

And we detect a certain mockery of the most venerable traditions of French declamation when choruses sing at top speed in an even-note patter style. Such levity struck a very responsive chord in the declining years of the Second Empire, when outward splendor and frivolity at the court of Napoleon III masked growing internal weakness. Offenbach was even made Chevalier de la Légion d'Honneur in 1862. But when the Empire ended in the catastrophic events of 1870–71,[15] he was so identified with the old regime that the continuation of his career seemed doubtful. Though two more operettas, *La Jolie Parfumeuse* (The Pretty Perfume Seller, 1874) and *La Boulangère a des écus* (The Baker Has Money) were a moderate success, his subsequent directorship of the Théâtre de la Gaité ended in disaster.

After a concert tour of the United States in 1875–76 Offenbach returned to Paris in broken health and died in 1880 while struggling to finish his most ambitious work, *Les Contes d'Hoffmann* (The Tales of Hoffmann); with the orchestration completed by Ernest Guiraud, this full-fledged opera was first presented at the Opéra comique in February 1881. The libretto of *Les Contes d'Hoffmann* is a clever conflation of three short stories by E. T. A. Hoffmann, adapted by Jules Barbier and Michel Carré from their earlier stage play, *Fantastiques d'Hoffmann* (1851). In a "framing" device Hoffmann himself becomes a character in the drama, relating the individual tales (of which he has become the protagonist) to his drinking companions. These bittersweet flights of fancy are given a remarkably varied musical setting by Offenbach. The dialogue is carried on in recitative that ranges from a rapid-fire *secco* style to dramatic declamation with florid orchestral accompaniment. There are operetta-like strophic songs with snappy choral refrains and swift-moving patter choruses reminiscent of Rossini. The air of Dapertutto, "Scintille diamant" in Act II, is a semiserious imitation of the gently chromatic sentimental aria then current in French opera; and the languorous motion in 6/8 meter of the famous Barcarolle at the beginning of that act is the epitome of the innocuous sort of musical expression favored in the opéra lyrique. This piece, best-known of all Offenbach's music, but hardly representative of his style, was borrowed from his unsuccessful romantic opera *Die Rheinnixen* (Vienna, 1864).

Another sort of divergence from the norms of opéra lyrique can be seen in the eternally popular *Carmen* of Georges Bizet (1838–75). Yet another product of the Paris Conservatoire, Bizet in his short life produced a considerable quantity of music in various categories: a Symphony in C (1855), two often-played orchestral suites (the second compiled by Ernest Guiraud after Bizet's death) that began as incidental

---

15. As victorious German troops occupied Paris, the French were bitterly divided against themselves; in 1871 the newly created Republican government even laid siege to the city to wrest it from the control of communards, and the loss of life in this operation exceeded that of the effort to resist the Germans.

Carmen, Act I. Elaina Obratsova sings the title role in this Metropolitan Opera production.

music to Alphonse Daudet's play *L'Arlésienne,* and a good number of compositions for piano. His career as an opera composer began with *Les Pêcheurs de perles* (The Pearl Fishers) in 1863. Neither this nor his dramatic works that followed it attracted much attention until *Carmen* had its premiere in 1875, some three months before the composer's death. First performed at the Opéra comique with spoken dialogue, the work was greeted with hostility by the public and the press: its plot and action were judged much too realistic—even indecent—and Bizet's music was declared unmelodious or even "Wagnerian". Fitted out with recitatives by Guiraud, *Carmen* played to a much more receptive audience in Vienna later in 1875 and soon became a staple in the international opera repertory.

As in Massenet's *Manon* and Puccini's *Manon Léscaut,* the heroine in *Carmen* is very much the center of attention. But the Spanish gypsy Carmen is utterly unlike the pathetic Manon: bold, seductive, mysterious, and pitiless, she captivated contemporary audiences while shocking them. Another powerful attraction of this opera was the generous local color of Bizet's score. There are songs and dances imitative of Gypsy music, a seguidilla (a Spanish dance similar to the bolero), and the well-known Habanera sung by Carmen in the first act. The musical style of *Carmen* for the most part should have been rather familiar to nineteenth-century listeners in France. Even the suave manner of the opéra lyrique is sometimes in evidence. An example is the air of Micaela (an ingenuous woman after the fashion of heroines in opéra lyrique), "Je dis que rien ne m'épouvante," in Act III; its gentle motion in 9/8 meter and a sweetly singing obbligato accompaniment in the upper instruments would sound quite at home in an opera of Thomas or Gounod. There are also clear signs of Italian influence. The very famil-

Example X–21: BIZET, *Carmen,* Act II, Toreador Song

iar refrain to the Toreador Song in Act II—which one might expect to
sound particularly Spanish—has the unadorned marchlike accompaniment that was a tradition in heroic tenor arias of Italian opera since early
Verdi (Example X–21). The only thing that is un-Italian about this
passage is the French text and the peculiarities of its declamation: the
melisma on *gar-* in the second measure, and the placement of the mute
-de at a rhythmically prominent point impart a distinctively French flavor to this phrase. And in more important ways *Carmen* brought to
native French opera strengths akin to the best of Verdi: a swift and vivid
drama, a sharp musical delineation of character, and, above all, a wonderfully varied and colorful treatment of the orchestra.

The Spanish flavor of *Carmen* was a relatively mild example of the
exoticism that was taking hold in French opera. In 1872 *Princesse jaune*
(The Yellow Princess) of Camille Saint-Saëns (1835–1921) was one of
the earliest examples of a fashionable Oriental subject, and many other
followed, such as *Salammbô* (1890) of Ernest Reyer (1823–1909). (The
most famous of them, however, was produced in Italy: Puccini's *Madama
Butterfly.*) What was much less the fashion in *Carmen* was its realistic
plot, based upon a novella of Prosper Mérimée: its serious depiction of
ordinary people, including women who smoke cigarettes in public, and
its tingling mixture of eroticism and violence. Apparently influenced
by the candid and minute representation of ordinary life in the writings
of Honoré de Balzac and Émile Zola, the drama of *Carmen* was in turn
an important model for works such as Gustave Charpentier's *Louise*
(1900) and for *verismo* in Italian opera of the end of the century.

From about 1860 Wagner and Wagnerism were increasingly an issue in the cultural life of Paris. A year before the disaster of *Tannhäuser* in 1861, several works of Wagner, including the Prelude to *Tristan und Isolde,* were heard there in concert performances. After 1861 Parisian theaters generally shunned Wagner's operas until nearly the end of the century; only *Lohengrin, Die Walküre,* and a short run of *Rienzi* were heard there until 1895. Aside from the pilgrimages to Munich or Bayreuth made by a few enthusiasts, the French were exposed only to bits and pieces of his works, occasionally played at concerts such as those of the Société des nouveaux concerts, founded in 1881 by Charles Lamoureux, or at private soirées. Ignorance of Wagner's music dramas did not, however, prevent a rising tide of Wagnerism in Parisian literary and artistic circles. The Symbolist poets, especially Baudelaire and Mallarmé, had some acquaintance with the composer's prose works, and proclaimed the indebtedness of their literary theories to what they imagined to be the composer's system. The *Revue Wagnérienne,* founded in 1885, was more a literary enterprise than a musical one; among its contributors were the writers Mallarmé, Paul Verlaine, Villiers de L'isle-Adam, and J. K. Huysmans. Even painters, such as Odilon Redon, Fantin-Latour, and the young Cézanne, sought to join the Wagnerist camp by depicting scenes from the master's works—works of which they could have had no direct experience.

Opera itself seemed rather less responsive to the blandishments of Wagnerism than the other arts in France. Until the end of the century the musical and dramatic manner of the opéra lyrique remained dominant. But in 1884 the plot (if not the music) of Ernest Reyer's *Sigurd* showed a clear debt to *The Ring.* And one younger French composer of opera who quite deliberately adopted the Wagnerian manner was Emmanuel Chabrier (1841–94). His *Gwendoline* (1886) has a prominent love duet often thought to be reminiscent of *Tristan,* and a general conflagration at the end recalls the *Ring.* Some of the writing in this opera is studiously chromatic. But it seems clear that an imitation of Wagner's harmonic style is not Chabrier's normal mode of musical discourse. More usual and more innovative than his chromaticism is a coloristic use of augmented triads and the juxtaposition of root-position chords in nonfunctional successions—techniques that might remind us more of Debussy than of Wagner.

As an assistant conductor of the concerts of Lamoureux, Chabrier shared his enthusiasm for Wagner's music with another young conductor of this series, Vincent D'Indy (1851–1931). This staunch admirer of the Wagnerian music drama wrote the librettos for his operas *Fervaal* (1897) and *L'Etranger* (1903). *Fervaal,* a mystical, symbolic treatment of a Celtic subject, has continuous music from beginning to end. As in much French opera of the period, there is some distinguishable recitative: a flexible, melodically limited declamation closely bound to tex-

Example X–22: D'INDY, *Fervaal,* Act I

tual rhythms. This kind of singing merges into a more expansive lyrical style in which—as in Wagner's late works—the text is nonetheless set almost strictly syllabically. In Example X–22 the Druidic priest Arfagard announces plans for war in this more melodic style. This example also shows something of the eclecticism of D'Indy's harmonic style. In the first two measures diatonic chords with roots a tritone apart (G and Db) are juxtaposed, and a B-major sonority (at "guerre") is answered by an altered seventh sound and an augmented triad. Such harmonic procedures became standard from about that time in the works of Debussy. But in the final measures of the example D'Indy launches into a linear chromatic progression that sounds straight out of *Tristan.* Such a mixture of "impressionist" sounds with Wagnerian chromaticism is symptomatic of the posture of music in France at the century's end; even when a capitulation to the spirit and manner of Bayreuth seemed most imminent, French composers always seemed able to preserve certain traits that were very much their own.

CHAPTER XI

Nationalist Music

Nationalism, an increasingly influential force in the life and culture of nineteenth-century Europe, decreed that one's primary loyalties were owed not to a dynastic state or even to a religious community, but to an ethnically homogeneous nation, to a "people." A corollary of a nationalist point of view holds that products of culture should reflect the character of the nation from which they arise. Throughout European history, political and social ideals had been supranational in scope. The Roman Empire was a persistent model for the formulation of ideas about the state, its influence extending from the medieval Holy Roman Empire as far as seventeenth-century visions of a united world civilization. European culture in the Middle Ages was marked by a unified religious outlook and a common language (Latin or Greek); for the Renaissance and all neoclassical cultures the civilization of ancient Greece and Rome provided a norm that transcended national differences. In England, physically isolated but more advanced than most nations in trade and industry, we can detect the first clear glimmering of nationalism. The Puritan Revolution of the seventeenth century stirred (in Milton and others) strong sentiments of national solidarity; England came to be seen as a single people, united like the tribes of ancient Israel in common purposes and beliefs.

During the second half of the eighteenth century nationalist impulses were felt in several countries: in Rousseau's notions of popular sovereignty and *volonté générale* (which seems close to a *volonté nationale*), in the celebration of a "folk" product in the poetic collections published by Percy and Herder. The Revolutions in America and France proved to be powerful coalescing forces in those countries, consolidating national identities in a spirit of patriotic fervor. During the nineteenth century, the "age of European nationalism," the long struggle for freedom and unification in Germany and Italy reflected a growing conviction that states ought to be coterminous with nationalities or languages. And again, political unrest and revolution proved to be both an impetus for and an instrument of nationalist movements. The uprisings that shook much of Europe in 1830 and in 1848 took on an intensified coloration of national patriotism as they spread outward from the epicenter in Paris. Particularly in 1848, French political developments were followed with fascination in Dresden, Buda-Pest, and Prague, inspiring enthusiasm for German, Hungarian, and Bohemian autonomy and unity.

Movements toward national identity were felt in literature and the arts at least as soon as in politics. Early in the nineteenth century a quickening interest in "peripheral" languages such as Czech, Hungarian, and Russian as literary vehicles, and a new pride in local history, customs, and lore began to replace the classicism and Francophilia that had dominated European culture since the seventeenth century. In music the new spirit was revealed in various ways, e.g. in Wagner's glorification of Germanic myth and Verdi's use of historical and literary subjects to serve present political ends. More specifically, nationalism could be seen in a new enthusiasm for folk song and dance, for the special musical idioms that were thought to characterize a people. These indigenous musical traits were sometimes quite consciously taken up by composers and incorporated into the traditional genres of art music, resulting in special local or "nationalist" adaptations of a general style. Thus the use of old English songs in ballad opera, Weber's appropriation of the *Männerchor* style in *Der Freischütz,* and even the imitation of the choruses from the fêtes in opéra comique might be considered evidences of musical nationalism.

A similar impulse can be seen in the cultivation of the waltz in Vienna. Having its origins in various peasant dances collectively known as *Deutsche* or *Ländler,* this dance moved from cobbled village squares in the Austrian Alps and surrounding regions to the polished ballroom floors of the Imperial city late in the eighteenth century. Although in the process the waltz exchanged its leaping and stamping motions for a more decorous gliding effect, its local and plebeian associations remained a powerful attraction. In the first two decades of the nineteenth century the waltz spread rapidly throughout Europe to become the most popular of all ballroom dances. Beethoven, Schubert, and Hummel all provided sets of them (under varying titles), clearly intended for dancing, but showing a heightened level of artistic cultivation. In Weber's rondo *Aufforderung zum Tanz* (Invitation To The Dance, 1819), one of the best-known piano compositions of the earlier nineteenth century, the waltz became a concert piece, at the same time assuming its later characteristic shape as a series of individual dances with an introduction and coda. Throughout the century the waltz made frequent appearances in "serious" music such as the *Symphonie fantastique* of Berlioz, Chopin's Waltzes, the second-act finale of Gounod's *Faust,* and the *Liebeslieder Walzer* of Johannes Brahms.

As the initial rage for the waltz began to subside in France and England, it took on new splendor and popularity in its birthplace, Vienna. In the hands of Joseph Lanner (1801–43) and Johann Strauss the elder (1804–

49), both of them composers, conductors, and violinists, the familiar physiognomy of the "Viennese waltz" took shape: a series of five to seven dances, each consisting of two eight-bar or (later) sixteen-bar sections, the whole framed by an introduction and coda. In addition to the distinctive waltz rhythm, this music featured violinistic devices such as playing on open strings, double stops in thirds, and frequent portamento—a nostalgic reminiscence of the sounds of folk playing shifted into the ballrooms and open-air concerts of the capital city. These dances began to be published in the 1820s, often with titles referring to the place or occasion for which they were composed; examples are Strauss's *Täuberln-Walzer* (named for the inn "Zu den zwei Tauben," 1826), and Lanner's *Der Schönbrunner* (1842). Even more renowned than Strauss was his son, the younger Johann Strauss (1825–99), who together with his brother Josef Strauss (1827–70) raised the Viennese waltz to even greater heights of popularity. The apogee of the genre occurred in the 1860s with celebrated works such as *An der schönen blauen Donau* (On the Beautiful Blue Danube) and *Geschichten aus dem Wienerwald* (Tales from the Vienna Woods), both by the younger Johann Strauss. In this music, adaptable for varying ensembles and performed in taverns, ballrooms, and concert halls, we detect an amalgam of popular and cultivated idioms that unites various strata of society in strong sentiments of local patriotism.

Johann Strauss the Younger and his Ensemble, from a contemporary print.

HUNGARY

The effects of nationalism in music were of course much more prominent in newly emerging nations than in the established ones. This was the case in Hungary, which, like many nations in Europe, gradually found its identity in the course of the nineteenth century. This area, occupied for many hundreds of years mainly by the Magyars, fell under Turkish domination in the sixteenth and seventeenth centuries and was ruled by the Austrian Hapsburgs in the eighteenth. In the 1830s there began a movement toward reform and independence that, despite periods of repression, was essentially complete by 1867. Under Austrian rule Western art music had flourished among the Hungarian nobility. Michael Haydn (1737–1806) and Carl Ditters von Dittersdorf (1739–99) were both employed at Nagyvárad (now Oradea Mare in Romania), and Joseph Haydn spent much of his long career at the court of Eszterháza, where the first regular opera theater in Hungary was established in 1768 under his direction.

In the later eighteenth century a musical idiom with its roots in indigenous folk music gained wide currency in Hungary: this was the *Verbunkos,* a style of dance music sometimes used for military recruiting (its name derives from the German *Werbung,* "recruiting").

Characteristic of this style were alternating slow and fast sections *(lassu* and *friss),* sharply accentuated rhythms with many dotted figures and triplets, and colorful violinistic ornamentation and paraphrase. A distinctive cadential pattern in the *Verbunkos* is a sort of *cambiata* figure in dotted-note rhythms called the *Bokázo* (Example XI–1). Associated largely with Gypsy musicians (though not created by them), this idiom was taken up by many others, until in the hands of violinists such as

Example XI–1: Verbunkos (Bokázo)

János Bihari and A. G. Csermák it became in the early nineteenth century something of a national style. The natural descendent of the *Verbunkos,* and in its early forms nearly indistinguishable from it, was the *Csárdás.* This dance, whatever its roots in folk music, was first known about 1840 almost exclusively in the fashionable ballrooms of the Hungarian capital, Pest. Another indigenous sort of Hungarian music was the *Magyarnóta,* a "popular art song" of the later nineteenth century that combined elements of folk melody with the standard harmonizations of Western art music.

Art music of a distinctly Hungarian cast came into prominence, mainly in the capital, in the 1830s. A national theater was established there in

1837, and a conservatory opened in 1840. The leading musician associated with this movement was the versatile Ferenc Erkel (1810–93), a pianist, composer, and conductor generally regarded as the founder of Hungarian opera. Beginning with *Mária Bátori* in 1840, Erkel (sometimes in collaboration with various of his four composer-sons) wrote a series of nine operas drawn mainly from local history. In these works a rather conventional structure of recitatives, arias, choruses, and divertissements is embellished at important points with the distinctive sounds of the *Verbunkos* and *Csárdás*. In the third act of *László Hunyadi* (1844), for example, there is a *Fidelio*-like scene in which the political prisoner Hunyadi languishes in a dungeon; his identity as a national hero is emphasized in the introductory *lassu*-like music (Example XI–2).

Example XI–2: ERKEL, *László Hunyadi,* Act III

Traditional Hungarian idioms came to be known in the rest of Europe when they were taken up by foreign composers. Beethoven and Schubert both made isolated attempts to imitate the *Verbunkos* style. The leading adapter and disseminator of this music, however, was Franz Liszt, who first showed an interest in the music of his native country upon his triumphal visit to Pest in 1839.[1] During the next eight years he wrote a series of National Melodies and Rhapsodies whose revisions are the well-known Hungarian Rhapsodies. These works show a splendid pianistic imitation of the sound of the Gypsy orchestra of violins, woodwinds, and cimbalom (an ancient Hungarian dulcimer). The extravagant ornamentation in this style, associated mainly with the solo violin in the *lassu* sections, accorded well with Liszt's proclivities for virtuoso improvisation. Example XI–3a shows the eight-bar theme from the beginning of the Hungarian Rhapsody No. 9, *Le Carnaval de Pesth.*

---

1.   See above, p. 183.

This theme is followed by a series of ornamented variations, one of which is shown in Example XI–3b.

Example XI–3: LISZT, *Hungarian Rhapsody No. 9*
    a. Mm. 20–27

    b. Mm. 53–60

In this variation the initial melodic motion from e♭′ to b♭′ is replaced with a brilliant two-and-one-half octave skittering gesture; this, and the wide-leaping figure that follows, are probably meant to evoke the musical idiom of the cimbalom played with hammers. A less pronounced imitation of Hungarian sounds can be heard in the construction of this melody. The scales in *Verbunkos* music often included a lowered second and raised fourth degree. Here the persistent A♮, while really occurring only as a passing tone between the normal fourth, A♭, and the fifth, B♭, nevertheless adds to this music a lingering aroma of exoticism. Liszt later incorporated the "Hungarian manner" into such diverse works as the *Missa solemnis* (1856) and his oratorio, *Die Legende von der heiligen Elisabeth* (1857–62). It was in works such as these, and in the popular Hungarian Dances of Brahms (written for piano four-hands and later transcribed for both solo piano and orchestra) that adaptations of Hungarian music were disseminated; European familiarity with the genuine article awaited the researches of Zoltán Kodály and Béla Bartók in the next century.

BOHEMIA

> I had frequently been told, that the Bohemians were the most musical people of Germany, or, perhaps, of all Europe; and an eminent German composer, now in London, had declared to me, that if they enjoyed the same advantages as the Italians, they would excel them.[2]

Thus Charles Burney, the indefatigable English music historian and traveler, spoke after his visit to Prague in 1772. As Burney also observed, however, Bohemia had been repeatedly scourged by the wars that ravaged central Europe, most recently the Seven Years' War, in which Frederick the Great scored a decisive victory over the Austrians in the Battle of Prague in 1757.

> And even in the short intervals of peace [he reported] their first nobility are attached to the court of Vienna, and seldom reside in their own capital; so that those among the poorer sort, who are taught music in their infancy, have no encouragement to pursue it in riper years.

Since 1526 Bohemia had been part of the Holy Roman Empire ruled by the Austrian Hapsburgs. During much of the sixteenth century the Emperors often chose to live in Prague; members of the nobility built palaces there to be close to the center of power, and resplendent musical establishments arose among families such as the Kinskys (later patrons

---

2. Charles Burney, *An Eighteenth-Century Musical Tour in Central Europe and the Netherlands,* ed. Percy A. Scholes (London, 1959), p. 131.

of Beethoven) and Czernins. By the time of Burney's visit, however, Vienna had become the established center of the Holy Roman Empire. The former glory of Prague was rather dimmed, and Bohemian musicians characteristically made their careers elsewhere: the Stamitz father and sons in Mannheim, the Benda brothers in Berlin and Gotha, J. L. Dusík in London and elsewhere, and a large contingent of composers and players, including Johann Baptist Vanhal and Leopold Kozeluch, in Vienna.

In the nineteenth century only small steps toward independence and national integrity were taken in Bohemia. While the successive uprisings that rocked many European capitals stirred great excitement in Prague, all attempts to loosen the hold of Hapsburg domination failed; until the end of the century a minority German population and its language dominated this land composed mainly of Slavs whose natural language was Czech. It was not until 1918 that present-day Czechoslovakia was formed from the unification of Bohemia with Moravia and Slovakia. In the earlier nineteenth century, despite systematic attempts to suppress the use of Czech, there was a modest flowering of literature in that language. The numerous translations into Czech and the Czech–German dictionary of Joseph Jungmann (1773–1847) served to confer a sort of legitimacy upon the language, and the distinctly nationalist writings of John Kolar (1793–1852) raised Czech poetry to a level that has rarely been surpassed.

TOMÁŠEK AND SMETANA

The first Bohemian composer of international reputation to carry out his career mainly in his native country was Václav Jan Tomášek (1774–1850).[3] He became the center of a circle in Prague that included a number of younger musical countrymen such as the composers Jan Bedřich Kittl (1806–68) and Jan Václav Voříšek (1791–1825), together with German-Bohemians like the pianist Alexander Dreyschock (1818–69) and Eduard Hanslick, later the magisterial music critic of Vienna. Though Tomášek set some Czech texts to music and made a few attempts to incorporate Bohemian folk melodies into his compositions, his outlook and that of his followers was essentially cosmopolitan, and his influence upon the "mainstream"—Schubert and others—considerable. It was not until the later stages of the career of Bedřich Smetana (1824–84) that Bohemia had a native composer who sought to create a distinctively national musical art.

Smetana was an émigré composer and pianist working in Sweden when the defeat of Austrian forces at the hands of Napoleon III in 1859

3. See above, p. 103.

Teresie Rückaufova as Marenka in Smetana's *The Bartered Bride,* 1866.

seemed to signal a relaxation of Hapsburg control in Bohemia. A Provisional Theater for the performance of plays and operas in the Czech language was built, and in 1862 Smetana settled in Prague with the intent of contributing to a nationalist musical culture. During the following twenty years he composed eight operas to Czech librettos. *The Brandenburgers in Bohemia* (1863), *Dalibor* (1867), and *Libuše* (1872) are serious works on subjects drawn from Bohemian history and legend. Somewhat conservative in musical style, these operas have evoked comparisons with *Fidelio* and *Der Freischütz*. Better received than these, however, were Smetana's comic operas, *The Bartered Bride* (1866 with three subsequent revisions), *The Two Widows* (1874), and *The Secret* (1878). Somewhat to the composer's chagrin, all of his other operas were overshadowed in the public's estimation by the lighthearted comedy, *The Bartered Bride*. Like Otto Nicolai's *Die lustige Weiber von Windsor,* Smetana's masterpiece borrows freely from the operatic fashions of an earlier age: styles of recitative and aria often recall Mozart (a "stuttering" song in Act II seems explicitly derivative of the duet of Papageno and Papagena in *Die Zauberflöte*), and the harmonies and instrumental colors, insofar as they depart from classical norms, seem reminiscent of Schubert. There are some gestures towards musical "local color"; in the first act a Polka (adapted from an earlier piano composition and added in 1870 for the Vienna premier) reminds us that this dance is of Bohemian origin; another Bohemian dance, the hemiola-laden Furiant, is heard in the second act.

In his earlier career Smetana, an ambitious pianist, composed a great deal of piano music in the genres then fashionable: variations, etudes, programmatic pieces, a great many dances, and a single sonata, in G minor (1846)—all very much influenced by Liszt. It was in Smetana's orchestral music, however, that the example of the Hungarian expatriate was most telling; Smetana was one of the first to follow his lead in composing symphonic poems: the earliest were *Richard III* (1858), *Wallenstein's Camp* (1859), and *Hakon Jarl* (1861). These works contain rather broad programmatic references to incidents in the dramas of Shakespeare, Schiller, and Oehlenschlager from which their titles derive; they also show, in a somewhat conservative stylistic context, a very sure hand in orchestral writing.

Most significant of Smetana's music for orchestra is surely his epic cycle of six symphonic poems, *Ma Vlast* (My Fatherland, c. 1872–79), individually titled *Vyšehrad, The Moldau, Šarka, From Bohemia's Woods and Fields, Tabor,* and *Blanik.* The episodes from the life and legend of Bohemia represented in these compositions, closely connected with Smetana's opera *Libuše,* were described by the composer:[4] a splendid medieval castle scene, the stately flow of the Moldau river, the triumph of an Amazon-like Bohemian maiden (Šarka) over her enemies, and the military exploits of the followers of John Huss. This music abounds with programmatic devices, with imitations in sound of clamorous battle, of dancing rivulets flowing into the Moldau, and of peasant gatherings along its banks. There is vigorous "peasant music" with polka rhythms, and one form of the principal theme of *The Moldau* suggests folk origins in its combination of a major third and minor sixth (Example XI–4). Throughout, Smetana shows a splendid gift for extended melodic line and for idiomatic and varied orchestration. And a full fugal exposition of a chromatic subject for *con sordino* strings in *From Bohemia's Woods and Fields* (mm. 74ff.), apparently meant as an illustration of "a gentle breeze [that] rustles through the grove," demonstrates a mastery of traditional contrapuntal writing as advanced as the century has to offer.

Of Smetana's small number of chamber compositions the best known is his String Quartet in E minor of 1876. Entitled *From My Life,* this

Example XI–4: SMETANA, *The Moldau,* mm. 72–80

Allegro (a 2 batti) commodo non agitato

---

4.   In a letter of 1879 to F. A. Urbánek.

programmatic work is an intensely personal document; the composer tells us in a letter of 1878 that the four movements illustrate the longings and revelry of his youth, his first love, and his final despair at the prospect of deafness.[5] His first string quartet, this piece shows great expressive range and a remarkably facile command of the medium. Certain mannerisms, especially harmonic shifts by thirds, may remind us of Schubert. But a more probable influence, surely, were the late quartets of another deaf composer, Beethoven. Smetana's second movement, *Allegro moderato a la Polka,* is a violent dance similar in tone and texture to the finale of Beethoven's String Quartet in C♯ minor, Op. 131. A compulsive working of sharply accented short motives and a predilection for emphatic unison playing, moreover, seem plainly reminiscent of Beethoven's late style.

Smetana is often considered the founder of Bohemian nationalist music. If there is any truth in this, it is not because there was a recognizable Bohemian style after which Smetana fashioned his own. Something like the reverse seems to have occurred: his personal idiom comprised of diverse elements, some of them imitative of Bohemian folk styles, came to be accepted as uniquely representative of his nation's musical culture.

DVOŘÁK

When Smetana became director of Prague's Provisional Theater in 1866 the principal violist of the orchestra there was a young musician from a village to the north, Antonín Dvořák (1841–1904). Having received a thorough church musician's education at the Prague Organ School, Dvořák began to show his great facility as a composer in the later 1860s: by 1875 he had to his credit four operas (three Czech librettos and one German one), five symphonies, and a great many chamber compositions including seven string quartets.[6] Like other Bohemian musicians who remained at home, Dvořák at first attracted little attention outside his country; then in 1874 his winning of an Austrian State Stipendium brought wider recognition, and, more important, lasting support from Brahms and Hanslick. Brahms urged his own publisher, Simrock of Berlin, to print Dvořák's works, and introduced them himself to leading European musicians. Hanslick guided the career of his young coun-

---

5.   See John Clapham, *Smetana* (London, 1972), p. 67.

6.   Dvořák's first four symphonies and first six string quartets were not published during his lifetime and are often not included in the numbering of his works. The most reliable designations for Dvořák's compositions are the "B" numbers from J. Burghauser, *Antonín Dvořák: thematický katalog, bibliografie, přehled života a díla* (Prague, 1960).

tryman with fatherly advice and favorable notices. Partly through the efforts of these powerful advocates, Dvořák achieved a considerable reputation by the time of his first maturity as a composer. With later travels to England and Russia, and a three-year sojourn in the United States (1892–95), he would cement his position as one of the world's most admired composers—a nearly unheard-of achievement, at the time, for an artist from a "peripheral" nation.

Dvořák's earliest style, until about 1875, often showed a certain naïve dependence upon classical models found in the music of Beethoven and Schubert. This seems particularly true in the early chamber music, where clear, traditional forms are subject only to local disturbances. In the String Quartet in A minor, Op. 16 (1874), for example, a motion from the tonic to the flat tonic is accomplished with a very Schubertian treble pivot tone (Example XI–5). But when he was very young, Dvořák was

Example XI–5: DVOŘÁK, String Quartet Op. 16 (B. 45), first movement, mm 267–74

also exposed to a new musical intoxicant. In 1863 Wagner appeared in Prague to conduct his *Faust Overture,* the Overture to *Tannhäuser,* the Preludes to *Tristan* and *Die Meistersinger,* and parts of *Die Walküre;* the impressionable Dvořák played in the viola section, and the first of his sporadic attempts to write in a Wagnerian manner date from this time. But Dvořák was never very comfortable in this very consciously adopted idiom. Of two early operas composed under the spell of Wagner, one, *Alfred* (1870), was never performed or published, and the other, *King and Charcoal Burner* (1871), Dvořák withdrew during rehearsal and completely revised the work in the retrospective manner of Lortzing. Dvořák's early symphonies, particularly the second in B♭, of 1865, have patches of advanced orchestration that seem clearly in Wagner's debt— and oddly incongruent with their own four-square rhythmic patterns.

Another strong ingredient in the formation of Dvořák's style was the folk music of his native Bohemia and surrounding regions. Like Chopin, he initially struck the wider public as a sort of romantic exotic. The first works of his published in 1878 by Simrock were the *Moravian Duets* for two voices and piano, and the *Slavonic Dances,* Op. 46, for two pianos, together with a transcription for orchestra. The *Slavonic Dances* (and the subsequent second set, Op. 72 of 1886–87), gained an immediate popularity that they have retained until the present day. Each consists of a series of contrasting sections, the first of which serves as a ritornello. They are all in 2/4 or 3/4 meter; the duple ones characteristically move in vigorous even eighth-note rhythms, and those in triple meter often have the hemiola effects of the Furiant. Simple triadic patterns dominate the melodies of these pieces, combining with their rhythmic construction to impart an appealing impression of "folklike-

Example XI–6
  a. Moravian Dance, mm. 1–4

  b. DVOŘÁK, *Slavonic Dance* Op. 46, No. 3 (B. 83), mm. 1–8

ness." Some of this music is apparently very close to specific folk dances and songs. A dance tune nearly identical to the first melody of the *Slavonic Dance* No. 3, for example, was found by František Bonus in the area of Tichá and Frenštát in Moravia (cf Example XI–6a and b).[7] In many other cases only general features of folk music that Dvořák knew were absorbed into his style; their influence often seems pervasive even when specific models cannot be shown. Thus movements of symphonies and chamber works easily fall into rhythmic patterns of the Furiant or the melancholy Dumka (originally a Slavic sung lament), and many of Dvořák's melodies assume a plain triadic shape, a modal coloring, or the configurations of the "gapped scale," all reminiscent of folk sources.

Dvořák's very ample *oeuvre* is well distributed throughout the traditional musical genres. Although recent audiences have shown more interest in his instrumental music than in his vocal compositions, his works include substantial numbers of songs, choral compositions, and operas. His once-popular *Stabat mater* (1876–77) for soloists, chorus, and orchestra shows an effective handling of these forces in an international and rather conservative stylistic context: the harmonies are roughly Mendelssohnian and there is a good bit of able counterpoint including a final fugal *Amen.* His oratorio *St. Ludmila,* written for the Leeds Music Festival in 1886, and his cantata *The Spectre's Bride* (1885), both of them following in a sort of modernized Handelian tradition, became favorites of choral societies in England and in such places as Providence, Rhode Island, and Milwaukee, Wisconsin.

Beginning in the early 1870s Dvořák worked persistently at the composition of opera. Early abortive attempts to imitate Wagner gave way to a retrospective style of comic opera in such works as *The Stubborn Lovers* (1874) and *The Cunning Peasant* (1877), works for which he found a ready model in Smetana's *The Bartered Bride* of the previous decade. Another serious opera, *Dimitrij,* followed in 1882; its story, a sequel to *Boris Godunov,* provided the composer with an opportunity to make effective use of his "generalized" folk idiom in portraying conflict between the Russian and Polish people. In his final operas, *Kate and the Devil* (1898–99), *Rusalka* (1900), and *Armida* (1902–3), Dvořák seemed once again attracted to a Wagnerian ideal: the music is thoroughly continuous and the orchestra increasingly prominent. *Rusalka,* the only one of Dvořák's operas to make its way outside Czechoslovakia, has a fairytale plot reminiscent of E. T. A. Hoffmann's *Undine.* Its music is an amalgam of folklike melodies with full and colorful orchestration, together with an occasional nod toward Wagnerian chromaticism and, as in the second-act duet between the water spirit Rusalka and her mor-

---

7.   Antonín Sychra, *Antonín Dvořák. Zur Aesthetik seines symphonischen Schaffens* (Leipzig, 1973), pp. 22–23.

tal lover, some florid Italianate singing. These seemingly diverse elements, however, are skillfully assimilated so that the final effect of the opera is a unified one.

Viewed in the wider context of European music of the later nineteenth century, Dvořák's work is of a conservative cast, and he made his mark most decisively as a composer in the traditional large instrumental genres: the symphony, the string quartet, and chamber compositions with piano. A surprisingly high proportion of his most durable works were composed during the three years he lived in New York as director of the National Conservatory of Music. Most acclaimed of all is his Ninth Symphony in E minor, Op. 95 (B. 178), *From the New World* (1893). Formally very traditional, it has outer movements with sonata-allegro shapes, an episodic slow movement, and a scherzo and trio. An effective irregularity in the first movement is the transposition of the second group of themes to G♯ minor / A♭ major—a major third higher than expected—in the recapitulation. Perhaps less felicitous is the reintroduction of the famous opening melody of the second movement into the development section of the last. Many of the familiar melodies of this symphony have a modal coloring, most often effected simply through the use of the flat seventh in minor; sometimes their folklike sound is enhanced with a drone accompaniment or a harmonization of stark root-position sonorities (Example XI–7a and b).

Autograph first page of Dvořák's Symphony in E minor, Op. 95, *From the New World*, 1893.

Example XI–7: DVOŘÁK, *Symphony From the New World*
   a. First movement, mm. 99–106

   b. Fourth movement, mm. 10–17

Many have been tempted to see in this music specific influences from Dvořák's American surroundings. This tendency was encouraged by certain remarks by the composer himself, who said in a letter of April 1893 that "those with sensitive noses will detect (in the *New World Symphony*) the influence of America".[8] The similarity of the first theme in G major of the first movement to the spiritual *Swing Low, Sweet Chariot* has often been noted. Dvořák did make a point of acquainting himself with native American music; he listened with great interest to the black singer Harry Thacker Burleigh, and in one of his visits to the Czech community in Spillville, Iowa, he arranged to observe the singing and dancing of a local Indian band. But it is difficult to establish that such contacts exerted any important influence upon his style.

Another celebrated work of Dvořák's American period is the Cello

8.   Ibid., p. 258.

Example XI–8: DVOŘÁK, Cello Concerto, Op. 104, first movement, mm.
1–6

Concerto in B minor, Op. 104 (B.191). He wrote only two other concertos: an early piano concerto in G minor (Op. 33; B.63) and a violin
concerto in A minor (Op. 53; B.108),[9] neither of which has ever gained
a firm place in the repertory. The Cello Concerto is widely regarded as
the finest example of its genre. It abounds with appealing melodies which,
like the very first one (Example XI–8) often have Dvořák's customary
modal flavor. This tune is particularly striking when the solo cello first
states it, with its flat seventh still intact, but in major. Here begins a
solo part treasured by all cellists: brilliant, sonorous, and thoroughly
idiomatic for the instrument. It seems to be the work of the composer
alone—Dvořák firmly rejected the alterations suggested by his cellist
friend to whom the concerto is dedicated, Hanuš Wihan. In 1895, after
returning to Prague from New York, Dvořák revised the last movement, substituting an extended slow coda, almost entirely over a tonic
pedal, for what had been a much more customary four-measure final
cadence.[10] Through this addition the movement acquires an odd shape;
but it is effective as a peroration to the entire work, and it is some of
the composer's most impressive music.

In certain ways Dvořák's musical style was always retrospective.
Tonality here is usually quite clear and unencumbered with chromatic
elaboration. Large-scale movements normally modulate to the expected
keys, and metric patterns are surprisingly regular, falling largely into
four-measure modules. But Dvořák's melodic inventiveness and talent
for orchestral variety, in addition to his musical "local color," held a
powerful attraction for a European culture that found the audacities of
Wagner and his followers barely assimilable. And within Bohemia,
Dvořák, like Smetana, was regarded as a genuine representative of a
nationalist art.

No other Bohemian composer of this period, within his own country
or elsewhere, enjoyed anything approaching the esteem of Smetana and
Dvořák. A worthy colleague of theirs, Zdeněk Fibich (1850–1900), was
a prolific and able composer who produced works in all the standard

---

9.   Dvořák also attempted an earlier cello concerto (in A major) in 1865, but left it
     unorchestrated.
10. He added these solemn strains in memory of his recently deceased sister-in-law
     Josephina Kaunitzová.

categories. In his trilogy of melodramas *Hippodramie* he brought this genre—which had previously been most extensively cultivated by his countryman Georg Benda—to new heights of dramatic power. But his training was mainly German and his music had nothing about it that seemed expressly Bohemian. He has been as fully ignored in his own country as in Europe at large.

POLAND

From the later Middle Ages until the late eighteenth century the kingdom of Poland was a very considerable one that included substantial portions of the present-day Soviet Union, Germany, and Czechoslovakia. In three successive partitions in the later eighteenth century, Russia, Prussia, and Austria appropriated more and more of Poland until in 1796 nothing remained. Polish generals participated eagerly in Napoleon's campaigns, especially against Russia, and were temporarily rewarded with the establishment of the Grand Duchy of Warsaw—which was promptly reappropriated by the Russians as they pursued the retreating French in 1812. The Congress of Vienna confirmed the division of Poland among the partitioning powers with the lion's share going to Russia. For the remainder of the century Poland remained effectively a Russian province; insurrections in 1830–31 (during which Chopin quit the country) and 1863 served mainly to tighten czarist control. Frustrated nationalist passions fueled a Romantic movement in Polish literature in which writers such as Adam Mickiewicz, Julius Slowacki, and Sigismund Krasinsky lamented their country's sorrows in strains akin to the poetry of Byron and Victor Hugo.

Poland had been an active participant in European art music since the sixteenth century. All the usual forms of church music were cultivated, particularly in the cathedral at Krakow. In the late sixteenth and earlier seventeenth centuries Italian composers of the rank of Luca Marenzio (c. 1553–99) and Tarquinio Merula (c. 1594–1665) spent time in Poland, mingling with local musicians and exerting a palpable influence on the development of Polish music. The Polish court sponsored Italian opera as early as 1633, and in the following century there was healthy activity in the composition of both opera and (as recent discoveries have shown) the symphony. At the turn of the nineteenth century the patriotic sentiments of oppressed Poles were perceivable in music as well as poetry; national dances such as the polonaise, krakowiac, and mazurka appeared in collections of folk music, and by Chopin's generation their distinctive rhythms were well absorbed into the styles of serious Polish composers.[11]

11. See above, pp. 198–99.

A predecessor of Chopin's on the Polish scene was the gifted pianist
and composer Maria Agata Szymanowska (1789–1831), born and educated in Warsaw, and from the time of her Parisian debut in 1810 a
well-known figure on European concert stages. Schumann spoke
enthusiastically of the piano etudes of the "gentle Szymanowska," not-
ing a similarity between her music and that of John Field.[12] Her compositions are mainly of the shorter variety: etudes, preludes, waltzes,
polonaises, and twenty-four mazurkas published in 1824, just as the
very youthful Chopin began his first experiments with the genre. The
comparison with Field is perhaps most apt in Szymanowska's nocturnes. The one in B♭, published posthumously in St. Petersburg, has
the simple arpeggiation, atmospheric pedal points, and ornamented
melody we associate with Field. But its overall structure is more elaborate than most of the Irishman's nocturnes: it is built on a rondo plan
in which the first theme reappears in ever-varied guises. And some of
the ornament sounds more like Chopin than Field, as in the final measures where two-note slurs (in imitation of bells) span double octaves
(Example XI–9).

Example XI–9: SZYMANOWSKA, Nocturne in B♭, mm. 57–61

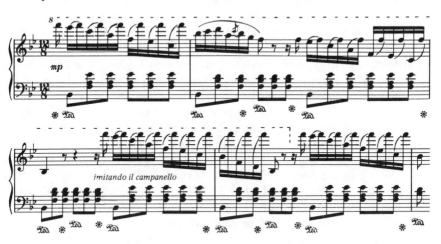

During the middle years of the nineteenth century Poland produced
several other prominent instrumental performers and composers. Two
of Chopin's fellow students with Józef Elsner at the Warsaw Conservatory were Julian Fontana (1810–65) and Antoni Orlowski (1811–61),
both of whom also fled the country in 1830–31. Fontana had a peri-

12. Robert Schumann, *Gesammelte Schriften über Musik und Musiker,* ed. M. Kreisig
(Leipzig, 1914), 1, pp. 206 and 215.

patetic career as a pianist in France, England, New York, and Havana, served as copyist and agent for Chopin in Paris, and composed a good number of piano pieces, some of them modeled on Polish folksongs and the music of American blacks. Orlowski was a pianist, violinist, conductor, and composer of stage music who spent most of his career in Rouen. A Polish violinist of the period who achieved considerable international acclaim was Karol Józef Lipiński (1790–1861). Like most virtuosos of his generation Lipiński was powerfully influenced in his earlier years by Paganini; in 1829 he was pitted in direct competition with the Italian virtuoso when he appeared in Warsaw. After extensive touring Lipiński settled down in 1839 as Konzertmeister in Dresden, where he conducted the Saxon court orchestra, taught several impor- tant students (one was Joseph Joachim), and composed orchestral music and violin pieces in traditional styles.

Perhaps the most celebrated violinist of the nineteenth century, after Paganini, was Henryk Wieniawski (1835–80).[13] After early training in Paris and exhaustive world tours as a virtuoso performer beginning at the age of thirteen, he settled in St. Petersburg in 1860 to play, conduct, teach, and compose. His richness of tone and electrifying technique set something of a new standard for violinists up to the present day; his special bowing technique (with a firm wrist and high elbow) developed into a Russian tradition. Wieniawski's career as a performer resembled those of the Paris-based piano virtuosos of the 1830s and 1840s: he trav- eled very widely, performing his own compositions that were designed to exhibit his special powers. This tradition has continued to flourish among Slavic musicians (mainly pianists) such as Anton Rubinstein and Sergey Rachmaninov well into the present century.

Some of Wieniawski's compositions have survived as a stable part of the violin repertory. Among these are the eight Etudes-Caprices Op. 18 for two violins (1863), reminiscent of Paganini's Capriccii Op. 1, and several mazurkas and polonaises—the requisite tribute to the com- poser's native country. There are 24 published *opera,* all for violin and piano or violin and orchestra. Most widely admired of all are his two violin concertos, particularly the second in D minor, composed in 1862. This work shows the mixture of caloric cantabile melody and technical fireworks that are a norm of virtuoso concertos of the time. But, espe- cially in the first movement, the orchestra is more than usually integral to the proceedings, often carrying significant thematic matter during the violin's pyrotechnics. And there are convincing unifying devices here that suggest large-scale cyclic form: the first movement omits a formal recapitulation and leads directly into the second *(Romance),* and the lyrical second theme of the opening movement reappears in two

---

13. Wieniawski was a member of a musical family that included his younger brother Józef, a pianist, and his nephew Adam, a composer.

episodes in the *á la Zingara* finale.

The central figure in Polish opera of the earlier nineteenth century was Karol Kazimierz Kurpinski (1785–1857), who was conductor at the Warsaw National Theater from 1824 to 1840, and the composer of some twenty-four works for the musical stage. These are mainly one- or two-act operas closely patterned after Viennese and French comic opera from the turn of the century, but with a strong additive of Polish folk music. One of these works, *Zamek na Czorsztynie* (The Castle of Czorsztyn) is still occasionally heard. Better known is the slightly later contribution of Stanislaw Moniuszko (1819–72), who after musical studies in his native Minsk, in Warsaw, and from 1837 to 1840 in Berlin, settled in Warsaw and produced his most highly regarded work *Halka* (first version, 1847). This estimable work shows clear dependence, both dramatic and musical, upon Italian serious opera of the generation just past, that of Rossini and Bellini. In Halka's aria from the beginning of Act II the rhythmic regularity and occasional florid ornament of the upper range of the melody betray Italian parentage. The frequent construction of scenes from recitatives and arias is, if anything, less flexible than the *scena ed aria* in mature Bellini; the orchestration and harmonic language, however, are richer and more varied. In this work and his later operas Moniusko's subjects and settings were Polish, and he injected into them a strong additive of musical local color (see Example XI–10). But in Europe at large, and to a great extent in Poland itself, his works

Example XI–10: MONIUSZKO, *Halka,* Act II

suffered from the widespread conviction that the only true representative of Polish music was Chopin.

RUSSIA

Russia of the late nineteenth century, nearly coterminous with the present-day Soviet Union, emerged as the largest country in the world—accounting for one-sixth of the earth's land area—by a gradual process of agglomeration of many independent states. From a nuclear principality of Moscow, founded, it seems, by Norsemen in the ninth century, and subject to continuous domination by warlike Asian Tatars from the thirteenth to the fifteenth centuries, the nation began to take decisive shape in the later fifteenth and sixteenth centuries. During this period Ivan III (the Great), his son Basil, and his grandson Ivan IV (the Terrible), adopted the title "czar" (or "tsar," short for "Caesar"), subdued their neighbors, and established monarchical control over most of present-day European Russia. Subsequent expansion took place mainly on three fronts: against Scandinavian control of the Baltic areas (Lithuania and Finland), against the Turks in the lands bordering the Black Sea, and last of all, in the late nineteenth century, into the vast lands of central Asia reaching to the frontier of China.

Partly because Russia had always rested solidly within the fold of the Eastern Orthodox Church, ties with Western civilization formed slowly. Peter the Great (1689–1725) was the first czar with extensive connections in the West, and he set about vigorously to enforce European models in municipal government, organization of the army, ship building, and styles of dress. And during the reign of Catherine II (1762–96), the great empress of German ancestry, a determined effort was made to import the principles and practices of the European Enlightenment. The enormous estates of the Church were broken up, the secular philosophy of the French Encyclopedists was encouraged (Diderot was even invited to complete his *magnum opus* in St. Petersburg), and Italian and French comic opera became a favorite court entertainment. It was during this period that Russia first became a great European power. The Francophilia that was in its final stages elsewhere in Europe now took firm hold, so that for much of the nineteenth century French was the preferred language of educated Russians.

In the western reaches of the lands that at one time or another belonged to Russia, particularly Latvia and Lithuania, the styles of Catholic church music then current dated back to the late Middle Ages. In Lithuania, Italian opera and other secular forms of Western music had been known since the seventeenth century. In Russia proper church music was confined to monophonic Byzantine chant until the seventeenth century, and secular art music hardly existed until the eighteenth. Then beginning in the 1730s visiting troupes of Italian players presented opera in St. Petersburg and Moscow; in 1735 the Empress Anne named the Neapolitan Francesco Araia *maestro di cappella,* and in succeeding years a long line of distinguished Italian composers occupied this position: Baldassare Galuppi, Tommaso Traetta, Giovanni Paisiello, Domenico Cimarosa, and others. Throughout the nineteenth century St. Petersburg was to be a routine (and particularly lucrative) stop on the tours of traveling European musicians, among them Clementi, Field, Spohr, Angelica Catalini, Berlioz, Liszt, and Clara Schumann.

In the eighteenth century Italian operas composed for the court were sometimes later heard in Russian translation in public theaters in Moscow and St. Petersburg, but genuine Russian opera sprang from different sources. In the last years of the century about 100 indigenous operas by Russian composers were performed. Their construction, like that of German Singspiel and French opéra comique of a half-century earlier, consisted of an alternation of spoken dialogue and simple songs together with occasional choruses. The librettos were peopled with lower- and middle-class characters (several written by Catherine II herself have more lofty subjects), and the music, much of it now lost, made extensive use of Russian folk tunes. The composer-compilers of the genre remained distinctly obscure. The only well-known Russian composer of the period, Dmitry Bortnyansky (1751–1825), was almost completely aloof from this movement; educated in Italy, he returned to direct the Imperial chapel choir and compose church music and opera very much in harmony with his Italian and French models.

In the first half of the nineteenth century Russia was ruled by two czars with very long reigns, Alexander I (1801–25) and Nicholas I (1825–55), who steered an uncertain and vacillating course in respect to liberalizing and Westernizing pressures. The first dozen years of Alexander I's reign were dominated by the Napoleonic Wars, culminating with the sack of Moscow and the defeat of the French. At about that time the liberal institutions he had earlier established in education, civil freedoms, and government were largely abandoned, and his successor, Nicholas, set out to suppress all ideas that seemed either revolutionary or foreign. In an atmosphere of repression and disappointed hopes there arose a group of young Russian writers who lamented the backwardness of their country and venerated things Western, showing a particular fondness for the Romantic poets of England and Germany. A prominent member of the group was the playwright Alexander Griboyedov (1795–1829), a brilliant satirist of the Russian social order. But the towering literary figure of the period was Alexander Pushkin (1799–1837), who took on a stature in Russian letters equivalent to that of

Goethe in Germany. His earlier works, heavily indebted to Byron, included an *Ode to Liberty* that together with his associations with the radical "Decembrist" movement forced him for a time into exile.

Russian concert life had its real beginnings in the early nineteenth century as a response to increasing contacts with the West. The practice of Lenten concerts was firmly established in St. Petersburg and Moscow in the first decades of the century, and benefit concerts—for the benefit of the principal performers—became common soon thereafter. Some of the most exalted of the nobility maintained private orchestras and even musical theaters. A very large share of the musical life of the country, however, was represented by amateur music making. Pianos and other domestic musical instruments (and teachers with German or Italian names) were increasingly in demand in higher social circles.[14] While most of the diversionary music in Russian parlors was imported, there emerged a new hybrid genre of song called the *bytovoy romance* that combined characteristics of airs from German and French comic opera with elements of Russian folksong, and came to figure heavily in the melodic style of nineteenth-century Russian opera.[15]

GLINKA AND DARGOMĬZHSKY

During the first quarter of the nineteenth century several native composers made determined efforts to produce opera of a distinctly Russian character. Notable among these was Stepan Ivanovich Davidof (1777–1825), best known for *Rusalka* (1803), an adaptation of a German Singspiel in which he provided new "Russian" music for the last part of the work. An Italian composer resident in Russia, Catterino Cavos (1776–1840), enthusiastically grasped hold of this new fashion and wrote a series of operas on Russian subjects; most admired of them was *Ivan Susanin* (1815), in which he made considerable use of Russian folk tunes. The composer usually acknowledged as the founder of Russian opera, however, is Mikhail Ivanovich Glinka (1804–57), who after a modicum of musical training in Italy and Germany produced the first important Russian opera, *A Life for the Czar* (1836). It is based on the same episode in Russian history as Cavos's *Ivan Susanin:*[16] "the Troublous Times" of 1605–13, in which years of turmoil are concluded with the elevation of

---

14. An early beneficiary of this new market was the musician and piano manufacturer Muzio Clementi, who visited Russia in 1802–3 and 1806. He wrote home to his business partner, "in Moscow they want instruments extremely and the people in general are much richer than in the capital [i.e. St. Petersburg]." Leon Plantinga, *Clementi; His Life and Music* (London, 1977), p. 192.

15. Gerald R. Seaman, *History of Russian Music* (New York, 1967), 1, p. 127.

16. *Ivan Susanin* was in fact its original title, and it is given under this name in the present-day Soviet Union.

Czar Michael, first ruler of the Romanov dynasty. In the opera Ivan Susanin is a heroic peasant who gives his life for the new czar by misleading the invading Polish forces.

In its overall shape *A Life for the Czar* rather resembles current styles in Italian and French serious opera. It begins with the chorus–slow aria–scene for chorus and soloists characteristic of Rossini's Introductions. The extensive dancing (especially in the second act portraying the Polish faction) and carefully crafted, expressive recitative suggest influence from the current French grand opera (this is the first Russian opera in which all the text is sung). But the work also shows distinctly "nation-

Example XI–11: GLINKA, *A Life for the Czar,* Wedding Chorus

Ro - zy - gra - li - sya, ras - plya - sa - lis' Kras - ny dye - vi - tsy v ti - ri - mu.
The beau - ti - ful girls___ fro - lic and dance___ in the cham - ber

Kak ad - na si - dit, ni ig - ra - yet, pri - go - ryu - ni - las', slyo - zy l'yot,___
Yet one___ sits,___ does___ not play, be - comes sad,___ tears she sheds,___

___ slyo - zy gor' - ki - ye!
___ bit - ter tears!

alist" traits. There are two certifiable Russian popular songs: Ivan Susanin's melody in No. 3 and the entr'acte to Act IV.[17] Many of the other melodies sound like Russian folksongs because Glinka had in effect mastered the idiom (in the 1820s he had published a number of such frank imitations of folksong with piano accompaniment). One such is the Wedding Chorus toward the end of Act III. It consists of two alternating strains, the second of which is shown in Example XI–11. The irregular repetition of tiny melodic modules (here it seems irregular largely because of the 5 / 4 meter) is a characteristic of Russian folk music familiar to Western listeners from Stravinsky's later *Petrushka* and *Les Noces*. The pentatonic construction of the melody (except at its end) from the tones G–C–D–E–G seems to have been common in Russian wedding songs.[18] In the example shown, "folklikeness" is also enhanced by the unison accompaniment. But more often in *A Life for the Czar* Glinka writes the standard harmonizations of Western art music, and in some places choruses of peasants sing in fugal imitation.

Glinka's second opera, *Ruslan and Lyudmila* (1842), a sprawling drama of mythical enchantment adapted from Pushkin's poem of the same name, makes much more extensive use of folk melody; tunes in it have been traced to Caucasian, Arabian, Persian, Finnish, and Turkish sources. And despite its eclecticism and disorganization, it became a model for a prominent strain of orientalism and "magic" themes in Russian dramatic music later in the century.[19] A special musical technique developed in this work presents constant repetitions of a simple tune against a perpetually changing accompanimental background. This procedure, related to the incessant repetition of motives in Russian folksong, was used again to good effect in Glinka's orchestral composition *Kamarinskaya* (1848).

An influential younger colleague of Glinka's was Alexander Sergeyevich Dargomïzhsky (1813–69), a composer of opera, songs, and orchestral pieces that contribute significantly to the profile of Russian nationalist music. After the near failure of his first opera, *Esmeralda* (1841), a work much indebted to French grand opera, Dargomïzhsky resolved to pursue a kind of musical realism in the exacting declamation of Russian poetry and the adoption of melodic idioms of Russian folksong. He set out to realize his intentions in a series of songs and romances, and to some extent in his opera *Rusalka* (1855), in which there is constant emphasis on peasant life and music, here cast in the set ensembles, choruses, and dances of grand opera. The purest illustration of Dar-

17. Glinka identifies these songs in his *Memoirs,* trans. Richard B. Mudge (Norman, Oklahoma, 1963), p. 101.
18. See Seaman, *History of Russian Music,* 1, p. 174.
19. See David Brown, *Mikhail Glinka: A Biographical and Critical Study* (London, 1974), p. 201.

A page from Pushkin's manuscript of *The Stone Guest* with a drawing by the poet.

gomïzhsky's program is his final opera, never quite finished, *The Stone Guest* (first performed in 1872 in a version completed by César Cui and Nikolay Rimsky-Korsakov). This work is a setting, with very few textual changes, of Pushkin's play on the Don Juan theme. It is written almost throughout in a style of dramatic declamation that falls between recitative and arioso singing, and is given a flexible, ever-changing accompaniment tinged with modal coloring. This kind of writing was surely influential for later Russian works such as Musorgsky's *Boris Godunov,* and perhaps even for one as seemingly remote as Debussy's *Pelléas et Mélisande.*

In the mid-nineteenth century musical culture in the capital city, St. Petersburg, somewhat resembled that of London a century earlier. Its most prestigious musical institution by far was the court opera, whose personnel and repertory were entirely Italian. There was also a Russian Opera (corresponding to English-language opera at London's Haymarket and Drury Lane theaters), a much less glamorous institution whose productions, though sung in Russian by local singers, were mainly adaptations of French, German, and Italian comic operas. Only a few Russian works were added to this repertory, such as Glinka's *A Life for the Czar* and *Ruslan and Lyudmila,* Dargomïzhsky's *Rusalka,* and *Askold's Tomb* by Alexei Verstovsky. Here too, the players in the orchestra were almost exclusively Italian. The musicians of the two theaters were also mainly responsible for the concerts in the city, largely limited to the Lenten period.[20] Russia produced very few professional musicians because there were virtually no institutions for musical education in the land,

---

20. See the informative study of Robert C. Ridenour, *Nationalism, Modernism, and Personal Rivalry in Nineteenth-Century Russian Music* (Ann Arbor, 1981), pp. 5–18.

and because, as was also true in eighteenth-century England, professional music making was simply not a socially acceptable pursuit for the well-born.

The death of Czar Nicholas I and accession of his son Alexander II in 1855 inaugurated a new period of optimism and growth in Russia. Many liberal measures were enacted, such as the final freeing of the serfs, reform of the judicial system, and the development of local self-government. A splendid flowering of Russian letters showed a new national consciousness: works on Russian history and language appeared, and, above all, there arose a small galaxy of novelists of the rank of Fyodor Mikhailovich Dostoyevsky (1821–1881), Ivan Sergeyevich Turgenev (1818–1883), and, a bit later, Count Leo Tolstoy (1828–1910). Music soon participated in this cultural quickening. In 1858 the pianist and composer Anton Rubinstein (1829–94) founded a Russian Musical Society that sponsored regular concerts in St. Petersburg; under its auspices Russia's first conservatory of music was opened in that city in 1861. In 1860 the new Maryinsky theater was built for the Russian Opera, and by degrees this institution began to rival the splendor of the Italian court opera.

There was a curious ambiguity in outlook among educated Russians in the later 1850s and 1860s. Most agreed that freedom from their country's provincialism was to be had by adopting the ways of the West; but among the same groups there was a heightened interest in cultivating what was specifically Russian in letters and the arts. Rubinstein's Russian Musical Society and its conservatory became a focal point in the controversies surrounding this issue. The most feared music critic in St. Petersburg in the 1860s, Alexander Serov (1820–71), described Rubinstein as a "backward classicist with German training"[21] and systematically condemned both the concerts and the conservatory sponsored by his society as "foreign." But the repertory of these concerts and the curriculum of the conservatory, both weighted heavily toward the Austro-German tradition of Mozart, Beethoven, Mendelssohn, and Schumann, was also criticized as simply old-fashioned. Serov was an enthusiast for Glinka and contemporary Russian music, but also for Berlioz, Liszt, and Wagner; thus he and like-minded critics—another prominent one was Vladimir Stasov (1824–1906)—found Russia's leading musical institutions seriously deficient on at least two counts. The positive theoretical principle espoused by these critics was the doctrine of "realism" deriving mainly from the literary critic Vissarion Belinsky, a doctrine that survives in present-day Soviet realism and is as difficult now as then to apply to music.

21. Ibid., p. 89.

"THE FIVE"

Both Serov and Stasov were associated with a school of composers who had in common a general advocacy of Russian music and an opposition to Russia's musical establishment.[22] This group, named *moguchay kuchka* ("mighty handful") by Stasov—often called "The Five" in English— was organized and led by Mily Alexeyevich Balakirev (1837–1910); the other members, all in a sense musical amateurs, as Russian musicians tended to be, were: César Cui (1835–1918), a military engineer; Alexander Porfir'yevich Borodin (1833–87), a chemist and medical researcher; Modest Petrovich Musorgsky (1839–81), an army officer and civil servant; and Nikolay Andreyevich Rimsky-Korsakov (1844–1908), a naval officer. In the years of their effective association, the early 1860s, all were very young men who in their idealism and enthusiasm might remind us of the *Harmonischer Verein* of Carl Maria von Weber or the group of musicians gathered around Schumann's *Neue Zeitschrift für Musik.*

Balakirev's formal education in music was scanty. As a boy he studied piano with his mother and for a short time with Alexander Dubuque, a student of John Field; he later had some instruction from the German pianist Karl Eisrich and the noted critic and musical scholar Alexander Ulibishev. A meeting with Glinka in 1855 seemed to determine his course as a future champion of Russian music. In the following years the other members of The Five one by one fell under his spell; by sheer force of personality he dominated the group, correcting and revising the others' compositions and shaping their musical opinions. In 1862 he broadened the sphere of his influence by participating in the establishment of the New School of Music, a rival institution to the St. Petersburg Conservatory. In view of his standing as leader of The Five, however, Balakirev's own compositions seem surprisingly little touched by Russian nationalist principles. In his two overtures on Russian themes (1858 and 1864, both later revised) and some of his songs he appears dependent upon Glinka's manner of treating Russian folk music and folklike music. But the Overture and Incidental Music to *King Lear* (1861) makes use of old English songs, the symphonic poem *In Bohemia* (composed in 1867 as "Overture on Czech Themes," revised in 1906) makes use of Bohemian ones, and a favorite genre among his piano compositions was the Polish mazurka. Otherwise his music seems to fall easily into the European traditions of, say, Meyerbeer and Berlioz. One aspect of his style clearly took root among his compatriots: that particular clarity and brilliance of orchestral sound (derived in part, perhaps, from Berlioz, who conducted his works in Russia with great suc-

22. Stasov and Serov later parted company in a bitter controversy over differing evaluations of Glinka's two operas. See Richard Taruskin, "Glinka's Ambiguous Legacy and the Birth Pangs of Russian Opera," *Nineteenth-Century Music,* 1 (1977): 142–62.

cess in 1847 and 1867) that also distinguishes the music of Rimsky-Korsakov and, later, of his pupil Igor Stravinsky.

Of "The Five" the least known in modern times is César Cui, the composer and critic of Lithuanian birth and French descent who was the first to join Balakirev's coterie. For much of his life Cui wrote journal articles on music in which he stoutly espoused the principles of The Five, castigating the foes and glorifying the friends of Russian musical nationalism. His music, however, seems even more incongruent with these principles than does Balakirev's. Of his half-dozen full-length operas and numerous shorter dramatic works, the great majority draw on subjects from Western literature, and only in isolated spots (as in his first opera, *The Prisoner in the Caucasus,* 1858) is there any sign of an influence from Russian folk music. His style, like Balakirev's, seems to derive mainly from French sources such as Meyerbeer, Auber, and perhaps Adolphe Adam. An uncertain orchestrator, Cui was perhaps at his best in composing short piano and chamber compositions, such as the Five Pieces for Piano, Flute, and Violin, Op. 56, which have a certain grace and lyricism despite chromatic coloring that sounds to modern ears like dated parlor music.

Alexander Borodin's career provides a clear example of the special problems facing composers of the Russian school: a lack of methodical early training in music, demanding nonmusical professional activities, and an ambiguous feeling about Western styles as opposed to specifically Russian ones. After self-directed early efforts to learn cello playing and composition, Borodin entered medical school at the age of seventeen; thereafter his life as a musician was always subordinate to his distinguished scientific career, and some of his finest compositions were written sporadically over long stretches of time. From 1859 to 1862 he pursued his studies in Germany, absorbing in his spare time the musical styles of Schumann, Mendelssohn, and Chopin; back in St. Petersburg in 1862 he became a dedicated member of Balakirev's circle and immediately began ambitious projects in composition under the latter's tutelage. The songs and piano pieces Borodin had written up to this time were in a cosmopolitan parlor style familiar all over Europe—sometimes superimposed over melodic inflections of Russian folksong. The chamber music from this period and later (String Quintet in F minor, 1854; Piano Trio in D, 1861; String Quartets in A and D, 1879 and 1881) show a continuing influence of Mendelssohn. But in 1862, under Balakirev's somewhat fanatical direction, he began work on his First Symphony, in E^b, a composition of considerable merit that occupied him until its public premiere in 1869.

Several of Borodin's mature compositions are historically intertwined. Cheered by the success of his first symphony in 1869, he began work on a second one, as well as an opera, *Prince Igor,* whose libretto he himself constructed from the medieval Russian epic *The Lay of Igor's Campaign*. As work on the opera flagged, parts of its music were bodily transferred to the symphony. In 1872 both projects were interrupted as he entered into a characteristic collaboration with other members of The Five to compose an opera-ballet, *Mlada*. When this undertaking foundered, the music Borodin had composed for it was simply moved to the newly-revived *Prince Igor*. The symphony was finally performed in a first version in 1877; it was heard in its present form, with improvements in orchestration evidently suggested by Rimsky-Korsakov, two years later. This is an imposing work, full of attractive melodies and arresting orchestral effects. The winds are treated with special ingenuity, as in the striking repeated-note ostinato by the horns in the scherzo, and the delicate exchanges between instruments in the slow movement. While the melodic and harmonic style here are for the most part neither very advanced nor very "Russian," Borodin's penchant for a generalized exoticism can be noted in the second theme of the slow movement, where both the first and second scale-degrees (F♯ and G♯) are variable (Example XI–12).

Example XI–12: BORODIN, Symphony No. 2, third movement, mm. 62–66

When Borodin died in 1887 *Prince Igor* was not yet finished. The parts left uncomposed were completed and most of the work orchestrated by Rimsky-Korsakov and his pupil Alexander Glazunov for its premiere in 1890. In some respects *Prince Igor* follows in the nationalist tradition of Glinka. The folklike simplicity and modal inflection of the crowd scenes at the beginning and end make them believable as representations of the Russian people. And occasionally there are attempts at that flexible, quasi-recitativelike declamation cultivated by Glinka and Dargomïzhsky; an example is Vladimir's singing above a continuously falling bass line just before his serenade in Act II. But in its overall construction, the work falls largely into the familiar scenes and numbers of Italian and French opera. The style of melody is eclectic, but shows a particular allegiance to the Italian manner; Igor's impressive aria in Act II fleetingly sounds for all the world like "Amami, Alfredo" in *La Traviata* (Example XI–13). The sections depicting the fierce Polovtsi warriors are the most memorable in this opera. The savage exoti-

Example XI–13: BORODIN, *Prince Igor,* Act II

cism of the Polovtsian Dances at the end of the second act, while perhaps
more attributable to Borodin's active imagination than to his knowledge of Tatar folk music, has had a lasting appeal, and it is the only part
of *Prince Igor* regularly heard outside Russia.[23]

MUSORGSKY

Most highly regarded, these days, of the Russian composers of this
period is Modest Musorgsky, whose tragically disordered life and premature death resulted in a scattered oeuvre, with a great many works
left incomplete. Except for some instruction from Balakirev after 1857,
his musical education was effectively finished when he stopped taking
piano lessons in 1854, at the age of fifteen. It was then as a young army
officer and amateur musician that he was drawn into the circle around
Balakirev. After resigning his commission in 1858 he remained unem-
ployed for some five years, spending some of this time managing his

23. The composer's fleeting encounter with Arab music is described in Gerald Abra-
     ham, "Arab Melodies in Rimsky-Korsakov and Borodin," *Music and Letters,* 56
     (1975): 313–18.

An architectural project by Victor Hartmann for the "City-Gate of Kiev" (No. 10 of Musorgsky's *Pictures at an Exhibition*)

family's estate; thereafter he held one or another civil service position for nearly the rest of his life. During all these years he moved about restlessly in St. Petersburg, living with friends or, for a time, in a commune, succumbing progressively to the alcoholism that hastened his death in 1881 at the age of forty-two. Most of Musorgsky's music remained in manuscript at this time, and much of it, in the opinion of his colleagues, was unfit to print or perform because of crudeness of part-writing and faulty orchestration. Shortly after Musorgsky's death, Rimsky-Korsakov set about completing, revising, and in some cases rewriting a great portion of Musorgsky's music for publication, and for many years most of the composer's work was virtually unknown except in those well-doctored versions. It was not until 1928–39 that an accurate complete-works edition was published in Moscow. In the years that followed, Musorgsky's music in its original form has begun to gain currency.

This composer's earlier works—almost nothing survives from before 1858 or so—were largely for piano solo or voice and piano. Most of the early piano music is inconsequential: two sonatas have not survived,[24] and the few pieces we know of are short and largely featureless. In view of Musorgsky's very modest oeuvre as a piano composer, the suite *Pic-*

24. Incipits for the movements of an early sonata in E♭ are preserved in the composer's letter to Balakirev of August 13, 1858. See Jay Leyda and Sergei Bertensson, eds., *The Musorgsky Reader* (New York, 1947), p. 11.

tures at an Exhibition of 1874 is an extraordinary achievement. Musorgsky always responded most readily to dramatic scenes and visual stimuli; here he attempts a musical representation of an exhibition of the paintings of his recently deceased friend Victor Alexandrovich Hartmann. The ten discrete individual scenes, depicting subjects such as a gnome, an old castle, the Tuileries Gardens, a ballet of unhatched chicks, catacombs, and the city gates of Kiev, are connected by the recurring "Promenade"—an imposing chordal passage that sounds more like a stately procession than the strolling of gallery visitors. But many of the sketches seem ingeniously apposite: the bustling movement of the *Market Place in Limoges,* the French-sounding manner of the Tuileries music, the slow lumbering of a Polish oxcart in *Bydlo* (the modal construction here is unsettlingly similar to that of the *Old Castle*). The piano writing, though sometimes awkward, is effective. Only the final movement, *The Bohatyr Gate of Kiev,* sounds like a piano transcription of an orchestral piece, and only here does the popular orchestration by Maurice Ravel seem a distinct improvement upon the original.

During the period beginning in 1863, when he lived in an artists' commune in St. Petersburg, Musorgsky was thoroughly exposed to current fashions in literary theory and aesthetics such as the "realism" espoused by Nikolai Gavrilovich Chernishevsky and exemplified in the novels and stories of Turgenev and Grigorovich. The arts, according to this doctrine, must eschew their own conventions in order to present their subjects in a direct and unadorned fashion; and proper subjects for artistic treatment are to be the real stuff of ordinary life—the Russian peasant, newly freed, became a favorite object of literary scrutiny. Musorgsky, under the influence of these ideas and (a little later) of Dargomïzhsky's techniques of declamation in *The Stone Guest,* was fired with enthusiasm for achieving something analogous in his compositions. This led to concerted attempts to compose opera: a setting of *Salammbô,* after Flaubert, and of Gogol's *The Marriage,* for example, both of which remained incomplete. But the immediate proving ground for Musorgsky's ideas was the song, and in such works as *Darling Savishna, The Seminarist,* and *You Drunken Sot* (all 1866) he devised a severely naturalistic declamation that persisted in his later songs such as *The Nursery* (1870–72) and, in modified form, was to prove useful at the most dramatic points of his great opera *Boris Godunov.*

It was also mainly in his songs that Musorgsky developed his rather idiosyncratic harmonic style, an improvisational idiom in which traditional sounds are often combined in unorthodox ways. Example XI–14 shows an excerpt from *Serenade* in *Songs and Dances of Death,* 1875. This passage is set entirely over a tonic pedal point, a device Musorgsky used a great deal. The upper voices in the piano descend in the course of this phrase from an open-position A-major sound (initially with an

Example XI–14: MUSORGSKY, *Songs and Dances of Death: Serenade*

Pri - stal'-nykh glaz, go - lu - bo - ye_ si - ya - n'ye
The_____ in - tent eye, ra - di - ant - ly_ blue_____

added seventh) to a close-position one. In the course of this motion there are several familiar sonorities whose usual resolution is denied, especially the opening dominant seventh and the inverted augmented sixth in m. 3. Part of the obscurity here results from the unorthodox chord spelling that abounds in the music of The Five: the augmented sixth would behave more nearly normally as a dominant seventh if the D♯s were changed to E♭s. But the harmonic syntax here nonetheless remains eccentric.

Throughout his active career Musorgsky had at least one operatic project in motion. After *Salammbô,* a somewhat conventional "magic" drama, and *The Marriage,* an extreme experiment in realistic declamation, he attempted several works on Russian subjects; two major efforts, *Khovanshchina,* with a libretto by the composer, and *Sorochintsy Fair,* a comic opera after Gogol, were left unfinished at the composer's death. Thus Musorgsky's only completed opera is *Boris Godunov.* The history of its composition, revision, and performance is a tangled one. Of two versions by Musorgsky alone (1869 and 1873) only the second was performed in his lifetime; like most of Musorgsky's music, this work was subject, after the composer's death, to vigorous revision by Rimsky-Korsakov, and it is mainly in this guise that modern operagoers know *Boris Godunov.* Rimsky-Korsakov made Musorgsky's rather rough-hewn orchestration smoother, more brilliant, and more conventional. Details of part-writing, harmony, and melody were also changed throughout, substantially modifying the primitive strength of the original.[25]

Musorgsky constructed his own libretto for *Boris Godunov* from two sources: Pushkin's play of the same name (1825) and (to a much lesser extent) the *History of the Russian State* (1818) by Nikolai Mikhailovich

---

25. In recent years Musorgsky's own *Boris* has been heard on stages in Leningrad, London, and New York. A full score has been published in a scholarly edition by David Lloyd-Jones (Oxford, 1975), and a recording put out by EMI records.

George London singing the title role in a Bolshoi production of *Boris Godunov*.

Karamzin. Pushkin's work is a loosely constructed series of twenty-four scenes that chronicles—avowedly in a Shakespearian manner—events in Russian history from the early seventeenth-century "Troublous Times" from which the libretto of Glinka's *A Life for the Czar* also derives.[26] Musorgsky fashioned seven (later nine) scenes of his own from this source, freely altering Pushkin's blank verse and sometimes changing the order of events. In a few cases incidents not included in the play were taken from Karamzin. One such is the final scene in the forest near Kromy, an episode that Musorgsky added in 1873 (the first version had ended in the previous scene with the death of Boris).

The opera, like the play (and somewhat like Shakespeare's chronicle plays), consists of a series of tenuously connected episodes spanning several years of history. The two scenes of the Prologue show crowds of Russian people (an ever-present force in the opera) first reluctant and then accepting Boris's accession to the Czar's throne. The last act shows the powerful, fickle crowd again, now hostile to Boris (who, in Musorgsky's two versions of the opera, is about to die or has just done so) and welcoming the pretender Grigory. In the intervening acts, scenes widely separated in time and place establish the pretender's plot and present the guilt-ridden, fearful Boris in his role as czar and father. Musorgsky himself, however, is responsible for injecting one or two unifying devices into this loose assemblage of tableaux. In Act IV, for example, it is the composer who reintroduced the monk Pimen who tells of a miracle at the tomb of the rightful heir to the throne, Dmitry, whom Boris had murdered. This precipitates Boris' near-madness and death, just as the threatening report of the treacherous Lord Shuisky in Act II had triggered his hysterical hallucinations of the dead Dmitry's presence.

---

26. Gerald Abraham provides a full discussion of the relationship between the play and the libretto in *Slavonic and Romantic Music* (New York, 1968), pp. 178–87.

Example XI–15: MUSORGSKY, *Boris Godunov,* Prologue, Scene 2

Most impressive of the connective devices supplied by the composer in this opera are musical ones: specific melodic and harmonic motives have a subtle and reasonably consistent association with dramatic acts and persons. Boris's varying frames of mind are represented by several characteristic phrases, such as the music he sings upon his first appearance in the Coronation Scene (Scene 2 of the Prologue) and again shortly after his entry in Act II. In the first case he prays for wisdom as he ascends the throne; in the second he contemplates his son's taking a similar step. The most distinctive progression in these passages is a cadential melodic motion descending downward from the sixth degree, harmonized in the Prologue with a striking diatonic sequence that avoids expected dominant–tonic relationships (Example XI–15). Upon its recurrence in Act II the accompaniment presents a more extended (and conventional) sequence of parallel tenths between melody and bass (see ARM 20). Both seem to exude the world-weariness of the troubled Boris. Another musical phrase, used to even more specific dramatic purpose, is the "Dmitry motive"; Example XI–16 shows its first occurrence in Act I, Scene 2, where Grigory conceives the notion of impersonating the Czarevich Dmitry. Henceforth the motive is used to identify both Grigory and the dead Dmitry, as, for example, in Act II where

Example XI–16: MUSORGSKY, *Boris Godunov,* Act I, Scene 2

Shuisky tells Boris of the Pretender's plot (ARM 20, p. 420), thus providing eerie reinforcement to Boris's superstitious fear that the Pretender is really the murdered Dmitry returned to life.

Act II (given in ARM 20 beginning with Boris's entrance) takes place
in the czar's living quarters in the Kremlin. It shows an adroit mingling
of two very different worlds in which Boris lives: the private man's
peaceful domesticity and the tyrant's nightmare of suspicion and guilt.
In the earlier part of the act Boris's children are engaged in their own
pursuits; this provides an opportunity for the childlike games and songs
for which Musorgsky had shown a special talent in his song cycle *The
Nursery*. (These sections were mainly added in the second version of
Boris in 1873). Boris's entrance marks the impinging of the one world
upon the other. After initial exchanges with his children he falls prey to
his own morbid meditations, leading to visions of the bloody corpse of
Dmitry. This is interrupted by a great alarm from the next room caused,
as it turns out, by an irate parrot escaped from its cage. The feared
Shuisky is announced, but Boris's little son Feodor appears instead, to
give a charming account of the parrot incident. At last Shuisky does
enter, and the act moves to its dramatic climax in Boris's renewed hal-
lucinatory visions.

This act is distinguished by an amalgamation of musical styles—from
realistic, speechlike declamation to genuinely lyrical melody—roughly
parallel to its widely differing dramatic elements. Always syllabic, and
flowing readily from one style of melody to another, the singing is
responsive to the finest shades of thought and feeling in the text. In
Boris' monologue (beginning with the Moderato) thoughts of his children, of sanguine astrologers' reports, and even, for some reason, of
the inevitable consequences of sin, produce a smooth melodic motion
with hints of metrical periodization; the two visions of the corpse are
conveyed in a fragmented, gasping declamatory style, its effect augmented by obsessively repeated accompanimental figures. Still different
is Feodor's set piece about the parrot, a song with repetitive melodic

cells and a modal construction reminiscent of Russian folksong.[27] The final section of the act is one of the great "mad scenes" in opera. Boris's frenzy takes place on a darkened stage with the incessant ticking of a clock (represented by alternating bass tones a tritone apart), moonlit glimpses of the clock's puppet-figures that Boris mistakes for the murdered Dmitry, and a fearful whirring violin figure that seems to blend the internal and external events in Boris's consciousness hopelessly, creating a scene of phantasmagoric terror worthy of Dostoyevsky.

RIMSKY-KORSAKOV

Youngest of the group of composers around Balakirev was Nikolay Andreyevich Rimsky-Korsakov, first a naval officer, then an inspector of naval bands, and after 1871, with very little professional training in music, professor of composition at the St. Petersburg Conservatory. As an adolescent amateur musician he fell strongly under Balakirev's spell and quickly acquired such proficiency in writing for instruments that he became something of an official orchestrator for the group. Early on he scored works by Cui and Dargomïzhsky; the years 1881–83 were mainly spent revising and orchestrating major portions of Musorgsky's music, and upon Borodin's death in 1887 he, together with Glazunov, assumed the task of completing and orchestrating *Prince Igor*. Rimsky-Korsakov's special orchestral sound is known in the Western world largely through three compositions of 1888–89: the *Capriccio Espagnol,* the symphonic suite *Sheherazade,* and the *Russian Easter Festival Overture.* The particular brilliance, clarity, and vivid tone colors that one hears occasionally in the compositions of other members of The Five, especially in Balakirev's music, are highly developed and consistent in Rimsky-Korsakov's mature works.

This orchestral technique characteristically casts the principal melodic line in very bold relief with inventive doublings and an avoidance of competing activity in the middle and lower ranges. Bass support tends to be unobtrusive, and the accompanying parts of the orchestra often supply splashes of punctuating color rather than integral part-writing. One of many possible examples of this is the whole of the third movement of *Sheherazade.*[28] It has two related melodies, each repeated a good many times. The first is played initially by first and second violins in unison, next oboe and cellos, then English horn and cellos, solo clarinet

27. Musorgsky of course employed a genuine well-known Russian folksong in the Coronation Scene in the Prologue, *Slava Bogu na nebe,* the tune Beethoven had already used in his second Razumovsky Quartet, Op. 59, No. 2.

28. In his autobiography, Rimsky-Korsakov provided programmatic titles for the four movements of this work. The third is called "The Prince and the Princess."

and cellos, violins and clarinets, and finally, first violins alone. A subdued and extremely simple accompaniment in sustained chords interferes not in the least with the listener's concentration upon the changing colors of the melody. Only in the rushing flourishes between phrases (played alternately by clarinet, violins, flute, and later harp) does any part of the texture other than melody call attention to itself.

In the next section of this movement the second melody is treated similarly, elaborating this mosaic of ever-shifting colors (see Example XI–17). Here the melody is played in triple octaves by first and second clarinets and piccolo. The rest of the orchestra contributes sharp points of instrumental color: a rhythmic dominant ostinato in the first trumpet acting in concert with the percussion instruments—here the traditional ones of "Turkish music"—and quiet tonic arpeggiations added by the harp, bassoons, and lower strings.

Rimsky-Korsakov calculated such effects with care. Many of his special techniques in instrumental writing are detailed in his excellent treatise on orchestration, compiled from 1873 until his death (he illustrates one procedure for writing woodwinds in triple octaves in the excerpt shown in Example XI–17.)[29] In both theory and practice his orchestration is bound up with a particular view of musical texture: an intense melody is supported by blocks and strata of sound, not by competing melodic lines. And the instrumental colors of these components are essential; he maintained in the Preface to his treatise, "It is a great mistake to say: this composer scores well, or, that composition is well orchestrated, for orchestration is *part of the very soul of the work.*"[30] In this view of the relation of color to line he was much closer to Berlioz than to Wagner, and his handling of the orchestra was to exert a powerful influence in the new century: on the music of Glazunov, Prokofief, and Stravinsky, and even of Debussy and Ravel.

His reputation in the West notwithstanding, Rimsky-Korsakov invested the major portion of his compositional energies in the writing of operas—fifteen in all—for most of which he composed his own librettos. Like his colleagues, he was fascinated with events of Russian history and literature, and looked to Glinka as his guide. While his first opera, *The Maid of Pskov* (1872), is based on the life of Ivan the Terrible (who also appears in a nonsinging role in *The Czar's Bride,* 1899), Rimsky-Korsakov was later drawn increasingly to subjects of fantasy and enchantment—to the Glinka of *Ruslan and Lyudmila* rather than *A Life for the Czar. Snow Maiden* (1881), with a libretto after Ostrovsky's dramatic poem based on old Slavonic mythology, shows the composer in the first embrace of the primitive pantheism that attracted him the rest

---

29. Nicolas Rimsky-Korsakov, *Principles of Orchestration,* ed. M. Steinberg, trans. E. Agate (New York, 1912), 1, p. 51; 2, p. 67.

30. Ibid., 1, p. 2.

of his life. *Sadko* (1896), regarded by many as his finest opera, draws its story of sea gods, nymphs, and associated mortals from Russian legend going back to the Middle Ages. In his *Legend of the Invisible City of*

Example XI–17: RIMSKY-KORSAKOV, *Sheherazade,* third movement, mm. 106–12

Kitezh and the Maiden (1905), a tale of pantheism and enchantment is overlaid with Christian mysticism, and in his final opera, *Coq d'Or* (after Pushkin), a fairy-tale fantasy is mixed with a certain self-conscious irony. Two enduring traits of Russian opera are to be seen almost throughout these works: they are constructed as a series of static tableaux rather than goal-directed drama, and, within this structure, crowd scenes assume great importance.[31]

The musical style of Rimsky-Korsakov's operas is remarkably various. At one extreme is the stark, realistic declamation derived from Dargomïzhsky's most severe manner in *The Stone Guest*. The only pure example of this in Rimsky-Korsakov is the one-act *Mozart and Salieri* (1897), but stretches of it occur in the two operas after stories of Gogol, *May Night* (1879) and *Christmas Eve* (1895). At the other extreme is the ornate post-Wagnerian chromaticism of *Kashchei the Immortal* (1901). Certain characteristic melodic turns persist through it all, especially a disjunct cadential formula emphasizing the sixth degree of the scale.[32] And throughout the operas beginning at least with *Sadko*, Rimsky-Korsakov's skills as an orchestrator enabled him to provide specially vivid musical evocations of the strange events and places in which he specialized.

The issues in Russian music in the later nineteenth century were much less clear than is often believed. The customary portrait of a group of nationalist composers urging in precept and practice the virtues of a distinctly Russian musical art, in opposition to the cosmopolitan tendencies of the Russian Musical Society and the St. Petersburg Conservatory, is, even among generalizations, unusually misleading. The membership of the nationalist group, in the first place, is not unambiguous. The integrity of the "mighty handful" christened by Stasov was badly undermined by differing tastes and shifting alliances; it threatened to dissolve entirely after 1867—particularly as its leader, Balakirev, now was conducting the concerts of the supposed adversary, the Russian Musical Society. And in 1871 another of the group, Rimsky-Korsakov, as a professor in the Conservatory began to place his imprint upon a whole generation of musicians in that institution. In the practice of their craft as composers, moreover, this group showed no very distinct unity of style or idea; the music of Balakirev, as we have noted, shows little allegiance to nationalist doctrine, and that of Cui, almost none. If The Five were united in anything, it was probably in the traditional enmity of those outside the establishment toward those inside; and if there was any real content to their opposition, it had as much to do with the old-fashioned cast of the repertory and teaching at the Conservatory as with its purported "foreignness."[33]

31. An expert and readable account of Rimsky-Korsakov's operas can be found in Gerald Abraham, *Studies in Russian Music* (London, 1936), chapters 8–14.

32. See ibid., pp. 203ff. and 237–38.

33. Robert C. Ridenour provides a good corrective to prevailing views of Russian music of this period in *Nationalism, Modernism, and Personal Rivalry*. An unseen force in determining the conservative policies of the Russian Musical Society and its Conservatory was the Grand Duchess Elena Pavlovna, its principal patron; her death in 1873 led to a change in its orientation.

TCHAIKOVSKY

The leading standard bearer for the "cosmopolitan" or "European" faction in Russian music, in the usual view, was Pyotr Il'yich Tchaikovsky (1840–93), a student of Anton Rubinstein and graduate of the St. Petersburg Conservatory. Yet his identification with such a faction is tenuous. In 1868 and again in 1882 he fell under the spell of Balakirev, whose influence is strongly felt in Tchaikovsky's overture *Romeo and Juliet* (first version, 1869) and his *Manfred Symphony* (1885). Tchaikovsky maintained an interest in indigenous Russian music all his life; he arranged and published a collection of folksongs in 1868–69 and used folk melodies in his works from nearly all periods. His operas show about as much dependence upon Russian literary and historical sources as do those of The Five. Perhaps the real factors in his consignment to the "European" camp were external ones: during the heyday of The Five, the early 1860s, Tchaikovsky was a student at the rival institution, the Conservatory; immediately after graduation he further distanced himself from them by taking a position at the new conservatory founded by Nikolay Rubinstein in Moscow; and for much of his later career he traveled frequently in the West and established a reputation there unapproached by any other Russian musician.

Before his move to Moscow in 1866 Tchaikovsky produced little music of note: only a few tentative orchestral pieces, including an overture to Ostrovsky's play *The Storm*. Once in Moscow he settled down to serious composition, and by 1872 had produced his first two symphonies and three operas. Of the latter he saved only one, *Oprichnik* (1872), destroying the other two after transferring some of their music to other compositions. Most promising, perhaps, of these early works is the Second Symphony in C minor (the *Little Russian*), an essay in "nationalist" music that inaugurates a period of intense preoccupation with Russian musical idiom, probably owing a good deal to his contacts with Balakirev. Ukranian folksongs provide the principal thematic materials for three of its four movements; the one used in the finale, *The Crane,* bears a striking family resemblance to *Slava* (used by Beethoven and by Musorgsky in *Boris Godunov*) as well as to the Promenade theme of *Pictures at an Exhibition*. Tchaikovsky typically subjects these tunes to a variation treatment popularized by Glinka: many repeated statements of the melody with changing instrumental colors and accompanimental patterns. In this symphony we also hear stylistic traits that will long endure in his works, such as the deft and colorful obbligato lines for the woodwinds in the Scherzo and the *fortissimo* punctuating orchestral strokes that threaten to grow tiresome in that movement and the finale.

Tchaikovsky was also strongly touched by his traditional conservatory training. This is evident from the first in harmony and part-writ-

Tchaikovsky at the age of 33.

ing marked by both professionalism and a certain conventionality. And that experience was also a factor, no doubt, in the formation of an indelible streak of neoclassicism in Tchaikovsky's musical thought. A fascination with traditional large-scale genres of instrumental music—and the ever-renewed struggles with form they entail—together with a certain conscious archaism of style reminiscent of Schumann and even of Mozart are a permanent feature of his work. This can be seen in all three of his string quartets, especially the first one in D major (1871), where unadorned Classical structure is combined with the lyrical melody for which Tchaikovsky had a special gift (the very familiar Andante Cantabile from this composition, later arranged for cello and string orchestra by the composer, once again draws its melody from a folksong[34]). Two other well-known instrumental compositions that show the composer's marked fondness for styles of the past are the Variations on a Rococo Theme for cello and orchestra (1876) and the Serenade for Strings (1881).

Another very prominent factor in Tchaikovsky's style is his proclivity for current fashions in music for the salon and dance. Much of his output of songs and piano music has strong affinities with these semi-popular styles. An example is his best-known song, the setting of Goethe's venerable *Nur wer die Sehnsucht kennt*, familiar in English as *None but the Lonely Heart;* it has the sweeping melodic line and slightly overripe secondary sevenths of the drawing-room romance—a style of writing that one often hears in Tchaikovsky, as in the exceedingly poignant Andante theme of the first movement of the Sixth Symphony.

34. See David Brown, *Tchaikowsky: a Biographical and Critical Study, I: The Early Years, 1840–1874* (New York, 1978), p. 218ff.

Tchaikovsky's talent for dancelike music yielded better results. His three ballet scores, *Swan Lake* (1876), *The Sleeping Beauty* (1889), and *The Nutcracker* (1892), have remained staples of the repertory because they are so well conceived for the classical ballet: the music is cleverly evocative and full of contrasts of color and rhythm—the composer himself regarded *The Sleeping Beauty* as one of his best compositions. Echoes of the dance can be heard throughout Tchaikovsky's oeuvre, sometimes working at cross-purposes with his efforts toward elaborately reasoned symphonic structures, but more often showing him at his unselfconscious best.

The central pursuit of Tchaikovsky's life, it seems safe to say, was the composition of opera. He was always searching restlessly for promising subjects for librettos, and there were few years in his maturity when he did not have an opera underway. After abandoning his first two works in the genre, he turned to a familiar episode from Russian history, the reign of Ivan the Terrible (the subject of two of Rimsky-Korsakov's operas) and composed *The Oprichnik* (1872) to his own libretto. Avowedly opposed to the "realist" doctrine of Dargomïzhsky and Musorgsky, he modeled his work after pan-European traditions, especially the grand opera of Meyerbeer.[35] His next opera, *Vacula the Smith* (1874), however, is an admirable work with clear Russian lineage; its subject drawn from Gogol, it is full of the idiom of Russian folk music and owes a considerable debt, both dramatically and musically, to Glinka's *Ruslan and Lyudmila*.

Of Tchaikovsky's ten operas, only two, *Eugene Onegin* (1878) and *The Queen of Spades* (1890), have any currency in the West; the first of these is firmly installed in the repertory. *Eugene Onegin* is a warm domestic drama, or, as Tchaikowsky called it, series of "lyric scenes," its subject drawn from a verse-novel of Pushkin, that inexhaustible poetic wellspring for Russian opera. Its central character, Tatyana, was one for whom Tchaikovsky felt special sympathy;[36] she emerges as a fully convincing heroine—her ingenuous charm might remind English readers of Maggie in Eliot's *The Mill on the Floss,* or Hardy's Tess—whose vividness is ample recompense for an absence of developed plot or scenic effects. Divided into the conventional numbers (scenes, arias, ensembles, and choruses), it presents a series of vignettes with music well adapted to the dramatic purpose at hand. Particularly impressive is the famous Letter Scene (No. 9), in which Tatyana's shifting moods are well reflected in a flexible vocal line ranging from free *parlando* to expressive lyricism. At its high point Tchaikovsky writes a melody whose shape might come

---

35. See Gerald Abraham, "Tchaikowsky's Operas" in *Slavonic and Romantic Music*, pp. 128ff. This essay remains the most useful discussion of its subject.

36. By his own testimony he mingled feelings for Tatyana with the conduct of his real life, leading to a disastrous (and very brief) marriage in 1877.

Example XI–18: TCHAIKOVSKY, *Eugene Onegin,* No. 9

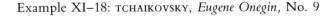

straight out of Verdi (Example XI–18); but its basis in the natural minor scale and harmonic emphasis of the flat sixth degree (the sonority in the second measure, set over a tonic pedal, might be called a "neapolitan sixth to the dominant") gives it a special and distinctly Russian flavor.[37] This scene is slightly marred—less so than much of the opera—by Tchaikovsky's tendency to clutter the orchestral part with perpetual obbligato accompaniments.

If the overall structure and some of the music of *Eugene Onegin* may remind us of French opera in the time of Meyerbeer and just after, Tchaikovsky's next opera, *The Maid of Orleans* (after Schiller's play on Joan of Arc) seems in its light style and decorative chromaticism still more indebted to the opéra lyrique of, say, Thomas and Massenet. In *Mazeppa* (1883), again after Pushkin, Tchaikovsky returned to a subject from Russian history (this time from the beginning of the reign of Peter the Great) and, at points, to a "Russian" musical idiom reminiscent of Glinka. *The Queen of Spades* (1890), once more deriving from Pushkin, is a little drama of macabre wit for which Tchaikowsky wrote music of very disparate kinds. Some of the score approaches the rhetorical pathos of the Fifth and Sixth Symphonies that date from the same period. But here, more than in any other of the operas, Tchaikovsky also indulged his fondness for retrospection: a pastoral cantata in neoclassic style is inserted into Scene 3, and there are quotations (some acknowledged and some not) of music by Grétry, Mozart, and Bortnyansky.[38] This is done as a nostalgic evocation of the bygone days of Catherine the Great, very much as Strauss was to recall the time of Maria Theresa in *Rosenkavalier.*

However central his operas were to Tchaikovsky's career in Russia, he is best known elsewhere for his orchestral music, the symphonies

37. Abraham points out that the last portion of this melody occurs throughout the opera. Gerald Abraham, *"Eugene Onegin and Tchaikowsky's Marriage," On Russian Music* (London, 1939), pp. 232–33. Its beginning shows a drooping gesture often to be heard in Tchaikovsky, as in the opening of the finale of the Sixth Symphony—here harmonized with a series of seventh chords whose bald parallel motion is camouflaged by systematic voice exchanges.

38. See Abraham, *Slavonic and Romantic Music,* pp. 171–72.

and concertos. He wrote two full-length piano concertos and a third in one movement adapted from a projected symphony. Of these only the first concerto in B♭ minor, Op. 23, is heard very often—and it is heard very often indeed. Tchaikovsky first played it through early in 1875 for Nikolay Rubinstein, who, the composer reports, condemned it as worthless, trivial, and unperformable. He nonetheless completed the score and dedicated it to Hans von Bülow, who gave it its premiere performance in Boston later that year. It quickly became a favorite of pianists and audiences alike. Neither seemed to worry much about its famous structural anomaly: the opening grandiloquent theme, huge in the extreme, appears in the wrong key (D♭ major), then disappears never to return. In fact it is probably that theme, first played by the strings with broadly spaced fortissimo accompanying chords in the piano, that is chiefly responsible for the piece's popularity (it alone was pressed into service in the cinema). Attractive and original things happen later in the composition; the two halves of the pastorale-like slow movement are separated by a flute *scherzando* contrasting section. And the last movement is one of Tchaikovsky's "Russian finales," whose vigorous main theme, derived from a Ukrainian folk tune, takes on added brightness in exchanges between soloist and orchestra. Equally popular is the composer's single Violin Concerto, Op. 35 (1878), where his talent for dramatic, expressive melody and an artful transformation of Russian folk idiom (Hanslick called the finale of this piece "odorously Russian") seem particularly well adapted to the genre of the solo concerto.

In the last years before his tragic death (its cause now hotly debated) in 1893, Tchaikovsky made repeated foreign tours in which he appeared as conductor on the principal concert stages of Europe and the eastern United States. In this way his works, particularly those for orchestra, achieved a much wider exposure than the music of any other Russian composer of the time. Central to his concert repertory were the six symphonies, whose composition was spread out about evenly throughout his career from 1866 to 1893. In these works he struggled ceaselessly with the opposed demands of formal traditions he had learned in the conservatory and his own predilection for an emotional and expressive progression of events corresponding to an unspoken program. In a frank self-appraisal in 1878 (the time of the Fourth Symphony) he acknowledged the continuing rightness of a much earlier criticism of his style made by Balakirev: "There is frequently *padding* in my works; to an experienced eye the stitches show in my seams."[39] These compositions have an episodic character akin to typical structures in opera by Tchaikovsky and his Russian contemporaries; in the last three symphonies this is offset by cyclic procedures with a vague dramatic import, particularly in the use of recurring "motto themes."

39.   Quoted from Abraham, "Tchaikowsky Revalued," *Studies in Russian Music,* p. 342.

Example XI–19: TCHAIKOVSKY, Fifth Symphony, fourth movement, mm. 1–4

In the Fifth and Sixth Symphonies Tchaikovsky reaches the pinnacle of the rhetorical expressiveness that characterizes much of his later work. The dynamic range of the orchestral writing is extreme, and the building of climaxes is extended to a point bordering on hysteria. The famous "brooding melancholy" of these compositions, especially the Fifth Symphony, is largely due to Tchaikovsky's talent for manipulating darker tone colors. The motto theme of the Fifth, occurring in all four movements, provides an example. At the start of the first movement it is sounded by the clarinets far down in their chalumeau register against low strings, and the finale begins with the tune played so low by the violins that the violas and cellos must supply one of its pitches (Example XI–19). Another orchestral technique contributing to the special sound of these pieces is the creation of a backdrop of wind sound through repeated patterns, often highly rhythmical ones, played by brass and woodwinds together; this produces a thickness and busyness very useful in creating climax. And Tchaikovsky's particular love for arresting trumpet and horn calls is everywhere evident. The beginning of the Fourth Symphony (ARM 21) may provide a clue to the origins of this predilection: it opens with a powerful horn call, darkened at its initial appearance by the addition of bassoons, that bears a clear melodic resemblance to the opening of Schumann's First Symphony (which in turn recalls the beginning of Schubert's Great C-major). But Tchaikovsky has transformed the magic of the Romantic horn call into something imperious and urgent—he felt beckoned, not by the green fields of youthful enchantment, but by a somber and inexorable fate.

SCANDINAVIA

Throughout history three of the four Scandinavian countries, Norway, Sweden, and Denmark, have been closely related through a common cultural and linguistic heritage. Finland, settled in the early Middle Ages by nomadic tribes, related to the Magyars of the Danube basin, who spoke a Finno-Ugric language quite unrelated to those of their European neighbors, have always maintained a certain orientation towards the East. Since the late Middle Ages Norway had been under the control of Denmark; Finland, subject to the Swedish crown, was the traditional battleground in the wars between Sweden and Russia. Then in the course of the shifting alliances of the Napoleonic Wars Sweden relinquished control of Finland, which in 1809 became a semi-independent Grand Duchy of Russia. Denmark, as a punishment for siding with the French, was forced to cede Norway to Sweden in 1814. These governmental arrangements, often uneasy, lasted for the rest of the century.

Finland was very largely an agrarian country during the nineteenth century, and its small middle and upper classes, concentrated at the southwest coast, consisted mainly of Swedish residents. It was only in the second half of the century that something like a nationalist movement began to assert itself in matters of politics and language. A modest body of indigenous Finnish literature, written mainly by amateurs, took shape later in the century; its leading representative was the novelist and short-story writer Juhani Aho (1861–1921). While Finland had relatively rich and varied traditions in folk music, art music remained very much under the influence of German practice. The principal teachers of music in the country were German born. Finnish musicians such as Robert Kajanus (1856–1933), founder and leader of the Helsinki Orchestral Society, and Martin Wegelius (1846–1906), pianist, teacher, conductor, and composer, were trained in Germany. While Kajanus composed some mildly "nationalist" music in the 1880s (two Finnish Rhapsodies in 1882 and 1889), the growth of a significant body of music of a specifically Finnish cast awaited the appearance of his protégé, Jean Sibelius (1865–1957).

From the seventeenth century the rich musical life in Sweden was also very much dependent upon that of Germany, particularly after the Thirty Years' War (1618–48), during which many German musicians and instrument builders took refuge in the country. During the following century Stockholm developed a concert life and operatic practice comparable to that of smaller courts in Germany; the court opera was mainly Italian with some German additions, and the instrumental repertory favored works of Germans, supplemented occasionally by those of Swedish composers such as Ferdinand Zellbell (1719–80). During the early part of the nineteenth century concert societies sprang up in several of Sweden's major cities, and the number of native composers increased appreciably. The prevailing musical style was largely conservative. The choral pieces and songs of the able composer Adolf Fredrik Lindblad (1801–78), some of them modeled after Swedish folk melodies, elicited praise outside Sweden, but criticism for excessive harmonic complexity at home. His Symphony in C, performed in Leipzig in 1839, received a warm notice from Schumann,[40] but in Sweden his instrumental music was mainly ignored.

The most important Swedish composer of the nineteenth century in the opinion of many, Franz Berwald (1796–1868), was scarcely recognized in Sweden or elsewhere. After middling success as a youthful violinist he moved to Berlin in 1829 (where he became a successful purveyor of orthopedic devices), and lived abroad for most of the next twenty years. After his return to Sweden in 1849 he pursued various other careers while attempting vainly to achieve success as an opera composer. But his works that now seem most worthy of note are the instrumental compositions, particularly his four symphonies. These pieces, all composed from 1842 to 1845, reveal a forceful and independent musical mind operating within well-circumscribed boundaries of the German symphonic tradition.[41] The *Sinfonie singulière,* rediscovered in the twentieth century and perhaps the most striking of the four, is written in a style that will remind the modern listener of Schubert of

Example XI–20: BERWALD, *Sinfonie singulière,* fourth movement, mm. 233–45

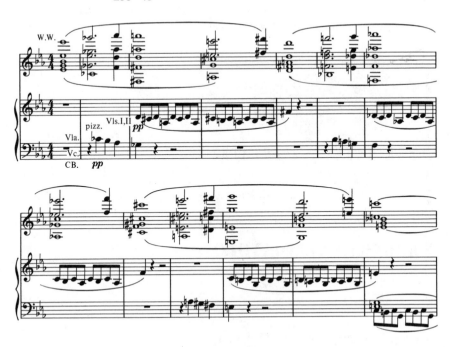

---

40. Robert Schumann, *Gesammelte Schriften,* 2, pp. 502–3.

41. A collected edition of the works of Berwald has been launched by Monumenta Musicae Svecicae in Stockholm; by 1982 it has reached 14 volumes, together with a volume of documentary materials on Berwald's life.

the Great C-major Symphony or Mendelssohn's mature orchestral music. The instrumental textures are clear and classic, and the formal procedures largely traditional. In this work and others, however, the Scherzo—this one an agile, gossamer movement alla Mendelssohn—is enfolded within the two halves of the Adagio. Most disturbing to his audiences, and seemingly most attractive to his present-day admirers, are Berwald's occasional harmonic audacities. These often take the form of strong local motions in the "flat direction"; the Adagio of the *Sinfonie singulière* introduces a jolting Neapolitan sixth in major in the second measure. Berwald's tonal adventures are often combined with his strong predilection for harmonic sequence: Example XI–20, from the finale of the *Sinfonie singulière,* shows a sequence that moves, with perfect metrical regularity, downward by semitone from E♭ to C.

After the mid-nineteenth century the newly reorganized Stockholm Conservatory provided improved opportunities for musical education. Many Swedish musicians also sought professional training abroad, especially in the circle of Schumann and Mendelssohn and their followers at the Leipzig Conservatory. Newly founded symphony orchestras in various Swedish cities played works by Fredrik Vilhelm Norman (1831–85) and Andreas Hállen (1846–1925), both of them trained in Leipzig. A musician of very great influence in the later century was

An advertisement of Jenny Lind's London appearance in Meyerbeer's *Robert-le-Diable,* 8 May 1847.

Johann August Söderman (1832–76), a conductor at the Stockholm Royal Opera and the composer of a series of Swedish works for stage that were performed alongside the standard Italian and French repertory. Most advanced in style of his compositions, however, are the ballads for solo voice and orchestra, *Qvarnruinen, Arme Peter,* and others, in which declamatory singing is accompanied by a very full orchestral sound and quasi-Wagnerian chromaticism. But the only Swedish musician of the century to make a lasting impression in the world at large was the brilliant soprano Jenny Lind (1820–87); she made her career first in opera (until about 1849) and later as an oratorio singer and recitalist, delighting audiences throughout Europe, England, and America until after 1880.

Art music in Norway remained mostly at an amateur level until the nineteenth century. But after Norway's annexation by Sweden in 1814, stirrings of patriotic sentiment led a growing musical art in distinctly nationalist directions. The poet Henrik Wegeland (1808–45) glorified the life and spirit of the old Vikings, and a lively interest in national lore led to the influential edition of Norwegian folk songs by L. M. Lindeman in 1841. The first disseminator of a Norwegian musical idiom was the spectacular violinist from Bergen, Ole Bull (1810–80). On concert stages from Vienna to Chicago he improvised in the style of the Norwegian folk dance, the *Slåtter,* using an instrument modified to resemble a peasant fiddle in tone quality and ease in playing multiple stops. Some of his compositions, too, such as *Souvenirs de Norvège,* were consciously modeled on Norwegian folk music. His consumate skills as a performer (Schumann compared him favorably with Paganini[42]) and his tireless international campaigning for his country's independence from Sweden made him the best-known Norwegian of his generation.

While Norway was under the political domination of Sweden, it was, for most of the nineteenth century, culturally subservient to Denmark. Copenhagen was the main center of learning and the arts for the entire area, and not much effort was made until well after mid-century to establish institutions like opera and orchestral music in Norway—the first Norwegian opera, *Fredkulla* (The Peacemaker), was composed by Martin Andreas Udbye in 1858, and Otto Winter-Hjelm produced the first Norwegian symphony three years later. Then in the latter part of the century two composers came into prominence, Johan Svendsen (1840–1911) and Edvard Grieg (1843–1907), who brought world attention to Norway's music comparable to that which the acerbic plays and poetry of Henrik Ibsen attracted to its literature.

Svendsen was another in the long procession of Scandinavian musicians trained at the Leipzig Conservatory. He was there during some of

---

42. Robert Schumann, 2, p. 357.

the institution's more luminous years in the 1860s; he studied violin with Ferdinand David, theory with Moritz Hauptmann, and composition with Carl Reinecke. While he spent most of his notable career as a conductor and composer outside Norway (in Leipzig, Paris, and from 1883 until his death in Copenhagen), he together with Grieg was always seen as representative of a "nationalist-Romantic" movement in Norwegian music. His greatest strength was orchestral composition. His two symphonies (1866 and 1877) show a Mendelssohnian clarity of form together with orchestral colors suggesting the influence of Berlioz and Wagner (with whom he was closely associated in Bayreuth in the 1870s). His two concertos, for cello and violin, show similar traits of meticulous craftsmanship, but lack the virtuoso flair often thought essential to the category. Specifically "nationalist" characteristics occur in his music to only a modest degree, as in the orchestral adaptations of Norwegian folksongs in *Norsk Kunstnerkarneval* (c. 1874) and the four Norwegian Rhapsodies (c. 1876). It is unfortunate that the only composition of his currently performed is the rather slight Romance for violin and orchestra (1881), where the principal interest resides in a tentative exploration of Wagnerian chromaticism in the alternating slow sections.

Edvard Grieg, born in Bergen three years later than Svendsen, entered the Leipzig Conservatory at the age of fifteen. Though later bitterly critical of his experience there, some of what he learned—such as an intimate acquaintance with the music of Schumann—had a lasting effect on his compositional style. Another, more potent influence was Norwegian folk music, first brought to his attention in 1864 and 1865 by contacts with Ole Bull and the ardent young nationalist composer Rikard Nordraak (1842–1866), and a little later by his encounter with Lindeman's collection of folksongs. From this time on Grieg resolved to cultivate a specifically Norwegian idiom, and his music reflects this with some consistency. In 1869 he set a series of Lindeman's tunes as his Opus 17, *Norwegian Folk Melodies and Dances*. The melodies show certain consistent traits such as a construction from often-repeated cells, use of the lowered seventh in minor, and—most distinctively—an ambiguity between the natural and sharp fourth. Grieg harmonizes much of this music with drone pedals (Example XI–21); this simple, folklike effect consorts oddly with the mildly chromatic style of nineteenth-century art music also present in the set. The raised fourth, in particular, has a dramatically different significance in these two contexts. In one case it threatens the tonal orientation of the music; in the other it is but a harmless ornamental lower neighbor to the dominant. This sort of ambiguity, reflecting an ongoing attempt to reconcile two radically different musical worlds, is central to Greig's style.

In his years at the Leipzig Conservatory Greig did not, for one reason or another, gain confidence in handling the traditional large forms. His

Example XI–21: GRIEG, *Leaping Dance,* Op. 17

single very early symphony he regarded as a failure, and his later sporadic attempts at chamber music (he completed a string quartet, three
violin sonatas, and a cello sonata) produced pieces with certain attractive passages but little long-term coherence. In view of this it may seem
remarkable that his only completed concerto, the youthful Piano Concerto in A minor (1868, the orchestral part revised in 1906–7), has become
one of the most popular compositions of its genre. But the nineteenth-
century concerto was the one large form in which neither formal cohesion nor elaborate detail was much of an issue. Grieg's concerto, very
obviously patterned after Schumann's piano concerto in the same key,
shows few of the textural and rhythmic intricacies of its model. Its
combination of bravura piano playing and lyrical episodes is simple and
broadly drawn; with the spicy addition of a vaguely folklike main theme
in the last movement it has everything that was expected of a solo concerto of its time. Of Grieg's other compositions for large forces, most
successful is the incidental music for Björnstjerne Björnson's *Sigurd Jor-
salfar* (1872) and Ibsen's *Peer Gynt* (1876); he arranged parts of the latter
into two orchestral suites whose spritely tunes and evocative color have
won them a permanent place in the orchestral repertory.

Grieg's strong points—a pronounced gift for lyrical melody and a
certain adventurousness of harmonic style—are most conspicuous in his
songs. There are 140 of them, rather evenly spread throughout his career,
composed to German, Danish, and Norwegian texts. Some have a very
pronounced folklike character (though only one, the well-known *Sol-
veig's Song* to a poem by Ibsen, uses an actual folk melody). *Hidden Love*
(Op. 33, No. 2), its text by Björnson, has the persistent pedal points
and repeated motives that marked his settings from Lindeman's collection. Others, such as the setting of Vinje's *Beside the River* (Op. 33, No.
5), has a harmonic subtlety and an interplay between voice and piano
reminiscent of Schumann of 1840. In his late song cycle *Haugtussa* (Op.
67, 1895) Grieg reaches the most advanced stage in his harmonic style.
Not all of the cycle seems successful; the unrelieved chromatic inner
motion of *The Tryst* (No. 4), for example, cloys. But nonfunctional
seventh chords and augmented triads in *Love* are close to the harmonic
idiom of Debussy (Example XI–22).

Example XI–22: GRIEG, *Love,* Op. 67, No. 5

ge - hö - ret ein - zig nur dir, nur dir!____
be - longs a - lone to you, on - ly you!____

Copenhagen in the later eighteenth century was a sophisticated cultural center where opera, symphonic music, and church music flourished under the auspices of the court. But the turmoil of the Napoleonic
wars and their aftermath dealt harshly with Denmark, and the arts were
slow to recover. The leading figure in Danish music during these lean
years was Christoph Ernst Friedrich Weyse (1774–1842), an organist
and a composer of church cantatas and Singspiele of a conservative cast.
About mid-century there was a quickening of concert life. In 1849 the
Musikforeningen, an organization that supported an orchestra and a
chorus, came under the direction of Niels Gade (1817–90), a versatile
musician and prolific composer who became virtually the sole arbiter
of musical taste in Denmark until his death. Several other concert societies were begun in succeeding years, so that by the last quarter of the
century Copenhagen was again the center of musical performance in
Scandinavia.

Nineteenth-century composers in Denmark never developed a very
distinct profile, and "nationalist" music scarcely existed there. Danish
operas, such as *Lulu* (1824) by Friedrich Kuhlau (1786–1832), who is
mainly known for his piano music, and *Ravnen* (1832) by J. P. E. Hartmann (Gade's father-in-law) are derivative of Weber; no notable progress in operatic composition was made until the very end of the century
in the works of Peter Lange-Müller (1850–1926). Gade himself showed
some early interest in regional musical idioms in his overture *Echoes of
Ossian* (1840), but no more so than had Mendelssohn in his overture on
a similar subject, *The Hebrides* (1830). Gade's energetic First Symphony
(1842) is a well-made composition that suggests a strong influence from
Mendelssohn (Schumann also heard in it echoes of Schubert[43]), and his
later music—there were seven more symphonies—seems very much

43. Ibid., 2, p. 159.

the same. Yet he showed a certain individual bent in his cultivation of an unusual genre for his century, the secular cantata; two popular examples for soloists, chorus, and orchestra were on Danish subjects: *The Erl-King's Daughter* (1853) and *Baldur's Dream* (1858).

ENGLAND

England in the nineteenth century enjoyed unprecedented industrial and mercantile successes, reaching the zenith of her international influence and the greatest extension of her empire. The social ills that followed in the wake of a burgeoning Industrial Revolution are well known; yet redress was not sought in political revolution, as in most of Europe, but through a gradual and fairly orderly process of improvement. In this climate English science and letters flourished. The period produced reflections on society and science by minds of the caliber of Arnold, Bentham, J. S. Mill, Huxley, and Darwin; it also witnessed the flowering of Romantic poetry and the novel.

There was no comparable cultivation of original work in the other arts in nineteenth-century England. The landscape painting of Constable and Turner was something of an isolated highpoint. In respect to music, Britain remained as it had been in the eighteenth century, a nation of consumers rather than producers. From about the 1780s until the end of the nineteenth century London had as rich a musical life as any city in the world: opera in Italian and English was regularly performed in at least three theaters, and each season multiple series of concerts competed for the attention of an enthusiastic public. The orchestra of the Philharmonic Society was formed in 1813, and in 1852 the New Philharmonic Society was established. Orchestras in other cities sprang up, such as that founded by Charles Hallé in Manchester in 1858. Chamber music and recitals were heard in public as early and as often in England as anywhere in Europe, and later in the century music was performed in mammoth buildings, viz. the Crystal Palace and Royal Albert Hall (opened, respectively, in 1852 and 1871). But amidst all this musical activity the work of English composers could never rival the prestige of the German and Italian repertory. English music was expected to imitate continental models, and for the most part it did so.

Italian opera, the traditional musical preserve of England's aristocracy, continued throughout the century to play at King's Theater (after Queen Victoria's accession in 1837 called Her Majesty's Theater) in the Haymarket and (from 1847) at Covent Garden. So essential was the "Italianness" of the institution that an opera by a British composer on a Shakespearian subject, Michael Balfe's *Falstaff* (1838), had to be composed to an Italian libretto, and the first performances of Wagner's operas (beginning in 1870) were in Italian translation.

First edition of "Home Sweet Home" from Henry Bishop's opera *Clari, or the Maid of Milan,* 1823.

The more plebeian English drama with music, some of which may legitimately be called opera, was heard at the Drury Lane Theater, until 1847 at Covent Garden, and at various smaller theaters. Until the mid-1830s, the leading composer of these productions was Henry Bishop (1786–1855), whose musical numbers included tuneful "airs" and "ballads" (one is "Home, Sweet Home," from *Clari,* 1823) and occasional imitations of the aria style of Rossini or Weber; he was also responsible for mutilating works such as *Don Giovanni* and *The Barber of Seville* for performance on the English-language stage. Following the great London successes of Weber's *Freischütz* and *Oberon,* the latter commissioned by Covent Garden in 1826, English operas began to show signs of greater musical sophistication. This can be seen in the works of the prolific Michael Balfe (1808–70), and in those of the eclectic Edward Loder (1813–65), who in *Raymond and Agnes* (1855) seems to have added *Fidelio* to the usual repertory of continental models to be imitated. In all these works the structure is basically the same: spoken drama predominates, giving rise at various points to musical set pieces such as airs, ensembles, and choruses, as well as occasional recitative and melodrama.

The most distinctive English musical drama of the century is to be found in the operettas of Gilbert and Sullivan. Arthur Sullivan (1842–1900), one of a very long procession of English music students to study at the Leipzig Convervatory, entered there together with Grieg in 1858 and remained until 1861; in succeeding years he maintained an active life as organist, conductor, and composer of "serious" music while creating nearly single-handedly the tradition of the English operetta. In 1875 he first entered into collaboration with W. S. Gilbert to produce a one-act "afterpiece" to an opera of Offenbach. This was *Trial by Jury,* to be followed by such memorable works as *H. M. S. Pinafore* (1878), *The Pirates of Penzance* (1879), *The Mikado* (1885), and *The Yeoman of the Guard* (1888). The broad parody and witty absurdities of Gilbert's texts are matched by Sullivan's dazzling array of borrowed and adapted styles, from solemn Handelian recitative to Gounod-like sentimental airs. The most fertile source for Sullivan's invention, however, is the Italian opera (especially Rossini) he had learned as a young organist at Covent Garden. The marching rhythms of many of his choruses come straight from this tradition;[44] the familiar one in *The Pirates of Penzance,* "Come Friends Who Plow the Sea" (still more familiar as "Hail, Hail, the Gang's All Here") is cut from the same cloth as the Anvil Chorus in *Il Trovatore.* And the characteristic patter songs—a particularly delightful one is the trio "My Eyes are Fully Open" in *Ruddigore*—have their stylistic origins in *The Barber of Seville* and, more remotely, in the basso-buffo singing characteristic of eighteenth-century Italian comic opera.

Instrumental music heard in nineteenth-century Britain was still mainly written by foreigners. Some, like Clementi, J. B. Cramer, Ignaz Moscheles, and Julius Benedict, were long-term residents of the country. Others, such as Spohr, Mendelssohn, Berlioz, and Liszt, following in the tradition of Haydn, presented their music on visits to England. But the composer whose instrumental compositions were performed most frequently of all, Beethoven, managed to endear himself to English audiences without setting foot in the country. Of native English musicians the outstanding instrumental composer of the first half of the century was William Sterndale Bennett (1816–75), the first distinguished student of the Royal Academy of Music, and from 1837 a teacher there. Bennett was a brilliant pianist whose playing of his own concertos impressed audiences in both England and Germany. He wrote piano miniatures of considerable charm; some of them, such as the Impromptus, Op. 12 (1836), seem derivative of Mendelssohn, Bennett's early friend and supporter. More so are his concert overtures, especially his popular *The Naiads* (1836), a piece stylistically very close to Mendelssohn's *Die schöne Melusina* (1833). Schumann praised Bennett and his music enthusiastically in 1837–38: "He has in a word the most ennobled taste, the liveliest sense of what is genuine and true."[45] But the promise he showed at that time was little realized; in later years his compositions were few and stylistically static.

Two English composers of the later century, Hubert Parry (1848–

---

44. As does the rhythmic accompaniment to Sullivan's hymn *Onward, Christian Soldiers.*
45. Robert Schumann, 1, p. 289.

1918) and Charles Stanford (1852–1924), both teachers at the Royal College of Music at its founding in 1883, were scholarly musicians of great distinction. Whereas Mendelssohn's instrumental style was a dominant force in mid-nineteenth-century England, the clearest influence for composers of this new generation was apparently Brahms. Parry's orchestral music (including four symphonies) and chamber compositions, mainly concentrated in the early part of his career, show this distinctly. Stanford (also a graduate of the Leipzig Conservatory) was a prolific composer in all the standard genres except opera; his high level of craftsmanship and conservative leanings were a shaping force in English music at the century's end. A strong individual voice among English instrumental composers, however, was not heard until the maturity of Edward Elgar (1857–1934). His only major composition written in the nineteenth century, the *Enigma Variations* (1899), has proved the most durable of his works (with the possible exception of the first of the *Pomp and Circumstance Marches* [1901] played at most American academic commencement ceremonies). Some of its orchestral textures and variation technique recall works of Brahms such as the *Variations on a Theme by Haydn* (1873); but its harmonic vocabulary includes chromatic elements that are a personal adaptation of the mature Wagnerian style.

The usual factors in the growth of cultural nationalism—status as a developing nation, struggle against a foreign oppressor, feelings of cultural inferiority—were of course lacking in England. It was mainly in a quickening of interest in the "Celtic fringes" that certain nationalist traits appeared in music, and this occurred only late in the century. Charles Stanford, who was born in Dublin, occasionally featured Irish folktunes in his music, notably in his Third Symphony (*The Irish,* 1887). Alexander Mackenzie (1847–1935), the distinguished principal of the Royal Academy of Music after 1888, celebrated his northern heritage in descriptive instrumental music such as the *Scottish Piano Concerto,* first performed by Ignaz Paderewski in 1897; *The Land of the Mountain and Flood* and *Highland Memories* by Hamish MacCunn (1868–1916) were popular orchestral pieces in London at the end of the century.

It was in church music and choral singing that English musical life of the nineteenth century showed most individuality. After a serious decline in the level of support and quality of music in the Church of England in the late eighteenth and early nineteenth centuries, the religious revival and general spirit of reform of Victorian times produced a surge of new vitality. Choirs in the thirty-odd cathedrals in Britain (notably at St. Paul's in London after John Stainer became organist in 1872) were expanded, and enormous numbers of new anthems were composed for their use. The century's leading composer of music for the church was Samuel Sebastian Wesley (1810–76), a member of the prominent family of English churchmen and musicians. During his career of restless moving

The audience, chorus and orchestra depicted during a concert in the central transept of the Crystal Palace, London. Woodcut, 1857.

from one church position to another in Hereford, Leeds, and Gloucester, he produced a large number of anthems still in use (best known perhaps is *The Wilderness and the Solitary Place*), some short and expressive on the model of Mozart's *Ave verum corpus,* and some longer and multisectional. Their style, though reminiscent of Mendelssohn's and Spohr's oratorio writing, also has some of the four-square solidity of the Protestant hymns in which his family excelled. An eloquent and irritable spokesman for the improvement of church music and the church musician's lot, Wesley did not live to hear the distinctive sort of singing that never fails to impress visitors to English cathedrals and some college chapels: that wonderfully precise enunciation and straight tone, especially in boys' voices, was a product of the final two decades of the century.

Ever since the time of Handel the oratorio had been a sustaining force in English musical life. Extravagant commemorative performances of Handel's works beginning in 1784 provided steady nourishment for the public appetite for this genre. At the end of the eighteenth century both Drury Lane and Covent Garden supplemented their opera seasons with substantial series of oratorio performances. But oratorios became the special province of the amateur choral societies that flourished throughout the nation during all of the nineteenth century. Many of these were modest organizations of no more than local significance; but the choral festivals of Birmingham, Leeds, and especially the triennial Handel Festival at the Crystal Palace, were the grandest musical events in England. At the beginning of the century the works of Handel dominated the repertory, with occasional performances of Haydn's two oratorios and those of native composers such as William Crotch (1775–1847). Spohr's *The Last Judgment* and Mendelssohn's *Elijah,* the latter premiered at Birmingham in 1846, offered the first serious competition to Handel's works, and in 1882 Gounod's *La Rédemption* injected yet another note into the standard repertory. One or another of these imports usually exerted a strong influence on English composers of this genre: among them were Henry Hugo Pierson (*Jerusalem,* 1852), Frederick Ouseley (*The Martyrdom of St. Polycarp,* 1855), and Hubert Parry (*Judith,* 1888).

A related category intended for the same performing groups was the sacred cantata. Most of these works were by Englishmen and virtually all English composers of the second half of the century wrote them because they provided the only commercially viable outlet for their skills. Though their structure of narrative recitative interspersed with solos and choruses was similar to that of the oratorio, the cantatas were often deliberately written in a style simple enough for satisfactory performance by amateurs. A popular example was Bennett's *The Woman of Samaria* (Birmingham Festival, 1867). This episode in the life of Christ is narrated in plain recitative set to the text of the Authorized Version of the Bible. The set pieces have a newly composed text and are mainly

Example XI–23: WILLIAM STERNDALE BENNETT, *The Woman of Samaria*

the i - mage of th'in - vi - si - ble God,

i - mage, i - mage of th'in - vi - si - ble God,

i - mage, the i - mage of God,

the i - mage of the in - vi - si - ble God,

in a simple diatonic style; occasional patches of chromatic coloring (see Example XI–23) are never complex enough to throw anyone off. Works such as this exude a certain studied innocence and easy sentiment that were important components of the Victorian sensibility.

SPAIN

The nineteenth century in Spain was a period of almost unremitting turmoil and confusion. A favorite battleground of the French and English during the Napoleonic Wars, and thereafter the nearly continuous victim of alternating despotic misrule and political anarchy, the nation suffered a sad and irreversible decline from its former glories in almost all areas. After two centuries of a flourishing indigenous musical culture, art music in eighteenth-century Spain fell strongly under Italian domination. The favored musical posts in both court and church were occupied by such Italians as Domenico Scarlatti, Gaetano Brunetti, Luigi Boccherini, and the famed castrato Farinelli. In the nineteenth century musical institutions shared to some extent the fate of other sectors of the nation's life, and support for the arts, whether native or imported, was very limited. A musical conservatory was founded in Madrid in 1830, however, at the behest of the new queen from Naples, Maria Cristina. Modeled after the Neapolitan conservatories, and directed in its first years by the Italian singer Francesco Piermarini, this institution consolidated the hegemony of Italian music in Spain. The most admired Spanish composer of the first half of the century, Ramón Carnicer (1789–1855), wrote his operas in an Italian style to Italian librettos, several of them, such as *Cristoforo Colombo* (1831), by Felice Romani.

In the later eighteenth century a modest form of native dramatic music had made an appearance in Spain: the *tonadilla,* a brief dramatic skit with simple music (often folklike) that resembled the earliest stages of the Italian opera buffa. After its demise in the first decade of new century there was almost no Spanish drama with music until the later 1840s, when a new form of populist musical entertainment, the *zarzuela,* took shape. Consisting of one to three short acts, these plays presented lower-class life and concerns in a mixture of speaking, singing, and dancing in which popular songs and dance tunes were a prominent feature, as was the parody of Italian opera. By the century's end these entertainments were so firmly established that eleven theaters in Madrid presented them exclusively. Leading composer-compilers of the genre were Pascual Juan Arriete, Francisco Asenjo Barbieri (also a leading historian of Spanish music), and Federico Chueca.

Among Spanish practitioners of "serious" music, several performers achieved world reputations, e.g. Fernando Sor (1778–1839), a founder of classical guitar playing, and, above all, the violinist-composer Pablo Sarasate (1844–1908), one of the greatest virtuosos of the century, whose *Zigeunerweisen* are still a staple of the violin repertory. Though foreign composers, beginning with Rossini in *The Barber of Seville,* and continuing with Liszt, Bizet, and Glinka, had frequently seized upon the idioms of Spanish folk music. nothing resembling a nationalist movement in Spanish art music appeared until the very end of the century. Isaac Albéniz (1860–1909), a disciple of Liszt and initially a composer in an international salon style, turned his attention toward the sounds of Spanish folk music in the 1890s; as a resident of Paris he interested Debussy and Ravel in the rhythms of the bolero and fandango, and contributed to the evolving Impressionist style. His masterpiece is *Suite Iberia* (1906), a compendium of Spanish musical idiom and original pianistic effects. Albéniz's younger colleague Enrique Granados (1867–1916), early influenced by Grieg and Schumann, composed a series of piano miniatures *(Danzas españolas)* and songs *(Colección de tonadillas)* in the 1890s that sensitively blend a variety of Spanish musical styles with the common techniques of late-nineteenth-century art music. His most substantial work, *Goyescas* (1911), recalling Musorgsky's *Pictures at an Exhibition,* is a series of six pieces illustrative of paintings of Goya, written in an improvisatory, individual style with somewhat abstract references to Spanish folk music. The last and best of the troika of Spanish nationalist composers was Manuel de Falla (1876–1946), at once the most technically accomplished of the three and the most devoted to his heritage in Spanish music. His dramatic and orchestral works, Spain's finest contribution to the art in modern times, belong to the history of twentieth-century music.

CHAPTER XII

Crosscurrents in the Late Century

Composers in the second half of the nineteenth century were faced with an unprecedented array of seemingly opposed ideas and ideals concerning the arts. The Romantic insistence upon originality was, if anything, heightened by a renewed belief in progress, that compulsive faith of a Europe in the throes of industrialization and burgeoning technology. At the same time history and tradition took on new importance, whether in the guise of a Nazarene longing for earlier and simpler times or in a passion for scientific certainty in understanding the past, shown by historians such as Leopold von Ranke and his followers. In works of art the unique gemlike miniature remained an ideal—an ideal not to be entirely sacrificed to the powerful competing demand for breadth of vision, for monumentality. The essential ideality of art urged by neo-

Jean-François Millet, *The Gleaners*, 1857.

Platonist views such as Schopenhauer's was still a dominant force; but it was opposed by a rising tide of realism in which plain depictions of life were expected to make a social point, as in the "working scenes" of the painters Jean-Gustave Courbet and Jean-François Millet, and, according to George Bernard Shaw, in an allegory of class struggle in the *Ring of the Nibelung*.

LISZT AND THE "NEW GERMAN SCHOOL"

A composer peculiarly susceptible to this welter of competing notions was Franz Liszt, who gave up his career as the world's most celebrated virtuoso in 1848 to settle (like Goethe before him) at the court of Weimar; there he became a tireless champion of avant-garde music, conducting performances of Wagner's works despite intense political pressure, and those of Berlioz in the face of public apathy. In the midst of all this activity he enjoyed the most fruitful decade of his life as a composer. During this period he was also busy as a collaborative writer on musical subjects, producing (with the extensive help of the Princess Sayn-Wittgenstein) monographs on the works of Wagner, Berlioz, Chopin, and music of the Gypsies.

Liszt was preoccupied with questions about the future of instrumental music at a time when there was a widespread feeling that its traditional forms were exhausted—though Hanslick, for one, disagreed, and Wagner seemed to deny that instrumental music had a future in any case. The genre as a whole did seem to have reached a kind of closure. Composers had departed ever further from a classical ideal in which the essential traits of a composition are those prescribed by its kind, i.e. in which a piece of music is largely defined by a class of things it represents (sonata, fugue, or Lied for example). In their increasing predilection for the unique, for the expression of special states of mind, and for the most subjective impressions, composers had largely either abandoned sturdy old categories such as symphony and sonata or subjected them to very radical modification. And by mid-century no commanding new types had appeared to take their place.

To give up the refuge of established genres in favor of something new and special is to risk misunderstanding and alienation from one's audience. It was largely in an attempt to evade this difficulty that Schumann, Berlioz, and others had resorted to programs, evocative titles, and the association of music with literary models. And now, after mid-century, there was at hand powerful new justification for such things in Hegelian philosophy.

A dominant strain of Romantic aesthetics, led by E. T. A. Hoffmann and Schopenhauer, had maintained that music of the highest sort was necessarily "pure" instrumental music, that its transcendental qualities were dimmed by an association with texts or literary counterparts. The philosophy of Hegel and the Hegelians, now in the ascendent, held otherwise. In his *Lectures on Aesthetics*[1] Hegel had subscribed to a common view that the arts were alike as to content (for him their content was that entity that pervades his thought as a whole, "spirit"), and different only as to sensuous form. He then described an orderly progression, abstractly theoretical, but also in a sense historical, from "symbolic" to "classical" to "romantic" art, in which the principal distinctions had to do with changing relationships between spiritual content and sensuous form. The representative symbolic and classical arts were, respectively, architecture and sculpture. There were three characteristically romantic arts: painting, music, and poetry, in ascending order of spirituality—i.e., in domination of spiritual content over form. Poetry, the "highest" of the romantic arts, could only enhance the value and effect of music when the two are brought together. Hegel repeatedly expressed his higher regard for music whose spiritual content was strengthened and clarified by an association with poetry, and this view was reinforced in writings of his followers, such as Friedrich Theodor Vischer's *Aesthetik oder Wissenschaft des Schönen* (1846–57).

Liszt now enthusiastically entered the debate about whether music is well or badly served in being joined to poems, narratives, or scenes. His engagement with these issues as a composer led to the creation of some of his most impressive music. The *Faust Symphony* (1857, with several subsequent revisions), dedicated to Berlioz and plainly influenced by his *La Damnation de Faust,* is a massive composition for orchestra and chorus whose three parts offer a portrayal of the three main figures in Goethe's play, Faust, Gretchen, and Mephistopheles. Musical characterization of a high order is coordinated with an advanced stage of Liszt's technique of "thematic transformation," in which virtually all the music is derived from a small number of melodic kernals. During the years 1848 to 1857, he also composed twelve orchestral compositions called "symphonic poems" (in 1857 Wagner publicly hailed the name and the genre as Liszt's innovations[2]). None of them is cast in the usual forms of the symphony or overture, and all have a connection of one sort or another with an extramusical program. Like the writing of his literary works, however, the assignment of programmatic references to these pieces seems to have been something of a joint effort with the princess.

Liszt's symphonic poems come in a wide variety of shapes and sizes,

---

1. This work, consisting of lectures compiled and published after Hegel's death by his students, seems more readable than many of the philosopher's original writings. They have been newly translated by T. M. Knox as *Aesthetics: Lectures on Fine Art,* 2 vols. (Oxford, 1974–75). The most pertinent sections for this discussion are part of the Introduction (I, pp. 69–82) and the chapter on Music (II, pp. 888–958).

2. Wagner, *Gesammelte Schriften und Dichtungen,* 5, p. 188.

lasting from ten minutes *(Hamlet)* to about forty *(Ce qu'on entend sur la montagne)*. Several are highly episodic in construction, and some make extended use of recitativelike passages—a customary way, after the example of Beethoven's Ninth Symphony, of reaching toward a "meaning" normally outside the bounds of instrumental music. The best-known of them, *Les Preludes,* illustrates the tenuous connection between the program and the work that is fairly characteristic of these pieces. It was originally conceived in 1848 as an overture to a choral work, *The Four Elements,* with a text by Joseph Autran. When first performed in 1854 it sported its present title, derived from a meditation of Lamartine, and the score published two years later included a rather vaporous summary of that poem calculated to emphasize its points of congruence with the composition.

Les Preludes is tightly constructed, opposing the tonalities of C major and E major, and returning to C by way of A major, showing again the fondness for third relations we have noted in Liszt's piano music. Two of its three principal melodic themes are clearly derived from the recitativelike cell-motive with which the composition begins. Although Liszt felt sufficiently uncertain of his skills as an orchestrator during this period to enlist the aid of the young musicians August Conradi and Joachim Raff to help him, the treatment of the orchestra here is competent and mainly conventional. But two passages, mm. 155ff. and 344ff., respectively emerge as strongly derivative of Berlioz's bold parallel motion in the first movement of *Symphonie fantastique* and the brilliant violin obbligato figures in Wagner's overture to *Tannhäuser*—both of which Liszt had recently transcribed for piano.

Liszt's other symphonic poems differ in important ways from *Les Preludes. Hamlet* (1858), composed as a musical illustration of the Shake-

Example XII–1: LISZT, *Hamlet,* mm. 1–8

Liszt conducting a music festival in Pest. Woodcut, 1865.

spearian character (with two brief contrasting references to Ophelia), is written in a strongly chromatic style, signaled from the beginning in its *Tristan*-like opening (Example XII–1). Its orchestration, making use of muted horns, bass trombone, and tuba, is advanced and sure-handed. While somewhat unclear as to intent and manifestly indebted to Berlioz's programmatic orchestral works such as the *Symphonie fantastique*, the overture *King Lear*, and *Harold in Italy*, and even to Mendelssohn's overtures, Liszt's symphonic poems[3] seemed to offer a new point of departure, a reassurance to younger composers that it was possible to explore an expanding world of orchestral sounds in fresh shapes, with a new measure of liberation from the overpowering legacy of Beethoven.

In 1861 Liszt left Weimar and moved to Rome, where in 1865 he took minor orders in the Catholic Church. Then in 1869 he began the final period of his career, his "vie trifurquée" as he called it, moving methodically between Rome, Weimar, and Budapest. During this time

3. In 1882 Liszt added a thirteenth symphonic poem, *Von der Wiege bis zum Grabe* (From the Cradle to the Grave).

he received piano students from the entire Western world; among them were giants of the following generation such as Emil Sauer, Moritz Rosenthal, Alexander Siloti, and Eugen D'Albert. And Liszt exerted an oraclelike attraction for younger composers; Anton Rubinstein, Borodin, Grieg, and Debussy all made the pilgrimage to Rome or Weimar. Always of a visionary turn of mind, Liszt in his latest years concentrated his efforts as a composer upon sacred music. Two large-scale oratorios, *Die Legende der heiligen Elizabeth* and *Christus,* and three Masses with chorus and orchestra were finished in the 1860s. The remaining years of the composer's life saw an unbroken succession of motets and settings of liturgical texts. In these works Liszt sought to fulfill an earlier avowed aim to introduce into sacred music artistic standards comparable to those of secular composition. Some of his later sacred works, such as the *Via Crucis* (1879) for soloists, chorus, and orchestra, were the proving ground for his most radical harmonic experiments; Example XII–2 shows a level of chromaticism that threatens the boundaries of tonality.

Example XII–2: LISZT, *Via Crucis,* No. 4.

During his years in Weimar Liszt became a central figure in what was seen as an evolving polarization of German music. Partly because of the aesthetic stance of his purported writings, but more particularly because of his championship of the works of Wagner, he was widely praised or blamed as a leader, along with the banished Dresden kapellmeister, of a "New German School." This name had strong connotations of political liberalism and German nationalism. A widespread knowledge of Wagner's participation in the Dresden uprising of 1849 and his subsequent banishment established this connection, and his revolutionary writings from around 1850, *Art and Revolution, The Artwork of the Future,* and *Opera and Drama,* confirmed it. This seemed to some a movement perfectly attuned to the times: it proposed an indigenous German musical drama to supplant Meyerbeer and the Italians, and, in the works of Liszt, a rebirth of instrumental music aesthetically akin to it, in which formal shapes would be responsive to a poetic idea or program. A few liberal newspapers in Germany cautiously supported the cause, but its chief organ was Schumann's old journal, the *Neue Zeitschrift für Musik* of Leipzig, now edited by Franz Brendel. Some of Wagner's own essays were published in the journal, beginning with the infamous *Judaism in Music* in 1850. Other writers quickly took up the cudgels on behalf of the "new music": Liszt's student, Hans von Bülow, Wagner's former associate at Dresden Theodor Uhlig, and Brendel himself, who declared in his opening editorial of 1852, "These pages henceforth have the task of furthering in every possible way that transformation which the art is just now entering."[4]

BRAHMS

The following year the *Neue Zeitschrift,* in a magnanimous gesture, nonetheless printed an article by its former editor, Schumann, in which a young composer quite outside the Wagner-Liszt circle was hailed as something of a musical Messiah. After praising the work of a long list of promising composers, including Joseph Joachim, Theodore Kirchner, and even F. E. Wilsing—but with no mention of Wagner or Liszt or any of their group—Schumann continued:

> I thought that after these developments one would and must suddenly appear who is called to embody the highest expression of the time in ideal fashion, one whose mastery would not unfold in slow stages, but like Minerva, spring fully-armed from the head of Cronus. And he has come.[5]

Schumann was speaking of Johannes Brahms (1833–97), at the time an unknown musician of twenty. Such an introduction naturally set up Brahms as a rival to the "New German School," and fuel was added to the flame in 1860 when Brahms and Joachim publically declared their opposition to the policies of Brendel's paper and the music it cham-

---

4. *Neue Zeitschrift für Musik,* XXXVI (1852): 4.
5. Schumann, *Gesammelte Schriften,* 2, p. 301. Schumann got his mythology slightly wrong here: it was from the head of Jupiter (or Zeus) that Minerva (or Athena) sprang.

pioned. Brahms paid little attention to this perceived polarity in succeeding years, even when Wagner attacked him in print in 1869 and 1879.[6]

Brahms, the son of a humble musician in Hamburg, studied piano and composition there with Eduard Marxsen (1806–87). In 1853, while on tour with the Hungarian violinist Eduard Reményi, he spent some weeks in Weimar with the Liszt entourage, and shortly thereafter met the Schumanns in Düsseldorf. By training and temperament he was much more inclined toward the aesthetic views of the latter, and the influence of Schumann—i.e. Schumann in his final and most classicist period—remained with Brahms for the rest of his life. His earliest compositions, heavily weighted toward piano music, include the three piano sonatas, Opp. 1, 2, and 5 of 1852–53. These pieces, apparently among those that so impressed Schumann, may seem in retrospect a bit diffuse and eclectic, especially the Sonata in F♯ minor, Op. 2. But some of the hallmarks of Brahms's mature style are already clearly visible: a preference for dense sonorities with many parallel sixths and thirds, frequent pedal points, harmonies that tend to turn toward the "flat side," and a fondness for metric displacement. The beginning of the Scherzo of the Sonata in C, Op. 1 (See Example XII–3), shows pedals on the tonic (E) and then the dominant (B), the characteristic parallel $^6_4$ chords in the treble (doubled below), and a hemiola-like metrical ambiguity in m. 3. These early pieces provide some justification for Schumann's colorful metaphor: essential traits of Brahms's music appeared early and "fully armed."

Example XII–3: BRAHMS, Sonata in C, Op. 1, Scherzo

Allegro molto e con fuoco

At the time of Schumann's illness and death Brahms formed a strong attachment to Clara Schumann, and spent the years 1854–59 wandering restlessly between her home in Düsseldorf, his native Hamburg, the court at Detmold where he found temporary employment, and the cities where one or the other of them was appearing as pianist. These years

6.   *Ueber das Dirigieren* (On Conducting) and *Ueber das Dichten und Komponieren* (On Writing Poetry and Music).

saw only a few new compositions. In two orchestral serenades (Opp. 11 and 16) Brahms explored the possibilities of the instrumental ensemble available to him at Detmold. A more substantial composition, one that occupied Brahms's attention intermittently during all of 1854–58, was first projected as a two-piano sonata, and then as a symphony. But the pianistic nature of the work finally led him to finish it as a piano concerto—yielding, meanwhile, a discarded marchlike slow movement in B♭ minor that was to become the first section of the impressive chorus "Denn alles Fleisch es ist wie Grass" in the *German Requiem* (1868).[7]

This concerto in D minor, published in 1861 as Opus 15, was premiered in Hannover in 1859 with Joachim conducting and the composer at the piano. There it was a *succès d'estime,* but another performance in Leipzig a few days later was hissed. This was clearly not what the audience expected of a piano concerto. It betrays its symphonic origins in a complex interweaving of materials in which soloist and orchestra participate equally, and there are only isolated spots of virtuoso display by the pianist (for instance the octaves at the end of the first movement). Brahms's opulent keyboard textures, persistent contrapuntal elaboration, and rhythmic intricacies were apparently not sufficient recompense for a lack of pianistic brilliance. And there is a certain unrelieved gravity about the work, a sameness of tone exacerbated by the common tonic, D, in all three movements.

After a three-year interlude (1859–62) spent in Hamburg conducting a women's chorus and working steadily at new compositions (the *Var-*

The Vienna *Staatsoper;* a photograph taken at the end of the nineteenth century.

7.   This theme, frequently called a sarabande, lacks the distinctive rhythm of that dance.

iations and Fugue on a Theme of Handel were completed in addition to several chamber works and a good many pieces for his chorus), the thirty-year-old Brahms moved to Vienna, where after some indecision he was to remain for the rest of his life. Vienna during the final slow decline of the Hapsburg monarchy remained a place of great cultural vitality. During Brahms's first years there the medieval ramparts of the city were torn down and replaced by the Ringstrasse and the huge buildings flanking it, including the new Hofoper (now the Staatsoper), opened in 1869. This imposing place was only one of several theaters in Vienna that staged operas for the remainder of the century. There was also the old Burgtheater, the Theater an der Wien that specialized in operetta, and the more modest Theater in der Josefstadt. The Vienna Philharmonic Orchestra began giving regular concerts in 1860, and in 1870 a resplendent new concert hall, the Grosser Saal of the Musikverein, was opened. But the city also retained something of the social ambience that had prevailed during the Congress of Vienna: a characteristic mixture of hedonism and *Gemütlichkeit* was reflected in the craze for the waltz and operetta, the countless beer halls and coffee houses with music, and the frequent outdoor concerts.

Brahms's first employment in Vienna was a single season (1863–64) as conductor of the Wiener Singakademie, a choral group whose focus he promptly shifted toward older music. Then from 1872 to 1875 he was conductor of both the choral and orchestral concerts of the venerable Gesellschaft der Musikfreunde (Society of the Friends of Music), an organization that presided over concerts, a library, and a conservatory of music. Except for these two brief engagements Brahms never held an official post in Vienna. He taught privately from time to time and made occasional short tours as a pianist (later as a conductor of his own works). Otherwise he devoted himself entirely to composition, and his growing fame allowed him to do so comfortably, living in the city in the winter and spending summers in picturesque surroundings at Baden-Baden, at a lake in Bavaria, or in the Swiss Alps.

In the city of Mozart, Beethoven, and Schubert, Brahms applied himself studiously to perpetuating their legacy. Taking scant notice of the persistent clamor for novelty heard from many quarters, especially in Germany, he continued to write in the traditional forms, the chamber sonata, the concerto, the Lied, and eventually the symphony. There were clear periods of concentration on one genre or another. The years until 1865, for example, saw a continued flowering of chamber music that had begun about 1860; during this period Brahms completed his two String Sextets, the first two of his three Piano Quartets (in G minor and A major), the Piano Quintet, the first Cello Sonata (E minor), and the Horn Trio. In these works Brahms faced the grave problem confronting all composers of large-scale instrumental music in his era: how does one write original and effective sonatas and quartets—not to speak of symphonies—after Beethoven? Schubert and Schumann had been troubled by this question, and in formulating his own solutions it is clear that Brahms learned from them both. In matters of melody, texture, and rhythm Schumann's music appears to have been continuously influential. As to formal structures, particularly in respect to sonata-allegro form, the importance of Schubert's example becomes increasingly plain.[8] But certain salient traits of his music belong to Brahms alone: extensive patches of rigorous counterpoint, for example, and an unfailing tightness of construction.

One of the most admired of these chamber works is the Piano Quintet in F minor, Op. 34. Having existed in two previous incarnations as a string quintet and a two-piano sonata, this composition was finished in its present form in late 1865. By this time Brahms's mastery of extended formal structures is fully evident. In the first movement the largest tonal motions are intricately reflected at a local level: an emphasis of the lowered sixth (D♭) in the opening theme and the transitional material (Examples XII–4a and b) is a harbinger of the C♯ minor / D♭ major

The first autograph page of Brahms's Piano Quintet.

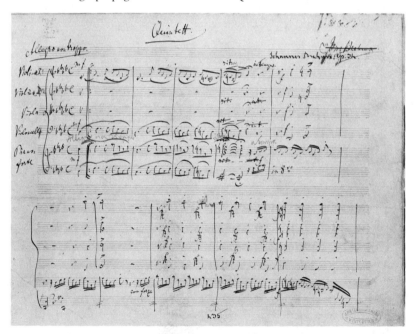

8.   An impressive and largely convincing treatment of this subject is James Webster, "Schubert's Sonata Form and Brahms's First Maturity," *Nineteenth-Century Music,* II (1978): 18–35, and III (1979): 52–71. A broader view of this subject might take into account the sonata movements of Schubert's contemporaries such as Clementi, Dusík, and Hummel; some of Schubert's departures from classic norms were also widely practiced by these composers (see above, pp. 92–96 and 101–2): among these are the use of lyrical, quasi-closed themes and multiple secondary keys. And there is reason to believe that Brahms was acquainted with their music earlier than with Schubert's. See Max Kalbeck, *Johannes Brahms* (Berlin, 1904ff.) I, p. 23.

secondary key area in which the exposition ends. Here Brahms departs from the Schubertian model, which after such an excursion normally put the last section of the exposition in the dominant, thus "resolving" the lowered sixth downward. The equivalent of that motion does appear in Brahms's recapitulation, however, where the corresponding music begins in F♯ minor (m. 195) and at m. 208 simply drops to the tonic F minor. This upper-semitone relationship to both the dominant and tonic is powerfully reinforced in the third movement, the Scherzo in C minor; it begins with a large gesture in which A♭ moves to G over a tonic

Example XII–4: BRAHMS, Piano Quintet, Op. 34, first movement
    a. Mm. 1–4

    b. Mm. 23–26

pedal, and ends with a merciless hammering on D♭–C.

Brahms's mature grasp of large forms in the chamber music of this period is also shown in intricate thematic interrelationships. Every bit as adept at thematic transformation as Liszt, to whom the invention of this device is often ascribed, he characteristically creates subtle points of similarity among all the principal melodic motives of a movement. In the first movement of the Piano Quintet we have noted a tonal relationship between the opening melody and the transitional material (Example XII–4); the closing theme in D♭ major derives its shape and initial rhythm quite obviously from that opening melody as well (Example XII–5), and the dotted rhythm that follows is related to the transitional material. In movements of this sort the traditional distinctions between exposition and development are blurred; the development section and coda, those traditional areas for working out the potentialities of musical materials, here continue processes that were started at the beginning.

Example XII–5: BRAHMS, Piano Quintet, Op. 34, first movement, mm. 74–78

In 1866–72 Brahms wrote vocal music almost exclusively. Those years saw the completion of some fifty-six Lieder and a great deal of music involving chorus: the Twelve Songs and Romances Op. 44 (1866), the cantata *Rinaldo* (1868), the *Alto Rhapsody* for alto solo, four male voices, and orchestra (1869), the *Schicksalslied* and *Triumphlied* (both 1871), and the most significant composition of this period, the *German Requiem.*

Brahms's *German Requiem,* a composition in seven movements for soprano and baritone solo, chorus, and orchestra, is not composed to the traditional text of the Requiem Mass, but to one compiled from the Old and New Testaments by the composer. Like a number of his major works, it was very long in the making. Some of the second movement, as we have seen, existed as early as 1854 in the complex of music destined for the First Piano Concerto; the fifth movement, for soprano solo and chorus, was newly added in May 1868, after the piece had already been performed in a six-movement form. This composition, like most with religious texts in the nineteenth century, has about it a certain air of antiquarianism: contrapuntal textures abound, and at spots the choral writing resembles the ancient "points of imitation" technique (in the first movement, for example, the sections beginning with "werden mit Freuden" and "und kommen mit Freuden"). The third and sixth movements finish with genuine fugues; the former is the famous one set entirely over a D pedal point in the timpani and basses—the very low DD being sustained by contrabasses with their lowest string tuned downward one step. A very different sort of movement is the fourth, often heard as a separate anthem, "Wie lieblich sind deine Wohnungen" ("How lovely are thy dwelling places"); its easy lyricism and tonal simplicity have many models in the sacred music of Mendelssohn, for example "He Watching over Israel" from *Elijah*.

The most idiosyncratic movement of this composition is the second, "Denn alles Fleisch es ist wie Gras" ("For all flesh is as grass"). It falls into two very distinct large sections, in B♭ minor and B♭ major, of which only the first uses preexistent music. This first section has a shape that can be shown thus:

A	*B*	*A*
a b a b		*a b a b*
i	VI	i

Each of the *a*'s and *b*'s consists of two components, one for the instruments and one for the chorus (Example XII–6); the instrumental motives, as in many a chorus of Bach, are put to use as ritornellos between successive entrances of the vocal parts. The dirgelike *a* for the voices, utterly different from any other choral writing in the composition, is chanted in unison like a recurrent cantus firmus with archaic Phrygian coloring. That lowered second degree (C♭), a favorite device of Brahms that recurs, for example, in the slow movement of the Fourth Symphony, also provides here a tonal bond with the G♭ major key of the *B* section. And the tune would have had other connotations for German audiences: it is nearly identical with the well-known chorale melody "Wer nur den lieben Gott lässt walten" ("He who but lets God hold sway"). Skillfully combining various older techniques with Brahms's evolving personal style, this composition served more than any other to establish him in

Example XII–6: BRAHMS, *A German Requiem*, second movement
   a. Mm. 22–26

   b. Mm. 33–35

this period as one of the leading composers of Europe.

In 1873 Brahms began once again to write instrumental music. His two String Quartets, Op. 51, were completed that year, and by 1877 he had also finished the Piano Quartet Op. 60, his final String Quartet, Op. 67, and the first two symphonies. But the first signal achievement of this new burst of composition for instruments was the *Variations on a Theme by Haydn* for two pianos (Op. 56b) and the slightly later version for orchestra (Op. 56a) of 1873. Its theme, the so-called St. Anthony Chorale (whose attribution to Haydn is now much doubted) may have fascinated Brahms with its metrical oddities; the first section of its binary form consists of two five-measure phrases, and ambiguities in groupings of subphrases abound. Rhythmic and metrical subtleties are a prime feature of the eight variations that follow, though the overall dimensions of the sections of the theme are maintained precisely except for the single extra measure in Variation 4. The last measures of Variation 7 (given in Example XII–7 together with the corresponding section of the theme) show Brahms's rhythmic subterfuges at their most elaborate. While the left hand of the second piano maintains the 6 / 8 meter intact the other parts of the texture fall into three separate patterns, all

Example XII–7: BRAHMS, *Variations on a Theme by Haydn*
  a. Theme

  b. Variation 7

of which reinforce a 3/4 meter beginning in the *middle* of each 6/8 measure. Complications mount in m. 318. In the first piano the right hand now falls into groups suggesting 2/4, while the left alternates between 6/8 and 3/4, and the right hand in the second piano executes a "written-out retard."

These eight variations are followed by a finale that is itself a set of variations over a five-measure ground bass derived from the original theme. There are seventeen statements of this ostinato figure, sometimes in the bass and sometimes in the upper parts, in the course of a dazzling display of shifting variation techniques. For Brahms, as for Beethoven in his late years, the circumscribed arena of variation writing was a vital testing ground for the development of style. These variations of Brahms are vastly less abstract than, say, the *Diabelli Variations* or the variations of the String Quartet Op. 131. More dependent upon Bach, perhaps, than upon Beethoven, they seek new levels of intricacy in the employment of received techniques rather than using the form as a point of departure for the exploration of uncharted territory.

The brilliant artistic and popular success of the orchestral version of the *Variations on a Theme by Haydn* seems to have emboldened Brahms to finish, at last, his First Symphony, now almost twenty years underway. A start was made on the first movement as early as 1855, and a version of it (apparently without the introduction) was complete by 1862 when he gave it to Clara Schumann for her comments. But there was no decisive progress on the other movements until the summer of 1874, and the symphony was finally finished only in September 1876. Timidity about writing for orchestra was hardly a reason for the delay, for in addition to the *Haydn Variations* Brahms had already composed two orchestral Serenades, Opp. 11 and 16, the Piano Concerto in D minor, and extensive orchestral music in the *German Requiem,* the cantata *Rinaldo,* and other concerted works. It was the idea of the *symphony,* with the long shadow cast over it by Beethoven, that intimidated Brahms. Early in the 1870s he is reported to have told the conductor Hermann Levi, "I will never finish a symphony. You have no idea how it affects one's spirits to hear continually the marching of a giant behind him."[9]

If only for its complexity and monumentality, this First Symphony in C minor, Op. 68, inevitably invited comparisons with Beethoven. And its tonality was that of Beethoven's Fifth, moving to the raised third for the second movement like Beethoven's Third Piano Concerto in the same key. But what occasioned most comment was the chorale-like first theme of the finale that reminded many listeners of the *Freude* theme from Beethoven's Ninth—particularly as it emerges, like Bee-

9.   Kalbeck, 1, p. 165.

thoven's tune, from a long and portentious introduction.[10] Brahms's finale is a large-limbed, intricately structured sonata-allegro form that makes a determined feint toward a rondo shape by introducing a full statement of the first theme in tonic at the beginning of the development:

Intro	Exposition	Development	Recapitulation	Coda
(a) (c) x	a trans. b c	a (a) (trans.)	x b c	(a)
i I	I V iii	I ♭III	I I i	i I

However Beethoven's example may have weighed on Brahms's mind, other forces also seem to be at work here. The double secondary keys (the motion to E minor reflecting the larger tonal contrast of C–E between the first two movements) and the omission of the first theme in the recapitulation suggest a continued influence, in matters of form, from Schubert. And in the development there is a fugal section (mm. 234ff.), based on material from the transition, that exceeds in scope and complexity any contrapuntal passage in the Beethoven (or Schubert) symphonies; it recalls, if anything, another symphonic finale in C major, that of Mozart's *Jupiter Symphony*.

Brahms's Second Symphony, Op. 73 in D major, followed hard on the heels of the First; this fact, together with its more idyllic nature, has led many to see these two works as a pair corresponding to Beethoven's Fifth and Sixth Symphonies. But in its overall dimensions the Second Symphony is fully as spacious as the First, and its slow movement and finale as fully elaborated as anything in Brahms. The Third Symphony, Op. 90 in F major, and the Fourth, Op. 98 in E minor, followed as another chronological pair in 1883 and 1885. In both these works the center of gravity is shifted dramatically toward the end. The finale of the Fourth is an overwhelming passacaglia-like structure consisting of thirty variations and a coda on a basso ostinato theme (Example XII–8) much like that of the final chorus in Bach's Cantata No. 150, *Nach dir, Herr, verlanget mich*.[11] The internal movements of this composition,

Example XII–8: BRAHMS, Fourth Symphony, last movement, ostinato theme

Allegro energico e passionato

10. The other theme that aroused much comment, especially when the symphony was played in England, is the C-major horn call (*x* in the schematic outline) whose first measures closely resemble the "Westminster rounds" that sound from Big Ben. The similarity is probably coincidental.
11. Bach called this chorus "Ciacona." Another suggested model for this movement is the Thirty-two Variations in C minor, WoO 80, of Beethoven.

too, differ formally from those of the other symphonies. While the other slow movements are all clear-cut ternary forms, the Andante moderato of the Fourth, with its lugubrious phrygian opening, is a full sonata-allegro. What follows is the only movement in Brahms's symphonies approaching a scherzo. Its bumptious leaps with full orchestration, accented at strategic points by a jangling triangle, provide a comic flavor very rare in this composer's oeuvre.

Between his "two pairs" of symphonies Brahms undertook a very different sort of large-scale composition, the Violin Concerto in D, Op. 77, written in 1878. This work presented him with altogether new problems: nonviolinist that he was, he had never before undertaken to write the florid soloistic string music expected in such a piece. He appealed to his friend Joseph Joachim, the violin virtuoso, for help; Brahms sent a letter together with the solo part of the first movement in August 1877, requesting that he "say a word, or perhaps write it into the score: 'difficult,' 'awkward,' 'impossible,' or the like. The whole thing has four movements; I have included the beginning of the last one—so that inept figurations might be forbidden me from the start!"[12] Despite this show of docility, Brahms accepted few of the suggestions Joachim made in the autograph of the violin part, the autograph score,[13] and in the correspondence between the two men that followed. In several cases the composer agreed to reduce the dynamic level of the orchestra when the soloist was playing; but most of Joachim's suggestions for changes in violin figuration failed to convince Brahms. A tricky place in the solo part near the end of the finale (mm. 325–26), where the solo violin

Example XII–9: BRAHMS, Violin Concerto, Op. 77, finale
  a. Brahm's solution

  b. Joachim's suggestion

12. Andreas Moser, ed., *Johannes Brahms im Briefwechsel mit Joseph Joachim* (Berlin, 1908).

13. These autographs are, respectively, in the Deutsche Staatsbibliothek in East Berlin and the Library of Congress. The latter was published in facsimile by the Library of Congress in 1977.

ushers in a restatement of the first theme, offers a sample of their nego-
tiations. Brahms wrote three alternative versions of these measures in
the autograph score, the third of which is shown in Example XII–9a; a
hand thought to be Joachim's crossed them all out and neatly wrote in
a fourth (Example XII–9b). The published version—surely to the
advantage of this passage—reverts to the triplets of Brahms's own (third)
version. However much has been made of the collaboration of the two
artists in producing this concerto, the composition, including the solo
part, is overwhelmingly the work of Brahms.

By the time the concerto was premiered in Leipzig on New Year's
Day 1879 (Joachim playing solo violin and Brahms conducting), a very
substantial change had been made: a projected Adagio and Scherzo had
been replaced with a new slow movement so that the work now had
the standard three-movement concerto form.[14] It opens with an expansive and impressive example of first-movement form in a Classic concerto (ARM 22); the double exposition can be outlined thus:

	Orchestra						Soloist and orchestra							
measure	1	17	41	61	69	78	90	136	164	178	198	206	236	246
motive	a	a^1	b	b^1	b^2	c	(a)	a	a^1	b	b^1	Sb	b^2	c
key	I			∿∿∿	∿∿∿	i	i	I	v	V		∿∿∿	V	v

Although Brahms had written only one concerto up to this time, the
protean and problematic D-minor Piano Concerto, in this work he seems
well in command of the genre. The orchestral exposition, remaining in
the tonic, presents an unbroken series of short motives; the following
exposition for soloist and orchestra, modulating to the dominant, presents them again in order, in addition to a seemingly new one *(Sb)* first
introduced by the solo violin. All these features had been standard in
the piano concertos of Mozart. But the opening measures of this concerto suggest an influence more proximate than that of Mozart. A melody built almost exclusively upon the pitches of the tonic triad is
reminiscent of many opening themes of Beethoven, particularly those
of his middle period, as in the *Eroica* Symphony and the *Leonore* Overtures Nos. 2 and 3; here the resemblance seems closest to the first theme
of Beethoven's Fifth Piano Concerto, the *Emperor* (Example XII–10),
which, like Brahms's melody, adds the lower sixth to the triad.[15] When
the soloist enters with cadenzalike material in Brahms's concerto (m.
90) we are again reminded of Beethoven, whose solo parts in the Violin
Concerto and *Emperor* Concerto begin similarly. And Brahms's first
movement ends like that of Beethoven's Violin Concerto: a *dolce* state-

---

14. It has been speculated, without convincing evidence, that the two discarded inner
    movements were used in the Second Piano Concerto in B♭.
15. And the distinctive pause on the fifth of the dominant at the end of the first phrase
    recalls the first theme of Beethoven's Violin Concerto.

Example XII–10
   a. BEETHOVEN, Piano Concerto No. 5, first movement

   b. BRAHMS, Violin Concerto, first movement

ment of a principal theme (Beethoven uses his second one, Brahms his first) gradually gains momentum for a brilliant finish. Other details, too, suggest a dependence upon Beethoven; one is the cadence before *b* (mm. 38–41), where the descending scale in even eighth-note motion leading to the tonic seems directly borrowed from the similarly placed cadence (mm. 77–83) in the first movement of the *Eroica* (see ARM 2).

There are also important ways in which Brahms departs from his models in concerto writing. The relationship of tutti and solo sections, for one thing, differs from the usual practice in either Mozart or Beethoven. After the initial orchestral exposition Brahms writes genuine tuttis at certain accepted structural points, marking the endings of the second exposition, the development, and the recapitulation, in addition to a brief one within the development (mm. 340–48), thus:

First Exp.	Second Exp. *T*	Development *T* (with *T*)	Recapitulation *T*

But Mozart and Beethoven had habitually included a number of shorter tuttis within the second exposition and recapitulation as well, forcefully underscoring the comings and goings of the soloist. Brahms's texture is more continuous. The soloist and orchestra more often interact than compete against each other. The closest approach to a tutti in the second exposition is b^1 at m. 198 (and at the corresponding point, m. 437, in the recapitulation). Here the orchestra plays alone for six measures; but the music is *pianissimo* and takes up the figuration the violin had just left off (and is about to resume again), quite vitiating the usual dramatic punctuating effect of a tutti.

In the music of the tuttis proper, too, Brahms departs from normal practice. It had been usual in the Classic concerto to earmark certain passages in the orchestral exposition for later use in the tuttis; most common of these were the opening motive and some forceful modulatory section, usually from the transition. Brahms uses such materials, but never in the straightforward form familiar from Baroque and Classic concertos. For the tutti following the second exposition (mm. 272–304) he writes what seems to have been characteristically solo music: the cadenzalike elaboration of *a* with which the soloist had entered, as well as the soloist's new theme, *Sb*. The internal tutti in the development (mm. 340–48) is a contrapuntal, abstract treatment of *b;* its accented quarter notes reproduce the rhythm of this motive, while the sixteenth-and-eighth figure (initially in the bass) derives from a counterpoint to it played earlier by the soloist (beginning in m. 312). The tutti at the end of the development (mm. 381–89) is the most nearly normal one, presenting the opening theme in the tonic, but adding a counterpoint first heard in the violas during the soloist's version of that theme in m. 136. Then in the final tutti (mm. 513–25) we hear the first theme again; but this time it is deflected toward ♭VI through a gigantic deceptive cadence, barely managing to right itself in time for the soloist's cadenza. In no case do we hear that return of unaltered music in the expected key, instantly recognizable and definitive of form, that had always been a hallmark of the concerto.

The solo part of this work features some of the wide-ranging virtuoso writing expected in a violin concerto. The figuration into which the opening solo dissolves in m. 102[16] and the ornament added to *a* in the development (mm. 348ff.), for example, show the characteristic mobility and brilliance produced by passing rapidly from one string to another. But most of the violin figuration consists of more generalized arpeggio and scale patterns (some of which violinists still find awkward), and there are none of the special gymnastic feats that had been standard fare in violin concertos since Paganini. Brahms's solo part is more consistently thematic than is usual. And sometimes it blends into the texture in a distinctly unsoloistic way, as in the *b²* music (mm. 236 and 479), where it does little but provide an upper dominant pedal.

Many of the identifying features of Brahms's style are plainly to be heard in this concerto. A fondness for low-lying sonorities, for example, is evident in the first measures of the orchestral exposition, where, as in the entire first movement of the *German Requiem* and in the Serenade Op. 16, the violas assume a melodic role in their own range. Sometimes the solo part, too, lies unusually low; an example is the recurrence of the energetic *a* in the recapitulation, where the violin, now playing a fifth lower, sounds dark and inevitably fuzzy. Such a consideration may have contributed to one of the few formal irregularities of the movement. In the recapitulation, *Sb* (m. 445) is first heard not in the tonic but the major mediant, i.e. a third instead of a fifth lower than in the exposition, in a brighter-sounding range of the violin. (The orchestra thereupon turns the melody back, Schubert-like, to the tonic.)

The harmonic style of this composition, too, is vintage Brahms. The composer's fascination with pedal points is shown when the first thirty measures of the solo part, set in the parallel minor, sound over a tonic

---

16. This is one passage where the autograph shows that Brahms accepted a suggestion of Joachim; the third note of the sextuplets in mm. 102–4 was originally an a′; the repeated d′ (on the open string) can be attributed to the violinist.

pedal; all later passages derivative of this music (the tutti at the end of the exposition and mm. 361ff. in the development) are treated similarly. This tonic pedal naturally leads the composer to dwell on harmonies consonant with it; rather than the obvious subdominant there is an immediate emphasis upon the sixth (B♭) of the parallel minor. This pitch represents an inflection of the conspicuous major sixth of the opening motive, and in retrospect we recognize its participation in various motions in the flat direction in the first exposition, especially in a and b^2. By according an equal standing to the minor form of each tonality falling within his orbit Brahms constantly creates fresh available keys farther down the circle of fifths. This is particularly clear in the development, where C minor, the key that dominates the center of this section, is reached by simple moves from the minor dominant (a) to its relative major (C) and *its* parallel minor. Then the internal tutti of the development at mm. 340–48, a sort of harmonic denouement of the movement, dissolves this stable tonality and leads a tortuous course back to the sharp side and the dominant of D. Harmonic tempo here is extremely quick, but the individual motions by fifth and third or through mode change are largely conservative. Brahms's musical thought always seemed well insulated from the Wagnerian chromaticism brewing in the world around him.

The rhythmic ambiguities one comes to expect of Brahms appear promptly in this piece. Within a (mm. 21ff.) we are introduced to a disturbance of the 3/4 meter (itself unusual in a first movement) that will be heard many times, viz. a pairing of measures that implies 3/2:

This hemiola effect is again very prominent in the soloist's new theme, *Sb*. Another favorite rhythmic stratagem of Brahms can be heard in the continuation of b (mm. 53ff.) and at b^2 (m. 69ff.), where in each case a figure of five quarter notes is repeated with ever-shifting accentuation within the 3 / 4 measure. For a familiar example of yet another sort of metrical displacement one can turn to the last movement, where the soloist's very regular first theme is "foreshortened" upon repetition by the orchestra (Example XII–11). This severely disturbed phrase places the strong accent a half-beat too soon—and then in righting itself adds an entire measure to its length. But such manipulation of rhythm and meter can have the force it does in Brahms's music only because there is an underlying regularity to be disrupted; in this respect, too, Brahms works from within a tradition, expanding its boundaries while leaving it clearly intact.

We have seen that some motives of this movement are related through similar harmonic traits (especially a bending toward the "flat side") and that others share certain rhythmic peculiarities. Such interrelationships

Example XII–11: BRAHMS, Violin Concerto, third movement
  a. Mm. 1–8, solo violin

  b. Mm. 21–35, violins I and II

reach very far. A basis for them is established in the two parts of *a:* a triadic motive in the lower strings (joined by bassoons and horns) followed by a stepwise one, first rising and then falling, in the oboes. The motive a^1 (m.18) derives quite audibly from these two motions of the second part of *a;* *b* (m.41) is similarly derived from *a,* but uses the rhythm of a^1 and adds a downward leap of a fourth to produce an incipient compound melody; b^1 (m.61) is an expanded version of the disjunct downward leaps of *a.* The stepwise motion of b^2 (m.69) is a virtual quotation of *b* (m.41). The only motive of the orchestral exposition seemingly unrelated to the others is *c* (m.78). Its emphatic homophonic triads, however, reappear in the second exposition in the soloist's elaboration of a^1 (mm. 164 ff.), creating, thus, a bond between those two bits of melody. And the celebrated new motive in the second exposition, *Sb* (m. 206), shows a physiognomy like that of *b,* with the compound feature now clarified (the functional part of this melody is its lower component, d″–c♯″–b′–a′, that forms parallel sixths with the bass). Although such elaborate interrelationships are not immediately recognizable to many listeners, upon repeated hearings they seep into the consciousness and contribute to the satisfying sense of unity this movement projects. The procedure operating here is like the thematic transformation associated with the music of Liszt; but it has its roots further back, surely, in tightly interconnected pieces of Beethoven such as the first movement of the Sonata Op. 31, No. 2.[17]

17. See above, pp. 32–37.

The second movement that Brahms substituted for the two original middle movements of this concerto is an Adagio in F of modest proportions, constructed on a ternary plan like that of the slow movements of the first three symphonies. But the central section offers a degree of contrast in character and key (F♯ minor) that is rare in Brahms. The finale is a brilliant rondo whose memorable first theme (see Example XII–11) is often cited as an example of Brahms's penchant for Hungarian idioms. The strong dotted rhythms, the offbeat *sforzato* in m. 3, and the decisive turn to the relative minor might be thought reminiscent of the *verbunkos* style. But the resemblance is faint in comparison to pieces such as Brahms's *Hungarian Dances* for piano four-hands of 1852–69. A notable formal feature of this finale is an outsized coda (recalling many of Beethoven's rondo finales such as that of the *Waldstein* Sonata or the Third Piano Concerto); here we are given that first theme in another rhythmic transformation, the dotted rhythms now smoothed out and the tempo very much quickened (Example XII–12).

Example XII–12: BRAHMS, Violin Concerto, third movement

Brahms's compositions for solo piano were largely written in the earlier years, when he was regularly active as a pianist. The three sonatas, the variations after Handel, Paganini, and Schumann, and the four Ballades Op. 10 were composed by 1864. All of these pieces show virtuoso keyboard writing appropriate for the ambitious young pianist. Thereafter piano compositions were few and far between until a late burst of activity in 1892–93 produced the Fantasias Op. 116, the three Intermezzos Op. 117, and the ten pieces (named "intermezzo," "ballade," "romance," and "rhapsody") of Opp. 118 and 119. Midway between the early and late piano music are the isolated eight pieces (Capriccios and Intermezzos) of Op. 76 and the two Rhapsodies Op. 79 of 1878 and 1879. No very clear intent is discernible in the naming of these compositions, except, perhaps, that intermezzos tend to be quiet pieces, and rhapsodies more passionate and rhetorical.[18] In all of them episodic structures predominate, with occasional approximations of sonata form in the longer ones. The Rhapsody in B minor, Op. 79, No. 1, for example, is a very extended *ABA* structure in which the *A* section itself has the shape of a miniature sonata-allegro form that explores two secondary key areas, F♯ minor and D minor. The harmonic style here shows Brahms's most advanced manner; modulating mainly by thirds, the piece never achieves an authentic cadence in the tonic until the end of *A*. The other Rhapsody of Op. 79, in G minor, is a straight sonata-allegro form in which an unremittingly dark color is abetted by putting all the themes in minor. And again Brahms conscientiously obscures the tonality, this time with an opening deceptive cadence followed by a series of dominant–tonic motions that fleetingly imply in turn F, C, G, A, and E (Example XII–13). This technique may have been learned from Schumann, as in his *Grillen* from the *Fantasiestücke*, Op. 12 (ARM 14C). Both of these Rhapsodies show Brahms's characteristic full-bod-

Example XII–13: BRAHMS, Rhapsody Op. 79, No. 2, mm. 1–8

---

18.   These titles come from disparate sources: "capriccio" was a name applied to keyboard pieces from the early seventeenth century; "intermezzo" had been used by Mendelssohn and Schumann, and "ballade" of course by Chopin. "Rhapsody," after Liszt's *Hungarian Rhapsodies,* was associated with Magyar or Gypsy idioms; Brahms may have had in mind instead the Rhapsodies of Tomášek (see above, p. 103).

ied sonorities for piano, with widely spaced chords, expansive figurations, and a special emphasis on the lower register.

The two hundred Lieder Brahms composed were rather evenly distributed throughout his career, from the *Sechs Gesänge* Op. 3 of 1853 to
the *Vier ernste Gesänge* of 1896. His choice of texts for his songs has
been much criticized. Many are the work of minor poets, including his
friend Klaus Groth and his biographer Max Kalbeck. He first attracted
public notice as a Lieder composer with the fifteen Romances from
Ludwig Tieck's *Wundersame Liebesgeschichte der schönen Magelone und des
Grafen Peter von Provence* (Wondrous Love Story of Fair Magelone and
Count Peter of Provence) composed in 1861–68; this remained his most
extensive musical setting of texts by any major writer. Tieck's work is
a novellike prose narrative, based on a medieval romance, with seventeen interspersed poems that reflect on the events of the story. As these
poems (like those of *Wilhelm Meister*) are spoken by various characters
in varying circumstances, there is no continuity of meaning among the
verses themselves: in only a very loose sense can they be said to comprise a cycle. In his settings Brahms seemed to respond to the conscious
archaism of his textual source in adopting a modified ballad style. The
songs are mainly through-composed, freely changing texture and figuration in response to changes of mood and meaning in the poetry. And
the piano accompaniments are often dramatic and mildly pictorial, with
the wide-ranging figurations familiar from Brahms's solo keyboard
music. But the vocal parts have almost none of the recitativelike declamation common to the ballade. They resemble loosely constructed arias
in which words are sometimes repeated with a prolixity foreign to any
tradition of German song. Perhaps the most satisfying song of the set
is the one that is least changeable and least dramatic, *Ruhe, Süssliebchen;*
in this lullaby Brahms's sonorous textures and extended pedal points
produce an impressive lyricism.

These sprawling, through-composed works are not typical of Brahms's
Lieder style, however; more usual are compact, tight-knit songs in
strophic, modified strophic, or simple episodic forms. Many effect a
similarity to folksong. One example is *Therese,* Op. 86, No. 1 (1878),
set to an ingenuous poem by Gottfried Keller in which a woman gently
turns away the loving glances of a very much younger man. Brahms
fits the three stanzas into a bar-form *(AAB)* with an aggressively simple
melody; its simplicity is first matched by the piano part, and then, in
the final stanza, contradicted by thick textures and chromatic motion.
Much more successful, surely, is *Guten Abend, gute Nacht* (its text from
Des Knaben Wunderhorn), the famous lullaby of 1868 in which nothing
intrudes upon an atmosphere of perfect naïvete. At the opposite extreme
are a few highly sophisticated songs in which the full force of the composer's musical craft is brought to bear upon a brief moment of lyrical
expression. A fine example is *Der Tod, das ist die kühle Nacht,* Op. 96,

Example XII–14: BRAHMS, *Der Tod, das ist die kühle Nacht,* mm 6–11

No. 1 (1884), one of Brahms's half-dozen settings of poems by Heine. Here the poet (for once with no apparent insincerities) likens death to the cool night and life to the oppressive day. Brahms, often responsive to thoughts about death, provided a through-composed setting whose very spareness enhances its special harmonic effects, as in the musical representation of the coming of sleep—i.e. death—(see in Example XII–14). Here chromatic stepwise motion through seventh chords and augmented sixths is broken at a crucial point in the text *(schläfert,)* "growing sleepy") by the surprising move of a descending tritone in the bass.

The years 1884–86 saw a great outpouring of songs by Brahms; in all there were about thirty-five, set to verses by diverse poets (most of them very minor), and published in small collections as Opp. 94–97 and 105–7. Thereupon followed a decade in which he wrote no original songs, though his arrangements of German folksongs *(49 Deutsche Volkslieder)* appeared in 1894. Then in the spring of 1896, with only a year to live, he made his final and best contribution to song writing, the *Four Serious Songs,* Op. 121. As in the case of the *German Requiem,* Brahms himself compiled the texts from the Old and New Testaments in Luther's translation. And again the subject is death, a subject much on the mind of this north German Protestant. In the first two songs *(Denn es gehet dem Menschen* and *Ich wandte mich,* both with texts from Ecclesiastes) the mood is one of unrelieved pessimism, but in the third *(O Tod,* the text from Ecclesiasticus) the opening words "O Death, how bitter thou art" are later remarkably emended to "O Death, how welcome thou art to the needy"; the last song is an encomium to love, presumably as the conqueror of death, in the words of I Corinthians: "Though I speak with the tongues of men and angels, and have not love, then I am as sounding brass." Brahms's music to these texts mingles an austere cantatalike declamation with the lyric expression of the Lied. His setting of the two textual fragments from *O Tod* translated above shows the one transformed into the other (Example XII–15). The falling thirds of the opening (exactly the pitches of the beginning of the Fourth Symphony) are approximately inverted and adjusted to the major mode; the solemn chordal interjections of dramatic recitative are replaced by a rich accompanimental pattern of descending tenths in the outer parts imitated sequentially, in diminution, in the alto and tenor registers. The musical metamorphosis is as striking as the textual one, and a convincing counterpart to it.

Example XII–15: BRAHMS, *O Tod*
  a. Mm. 1–5

  b. Mm. 19–24

Brahms at the piano. A drawing by Willy von Beckerath based on sketches made a scant year before the composer's death.

In 1879 the University of Breslau conferred upon Brahms an honorary doctorate with the citation *Artis musicae severioris in Germania nunc princeps* ("Now the first among contemporary masters in Germany of music in the strict style"). This reflected a very widespread view that Brahms's chief virtues were those of a great craftsman and conservator of tradition. And, indeed, the degree of filial piety Brahms showed toward his musical inheritance was probably unmatched among composers of his century. In his spare time he was an avid collector of older music, autograph scores of the masters, folk music, and theoretical treatises of the eighteenth and nineteenth centuries. He had frequent exchanges with the foremost musical scholars of his day, Philipp Spitta, Friedrich Chrysander, C. F. Pohl, and Gustav Nottebohm (specialists, respectively, in Bach, Handel, Haydn, and Beethoven). Brahms himself prepared editions of the Mozart Requiem and the works of Couperin, and collaborated with Clara Schumann in publishing the collected edition of the works of Robert Schumann. His own music, whatever its innovations in rhythm, texture, and harmony, is consistently informed with the techniques and spirit of this legacy. He was the last great representative of a Classic-Romantic tradition in music to remain unequivocally within the fold.

BRUCKNER

Another composer with powerful ties to the past who lived in Vienna during virtually all of Brahms's residence there was Anton Bruckner (1824–96). The son of a village schoolmaster in northern Austria who himself plied the same trade during his early adulthood, Bruckner became organist at the cathedral of Linz at the end of 1855 and professor at the Vienna Conservatory in 1868. At this time, he also held posts as organist at the Imperial Chapel and as organ teacher at a teachers' training college in Vienna, making this city his home for the rest of his life. Bruckner lived a lifetime of pious devotion to the Catholic Church, and a large proportion of his oeuvre, especially from his earlier years, consists of sacred music. The sacred works through the 1840s are archaic and eclectic, but they show a dominant influence of Mozart's church music—of a style, that is, that was old fashioned even for Mozart. His Requiem Mass of 1848–49, for example, especially the *Dies irae,* emphatically recalls Mozart's Requiem. Only very occasionally, as in the altered sevenths at "culpa rubet vultus meus," does the mask slip to reveal this as a work written in the mid-nineteenth century.

More lasting in Bruckner's sacred music was the influence of the Caecilian movement, which urged the emulation of yet older styles of church music. In the wake of historical researches in the earlier part of the

Anton Bruckner; a painting by Ferry Beraton.

century by scholars such as Raphael Georg Kiesewetter and Giuseppe
Baini—and of the Romantic adulation of early music in writings like A.
F. J. Thibaut's *Ueber Reinheit der Tonkunst* (On Purity in Music, 1825)—
this movement sought to reinstate the authentic singing of Gregorian
chant and the sacred polyphonic style of the sixteenth century. Imita-
tion of sacred polyphony alla Palestrina was a prominent element in
Bruckner's church music nearly all his life. It dominates the eight-voice
Mass in E of 1866 (with revisions in 1876 and 1882), for example; but

Example XII–16: BRUCKNER, Mass in E, Kyrie, mm. 86–95

here, as in many of Bruckner's sacred works, this sort of writing mixes uneasily with passages in a more modern style. In the Kyrie (see Example XII–16) there is an abrupt shift from elaborate imitative counterpoint (distinguishable from the genuine historical article only by certain impermissible leaps and the pedal point in the bass) to homophonic declamation in functional seventh chords. In a few works, mainly those for voices alone such as *Pange lingua* (1868), *Os justi* (1879), or the exquisite *Christus factus est* (his third setting of this text, 1884), the archaic style is nearly consistent. Other sacred compositions stand at the opposite extreme: the *Te Deum* (1884) and Psalm 150 (1892) are massive works in Bruckner's own late Romantic idiom.

Among his contemporaries as well as with posterity Bruckner's reputation has rested largely upon his symphonies. There are nine numbered ones, of which the last is unfinished; in addition there are two early works in F minor and D minor (the latter called by Bruckner *Die Nullte*, i.e. "No. 0"). Of the numbered symphonies all but the first date from the composer's years in Vienna. But their acceptance in Viennese musical circles was slow in coming: the First (1856–66) and Second (1871–72) were rejected out of hand by the Vienna Philharmonic Orchestra, and the premiere of the Third in 1877, with Bruckner conducting, was greeted with whistling and catcalls. The Viennese audience were perhaps put off by a certain starkness of orchestral color, the unaccustomed juxtaposition of blocks of unlike material, and, most of all, by the great length of the work. But there were external reasons as well for their displeasure: the composer had declared his admiration for Wagner and dedicated this symphony to him, thus quite unintentionally becoming a focal point in the bitter conflict between the adherents of Wagner and Brahms. Hanslick, previously friendly, now was merciless in his criticism, and the chronically conservative Viennese musical public generally shared his opinion. Bruckner had to wait until the final decade of his life for public recognition; in the meantime his insecurity led him to accept one revision after another of his symphonies by well-intentioned disciples, so that even now there is massive confusion as to the authentic texts of these works.

Bruckner's symphonies fall into certain regular patterns. All the complete ones have four movements of outwardly traditional types, the first and last normally cast in extended sonata-allegro shapes. The relationship of these outer movements is further emphasized in a certain similarity of musical materials and, beginning with the Third Symphony, a return of the opening theme at the end of the composition. The slow movements usually present two principal themes, varied in alternation as in the slow movement of Beethoven's Ninth. In the scherzos we hear echoes of upper Austrian folk music and the only suggestions of levity to be found in Bruckner's works. A hallmark of the symphonies is the "beginning out of nothing": the first movements in nearly every case grow out of a soft and indistinct harmonic figure or *tremolando* in the strings, as in a vision of the gradual emergence of form out of chaos. Most conspicuous of all is the sheer bigness of these works, a monumentality achieved mainly through a slowing of usual musical processes, through great stretches of leisurely development and expansive sections of static harmony.

The Third Symphony in D minor is the first that is representative of the mature Bruckner. Its unfortunate premiere in 1877 was preceded by a period of composition and revision stretching over almost five years. And the form in which it is usually performed at present incorporates further major revisions, undertaken with the help of Franz Schalk in 1889–90. This symphony shows more clearly than any other Bruckner's fixation upon the symphonies of Beethoven, particularly the Ninth in the same key of D minor. It begins unmistakably like Beethoven's Ninth: a single *pianissimo* chord building in the strings and winds forms a static backdrop to a falling figure constructed from its open fifth and octave (Example XII–17).[19] Listeners have ample opportunity to appre-

Example XII–17: BRUCKNER, Third Symphony, first movement, mm. 5–11

---

19. It has also been said that Bruckner's opening recalls the beginning of Wagner's Overture to *The Flying Dutchman*. See Dika Newlin, *Bruckner, Mahler, Schoenberg*

ciate the similarity, as this music is played twice more, at the beginning of the recapitulation and in the coda. But there is a crucial difference between this passage and its model. Beethoven's hollow opening sonority turns out to be dominant, recognizable as such when it finally resolves with a great forward thrust to the tonic; Bruckner's is tonic from the beginning, establishing at the outset a static quality that marks much of his symphonic writing. In the remainder of this movement a fairly normal if outsized sonata-allegro from unfolds. A secondary subject in the relative major features a rhythm that is ubiquitous in Bruckner: ♫♪ ♫. The only real irregularities are a persistent challenge to the primacy of the keys of D minor and F major by E major, and an unexpected *fortissimo* statement of the first theme in tonic in the middle of the development.

Bruckner's Fourth Symphony in E♭, *The Romantic,* finished in 1874 and revised, with a new Scherzo, in 1878–80, has long been one of his most popular and accessible works. The first movement has a particularly arresting "beginning out of nothing": a horn call, above *tremolando* strings and a tonic pedal, whose effect is redoubled in the recapitulation by an added triadic figure for muted violins and flutes. The initial contrasting key turns out to be D♭, but by the end of the exposition Bruckner brings the music around, in Schubertian fashion, to the dominant. This formally orthodox and fairly economical movement acquires some of Bruckner's characteristic spaciousness only by the addition of a sizable coda. The slow movement, constructed according to the usual *ABABA* plan, is a leisurely Andante that seems to suffer from too great a similarity between its two themes. The energetic scherzo features an ingenuous Ländler-like trio and benefits from effective truncation of the main section upon repetition. In the finale, subtle reminiscences of earlier melodic shapes (such as an emphatic reference to the lowered sixth degree that colors the opening theme of the first movement) contribute to an impression of dramatic closure.

One apparent objective in the successive revisions of the Third Symphony was the expunging of certain specific resemblances to compositions by Wagner. (Some remain, as in the chromatic sequential buildup to the entry of the opening theme in the development section of the first movement.) But however closely the two composers were associated in the minds of the Viennese public, similarities to Wagner's music are always easy to spot in Bruckner's symphonies because their styles are fundamentally dissimilar. Bruckner's writing tends to be more diatonic, with frequent Schubertian shifts by thirds. And the formal patterns of his music are usually easily detectable: movements fall into large tonally unified blocks, sometimes separated by conspicuous pauses.

(New York, 1978), p. 84. But this resemblance is surely only another sign of the widespread influence of Beethoven's last symphony.

In addition to long-drawn seamless Wagnerian melody, there are frequent square-cut choralelike themes, notably in finales. The orchestration in his symphonies (especially before his disciples touched it up) is more modest than Wagner's: the first two employ the instruments of Beethoven's Fifth except for two extra horns, and the most notable addition thereafter is the four Wagner tubas in the Seventh, Eighth, and Ninth. Bruckner's handling of this orchestra is traditional: instead of the brilliant mixing and coloristic figurations of Berlioz and the mature Wagner there is an emphasis on the primary colors of the orchestral choirs that reminds us of the composer's continuing attachment to the organ. Bruckner seems to have made his first acquaintance with Wagner's music as late as 1862. However stunning the experience, Bruckner never became the "Wagnerian symphonist" he was alleged to be; the two composers remained nearly as unalike in their music as in their personalities.

In important ways, Bruckner's symphonies are *sui generis*. They are the first to attempt a further enlargement of scale in the symphony after Beethoven's Ninth, and thus to challenge the commonly held view, enunciated by Wagner, that the idea of the symphony had reached its apotheosis and closure in that work. And the static spaciousness, that majestic slowness of Bruckner's symphonic works, has led many to feel in them intimations of a metaphysical order, a reflection of the religious fervor and awe that was always foremost in the mind of their composer. A specific formulation of this view is given by the Swiss music theorist and Bruckner scholar Ernst Kurth, who, in a strongly idealist vein, saw in these symphonies the ultimate demonstration of musical form as the perceptible embodiment of "psychic energy"—an extension of Schopenhauer's "immediate representation of the Will."[20]

LEIPZIG

If Vienna was one center of hospitality to various strains of musical conservatism in the later nineteenth century, Leipzig was another. A guiding spirit there for the last four decades of the century was Carl Reinecke (1824–1910), professor and later director of the Conservatory and from 1860 until 1895 conductor of the Gewandhaus orchestra. Intent upon perpetuating the legacy of the Classic style in both his composing and teaching, Reinecke produced a good deal of well-crafted chamber music, three symphonies, four piano concertos, and nine programmatic overtures. This music, often reminiscent of Mendelssohn, was widely respected in its day—unlike Reinecke's six operas, which despite certain Wagnerian traits were nearly ignored. In addition to the long procession of Reinecke's prominent students from Scandinavia, Britain, and

20.   Ernst Kurth, *Bruckner,* 2 vols. (Berlin, 1925), especially 1, pp. 233ff.

the United States, two Germans who deserve mention are the distinguished conductor-composer Felix Weingartner (1863–1942) and the composer Max Bruch (1838–1920), noted in his lifetime for his secular choral music, but now remembered almost exclusively for his two somewhat Brahmsian violin concertos in G minor (1868) and D minor (1878).

PARIS

Paris in the late century presented something of a microcosm of musical Europe, together with certain enduring traits of practice and taste that were specifically French. Opera, as always, quite overshadowed all other forms of music in the French imagination. As we have noted in Chapter X, opera in France for the most part maintained its special identity in the face of challenges from both Italian *verismo* and Wagnerism. It was in areas where the French felt less self-sufficient, especially in instrumental music, that we see something of the variety and conflict that characteristized musical life in Europe at large. There were pockets of enthusiasm for music of the classical German tradition, for Beethoven, Mendelssohn, and to some extent Schumann; chamber-music societies that sprang up after mid-century, such as the Société des derniers quatuors de Beethoven, frankly acknowledged their orientation toward an art form that had never taken solid root in France. The music of Wagner was given a hearing, not on the opera stage, but piecemeal at the orchestral concerts of the conductors Pasdeloup, Colonne, and Lamoureux. Another strain of European music was taken up by oratorio societies modeled after those in England: in the 1870s a Société de l'harmonie sacrée, for example, performed works of Handel as well as the *St. Matthew Passion*. Church music too was subject to the same pressures in France as elsewhere, and the French Caecilian movement was more vigorous than any other. In the second half of the century two schools of music were founded in Paris to advance the cause of plainsong and traditional polyphony: the École Niedermeyer at mid-century and the Schola cantorum in 1894.

In 1871, in the wake of the humiliations of the Franco-Prussian War, a Société nationale de musique was established in Paris for the express purpose of performing nonoperatic music by French composers. The founders of this institution that was to provide a major impetus for new French music were the singing teacher Romain Bussine (1830–99) and the composer Camille Saint-Saëns (1835–1921). Saint-Saëns, a prominent figure in the Parisian musical scene for a prodigious number of years, was trained as an organist and composer at the Conservatoire, taught in the earlier 1860s at the École Niedermeyer, toured extensively as a pianist, and composed prolifically in all the standard genres. Early

Example XII–18: SAINT-SAËNS, Piano Concerto in G minor, opening

known as a champion of modern music, he campaigned for the works of Wagner and Liszt when they were the object of scorn in France. He was one of the first among the French to follow Liszt's example in composing symphonic poems *(Le rouet d'Omphale,* 1872; *Danse macabre,* 1874). But by gradual stages he came to be identified with the forces of conservatism and the French musical establishment, so that the young Debussy could exclaim in 1901, "How is it possible to go so completely wrong? Saint-Saëns knows the world's music better than anyone. How could he forget that he made known and compelled recognition for the turbulent genius of Liszt? How could he forget his worship of the elder Bach?"[21] Saint-Saëns's style, though markedly eclectic, was indeed largely conservative. Of all French composers of his time he was most dedicated to the Viennese Classic tradition of the symphony, concerto, and chamber sonata. His harmonic language is almost always solidly diatonic, with a great deal of root movement by thirds. A continuing interest in Baroque counterpoint can be seen in the Bachian opening (see Example XII–18) of the second of his five piano concertos (1858)—an effect that seems quite nullified by the sophisticated frivolity of the second and third movements. Much more convincing is the mixture of old and new in his Third Symphony, the *Organ Symphony* (1886); here fugal sections seem well at home in a cyclic work featuring the huge sounds of the organ heard in a concertato role against the orchestra.

Always perceived as more forward looking was the Belgian-born organist and composer César Franck (1822–90), who in his successive positions at the basilica of St. Clotilde, the Jesuit College of Vaugirard, and the Conservatoire gathered about him a group of faithful students (the "bande à Franck") who campaigned fiercely for the cause of avant-garde French music. When Frank became president of the Société nationale in 1886 these disciples, including the composers Henri Duparc (1848–1933) and Ernest Chausson (1855–1899), contributed to a bitter polarization between themselves and the "reactionaries" led by Saint-Saëns—a schism akin to the Wagner–Brahms factionalism in Vienna. Franck, like Brahms, remained aloof from such controversies.

---

21. Claude Debussy, *Monsieur Croche the Dilettante Hater* (London, 1927), p. 21

In his earlier career Franck's output was meager. An unsuccessful oratorio, *Ruth* (1846), consumed his best efforts for several years, but the most promising compositions before 1865 are probably the ambitious *Six Pieces for Organ,* Opp. 16–21 (1862). These are large-scale works, usually in several movements, that range from Bachian fugal exercises to serious Liszt-like attempts to simulate the orchestra at the organ (the second composition of the set is *Grande Pièce symphonique,* Op. 17). Little is to be seen, as yet, of Franck's famous chromaticism: the most common nondiatonic procedures here are a liberal use of diminished seventh chords in modulatory passages. In 1874 Franck heard the Prelude to *Tristan* for the first time; this experience seems to have been a key factor in his conversion to a strongly chromatic idiom, immediately evident in his organ compositions and the symphonic poem *Les Eolides* of 1875–76. In the *Pièce héroique,* Op. 37, the third of his *Trois Pièces* for organ of 1878 (Example XII–19), there is a descending sequence with four melodic lines (one in the right hand and three in the left), in which the chromatic motion is unbroken. But at two points there is a strong implication of standard tonal function: measures 6 and 8 outline dominant–tonic progressions to E♭ minor and C♯ minor respectively. However clearly this harmonic language seems to belong to a post-*Tristan* era, its tonal roots are relatively clear, and any assessment of its debt to Wagner must take into account the passage's striking similarity to the descending sequence in Chopin's Prelude in E minor of the later 1830s.[22]

Example XII–19: FRANCK, *Pièce héroique,* mm. 5–10

22. See above, p. 197–98.

Franck's last dozen years were his most productive ones. During this period he wrote most of the music for which he is best remembered: the oratorio *Les Béatitudes* (1879), the Piano Quintet (1879), the Symphonic Variations for piano and orchestra (1885), the Symphony in D minor (1888), the Violin Sonata in A (1886), and his single String Quartet (1889). In these late instrumental works he struggled with an acute form of a problem familiar to many nineteenth-century composers: that of adapting the procedures of the sonata to a seemingly alien musical language. The pervasive chromaticism of much of Franck's writing would appear particularly inimical to the tonal implications of sonata form, and indeed at crucial junctures in his chamber music and symphony he simply abandons it. The first movement of the Symphony in D minor has an overall tonal plan as clear and regular as anything in Mozart because the main points at which the form is articulated (such as the first and second themes in both exposition and recapitulation) are tonally solid; the *Tristan*-like chromatic wandering is restricted to the traditional areas of instability. This symphony also provides an example of the cyclic form which Franck cultivated perhaps more assiduously than any of his contemporaries: its finale reintroduces all the principal themes of the other two movements.

The most individual voice among French composers of the late nineteenth century was that of Gabriel Fauré (1845–1924). Though a student and lifelong associate of the conservative Saint-Saëns, Fauré carved out a personal style that had little to do with either the emergent French classicism or the chromatic idiom of Wagner and Franck. His piano works of the 1880s, nocturnes, impromptus, and barcarolles, betray a considerable debt to Chopin. But occasional harmonic turns show a strongly individual bent, as in the ambitious Ballade in F♯ major, Op. 19, where there are patches of nonfunctional linear writing and tentative approaches to the whole-tone scale (Example XII-20). Fauré's best-known large-scale work, the *Requiem* (1894), was some twenty years in the making; its style varies from the mildly chromatic idiom of contemporary French church music (for example the *Pie Jesu*) to a simulation of *stile antico* polyphony (parts of the Offertory), but there is little sign here of this composer at his most original.

Example XII–20: FAURÉ, Ballade, Op. 19

The real proving ground for Fauré's stylistic innovations and the field of his greatest accomplishment was the French song, or, as it was by this time called, the *melodie*. A tradition of French accompanied song with some artistic ambition had begun to take shape only in the later 1830s, mainly, it appears, in response to a burst of enthusiasm in France for the Lieder of Schubert. A signal early achievement in the genre was the first version, for voice and piano, of Berlioz's *Nuits d'été* (1841). Thereafter most of the major French composers cultivated the *mélodie*: Gounod, Massenet, Saint-Saëns, and Lalo all left substantial numbers of them, which now reveal an influence from Schumann as well as Schubert. Fauré composed some 107 songs, about half of them appearing in three collections of twenty each published in 1879, 1897, and 1908. These volumes chronicle a growing sensitivity to textual-musical relationships and an increasingly individual harmonic style that strains the limits of tonal syntax.

Most prized among Fauré's songs is a cycle standing outside the three main collections, *La Bonne Chanson* (1894), set to nine poems from the series with that title by Paul Verlaine. The music put to these delicate love lyrics is highly sensitive to their rhythmic and tonal inflections; the piano accompaniments, in accord with long-standing traditions of the Lied, is homogeneous in figuration and sometimes mildly illustrative of textual meanings. What is genuinely new is the harmonic language. Root progression by thirds has overwhelmed the standard motion by fifths; the usual sounds of a tonal syntax are more often than not deprived of their expected function, so that a traditional dominant–tonic ending in the seventh song, *Donc, Ce Sera Par Un Claire Jour d'été,* sounds oddly out of place. Most disruptive to a sense of tonality is Fauré's use of highly implicative sonorities such as dominant sevenths and ninths in new contexts. In the first song, (see Example XII–21), there is an alternation of a dominant ninth on A♭ with a C-minor chord in first inversion. In addition to this root movement by third, both the seventh and ninth resolve upward (G♭–G♮ and B♭–C). The ambiguity of G♭ / G♮

Example XII–21: FAURÉ, *Une Sainte en son auréole*

Claude Monet, *The Luncheon*, 1872–74; an early example of Impressionistic painting.

between these two sonorities, moreover, contributes to a whole-tone progression in the melodic line from g♭′ to ″C. This is the language of musical impressionism at its birth. *La Bonne Chanson* was published in the year of the sensational premiere of Debussy's *Prélude à l'après-midi d'un faune;* its composer has been given insufficient credit for his contribution to the dominant idiom of modern music in France.

THE CENTURY'S END IN GERMANY AND AUSTRIA

The musical world of Germany and Austria at the end of the century was marked by conflict and uncertainty. The aesthetic stance of the New German School was increasingly accepted as fashionable and progressive; Brahms was the only composer of first rank to challenge it. But the precepts of Wagner and Liszt had about them a vagueness that left even the most willing of followers without direction. The Wagnerian music drama seemed to have been exhausted by Wagner, and the new gospel for instrumental music amounted to little more than a prescription for a structure based on a "poetic idea" rather than on inherited musical forms. Some young composers emerging into this confusing world sought refuge in techniques of the past. One was the Bavarian Max Reger (1873–1916), who fluctuated between a Brahmsian adherence to the canons of Viennese Classicism and (especially in his organ works) a hybrid polyphonic style with Baroque rhythmic patterns and post-Wagerian chromatic harmony; this music has never made much of an impression outside Germany. Only one figure was widely perceived as a worthy heir to the New German mantle: Richard Strauss (1864–1949), who confidently took up Liszt's notion of the symphonic poem, and who in the new century was to forge almost single-handedly a new course for German opera.

Strauss began his musical career in the hothouse musical atmosphere of the Munich Court Opera, where his father was principal horn player. He early came under the tutelage of the conductor there, Hermann Levi, who was then emerging as a leading exponent of Wagner's music. Then at about the age of twenty he became a protégé of Hans von Bülow, conductor of the famed Meiningen Court Orchestra. After briefly succeeding Bülow in that post and conducting regularly at Munich and Berlin from 1886, Strauss became one of a new breed of musician, the cosmopolitan professional conductor—a latter-day counterpart to the piano and violin virtuosos who had flourished since the 1830s. At the same time he composed continuously, producing in the 1880s a succession of instrumental works of a rather conservative cast reminiscent of Mendelssohn and Schumann. But certain of these compositions, particularly the *Burlesque* for piano and orchestra and the "symphonic fantasy" *Aus Italien* (both 1886), show flashes of brilliant and evocative orchestral writing that point firmly toward Strauss's future.

In the mid-1880s Strauss's adherence to the Wagner-Liszt camp was consolidated by his association at Meiningen with the ardent Wagnerite

The young Richard Strauss; a photograph dated 1888.

Alexander Ritter,[23] and in 1889 he won the support of Cosima Wagner. This led to a triumphant performance at Weimar of his tone poem (as he chose to call it) *Don Juan* (1889). Following hard on the heels of his *Macbeth* (1888), this was the second in a series of seven imposing compositions of this genre that Strauss produced in the decade 1888–98. All are in one continuous movement after the Lisztian model, and all have programmatic connections with varying degrees of explicitness. To the score of *Don Juan* Strauss attached selected lines from Nicolaus Lenau's poem of that name in which the protagonist is presented as a Byronic sensualist-hero, simultaneously driven by passion and afflicted with satiety and emptiness. There is no narrative in the quoted portions of the poem, and it is left to the listener to make any connections between musical and literary events.

The structure of *Don Juan* bears some resemblance to both sonata-allegro and rondo form. After a reasonably orderly exposition in the principal keys of E and B (see ARM 23, mm. 1–17 and 90ff.) there follows a restatement of the first theme in the tonic (m. 168), a developmentlike section in which two new ideas are introduced (mm. 251 and 314), and a truncated recapitulation, centered about E major, that draws freely on all this material. The piece opens with an arresting motto theme of a sort that is something of a Straussian trademark; similar terse and summary beginnings are to be heard in the tone poems *Till Eulenspiegels lustige Streiche* (1895), *Ein Heldenleben* (Life of a Hero) (1898), and especially in *Also sprach Zarathustra* (1896), familiar to many from the film *2001: A Space Odyssey*. In *Don Juan* the opening owes much of its effect to the striking ascending motion C–E, the latter being the tonic (see Example XII–22). This device is reminiscent of a favorite practice of Berlioz in which the climax of a phrase is intensified by a sudden turn to a remote sonority.

Example XII–22: STRAUSS, *Don Juan,* opening

---

23. Romain Rolland, the distinguished French critic and friend of Strauss, reports the composer's own estimate of his debt to Ritter: "It was he who, by dint of years of lessons and affectionate advice, made me a musician of the future *(Zukunftsmusiker)*, and put me on the path along which I now walk independently and alone." *Richard Strauss and Romain Rolland: Correspondence, Diary, and Essays,* ed. Rollo Myers (Berkeley, 1968), p. 176.

Another crucial factor in this excerpt is of course the sheen and potency of the orchestral sound. The violins and high winds rise to their most brilliant upper register while the brass play carefully spaced chords that add great power without muddiness. A drive for strength and variety of sound in the tone poems led Strauss to call for increasingly large instrumental forces. *Till Eulenspiegel* requires a phalanx of sixteen woodwinds, eight horns, and six trumpets; the orchestra for *Ein Heldenleben* is even a bit larger, and both are comparable with the vast ensemble needed for Wagner's *Ring*. Strauss explored the potentialities of this expanded orchestra as Liszt had experimented with the newly strengthened piano in the 1830s and 1840s. Thematic material is itself calculated primarily for orchestral effect; musical figures are heard not as melodies or accompanimental patterns, but as splashes of instrumental color. Hanslick, who could hardly be expected to approve, called *Don Juan* "a tumult of brilliant daubs, a faltering tonal orgy, half bacchanale, half witches' sabbath."[24] But Strauss's orchestral technique was founded on a scrupulous study of the capabilities of modern instruments, singly and in combination. This is clear from his meticulous revision of Berlioz's *Traité d'instrumentation,* published in 1904. We can also conclude from this publication what we might in any case have assumed, viz. that most of Strauss's ideas about the orchestra had a single source of inspiration: almost all his additions to Berlioz's text are illustrations from the music of Wagner.

Hanslick's other objection to Strauss's tone poems is directed toward their apparent dependence upon programs or poetic ideas: "The basic characteristic of Strauss as a symphonist is that he composes with poetic rather than with musical elements and, through his emancipation from musical logic, takes a position adjacent to music rather than squarely in it."[25] This familiar-sounding reproach (that might be mistaken for Fétis's attacks on Berlioz's *Symphonie fantastique* sixty years earlier) was written about *Tod und Verklärung* (Death and Transfiguration) in 1893; at this point the final degree of onomatopoetic depiction in *Till Eulenspiegel* and *Don Quixote,* with its famous imitation of whirring windmills and bleating sheep, were yet to come. But Strauss always insisted that his music should be graspable without the programs. Indeed, all the tone poems can also be related to standard musical shapes: the sonata-allegro form, the rondo, or, in the case of *Don Quixote,* variation form. And even as a composer of program music, Strauss's central aims and methods were not very far removed from traditional enterprises of Romantic composers: the evocation of feeling and the portrayal of character.

Another factor surely contributed to the dramatic polarization of

---

24.   Eduard Hanslick, *Music Criticisms,* ed. H. Pleasants (Baltimore, 1950), p. 292.
25.   Ibid., p. 294.

opinion about Strauss and his music. The very monumentality of his works, his apparent congeniality of outlook with both Nietzsche and Wagner, and his willingness to portray himself as hero in the outsized *Ein Heldenleben* formed a composite image that inspired both admiration and distaste. Whether accurate or not, this image seemed to accord well with his status as the leading composer of the powerful young German Empire. It remained to be shown in the next century how many other facets there were to his character and work.

Another of the late century's constellation of younger composers who provided a certain continuity between the central Austro-German musical tradition and emerging styles of the 1900s was Gustav Mahler (1860–1911). Like Strauss, Mahler first made his mark as a conductor. After his student days at the Vienna Conservatory, he held successive posts at Kassel, Prague, Leipzig, Budapest, and Hamburg before returning to Vienna to conduct the Court Opera in 1897; and from 1898 to 1901 he assumed the directorship of the Vienna Philharmonic orchestra as well. In these positions Mahler created the most brilliant and controversial chapter in the history of musical performance in Vienna. He provided vivid interpretations of all the principal Austro-German masters from Mozart to Wagner. Seeing the interpreter's role as a creative one, he freely touched up what he saw as weaknesses in the orchestration of Schumann and even Beethoven; he reconstructed Weber's opera *Die drei Pintos* from the composer's sketches (adding music where necessary from other minor works of Weber), installing it in the repertory; and introduced the now-common practice of injecting the *Leonore Overture No. 3* before the final scene of *Fidelio*.

Mahler's achievement as a composer lay almost exclusively in two areas: the symphony and the song with orchestral (or sometimes piano) accompaniment. For him the two genres were intimately connected. Whether concealed or revealed, literary ideas and images played a huge part in his musical imagination. In the convoluted process of structuring and revision through which the massive symphonies took shape, his songs became a reservoir of poetic and musical ideas from which he drew at will. Three early works were seminal in the formulation of his style and way of working: the gigantic cantata *Das klagende Lied* (The Song of Lament, 1880), the song cycle *Lieder eines fahrenden Gesellen* (Songs of a Wayfarer, 1885), and a series of nine songs on texts from Arnim and Brentano's *Des Knaben Wunderhorn* (The Youth's Magic Horn). The latter two collections, first written for voice and piano and most of them subsequently orchestrated, were probably conceived for orchestra from the first. *Das klagende Lied* and the *Lieder eines fahrenden Gesellen* are both set to Mahler's own words. These poetic texts, like his reversion to the old *Wunderhorn* collection, show a retrospective attachment to earlier strata of German Romanticism: to a double-edged symbolism in which nature is both nurturing and threatening, to a

Auguste Rodin's *Head of Mahler,*
1909.

Hoffmannesque indulgence in the bizarre and gruesome, to a portrayal of the artist—in the *Lieder eines fahrenden Gesellen* this figure is unmistakably Mahler himself—as a tender plant in an alien world. The style of this early music is eclectic: influences from Schubert and Weber are detectable side-by-side with reminiscences of Berlioz and Wagner. The orchestral writing is strikingly individual from the outset. At times it becomes a vehicle for a kind of sardonic irony as Mahler satirizes the very musical ideas he is presenting by clothing them in odd instrumental colors.

Mahler's first three symphonies (and to a lesser extent the Fourth as well) represent an unbroken extension of the musico-poetic world of those three early works. The First Symphony in D major, first performed in Budapest (1889) as a tone poem in five movements, acquired its present four-movement shape and its new name through revisions carried out in the 1890s. At every step of the way the work was heavily laden with programmatic associations, some literary and some autobiographical. The sketchy explanations provided by the composer for certain performances, and the much fuller ones left by his close friend Natalie Bauer-Lechner,[26] show a continuation of the idea of the *Lieder eines fahrenden Gesellen:* a hero's progress through the trials of life and death. All the movements but the last incorporate music from Mahler's previously composed songs, the principal source being the *Lieder eines fahrenden Gesellen.*

26. Natalie Bauer-Lechner, *Recollections of Gustav Mahler,* trans. Dika Newlin, ed. Peter Franklin (Cambridge, 1980). See also Henry-Louis de la Grange, *Mahler* (Garden City, N.Y., 1973) I, pp. 747–52. The title that Mahler for a time attached to the symphony, *Titan* (after Jean Paul's novel), was applied *ex post facto* and soon discarded.

Example XII–23: MAHLER, *Ging heut' morgens*

Ging heut' mor - gens ü - bers Feld, Tau noch auf den Grä - sern hing;

The third movement, a funeral march, suggests a further dependence upon both Beethoven's and Berlioz's symphonic portrayals of heros. But Mahler characteristically gives this music an ironic twist: the principal theme, played in imitation of a rustic wind band, is the round *Frère Jacques* put into the minor mode—thus providing an irreverent new twist to an old poetic identification of sleep and death. And the extent to which the specter of Beethoven's achievement continued to haunt symphonic composers of the period can be seen by a glance at the symphony's opening. Like Bruckner's Third, it begins with an unmistakable recollection of the archetypal symphony in D minor / D major, Beethoven's Ninth: for 56 measures a sustained *pianissimo* A sounds in the strings as other figures played against it gradually gather force, leading to an integral first theme. But there are significant differences. The sustained A in the violins is at first a very high ghostly-sounding harmonic; and the conclusion to which this portentious introduction leads is not the high-minded drama of Beethoven's Ninth, but the jocular melody borrowed from Mahler's song *Ging heut' morgens übers Feld*[27] (Example XII–23) that is the principal theme of the entire movement, introducing thus another of the composer's juxtapositions of the exalted and the ordinary.

Mahler's Second Symphony has many features in common with the First. It too began life as a tone poem; it shows programmatic connections with early nineteenth-century literary sources as well as events in Mahler's own life, and makes use of some of the composer's preexistent songs. The huge first movement, composed in 1888, is another funeral march that existed for a time as an independent tone poem called *Totenfeier* (Funeral Celebration), after the poem of that name by Adam Mickiewicz. Mahler also explained, "I have called the first movement Totenfeier and, if you are interested, it is the hero of my first D-Major Symphony who is being carried to his grave . . ."[28] The other four movements were attached much later; Mahler's *Wunderhorn* songs from this period, *Des Antonius von Padua Fischpredigt* and *Urlicht,* were pressed into service for the scherzo-like third movement and the choralelike fourth (in the latter movement, for the first time in the Mahler sym-

---

27. "This Morning I Set Off across the Fields." Mahler associated this opening with a vision of the hero in an awakening spring landscape.

28. De la Grange, I, p. 784.

A sketch-page of Mahler's Second Symphony, first movement, showing the end of the Development and the beginning of the Recapitulation.

phonies there is a vocal part, an alto solo). The finale was added in 1894. Presenting an apocalyptic vision of the Day of Judgment and the Resurrection, it is an extended composition for two soloists, chorus, and orchestra, on the text of Klopstock's hymn *Auferstehung* (Resurrection), as emended and enlarged by the composer.

This striving for a monumental, overwhelming synthesis of musical types and programmatic associations was continued in the Third Symphony (1896), a six-movement work (a seventh was transferred to the Fourth Symphony) that Mahler projected as a panegyric to all of creation, from inanimate nature to the angels. For this undertaking he prescribed perhaps the most imposing musical forces yet required for a symphony: an orchestra with 8 horns, 5 clarinets, 4 each of oboes, flutes, and bassoons, a huge battery of percussion, two separate choruses, and an alto soloist. Such Titanism is very much of a piece with Mahler's view of music and of the symphony. Fired with Schopenhauer's vision of music as an immediate reflection of the primal substance, the "Will" of the universe, he set about quite literally to portray the entire world of nature and human experience in the symphony. With perfect sincerity and unflagging devotion he pursued his quest into the new century, completing, in all, nine symphonies and beginning a tenth. While the strategy varied (only the Eighth again resorts to the use of giant forces including choruses), that central cosmic goal remained constant.

Mahler's symphonies nonetheless maintained certain distinct ties with the traditions of the genre. However overpowering the orchestral forces he assembled, his writing for instruments tended increasingly toward sophistication and selectiveness; variety and novelty of color were more the point than volume of sound. And whatever programmatic ideas were in force, the movements often assume traditional shapes: the first movements of the first four symphonies all resemble sonata-allegro forms, and internal movements frequently have an episodic plan such as the scherzo-trio. Mahler's harmonic language, like that of Strauss and Bruckner, remains solidly tonal. Though there are episodes of chromaticism, diatonic syntax predominates strongly, with a fondness shown for the large-scale movement by thirds that by now seems more the rule in European music than the exception. One recurrent harmonic device is novel: the so-called progressive tonality by which compositions begin in one key and end in another. This seems to have happened fortuitously in *Das klagende Lied* when Mahler deleted its original first section, *Waldmärchen*. In the Second (C–E♭) and Fourth (G–E) symphonies the move is deliberate, and it recurs in the Fifth, Seventh, and Ninth, underscoring Mahler's conception of the symphony as a lifelike organism that progresses and evolves, with no guarantee of a return to its origins.

In Vienna the convergence of the crosscurrents of late-nineteenth-century musical culture seemed to create a special turbulence. Wagner and Wagnerism remained a burning issue because of the ever-present activities of Hanslick and Brahms; Bruckner and, later, Mahler attracted controversy as they pursued relentlessly what each conceived to be a proper course for large-scale instrumental composition after the intervention of Wagner and Liszt. A quieter figure in Vienna who in a very different way explored possible continuations for seemingly exhausted traditions was Hugo Wolf (1860–1903). A friend of Mahler's and fellow Wagner-enthusiast during their student days in Vienna, Wolf stayed on in that city, leading a bohemian existence reminiscent of Schubert's life there, composing in various genres but making his mark in a single one, the Lied.

Wolf's art was firmly anchored in the central traditions of the German Lied. The eighty-odd songs he composed before 1880 (only three of which he chose to publish) are nearly all set to earlier nineteenth-century poetry by Goethe, Lenau, Hebbel, Heine, and others. Their musical style owes something to Schubert and much to Schumann: in vocal writing, types of accompanimental figuration, and harmonic practice. But on occasion the young Wolf breaks sharply from their example. In his Heine settings (1878), where one might expect the shadow of Schumann to loom largest, Wolf seems more than usually independent. *Ich stand in dunkeln Träumen,* for example, begins and ends with a canonic passage in the piano that conceals its tonal orientation until nearly the end (Example XII–24a). This is the beginning of a complex imitative relationship in which the piano frequently mirrors the vocal

Hugo Wolf; an etching by William Unger.

line in diminution (a practice Brahms favored). Both elements can be seen as textual interpretation: the nebulous framing music as a counterpart to the persona's eerie dream that forms the context of the poem; and the imitations as illustrative of its central event, the reciprocal gaze of the persona and the portrait of his beloved come to life. Example XII–24b shows an instance of this imitation as well as a sample of local text interpretation: the cross-relation at the word *leben* (at the point the picture comes alive) is more jarring then anything in Schumann's songs.

Example XII–24: WOLF, *Ich stand in dunkeln Träumen*
    a. Mm. 1–8

b. Mm. 17–23

The year 1888 was one of phenomenal productivity for Wolf in which his output of songs compared with that of Schumann in 1840. This year also marked the beginning of his orderly construction of "songbooks": those massive collections of up to fifty songs each that were unified by textual source. First were the *Gedichte von Eduard Mörike,* the *Gedichte von Joseph v. Eichendorff,* both published in 1889, and the *Gedichte von J. W. von Goethe* of 1890. Next Wolf turned to Spanish and Italian poetry in the translations of Paul Heyse and Emanuel Geibel; the *Spanisches Liederbuch* and *Italienisches Liederbuch* appeared in 1891 and 1892. Such an arrangement of his work reflected more than a passion for order. Grouping his songs as he did was one way in which Wolf showed his intense belief in the primacy of the poetic text: the volumes of songs were meant as a tribute to the poet fully as much as to the composer. They also provided something of a substitute for the large-scale compositions Wolf always longed to produce but could not.

The Mörike, Eichendorff, and Goethe volumes all show the composer's continued preoccupation with poetry from earlier in the century. But in the case of Mörike Wolf was drawn to a poet whose oeuvre, though largely complete by 1840, strikingly prefigured later poetic strains. Ambiguities of literal meaning and complex associations of sound and sense anticipate the manner of the symbolists Baudelaire, Verlaine, and Mallarmé, as well as later German poets such as Hofmannsthal and Stephan Georg. This elusive poetry called forth Wolf's best efforts; the finest of his Mörike settings achieve an extraordinary congruity of mood and nuance between the poetry and music.

One such is *Das verlassene Mägdlein* (The Forsaken Maiden; ARM 24b). This poem recounts the musings of a servant girl who rises early to kindle a fire, and, gazing into the fire, recalls dreams of her faithless lover. Wolf set the four stanzas of the poem to music that has roughly the shape *a b a* (he seldom wrote purely strophic music for strophic poems); the music of the first stanza recurs in the last. But the dominant rhythm of the first stanza, ♩ ♫ | ♪.♪ , also governs the motion of the second, though the melody is quite different. That rhythm plays upon a conflict, very common in German poetry, between the formal poetic meter of the poem and its ordinary speech rhythms. The trochaic meter, alternating four and three stresses per line, several times forces an unaccented syllable into an accented position; examples are the first syllables of "Eh' die Sternlein schwinden" and "So kommt der Tag heran." Wolf's initial rhythm in the first two stanzas holds obstinately to the formal poetic meter, placing a false stress, for example, on *"ich* schaue so darein." This creates a repetitive sing-song quality strikingly evocative of the dull melancholy of the girl's morning activities. In the third stanza, when the dream is remembered and the lover introduced, this "framing" rhythm is in the passion of the moment replaced by speechlike declamation; the accompaniment, however, holds to the old rocking motion, retaining a connection with humdrum reality, a reality that returns with renewed force in the final stanza.

This song shows something of the remarkable battery of original harmonic techniques that Wolf brought to his interpretive task. The home key of A minor only gradually comes into view in the first eight measures as morning dawns. The key is brightened to A major as the flames cast their glow. The drama of the central portion of the poem is articulated by two new keys on the flat side: A♭ upon the persona's first revelation of her feelings ("Ich schaue so darein") and B♭ for the dream and the lover ("Plötzlich, da kommt es mir"). And Wolf underscores the insubstantiality of this reverie by a very persistent introduction of tonally indeterminate augmented triads; in the piano interlude before the third stanza they are used exclusively, quite obliterating the tonal center, and in the following music they act vaguely as a substitute dominant to B♭.

A prominent use of augmented sonorities was only one way in which Wolf stretched the bounds of the tonal system.[29] Like Fauré he also experimented extensively with the placement of functional sounds in nonfunctional contexts; *An eine Aeölsharfe,* for example, begins with a remarkable series of chords that are written as either dominant sevenths or augmented sixths, but resolve like neither. Other Mörike settings

---

29. A valuable treatment of Wolf's harmonic practice is Deborah Stein, *Extended Tonal Procedures in the Lieder of Hugo Wolf* (Ph.D. dissertation, Yale University, 1982).

using similar techniques are *Seufzer* (ARM 24d), *Er ist's* (ARM 24a), and the splendid *Um Mitternacht* (ARM 24c). Wolf sometimes undermines the tonal system in more radical ways. A few songs, such as *In dem Schatten* from the *Spanisches Liederbuch,* can best be described as having two tonal centers, in this and most cases a third apart. And on occasion Wolf's songs show true "progressive tonality"; *Der Mond hat eine schwere klag'* from the *Italienisches Liederbuch,* for example, begins in E♭ minor, dwells on G♭, and ends in C♭. This exhaustive probing of the limits of tonality, carried out in a restless search for ever new expressive resources, led inevitably to the exhaustion and collapse of the system. Firmly rooted in the musical traditions of his century, Wolf, like Mahler and Strauss, extended certain facets of its practice to what seemed like a point of no return.

Europe at the century's end would have been scarcely recognizable to its inhabitants of 1800. Whole new nations had come into being in the unification of Germany and Italy and in the emerging independence of Hungary. And governments responding in varying degrees to the demands of an established middle class had replaced autocratic hereditary rule everywhere except in Russia, where a revolution was to be not long in coming.

Industry, technology, and science had made breathtaking gains. When Beethoven, at the beginning of our narrative, journeyed from Bonn to Vienna, he traveled by horse-drawn conveyance exactly as the Roman invaders of his homeland had done nearly two thousand years before. Richard Strauss could make the same trip in a fraction of the time by train. Ocean travel by steamship, instant communication by telegraph (and by telephone and radio, just now beginning), large-scale manufacturing with iron and steel machinery, the emergence of electric power and lighting, the recent discovery of bacteria and radioactivity—innovations like these had changed the life and mind of the continent.

Heady triumphs in the physical sciences during the later century encouraged a widespread belief that their methods and materials must be paradigmatic for all branches of knowledge: that even the riddles of human nature and human society must be subject to discoverable scientific laws. This view was central to a "positivist" outlook (named by Auguste Comte, who also coined the term "sociology") that came to dominate European thought in the later century. The mechanical processes of natural selection described by Darwin and A. R. Wallace in the 1850s reinforced a growing conviction that all life, including human life, can ultimately be explained through concepts such as "matter," "force," and "covering law." And underlying the economic theories of Karl Marx, which appeared about the same time, was a materialist conception of history that fit well with such a view; in Marx's scheme the social ideas and institutions of a given time were finally determined by the material basis of life, by the manner of production and distribution of goods. "Things are in the saddle," lamented Emerson, "and ride mankind."

Where such ideas are dominant one might expect a demythologizing of art; surely they create a climate inhospitable to Romantic notions about the primacy of the individual poetic sensibility, or a "spiritual content" of art, or a transcendental cognitive function of the artistic experience. And the later nineteenth century did see a new anti-Romantic emphasis in movements toward "realism" and "naturalism" in literature and the visual arts: especially in France in the novels of Zola and Maupassant, for example, and in the paintings of Courbet and Millet, minute and exacting observations of life are meant to make a social point without any intervening interpretive act by the artist.

It is difficult to see how we might recognize a clear counterpart to "realism" or "naturalism" in any repertory of music. One might cite various attempts at musical imitations of natural sounds, for example those in Berlioz's *Symphonie fantastique* and Strauss's *Symphonia domestica,* as exercises in musical realism. But even the most extreme of such references to extramusical objects or events fall far short of the specificity easily achieved by prose or painting; explicit denotation has never worked well in music. Nor did such onomatopoetic effects ever become a widespread and accepted means of musical expression, or a significant element in anyone's aesthetic canon. They remained isolated *jeux d'esprit,* well outside the mainstream of musical practice. "Natural" declamation in the operas of Dargomïzhsky and Musorgsky and *verismo* on the Italian operatic stage are also sometimes mentioned as examples of realism in music. In both cases the means and ends seem quite other than those of contemporaneous literature and painting: Puccini presents not ordinary life but heightened theatricality, and Musorgsky's recitative only revives (with a certain nationalist twist) principles of declamation as old as Gluck or even Peri.

It is difficult, indeed, to detect any important reflection in musical thought or practice of the positivist spirit of the later nineteenth century. And if this dominant intellectual stance made no very perceptible impact upon the art, one explanation may be found in the centrality and hugeness, at this juncture, of the figure of Wagner. Though Wagner was thought to represent all that was progressive in music, it is hard to imagine an artist or thinker less attuned to an age of materialist scientism than he. Wagner's views about art remained almost entirely within the fold of Romantic aesthetics. The very notion of a *Gesamtkunstwerk* presupposes a commonality of aim and effect in the arts that had been an article of faith in the first decades of the century. And Wagner's glorification of national myth and primitive poetry as the collective expression of a people stems from a yet earlier stratum of Romantic thought found in Herder and Bishop Percy. Then too, the old view of art as a subjective but universally significant product of the individual imagination reappears in full force with Wagner. When at the end of the century Mahler declared his fealty to Wagner even as he turned for ideas and texts to Schopenhauerian philosophy and *Des Knaben Wunderhorn*, he showed no inconsistency; nothing said or done by the sorcerer of Bayreuth had repealed the basic tenets of musical Romanticism.

If any area of music in the second half of the nineteenth century reflected something of the new scientific spirit, it was that of musical scholarship. The founding of the Bach Gesellschaft in 1850 and Friedrich Chrysander's launching of the collected Handel edition a decade later inaugurated a new era of activity in this field. Other composers for whom collected editions were completed by the end of the century or shortly thereafter were Palestrina, Mozart, Schumann, and Schubert. A tradition of publishing huge anthologies of early music began as early as 1839 with the twenty-eight volume *Musica sacra* of Franz Commer; R. J. van Maldeghem's *Tresor musical,* of a similar scope, was begun in 1865, and the first volumes of two of the great *Denkmäler* series (the *Denkmäler deutscher Tonkunst* and the *Denkmäler der Tonkunst in Oesterreich*) appeared in the 1890s.

At first a sort of Romantic historicism (and perhaps even a nationalistic pride) may have motivated much of this musicological activity. But by 1863 a new scholarly and objective stance was evident in Chrysander's *Jahrbuch für musikalische Wissenschaft* (Yearbook of Musical Science); the accurate and faithful rendition of the text advocated there resembles the ideal of a "true narrative" among the Berlin school of "scientific" historians led by Leopold von Ranke. The new *Wissenschaft* in music, under the leadership of Chrysander in Hamburg, Guido Adler in Vienna, and Philipp Spitta in Berlin, was to establish its firmest ties with other humanistic disciplines; it was nevertheless strongly colored, from the first, by current scientific demands for factual objectivity and accurate observation.[30]

Musical practice and its aesthetic foundations, however, seemed largely immune to the century's marked disjunction between an earlier Romanticism and idealism and a later positivism and realism. After 1850 music could be said to live a life somewhat detached from the rest of European culture;[31] it provided an escape into the noumenal quite at

---

30. One point at which science and music plainly intersected was in the study of acoustics and the physiological foundations of musical perception, a field greatly advanced by Hermann von Helmholtz in the 1860s and 1870s. The influential harmonic theories of Hugo Riemann (1849–1919) were consciously based on recent findings in this field. Another clear influence from nineteenth-century scientific method can be seen in the compilation of thematic catalogues of composers' music. The first important one was in fact done by a botanist: Ludwig von Köchel's chronological catalogue of the works of Mozart (1862).

31. Cf. Carl Dahlhaus, "Neo-Romanticism," *19th-Century Music,* III (1979): 97–105.

odds with current ways of thinking and feeling—a clear specimen of Marx's despised *phantasmagoria*. Thus a whole century's music—and in some respects that of a century and a half, reaching back to the mid-1700s—can be seen to show a general unity of style and idea.

As the century waned, it was clear that the end of this musical tradition was near. It was not only the tonal system whose resources seemed used up. The expansion and modification of traditional formal shapes, as well as their replacement with new large-scale organizations based upon extramusical associations, appeared to have been well explored. And sounds that could be had from the instruments of the orchestra, from the most overpowering masses to the most delicate combinations, seemed well charted. Radical new experiments underway in France, meanwhile, and more radical ones shortly to begin in Vienna, signaled the ending of a musical era in which innovation had occurred mainly within widely recognized boundaries. The passing of this old order marked the conclusion of a century—the only century the West has seen—when music has thrived in a public context, when a precarious balance could be maintained between the artist's drive for originality and the public's demand for accessibility. The success of this venture still resonates in our concert halls and opera theaters as modern audiences show an undiminished enthusiasm for the music of the nineteenth century.

Bibliography

This bibliography is of necessity very selective. Intended mainly for the English-speaking student, it includes works in other languages only if they are of special importance and nothing like their equivalent is available in English. A preference is also shown for writings that are fairly broad in scope; an occasional highly specialized technical study is listed, however, to give the more advanced student a glimpse of current trends in musical scholarship for this period. It seemed most convenient and useful to organize the principal listings by composer. In addition, a few general readings are suggested that bear on the subjects of the individual chapters. In all cases, an attempt has been made to indicate the existence of reprints and paperback editions. The latter are indicated by an asterisk preceding their date of publication.

The following are abbreviations for bibliographic references:

19CM	*Nineteenth-Century Music*
AcM	*Acta musicologica*
IRASM	*International Review of the Aesthetics and Sociology of Music*
JAMS	*Journal of the American Musicological Society*
JMT	*Journal of Music Theory*
MF	*Music Forum*
ML	*Music and Letters*
MMR	*The Monthly Musical Review*
MQ	*The Musical Quarterly*
MR	*The Music Review*
MT	*The Musical Times*
PMA	*Proceedings of the Musical Association*
PRMA	*Papers of the Royal Musical Association*

GENERAL

Abraham, Gerald. *A Hundred Years of Music.* 4th ed. London: Duckworth, *1974.

Breunig, Charles. *The Age of Revolution and Reaction, 1789–1850.* New York: W. W. Norton, 1970, *1977.

Dahlhaus, Carl. *Die Musik des 19. Jahrhunderts [Neues Handbuch der Musikwissenschaft VI].* Wiesbaden: Athenaion, 1980.

———, ed. *Studien zur Trivialmusik des 19. Jahrhunderts.* Regensburg: Bosse, 1967.

Einstein, Alfred. *Music in the Romantic Era.* New York: W. W. Norton, 1947.

Knepler, Georg. *Musikgeschichte des 19. Jahrhunderts.* Berlin: Henschelverlag, 1961.

Longyear, Rey Morgan. *Nineteenth-Century Romanticism in Music.* Englewood Cliffs, N.J.: Prentice-Hall, 1969. 2nd ed., *1973.

Nineteenth-Century Music. Berkeley: Univ. of California Press, 1977–.

Rich, Norman. *The Age of Nationalism and Reform, 1850–1890.* New York: W. W. Norton, 1970, *1976.

Tovey, Donald Francis. *Essays in Musical Analysis.* London: Oxford Univ. Press, 1935–39, *1981.

CHAPTER I, INTRODUCTION

Abrams, Meyer H. *The Mirror and the Lamp: Romantic Theory and the Critical Tradition.* New York: Oxford Univ. Press, *1953.

Babbitt, Irving. *Rousseau and Romanticism.* New York: Houghton Mifflin, 1919. Reprint, 1976, *1977.

Blume, Friedrich. *Classic and Romantic Music: a Comprehensive Survey.* Trans. M. D. Herter Norton. New York: W. W. Norton, *1970.

Dahlhaus, Carl. *Esthetics of Music.* Trans. William W. Austin. Cambridge: Cambridge Univ. Press, *1982.

Duckles, Vincent. "Patterns in the Historiography of Nineteenth-Century Music." *AcM* XLII (1970): 75–82.

Frye, Northrop, ed. *Romanticism Reconsidered.* New York: Columbia Univ. Press, *1963.

Harding, Rosamond E. M. *The Pianoforte: Its History Traced to the Great Exhibition of 1851.* Cambridge: Cambridge Univ. Press, 1933. Reprint, New York: Da Capo Press, 1973. Reprint, Gresham, 1979.

Jones, Howard Mumford. *Revolution and Romanticism.* Cambridge, Mass.: Harvard Univ. Press, 1974.

Lovejoy, Arthur Oncken. "On the Discrimination of Romanticisms." In *Essays in the History of Ideas,* 228–53. Baltimore: Johns Hopkins Press, 1948. Reprint, Greenwood Press, *1978.

Palmer, R. R. *The Age of the Democratic Revolution*. Princeton: Princeton Univ. Press, ★1959.

Praz, Mario. *The Romantic Agony*. Trans. A. Davidson. 2nd ed., London, New York: Oxford Univ. Press, ★1951.

Schafer, R. Murray, *E. T. A. Hoffmann and Music*. Toronto: Univ. of Toronto Press, 1975.

Scott, H. A. "London's Earliest Public Concerts." *MQ* XXII (1936): 446.

Wellek, René. "The Concept of Romanticism in Literary History." In *Concepts of Criticism*. New Haven: Yale Univ. Press, ★1963.

Young, Percy M. *The Concert Tradition*. London: R. and K. Paul, 1965, ★1981.

CHAPTER II, BEETHOVEN IN VIENNA, 1792–1808

Abraham, Gerald, ed. *The Age of Beethoven, 1790–1830*. New York: Oxford Univ. Press, 1982.

Barea, Ilsa. *Vienna*. New York: Knopf, 1966.

Branscombe, P. "Music in the Viennese Popular Theatre of the Eighteenth and Nineteenth Centuries." *PRMA* XCVIII (1971–72): 101.

Landon, H. C. Robbins. *Essays on the Viennese Classical Style*. New York: Macmillan, 1970.

Ratner, Leonard. *Classic Music: Expression, Form, and Style*. New York: Schirmer Books, 1980.

———. "Harmonic Aspects of Classic Form." *JAMS* II (1949): 159.

Rosen, Charles. *The Classical Style: Haydn, Mozart, Beethoven*. New York: Viking Press, 1971. Reprint, W. W. Norton, ★1972.

Rudé, George. *Revolutionary Europe, 1783–1815*. New York: Harper & Row, ★1966.

CHAPTER III, BEETHOVEN: THE LATE YEARS, 1809–27

Droz, Jacques. *Europe between Revolutions, 1815–1848*. Trans, Robert Baldick. London: Collins, 1967, ★1980.

Johnson, Douglas. "Beethoven Scholars and Beethoven's Sketches." *19CM* II (1978–79): 3.

Kissinger, Henry Alfred. *A World Restored*. New York: Grosset & Dunlap, 1964.

Lockhart, John G. *The Peacemakers, 1814–1815*. New York: G. P. Putnam's Sons, 1934. Reprint, Ayer Co., 1968.

May, Arthur James. *The Age of Metternich, 1814–1848*. New York: Holt, Rinehart and Winston, 1967.

Talmon, J. L. *Romanticism and Revolt. Europe 1815–1848*. London: Thames & Hudson, 1967, ★1979.

Treitler, Leo. "History, Criticism, and Beethoven's Ninth Symphony." *19CM* 3 (1979–80): 193.

CHAPTER IV, BEETHOVEN'S CONTEMPORARIES: INSTRUMENTAL MUSIC

Blom, Eric. "The Prophesies of Dussek." In *Classics: Major and Minor*. London, 1956. Reprint, New York: Da Capo Press, 1972.

Dale, Kathleen. *Nineteenth Century Piano Music*. London: Oxford Univ. Press, 1954. Reprint, Da Capo Press, 1974.

Ehrlich, Cyril. *The Piano: a History*. London: Dent, 1976.

Fuller, David. "Accompanied Keyboard Music." *MQ* 60 (1974): 222.

Kirby, Frank Eugene. *A Short History of Keyboard Music*. New York: Free Press, 1966.

Krebs, Harald. "Alternatives to Monotonality in Early Nineteenth-Century Music." *JMT* 25 (1981): 1.

Loesser, Arthur. *Men, Women and Pianos: a Social History*. New York: Simon and Schuster, 1954, ★1964.

Matthews, Denis, ed., *Keyboard Music*. New York: Praeger, 1972.

Newman, William S. "Beethoven's Pianos Versus his Piano Ideals." *JAMS* 23 (1970): 484.

———. *The Sonata Since Beethoven: the Third and Final Volume of a History of the Sonata Idea*. Chapel Hill: Univ. of North Carolina Press, 1969. Rev. 2nd ed., ★1972. Rev. 3rd ed. New York: W. W. Norton, 1983.

Ringer, Alexander. "Beethoven and the London Piano-forte School." *MQ* 56 (1970): 742.

CHAPTER V, THE LIED: SCHUBERT AND HIS PREDECESSORS

Brauner, Charles S. "Irony in the Heine Lieder of Schubert and Schumann." *MQ* 67 (1981): 261.

Citron, Marcia J. "Corona Schröter: Singer, Composer, Actress." *ML* 61 (1980): 15.

Kravitt, Edward F. "The Lied in 19th-Century Concert Life." *JAMS* 18 (1965): 207.

Schwab, Heinrich Wilhelm. *Sangbarkeit, Popularität und Kunstlied: Studien zu Lied und Liedästhetik der mittleren Goethezeit, 1770–1814*. Regensburg: Bosse, 1965.

Stein, Jack Madison. *Poem and Music in the German Lied from Gluck to Hugo Wolf*. Cambridge: Harvard Univ. Press, 1971.

Stevens, Denis, ed. *A History of Song*. London: Hutchinson, 1960. Rev. ed., New York: W. W. Norton, ★1970.

Wiora, Walter. *Das deutsche Lied: zur Geschichte und Ästhetik einer musikalischen Gattung*. Wolfenbüttel: Möseler, 1971.

CHAPTER VI, THE RISE OF NINETEENTH-CENTURY OPERA

Becker, Heinz. "Die historische Bedeutung der Grand Opera." In *Beiträge zur Geschichte der Musikanschauung im 19. Jahrhundert*. Ed. Walter Salmen. Regensburg: Gustav Bosse, 1965.

Dean, Winton. "Meyerbeer's Italian Operas." In *Music and Bibliography: Essays in Honour of Alec Hyatt King*. Ed. Oliver Neighbour. New York: K. G. Saur, Clive Bingley, 1980.

———. "Opera under the French Revolution." *PRMA* 94 (1967–68): 77.

Deane, B. "The French Operatic Overture from Grétry to Berlioz." *PRMA* 99 (1972–73): 67.

Dent, Edward J. *The Rise of Romantic Opera*. Ed. Winton Dean. Cambridge: Cambridge Univ. Press, 1976, ★1979.

Dudley, W. S. "Orchestration in the Musique d'Harmonie of the French Revolution." Ph.D. dissertation, University of California, Berkeley, 1968.

Garlington, Aubrey S., Jr. "August Wilhelm von Schlegel and the German Romantic Opera." *JAMS* 30 (1977): 500.

———. "E. T. A. Hoffmann's 'Der Dichter und der Komponist' and the Creation of the German Romantic Opera." *MQ* 65 (1979): 22.

———. "German Romantic Opera and the Problem of Origins." *MQ* 63 (1977): 247.

Longyear, Rey M. "Notes on the Rescue Opera." *MQ* 45 (1959): 49.

Rushton, Julian. "Philidor and the Tragédie Lyrique." *MT* 117 (1976): 734.

Weinstock, Herbert. *Donizetti and the World of Opera in Italy, Paris and Vienna in the First Half of the Nineteenth Century*. New York: Pantheon Books, 1964.

CHAPTER VII, PARIS FROM 1830   ₁848

Carse, Adam. *The Orchestra from Beethoven to Berlioz*. Cambridge: W. Heffer & Sons, 1948.

Crosten, William L. *French Grand Opera; an Art and a Business*. New York: King's Crown Press, 1948. Reprint, Da Capo Press, 1972.

Friedland, Bea. "Louise Farrenc (1804–1875): Composer, Performer, Scholar." *MQ* 60 (1974): 257.

Guichard, Léon. *La Musique et les lettres au temps du romantisme*. Paris: Presses universitaires de France, 1955.

Loesser, Arthur. *Men, Women, and Pianos: a Social History*. New York: Simon & Schuster, 1954, ★1964.

Pendle, Karin. "Eugène Scribe and French Opera of the Nineteenth Century." *MQ* 57 (1971): 535.

Primmer, Brian. "Unity and Ensemble: Contrasting Ideals in Romantic Music." *19CM* 6 (1982–83): 97.

Schrade, Leo. *Beethoven in France*. New Haven: Yale Univ. Press, 1942. Reprint, Da Capo Press, 1978.

Smith, Patrick. *The Tenth Muse: A Historical Study of the Opera Libretto*. New York: Knopf, 1970.

Stearns, Peter N. *1848: The Revolutionary Tide in Europe*. New York: W. W. Norton, 1974.

Suttoni, C. R. "Piano and Opera: a Study of the Piano Fantasies written on Opera Themes in the Romantic Era." Ph.D. dissertation, New York University, 1973.

CHAPTER VIII, SCHUMANN AND HIS GERMAN CONTEMPORARIES

Dörffel, Alfred. *Geschichte der Gewandhausconcerte zu Leipzig*. Leipzig, 1884. Reprint, Wiesbaden: Breitkopf & Härtel, 1972.

Forchert, Arno. "Adolf Bernhard Marx und seine Berliner *Allgemeine musikalische Zeitung*." In *Studien zur Musikgeschichte Berlins im frühen 19. Jahrhundert*. Ed. Carl Dahlhaus. Regensburg: Bosse, 1980.

Longyear, Rey M. "The German Romantic Efflorescence." In *Nineteenth-Century Romanticism in Music,* Ch. 6. Englewood Cliffs, N.J.: Prentice-Hall, ★1973.

Lovejoy, Arthur O. "The Meaning of 'Romantic' in Early German Romanticism." In *Essays in the History of Ideas,* Ch. 10. Baltimore: Johns Hopkins Press, 1948. Reprint, Greenwood Press, ★1978.

Mahling, Christoph Hellmut. "Zum 'Musikbetrieb' Berlins und seinen Institutionen in der ersten Hälfte des 19. Jahrhunderts." In *Studien zur Musikgeschichte Berlins im frühen 19. Jahrhundert*. Ed. Carl Dahlhaus. Regensburg: Bosse, 1980.

Neuls-Bates, Carol. *Women in Music: an Anthology of Source Readings from the Middle Ages to the Present*. Sections 22 and 23 on Fanny Hensel and Clara Schumann. New York: Harper & Row, 1982.

Newman, William S. *The Sonata Since Beethoven: the Third and Final Volume of a History of the Sonata Idea*. Chapel Hill: Univ. of North Carolina Press, 1969. Rev. 2nd ed. ★1972. Rev. 3rd ed., New York: W. W. Norton, 1983.

Plantinga, Leon. *Schumann as Critic*. New Haven: Yale Univ. Press, 1967. Reprint, 1977.

Silz, Walter, *Early German Romanticism, its Founders and Heinrich von Kleist*. Cambridge: Harvard Univ. Press, 1929.

Strunk, Oliver, ed., "Literary Forerunners of Musical Romanticism" and "Composer Critics of the Nineteenth Century." In *Source Readings in Music History from Classical Antiquity through the Romantic Era*, Ch. 17 and 18. New York: W. W. Norton, 1950. Also available as separate volume, *1965.

CHAPTER IX, WAGNER AND THE MUSIC DRAMA

Barzun, Jacques. *Darwin, Marx, Wagner*. Boston: Little, Brown, 1941, *1981.

Guichard, Léon. *La Musique et les lettres en France au temps du wagnérisme*. Paris: Presses universitaires de France, 1963.

Hobsbawm, E. J. *The Age of Capital, 1848–1875*. New York: Scribner, 1975.

Nietzsche, Friedrich. *The Birth of Tragedy*. Trans. Francis Golffing. Garden City, N.Y.: Doubleday, 1956.

Taylor, A. J. P. *The Struggle for Mastery in Europe, 1848–1918*. Oxford: Oxford Univ. Press, 1954.

Zuckerman, Elliott. *The First Hundred Years of Wagner's Tristan*. New York: Columbia Univ. Press, 1964.

CHAPTER X, ITALIAN AND FRENCH OPERA IN THE LATER NINETEENTH CENTURY

Bury, J. P. T. *Napoleon III and the Second Empire*. London: English Universities Press, 1964.

Chapman, Guy. *The Third Republic of France: The First Phase 1871–1894*. New York: St. Martin's Press, 1962.

Fulcher, Jane. "The Orpheon Societies: 'Music for the Workers' in Second-Empire France." *IRASM* 10 (1979): 47.

Guichard, Léon. *La Musique et les lettres en France au temps du wagnérisme*. Paris: Presses universitaires de France, 1963.

Kerman, Joseph. *Opera as Drama*. New York: Alfred A. Knopf, 1956; Random House, *1956.

CHAPTER XI, NATIONALIST MUSIC

Abraham, Gerald. *On Russian Music*. London: William Reeves, 1939. Reprint, Scholarly, 1976. Reprint, Irvington, 1982.

————. "Russia." In *A History of Song,* 338. Ed. Denis Stevens. London: Hutchinson, 1960. Rev. ed., New York: W. W. Norton, ★1970.

————. *Slavonic and Romantic Music.* New York: St. Martin's Press, 1968.

————. *Studies in Russian Music.* London: William Reeves, 1935. Rev. 1969. Reprint, Scholarly, 1976.

Andreis, Josip. *Music in Croatia.* Zagreb: Institute of Musicology, 1974.

Brown, David. "Balakirev, Tchaikovsky and Nationalism." *ML* 42 (1961): 227.

Brown, Malcolm H. *Papers of the Yugoslav-American Seminar on Music.* Bloomington, Indiana: Indiana Univ. Press, 1970.

Calvocoressi, M. D., and Gerald Abraham. *Masters of Russian Music.* London: Duckworth, 1936. Reprint, Johnson, n.d.

Cooper, Martin. *Russian Opera.* London: Max Parrish, 1951.

Foster, Myles Birket. *The History of the Philharmonic Society of London, 1813–1912.* London: John Lane, The Bodley Head, 1912.

Harley, John. "Music at the English Court in the Eighteenth and Nineteenth Century." *ML* 50 (1969): 332.

Horton, John. *Scandinavian Music: a Short History.* London: Faber & Faber, 1963.

Lange, Kristian, and Arne Østvedt. *Norwegian Music.* London: D. Dobson, 1958.

Ridenour, Robert C. *Nationalism, Modernism, and Personal Rivalry in Nineteenth-Century Russian Music.* Ann Arbor: UMI Research Press, 1981.

Rimsky-Korsakov, Nicolas. *Principles of Orchestration.* Ed. M. Steinberg. Trans. Edward Agate. New York: E. F. Kalmus, 1912. Reprint, Dover, n.d.

Seaman, Gerald R. *History of Russian Music,* Vol. 1. New York: Frederick A. Praeger, 1967.

Szabolcsi, Bence. *A Concise History of Hungarian Music.* Trans. Sára Karig. Budapest: Corvina Press, 1964. 2nd enl. ed., 1974.

Taruskin, Richard. "Glinka's Ambiguous Legacy and the Birth Pangs of Russian Opera." *19CM* 1 (Nov. 1977): 142.

————. "How the Acorn Took Root: A Tale of Russia." *19CM* 6 (1982–83): 189.

————. "Opera and Drama in Russia: The Case of Serov's *Judith.*" *JAMS* 32 (1979): 74.

Temperley, Nicholas, ed. *The Athlone History of Music in Britain: Vol. V, The Romantic Age, 1800–1914.* London: The Athlone Press, 1981.

Temperley, Nicholas. "Domestic Music in England, 1800–1860." *PRMA* 85 (1959): 312.

————. "Mendelssohn's Influence on English Music." *ML* 43 (1962): 224.

Véber, Gyvla. *Ungarische Elemente in der Opernmusik Ferenc Erkels.* Bilthoven: A. B. Creyghton, 1976.

Walker, Ernest. *A History of Music in England*. London: Oxford Univ. Press, 1952.

Zetlin, Mikhail. *The Five: The Evolution of the Russian School of Music*. Trans. George Panin. New York: International Universities Press, 1959.

CHAPTER XII, CROSSCURRENTS IN THE LATE CENTURY

Cooper, Martin. *French Music from the Death of Berlioz to the Death of Fauré*. London: Oxford Univ. Press, *1969.

Fay, Amy. *Music-Study in Germany*. Chicago: Jansen, McClurg, 1881. London: Macmillan, 1886. Reprint, 1965.

Gollwitzer, Heinz. *Europe in the Age of Imperialism, 1880–1914*. Trans. David Adam and Stanley Baron. London: Thames & Hudson, 1969, *1979.

Hughes, Gervase. *Composers of Operetta*. London: Macmillan, 1962.

Kravitt, Edward F. "The Influence of Theatrical Declamation upon Composers of the Late Romantic Lied." *AcM* 34 (1962): 18.

———. "The Joining of Words and Music in Late Romantic Melodrama." *MQ* 62 1976): 571.

———. "The Orchestral Lied: an Inquiry into its Style and Unexpected Flowering around 1900." *MR* 37 (1976): 209.

———. "Tempo as an Expressive Element in the Late Romantic Lied." *MQ* 59 (1973): 497.

McGrath, William. *Dionysian Art and Populist Politics in Austria*. New Haven: Yale Univ. Press, 1974.

May, Arthur J. *Vienna in the Age of Franz Josef*. Norman, Oklahoma: Univ. of Oklahoma Press, 1966.

Meister, Barbara. *Nineteenth-Century French Song: Fauré, Chausson, Duparc, and Debussy*. Bloomington: Indiana Univ. Press, 1980.

Morgan, Robert P. "Ives and Mahler: Mutual Responses at the End of an Era." *19CM* 2 (1978–79): 72.

Myers, Rollo. *Modern French Music*. New York: Praeger, 1971.

Newlin, Dika. *Bruckner, Mahler, Schoenberg*. New York: King's Crown Press, 1947. Rev. ed., New York: W. W. Norton, 1978.

Noske, Frits. *French Song from Berlioz to Duparc: The Origin and Development of the Mélodie*. 2nd ed. Trans. and ed. Rita Benton. New York: Dover, 1970.

Pleasants, Henry, ed. and trans. *E. Hanslick: Vienna's Golden Years of Music 1850–1900*. New York, 1950. Rev. as *E. Hanslick: Music Criticisms 1849–99*. [selected writings] 1963.

COMPOSERS

Balakirev, Mily

Collected Edition   M. A. Balakirev. *Complete Piano Works* (Moscow: State Music Publishers, 1952–).

Abraham, Gerald. "Balakirev: a Flawed Genius." In *Studies in Russian Music,* 311. London: Reeves, 1936. Reprint, Scholarly, 1976.

————. "Balakirev's Music to *King Lear,*" "Balakirev's Piano Sonata," "Balakirev's Symphonies." In *On Russian Music,* 179. London: Reeves, 1939. Reprint, Scholarly, 1976.

————. "Balakirev's Symphonies." *ML* 14 (1933): 355.

Calvocoressi, M. D. "Mily Balakiref." In *Masters of Russian Music,* 97. Ed. M.D. Calvocoressi and Gerald Abraham. London: Duckworth, 1936. Reprint, Johnson, n.d.

Davis, Richard. "Henselt, Balakirev and the Piano." *MR* 28 (1967): 173–208.

Garden, Edward. *Balakirev: A Critical Study of his Life and Music.* London: Faber and Faber, 1967.

Beethoven, Ludwig van

Collected Editions   L. van Beethovens Werke: Vollständige kritisch durchgesehene überall berechtigte Ausgabe 1–24 (Leipzig, 1862–65); 25 (Leipzig, 1888).

L. van Beethoven: Sämtliche Werke: Supplemente zur Gesamtausgabe. Ed. W. Hess. Wiesbaden, 1959–71.

L. van Beethoven: Werke: neue Ausgabe sämtlicher Werke. Ed. J. Schmidt-Görg and others. Munich and Duisburg: G. Henle, 1961–.

Works Catalogues   Hess, Willy. *Verzeichnis der nicht in der Gesamtausgabe veröffentlichten Werke Ludwig van Beethovens.* Wiesbaden: Breitkopf & Härtel, 1957.

Kinsky, Georg, and Hans Halm. *Das Werk Beethovens: thematisch-bibliographisches Verzeichnis seiner sämtlichen vollendeten Kompositionen.* Munich and Duisburg: G. Henle, 1955.

Anderson, Emily, ed. and trans. *The Letters of Beethoven.* New York: St. Martin's Press, 1961.

Arnold, Denis, and Nigel Fortune. *The Beethoven Companion.* London: Faber, 1971.

Berlioz, Hector. *Beethoven: a Critical Appreciation of Beethoven's Nine Symphonies and his Only Opera, Fidelio, with its Four Overtures.* Trans. and ed. Ralph DeSola [selections from *A travers chants*]. Boston: Crescendo Publishing Co., 1975.

Brandenburg, Sieghard. "The First Version of Beethoven's G major String Quartet, Op. 18, No. 2." *ML* 58 (1977): 127.

———. "The Historical Background to the 'Heiliger Dankgesang' in Beethoven's A-minor Quartet, op. 132." In *Beethoven Studies* 3. Ed. Alan Tyson. Cambridge: Cambridge Univ. Press, 1982.

Cooper, Martin. *Beethoven: the Last Decade, 1817–1827.* London: Oxford Univ. Press, 1970.

Forbes, Elliot, ed. *L. van Beethoven: Symphony No. 5 in C minor.* Norton Critical Score. New York: W. W. Norton, *1971.

Gossett, Philip. "Beethoven's Sixth Symphony: Sketches for the First Movement." *JAMS* 27 (1974): 248.

Grove, Sir George. *Beethoven's Nine Symphonies.* London: Novello, 1884. Reprint, New York: Dover, *1962.

Johnson, Douglas. "Beethoven's Sketches for the Scherzo of the Quartet, Op. 18, no. 6." *JAMS* 23 (1970): 385.

———, and Alan Tyson. "Reconstructing Beethoven's Sketchbooks." *JAMS* 25 (1972): 137.

Kerman, Joseph. "An die ferne Geliebte." In *Beethoven Studies* 1, 123. Ed. Alan Tyson. New York: W. W. Norton, 1973.

———. *Ludwig van Beethoven: Autograph Miscellany from circa 1786 to 1799.* London: Trustees of the British Museum, 1970.

———. *The Beethoven Quartets.* New York: A. A. Knopf, 1967, Reprint W. W. Norton, *1979.

Kerman, Joseph and Alan Tyson. *The New Grove Beethoven.* New York: W. W. Norton, *1983.

Kinderman, William. "The Evolution and Structure of Beethoven's 'Diabelli' Variations." *JAMS* 35 (1982): 306.

Kirkendale, Warren. "The 'Great Fugue' Op. 133: Beethoven's 'Art of Fugue.' " *AcM* 35 (1963): 14.

Kramer, Richard. "Notes to Beethoven's Education." *JAMS* 28 (1975): 72–101.

Landon, H. C. Robbins, ed. *Beethoven: a Documentary Study.* London: Macmillan, 1970.

Lang, Paul Henry, ed. *The Creative World of Beethoven.* New York: W. W. Norton, *1971.

Lockwood, Lewis. "Beethoven's Sketches for Sehnsucht (WoO 146)." In *Beethoven Studies* 1, 97. Ed. Alan Tyson. New York: W. W. Norton, 1973.

———. "On Beethoven's Sketches and Autographs: Some Problems of Definition and Interpretation." *AcM* 42 (1970): 32.

———. "The Autograph of the First Movement of Beethoven's Sonata for Violoncello and Pianoforte, Opus 69." *MF* 2 (1970): 1–109

———. " 'Eroica' Perspectives: Strategy and Design in in the First Movement." In *Beethoven Studies* 3. Ed. Alan Tyson. Cambridge: Cambridge Univ. Press, 1982.

MacArdle, Donald, and Ludwig Misch. *New Beethoven Letters.* Norman: Univ. of Oklahoma Press, 1957.

Mann, Alfred. "Beethoven's Contrapuntal Studies with Haydn." *MQ* 56 (1970): 711.

Mitchell, William J. "Beethoven's La Malinconia from the String Quartet, Opus 18, No. 6: Technique and Structure." *MF* 3 (1973): 269.

Newman, William S. *Performance Practices in Beethoven's Piano Sonatas: an Introduction.* New York: W. W. Norton, 1971.

Schenker, Heinrich. *Beethovens neunte Sinfonie.* Vienna: Universal-Edition, 1912.

Scherman, Thomas, and Louis Biancolli, eds. *The Beethoven Companion.* Garden City, New York: Doubleday, 1972.

Schindler, Anton Felix. *Beethoven as I knew Him.* Ed. D. W. MacArdle. Trans. Constance S. Jolly. Chapel Hill: Univ. of North Carolina Press, 1966. Reprint, New York: W. W. Norton, ★1972.

Schmidt-Görg, Joseph, and Hans Schmidt, eds. *Ludwig van Beethoven.* New York: Praeger, 1970.

Schrade, Leo. *Beethoven in France: The Growth of an Idea.* New Haven: Yale Univ. Press, 1942.

Solomon, Maynard. *Beethoven.* New York: Schirmer Books, 1977.

———. "Beethoven; the Nobility Pretense." *MQ* 61 (1975): 272.

———. "The Creative Periods of Beethoven." *MR* 34 (1973): 30.

———. "Beethoven's Tagebuch of 1812–1818." In *Beethoven Studies* 3. Ed. Alan Tyson. Cambridge: Cambridge Univ. Press, 1982.

Sonneck, Oscar George, ed. *Beethoven: Impressions of Contemporaries.* New York: G. Schirmer, 1926. Reprint, ★1967.

Sterba, Editha and Richard. *Beethoven and His Nephew: a Psychoanalytic Study of their Relationship.* New York: Pantheon, 1954, 1981.

Thayer, Alexander W. *Thayer's Life of Beethoven.* Rev. Elliot Forbes. Princeton: Princeton Univ. Press, 1964, ★1967.

Tovey, Donald Francis. *A Companion to Beethoven's Pianoforte Sonatas: Bar-to-Bar Analysis.* London: Associated Board of the Royal Schools of Music, 1931. Reprint, New York: AMS Press, 1976.

Tyson, Alan. "A Reconstruction of the Pastoral Symphony Sketchbook." In *Beethoven Studies* 1, 67. Ed. Alan Tyson. New York: W. W. Norton, 1973.

———. "The Authors of the Op. 104 String Quintet." In *Beethoven Studies* 1, 158. Ed. Alan Tyson. New York: W. W. Norton, 1973.

———. "The Problem of Beethoven's 'First' *Leonore* Overture." *JAMS* 28 (1975): 292.

———, ed. *Beethoven Studies,* 1. New York: W. W. Norton, 1973; 2. London: Oxford Univ. Press, 1977; 3. Cambridge: Cambridge Univ. Press, 1982.

Winter, Robert. "Plans for the Structure of the String Quartet in C sharp minor." In *Beethoven Studies* 2, 106. Ed. Alan Tyson. London: Oxford Univ. Press, 1977.

Bellini, Vincenzo

Brauner, Charles S. "Textual Problems in Bellini's *Norma* and *Beatrice di Tenda.*" *JAMS* 29 (1976): 99.

Brunel, Pierre. *Vincenzo Bellini.* Paris: Fayard, 1981.

Lippmann, Friedrich. "Vincenzo Bellini." In *The New Grove Masters of Italian Opera*, 155. New York: W. W. Norton, ★1983.

———. "Vincenzo Bellini und die italienische Opera seria seiner Zeit," *Analecta musicologica* 6 (1969): 365.

Orrey, Leslie. *Bellini.* London: Dent, 1969.

———. "The Literary Sources of Bellini's First Opera." *ML* 55 (1974): 24.

Berlioz, Hector

Collected Editions *Hector Berlioz: Werke.* Ed. C. Malherbe and F. Weingartner. Leipzig, 1900–10.

New Berlioz Edition. Ed. H. Macdonald and others. Kassel, 1967–.

Works Catalogue Hopkinson, Cecil. *A Bibliography of the Musical and Literary Works of Hector Berlioz, 1803–1869, with Histories of the French Music Publishers Concerned.* 2nd ed. Tunbridge Wells: R. Macnutt, 1980.

Barzun, Jacques. "Berlioz a Hundred Years After." *MQ* 56 (1970): 1.

———. *Berlioz and the Romantic Century.* Boston: Little, Brown, 1950. 3rd ed., 1969.

Berlioz, Hector. *Mémoires* (Paris, 1870). Trans. David Cairns. London, 1969. Reprint as *The Memoirs of Hector Berlioz.* New York: W. W. Norton, ★1975.

Bloom, Peter. "A Return to Berlioz' *Retour à la vie.*" *MQ* 64 (1978): 354.

———. "Berlioz à l'Institut Revisited." *AcM* 53 (1981): 171.

———. "Orpheus' Lyre Resurrected: a tableau musical by Berlioz." *MQ* 61 (1975): 189.

Cairns, David. "Berlioz and Virgil." *PRMA* 95 (1968–69): 97.

———. "Spontini's Influence on Berlioz." In *From Parnassus: Essays in Honor of Jacques Barzun*, 25. Ed. Dora B. Weiner and William R. Keylor. New York: Harper & Row, 1976.

Citron, Pierre, ed. *Correspondance générale* I, 1803–1832; II, 1832–1842. Paris: Flammarion, 1972, 1975.

Cone, Edward T., ed. *Berlioz: Fantastic Symphony.* Norton Critical Score. New York: W. W. Norton, ★1971.

Crabbe, John. *Hector Berlioz: Rational Romantic*. London: Kahn and Averill, 1980.

Dickinson, A. E. F. "Berlioz's Songs." *MQ* 55 (1969): 329.

Elliott, John R., Jr. "The Shakespeare Berlioz Saw." *ML* 57 (1976): 292.

Friedheim, Philip. "Radical Harmonic Procedures in Berlioz." *MR* 21 (1960): 282.

Holoman, Dallas Kern. *The Creative Process in the Autograph Musical Documents of Hector Berlioz, ca. 1818–1840*. Ann Arbor: UMI Research Press, 1980.

————. "The Present State of Berlioz Research." *AcM* 47 (1975): 31–67.

Hopkinson, Cecil. "Berlioz and the Marseillaise," *ML* 51 (1970): 435.

Macdonald, Hugh. *Berlioz Orchestral Music*. London: BBC, 1969.

————. "Berlioz's Self-borrowings." *PRMA* 92 (1965–66): 27.

————. "Hector Berlioz 1969: a Centenary Assessment." *Adam* 34 (1969): 35.

————. "The Original 'Benvenuto' Cellini." *MT* 107 (1966): 1042.

Newman, Ernest. *Berlioz, Romantic and Classic: Writings by Ernest Newman*. Ed. Peter Heyworth. London: Gollancz, 1972.

Plantinga, Leon. "Berlioz's Use of Shakespearian Themes." *Yale French Studies* 33 (1964): 72.

Primmer, Brian. *The Berlioz Style*. London: Oxford Univ. Press, 1973.

Rushton, Julian. "The Genesis of Berlioz's 'La Damnation de Faust.' " *ML* 56 (1975): 129.

Temperley, Nicholas. "The Symphonie Fantastique and its Program." *MQ* 57 (1971): 593.

Berwald, Franz

Collected Edition   *Franz Berwald. Sämtliche Werke*. Editionsleitung Berwald-Kommittén. Kassel: Bärenreiter, 1966–82.

Berwald, Franz. *Franz Berwald: die Dokumente seines Lebens*. Ed. Erling Lomnäs and others. Kassell: Bärenreiter, 1979.

Layton, Robert. *Franz Berwald*. Forward by Gerald Abraham. London: A. Blond, 1959.

Bizet, Georges

Curtiss, Mina. *Bizet and his World*. New York: A. Knopf, 1958, ★1974.

————. "Bizet, Offenbach, and Rossini." *MQ* 40 (1954): 350.

Dean, Winton. "Bizet's Self-borrowings:" *ML* 41 (1960) 238.

————. *Georges Bizet: His Life and Work*. London: J.M. Dent, 1948. 3rd ed., 1975.

————. "The True Carmen?" *MT* 106 (1965): 846.

Klein, John W. "Georges Bizet's Tragic Son." *ML* 49 (1968): 357.

Shanet, Howard. "Bizet's Suppressed Symphony." *MQ* 44 (1958); 461.

Tiersot, Julien. "Bizet and Spanish Music." *MQ* 13 (1927): 566.

Borodin, Alexander

Abraham, Gerald. "Arab Melodies in Rimsky-Korsakov and Borodin." *ML* 56 (1975): 313.

————. "Borodin as a Symphonist," *"Prince Igor."* In *Studies in Russian Music,* 102, 119. London: William Reeves, 1936.

————. *Borodin: The Composer and his Music.* London: William Reeves, 1927. Reprint, AMS Press, n.d.

————. "The History of Prince Igor," "Borodin's Songs." In *On Russian Music,* 147, 169. London: William Reeves, 1939.

Bobéth, Marek. *Borodin und seine Oper Fürst Igor: Geschichte, Analyse, Konsequenzen.* Munich: Katzbichler, 1982.

Calvocoressi, M. D. "Alexander Borodin." In *Masters of Russian Music.* Ed. M. D. Calvocoressi and Gerald Abraham, 155. London: Duckworth, 1936.

————. "Borodin Revisited." *MT* 65 (1924): 1086.

Findeyzen, N. "Borodin's Musical Legacy." *MMR* 57 (1927): 34, 74.

Lloyd-Jones, David. "The Bogatyrs: Russia's First Operetta." *MMR* 89 (1959): 123.

————. "Borodin in Heidelberg." *MQ* 46 (1960): 500.

————. "Borodin on Liszt." *ML* 42 (1961): 117.

Brahms, Johannes

Collected Edition   *Johannes Brahms sämtliche Werke.* Ed. H. Gál (I–X) and E. Mandyczewski (XI–XXVI). Leipzig, 1926–27.

Works Catalogues   Ehrmann, Alfred von. *Johannes Brahms: thematisches Verzeichnis seiner Werke.* Leipzig: Breitkopf & Härtel, 1933.

Hofmann, Kurt. *Die Erstdrucke der Werke von Johannes Brahms.* Tutzing: Hans Schneider, 1975.

McCorkle, Donald, and Margit, eds. *Thematisches Verzeichnis.* Munich: Henle, in prep.

Barkan, Hans, ed. *Johannes Brahms and Theodor Billroth: Letters from a Musical Friendship.* Norman, Oklahoma: Univ. of Oklahoma Press, 1957.

Bickley, Nora, trans. *Letters From and To J. Joachim.* London: Macmillan, 1914.

Boyer, Thomas. "Brahms as Count Peter of Province: A Psychosexual Interpretation of the *Magelone* Poetry." *MQ* 66 (1980): 262.

Clapham, John. "Dvořák's Relations with Brahms and Hanslick." *MQ* 57 (1971): 241.

Dale, Kathleen. *Brahms: a Biography with a Survey of Books, Editions & Recordings.* Hamden, Connecticut: Shoe String Press, 1970.

Dunsby, Jonathan. *Structural Ambiguity in Brahms: Analytic Approaches to Four Works.* Ann Arbor: UMI Research Press, 1981.

Forte, Allen. "Motive and Rhythmic Contour in Brahms's Alto Rhapsody." *JMT* 27 (1983).

———. "Motivic and Structural Levels in the First Movement of Brahms's C minor String Quartet." *MQ* 69 (1983).

———. "The Structural Origin of Exact Tempi in the Brahms Haydn Variations." *MR* 18 (1957: 138.

Fox Strangways, A. H. "Brahms and Tieck's 'Magelone.' " *ML* 21 (1940): 211.

Frisch, Walter. "Brahms, Developing Variation, and the Schoenberg Critical Tradition." *19CM* 5 (Spring 1982): 215.

Gál, Hans. *Johannes Brahms: His Work and Personality.* Trans. Joseph Stein. Westport, Connecticut: Greenwood Press, 1977.

Geiringer, Karl. "Brahms and Wagner, with Unpublished Letters." *MQ* 22 (1936): 178.

———. *Brahms, His Life and Work.* Trans. H. B. Weiner and B. Miall. Boston: Houghton Mifflin, 1936. Rev. ed., 1947.

Harrison, Max. *The Lieder of Brahms.* New York: Praeger, 1972.

Harrison, Julius A. *Brahms and his Four Symphonies.* London: Chapman & Hall, 1939.

Horton, John. *Brahms Orchestral Music.* Seattle: Univ. of Washington Press, 1969.

Kalbeck, Max. *Johannes Brahms.* Berlin: Deutsche Brahms-Gesellschaft, 1904–14. Reprint, 1976.

Kinsey, Barbara. "Mörike Poems Set by Brahms, Schumann and Wolf." *MR* 29 (1968): 257.

Kirby, Frank. "Brahms and the Piano Sonata." In *Paul A. Pisk: Essays in his Honor,* 163. Ed. John Glowacki. Austin: Univ. of Texas Press, 1966.

Kross, Siegfried. "Brahms and E. T. A. Hoffmann." *19CM* 5 (1981–82): 193.

Litzmann, Berthold, ed. *Letters of Clara Schumann and Johannes Brahms, 1853–1896.* New York: Longmans, Green, 1927, ★1974.

McCorkle, Donald M. *Brahms: Variations on a Theme of Haydn, Opp. 56a and 56b.* Norton Critical Score. New York: Norton, ★1976.

——— and Margit. "Five Fundamental Problems in Brahms Source Research." *AcM* 48 (1976): 253.

Mason, Daniel G. *The Chamber Music of Brahms.* London and New York: Macmillan, 1933. 2nd ed., 1950.

Musgrave, Michael. "The Historical Influences in the Growth of Brahms's Requiem." *ML* 53 (1972): 3.

Redlich, Hans F. "Bruckner and Brahms Quintets in F," *ML* 36 (1955): 253.

Sams, Eric. *Brahms Songs*. London: British Broadcasting Corp., 1972.

Schoenberg, Arnold. "Brahms the Progressive." In *Style and Idea*. New York: Philosophical Library, 1950.

Truscott, Harold. "Brahms and Sonata Style." *MR* 25 (1964): 186.

Webster, James. "Schubert's Sonata Form and Brahms's First Maturity." *19CM* 2 (July 1978): 18, and 3 (July 1979): 52.

Bruckner, Anton

Collected Editions A. *Bruckner: Sämtliche Werke*. Ed. Haas, Nowak, Oeser, Orel (volumes published separately, Vienna, Leipzig, Wiesbaden).

Anton Bruckner: Gesamtausgabe. Ed. L. Nowak and F. Grasberger. Vienna, 1951–.

Cooke, Deryck. "The Bruckner Problem Simplified." *MT* 110 (1969): 20, 142, 362, 479, 828.

Dawson-Bowling, Paul. "Thematic and Tonal Unity in Bruckner's Eighth Symphony." *MR* 30 (1969): 225.

Doernberg, Erwin. *The Life and Symphonies of Anton Bruckner*. London: Barrie & Rockliff, 1960. Reprint, 1968.

Engel, Gabriel. *The Symphonies of Anton Bruckner*. Iowa City: Bruckner Society, 1955.

Grant, Parks. "Bruckner and Mahler: the Fundamental Dissimilarity of their Styles." *MR* 32 (1971):36.

Hawkshaw, Paul. "The Date of Bruckner's 'Nullified' Symphony in D Minor." *19CM* 6 (1982–83):252.

Howie, A. C. "Traditional and Novel Elements in Bruckner's Sacred Music." *MQ* 67 (1981): 544.

Kirsch, Winfried. "Die Bruckner Forschung seit 1945." *AcM* 53 (1981): 157, and 54 (1982): 208.

Kurth, Ernst. *Bruckner*. 2 vols. Berlin: Max Hesses, 1925. Reprint, 1971.

Redlich, Hans F. "Bruckner and Brahms Quintets in F." *ML* 36 (1955): 253.

———. *Bruckner and Mahler*. London: J. M. Dent, 1955. Rev. ed., 1970.

———. "Bruckner's Forgotten Symphony (No. "O")." *Music Survey* 2 (1949): 14.

Schönzeler, Hans Hubert. *Bruckner*. London and New York: Grossman, 1970.

Simpson, Robert. *The Essence of Bruckner: an Essay towards the Understanding of his Music*. London: Victor Gollancz, 1967.

———. "The Seventh Symphony of Bruckner." *MR* 8 (1947):178.

Wolff, Werner. *Anton Bruckner: Rustic Genius*. New York: E. P. Dutton, 1942.

Chabrier, Emmanuel

Delage, Roger. *Chabrier*. Geneva: Editions Minkoff & Lattès, 1982.

———. "Ravel and Chabrier." *MQ* 61 (1975): 546.

Myers, Rollo. *Emmanuel Chabrier and his Circle*. London: Dent, 1969.

Prod'homme, J.-G. "Chabrier in his Letters." *MQ* 21 (1935): 451.

Cherubini, Luigi

Damerini, Adelmo, ed. *Luigi Cherubini nel II centenario della nascita*. Florence: L. S. Olschki, 1962. Incl. cat. of works, critical bibliography, and essay on Cherubini's early career.

Deane, Basil. *Cherubini*. London: Oxford Univ. Press, 1965.

Ringer, Alexander Lothar. "Cherubini's *Médée* and the Spirit of French Revolutionary Opera." In *Essays in Musicology in Honor of Dragan Plamenac*, 281. Ed. Gustave Reese. Pittsburgh: Univ. of Pittsburgh Press, 1969. Reprint, 1977.

Selden, Margery S. "Cherubini: the Italian 'Image.' " *JAMS* 17 (1964): 378.

———. "Napoleon and Cherubini." JAMS 8 (1955): 110–15.

Chopin, Frédéric

Collected Edition   F. F. Chopin: *Dziela wszystkie* [Complete works]. Ed. I. J. Paderewski. Warsaw and Kraków, 1949–61.

Works Catalogues   Brown, Maurice J. E. *Chopin: an Index of his Works in Chronological Order*. London: Macmillan, 1960. 2nd ed., 1972.

Kobylańska, Krystyna. *Frédéric Chopin: Thematisch-Bibliographisches Werkverzeichnis*. Munich: Henle, 1979.

Abraham, Gerald. *Chopin's Musical Style*. London: Oxford Univ. Press, 1939. Reprint, Greenwood Press, 1980.

———. *Slavonic and Romantic Music*. New York: St. Martin's Press, 1968.

Belotti, Gastone. *F. Chopin l'uomo*. Milan: Sapere, 1974.

Golos, George S. "Some Slavic Predecessors of Chopin." *MQ* 46 (1960): 437.

Hedley, Arthur. *Chopin*. 3rd rev. by Maurice J. E. Brown. London: Dent, 1974.

————, ed. and trans. *Selected Correspondence of Fryderyk Chopin*. London: Heinemann, 1962.

Higgins, Thomas. *Frederic Chopin: Preludes, Opus 28*. Norton Critical Score. New York: W. W. Norton, ★1973.

Hipkins, Edith J. *How Chopin Played*. London: Dent, 1937.

Kallberg, Jeffrey. Review of: William G. Attwood, *The Lioness and the Little One: the Liason of George Sand and Frédéric Chopin* (New York: Columbia Univ. Press, 1980). In *19CM* 5 (1981–82): 244.

Murdoch, William David. *Chopin: his Life*. New York: Macmillan, 1935. Reprint, Greenwood Press, 1971.

Walker, Alan, ed. *Frédéric Chopin: Profiles of the Man and the Musician*. London: Barrie & Rockliff, 1966. 2nd ed., 1973, as *The Chopin Companion*.

Zebrowski, Dariusz, ed. *Studies in Chopin*. Warsaw: The Chopin Society, 1973.

Clementi, Muzio

<u>Collected Editions</u>   *Collected Works of Muzio Clementi*. New York: Da Capo Press, 1973 [reprint of *Oeuvres de Clementi* (Leipzig, 1803–1819)].

Spada, Pietro, ed., *The Complete Symphonic Works of Muzio Clementi*. Milan: Suvini Zerboni, 1977 [some works reconstructed].

<u>Works Catalogue</u>   Tyson, Alan. *Thematic Catalogue of the Works of Muzio Clementi*. Tutzing: Hans Schneider, 1967.

Badura-Skoda, Eva. "Clementi's 'Musical Characteristics' Opus 19." In *Studies in Eighteenth-Century Music: a Tribute to Karl Geiringer,* 53. Ed. H. C. Robbins Landon. London: Oxford Univ. Press, 1970.

Graue, Jerald C. "Muzio Clementi and the Development of Pianoforte Music in Industrial England." Ph.D. dissertation, University of Illinois, 1971.

Hill, John Walter. Review of Muzio Clementi: *Opere sinfoniche complete,* Ed. Pietro Spada. In *JAMS* 32 (1979): 577.

Plantinga, Leon. *Muzio Clementi: his Life and Music*. London: Oxford Univ. Press, 1977.

————. "Clementi, Virtuosity, and the 'German Manner.' " *JAMS* 25 (1972): 303.

Saint-Foix, Georges de. "Clementi, Forerunner of Beethoven." *MQ* 17 (1931): 84.

Cramer, J. B.

Brocklehurst, J. Brian. "The Studies of J. B. Cramer and his Predecessors." *ML* 39 (1958): 256.

Graue, Jerald C. "The Clementi-Cramer Dispute Revisited." *ML* 56 (1975): 47.

King, Alec Hyatt. "Mozart and Cramer." In *Mozart in Restrospect: Studies in Criticism and Bibliography,* 112. London: Oxford Univ. Press, 1955. 3rd ed., 1970.

Tyson, Alan. "A Feud between Clementi and Cramer." *ML* 54 (1973): 281.

Cui, César

Abraham, Gerald. "Heine, Queuille, and William Ratcliff." In *Musicae scientiae collectanea; Festschrift Karl Gustav Fellerer,* 12. Ed. Heinrich Hüschen. Cologne: A. Volk, 1973.

Calvocoressi, M. D. "César Cui." In *Masters of Russian Music.* Ed. M. D. Calvocoressi and Gerald Abraham, 147. London: Duckworth, 1936.

Czerny, Carl

Badura-Skoda, Paul, ed. *On the Proper Performance of all Beethoven's Works for the Piano. Czerny's Reminiscences of Beethoven and Chapters II and III from Volume IV of the Complete Theoretical and Practical Piano Forte School, op. 500.* Vienna: Universal Edition, 1970.

Czerny, Carl. *Erinnerungen aus meinem Leben.* Vienna, 1842. Trans. Ernest Sanders as "Recollections from my Life." *MQ* 42 (1956): 302.

———. *Letters to a Young Lady, on the Art of Playing the Pianoforte.* Trans. J. A. Hamilton. New York: Da Capo Press, 1982.

———. *School of Practical Composition, or Complete Treatise on the Composition of All Kinds of Music.* New York: Da Capo Press, 1979.

———. *A Systematic Introduction to Improvisation on the Pianoforte [Systematische Anleitung zum Fantasieren auf dem Pianoforte].* Trans. and ed. Alice Mitchell. London: Longman, 1983.

Dale, Kathleen "The Three C's: Pioneers of Pianoforte Playing." *MR* 6 (1945): 138.

Dargomïzhsky, Alexander

Collected Edition   Separate editions of romances and songs, symphonies, . . . Ed. M. S. Pekelis. Moscow and Leningrad, 1947–67.

Abraham, Gerald. "Dargomïzhsky's Orchestral Pieces," "Glinka, Dargomïzhsky and *The Rusalka.*" In *On Russian Music,* 43, 52. London: Wm. Reeves, 1939.

———. "The Stone Guest." In *Studies in Russian Music,* 68. London: Wm. Reeves, 1936.

Baker, Jennifer. "Dargomïzhsky, Realism and *The Stone Guest.*" *MR* 37 (1976): 193.

Smith Brindle, Reginald. "The Sagra Musicale Umbra at Perugia." *MT* 96 (1955): 661 [on *The Stone Guest*].

Taruskin, Richard. "Realism as Preached and Practiced: the Russian Opera Dialogue." *MQ* 56 (1970): 431.

Donizetti, Gaetano

Ashbrook, William. *Donizetti and his Operas*. Cambridge: Cambridge Univ. Press, 1982, ★1983.

Ashbrook, William and Julian Budden. "Gaetano Donizetti." In *The New Grove Masters of Italian Opera*, 93. New York: W. W. Norton, ★1983.

Dean, Winton. "Some Echoes of Donizetti in Verdi's Operas." *3° Congresso internazionale di studi verdiani*, 122. Milan: 1972.

Dent, Edward J. "Donizetti: an Italian Romantic." In *Fanfare for Ernest Newman*. Ed. Van Thal. London: A. Barker, 1955. Reprint in *Journal of the Donizetti Society* 2 (1975): 249.

Messenger, M. F. "Donizetti, 1840: 3 'French' Operas and their Italian Counterparts." *Journal of the Donizetti Society* 2 (1975): 99.

Weinstock, Herbert. *Donizetti and the World of Opera in Italy, Paris and Vienna in the First Half of the Nineteenth Century*. New York: Pantheon Books, 1964. Reprint, Octagon, 1979.

Dusík, Jan Ladislaus

Collected Editions   *Collected Works of Jan Ladislaus Dussek* (Leipzig, 1813–17). Reprint, Da Capo Press, 1976.

J. L. Dussek: Selected Piano Works. Ed. H. A. Craw. Madison, Wisconsin, 1977.

Works Catalogue   Craw, Howard Allen. *A Biography and Thematic Catalog of the Works of J. L. Dussek (1760–1812)*. Ph.D. dissertation, University of Southern California, 1964.

Grossman, Orin. *Collected Works of Jan Ladislaus Dussek*. Vol. I, introduction. New York: Da Capo Press, 1978.

———. "The Piano Sonatas of Jan Ludislav Dussek (1760–1812)." Ph.D. dissertation, Yale University, 1975.

Klíma, Stanislas V. "Dussek in England." *ML* 41 (1960): 146.

Ringer, Alexander. "Beethoven and the London Pianoforte School." *MQ* 56 (1970): 742.

Truscott, Harold. "Dussek and the Concerto." *MR* 16 (1955): 29.

Dvořák, Antonín

Collected Editions   A. *Dvořák: souborné vydání* [Complete Edition]. Ed. O. Šourek and others. Prague, 1955–.

Beveridge, David. "Sophisticated Primitivism: the Significance of Pentatonicism in Dvořák's *American* Quartet." *Current Musicology* 24 (1977): 25.

Works Catalogue   Burghauser, Jarmil. *Antonin Dvořák: thematický katalog, bibliografie, přehled života a díla* [Thematic Catalogue, Bibliography, Survey of Life and Works]. Prague: Státní nakladatelství krásné literatury . . . , 1960.

Clapham, John. *Dvořák.* New York: W. W. Norton, 1979.

————. "Dvořák on the American Scene." *19CM* 5 (Summer 1981): 16.

————. "Dvořák's Cello Concerto, a Masterpiece in the Making." *MR* 40 (1979): 123.

————. "Dvořák's First Contacts with England." *MT* 119 (1978): 758.

————. "Dvořák's Musical Directorship in New York." *ML* 48 (1967): 40.

————. "Dvořák's Relations with Brahms and Hanslick." *MQ* 57 (1971): 241.

————. "Dvořák's Symphony in D minor—the Creative Process." *ML* 42 (1961): 103.

————. "The Evolution of Dvořák's Symphony 'From the New World.' " *MQ* 44 (1958): 167.

————. "Indian Influence on Dvořák's American Chamber Music." In *Musica cameralis:* (Brno VI 1971): 174.

————. "The National Origins of Dvořák's Art." *PRMA* 89 (1962–63): 75.

Hanslick, Eduard. "Anton Dvořák." *Musical Review* I / 9 (New York, 11 Dec. 1879): 141.

Harrison, Julius. "Antonin Dvořák." In *The Symphony* I. Ed. Robert Simpson. Newton Abbot: David & Charles, 1972.

Layton, Robert. *Dvořák's Symphonies and Concertos.* London: BBC, *1978.

Šourek, Otakar. *Anton Dvořák; his Life and Works.* New York: Philosophical Library, 1954.

————. *Antonín Dvořák; Letters and Reminiscences.* Trans. Roberta Samsour. Prague: Artia, 1954. Reprint, Da Capo Press, 1983.

————. *The Orchestral Works of Antonín Dvořák.* Trans. Roberta Samsour. Prague: Artia, 1958. Reprint, Greenwood Press, n.d.

Fauré, Gabriel

Cooper, Martin. "Some Aspects of Fauré's Technique." *MMR* 75 (1945): 75.

Copland, Aaron. "Gabriel Fauré, a Neglected Master." *MQ* 10 (1924): 573.

Lockspeiser, Edward. "Fauré and the Song." *MMR* 75 (1945): 79.

Orledge, Robert. "Fauré's 'Pelléas et Mélisande.' " *ML* 56 (1975): 170.

————. *Gabriel Fauré*. London: Eulenburg, 1979.

Orrey, Leslie. "The Songs of Gabriel Fauré." *MR* 6 (1945): 72

Suckling, Norman. "The Unknown Fauré." *MMR* 75 (1945): 84.

Vuillermoz, Émile. *Gabriel Fauré*. Trans. Kenneth Schapin. Philadelphia: Chilton, 1969. Reprint Da Capo Press, 1983.

Field, John

Works Catalogue Hopkinson, Cecil. *A Bibliographical Thematic Catalogue of the Works of John Field, 1782–1837*. London: Harding & Curtis, 1961.

Branson, David. *John Field and Chopin*. New York: St. Martin's Press, 1972.

Nikolaev, Aleksandr Aleksandrovich. *John Field*. Trans. Harold M. Cardello. New York: Musical Scope Publishers, 1973.

Piggot, Patrick. *The Life and Music of John Field*. Berkeley: Univ. of California Press, 1973.

Temperley, Nicholas. "John Field's Life and Music." *MT* 115 (1974): 386.

————. "John Field and the First Nocturne." *ML* 56 (1975): 335.

Franck, César

Works Catalogue Mohr, Wilhelm. *César Franck*. 2nd ed. Tutzing: H. Schneider, 1969 [includes thematic catalogue of published works].

Davies, Laurence. *César Franck and His Circle*. London: Barrie & Jenkins, 1970.

————. *Franck*. London: Dent, 1973.

Franz, Robert

Works Catalogue Boonin, Joseph M. *An Index to the Solo Songs of Robert Franz*. Hackensack, N.J.: J. Boonin, 1970.

Porter, Ernest. "Robert Franz on Song." *MR* 26 (1965): 15.

————. "The Songs of Robert Franz," *MT* 104 (1963): 477.

Glinka, Mikhail

Collected Edition M. I. Glinka. *Polnoye sobraniye sochineniy*. Ed. V. Ya. Shebalin and others. Moscow, 1955–69.

Abraham, Gerald. "Glinka and his Achievement." In *Studies in Russian Music* 21. London: William Reeves, 1936.

————. "A Life for the Tsar," "Ruslan and Lyudmilla," "Glinka,

Dargomïzhsky and the Rusalka." In *On Russian Music,* 1–51. London: William Reeves, 1939.

Brown, David. *Mikhail Glinka: A Biographical and Critical Study.* London: Oxford Univ. Press, 1974.

Glinka, Mikhail Ivanovich. *Memoirs.* Trans. Richard B. Mudge. Norman, Oklahoma: Univ. of Oklahoma Press, 1963.

Gottschalk, Louis Moreau

Works Catalogues   Doyle, John G. *Louis Moreau Gottschalk, 1829–1869: A Bibliographical Study and Catalog of Works.* Detroit: Information Coordinators, 1983.

Offergeld, Robert. *The Centennial Catalogue of the Published and Unpublished Compositions of Louis Moreau Gottschalk.* New York: Stereo Review, 1970.

Howard, John T. "Louis Moreau Gottschalk, as Portrayed by Himself." *MQ* 18 (1932): 120.

Lindstrom, Carl E. "The American Quality in the Music of Louis Moreau Gottschalk." *MQ* 31 (1945): 356.

Gounod, Charles

Cooper, Martin. "Charles Gounod and his influence on French Music." *ML* 21 (1940): 50.

Curtiss, Mina. "Gounod before *Faust.*" *MQ* 38 (1952): 48.

Hannas, Ruth. "Gounod and Alfred William Phillips." *MQ* 45 (1959): 508.

Harding, James. *Gounod.* New York: Stein & Day, 1973.

Marix-Spire, Thérèse. "Gounod and his First Interpreter, Pauline Viardot." *MQ* 31 (1945): 193, 299.

Grétry, André-Ernest-Modeste

Collected Edition   *A.-E.-M Grétry: Collection complète des oeuvres.* Ed. F. A. Gevaert, A. Wotquenne, and others. Leipzig, 1884–1936.

Clercx, Suzanne. *Grétry, 1741–1813.* Brussels: La Renaissance du Livre, 1944. Reprint, AMS Press, n.d.

———. "Le rôle de l'Académie Philharmonique de Bologne dans la formation d'A. M. Grétry." *Quadrivium* 8 (1967): 75.

Pendle, Karin. "The Opéras Comiques of Grétry and Marmontel." *MQ* 62 (1976): 409.

Grieg, Edvard

Collected Edition   E. Grieg: Gesamtausgabe / Complete Works. Frankfurt a / M, 1977–.

Works Catalogue   Fog, Dan. _Grieg-Katalog: Verzeichnis der im Druck erschienenen Kompositionen von Edvard Grieg._ Copenhagen: Dan Fog, 1980.

Abraham, Gerald. _Grieg: a Symposium._ London: Lindsay Drummond, 1948. Reprint, Greenwood Press, 1972.

Dale, Kathleen. "Edvard Grieg's Pianoforte Music." _ML_ 24 (1943): 193.

Desmond, Astra. "Grieg's Songs." _ML_ 22 (1941): 333.

Grainger, Percy. "Personal Recollections of Grieg." _MT_ 48 (1907): 720.

Horton, John. _Grieg._ London: Dent, 1974, *1975.

Johansen, David Monrad. _Edvard Grieg._ Trans. Madge Robertson. Princeton: Princeton Univ. Press, 1938.

Hensel, Fanny Mendelssohn

Elvers, Rudolf. "Verzeichnis der Musik-Autographen von Fanni Hensel im Mendelssohn-Archiv zu Berlin." In _Mendelssohn Studien,_ (Berlin, 1972): 169.

———. _"Weitere Quellen zu den Werken von Fanni Hensel."_ In _Mendelssohn Studien_ 2 (Berlin, 1975): 215.

Hensel, Sebastian, ed. _The Mendelssohn Family (1729–1847)._ Trans. Carl Klingemann. New York: 1882.

Sirota, Victoria Ressmeyer. "The Life and Works of Fanny Mendelssohn Hensel." DMA dissertation, Boston University, 1981.

Hoffmann, E. T. A.

Collected Editions   E. T. A. Hoffmann: Musikalische Werke. Ed. G. Becking. Leipzig, 1922–27.

E. T. A. Hoffmann: Ausgewählte musikalische Werke. Ed. G. von Dadelsen and others. Mainz, 1970–.

Works Catalogue   Allroggen, Gerhard. _E. T. A. Hoffmanns Kompositionen: ein chronologisch-thematisches Verzeichnis seiner musikalischen Werke mit einer Einführung._ Regensburg: Gustav Bosse, 1970.

Garlington, Aubrey S. "Notes on Dramatic Motives in Opera: Hoffmann's _Undine._" _MR_ 32 (1971): 136.

Hoffmann, E. T. A. _Selected Writings of E. T. A. Hoffmann._ Ed. and trans. Leonard J. Kent and Elizabeth C. Knight. 2 vols. Chicago: Univ. of Chicago Press, 1969.

Schafer, R. Murray. _E. T. A. Hoffmann and Music._ Toronto: Univ. of Toronto Press, 1975.

Hummel, Johann Nepomuk

Works Catalogue   Zimmerschied, Dieter. *Thematiches Verzeichnis der Werke von Johann Nepomuk Hummel*. Hofheim am Taunus: F. Hofmeister, 1971.

Brock, David G. "The Church Music of Hummel." *MR* 31 (1970): 249.

Mitchell, Francis Humphries. "The Piano Concertos of Johann Nepomuk Hummel." Ph.D. dissertation, Northwestern University, 1957.

Sachs, Joel. "A Checklist of the Works of Johann Nepomuk Hummel." *Notes* 30 (1973–74): 732.

———. "Hummel and the Pirates: the Struggle for Musical Copyright." *MQ* 59 (1973): 31.

———. *Kapellmeister Hummel in England and France*. Detroit Monographs in Musicology, 6. Detroit: Information Coordinators, 1977.

d'Indy, Vincent

Davies, Laurence. "The French Wagnerians." *Opera* 19 (1968): 351.

Demuth, Norman. *Vincent d'Indy, 1851–1931: Champion of Classicism*. London: Rockliff, 1951.

Paul, Charles B. "Rameau, d'Indy, and French Nationalism." *MQ* 58 (1972): 46.

Le Sueur, Jean-François

Works Catalogue   Mongrédien, Jean. *Catalogue thematique de l'oeuvre complète du compositeur Jean-François Le Sueur (1760–1837)*. New York: Pendragon Press, 1980.

Barzun, Jacques. *Berlioz and the Romantic Century*. Boston: Little, Brown, 1950. 3rd ed., 1969.

Charlton, David. "Ossian, Le Sueur and Opera." *Studies in Music* 11 (1977): 37.

Mongrédien, Jean. *Jean François Le Sueur: Contribution à l'étude d'un demi-siècle de musique française: 1780–1830*. Berne: P. Lang, 1980.

Saloman, Ora. "La Cépède's 'La poétique de la musique' and Le Sueur." *AcM* 47 (1975): 144.

Liszt, Franz

Collected Editions   *Franz Liszt: Musikalische Werke*. Ed. F. Busoni, P. Raabe, and others. Leipzig 1907–36. Reprint, 1966.

Franz Liszt: New Edition of the Complete Works, 1st ser., ed. Z. Gárdonyi, I. Sulyok and I. Szelényi. Kassel and Budapest, 1970–.

Works Catalogue *Thematisches Verzeichniss der Werke, Bearbeitungen und Transcriptionen von F. Liszt.* London: H. Baron, 1965. Photo repr. of Leipzig: Breitkopf and Härtel, 1877.

Haraszti, Émile. *Franz Liszt.* Paris: A. and J. Picard, 1967.

――――. "Le Problème Liszt." *AcM* 9 (1937): 126–27.

Hugo, Howard E., ed. *The Letters of Franz Liszt to Marie zu Sayn-Wittgenstein.* Cambridge: Harvard Univ. Press, 1953.

La Mara [Ida Maria Lipsius], ed. *Letters of Franz Liszt.* Trans. Constance Bache. New York: C. Scribner, 1894.

Locke, Ralph P. "Liszt's Saint-Simonian Adventure." *19CM* 4 (Spring 1981): 209.

Longyear, Rey M. "The Text of Liszt's B Minor Sonata." *MQ* 60 (1974): 435.

Main, Alexander. "Liszt after Lamartine: 'Les Préludes.' " *ML* 60 (1979): 133.

――――. "Liszt's *Lyon:* Music and the Social Conscience." *19CM* 4 (Spring 1981): 228.

Perényi, Eleanor. *Liszt: the Artist as Romantic Hero.* Boston: Little, Brown, 1974.

Raabe, Peter. *Franz Liszt.* Stuttgart: J. G. Cotta, 1931. Rev. ed. Tutzing: Hans Schneider, 1968.

Searle, Humphrey. *The Music of Liszt.* London: Williams & Norgate, 1954.

Todd, R. Larry. "Liszt, Fantasy and Fugue for Organ on 'Ad nos, ad salutarem undam.' "*19CM* 4 (Spring 1981): 250.

Tyler, William R., trans. *The Letters of Franz Liszt to Olga von Meyendorf 1871–1886.* Cambridge: Harvard Univ. Press, 1979.

Walker, Alan. *Franz Liszt: the Man and His Music.* London: Barrie & Jenkins, 1970. 2nd ed. 1976.

――――. *Franz Liszt: The Virtuoso Years, 1811–1847.* New York: Knopf, 1983.

――――. "Liszt and the Schubert Song Transcriptions." *MQ* 67 (1981): 50.

Winklhofer, Sharon. "Liszt, Marie d'Agoult, and the 'Dante' Sonata." *19CM* 1 (July 1977): 15.

Loewe, Carl

Collected Editions *Carl Loewes Werke: Gesamtausgabe der Balladen, Legenden, Lieder und Gesänge.* Ed. M. Runze. Leipzig, 1899–1904. Reprint, 1970.

Althouse, Paul Leinbach. "Carl Loewe, 1796–1869: his Lieder, Ballads, and their Performance." Ph.D. dissertation, Yale University, 1971.

Brown, Maurice J. E. "Carl Loewe, 1796–1869." *MT* 110 (1969): 357.

Elson, James. "Carl Loewe and the Nineteenth Century German Ballad." *National Association of Teachers of Singing Bulletin* 28 (1971): 16.

Mahler, Gustav

<u>Collected Edition</u>   G. Mahler: *Sämtliche Werke: Kritische Gesamtausgabe.* Ed. Internationale Gustav Mahler Gesellschaft. Vienna, 1960–.

Bauer-Lechner, Natalie. *Recollections of Gustav Mahler*. Ed. Peter Franklin. Trans. Dika Newlin. Cambridge: Cambridge Univ. Press, 1980.

Bekker, Paul. *Gustav Mahlers Sinfonien*. Berlin: Schuster & Loeffler, 1921.

Blaukopf, Kurt, ed. and comp. *Mahler: A Documentary Study*. New York: Oxford Univ. Press, 1976.

Cooke, Deryck. *Gustav Mahler: an Introduction to his Music*. London: Faber & Faber, 1980.

De La Grange, Henry-Louis. *Mahler*. Vol. 1. New York: Doubleday, 1973.

Del Mar, Norman. *Mahler's Sixth Symphony—A Study*. London: Eulenburg Books, 1979.

Floros, Constantin. *Gustav Mahler*. Vols. 1 and 2. Wiesbaden: Breitkopf & Härtel, 1977.

Kennedy, Michael. *Mahler*. London: Dent, 1974, *1977.

McGrath, William. *Dionysian Art and Populist Politics in Austria*. New Haven: Yale Univ. Press, 1974.

Mahler, Gustav. *Selected Letters of Gustav Mahler*. Ed. Knud Martner. Trans. Eithne Wilkins, Ernest Kaiser, and Bill Hopkins. New York: Farrar, Straus and Giroux, 1979.

Mitchell, Donald. *Gustav Mahler: The Early Years*. London: Rockliff, 1958. Rev., ed. by Paul Banks and David Matthews. Berkeley: Univ. of California Press, 1980.

————. *Gustav Mahler: The Wunderhorn Years*. Boulder, Colorado: Westview Press, 1976.

Murphy, Edward W. "Sonata-rondo Form in the Symphonies of Gustav Mahler." *MR* 36 (1975): 54.

Redlich, Hans F. *Bruckner and Mahler*. London: Dent, 1955. Rev. ed., 1970.

Reilly, Edward R. *Gustav Mahler and Guido Adler: Records of a Friendship*. Cambridge: Cambridge Univ. Press, 1982.

Roman, Zoltan. "Structure as a Factor in the Genesis of Mahler's Songs." *MR* 35 (1974): 157.

Schoenberg, Arnold. "Gustav Mahler." In *Style and Idea*. New York: Philosophical Library, 1950.

Stein, Erwin. "Mahler and the Vienna Opera." *Opera* 4 (1953): 4, 145, 200, 281.

Truscott, Harold. "Some Aspects of Mahler's Tonality." *MMR* 87 (1957): 203.

Walter, Bruno. *Gustav Mahler*. Trans. James Galston. London: 1937. Reprint, *1973.

Wellesz, Egon. "The Symphonies of Gustav Mahler." *MR* 1 (1940): 2.

Werfel, Alma Mahler. *Gustav Mahler: Memories and Letters*. 3rd rev. and enl. ed., Ed. Donald Mitchell and Knud Martner. Trans. Basil Creighton. Seattle: Univ. of Washington Press, 1975.

Wiesmann, Šigrid, ed. *Gustav Mahler in Vienna*. London: Thames & Hudson, 1977.

Mascagni, Pietro

Lawrence, D. H. Introduction to *Cavalleria rusticana,* by Giovanni Verga. London: J. Cape, 1928.

Massenet, Jules

Budden, Julian. "Massenet and the French Tradition." *The Listener* 82 (1969): 865.

Harding, James. *Massenet*. London: J. M. Dent, 1970.

Méhul, Etienne-Nicolas

Charlton, David. "Motive and Motif: Méhul before 1791." *ML* 58 (1976): 362.

Ringer, Alexander. "A French Symphonist at the Time of Beethoven: Etienne-Nicolas Méhul." *MQ* 37 (1951): 543.

Mendelssohn, Felix

Collected Editions *Felix Mendelssohn-Bartholdy: Werke kritisch durchgesehene Ausgabe*. Ed. J. Rietz. Leipzig, 1874–77.

Leipziger Ausgabe der Werke Felix Mendelssohn Bartholdys. Ed. Internationale Felix-Mendelssohn-Gesellschaft. Leipzig, 1960–.

Dahlhaus, Carl, ed. *Das Problem Mendelssohn*. Regensburg: Gustav Bosse, 1974.

Devrient, Eduard. *My Recollections of Felix Mendelssohn-Bartholdy and his Letters to Me*. Trans. Natalia Macfarren. London: Richard Bentley, 1869. Reprint, New York: Vienna House, 1972.

Godwin, Joscelyn. "Early Mendelssohn and Late Beethoven." *ML* 55 (1974): 272.

Grossmann-Vendrey, Susanna. *Felix Mendelssohn-Bartholdy und die Musik der Vergangenheit*. Regensburg: Gustav Bosse, 1969.

Hiller, Ferdinand. *Mendelssohn Letters and Recollections*. Trans. M. E. von Glehn. 2nd ed. London: Macmillan, 1874. Reprint with intro. by Joel Sachs, New York: Vienna House, 1972.

Krummacher, Friedhelm. *Mendelssohn—der Komponist: Studien zur Kammermusik für Streicher*. Munich: W. Fink, 1978.

Kupferberg, Herbert. *The Mendelssohns: Three Generations of Genius*. New York: C. Scribner's Sons, 1972.

Mendelssohn, Felix. *Letters*. Trans. G. Selden-Goth. New York: Pantheon, 1945. Reprint, ★1969.

Moscheles, Felix, trans. and ed. *Letters of Felix Mendelssohn to Ignaz and Charlotte Moscheles*. Boston: Ticknor, 1888. Reprint, Freeport, N.Y., Books for Libraries Press, 1970.

Pritchard, Brian W. "Mendelssohn's Chorale Cantatas: an Appraisal." *MQ* 62 (1976): 1.

Seaton, Douglass. "The Romantic Mendelssohn: The Composition of *Die erste Walpurgisnacht.*" *MQ* 68 (1982): 398.

Thomas, Mathias. *Das Instrumentalwerk Felix Mendelssohn Bartholdys; eine systematisch-theoretische Untersuchung unter besonderer Berücksichtigung der zeitgenössischen Musiktheorie*. Göttinger musikwissenschaftliche Arbeit, 4. Kassel: Bärenreiter-Antiquariat, 1972.

Todd, R. Larry. *Mendelssohn's Musical Education: A Study and Edition of his Exercises in Composition*. Cambridge: Cambridge Univ. Press, 1983.

————. "Of Sea Gulls and Counterpoint: the Early Versions of Mendelssohn's *Hebrides* Overture." *19CM* 2 (March 1979): 197.

Werner, Eric. *Mendelssohn: A New Image of the Composer and his Age*. New York: Macmillan, 1963.

Wolff, Hellmuth Christian. "Mendelssohn and Handel." *MQ* 45 (1969): 175.

Mercadante, Saverio

Notarnicola, Biagio. *Saverio Mercadante, biografia critica*. Rome: F. Francioni, 1945. Rev. and enl. ed., 1948, as *Saverio Mercadante nella gloria e nella luce*.

Walker, Frank. "Mercadante and Verdi." *ML* 33 (1952): 311; 34 (1953): 33.

Meyerbeer, Giacomo

Becker, Heinz. *Giacomo Meyerbeer, Briefwechsel und Tagebücher*. Berlin: W. de Gruyter, 1960–.

Brent-Smith, A. E. "The Tragedy of Meyerbeer." *ML* 6 (1925): 248.

Cooper, Martin. "Giacomo Meyerbeer." In *Fanfare for Ernest Newman*, 38. Ed. Van Thal. London: A. Barker, 1955.

Dean, Winton. "Meyerbeer's Italian Operas." In *Music and Bibliog-*

raphy: Essays in Honour of Alec Hyatt King, 170. Ed. Oliver Neighbour. New York: K. G. Saur, Clive Bingley, 1980.

Istel, Edgar. "Act IV of *Les Huguenots.*" *MQ* 22 (1936): 87.

Klein, John W. "Giacomo Meyerbeer (1791–1864)." *MR* 25 (1964): 142.

Moniuszko, Stanislaw

<u>Collected Edition</u> S. Moniuszko: *Dziela* [Works]. Ed. W. Rudziński. Kraków, 1965–.

Jachimecki, Zdzislaw. "S. Moniuszko and Polish Music." *Slavonic Review* 2 (1924): 533.

————. "Stanislaus Moniuszko." *MQ* 14 (1928): 54).

Maciejewski, B. M. *Moniuszko, Father of Polish Opera.* London: Allegro Press, 1979.

Rudziński, Witold. *Moniuszko.* Kraków: Polskie Wydawnictwo Muzyczne, 1972 [in Polish; includes bibliography and discography].

Moscheles, Ignaz

<u>Works Catalogue</u> *Thematisches Verzeichniss im Druck erschienenen Compositionen von Ignaz Moscheles.* Leipzig, 1885. Reprint, 1966.

Moscheles, Charlotte. *Life of Moscheles: with selections from his Diaries and Correspondence, by his Wife.* Trans. of *Aus Moscheles Leben,* Leipzig, 1872. Adapted from German by A. D. Coleridge. London: Hurst and Blackett, 1873. Reissued as *Recent Music and Musicians as Described in the Diaries and Correspondence of Ignatz Moscheles.* New York: Da Capo Press, 1970.

Moscheles, Felix, ed. *Letters of Felix Mendelssohn to Ignaz and Charlotte Moscheles.* Boston: Ticknor, 1888.

Roche, Jerome. "Ignaz Moscheles: 1794–1870." *MT* 111 (1970): 264.

Musorgsky, Modest

<u>Collected Edition</u> M. P. *Musorgsky: Polnoye sobraniye sochineniy* [Complete Collection of His Works]. Ed. Pavel Lamm. Moscow: 1928–34. Reprint, 1969.

Brown, Malcolm Hamrick. *Musorgsky, in Memoriam, 1881–1981.* Ann Arbor: UMI Research Press, 1982.

Calvocoressi, M. D. *Modest Mussorgsky: his Life and Works.* Rev. by Gerald Abraham. London: J. M. Dent, ★1974.

Frankenstein, Alfred. "Victor Hartmann and Modeste Mussorgsky." *MQ* 25 (1939): 268.

Leyda, Jay, and Sergei Bertensson, eds. *The Musorgsky Reader: a Life of M. P. Musorgsky in Letters and Documents*. New York: W. W. Norton, 1947. Reprint, 1970.

Lloyd-Jones, David. *Boris Godunov: Critical Commentary*. London: Oxford Univ. Press, 1975.

Oldani, Robert W. "Boris Godunov and the Censor." *19CM* 2 (1978–79): 245.

Offenbach, Jacques

Faris, Alex. *Jacques Offenbach*. Boston: Faber & Faber, 1980.

Harding, James. *Jacques Offenbach: A Biography*. New York: Riverrun Press, 1980, ★1981.

Lamb, Andrew. "How Offenbach Conquered London." *Opera* 20 (1969): 932.

MacClintock, L., trans. *Orpheus in America: Offenbach's Diary of His Journey to the New World*. Bloomington, Indiana: Indiana Univ. Press, 1957.

Paganini, Niccolò

Collected Editions   *Edizione nazionale delle opere di Niccolò Paganini*. Rome: Istituto italiano per la storia della musica, 1976–80.

Courcy, Geraldine I. C. de. *Paganini, the Genoese*. Norman, Oklahoma: Univ. of Oklahoma Press, 1957. Reprint, 1977.

Kendall, Alan. *Paganini: A Biography*. London: Chappell, 1982.

Kirkendale, Warren. " 'Segreto comunicato da Paganini.' " *JAMS* 18 (1965): 394.

Pulver, Jeffrey. *Paganini, the Romantic Virtuoso.*London: H. Joseph, 1936. Reprint,1970.

Stratton, Stephen S. *Nicolo Paganini: his Life and Works*. London: "The Strad" office, 1907. Reprint, 1971.

Výborný, Zdeněk. "The Real Paganini." *ML* 42 (1961): 348.

Puccini, Giacomo

Works Catalogue   Hopkinson, Cecil. *Bibliography of the Works of Giacomo Puccini 1888–1924*. New York: Broude Bros., 1968.

Ashbrook, William. *The Operas of Puccini*. London: Cassell, 1968.

Carner, Mosco. "Giacomo Puccini." in *The New Grove Masters of Italian Opera,* 311. New York: W. W. Norton, ★1983.

———. *Puccini: a Critical Biography*. New York: Knopf, 1959. Rev. ed., 1974.

Greenfeld, Howard. *Puccini: a Biography*. New York: Putnam, 1980.

Macdonald, Ray S. *Puccini, King of Verismo*. New York: Vantage Press, 1973.

Marek, George R. *Puccini: a Biography*. New York: Simon and Schuster, 1951.

Sartori, Claudio, ed. *Puccini*. Milan: Ricordi, 1959.

Reicha, Anton

<u>*Works Catalogue*</u> Šotolová, Olga. *Antonín Reicha*. Prague: Editio Supraphon, 1977.

Newman, William. S. *The Sonata Since Beethoven: The Third and Final Volume of a History of the Sonata Idea*. Chapel Hill: Univ. of North Carolina Press, 1969. Rev. 2nd ed. ★1972. Rev. 3rd ed., New York: W. W. Norton, 1983.

Prod'homme, J.-G. "From the Unpublished Autobiography of Anton Reicha." *MQ* 22 (1936): 339.

Ries, Ferdinand

<u>*Works Catalogue*</u> Hill, Cecil. *Ferdinand Ries, A Thematic Catalogue*. Univ. of New England Monographs 1. Armidale, New South Wales: Univ. of New England, 1977.

Hill, Cecil. "Ferdinand Ries: a Preliminary List of Correspondence." *Fontes artis musicae* 23 (1976): 7.

McArdle, Donald W. "Beethoven and Ferdinand Ries." *ML* 46 (1965): 23.

Rimsky-Korsakov, Nikolay

Abraham, Gerald. "Arab Melodies in Rimsky-Korsakov and Borodin." *ML* 56 (1975): 313.

―――. *"Pskovityanka:* the Original Version of Rimsky-Korsakov's First Opera." *MQ* 54 (1968): 58.

―――. *Rimsky-Korsakov: A Short Biography*. London: Duckworth, 1945. Reprint AMS Press, n.d.

―――. "Rimsky-Korsakov as Self Critic" and "Rimsky-Korsakov's Songs." In *Slavonic and Romantic Music,* 195ff. New York: St. Martin's Press, 1968.

―――. "Rimsky-Korsakov's First Opera," "Rimsky-Korsakov's Gogol Operas," "Snow Maiden," "Sadko," "The Tsar's Bride," "Kitezh," and "The Golden Cockerel." In *Studies in Russian Music,* 142ff. London: William Reeves, 1936. Reprint, Scholarly, 1976.

―――. "Satire and Symbolism in *The Golden Cockerel." ML* 52 (1971): 46.

Feinberg, Saul. "Rimsky-Korsakov's Suite from *Le coq d'or." MR* 30 (1969): 47.

Garden, Edward. "Three Russian Piano Concertos," *ML* 60 (1979): 166.

Rossini, Gioachino

<u>Collected Editions</u>   *Quaderni: rossiniani.* 19 vols. Pesaro: Fondazione Rossini, 1954–76.

Editione critica delle opere di Gioachino Rossini. ed. B. Cagli, P. Gossett, A. Zedda. Pesaro: Fondazione Rossini, 1982.

Gossett, Philip. "Gioachino Rossini." In *The New Grove Masters of Italian Opera,* 1. New York: W. W. Norton, ★1983.

———. "Gioachino Rossini and the Conventions of Composition." *AcM* 42 (1970): 48.

———. "The Overtures of Rossini." *19CM* 3 (July 1979): 3.

———. "Rossini in Naples: Some Major Works Recovered." *MQ* 54 (1968): 316.

Michotte, Edmond. *Richard Wagner's Visit to Rossini (Paris, 1860).* Trans. Herbert Weinstock. Chicago: Univ. of Chicago Press, 1968.

Stendhal [Marie Henri Beyle]. *Vie de Rossini.* Paris, 1824. Rev. by Henri Prunières. Paris, 1922. Trans. Richard N. Coe. Seattle: Univ. of Washington Press, ★1972.

Weinstock, Herbert. *Rossini: a Biography.* New York: A. A. Knopf, 1968.

Rubinstein, Anton

Abraham, Gerald. "Anton Rubinstein: Russian Composer." *MT* 86 (1945): 361

Bennigsen, Olga. "The Brothers Rubinstein and their Circle." *MQ* 25 (1939): 407.

Maclean, Charles. "Rubinstein as Composer for the Pianoforte." *PMA* 39 (1912–13): 129.

Saint-Saëns, Camille

<u>Works Catalogue</u>   *Catalogue général et thématique des oeuvres de Saint-Saëns.* Paris: Durand, 1897. Rev. ed., 1908.

Fallon, Daniel. "Saint-Saëns and the *Concours de composition musicale* in Bordeaux." *JAMS* 31 (1978): 309.

Harding, James. *Saint-Saëns and his Circle.* London: Chapman & Hall, 1965.

Lyle, Watson. *Camille Saint-Saëns: His Life and Art.* London: Kegan Paul, 1923. Reprint, Greenwood Press, n.d.

Schubert, Franz

<u>Collected Editions</u>   *Franz Schuberts Werke: Kritisch durchgesehene Gesamtausgabe.* Ed. E. Mandyczewski, J. Brahms, and others. Leipzig, 1884–97. Reprint, 1964–69.

Franz Schubert: Neue Ausgabe sämtlicher Werke. Ed. W. Dürr, A. Feil, C. Landon, and others. Kassel, 1964–.

Works Catalogues   Deutsch, Otto Erich, ed. *Schubert: Thematic Catalogue of All His Works.* London: Dent, 1951.

————. *Franz Schubert: Thematiches Verzeichnis seiner Werke in chronologischer Folge.* Kassel: Bärenreiter, 1978.

Abraham, Gerald, ed. *The Music of Schubert.* New York: Norton, 1947. Reprint, 1969.

Armitage-Smith, Julian. "Schubert's *Winterreise,* Part I: the Sources of the Musical Text." *MQ* 60 (1974): 20.

Badura-Skoda, Eva, and Peter Branscombe, eds. *Schubert Studies: Problems of Style and Chronology.* Cambridge, New York: Cambridge Univ. Press, 1982.

Biba, Otto. "Schubert's Position in Viennese Musical Life." *19CM* 3 (November 1979): 106.

Brown, Maurice, J. E. *Schubert: a Critical Biography.* London: Macmillan, 1958. Reprint, Da Capo, 1977.

————. "Schubert: Discoveries of the Last Decade." *MQ* 47 (1961): 293.

————. "Schubert: Discoveries of the Last Decade." *MQ* 57 (1971): 351.

Brown, Maurice, J. E. with Eric Sams. *The New Grove Schubert.* New York: W. W. Norton, ★1983.

Chusid, Martin. *Schubert, Symphony in B minor ("Unfinished").* Norton Critical Score. New York: Norton, ★1968.

————. "Schubert's Overture for String Quintet and Cherubini's Overture to *Faniska.*" *JAMS* 15 (1962): 78.

Citron, Marcia J. "Schubert's Seven Complete Operas: a Musicodramatic Study." University of North Carolina, Ph.D. dissertation, 1971.

Cone, Edward T. "Schubert's Promissory Note." *19CM* 5 (Spring 1982): 233.

Coren, Daniel. "Ambiguity in Schubert's Recapitulations." *MQ* 60 (1974): 568.

Deutsch, Otto Erich, ed., *The Schubert Reader: a Life of Franz Schubert in Letters and Documents.* Trans. Eric Blom. New York: W. W. Norton, 1947.

————, ed. *Schubert: a Documentary Biography.* Trans. Eric Blom. London: J. M. Dent, 1946. Reprint, Da Capo, 1977.

————, ed. *Schubert: Memoirs by his Friends.* London: A. and C. Black, 1958.

Dürr, Walther. "Schubert and Johann Michael Vogl: A Reappraisal." *19CM* 3 (November 1979): 126.

Georgiades, Thrasybulos. *Schubert: Musik und Lyrik.* Gottingen: Vandenhoeck & Ruprecht, 1967.

Griffel, L. Michael. "A Reappraisal of Schubert's Methods of Composition." *MQ* 63 (1977): 186.

Landon, Christa. "New Schubert Finds." *MR* 31 (1970): 215.

Lewin, David. "*Auf dem Flusse:* Image and Background in a Schubert Song." *19CM* 6 (Summer 1982): 47.

Mann, Alfred. "Schubert's Lesson with Sechter." *19CM* 6 (Fall 1982): 159.

Newman, William S. "Freedom of Tempo in Schubert's Instrumental Music." *MQ* 61 (1975): 528.

Reed, John. " 'Die Schöne Müllerin' Reconsidered." *ML* 59 (1978): 411.

Rifkin, Joshua. "A Note on Schubert's Great C-Major Symphony." *19CM* 6 (Summer 1982): 13.

Sams, Eric. "Schubert's Illness Re-examined." *MT* 121 (1980): 15.

Solomon, Maynard. "Schubert and Beethoven." *19CM* 3 (November 1979): 114.

Webster, James. "Schubert's Sonata Form and Brahms's First Maturity." *19CM* 2 (July 1978): 18; 3 (July 1979): 52.

Winter, Robert. "Schubert's Undated Works, a New Chronology." *MT* 119 (1978): 498.

Schumann, Clara

Chissell, Joan. *Clara Schumann: A Dedicated Spirit*. New York: Taplinger, 1983.

Höcker, Karla. *Das Leben von Clara Schumann, geb. Wieck*. Berlin: Klopp, 1975.

Litzmann, Berthold, ed. *Letters of Clara Schumann and Johannes Brahms, 1853–1896*. New York: Longmans, Green, 1927, ★1974.

————. *Clara Schumann: an Artist's Life based on Material found in Diaries and Letters*. Trans. Grace E. Hadow. London: Macmillan, 1913. Reprint, 1972.

Pettler, Pamela Suskind. "Clara Schumann's Recitals, 1832–50." *19CM* 4 (1980–81): 70–76.

Suskind, Pamela. "Clara Wieck Schumann as Pianist and Composer: A Study of her Life and Works." Ph.D. dissertation, University of California at Berkeley, 1977.

Schumann, Robert

Collected Editions *Robert Schumann: Werke*. Ed. Clara Schumann, Johannes Brahms, and others. Leipzig, 1881–93.

Works Catalogue Hoffman, Kurt, and Siegmar Keil. *Robert Schumann: Thematisches Verzeichnis, sämtlicher im Druck erschienenen musikalischen*

Werke mit Angabe des Jahres ihres Entstehens und Erscheinens. Hamburg: Schuberth, 1982.

Abraham, Gerald, ed. *Schumann: a Symposium.* London: Oxford Univ. Press, 1952. Reprint, Greenwood Press, 1977.

Alf, Julius, and Joseph A. Kruse. *Robert Schumann, Universalgeist der Romantik: Beiträge zu seiner Persönlichkeit und seinem Werk.* Düsseldorf: Droste, 1981.

Chissell, Joan. *Schumann.* London: Dent, 1948. Rev. ed., 1967.

Dümling, Albrecht, ed. *Heinrich Heine, vertont von Robert Schumann.* Munich: Kindler, 1981.

Finson, Jon. "The Sketches for Robert Schumann's C Minor Symphony." *Journal of Musicology* 1 (1982): 395.

Hallmark, Rufus. *The Genesis of Schumann's 'Dichterliebe': a Source Study.* Ann Arbor: UMI Research Press, 1979.

———. "The Sketches for *Dichterliebe*." *19CM* 1 (1977–78): 110.

Lippman, Edward A. "Theory and Practice in Schumann's Aesthetics." *JAMS* 17 (1964): 310.

Maniates, Maria R. "The D minor Symphony of Robert Schumann." In *Festschrift für Walter Wiora,* 441. Ed. Ludwig Finscher and Christoph-Hellmut Mahling. Kassel: Bärenreiter, 1967.

Niecks, Friedrich. *Robert Schumann.* Ed. Christina Niecks. London: Dent, 1925. Reprint, AMS Press, n.d.

Plantinga, Leon. *Schumann as Critic.* New Haven: Yale Univ. Press, 1967. Reprint, 1977.

———. "Schumann's View of Romantic." *MQ* 52 (1966): 221.

Pleasants, Henry, ed. *The Musical World of Robert Schumann, a Selection from his own Writings.* New York: St. Martin's Press, 1965.

Roesner, Linda Correll. "Schumann's Revisions in the First Movement of the Piano Sonata in G Minor, Op. 22." *19CM* 1 (1977): 197.

———. "The Autograph of Schumann's Piano Sonata in F minor, Opus 14." *MQ* 61 (1975): 98.

Sams, Eric. *The Songs of Robert Schumann.* London: Methuen, 1969. 2nd ed., 1975.

Schumann, Robert. *Briefe.* Ed. G. Jansen. Leipzig: Breitkopf and Härtel, 1904.

———. *Early Letters.* Trans. May Herbert. London: George Bell, 1888.

———. Gesammelte Schriften über Musik und Musiker. Ed. M. Kreisig. Leipzig: Breitkopf and Härtel, 1914.

———. *Music and Musicians.* Trans. Fanny Raymond Ritter. London: Wm. Reeves, n.d.

———. *On Music and Musicians.* Ed. Konrad Wolff. New York: McGraw Hill, 1964, ★1982.

Siegel, Linda. "A Second Look at Schumann's *Genoveva*." *MR* 36 (1975): 17.

Thym, Jurgen. "The Solo Song Settings of Eichendorff's Poems by Schumann and Wolf." Ph.D. dissertation, Case Western Reserve University, 1974.

Walker, Alan, ed. *Robert Schumann: the Man and his Music*. London: Barrie & Jenkins, 1972. 2nd ed., 1976.

Walsh, Stephen. *The Lieder of Schumann*. New York: Praeger, 1972.

Wasielewski, Wilhelm von. *Life of Robert Schumann*. Trans. A. L. Alger, 1871. Reprint, Detroit: Information Coordinators, 1975.

Smetana, Bedřich

Collected Edition   *Souborná dila Bedřicha Smetany* [Smetana's Collected Works]. Ed. Nejedlý, Ostrčil, and others. Prague, 1924–.

Abraham, Gerald. "The Genesis of the Bartered Bride." *ML* 28 (1947): 36.

Clapham, John. " 'Dalibor': an Introduction." *Opera* 27 (1976): 890.

———. *Smetana*. London: Dent, 1972.

Tiersot, Julien. *Smetana*. Paris: Henri Laurens, 1926.

Spohr, Louis

Works Catalogue   Göthel, Folker. *Thematisch-Bibliographisches Verzeichnis der Werke von Louis Spohr*. Tutzing: Hans Schneider, 1981.

Berrett, Joshua, ed. *Louis Spohr 1784–1859: Three Symphonies 4, 6, 7*. Introductory essay, pp. xi–xxxi. New York: Garland, 1980.

Brown, Clive. "Spohr's 'Jessonda.' " *MT* 121 (1980): 94.

Gorrell, Lorraine. "The Songs of Louis Spohr." *MR* 39 (1978): 31.

Pleasants, Henry, ed. *The Musical Journey of Louis Spohr*. Norman: Univ. of Oklahoma Press, 1961.

Spohr, Louis. *Selbstbiographie*. 1860. English trans. as *Louis Spohr's Autobiography*. London: Reeves & Turner, 1865. Reprint, 1969.

Spontini, Gaspare

Abraham, Gerald. "The Best of Spontini." *ML* 23 (1942): 163.

Strauss, Johann (the younger)

Collected Edition   *Johann Strauss (Sohn). Gesamtausgabe*. Ed. Fritz Racek. Vienna: Universal, 1967–82.

Works Catalogues   Flamme, Chr., ed. *Verzeichnis der sämtlichen, im Druck erschienenen Kompositionen von Johann Strauss (Vater), Johann Strauss (Sohn), Josef Strauss und Eduard Strauss*. Walluf bei Wiesbaden: M. Sandig, 1972.

Weinmann, Alexander, ed. *Verzeichnis sämtlicher Werke von Johann Strauss, Vater und Sohn*. Vienna: L. Krenn, 1956.

Fantel, Hans. *Johann Strauss: Father and Son, and their Era*. Newton Abbot: David & Charles, 1971.

Gartenberg, Egon. *Johann Strauss; the End of an Era*. University Park, Penn.: Pennsylvania State Univ. Press, 1974.

Strauss, Richard

<u>Collected Edition</u>   *Richard Strauss Lieder Gesamtausgabe*. Ed. Franz Trenner. Fürstner: Boosey & Hawkes, 1964–65.

<u>Works Catalogue</u>   Mueller von Asow, E. H. *Richard Strauss: thematisches Verzeichnis*. Vienna: Doblinger, 1955–66.

Armstrong, Thomas. *Strauss' Tone Poems*. London: Oxford Univ. Press, 1931.

Birkin, Kenneth W. "Strauss, Zweig and Gregor: Unpublished Letters." *ML* 56 (1975): 180.

Del Mar, Norman. *Richard Strauss: a Critical Commentary on his Life and Works*. Philadelphia: Chilton Book, 1962–73. Reprint with corrections, 1978.

Jefferson, Alan. *The Life of Richard Strauss*. Newton Abbot: David & Charles, 1973.

————. *The Lieder of Richard Strauss*. New York: Praeger, 1972.

Kennedy, Michael. *Richard Strauss:* London: Dent, 1976.

Mann, William. *Richard Strauss: a Critical Study of the Operas*. London: Cassell, 1964.

Myers, Rollo, ed. *Richard Strauss & Romain Rolland: Correspondence*. Berkeley and Los Angeles: Univ. of California Press, 1968.

Newman, Ernest. *Richard Strauss*. London: J. Lane, 1908. Reprint, 1970.

Petersen, Barbara E. *Ton und Wort: the Lieder of Richard Strauss*. Ann Arbor: UMI Press, 1980.

Schuh, Willi and Franz Trenner. *Correspondence: Hans von Bülow and Richard Strauss*. Trans. Anthony Gishford. London: Boosey & Hawkes, 1955.

Strauss, Richard. *The Correspondence between Richard Strauss and Hugo von Hofmannsthal*. Trans. Hanns Hammelmann and Ewald Osers. London: Collins, 1961, *1981.

Tchaikovsky, Pyotr Il'yich

<u>Collected Edition</u>   *P. I. Tchaikovsky: Polnoye sobraniye sochineniy* [Complete Edition of Compositions]. Moscow and Leningrad, 1940–71.

<u>Works Catalogue</u>   Jurgenson, B. *Catalogue thématique des oeuvres de P. Tschaïkowsky*. New York: Am-Rus Music, n.d.

Abraham, Gerald, ed. *Tchaikovsky: a Symposium*. London: L. Drummond, 1945. Reprint, 1979.

————. "Tchaikovsky." In *Masters of Russian Music*. Ed. M. D. Calvocoressi and G. Abraham, 249. London: Wm. Reeves, 1936.

————. "Tchaikovsky Revalued." In *Studies in Russian Music,* 334. London: Wm. Reeves, 1936.

————. *The Music of Tchaikovsky*. New York: W. W. Norton, 1946, *1974.

————. "The Programme of the *Pathétique* Symphony" and *"Eugene Onegin* and Tchaikovsky's Marriage." In *On Russian Music,* 143, 225. London: Wm. Reeves, 1939.

Brown, David. *Tchaikovsky: I: The Early Years, 1840–1874.* New York: W. W. Norton, 1978.

————. *Tchaikovsky: The Crisis Years, 1874–1878.* New York: W. W. Norton, 1982.

Fiske, Roger. "Tchaikovsky's Later Piano Concertos." *Musical Opinion* 62 (1938): 17, 114, 209.

Friskin, James. "The Text of Tchaikovsky's B flat minor Concerto." *ML* 50 (1969): 246.

Garden, Edward. "Tchaikovsky and Tolstoy." *ML* 55 (1974): 307.

————. "Three Russian Piano Concertos." *ML* 60 (1979): 166.

Orlova, Alexandra. "Tchaikovsky: the Last Chapter." *ML* 62 (1981): 125.

Tchaikovsky, Peter Ilyich. *Letters to his Family: an Autobiography.* Trans. Galina von Meck. New York: Stein & Day, 1981.

Warrack, John. *Tchaikovsky*. London: Hamish Hamilton, 1973.

Weinstock, Herbert. *Tchaikovsky*. New York: A. A. Knopf, 1946. Reprint, Da Capo, 1980.

Westrup, Jack. "Tchaikovsky and the Symphony." *MT* 81 (1940): 249.

Thomas, Ambroise

Cooper, Martin. "Charles Louis Ambroise Thomas." In *The Music Masters,* Vol. 2, 189. Ed. A. L. Bacharach. London: Cassell, 1957–58.

Dean, Winton. "Shakespeare and Opera." In *Shakespeare in Music.* Ed. Phyllis Hartnoll. London: Macmillan, 1964.

Tomášek, Václav Jan

Kahl, Willi. "Das lyrische Klavierstück Schuberts und seiner Vorgänger seit 1810." *Archiv für Musikwissenschaft* 3 (1921): 56.

Loft, Abram, ed. "Excerpts from the Memoirs of J. W. Tomaschek." *MQ* 32 (1946): 244.

Simpson, Adrienne. "Beethoven through Czech Eyes." *MT* 111 (1970): 1203.

Simpson, Adrienne and Sandra Horsfall. "A Czech Composer Views his Contemporaries." *MT* 115 (1974): 287.

Verdi, Giuseppe

<u>Collected Editions</u>   The Works of Giuseppe Verdi. Ed. Philip Gossett and others. Chicago: Univ. of Chicago Press, and Milan: Ricordi, 1983–.

<u>Works Catalogues</u>   Chusid, Martin. *A Catalog of Verdi's Operas*. Hackensack, New Jersey: J. Boonin, 1974.

Hopkinson, Cecil. *A Bibliography of the Works of Giuseppe Verdi, 1813–1901*. 2 vols. New York: Broude Bros., 1973, 1978.

Badacsonyi, George. "Verdi's Two *Macbeths*." *Opera* 27 (1976): 108.

Baldini, Gabriele. *The Story of Giuseppe Verdi*. Cambridge: Cambridge Univ. Press, 1980.

Budden, Julian. *The Operas of Verdi*. 3 vols. New York: Praeger, 1973–82.

———. "The Two Traviatas." *PRMA* 99 (1972–73): 43.

Chusid, Martin. "Drama and the Key of F Major in *La traviata*." In *3° Congresso internazionale di studi verdiani*, 89. Milan, 1972.

———. "The Organization of Scenes with Arias: Verdi's Cavatinas and Romanzas." In *1° Congresso internazionale di studi verdiani*, 132. Venice, 1966.

———. "Rigoletto and Monterone: a Study in Musical Dramaturgy." *International Musicological Society Congress Report 11*, 325. Copenhagen: 1972.

Cone, Edward T. "The Stature of *Falstaff*: Technique and Content in Verdi's Last Opera." *Center* 1 (1954): 17.

Gossett, Philip. "Verdi, Ghislanzoni, and *Aïda*: the Uses of Convention." *Critical Inquiry* 1 (1974): 291.

Hopkinson, Cecil. "Bibliographical Problems concerned with Verdi and his Publishers." In *1° Congresso internazionale di studi verdiani*, 431. Venice: 1966.

Kerman, Joseph. "Verdi's Use of Recurring Themes." In *Studies in Music History: Essays for Oliver Strunk*, 495. Ed. Harold S. Powers. Princeton: Princeton Univ. Press, 1968.

Kimbell, David. *Verdi in the Age of Italian Romanticism*. Cambridge: Cambridge Univ. Press, 1981.

Lawton, David. "On the 'Bacio' Theme in *Otello*." *19CM* 1 (1977–78): 211.

Mendelsohn, Gerald. "Verdi the Man and Verdi the Dramatist." *19CM* 2 (1978–79): 110 and 214.

Noske, Frits. "Ritual Scenes in Verdi's Operas." *ML* 54 (1973): 415.

Osborne, Charles. *The Complete Operas of Verdi*. London: Victor Gollancz, 1969, *1977.

———. *Letters of Giuseppe Verdi*. London: Victor Gollancz, 1971.

Porter, Andrew. "Giuseppe Verdi." In *The New Grove Masters of Italian Opera,* 193. New York: W. W. Norton, ★1983.

———. *"Les vêpres siciliennes:* New Letters from Verdi to Scribe." *19CM* 2 (1978–79): 95.

———. "The Making of Don Carlos." *PRMA* 98 (1971–72): 73.

Rosen, David. "Verdi's 'Liber scriptus' Rewritten." *MQ* 55 (1969): 151.

Rosen, David and Andrew Porter, eds. *Verdi's* Macbeth: *A Sourcebook*. New York: W. W. Norton, 1984.

Sabbeth, Daniel. "Dramatic and Musical Organization in *Falstaff."* In *3° Congresso internazionale di studi verdiani,* 415. Milan: 1972.

Toye, Francis. *Giuseppe Verdi: his Life and Works*. London: W. Heinemann, 1931, 1946. Reprint, Vienna House, 1972.

Walker, Frank. *The Man Verdi*. New York: Alfred A. Knopf, 1962, ★1982.

Weaver, William. *Verdi: a Documentary Study*. London: Thames & Hudson, 1977.

Weaver, William, and Martin Chusid, eds. *The Verdi Companion*. New York: W. W. Norton, 1979.

Werfel, Franz, and Paul Stefan. *Verdi: the Man in his Letters*. New York: L. B. Fischer, 1942. Reprint, Scholarly, n.d.

Wagner, Richard

<u>Collected Editions</u> *Richard Wagners Werke*. Ed. M. Balling. Leipzig, 1912–29. Reprint, 1971.

R. *Wagner: Sämtliche Werke*. Ed. Carl Dahlhaus, Egon Voss, and others. Mainz, 1970–.

<u>Works Catalogue</u> Deathridge, John, Martin Geck, and Egon Voss, eds. *Richard Wagner Werk-Verzeichnis,* in prep.

Kastner, Emerich, ed. *Wagner-Catalog: Chronologisches Verzeichniss*. Offenbach a / M, 1878. Reprint, Hilversum: Frits Knuf, 1966.

Bailey, Robert. "The Structure of the Ring and its Evolution." *19CM* 1 (July 1977): 48.

———. "Wagner's Musical Sketches for *Siegfrieds Tod."* In *Studies in Music History: Essays for Oliver Strunk,* 459. Ed. Harold S. Powers. Princeton: Princeton Univ. Press, 1968.

Barth, Herbert, Dietrich Mack, and Egon Voss. *Wagner: a Documentary Study*. New York: Oxford Univ. Press, 1975.

Bergfeld, Joachim, ed. *The Diary of Richard Wagner, 1865–1882: the Brown Book*. Trans. George Bird. London: Victor Gollancz, 1980.

Burbridge, Peter, and Richard Sutton, eds. *The Wagner Companion*. New York: Cambridge Univ. Press, ★1979.

Burk, John Naglee, ed. *Letters of Richard Wagner: the Burrell Collection*. New York: Macmillan, 1950. Reprint, Vienna House, 1972.

Dahlhaus, Carl. *Richard Wagner's Music Dramas*. Trans. Mary Whittall. New York: Cambridge Univ. Press, 1979.

————. "Wagner and Program Music." *Studies in Romanticism* 9 (1970): 3.

Deathridge, John. *Wagner's Rienzi: a Reappraisal Based on a Study of the Sketches and Drafts*. Oxford: Clarendon Press, 1977.

Deathridge, John and Carl Dahlhaus. *The New Grove Wagner*. New York: W. W. Norton, *1984.

Debussy, Claude. "Richard Wagner." In *Monsieur Croche the dilettante Hater*. London: Noel Douglas, 1927. Reprinted in *Three Classics in the Aesthetic of Music*. New York: Dover, 1962.

Donington, Robert. *Wagner's 'Ring' and its Symbols: the Music and the Myth*. London: Faber & Faber, 1963. Revised ed., St. Martins Press, 1974.

Förster-Nietzsche, Elisabeth. *The Nietzsche-Wagner Correspondence*. Trans. Caroline V. Kerr. Intro. by H. L. Mencken. New York: Boni & Liveright, 1921. Reprint *1970.

Gál, Hans. *Richard Wagner*. Trans. Hans-Hubert Schönzeler. London: Victor Gollancz, 1976.

Gregor-Dellin, Martin, and Dietrich Mack, eds. *Cosima Wagner's Diaries*. Trans. Geoffrey Skelton. New York: Harcourt Brace Jovanovich, 1978–79.

Heckel, Karl, ed. *Letters of Richard Wagner to Emil Heckel, with a Brief History of the Bayreuth Festivals*. Trans. Wm. Ashton Ellis. London: Richards, 1899.

Holloway, Robin. *Debussy and Wagner*. London: Eulenburg, 1979.

Hutcheson, Ernest. *A Musical Guide to the Richard Wagner Ring of the Nibelung*. New York: Simon and Schuster, 1940. Reprint, 1972.

Jacobs, Robert, trans. *Three Wagner Essays* [*Music of the Future; On Conducting; On Performing Beethoven's Ninth Symphony*]. London: Eulenburg, 1979, *1982.

Lenrow, Elbert, ed. and trans. *The Letters of Richard Wagner to Anton Pusinelli*. New York: Knopf, 1932. Reprint, 1972.

Lippman, Edward A. "The Esthetic Theories of Richard Wagner." *MQ* 44 (1958): 209.

Mann, Thomas. "The Sufferings and Greatness of Richard Wagner." In *Thomas Mann: Past Masters and other Papers,* 15–96. Trans. H. T. Lowe-Porter. New York: A. A. Knopf, 1933.

Michotte, Edmond. *Richard Wagner's Visit to Rossini (Paris, 1860)*. Trans. Herbert Weinstock. Chicago: Univ. of Chicago Press, 1968.

Mitchell, William J. "The Tristan Prelude: Techniques and Structure." *MF* 1 (1967): 162–203.

Newcomb, Anthony. "The Birth of Music out of the Spirit of Drama." *19CM* 5 (Summer 1981): 38.

Newman, Ernest. *The Life of Richard Wagner.* 4 vols. London: Cassell, 1933–47. Reprint, 1976, ★1976.

———. *The Wagner Operas.* New York: Knopf, 1949. Reprint, 1963. [Published in England under the title *Wagner Nights.*]

———. *Wagner as Man and Artist.* London: Jonathan Cape, 1913. Reprint, 1969.

Nietzsche, Friedrich Wilhelm. *The Birth of Tragedy* and *The Case of Wagner.* Trans., commentary Walter Kaufmann. New York: Vintage Books, 1967.

Porges, Heinrich. *Wagner Rehearsing the "Ring": An Eye-Witness Account of the Stage Rehearsals of the First Bayreuth Festival.* Trans. Robert L. Jacobs. Cambridge: Cambridge Univ. Press, 1983.

Rayner, Robert Macey. *Wagner and Die Meistersinger.* London: Oxford Univ. Press, 1940.

Shaw, George Bernard. *The Perfect Wagnerite: a Commentary on the Nibelung's Ring.* London, 1898. Reprint, 1972.

Siegel, Linda. "Wagner and the Romanticism of E. T. A. Hoffmann." *MQ* 51 (1965): 597.

Skelton, Geoffrey. *Wagner at Bayreuth: Experiment and Tradition.* New York: Braziller, 1965. Rev. and Enl., 1976.

Terry, Edward M. *A Richard Wagner Dictionary.* New York: Wilson, 1939. Reprint, 1971.

Wagner, Richard. *Correspondence of Wagner and Liszt.* Trans. Francis Hueffer. London: H. Grevel, 1888. Reprint, Greenwood Press, n.d.

———. *Die Briefe Richard Wagner an Judith Gautier, mit einer Einleitung, "Die Freundschaft Richard Wagners mit Judith Gautier."* Ed. Willi Schuh. Erlenbach-Zürich, Leipzig: Rotapfel-Verlag, 1936.

———. *Family Letters of Richard Wagner.* Trans. Wm. Ashton Ellis. London: Macmillan, 1911. Reprint, New York: Vienna House, 1971.

———. *Gesammelte Schriften und Dichtungen.* Ed. W. Golfer. Berlin and Leipzig: Bong & Co., ca. 1926.

———. *My Life.* Trans. Andrew Grey. Ed. Mary Whittall. New York: Cambridge Univ. Press, 1983.

———. *Prose Works.* Trans. Wm. Ashton Ellis. London, 1892. Reprint, New York: Broude Bros., 1966.

———. *Richard to Minna Wagner: Letters to his First Wife.* New York: Scribner's, 1909. Reprint, New York: Vienna House, 1972.

———. *Richard Wagner to Mathilde Wesendonck.* Trans. Wm. Ashton Ellis. New York: C. Scribner's Sons, 1905. Reprint, Boston: Milford House, 1971.

———. *Wagner on Music and Drama: a Compendium of Richard Wagner's Prose Works.* Ed. Albert Goldman and Evert Sprinchorn. Trans.

Wm. Ashton Ellis. New York: Dutton, 1964. Reprint, Da Capo Press, 1981.

Westernhagen, Curt von. *The Forging of the 'Ring': Richard Wagner's Composition Sketches for Der Ring des Nibelungen.* Trans. Arnold and Mary Whittall. Cambridge: Cambridge Univ. Press, 1976.

―――. *Wagner: a Biography.* Trans. Mary Whittall. Cambridge: Cambridge Univ. Press, 1978.

Wolzogen, Hans Paul, Freiherr von. *Guide through the Music of R. Wagner's 'The Ring of the Nibelung.'* Trans. E. von Wolzogen. 3rd ed. Leipzig, 1877.

Weber, Carl Maria von

<u>Collected Edition</u>   *Carl Maria von Weber: Musikalische Werke: erste kritische Gesamtausgabe.* Ed. H. J. Moser. Augsburg and Cologne: Benno Filser, 1926.

<u>Works Catalogue</u>   Jähns, Friedrich Wilhelm. *Carl Maria von Weber in seinen Werken: Chronologisch-thematisches Verzeichniss seiner sämmtlichen Compositionen.* Berlin: Robert Lienau, 1871. Reprint, 1967.

Abraham, Gerald. "Weber as Novelist and Critic." *MQ* 20 (1934): 27.

Englander, Richard. "The Struggle between German and Italian Opera at the Time of Weber." *MQ* 31 (1945): 479.

Jones, Gaynor G. "Weber's 'Secondary Worlds': the Later Operas of Carl Maria von Weber." *IRASM* 7 (1976): 219.

Kirby, Percival R. "Weber's Operas in London, 1824–6." *MQ* 32 (1946): 333.

Warrack, John. *Carl Maria von Weber.* Cambridge: Cambridge Univ. Press, 1968. 2nd ed., 1976.

―――, ed. *Writings on Music: Carl Maria von Weber.* Trans. Martin Cooper. Cambridge: Cambridge Univ. Press, 1981.

Wolf, Hugo

<u>Collected Edition</u>   *H. Wolf: Sämtliche Werke.* Ed. H. Jancik and others. Vienna, 1960–.

Aber, A. "Hugo Wolf's Posthumous Works." *MR* 2 (1941): 190.

Austin, Frederic. "The Songs of Hugo Wolf." *PMA* 38 (1911–12): 161.

Legge, Walter. "Hugo Wolf's Afterthoughts on his Mörike-Lieder." *MR* 2 (1941): 211.

Mackworth-Young, G. "Goethe's Prometheus and its Settings by Schubert and Wolf." *PRMA* 78 (1951–52): 53.

Newman, Ernest. *Hugo Wolf.* London: Methuen, 1907. Reprint, 1966.

Pleasants, Henry, ed. *The Music Criticism of Hugo Wolf.* New York: Holmes & Meier, 1978.

Sams, Eric. *The Songs of Hugo Wolf.* London: Methuen, 1961. 2nd ed., 1981.

Stein, Jack M. "Poem and Music in Hugo Wolf's Mörike Songs." *MQ* 53 (1967): 22.

Thym, Jurgen. "The Solo Song Settings of Eichendorff's Poems by Schumann and Wolf." Ph.D. dissertation, Case Western Reserve University, 1974.

Walker, Frank. "Conversations with Hugo Wolf." *ML* 41 (1960): 5.

———. "The History of Wolf's 'Italian Serenade.'" *MR* 8 (1947): 161.

———. *Hugo Wolf: a Biography.* London: Dent, 1951. 2nd ed., 1968.

———. "Hugo Wolf's Spanish and Italian Songs." *ML* 25 (1944): 194.

Index

Page numbers in **boldface** refer to examples. Those in *italics* refer to illustrations.